INTERNATIONAL MANAGEMENT

Text and Cases

IRWIN TITLES IN INTERNATIONAL BUSINESS AND ECONOMICS

Appleyard/Field
International Economics
2nd Edition 1996

Ball/McCulloch
**International Business:
Introduction and Essentials**
6th Edition 1996

Bartlett/Ghoshal
**Transnational Management:
Text, Cases, and Readings in
Cross-Border Management**
2nd Edition 1995

Beamish/Morrison/Rosenzweig
**International Management:
Text and Cases**
3rd Edition 1997

Cateora
International Marketing
9th Edition 1996

Eun/Kesnick
**International Financial
Management**
1997

Grosse/Kujawa
**International Business:
Theory and Applications**
2nd Edition 1992

Hill
**International Business:
Competing in the Global
Marketplace**
2nd Edition 1997

Levich
International Financial Markets
1997

Lindert
International Economics
10th Edition 1997

Mueller/Gernon/Meek
**Accounting: An International
Perspective**
4th Edition 1997

Richard
Law for Global Business
1994

Robock/Simmonds
**International Business and
Multinational Enterprises**
4th Edition 1989

THIRD EDITION

INTERNATIONAL MANAGEMENT

Text and Cases

Paul W. Beamish
Ivey School of Business
The University of Western Ontario

Allen Morrison
The American Graduate School of International Management

Philip M. Rosenzweig
IMD

IRWIN

Burr Ridge, Illinois
Boston, Massachusetts
Sydney, Australia

IRWIN **Concerned about Our Environment**

In recognition of the fact that our company is a large end-user of fragile yet replenishable resources, we at IRWIN can assure you that every effort is made to meet or exceed Environmental Protection Agency (EPA) recommendations and requirements for a "greener" workplace.

To preserve these natural assets, a number of environmental policies, both companywide and department-specific, have been implemented. From the use of 50% recycled paper in our textbooks to the printing of promotional materials with recycled stock and soy inks to our office paper recycle program, we are committed to reducing waste and replacing environmentally unsafe products with safer alternatives.

Irwin Book Team

Publisher: *Rob Zwettler*
Executive editor: *Craig S. Beytien*
Editorial coordinator: *Kimberly Kanakes*
Marketing manager: *Michael Campbell*
Project supervisor: *Jim Labeots*
Production supervisor: *Pat Frederickson*
Designer: *Michael Warrell*
Director, Prepress Purchasing: *Kimberly Meriwether David*
Compositor: *Electronic Publishing Services, Inc.*
Typeface: *10/12 Times Roman*
Printer: *R. R. Donnelley & Sons Company*

Times Mirror
Higher Education Group

Library of Congress Cataloging-in-Publication Data

Beamish, Paul W.
    International management : text and cases / Paul W. Beamish, Allen
Morrison, Philip M. Rosenzweig. — 3rd ed.
        p.   cm.
    Includes index.
    ISBN 0-256-19349-5
    1. International business enterprises—Management.
    2. International business enterprises—Management—Case studies.
    I. Morrison, Allen J.   II. Rosenzweig, Philip M., 1955-
    III. Title.
    HD62.4.B4   1997
    658.049—dc20   96–33085

Printed in the United States of America
1 2 3 4 5 6 7 8 9 0 DOC 3 2 1 0 9 8 7 6

to my father
John Richard Beamish

International Management is intended as an *international* international management book. The first two editions were used in over 200 universities and colleges in over 20 countries. The third edition, we hope, will have even wider usage. Why our optimism with this edition? In brief, it is because the book focuses on issues of international management common to businesspeople everywhere.

International Management is about how firms become and remain international in scope. It is about the experiences of firms of all sizes, from many countries, as they come to grips with an increasingly competitive global environment. It is about the practice of management when a home-market perspective is no longer enough to achieve and sustain success. Through carefully selected comprehensive case studies and integrated text material, this book bridges both the internationalization process and multinational management.

	Internationalization	*Ongoing Multinational Management*
Small/Medium-Size Firms	Smaller domestic firms moving abroad	Global niche competitors
Larger MNEs	Larger firms moving into more markets	Large, full-scale global competitors

The focus of many texts is on the lower right-hand cell in the above matrix—ongoing management issues in the world's larger MNEs. This is an important area, but one that presupposes a body of knowledge that most students do not possess. The focus of the first half of the text material and cases in this book is on internationalization—developing an awareness of the impact of international forces on the firm's future and establishing and conducting transactions with firms internationally. It is about understanding the basic modes of involvement and deciding when each is most appropriate. For each mode, both inward- and outward-looking perspectives can be considered: licensing (as licensor and licensee), trade (exporting and importing), joint ventures (with foreign companies abroad and at home), and subsidiaries (establishing foreign affiliates and as part of a foreign-controlled affiliate). As the left-hand cells in the matrix suggest, these issues are relevant for firms of all sizes.

The first half of ***International Management*** helps to demystify international business so a meaningful study of multinational management can occur. In the second half of the book, focus is on how to establish a balance between the sometimes conflicting demands of the multinational headquarters, the multinational subsidiary, and the governments of all the countries in which the MNEs operate. The cases are not limited to the experiences of the world's largest MNEs—they are also about smaller companies that must be global to survive and about the management of small subsidiaries.

International Management is intended for use in international business and international management courses at the undergraduate, graduate, and executive levels. It can serve as the basis for an overarching course that deals with internationalization and multinational management, or for courses in each. The chapters of text material can (and should) be supplemented with readings of the instructor's choice. Many of the suggested supplementary readings are from *Journal of International Business Studies,* which provides blanket permission to photocopy articles for classroom use at no charge.

In response to suggestions from the users and reviewers of the second edition, this edition contains more cases (28 versus 26) and more chapters of text (12 versus 11). Eighteen of the 28 cases are new to the third edition and several others (Cameron series, Larson) have been significantly revised and updated. The new cases were selected on the basis of managerial relevance, overall fit with suggested themes, availability, and the evaluations we received from a survey of the faculty users of the earlier editions. In regard to new text material, Philip Rosenzweig has contributed a chapter on The Evolving Multinational. All other chapters have been revised and updated. All but one of the chapters were (co) authored by us or one of our current or past colleagues. This has allowed us the opportunity to shape the body of text material into an integrated whole.

The cases in ***International Management*** have been extensively classroom-tested by us and colleagues around the world in executive, MBA, and undergraduate programs. One measure of their quality is that a number of them have been translated—into Japanese, French, Chinese, Spanish, Russian, and Indonesian. As well, several have won awards. For example, the Russki Adventures case received the 1992 EFMD Entrepreneurship Case Competition Award in European Management.

A videotape containing material relevant to a number of the cases is available from Richard D. Irwin. Use of the video is preferable but not essential.

Acknowledgments

The individual we most wish to acknowledge is Harold Crookell, a coauthor on the first edition. He passed away suddenly in 1991 and is sorely missed by all who knew him. His spirit of intellectual curiosity and dedication to the improvement of international management permeate this volume.

The authors are deeply indebted to a number of colleagues and institutions for the intellectual and financial support we have received:

Faculty Contributors of Cases/Chapters

Jay Anand, Ivey Business School
Stewart Black, American Graduate School of International Management
James Bowey, Bishop's University
Jonathan Calof, University of Ottawa
Joseph DiStefano, Ivey Business School
Andrew Inkpen, American Graduate School of International Management
Stephen Jenner, California State University, Dominquez Hills
Bud Johnston, Ivey Business School
Peter Killing, IMD
Masaaki (Mike) Kotabe, University of Texas at Austin
Henry W. Lane, Ivey Business School
Donald Lecraw, Ivey Business School
Isiaih Litvak, York University
Shigefumi Makino, Chinese University of Hong Kong
Thomas A. Poynter, Principal, The Transitions Group, Inc.
Jean-Louis Schaan, University of Ottawa

Research Associates and Assistants

Azimah Ainuddin, Harry Cheung, Ken Coelho, Andrew Delios, Charles Dhanaraj, Gayle Duncan, Carl Fey, Chris Horman, Katherine Johnston, Joyce Miller, Detlev Nitsch, Professor Arvind Phatak, Benoît Raillard, Douglas Reid, Tanya Spyridakis, S.M. Steele, Ian Sullivan, Jan Visser, Shari Ann Wortel, Professor John Zerio.

Institutional Contributors

Richard Ivey School of Business, The University of Western Ontario, London, Canada
American Graduate School of International Management—Thunderbird, AZ, U.S.A.
IMD—International Institute for Management Development, Lausanne, Switzerland
Harvard Business School, Boston, MA, U.S.A.
The World Bank, Washington, D.C.
Pacific 2000 Program, Department of Foreign Affairs and International Trade, Canada

Institute Pengembangan Manajemen Indonesia; Jakarta (with funding provided by USAID)

The following people provided detailed reviews on the second edition:

Carol Howard, University of Hawaii at Manoa
Robert Vidal, University of Cincinnati
Leland Wooton, Southern Methodist University

Earlier evaluations had been received from:

George Gore, University of Cincinnati
Stephen Jenner, San Diego State University
Cynthia Pavett, University of San Diego
F. Derakhshan, CSUSB
David Hopkins, University of Denver
Robert Moran, American Graduate School of International Management
Ellen Cook, University of San Diego
Kenneth R. Tillery, Middle Tennessee State University

We are grateful to all of these individuals and have tried to be as responsive as possible to their suggestions.

We are also grateful to the following people for their suggestions regarding the cases:

John Banks, Jafor Chowdhury, Chris Demchak, John Dutton, Nick Fry, Ruth Gunn, Steven H. Hanks, Louis Hébert, Dale Kling, R. Kustin, Neng Liang, Behnam Nakhai, Kent Neupert, Mohammad Pourheydarian, Carol Sanchez, John Stanbury, Tom Voight, Patrick Woodcock, George Yates.

Input on the cases contained in the earlier editions had been received from:

Rafiq Ahmen, A. Ali, Joe Anderson, William J. Arthur, Edgar Barrett, Brad Brown, Marie Burkhead, Susan Crockett, L.R. Edleson, Sanjay Goel, Robert Grosse, S.D. Guzell, Mary Howes, S. Kumar Jain, Neng Liang, Clair McRostie, Alan Murray, R.F. O'Neil, Y.S. Paik, Les Palich, S. Porth, Rich Pouder, Krishnan Ramaya, Kathy Rehbein, Lawrence Rhyne, Kendall Roth, Bill Scheela, Jason Schweizer, Hendrick Seturie, Trudy Somers, William C. Sproull, Phil Van Auken, William A. Ward, Marion White, and Georgie Willcox.

Finally, we wish to express our appreciation to our colleagues at Ivey. Richard Ivey School of Business is the second-largest producer of management case studies in the world. Fifteen of the 28 cases in this edition originated at Ivey. Any ongoing undertaking of this magnitude requires a great deal of financial and intellectual support. We receive this at Ivey.

Paul W. Beamish
Allen J. Morrison
Philip M. Rosenzweig

C O N T E N T S

xi

PART III

CASES ON MULTINATIONAL MANAGEMENT

INTERNATIONAL MANAGEMENT

Text and Cases

I TEXT

1 THE INTERNATIONALIZATION PROCESS

Internationalization is the process by which firms increase their awareness of the influence of international activities on their future, and establish and conduct transactions with firms from other countries. International transactions can influence a firm's future in both direct and indirect ways. Business decisions made in one country, regarding such things as foreign investments and partnership arrangements, can have significant impact on a firm in a different country—and vice versa. The impact of such decisions may not be immediately and directly evident. The development of an awareness and appreciation for the role of foreign competition becomes an integral—and sometimes overlooked—part of the internationalization process.

Firms become international in scope for a variety of reasons—some proactive and some reactive. Collectively these include a desire for continued growth, an unsolicited foreign order, domestic market saturation, the potential to exploit a new technological advantage, and so forth. The dominant reason, however, relates to performance. There is clear evidence that among the largest multinational enterprises (MNEs), a strong correlation exists between improved performance and degree of internationalization (see Exhibit 1–1).

Internationalization has both *inward-looking* and *outward-looking* dimensions. The outward-looking perspective incorporates an awareness of the nature of competition in foreign markets, and includes the following modes of activities:

a. Exporting
b. Acting as licensor to a foreign company
c. Establishing joint ventures outside the home country with foreign companies
d. Establishing or acquiring wholly owned businesses outside the home country

These outward-oriented elements are similar to those in the stages model of international expansion. The stages model is an outward-looking perspective developed to

This chapter was prepared by Paul W. Beamish.

EXHIBIT 1–1   MNE Performance and Degree of Internationalization*

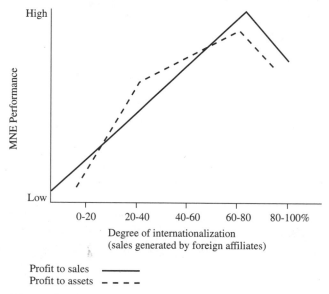

Profit to sales   ———
Profit to assets   - - - -

* Data are based on the 100 largest U.S. MNEs and the 100 largest European MNEs.

Source: J. M. Geringer, Paul W. Beamish, and R. daCosta, "Diversification Strategy and Internationalization: Implications for MNE Performance," *Strategic Management Journal* 10 (1989), pp. 109–19.

reflect the commonly observed pattern of increased commitment to international business. In the stages model,[1] a firm might progress from (a) indirect/ad hoc exporting—perhaps from unsolicited export orders—to (b) active exporting and/or licensing to (c) active exporting, licensing, and joint equity investment in foreign manufacture to (d) full-scale multinational marketing and production.

These are, of course, broad-based stages. In practice, there are many more subcategories. Within exporting, for example, firms may start with order-filling only. Soon after, however, they may be confronted with questions of whether to use exporting middlemen who take ownership (distributors) or those who are commissioned agents; and whether to export directly (either through the firm's own sales force, an export department, or a foreign sales company) or indirectly (through brokers or export agents).

Similarly, if an investment is to be made, there are questions regarding scale of investment (sales office, warehouse, packaging and assembly, or full-scale production), level of ownership (wholly, majority equity, equal, minority equity), and type

---

[1]See Franklin R. Root, *Entry Strategies for International Markets* (Lexington, MA: Lexington Books, 1987), p. 19.

EXHIBIT 1–2   The Foreign Direct Investment of MNEs

Choosing the Scale of Investment, Type of Partner, and Ownership Arrangement

Scale of investment: Sales office, Warehousing, Packaging and assembly, Full-scale production

Type of partners: Wholly owned (no partner), MNE partner, Private local partner, Local government partner, Local public as partner

Ownership arrangement: Majority owned, Equal ownership, Minority owned

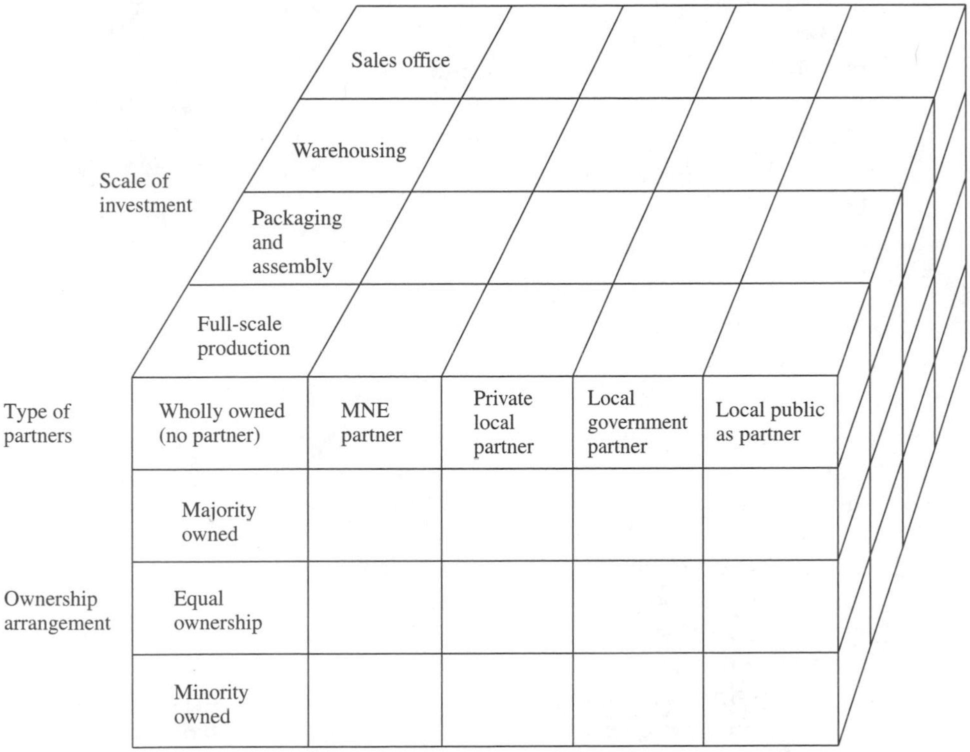

Note: While full-scale production via a wholly owned subsidiary is the most commonly studied form of MNE foreign direct investment (FDI), it is only one of at least 80 ($5 \times 4 \times 4$) regularly used forms of FDI.

of partner. As Exhibit 1–2 illustrates, there are numerous variations on the types of foreign direct investment possible.

The sequential approach in the stages model is intuitively appealing in that it suggests that as firms develop experience and confidence with international business, they will be willing to increase the scale of their investment and commitment in some sort of predictable fashion. The stages model also implies that over time, the firm's international operations will evolve toward modes such as wholly owned subsidiaries that promise greater risk (due to the required scale of investment) with the offsetting ability to exert greater control.

Not all firms follow such a path. Some start and stay with a particular mode or some skip stages, while others even change modes to a direction opposite to that suggested by the stages model. So while the stages model provides a useful way to organize our discussion, it is by no means reflective of, or appropriate for, all firms' approaches to international business. It is a descriptive model. It reflects what firms often do, not what they must or ought to do.

We also observe the formation of firms that, by necessity or design, are international from inception. These so-called "born globals" can take many forms, depending on the number of countries involved and the number of value chain activities that must be coordinated. (See Exhibit 1–3).

Internationalization affects firms in equally important ways from an inward perspective, which incorporates an awareness of the impact of global competitors on the ability of domestically oriented firms to compete. The related modes of activity include:

a. Importing/sourcing
b. Acting as licensee from a foreign company
c. Establishing joint ventures (JVs) inside the home country with foreign companies
d. Managing as the wholly owned subsidiary of a foreign firm

All of these modes and influences are relevant to the internationalization process and all are often overlooked. There are numerous reasons for considering importing rather than purchasing domestically, for considering foreign licensors or joint venture partners rather than strictly local ones, or if selling an entire business, considering foreign purchasers as an alternative to becoming the subsidiary of a domestic firm. Drawing upon resources and alternatives that are present elsewhere can help the firm see new opportunities, improve its bargaining power with local firms, make more informed decisions, and compete better at home.

Many firms have an appreciation for the nature and degree of competition in one or more foreign markets. Yet often they will not aggressively seek out markets that differ in language, geographic proximity, cultural similarity, and so forth. Some have suggested that for certain products, the world is a single market. The so-called Triad market (Japan, North America, and western Europe) is made up of 630 million buyers with similar tastes.[2] This view raises a number of issues to be explored in later chapters. Which products/services would fall into this category? How would a firm know that it may have a *globally* competitive product/service? If it did, how could it take the product/service effectively to numerous distant markets?

In terms of the new entrant to international business, how do managers make the decision to get involved internationally using *any mode?* Individual managers and groups of managers often possess distinct attitudes toward international business. These can range from being home-country oriented (ethnocentric),[3] to host-country

---

[2]See Kenichi Ohmae, *Beyond National Borders* (Homewood, IL.: Dow Jones-Irwin, 1987).

[3]See H.V. Perlmutter, "The Tortuous Evolution of the Multinational Corporation," *Columbia Journal of World Business*, January/February 1969, pp. 9–18; H.V. Perlmutter & D.A. Heenan, "How Multinational Should Your Top Managers Be?" *Harvard Business Review* 6 (1974), pp. 121–32; S. J. Kobrin, "Is There a Relationship Between a Geocentric Mind-Set and Multinational Strategy?" *Journal of International Business Studies* 3 (1994), pp. 493–511; and J. Calof and P. Beamish, "The Right Attitude for International Success," *Business Quarterly*, Vol 59, No.1, 1994, pp.105–110.

EXHIBIT 1–3   **Types of International New Ventures**

	Few	Many
Few Activities Coordinated across Countries (Primarily Logistics)	**New International Market Makers**	
	Export/Import Start-up	Multinational Trader
Coordination of Value Chain Activites	i	ii
	iii	iv
Many Activities Coordinated across Countries	Geographically Focused Start-up	Global Start-up
	Few	Many

Number of Countries Involved

Source: B. M. Oviatt and P. McDougall, "Toward a Theory of International New Ventures," *Journal of International Business Studies,* Vol 25, No. 1, 1994, p. 59.

oriented (polycentric), to world oriented (geocentric). There are two major risks associated with an ethnocentric, or home-country, focus. The first of these is a lack of awareness and appreciation for opportunities that exist external to the domestic market. The counterpoint to these potential opportunities is the potential threat of foreign competition in the home market. Numerous businesses have been hurt as a result of the naive view that if a product or service is NIH (not invented here), it won't be effective.

Relevant to all of the various perspectives and modes of involvement is the firm's need for methods of coming to grips with various international cultures. Firms do not typically have the resources available to develop a detailed understanding of numerous cultures. Yet to compete internationally, some degree of understanding is required. But how much? And which cultures does it make more sense to try to learn about?

There are still business people who persist in believing that international competition cannot affect them because they are too small, or because they are solely focused on the local market. Foreign competition affects every sector of the economy. Education is an important consideration at each stage of the internationalization process.

In the balance of this chapter, some of the issues we will deal with in the subsequent chapters and cases will be briefly considered.

The Global Business Environment

A key element of the internationalization process concerns *where* an organization chooses to do business outside its country. Many firms conduct an incomplete analysis of potential markets. This is due, in part, to a lack of awareness regarding global demographics.

Many criteria are available for assessing market compatibility. Chapter 2 provides some introductory material on population, gross national product, country growth rates, and so forth. Basic statistics on countries are included. This material is particularly useful when the firm is looking at opportunities on a worldwide (see Sterling Marking Products case), regional (see Nestlé Breakfast Cereal case), or national (see Technophar in Vietnam case) basis.

The World of International Trade

Chapter 3 presents an overview of the international trade environment, with particular emphasis on the need to appreciate the role of foreign competition in both the home market and foreign markets. A great deal of emphasis is placed on demystifying the nature of international business, in part through an overview of the trade framework.

The trade framework considers social, technological, economic, and political (STEP) environments, which make any country more or less attractive for international investment and trade. As part of this analysis, the distinctions between comparative and competitive advantage, theories of international trade, and the nature of exchange rates are reviewed.

Managing Export Operations

Exporting can often be the basis for all or part *of* an entire course on international marketing. This is because, as both the Neilson in Mexico case and the Cambridge Products series demonstrate, the export decision process is complex, requiring resolution of a number of fundamental questions. Firms of any size are faced with the same questions of where to expand (at home or abroad); if exporting, to which markets; the best way to enter these markets (i.e., what distribution arrangement, method of pricing, level of promotion, whether to adapt the product, and so forth); and the ongoing management of their foreign export operations. These questions are considered in detail in Chapter 4.

Global Sourcing Strategy

The decision to import a good or service must be made in the context of whether it would be better to purchase locally or to produce the product oneself. A firm with a home-country orientation may not even consider the possibility of importing. Not surprising, larger firms tend to have an advantage over smaller ones because they possess more resources with which to assess the importing alternative.

An excellent set of production and sourcing decisions that firms confront would include:[4]

1. From where should the firm supply the target market?
2. To what extent should the firm *itself* undertake production (degree of integration)?
3. To the extent that it does not, what and where should it buy from others?
4. To the extent that a firm opts to do at least some manufacturing, how should it acquire facilities?
5. Should the firm produce in one plant or many, related and autonomous?
6. What sort of production equipment (technology) should it use?
7. What site is best?
8. Where should research and development be located?

Importing should be a significant area of investigation, yet even purchasing texts frequently devote only limited space to international considerations. Of all the parts in the internationalization process, either from an outward or inward perspective, importing may well be the most underresearched. Although there has been recent progress,[5] much work remains. Chapter 5 deals with global sourcing strategy. It emphasizes logistical management of the interface of R&D, manufacturing, and marketing activities on a global basis.

Licensing

Our knowledge of international licensing is incomplete but growing. There are unresolved issues regarding the types of firms that license out; the predominant industries that are involved; the revenues generated; the extent to which they consider alternative modes; the countries they license to; whether they tend to consider it a stage in an internationalization process (or an end in itself); the costs of negotiating, administering, and policing license agreements; the frequency with which they lose proprietary advantages after licensing out; the most common terms in their license agreements; the areas in which there is the most disagreement; and so forth. Despite these limitations, we do know that firms license out their technology, trademarks, or other proprietary advantages in order to generate additional profits. Further, we know that licensing involves billions of dollars annually.

For the licensor, licensing is a chance to exploit its technology in markets that are too small to justify larger investments or in markets that restrict imports or FDI, or as a means of testing and developing a market. Firms are far more willing to license their peripheral technologies than their core technologies: no one wants to create a future competitor.

---

[4]See R.D. Robinson, *Internationalization of Business* (Chicago: The Dryden Press, 1984).
[5]See M. Leenders and D. Blenkhorn, *Reverse Marketing* (New York: The Free Press, 1988).

EXHIBIT 1–4   **A Typology of International Industrial Cooperation Modes***

Form of Cooperation	Equity or Nonequity	Length of Agreement	Transfer of Resources and Rights	Method of Transfer	Typical Compensation Method[†]
1. Wholly owned foreign subsidiaries	Equity	Unlimited	Whole range?	Internal to firm	Profits
2. Joint ventures	Equity	Unlimited	Whole range?	Internal to firm	Fraction of shares/dividends
3. Foreign minority holdings	Equity	Unlimited	Whole range?	Internal to firm	Fraction of shares/dividends
4. "Fade-out" agreements	Equity	Limited	Whole range? (for limited period)	Internal to firm changing to market	Fraction of shares/dividends
5. Licensing	Nonequity	Limited by contract	Limited range	Mixed**	Royalty as percent of sales
6. Franchising	Nonequity	Limited by contract	Limited + support	Market	Royalty as percent of sales and markups on components
7. Management contracts	Nonequity	Limited by contract	Limited	Market	Lump sum. Royalty.
8. Technical training	Nonequity	Limited	Small	Market	Lump sum
9. Turnkey ventures	Nonequity	Limited	Limited in time	Market	Lump sum
10. Contractual joint ventures	Nonequity	Limited	Specified by contract	Mixed	Function of the change in the costs and revenues of the venture, firm, or dominant partner
11. International subcontracting**	Nonequity	Limited	Small	Market	Markups
12. Strategic buyer-supplier coalitions**	Nonequity	Limited by contract but long-term	Limited + support	Mixed	Markups. Respective decreased costs/ increased revenues.

*Adapted from Peter J. Buckley and Mark Casson, *The Economic Theory of the Multinational Enterprise* (New York: St. Martin's Press, 1985), except where noted with double asterisk (**).

[†]Derived primarily from F. Contractor and P. Lorange, *Cooperative Strategies in International Business* (Lexington, MA: D. C. Heath, 1988).

        For the licensee, there are two principal advantages of licensing. The first is that it permits the acquisition of technology more cheaply than by internal development. Second, it allows the firm to acquire a technology that, when combined with other skills already present, permits it to diversify. It is important for technology buyers to (a) develop a minimum level of technical competence, (b) know their needs, and (c) consider alternative modes such as JVs.[6] This latter point is particularly relevant in the Cameron case.

---

     [6]See J. Peter Killing, "Technology Acquisition: License Agreement or Joint Venture?" *Columbia Journal of World Business,* Autumn 1980, pp. 38–46.

While there are typically lower levels of commitment associated with a licensing strategy, there are nonetheless risks for both parties. For the licensor there are the risks of losing a technological advantage, reputation, and potential profits. For the licensee, there are the risks that the technology will not work as expected or will cost more to implement than anticipated. Chapter 6 provides an introduction to the whole area of licensing.

The Design and Management of International Joint Ventures

International joint ventures are alliances formed by organizations from two or more countries. They are formed for a variety of reasons: to mesh complementary skills from different organizations, to assure or speed market access, to leapfrog a technological gap, to strategically respond to more intense competition, and so forth.

Joint ventures do not have to be physically located outside your home country to be "international." For an American, for example, an auto plant in the United States co-owned by American and Japanese partners is an "international" joint venture. In fact, given differences in language, culture, and management practices, such a joint venture would have greater international complexity than, for example, an American-Canadian joint venture physically located in Canada.

Joint ventures are one of many forms of cooperation, each of which has unique characteristics in terms of (a) whether it is equity-based, (b) the length of the agreement, (c) whether a whole range of resources and rights is transferred, (d) the method of resource transfer, and (e) the typical compensation method (see Exhibit 1–4). As the cases note, many firms often overlook the potential use of alternative cooperative approaches.

Chapter 7 considers why companies create joint ventures as well as providing some guidelines for their successful design and management. This serves as a useful basis for the internationalization case study Nora-Sakari, which looks at a proposed alliance. While this and other cases deal with proposals, they differ significantly in terms of country, scale, alliance type, motives for formation, and partner choice.

International Strategy Formulation

Chapter 8 looks at how international firms formulate product-market strategy to maximize the international competitiveness of the firm. The chapter and cases examine the pressures that exist for the multinational firm both to achieve global efficiencies and to be locally responsive. These pressures are easy to understand but difficult to deal with simultaneously.

At the same time as managers identify the incentives to become more international, they begin to run up against the sovereign interests of the various countries they may wish to do business in. The local governments will often use regulations to further their own in-terests in such things as employment, where production occurs, development of local businesses, foreign exchange controls, and so forth. This orientation must be balanced against the multinational's interest in operating efficiently and coordinating its global activities.

EXHIBIT 1–5   Multinational Management

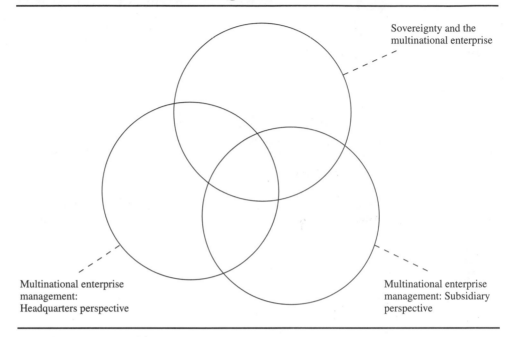

Sovereignty and the multinational enterprise

Multinational enterprise management: Headquarters perspective

Multinational enterprise management: Subsidiary perspective

If this were not enough, there are also pressures to adapt products to local conditions, perhaps organize to reflect a unique environment, and be generally responsive to the variety of differences that can exist between regions, countries, and cultures. Not surprisingly, subsidiary managers will often have very different ideas about how a subsidiary can best be managed. These in turn must be reconciled with the headquarters perspective and sovereignty concerns. All of the cases dealing with multinational management can be reviewed from the three perspectives noted in Exhibit 1–5. As you would expect, substantial overlap often exists.

The Impact of Globalization on the Organization of Activities

A major reason for the rise of multinational enterprises is their demonstrated ability to organize business activities on a multicountry basis. Organization involves both geographic configuration and international coordination and integration.

Chapter 9 introduces the organization structures through which international companies carry out their activities. The structures considered include the international division, area division, global product division, and the transnational option. Each structure represents a compromise—an attempt to balance the inherent strengths and weaknesses of the form chosen. Each structure must reconcile ease of administration with customer responsiveness, and parent company versus subsidiary perspectives. All of this must be done in the context of the sovereign concerns of different national governments, and sometimes widely different cultures.

The Evolving Multinational

Most multinationals undertake a series of foreign market entries over the course of years. Not surprisingly, they evolve in very different ways in order to reflect market complexity and the need to differentiate various subsidiaries.

The focus of Chapter 10 is on the evolving multinational enterprise. This evolving nature is considered along three dimensions: a geographic dimension, a line of business dimension, and a functional dimension. Insights are offered regarding factors that facilitate or impede evolution.

Emphasis then shifts to the ways in which evolution along these dimensions can be integrated. Of particular emphasis here is the way in which knowledge can be leveraged.

The Global Manager

Chapter 11 identifies and describes the skill set of the global manager. Effective global executives require the ability to: develop and use global strategic skills, manage change and transition, manage cultural diversity, design and function in flexible organization structures, work with others and in teams, communicate, and learn and transfer knowledge in an organization. This list can be viewed as a daunting challenge, or a lifelong opportunity.

The process of developing managers with these abilities involves human resource management policies and the managing of international assignments. This in turn is linked to selection, training, and repatriation.

Political Risk

Chapter 12 looks at political risk and how to manage government intervention. This relationship between a nation's sovereignty and multinational enterprises continues to be an important one for international managers. The Enron Development Corporation case focuses on the implications of the cancellation of a multibillion-dollar power plant project in India.

Conclusion

The chapters and cases that follow deal with issues of both internationalization and ongoing multinational management. They are intended to help build an understanding of the impact of global competition; an appreciation for the various modes of involvement; and a sensitivity to, and experience with, international management.

Supplementary Reading

Anderson, O. "On the Internationalization Process of Firms: A Critical Analysis." *Journal of International Business Studies*, Vol. 24, No. 2, 1993.

Calof, Jonathan, and Paul W. Beamish. "Adapting to Foreign Markets: Explaining Internationalization." *International Business Review*, Vol. 4, No. 2, 1995, pp.115–31.

Forsgren, M. *Managing the Internationalization Process*. London: Routledge, 1989.

Johanson, Jan, and Jan-Erik Vahlne. "The Internationalization Process of the Firm—A Model of Knowledge Development and Increasing Foreign Market Commitments." *Journal of Inter-national Business Studies*, Spring-Summer 1977.

———. "The Mechanism of Internationalization." *International Marketing Review*, 7(4), 1990, pp. 11–24.

Kogut, B., and H. Singh. "The Effect of National Culture on the Choice of Entry Mode." *Journal of International Business Studies,* Fall 1988.

Leenders, M., and D. Blenkhorn. *Reverse Marketing.* New York: The Free Press, 1988.

Ohmae, Kenichi. *Beyond National Borders.* Homewood, IL: Dow Jones-Irwin, 1987.

Robinson, Richard D. *Internationalization of Business*. Chicago: The Dryden Press, 1984.

Root, Franklin R. *Entry Strategies for International Markets.* Lexington, MA: Lexington Books, 1987.

Sullivan, Daniel. "Measuring the Degree of Internationalization of a Firm." *Journal of International Business Studies*, Vol. 25, No. 2, 1994, pp. 325–42.

Welch, L. S., and R. Luostarinen. "Internationalization: Evolution of a Concept." *Journal of General Management,* Winter 1988.

2   The Global Business Environment

Effective international management starts with a knowledge of key variables in the global economic environment. In any industry in any country, managers must have an overall knowledge of the wheres, whats, whys, and hows of the countries and regions of the world. This knowledge starts with the size and growth rates of country markets; their populations; their trade volumes, compositions, and growth rates; their natural resource bases and labor costs; and their financial positions. This knowledge can be used as a first cut to identify the threats and opportunities that might arise in their international operations. It can assist them to identify countries and regions to which they might export, from which they might import, and in which they might invest in production operations.

Although we live in the "information age," often—too often—we are ignorant of these basic facts: Which countries have the highest income (gross national product) per person in the world? Which are the 10 most populous countries in the world? Which countries with populations over 5 million grew the fastest over the past 10 years? Which countries have the largest markets? Which countries have the largest volumes of international trade? Which countries have had the highest growth rates in their trade volumes over the past decade? Which countries are among the top 10 as sources for foreign direct investment? As host countries?

The purpose of this chapter is to present data—population, GNP, purchasing power parity, and international trade statistics—to respond to some of these questions. It also highlights the problems and limitations of the data and shows how the data can be used by international managers to begin to address some of the basic decisions of international management. In subsequent chapters additional data on trade and foreign investment will be presented. It should be emphasized, however, that this publicly available data is only a start. Once the relevant publicly available data have been gathered, additional data often must be gathered, sometimes by first-hand research; all the data must be interpreted, and decisions reached using this data

---

This chapter was prepared by Paul Beamish and Donald Lecraw.

as inputs. There is the story of a salesperson who went to one country to investigate the market for shoes. The summary of the trip report was: "No market here; no one wears shoes." Several years later another salesperson went to the same country. The summary of this trip was: "Huge market here; no one wears shoes."

Population

From a mid-1990s base of 5.6 billion people, our world's population is expected to grow to 8.5 billion by the year 2025. These people are unevenly distributed, with over half the world's population in Asia Pacific countries and only 5 percent in North America. Nearly one in four people are currently located in industrialized (high-income) countries (Exhibit 2–1). This portion will drop to one in eight in the decades ahead. These population trends have enormous implications for global employment. For example, the current movement of high-volume, semiskilled manufacturing jobs from high-income to low-income countries can only increase. Real wages in low-income countries with large and/or fast-growing populations—such as India, the Philippines, Indonesia, Bangladesh, Kenya, Syria, and Nicaragua—will likely not rise dramatically. They will be low-wage countries into the foreseeable future. Exports of low-cost, labor-intensive products from these countries will continue to exert pressure on producers of competing products in high-income countries.

High population growth rates also have implications for the types of products that are and will be in demand. In 48 countries, 45 percent of the population is under the age of 15; in 62 countries, 3 percent or less of the population is over 65 years old. Conversely, in 24 countries, less than 25 percent of the population is less than 15 years old; and for 32 countries, at least 10 percent of the population is at least 65 years old.

Substantial variability exists among countries with respect to the concentration of the population within the country. In many African countries, over 90 percent of the population is in rural areas. In other countries—such as Singapore, England, Australia, the Netherlands, Venezuela, Uruguay, and Germany—over 85 percent of the population lives in urban areas. Urban concentrations provide an opportunity for international managers to focus their efforts on geographically concentrated consumers and access the country's labor force. Nowhere is this truer than in the 12 metropolitan areas where the population exceeds 10 million: Mexico City, Tokyo-Yokohama, São Paulo, New York, Calcutta, Shanghai, Bombay, Jakarta, Manila, Buenos Aires, Seoul, Rio de Janeiro, Los Angeles, and London. Beyond the concentration of the population in urban centers is the growth rates of these centers. In 15 countries, the urban population is growing faster than 6 percent per year. These high growth rates have implications for growth in demand for products and services to support the infrastructure, such as equipment and services to provide electricity, housing, roads, transportation, telecommunications, and all types of environmental cleanup. On the other hand, they have implications for the availability of urban labor.

One of the trends of the last decades is the increasing number of people who go abroad to find jobs and to increase incomes. Over 80 million people work outside their home country. International migration of this magnitude has a major impact on

EXHIBIT 2–1   Statistics on 209 Countries and Territories

Economy	Population (000s) 1994	GNP Millions of US$ 1994	GNP per capita (a) US$ 1994	GNP per capita (a) Real Growth Rate(%) 1985-1994	GNP at PPP (b) Millions of US$ 1994	GNP at PPP (b) per capita US$ 1994
Afghanistan	18,879	N.A.	c	N.A.	N.A.	N.A.
Albania	3,414	1,229	360	−6.0	N.A.	N.A.
Algeria	27,325	46,115	1,690	−2.4	145,642	5,330 d
American Samoa	53	N.A.	e	N.A.	N.A.	N.A.
Andorra	64	N.A.	f	N.A.	N.A.	N.A.
Angola	10,674	N.A.	g	−0.9	N.A.	N.A.
Antigua and Barbuda	65	453	6,970	2.7	N.A.	N.A.
Argentina	34,180	275,657	8,060	1.9	304,886	8,920
Armenia /h	3,773	2,532	670	−12.9	8,187	2,170
Aruba	69	N.A.	f	6.2	N.A.	N.A.
Australia	17,841	320,705	17,980	1.2	338,979	19,000
Austria	7,915	197,475	24,950	2.3	160,120	20,230
Azerbaijan /h	7,472	3,730	500	−12.2	12,852	1,720
Bahamas, The	272	3,207	11,790	−0.7	4,148	15,250 d
Bahrain	548	4,114	7,500	−0.9	6,614	12,070 d
Bangladesh	117,787	26,636	230	2.1	159,012	1,350
Barbados	261	1,704	6,530	−0.1	2,808	10,760 d
Belarus /h	10,163	21,937	2,160	−1.7	50,917	5,010
Belgium	10,080	231,051	22,920	2.3	206,136	20,450
Belize	210	535	2,550	5.3	N.A.	N.A.
Benin	5,246	1,954	370	−0.8	8,708	1,660
Bermuda	63	N.A.	f	−1.2	N.A.	N.A.
Bhutan	675	272	400	N.A.	N.A.	N.A.
Bolivia	7,237	5,601	770	1.9	18,237	2,520
Bosnia and Herzegovina	N.A.	N.A.	c	N.A.	N.A.	N.A.
Botswana	1,443	4,037	2,800	6.6	7,677	5,320
Brazil	159,143	536,309	3,370	−0.4	895,975	5,630
Brunei	279	3,975	14,240	−1.5	N.A.	N.A.
Bulgaria	8,818	10,255	1,160	−3.2	37,300	4,230 d
Burkina Faso	10,046	2,982	300	−0.2	7,735	770 d
Burundi	6,209	904	150	−1.0	3,601	580 d
Cambodia	9,968	N.A.	c	N.A.	N.A.	N.A.
Cameroon	12,871	8,735	680	−6.6	25,356	1,970
Canada	29,121	569,949	19,570	0.4	620,860	21,320
Cape Verde	381	346	910	1.8	705	1,850 d
Cayman Islands	30	N.A.	f	N.A.	N.A.	N.A.
Central African Republic	3,235	1,991	370	−2.8	3,429	1,060 d
Chad	6,183	1,153	190	0.9	4,575	740 d
Channel Islands	147	N.A.	f	N.A.	N.A.	N.A.
Chile	14,044	50,051	3,560	6.2	127,239	9,060
China	1,190,918	630,202	530	6.9	2,989,204	2,510
Colombia	36,330	58,935	1,620	1.9	216,890	5,970
Comoros	485	249	510	−1.3	548	1,130 d
Congo	2,516	1,607	640	−2.7	5,032	2,000
Costa Rica	3,304	7,856	2,380	2.8	19,031	5,760

EXHIBIT 2–1   *(continued)*

Economy	Population (000s) 1994	GNP Millions of US$ 1994	GNP per capita (a) US$ 1994	GNP per capita (a) Real Growth Rate(%) 1985-1994	GNP at PPP (b) Millions of US$ 1994	GNP at PPP (b) per capita US$ 1994
Côte d'Ivoire	13,780	7,070	510	−5.2	18,465	1,340
Croatia	4,780	12,093	2,530	N.A.	N.A.	N.A.
Cuba	10,951	N.A.	g	N.A.	N.A.	N.A.
Cyprus	734	N.A.	f	5.2	N.A.	N.A.
Czech Republic	10,295	33,051	3,210	−2.1	81,433	7,910
Denmark	5,173	145,384	28,110	1.3	107,598	20,800
Djibouti	566	N.A.	g	N.A.	N.A.	N.A.
Dominica	71	201	2,830	4.2	N.A.	N.A.
Dominican Republic	7,684	10,109	1,320	2.1	29,122	3,790
Ecuador	11,220	14,703	1,310	1.0	49,144	4,380
Egypt, Arab Republic	57,556	40,950	710	1.6	207,777	3,610
El Salvador	5,641	8,365	1,480	1.6	14,159	2,510
Equatorial Guinea	389	167	430	*1.6*	N.A.	N.A.
Eritrea	N.A.	N.A.	c	N.A.	N.A.	N.A.
Estonia /h	1,541	4,351	2,820	−6.4	N.A.	N.A.
Ethiopia	53,435	6,947	130	−0.6	21,908	410
Faeroe Islands	47	N.A.	f	N.A.	N.A.	N.A.
Fiji	771	1,785	2,320	2.0	4,310	5,590 d
Finland	5,083	95,817	18,850	−0.3	83,310	16,390
France	57,726	1,355,039	23,470	1.7	1,144,129	19,820
French Guinea	140	N.A.	e	N.A.	N.A.	N.A.
French Polynesia	215	N.A.	f	N.A.	N.A.	N.A.
Gabon	1,035	3,669	3,550	−2.3	N.A.	N.A.
Gambia, The	1,081	384	360	0.5	1,243	1,150 d
Georgia /h	5,450	N.A.	c	−18.6	6,322	1,160
Germany	81,141	2,075,452	25,580	1.9	1,613,894	19,890
Ghana	16,944	7,311	430	1.4	34,227	2,020 d
Greece	10,408	80,194	7,710	1.3	118,651	11,400
Greenland	58	N.A.	f	N.A.	N.A.	N.A.
Grenada	92	241	2,620	3.9	N.A.	N.A.
Guadeloupe	420	N.A.	e	N.A.	N.A.	N.A.
Guam	147	N.A.	e	N.A.	N.A.	N.A.
Guatemala	10,322	12,237	1,190	0.9	36,024	3,490
Guinea	6,501	3,310	510	*1.2*	N.A.	N.A.
Guinea-Bissau	1,050	253	240	1.9	945	900 d
Guyana	825	434	530	0.3	1,650	2,000 d
Haiti	7,035	1,542	220	−5.0	6,543	930 d
Honduras	5,493	3,162	580	−0.1	10,437	1,900
Hong Kong /i	5,833	126,286	21,650	5.3	134,626	23,080
Hungary	10,161	39,009	3,840	−0.9	64,116	6,310
Iceland	266	6,545	24,590	0.3	5,027	18,900
India	913,600	278,739	310	2.9	1,178,544	1,290
Indonesia	189,907	167,632	880	6.0	700,757	3,690
Iran, Islamic Republic	65,758	N.A.	g	−1.0	305,775	4,650
Iraq	19,951	N.A.	g	N.A.	N.A.	N.A.

EXHIBIT 2–1   *(continued)*

Economy	Population (000s) 1994	GNP Millions of US$ 1994	GNP per capita (a) US$ 1994	GNP per capita (a) Real Growth Rate(%) 1985-1994	GNP at PPP (b) Millions of US$ 1994	GNP at PPP (b) per capita US$ 1994
Ireland	3,543	48,275	13,630	5.2	51,551	14,550
Isle of Man	73	N.A.	e	N.A.	N.A.	N.A.
Israel	5,420	78,113	14,410	2.5	85,040	15,690
Italy	57,154	1,101,258	19,270	1.8	1,063,636	18,610
Jamaica	2,496	3,553	1,420	1.7	7,413	2,970
Japan	124,782	4,321,136	34,630	3.2	2,664,096	21,350
Jordan	4,217	5,849	1,390	−6.3	18,091	4,290 d
Kazakhstan /h	17,027	18,896	1,110	−6.5	48,186	2,830
Kenya	26,017	6,643	260	0.0	35,123	1,350
Kiribati	77	56	730	−1.0	N.A.	N.A.
Korea, Dem. Republic	23,472	N.A.	g	N.A.	N.A.	N.A.
Korea, Republic	44,563	366,484	8,220	7.8	469,694	10,540
Kuwait	1,651	31,433	19,040	−1.3	40,450	24,500 d
Kyrgyz, Republic /h	4,667	2,825	610	−5.4	7,981	1,710
Laos PDR	4,742	1,496	320	2.1	N.A.	N.A.
Latvia /h	2,583	5,920	2,290	−6.2	13,354	5,170
Lebanon	3,930	N.A.	g	N.A.	N.A.	N.A.
Lesotho	1,996	1,398	700	0.5	3,433	1,720 d
Liberia	2,941	N.A.	c	N.A.	N.A.	N.A.
Libya	5,222	N.A.	e	N.A.	N.A.	N.A.
Liechtenstein	31	N.A.	f	N.A.	N.A.	N.A.
Lithuania /h	3,706	4,992	1,350	−7.8	12,007	3,240
Luxembourg	401	15,973	39,850	1.3	12,467	31,090
Macao	395	N.A.	f	N.A.	N.A.	N.A.
Macedonia, FYR /j	2,093	1,653	790	N.A.	N.A.	N.A.
Madagascar	13,101	3,058	230	−1.7	8,778	670
Malawi	10,843	1,560	140	−2.0	6,506	600
Malaysia	19,498	68,674	3,520	5.7	167,878	8,610
Maldives	246	221	900	6.5	N.A.	N.A.
Mali	9,524	2,421	250	0.9	4,952	520
Malta	364	N.A.	e	5.3	N.A.	N.A.
Marshall Islands	52	88	1,680	N.A.	N.A.	N.A.
Martinique	375	N.A.	e	N.A.	N.A.	N.A.
Mauritania	2,217	1,063	·480	0.2	3,481	1,570 d
Mauritius	1,104	3,514	3,180	5.6	14,496	13,130
Mayotte	105	N.A.	e	N.A.	N.A.	N.A.
Mexico	91,858	368,679	4,010	0.6	647,599	7,050
Micronesia, Fed. Sts.	107	202	1,890	N.A.	N.A.	N.A.
Moldova /h	4,420	3,853	870	N.A.	N.A.	N.A.
Monaco	32	N.A.	f	N.A.	N.A.	N.A.
Mongolia	2,363	801	340	−3.3	4,773	2,020 d
Morocco	26,488	30,330	1,150	1.1	91,119	3,440
Mozambique	16,614	1,328	80	3.5	9,138	550 d
Myanmar	45,555	N.A.	c	N.A.	N.A.	N.A.
Namibia	1,500	3,045	2,030	3.4	5,925	3,950 d

EXHIBIT 2–1   *(continued)*

Economy	Population (000s) 1994	GNP Millions of US$ 1994	GNP per capita (a) US$ 1994	GNP per capita (a) Real Growth Rate(%) 1985-1994	GNP at PPP (b) Millions of US$ 1994	GNP at PPP (b) per capita US$ 1994
Nepal	21,360	4,174	200	2.2	23,069	1,080 d
Netherlands	15,391	338,144	21,970	1.9	278,269	18,080
Netherlands Antilles	197	N.A.	f	N.A.	N.A.	N.A.
New Caledonia	178	N.A.	e	N.A.	N.A.	N.A.
New Zealand	3,531	46,578	13,190	0.5	59,250	16,780
Nicaragua	4,275	1,395	330	−6.4	7,909	1,850
Niger	8,846	2,040	230	−2.2	7,077	800 d
Nigeria	107,900	29,995	280	1.2	154,297	1,430
Northern Mariana Islands	46	N.A.	g	N.A.	N.A.	· N.A.
Norway	4,318	114,328	26,480	1.4	91,196	21,120
Oman	2,073	10,779	5,200	0.6	18,968	9,150 d
Pakistan	126,284	55,565	440	1.6	279,088	2,210
Panama	2,585	6,905	2,670	0.0	15,717	6,080
Papua New Guinea	4,205	4,857	1,160	2.1	10,218	2,430 d
Paraguay	4,830	7,606	1,570	1.0	17,098	3,540
Peru	23,331	44,110	1,890	−2.5	86,091	3,690
Philippines	66,188	63,311	960	1.8	185,326	2,800
Poland	38,341	94,613	2,470	0.9	206,275	5,380
Portugal	9,832	92,124	9,370	4.0	121,917	12,400
Puerto Rico	3,645	N.A.	e	*1.7*	N.A.	N.A.
Qatar	537	7,810	14,540	−0.8	N.A.	N.A.
Reunion	643	N.A.	e	N.A.	N.A.	N.A.
Romania	22,736	27,921	1,230	−6.2	66,389	2,920
Russia /h	148,366	392,496	2,650	−4.4	780,405	5,260
Rwanda	7,750	N.A.	c	−2.2	N.A.	N.A.
St. Kitts and Nevis	41	195	4,760	4.7	383	9,330 d
St. Lucia	145	501	3,450	4.0	N.A.	N.A.
St. Vincent	111	235	2,120	4.4	N.A.	N.A.
São Tomé and Principe	125	31	250	−2.5	N.A.	N.A.
Saudi Arabia	17,498	126,597	7,240	−1.2	N.A.	N.A.
Senegal	8,102	4,952	610	−0.5	13,449	1,660
Seychelles	73	453	6,210	4.5	N.A.	N.A.
Sierra Leone	4,587	698	150	−1.9	3,532	770
Singapore	2,819	65,842	23,360	6.9	60,411	21,430 d
Slovakia	5,333	11,914	2,230	−3.3	35,518	6,660
Slovenia	1,995	14,246	7,140	N.A.	N.A.	N.A.
Solomon Islands	366	291	800	1.8	747	2,040 d
Somalia	9,077	N.A.	c	*−1.2*	N.A.	N.A.
South Africa	41,591	125,225	3,010	−1.4	N.A.	N.A.
Spain	39,551	525,334	13,280	2.7	555,296	14,040
Sri Lanka	18,125	11,634	640	2.8	57,094	3,150
Sudan	27,361	N.A.	c	*−0.2*	N.A.	N.A.
Suriname	418	364	870	0.6	1,538	3,680 d
Swaziland	906	1,048	1,160	−1.3	2,609	2,880
Sweden	8,735	206,419	23,630	0.0	155,920	17,850
Switzerland	7,127	264,974	37,180	0.5	173,828	24,390

EXHIBIT 2–1   *(concluded)*

Economy	Population (000s) 1994	GNP Millions of US$ 1994	GNP per capita (a) US$ 1994	GNP per capita (a) Real Growth Rate(%) 1985-1994	GNP at PPP (b) Millions of US$ 1994	GNP at PPP (b) per capita US$ 1994
Syrian Arab Republic	14,171	N.A.	g	−2.4	N.A.	N.A.
Tajikistan /h	5,933	2,075	350	−11.7	6,882	1,160
Tanzania /k	28,846	N.A.	c	1.1	N.A.	N.A.
Thailand	58,718	129,864	2,210	8.2	403,393	6,870
Togo	4,010	1,267	320	−2.7	4,251	1,060 d
Tonga	98	160	1,640	0.1	367	3,740 d
Trinidad and Tobago	1,292	4,838	3,740	−2.3	10,904	8,440 d
Tunisia	8,815	15,873	1,800	1.8	43,722	4,960
Turkey	60,771	149,002	2,450	1.5	280,154	4,610
Turkmenistan /h	4,010	N.A.	g	−1.5	N.A.	N.A.
Uganda	18,592	3,718	200	3.0	17,476	940 d
Ukraine /h	51,465	80,921	1,570	−5.1	171,378	3,330
United Arab Emirates	1,855	N.A.	f	0.2	N.A.	N.A.
United Kingdom	58,088	1,069,457	18,410	1.4	1,055,459	18,170
United States	260,529	6,737,367	25,860	1.3	6,737,280	25,860
Uruguay	3,167	14,725	4,650	3.0	21,694	6,850
Uzbekistan /h	22,349	21,142	950	−2.4	53,414	2,390
Vanuatu	165	189	1,150	−0.9	436	2,640 d
Venezuela	21,378	59,025	2,760	0.6	168,672	7,890
Vietnam	72,500	13,775	190	N.A.	N.A.	N.A.
Virgin Islands (U.S.)	104	N.A.	f	N.A.	N.A.	N.A.
West Bank and Gaza	2,063	N.A.	g	N.A.	N.A.	N.A.
Western Samoa	169	163	970	N.A.	N.A.	N.A.
Yemen, Republic	13,873	3,884	280	N.A.	N.A.	N.A.
Yugoslavia, Federal Republic	10,707	N.A.	g	N.A.	N.A.	N.A.
Zaire	42,552	N.A.	c	−0.8	N.A.	N.A.
Zambia	9,196	3,206	350	−1.3	9,196	1,000
Zimbabwe	11,002	5,424	490	−0.6	22,444	2,040

Note: Figures in italics are for years other than those specified; the number 0 or 0.0 means zero or less than half the unit shown and not known more precisely.

N.A. means not available.

a. Atlas method.

b. PPP = Purchasing Power Parity. PPP is an alternative measure of an economy's income level relative to others, calculated by using international prices to value domestic production.

c. Estimated to be low-income ($725 or less).

d. PPP figures obtained from regression estimates.

e. Estimated to be upper-middle-income ($2,896 to $8,955).

f. Estimated to be high-income ($8,956 or more).

g. Estimated to be lower-middle-income ($726 to $2,895).

h. Estimates for the economies of the former Soviet Union are preliminary and their classification is kept under review.

i. References to GNP relate to GDP.

j. Former Yugoslav Republic of Macedonia.

k. Data cover mainland Tanzania only.

Source: The World Bank, *World Bank 1996 Atlas*, 1996.

overall trade and balance of payments when the funds that workers remit to their home countries are considered. For example, the World Bank has estimated that Filipino workers abroad remit $8 billion per year, compared to exports of about $13.5 billion.

Countries

The 1991 *World Bank Atlas* provides statistics on 185 countries and territories. The 1996 *World Bank Atlas* provides statistics on 209 countries and territories. Country proliferation is relevant not just to mapmakers and statisticians. It has obvious and immediate implications for multinational enterprises and international traders and their need to coordinate with national governments, to define territorial scope of operations, to analyze foreign exchange rates, and so forth.

Country proliferation seems likely to continue. On January 1, 1993, the Czechoslovakian federation was split into the Czech Republic and Slovakia. Yugoslavia seems to be splintering into an indeterminate number of pieces. Separatist elements exist in many of the countries of Africa and Asia, such as Indonesia, the Philippines, and India. Whether due to differences in culture, ethnic origin, language, or religion, this trend complicates the life of the international manager.

Beyond the proliferation in the number of countries, many countries are also highly diverse in terms of religion, ethnic groups, language, and income level. This diversity has implications for effective management practices in all the functional areas as well as general management in many countries. For example, it is dysfunctional to combine all the diverse people of Indonesia together in one group. An oil company in Jakarta, under a government-mandated training program, assigned mostly workers from one part of Sulawesi for training. Its experience had been that these were the workers who were most responsive to training. Its workers from other regions struck the company and the government would not allow these training costs to be recovered. The department of geodesy and cartography of the state geological committee of the Russian Academy of Sciences has devised an "Ethnic and Linguistic Homogeneity Index" of most of the countries of the world. The index ranges from 100 for North and South Korea to 7 for Tanzania (Indonesia is 24). This index gives some idea of the diversity facing international managers within each country.[1]

Economic Development

Global economic activity continues to be dominated by a small number of countries. Yet the ranks of the traditional G7 nations (the United States, Japan, Germany, France, Italy, United Kingdom, Canada), the countries with the largest economies as measured by GNP, are under challenge. As of 1994, when measured using purchasing

---

[1]See *The New Book of World Rankings* and *The CIA World Factbook* (referenced at the end of this chapter) for these and other interesting statistics.

power parity, China, Indonesia, India, Mexico, and Brazil have economies that are larger than that of Canada and some of the other G7 countries.

The economic figures for many countries can serve as a useful approximation of reality, while for others they are notoriously inaccurate. Some countries intentionally understate their GNP to attract development aid. Others simply have poor tracking mechanisms. As well, wars and insurrections can dramatically reduce—or increase—economic activity.

The data on GNP are designed to capture the volume of goods and services produced and consumed in a country. Hence, GNP is a first rough measure of market size. In 1994, the GNP of countries ranged from $6.7 trillion for the United States to $4.3 trillion for Japan, $2.1 trillion for Germany, down to $31 million for São Tomé and Principe.

Beyond the *size* of an economy, its growth rate is also important, since it signals the speed at which markets are growing. Many of the fastest-growing economies continue to be concentrated on the Asia-Pacific Rim. And many of the slowest-growing economies continue to be concentrated on the African continent. Many of the economies that have experienced negative growth have been concentrated in central and eastern Europe. For example, the economies of Armenia, Azerbaijan, and Georgia *declined* by 14.3, 13.6, and 19 percent *per year* from 1985 to 1994. The economies of the countries of Central and South America, such as Chile, seem to be recovering from the depression of the 1980s, as many have started to grow dramatically. Within these geographical regions, however, growth is far from uniform.

GDP (or GNP) per capita figures can give an indication of the income levels of countries. Income levels in turn can indicate the types of products that may be in demand and wage levels. These figures must be interpreted with care, however. They have three major faults. GNP is a measure of the goods and services that are produced by the economy and sold via the market *as recorded by the government.* For developing countries, many goods and services are produced for self-consumption or bartered. Government reporting systems often do not record these transactions or the transactions of small producers. The so-called subculture economies (SCEs) often include indigenous peoples, people who do not participate in the official economy, people who produce mostly for themselves and their families, and those working under ill-structured manufacturing environments (for example, producers of handicrafts, cultural products, handmade clothing, and so on). In some countries, 20 to 30 percent of the population works in the SCE. A similar problem exists to a lesser extent in many high-income countries.

In addition to the SCE, the production and consumption of illegal goods and services are not reported to the government and, hence, do not appear in GNP statistics. Neither does production and consumption of goods and services that are not reported to the government in order to avoid sales and income taxes. Studies of several countries estimate that this "underground economy" may equal as much as 20 to 30 percent of reported GNP.

A second problem arises when GNP is compared among countries. The GNP of the United States is expressed in dollars, that of Japan in yen, Germany's in deutsche marks, and so on. Comparisons need to be made using a common measure. Most often a country's GNP in domestic currency is converted into U.S. dollars *at the prevailing exchange rate* (or using an average of the past several years). But unless the exchange rate is maintained at its long-run equilibrium value, this conversion can give misleading results. For example, from 1990 to 1994 the Philippine peso rose from 28 per dollar to 24.5 per dollar and the Philippine GNP in pesos rose from 1,077 billion to 1,694 billion. These numbers led to a rise in GNP (expressed in dollars) from $38 billion to $66.4 billion, a 75 percent increase in GNP and a 60 percent increase in GNP per capita in just four years. If U.S. inflation over this period of a total of about 15 percent is subtracted to give real growth expressed in dollars, these numbers are reduced to 60 percent and 45 percent. Yet real growth in the Philippine GNP and GNP per capita *totaled* 10.4 percent and 1.4 percent, respectively, over this period. The problem here and in other intercountry comparisons is that the real exchange rate of the Philippines appreciated by about 50 percent over the period.[2]

The final problem is that prices for the same product may not be the same among countries when expressed in a common currency. If a cup of coffee costs 5 cents in India and 5 dollars in Japan, one cup of coffee produced in India would add 5 cents to GNP, but the same cup of coffee produced in Japan would add 5 dollars to Japan's GNP. This effect lowers the GNP (and, hence, the GNP per capita) figures for countries with low prices relative to ones with high prices. This problem can be addressed by restating GNP figures of each country with the same prices for all goods and services. This method is called the purchasing power parity (PPP). If PPP is applied to relatively expensive high-income countries, it usually leads to a fall in reported GNP per capita. Using 1994 data, the GNP per capita of Switzerland on a PPP basis was $24,390 compared to $37,180 using the standard method. This implies that goods and services in Switzerland were on average 52 percent more expensive than in the United States.[3] When the price differences are removed, Switzerland's GNP falls by 53 percent. Using the PPP, in 1994 U.S. GNP per capita of $25,860 was still the highest in the world among countries with populations over one million, followed by Switzerland, Hong Kong, Singapore, Japan, and Canada. Conversely, the GNP per capita levels of low-income countries are raised under the PPP method, in some cases by as much as a factor of six.

The PPP method also addresses the problem of changing exchange rates, since it uses common prices in all countries. GNP measured at PPP gives a more realistic measure of the size of a country's markets and its income levels. Notice that it leads to a compression of the range of GNP per capita figures, i.e., the income gap between the richest and the poorest countries is reduced, as is the gap between the incomes of high-income countries.

A word of caution is necessary here. The PPP method uses cost comparisons for *average* consumers. It is not an appropriate measure to use when considering overseas operations or the living expenses of expatriate managers. For example, Indonesia's GNP per capita in 1994 as reported by the IMF was $880 and its PPP GNP per capita

---

[2]See Chapter 3 for a description of the real exchange rate.

[3]The news magazine *The Economist* regularly publishes its "Big Mac Index," which compares prices of a Big Mac among a number of countries as a measure of relative prices. Switzerland and Japan usually have the highest priced Big Macs.

was $3,690. This implies a price differential of over four times. Yet, for an expatriate manager living in Jakarta compared to costs of living in Des Moines, Iowa, housing, car, food, and education expenses are all substantially higher, with only women's and children's clothing, candles, ornamental fish, and flowers (except carnations) being markedly less expensive.

Beyond the average level of income, the distribution of income around this level also has important implications for international management. Indonesia's reported GNP per capita was $880 in 1994. Even adjusting for purchasing power parity to $3,690, Indonesia still appears to have a low level of income and, hence, little demand for luxury products. Yet Jakarta traffic is chronically jammed, and in the jam are a very high proportion of Mercedes and full-sized BMWs. Similarly, Gucci, Charles Jourdan, and Dior *each* have more than 15 stores in Jakarta.

Growth in GNP and GNP per capita reflect rising demand and rising income levels and, hence, market opportunities. These growth figures are usually more accurate than the data on the levels themselves. Increasing demand not only makes a country more attractive as a trade destination or investment site, it may also facilitate entry. Existing suppliers may face capacity constraints. Sales by a new competitor, although reducing the market shares of existing firms, may not reduce their absolute sales volumes. Hence, competitive reaction may be muted.

Some firms have been more astute than others at responding to the changing income levels in certain countries. Phillips has the major share of the electric lamps market in Indonesia. As electricity is extended into the countryside, it has introduced 15-watt bulbs priced at less than half the price of its 100-watt bulbs (even though the delivered cost is almost the same) to fit the income levels, demand characteristics, and voltage levels in these areas. Over time, it introduces higher-priced, higher wattage bulbs as income levels rise and as the people become accustomed to using (Phillips) electric lighting.

To this point, the analysis has been based on the *past* performance of the economy. This analysis is useful for many purposes, such as market size, income distribution, and wage rates. But as with many areas of business management and strategy, some indications of future performance are also useful. For example, for the 20 years through 1993, growth in the Philippines was low. In 1994, however, growth began to accelerate, reaching over 6 percent in 1996. Forecasting growth has proven to be difficult at best for economists. Through 1995, two organizations, the World Economic Forum and the Institute for Management Development, had joined together to construct a "World Competitiveness Report," which ranked countries based on hundreds of factors that are thought to contribute to future growth. In 1996, these two organizations split and each published rankings of its own. The overall rankings are in Exhibit 2–2. There are some significant differences between the two sets of rankings: New Zealand is ranked third by one method, eleventh in the other; the United States is first in one ranking, fourth in another; the Netherlands is seventeenth in one ranking, seventh in the other. But there is a rough correspondence between the two rankings. Beyond these overall rankings, the two reports also rank countries based on natural resource availability, labor costs and quality, political stability, tax rates, and so on. These reports can provide a wealth of data on current and future economic conditions in many countries in the world.

Exhibit 2–2   World Competitiveness Rankings

Economy	World Economic Forum Ranking	IMD Ranking	Economy	World Economic Forum Ranking	IMD Ranking
Singapore	1	2	Ireland	26	22
Hong Kong	2	3	Iceland	27	25
New Zealand	3	11	Jordan	28	—
United States	4	1	Egypt	29	—
Luxembourg	5	8	Indonesia	30	41
Switzerland	6	9	Philippines	31	31
Norway	7	6	Spain	32	29
Canada	8	12	Mexico	33	42
Taiwan	9	18	Portugal	34	36
Malaysia	10	23	Czech Republic	35	34
Denmark	11	5	China	36	26
Australia	12	21	Argentina	37	32
Japan	13	4	Peru	38	—
Thailand	14	30	Greece	39	40
United Kingdom	15	19	Colombia	40	33
Finland	16	15	Italy	41	28
Netherlands	17	7	Turkey	42	35
Chile	18	13	South Africa	43	44
Austria	19	16	Poland	44	43
Korea	20	27	India	45	38
Sweden	21	14	Hungary	46	39
Germany	22	10	Venezuela	47	45
France	23	20	Brazil	48	37
Israel	24	24	Russia	49	46
Belgium	25	17			

Note: The World Economic Forum ranked 49 countries; IMD ranked 46 countries.

Sources: World Economic Forum, *1996 World Competitiveness Report,* 1996. IMD, *The World Competitiveness Yearbook 1996,* 1996.

Trade, Natural Resources, and Foreign Investment

An analysis of the trade volumes, growth rates, composition, and destinations and sources can provide useful insights into emerging sources of supply, shifting comparative and competitive advantages, and new markets. Trade as a percentage of GNP is very important to some countries, such as Hong Kong, Ireland, the Netherlands, and Taiwan.[4] For other countries—particularly those with large domestic markets

---

[4]Again there is a problem with these figures. International trade takes place in international currencies. Hence there is *not* a problem with understating it or overstating it based on differing prices, the PPP problem described above. GDP and GNP figures, however, are over- and understated because of differing prices. This tends to overstate the trade exposure of low-cost, usually developing countries and understate the trade exposure of high-cost countries such as Switzerland and Japan.

such as the United States, Japan, and Brazil—trade as a percentage of GNP is much lower. Over the past decade, growth in trade has been highest in many of the countries of the Asia-Pacific Rim and has stagnated in many of the countries of Africa (see Exhibit 2–3).

By the mid-1990s, the United States still accounted for the largest share of world merchandise trade, with approximately 12.7 percent of world exports and 16.9 percent of world imports, followed by Germany and Japan (Exhibit 2–3). The United States also had by far the largest share of world trade in commercial services (Exhibit 2–4). Over the past two decades, the trade exposure of the United States, defined as exports plus imports as a percentage of GDP, has increased. But by the mid-1990s, the trade exposure of the United States was still below that of most major countries.

Over the past decades, there have been three trends in the trade of manufactured products. The volume of trade in manufactured products has risen dramatically. The number of source countries has risen as well. And the composition of the trade of many countries has changed. These trends have been driven by the spread of product and process technology, the fall of transportation costs relative to production costs, and the reduction of tariff and nontariff barriers to trade (until the past five years). Rising real wages in some high-income countries and in the NICs (newly industrializing countries) have led to labor-intensive products being produced in lower-income countries. Nontariff barriers to trade, such as quotas, have also provided incentives for firms to move production to countries that have not had quotas imposed on them. For example, one U.S. importer of jeans compared a list of all the countries on which the United States imposed quotas on jeans and a list of all low-wage countries. He then went to several countries in southern Africa (which did not face quotas) to find firms with supply capabilities. He now imports jeans from Botswana.

Another influence on the volume, patterns, and composition of trade has been the change in the trade strategies of many developing countries—most notably China, Brazil, and Mexico, and more recently India and Indonesia—toward export promotion. The large populations of these countries and the rapid growth of their labor forces imply that real wages will continue to be low for many years into the future. Hence, unlike the NICs, they should remain low-cost producers of labor-intensive products for many years to come.

Trade in services has increased as a percentage of international trade—and there is every likelihood that this trend will continue in the future. The United States leads the world in exports of services: financial services, visual and audio media, shipping, insurance, advertising, and so on. In the coming decades, tourism is likely to be the highest growth sector in trade. Already trade in tourism is *the* major export of many countries (Exhibit 2–4).

Over the past decades, the relative value of unprocessed natural resources in international trade has declined. But, over the past decade, a combination of technology transfer combined with relatively low labor and, in some cases, land costs has led to a rapid increase in the number of countries that have begun to export fresh and processed agricultural and fishery products. These products have often been sold as "off brands" or "house brands" to price-sensitive consumers in high-income countries. Examples are: canned sardines, tuna fish, and pineapple (Thailand and

EXHIBIT 2–3   Leading Exporters and Importers in World Merchandise Trade, 1993 ($ billions and percentage)

Rank				1993		Rank				1993	
1980	*1990*	*1993*	*Exporters*	*Value*	*Share*	*1980*	*1990*	*1993*	*Importers*	*Value*	*Share*
1	2	1	United States	$456.9	12.7%	1	1	1	United States	$589.4	16.9%
2	1	2	Germany	406.9	11.4	2	2	2	Germany	374.0	10.7
3	3	3	Japan	351.3	9.8	3	3	3	Japan	209.7	6.0
4	4	4	France	195.1	5.4	5	5	4	United Kingdom	201.8	5.8
5	5	5	United Kingdom	181.2	5.1	4	4	5	France	188.1	5.4
7	6	6	Italy	168.5	4.7	10	8	6	Canada	136.4	3.9
10	8	7	Canada	144.3	4.0	6	6	7	Italy	136.2	3.9
9	7	8	Netherlands	120.3	3.4	7	7	8	Netherlands	107.4	3.1
11	9	9	Belgium-Luxembourg	103.8	2.9	18	12	9	Hong Kong	100.3	2.9
24	11	10	Hong Kong	98.2	2.7	8	10	10	Belgium-Luxembourg	99.9	2.9
32	13	11	Korea	81.0	2.3	22	18	11	China	86.3	2.5
31	15	12	China	75.7	2.1	17	15	12	Singapore	80.0	2.3
13	14	13	Switzerland	74.9	2.1	20	14	13	Korea	79.1	2.3
26	18	14	Singapore	72.0	2.0	12	11	14	Spain	74.8	2.1
23	12	15	Taiwan	69.2	1.9	11	13	15	Switzerland	72.7	2.1
21	17	16	Spain	58.7	1.6	21	21	16	Mexico	65.4	1.9
30	21	17	Mexico	51.9	1.4	23	16	17	Taiwan	53.0	1.5
12	16	18	Sweden	49.3	1.4	16	19	18	Austria	47.1	1.3
40	26	19	Malaysia	45.9	1.3	19	20	19	Australia	42.4	1.2
6	19	20	Saudi Arabia	44.9	1.3	13	17	20	Sweden	41.6	1.2
8	10	21	Russia	44.0	1.2	47	22	21	Thailand	40.6	1.2
18	22	22	Australia	42.2	1.2	9	9	22	Russia	33.1	0.9
33	20	23	Austria	39.3	1.1	51	31	23	Turkey	29.8	0.9
22	25	24	Brazil	38.8	1.1	24	23	24	Denmark	29.3	0.8
35	23	25	Denmark	37.1	1.0	39	32	25	Indonesia	28.4	0.8
19	28	26	Indonesia	36.6	1.0	14	28	26	Saudi Arabia	25.9	0.7
48	31	27	Thailand	36.4	1.0	15	30	27	Brazil	25.7	0.7
29	24	28	Norway	32.0	0.9	33	29	28	India	24.0	0.7
46	29	29	Ireland	28.7	0.8	28	26	29	Norway	24.0	0.7
16	30	30	South Africa	24.1	0.7	46	27	30	Portugal	22.3	0.6
37	27	31	Finland	23.1	0.6	38	33	31	Ireland	20.6	0.6
45	35	32	India	22.7	0.6	44	38	32	Israel	20.4	0.6
39	34	33	Iran	18.1	0.5	36	36	33	Iran	19.3	0.6
—	—	34	Turkey	15.6	0.4	25	37	34	South Africa	18.3	0.5
58	37	35	Portugal	15.4	0.4	—	—	35	Philippines	17.6	0.5
—	—	36	Israel	14.8	0.4	—	—	36	Poland	17.1	0.5
27	36	37	Venezuela	14.0	0.4	30	25	37	Finland	16.7	0.5
34	38	38	Poland	13.6	0.4	42	34	38	Greece	15.6	0.4
—	—	39	Argentina	13.1	0.4	—	—	39	Argentina	15.5	0.4
—	—	40	Ukraine	12.8	0.4	40	24	40	Malaysia	12.5	0.4
			Total	$3,372	94.1%				Total	$3,242	92.5%
			World	$3,584	100.0%				World	$3,505	100.0%

Note: Figures for 1993 are estimates.

Sources: GATT, *International Trade Annual,* 1992. World Bank, *World Tables,* 1995.

EXHIBIT 2–4   Leading Exporters and Importers in World Trade in Commercial Services, 1993 ($ billions and percentage)

Rank				1993		Rank				1993	
1980	*1990*	*1993*	*Exporters*	*Value*	*Share*	*1980*	*1990*	*1993*	*Importers*	*Value*	*Share*
2	1	1	United States	$298.6	16.4%	4	2	1	United States	$237.8	12.1%
6	5	2	Japan	203.7	11.2	3	1	2	Japan	207.6	10.6
1	2	3	France	187.5	10.3	2	4	3	France	182.5	9.3
3	3	4	United Kingdom	164.0	9.0	5	5	4	United Kingdom	178.2	9.1
4	4	5	Germany	156.0	8.6	1	3	5	Germany	152.2	7.8
8	9	6	Belgium-Luxembourg	120.5	6.6	9	8	6	Belgium-Luxembourg	109.3	5.6
5	6	7	Italy	87.9	4.8	7	6	7	Italy	103.6	5.3
7	7	8	Netherlands	64.9	3.6	32	23	8	Singapore	62.9	3.2
12	11	9	Switzerland	45.0	2.5	19	13	9	Taiwan	38.3	2.0
9	8	10	Spain	39.0	2.1	6	7	10	Netherlands	38.0	1.9
10	10	11	Austria	38.5	2.1	21	20	11	Denmark	30.9	1.6
17	16	12	Denmark	35.4	1.9	17	11	12	Spain	30.6	1.6
15	13	13	Singapore	24.7	1.4	10	9	13	Canada	28.4	1.4
14	12	14	Canada	20.6	1.1	16	18	14	Austria	27.7	1.4
13	15	15	Sweden	18.3	1.0	12	10	15	Sweden	26.4	1.3
30	22	16	Taiwan	16.5	0.9	13	12	16	Switzerland	26.3	1.3
20	19	17	Korea	15.8	0.9	14	15	17	Australia	24.7	1.3
21	14	18	Hong Kong	15.8	0.9	8	16	18	Saudi Arabia	21.4	1.1
23	20	19	Australia	15.6	0.9	15	21	19	Mexico	20.5	1.0
28	27	20	China	15.3	0.8	22	30	20	Brazil	20.2	1.0
11	17	21	Norway	12.4	0.7	25	19	21	Korea	19.4	1.0
33	21	22	Thailand	12.1	0.7	11	17	22	Norway	17.7	0.9
18	18	23	Mexico	11.8	0.7	40	33	23	China	15.8	0.8
57	23	24	Turkey	9.7	0.5	—	—	24	Indonesia	15.4	0.8
16	38	25	Saudi Arabia	9.2	0.5	41	25	25	Thailand	14.4	0.7
22	24	26	Greece	9.1	0.5	—	—	26	Russia	13.0	0.7
31	28	27	Portugal	7.8	0.4	42	37	27	Ireland	13.0	0.7
29	25	28	Egypt	7.5	0.4	28	26	28	Malaysia	12.8	0.7
35	32	29	Philippines	7.4	0.4	35	24	29	Finland	11.3	0.6
41	31	30	Malaysia	7.3	0.4	31	22	30	Hong Kong	10.0	0.5
25	30	31	Israel	6.8	0.4	30	29	31	India	9.9	0.5
26	33	32	India	6.3	0.3	36	28	32	Israel	9.6	0.5
—	—	33	Kuwait	6.2	0.3	26	38	33	Argentina	8.5	0.4
—	—	34	Russia	6.0	0.3	20	31	34	South Africa	8.1	0.4
27	29	35	Finland	5.9	0.3	—	—	35	Venezuela	8.0	0.4
39	37	36	Ireland	5.2	0.3	47	34	36	Portugal	7.8	0.4
34	36	37	Brazil	4.9	0.3	—	—	37	Turkey	7.8	0.4
—	—	38	Indonesia	4.8	0.3	38	40	38	Poland	6.1	0.3
32	35	39	Poland	4.4	0.2	44	36	39	New Zealand	5.9	0.3
24	34	40	South Africa	4.2	0.2	46	39	40	Greece	5.5	0.3
			Total	$1,733	96.1%				Total	$1,766	90.1%
			World	$1,804	100.0%				World	$1,960	100.0%

Note: Figures for 1993 are estimates.

Sources: GATT, *International Trade Annual,* 1992. World Bank, *World Tables,* 1995.

Indonesia), orange juice (Brazil), apple juice (many countries), and fresh flowers (several countries in South America, the Near East, and Africa). In the years to come, it is likely that this trend will continue and that greater volumes of an increased variety of agricultural products will be exported from a wider number of countries. The other factor in trade in agricultural products over the past 15 years has been the transformation of the EU (European Union) as a whole from the largest importer to the largest exporter of agricultural products. (This development was the root cause of one of the major points of friction in the Uruguay round of the GATT negotiations. See Chapter 4.)

Foreign direct investment has become one of the major means by which companies operate internationally and by which countries are linked. Foreign direct investment (FDI) not only influences the flow of capital but also the flows of product and process technology and trade patterns and volumes. Foreign investment often flows in response to market opportunities, factor costs (such as wages), natural resource availability and cost, the political and economic stability of countries, and the international debt position of the host country. Inflows of FDI not only affect the flows of imports into a country but often, at a later time, affect its exports. Hence, monitoring the volumes and industry composition of FDI is often an early warning signal concerning future exports.

Several other features of FDI flows are of note. They are highly concentrated among relatively few countries. About three-fourths of the flows of FDI are among the high-income countries, especially within the triad of Europe, Japan, and North America. Of the FDI that flows to lower-income countries, about two-thirds is concentrated among 10 countries.[5] FDI flows tend to be more volatile over time, both in aggregate and at the country level, than are GDP, domestic investment, and trade. FDI flows declined from 1979 to 1982 as world economic growth stagnated. Starting in 1986, however, FDI boomed, growing at 28.3 percent annually through 1990, compared to growth rates of 13 percent for merchandise exports and 12 percent for nominal GDP. This increase was largely fueled by substantial increases in outward investment from Japan. In the early 1990s, FDI outflows declined, but they have recovered over the 1993 to 1995 period. By 1992 (the latest year for which data is available), global sales generated by foreign subsidiaries of multinational enterprises (MNEs) totaled $5.2 trillion, compared to world exports of goods and services (excluding factor payments) of $4.9 trillion. About a third of international trade is estimated to be intrafirm, i.e., between subsidiaries of MNEs in different countries.

Another feature of FDI is that the number of firms that have become multinational enterprises (MNEs) has increased steadily over the decades and the number of home countries in which MNEs are based has increased as well. These trends have increased the complexity of the world competitive environment. In the second half of the 1980s, Japan became the largest source country for FDI, overtaking the United States and Britain. In the mid-1990s, the United States regained first place among outward investing countries. The United States also became the largest host country for inward FDI (Exhibit 2–5).

---

[5]Note, however, that the United Nations (UNCTAD), the organization that collects these statistics, still lists Singapore, Hong Kong, Korea, and Taiwan as low-income countries.

Exhibit 2–5   FDI Statistics

	France	*Germany*	*Japan*	*United Kingdom*	*United States*	*Developing Economies*
Outflows of FDI (1989–94, $ billions)	153	124	171	140	240	125
Share of FDI outflows (1983–88, percent)	6	8	15	20	15	6
Share of FDI outflows (1989–94, percent)	12	10	13	11	19	10
Inward stock of FDI (1994, $ billions)	142	132	17	214	504	584
Percentage of world total, inward FDI stock (1994)	6	6	1	9	22	25
Outward stock of FDI (1994, $ billions)	183	206	278	281	610	148
Percentage of world total outward FDI stock (1994)	8	9	12	12	26	6

Source: United Nations, *World Investment Report,* 1995.

The Environment

The days of uncontrolled international economic growth with little consideration for the environment are over. For example, in 1993, progress on signing a North American Free Trade Agreement was in jeopardy due to U.S. concerns over whether Mexico would legislate (and enforce) environmental protection measures.

For the multinational enterprise and its managers, the task of doing business internationally has become more complicated as everyone becomes aware of the impact of economic development on the environment. Waste creation (and disposal), water supply, air quality, overfishing and overlogging, acid rain, and so forth, variously affect businesses no matter where they are located. As an example, in the Philippines some Japanese companies have complained that new environmental standards for new investments are more stringent than they are in Japan—and that even if they were willing to bear the costs of meeting them, the government does not have the equipment to test for compliance to these standards. In addition, the number of constituencies that multinational firms are potentially answerable to has increased dramatically with the heightened awareness of our interconnectedness. This has raised both ethical and legal problems for MNEs. As but one of many examples, Indonesia has relatively loose standards for water discharge from rayon plants in order to encourage investment, employment, and output in this industry to supply its downstream textile industry at low cost. What are the legal and ethical responsibilities of MNEs when choosing their technology in undertaking such an investment?

Summary

These are only a few of the facts that are useful and relevant for international managers. They can provide but a start for an understanding of the international environment in which international managers must operate. Beyond these basics, an international manager needs more product-specific information. For example, if the manager works for a garment producer, information on the top exporters and importers and the growth rates of these imports and exports of textiles and garments is needed. Which country had the largest increase in garment exports over the past 10 years? Which country's exports are most highly concentrated in garments? Which countries are gaining comparative advantage in textiles and garments and which ones are losing it? How are markets and production of textiles segmented worldwide? And so on.

Also, as described in more detail in the next chapters, increasing international trade and investment are no longer undertaken on a country-by-country basis, but rather are undertaken on a regional, even global basis. This complicates the analysis manyfold.

An incredible amount and variety of data are available to managers. Knowledge of appropriate international data and the skills to interpret this data are an important start in reaching effective international management decisions.

Supplementary Reading

CIA. *The CIA World Factbook.*Washington, D.C.: CIA, annual editions; also available on CD-ROM and at http://www.odci.gov/cia.

IMD. *The World Competitiveness Yearbook 1996.* Lausanne: IMD, 1996; a summary is also available at http://www.imd.ch.

World Economic Forum. *1996 Global Competitiveness Report.* Geneva: World Economic Forum, 1996.

Kurian, George. *The New Book of World Rankings.* 3rd ed. New York: Facts on File, 1991.

Kidron, Michael, and Ronald Segal. *The State of the World Atlas.* 5th ed. New York: Penguin Books, 1995.

The World Bank. *The World Bank Atlas.* Washington, D.C.: The World Bank, annual editions.

Dreifus, Shirley B., and Michael Moynihan. *The World Market Atlas.* New York: Business International Corporation, annual editions.

3   THE WORLD OF INTERNATIONAL TRADE

International trade has been carried on between countries and geographical regions for thousands of years. Over the centuries, international trade, although periodically interrupted by wars and natural disasters, has gradually expanded, usually at a faster pace than the expansion of world output. The impetus for the existence and expansion of international trade is the same as that for any commercial transaction: value creation. International trade creates value for both producers and consumers. International trade increases demand for exportable products, thereby raising prices and volumes. It increases the supply of importable products, thereby reducing prices and increasing product availability and variety for consumers. International trade increases the efficiency of resource allocation worldwide, reduces production costs through economies of scale, and lowers input costs.

International trade can also lead to increased exposure for both firms and countries to the forces in the international economy: changes in prices and demand in export markets, changes in prices and supply of imported products, and changes in exchange rates. The increased openness to the international economic environment can increase the variability of a firm's profits and of a nation's GNP growth rate and hence increase the risks of a firm's operations and reduce the stability of a country's economy. International trade can also lead to disruption and restructuring as domestic firms are forced to compete with less expensive or higher quality imported products. On the other hand, international trade can allow firms to diversify away from dependence on demand in one country and can allow a country to diversify its economy through exports.

Every major firm is affected by international trade in one way or another: as an exporter; as an importer; as a competitor with imports; or as a financial institution involved in trade finance, foreign exchange markets, and international debt management. Similarly, the economies and firms in every country are impacted by international trade flows—and there is every likelihood that these effects will increase into the foreseeable future.

This chapter was prepared by Donald J. Lecraw.

A knowledge of international trade—the forces behind it and the means by which it is carried out—is essential to all business managers, not just to those directly engaged in international business operations. International trade, exporting and importing, is often the first form of international operations for firms in the manufacturing, natural resource, energy, and agricultural sectors. In 1994, world trade exceeded $4.2 trillion, up from $1.8 trillion in 1984.

International trade is inextricably linked with foreign direct investment, international technology transfer, and international finance: International trade often leads to foreign direct investment, which in turn often changes trade flows and patterns. Trade also leads to international financial flows and, in turn, trade is affected by foreign exchange availability and exchange rate movements. Technology transfer is often accomplished through international trade in capital goods and, in turn, technology transfer leads to trade in raw materials and semifinished and final products.

The International Trade Environment in the Late 1990s

In the 1970s, international trade was one of the major driving forces behind world economic expansion. The real value (the volume) of world exports expanded nearly threefold (10.2 percent per year on average) between 1970 and 1980 (from $700 billion to $2 trillion in constant 1980 dollars). This expansion was fostered by falling tariff and nontariff barriers to trade in most countries, decreased transportation and communication costs, and by the export-oriented growth strategies of many countries during this period. During the global recession in the early 1980s, world trade declined in real terms by a greater amount than did world GDP. The decline in world trade worsened the recession in many countries. From 1984 to 1994, however, world export volume grew by almost 70 percent. (See Exhibit 3–1 for the growth rates in international trade and world output. Notice that when world output growth is relatively high, the growth of trade exceeds it—and vice versa.)

As shown in Exhibit 2–3 on page 28, measured in terms of combined imports and exports, the United States is the largest trading nation in the world, with 14.0 percent of world exports and 15.1 percent of world imports in 1993. The relative trading power of the United States, which had fallen over the past several decades, improved in the early 1990s. The positions of Italy, Canada, the Netherlands, and Belgium also have improved, while those of Russia, Saudi Arabia, and Sweden have fallen. The most dramatic changes come from export-oriented newly industrializing countries (NICs), such as Korea, Singapore, and Taiwan. Countries of the ASEAN (Association of Southeast Asian Nations) region, such as Thailand and Malaysia, have made dramatic improvements, as have Latin American countries like Mexico. The effects of China's "open door policy" are also evident.

The rise in the real value of the U.S. dollar from 1978 through early 1985 had a severe negative impact on U.S. exporters and import-competing industries.[1] The fall of

---

[1]The concept of the "real value" of a currency is treated further on in this chapter. In short, the real value of a country's currency (its real exchange rate) increases (decreases) if changes in its nominal exchange rate are greater (less) than the differential inflation rates between it and its trading partners (when exchange rates are expressed in terms of the amount of foreign currency that can be purchased with one unit of domestic currency).

**EXHIBIT 3–1   Volume of World Trade and Output, 1980–1993
(average annual percentage change)**

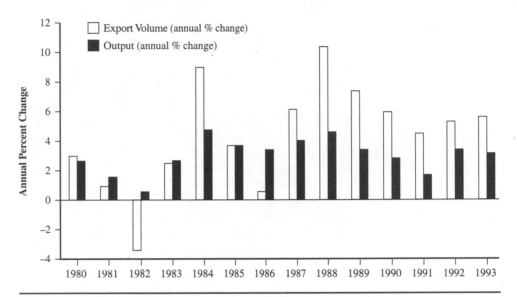

Source: IMF, *International Financial Statistics Yearbook,* 1995.

the U.S. dollar from 1985 to 1988 led to a strong recovery of U.S. exports and a reduction in the growth rate of imports. Export volume increased by 68 percent from 1985 to 1991, while import volume increased by 20 percent. In early 1993, the U.S. economy was expanding while the economies of its major trading partners—such as Canada, Germany, and Japan—continued with slow or negative growth. This situation led to increased trade deficits as import growth exceeded export growth. By 1994, the trade deficit of the U.S. had increased to $166 billion.

Until the early 1980s, the U.S. current account was roughly in balance. Since 1982, however, its trade deficits have led to substantial current account deficits totaling $1,260 billion over the 1982 to 1995 period. Current account deficits translate roughly into surpluses on the capital account. Hence, the United States went from being a net creditor with the rest of the world of about $400 billion to a net debtor of about $900 billion in 1994. If the United States is to stop going further and further into debt with the rest of the world, its trade balance will have to improve in the last half of the 1990s following its deterioration in the first half of the 1990s. The trade deficit will have to become a trade surplus to compensate for the interest and dividends on its accumulated international debt and net inward foreign direct investment. The longer this reversal from a trade deficit to a trade surplus is delayed, the greater the eventual surplus will have to be—otherwise U.S. international indebtedness will continue to rise.

As the trade deficit in the United States declined starting in the late 1980s through the early 1990s, its trading partners had to absorb about a $90 billion annual turnaround on their trade accounts through increased import growth rates and decreased export growth rates. This had a depressing effect on their economies, while at the same time it spurred U.S. economic growth. The deterioration of the U.S. trade account from 1991 to 1995 reduced U.S. economic growth and increased growth for its trading partners. If the U.S. trade deficit is to become a trade surplus, the trade accounts of its partners will have to accommodate this through substantial increases in import growth rates and a slowing of export growth rates. Most developing countries are not in a position to increase imports or decrease exports; they have debt problems of their own. If anything, their goals are to accelerate export growth. The oil exporters will not absorb it; oil prices will be stable at best and U.S. imports of oil will continue to rise.

That leaves Japan, some European countries, Canada and the NICs of Asia—such as Taiwan, South Korea, Singapore, and Hong Kong—to make the adjustment. Yet no country wants to reduce export or increase import growth rates for fear of reducing its own economic growth rate. One reaction to the U.S. trade and international debt problems has been a rise in protectionism, as each country has tried to shift the adjustment costs onto someone else. From 1980 to 1988, the percentage of U.S. imports under some form of nontariff restraint rose from 8 to 24 percent. These trade restraints cost U.S. consumers tens (some say hundreds) of billions of dollars per year. The United States has also enacted trade legislation that requires the government each year to assemble a "hit list" of countries that are not dealing fairly with American exports, investments, or intellectual property (patents and trademarks). This list is then used as a basis of negotiations with these countries, and in the event the outcomes of these negotiations are not satisfactory, used to impose trade sanctions. The rancor of the trade disputes between the U.S. and Japan and China was in part due to the United States' mounting trade deficits.

Major political leaders may also have significant implications for the world trade environment. The Uruguay round of GATT negotiations resulted in the establishment of the World Trade Organization (WTO) and produced some of the most basic changes to the GATT since it was implemented in 1947. In North and South America, the Free Trade Area of the Americas (FTAA) is under negotiation among 34 nations in the American hemisphere for completion in 2005. Yet in the political campaign of 1996, NAFTA itself has come under attack by some U.S. politicians as being detrimental to U.S. interests.

The gains from the negotiation and implementation of trading agreements such as GATT, NAFTA, and FTAA can be great. The conclusion of the Uruguay round of negotiations is expected to result in global income gains of $230 billion per year by the year 2005 (in 1992 dollars). More than half of this income gain is expected to go to developed countries, and one-third of the gain will accrue to developing countries. Most of the reductions in protection were in the manufacturing sector. Services received almost no liberalization, while agriculture received some limited reduction in protection.

Liberalization in the agriculture sector would affect the European Community to a large degree. Prior to the conclusion of the Uruguay round, trade-distorting policies in the European Union under the Common Agricultural Policy (CAP) turned the EU from the largest net importer of food products to the largest net food exporter in less than two decades. The CAP cost the EU between $40 billion and $50 billion per year in direct subsidies. The CAP cost consumers in the EU countries roughly an equal amount in higher prices and added 4 percent to the unemployment rate in Europe. In the late 1980s, it precipitated the largest trade war in 40 years, as the United States and Canada responded to agricultural subsidies in Europe with massive increases in the subsidies to their own farmers.[2]

The Uruguay round of the GATT resulted in some reductions in agriculture protection. Nontariff barriers to trade in agriculture were converted to tariff equivalents, which were scheduled for reduction in the future. The extension of GATT over trade in agricultural products was important in placing agricultural trade under firmer international regulations, and for setting the stage for future gains over time and in later negotiations. The establishment of the WTO also helps to alleviate fears of the development of a "fortress Europe" for exporters from Japan and North America.

Prior to the Uruguay round, North America's other large trading partner, Japan, had reduced its explicit tariff and nontariff barriers to trade on most products to levels below those in most other countries and had ceased its policy of undervaluing its exchange rate (to increase exports and reduce imports). In the first half of the 1990s, the yen continued its appreciation against major currencies in the world, and especially against the U.S. dollar. By the end of 1995, 100 yen could purchase $1 U.S., a marked change from the 240 yen required for $1 U.S. in 1985. Despite the appreciation of the yen, however, Japan has continued to run ever increasing merchandise trade surpluses. Japan's real exchange rate appreciated by over 60 percent from 1985 to 1994. Over the same period, however, although export volume grew by less than 20 percent while import volume doubled, its trade surplus rose from $56 billion to $146 billion. These mounting trade surpluses have often brought Japan's trading policies under the scrutiny of its major trading partners.

Japan's domestic market structure and its international trade are dominated by large trading houses and industrial groups. (For details, see the note on *keiretsu* appended to the Northern Telecom in Japan case.) Its distribution channels for manufactured products have proven difficult at best for Western exporters to penetrate. The Japanese government has also continued to follow a mercantilist trade strategy toward high-technology trade products in emerging industries, such as telecommunications and computers, through a combination of direct subsidies, market protection, and government purchasing regulations. Under duress, Japan has agreed to replace quantitative restrictions on rice imports with tariffs, but the replacement process has been slow and the initial tariffs were on the order of 700 percent.

One view of Japan's future trade and economic strategies has been graphically expressed by Mr. Morita (chairman of the board of Sony) and Mr. Ishihara (an

---

[2]Direct agricultural subsidies took up to two-thirds of the European Union budget. Direct agricultural subsidies *per farmer* in 1989 ranged from $4,000 in Australia to $10,000 in the EC, $16,000 in Canada and Japan, $21,000 in the United States, and $30,000 in Sweden. (As quoted in Clayton Yeuter, "Back 40 Blues," *The World in 1990.* London, Economist Publications, 1990.) These subsidies do not include subsidies via artificially high prices, which are more prevalent in Europe, Canada, and Japan than in the United States.

elected official) in *The Japan That Can Say "No."* They foresee a Japan that is largely independent of U.S. economic and political pressures and has reoriented itself toward leading a trading bloc of the countries of the Asia-Pacific Rim, including China. Although there have been proposals for the formation of a formal East Asian trading bloc with Japan as a major player, as yet these have not come to fruition. However, Japan's foreign direct investment and trade activities in Southeast and East Asia are contributing to the economic integration of the national economies of this region.

Among developing countries, there are also major pressures on the trade system. In general throughout the 1980s and the first half of the 1990s, the governments of most developing countries moved toward a more liberal position in international trade, both to expand exports and to open their economies to imports. Developing countries have often faced export markets made difficult to penetrate by tight regulations, and this difficulty has contributed to pressure and discontent with the international trade system on the part of developing countries, particularly as it applies to trade in labor-intensive products such as textiles, clothing, and footwear.

The conditions of trade established during the Uruguay round help to alleviate some of the pressure and discontent with international trade. Developing countries such as Indonesia, Malaysia, the Republic of Korea, and Thailand stand to benefit most from the new trading agreements. These countries, which are highly competitive exporters of textiles and clothing, have been committed to the liberalization of trade in agriculture and manufacturing. The elimination of the Multifibre Arrangement (a voluntary export restraint agreement), for example, enables these countries to expand their production of low-cost, labor-intensive products. Countries in South Asia (India, Nepal, Pakistan, and Bangladesh) are similarly expected to benefit from the Uruguay round; however, China, Taiwan, and Russia are not expected to gain as much because they are not WTO members.

There are other areas of uncertainty—both opportunity and risk—for firms engaged in international trade: the drive for modernization and deregulation in the economies of the People's Republic of China and in India; continued economic and political reforms in the eastern European countries; the reversion of Hong Kong to Chinese political control; and the emergence of Japan as a leading country for technology generation, trade, international capital, and foreign direct investment. Yet, it is within this environment that firms must compete in world trade markets if they are to survive, much less prosper.

In short, the pressures on the international trading system during the remainder of the 1990s are enormous. These pressures were felt during the Uruguay round of trade negotiations. The negotiations were marked by the division of the participants over some issues, including trade in agricultural products, intellectual property (patents and trademarks), trade in services, trade-related investment measures, and further market access for developing countries. Headway was made on several of these issues, while other issues such as services received little in reduction of protection and remain fresh territory for future negotiations.

This is the world of international trade.

A Framework for International Trade

The international trading environment is complex and ever changing. To manage international trade operations within this environment, a framework of analysis is useful. A framework can be used to disentangle the many factors that drive international flows of goods and services. This section presents one possible framework for analyzing a firm's international trade environment.

To simplify the exposition of this framework, the initial viewpoint will be of a firm with production operations in a single country as it analyzes trade operations with another country. Although this viewpoint is obviously unrealistic in a world of global competition with complex trading arrangements and in which some 33 percent of international trade is carried out by multinational enterprises (MNEs) at the intrafirm level, it can serve as a reasonable starting point for our analysis. Further on, this simple framework will be expanded to include multicountry and multifirm trade. Subsequent chapters will describe global sourcing and the complex trade and investment relationships that exist within and between multinational enterprises.

An Overview of the Trade Framework
A Framework for Trade Analysis

1. The Social, Technological, Economic, and Political (STEP) system and how this system affects the firm's comparative and competitive advantage.
2. Countries abroad as markets for exports and sources of imports.
3. Tariff and nontariff barriers to trade and government incentives to promote trade.
4. Linking producers and buyers through trade intermediaries.

The Step System and Comparative and Competitive Advantage

Each firm operates within the social, technological, economic, and political (STEP) environment of the country in which it produces. The STEP environment has a strong influence on the firm: the cost, quality, and range of products it produces, domestic demand for its products, the product and process technology it uses, its efficiency and scale of operations, the cost and availability of natural resources and factor inputs, such as capital and labor, the range of support industries, and how and where it markets its products. The firm's STEP environment influences the *comparative* advantage of the products it produces relative to products produced by other firms abroad. The firm's STEP environment may also influence its *competitive* advantage in the national market and abroad. Trends in this STEP environment relative to the trends in the STEP environment of other countries have a strong influence on a firm's ability to enter or to continue international trading operations.[3]

---

[3]See Paul Beamish, "European Foreign Investment: Why Go to Canada," *European Management Journal,* Vol. 14, No. 1, 1996, for an application of the STEP analysis.

For example, Singapore's rapid economic development over the past 15 years has led to a substantial rise in real wages relative to those in most other countries. In response to this change in Singapore's comparative advantage in labor-intensive products, firms in the export-oriented, labor-intensive garment industry became less and less competitive on world markets, that is, they lost their comparative advantage arising from Singapore's past relatively low labor costs and high worker efficiency. In response to this change, some firms have changed their *comparative* advantage in the production of low-cost, low-quality, standardized garments to a *comparative* advantage in high-quality designer garments (based on Singapore's relatively low-wage skilled workers). Alternatively, other firms have invested abroad. To do this, they have utilized their competitive advantage in managing a low-wage labor force and in their channels of distribution from Singapore to other lower-wage countries onto export markets. Firms that could not respond to these changes in Singapore's comparative advantage with changes in their competitive advantage have gone out of business. Changes in all the elements of the STEP system in which the firm operates can have similar effects on its ability to export or to compete with imports. In other countries, social pressures have led to implementation of strict environmental protection measures. These measures have changed the comparative advantage of heavy, pollution-intensive industries, such as steel, chemicals, and pulp and paper, in these countries. Government policies and economic forces can influence the location of technology generation and its diffusion within the country and worldwide by subsidizing these industries in a number of ways. These policies have changed the comparative advantage of some countries in technology-intensive industries.

The STEP system in which a firm operates—and how it responds to and influences comparative and competitive advantage—forms the first block in the analytical framework. This emphasis on the effects of a firm's external environment on its ability to trade is not meant to be deterministic, however. A firm can develop a competitive advantage that enables it to export even though the STEP system in its home country places it at a comparative disadvantage. Kaufman Shoes in Canada exports work boots and after-ski boots worldwide. Kaufman has developed a competitive advantage based on quality, style, and design that has allowed it to compete internationally even though the shoe industry as a whole in Canada is at a comparative disadvantage in international trade. Similarly, in the mid-1980s, Proton component televisions were developed in Taiwan by contracting for state-of-the-art U.S. design technology. By this means Proton developed a competitive advantage at the very top end of the line in televisions, despite Taiwan's comparative disadvantage in state-of-the-art technology generation (as opposed to technology transfer and adaptation). For both these firms, however, the STEP systems in which they operate do not foster their competitive advantage; rather, they detract from it. Kaufman must constantly strive to maintain its competitive advantage in quality, design, and style over firms in lower-wage countries whose skills on these dimensions are increasing year by year. Similarly, when Proton failed to continue to upgrade its technology by further purchases from abroad, firms in Japan, the United States, and Europe with in-house technology generation capabilities (which Proton lacked) matched its quality at a lower price.

A competitive advantage based on government subsidies (when the country does not have and cannot develop a comparative advantage in the firm's products) is always at risk if funding for these programs is reduced or they are terminated. The budget constraints under which many countries are operating in the 1990s have placed, and will continue to place, pressure on subsidies that come out of the government budgets. As an extreme ex-ample, Indonesia has fostered the development of a main-frame aircraft producer, IPTN, through heavy direct government subsidies and a monopoly on the captive market in Indonesia. When these subsidies were terminated and the domestic market dried up, IPTN faced extreme difficulties. A similar conclusion would hold for agribusiness firms in Europe and Japan, for example, which rely on heavy government protection and subsidies.

Conversely, a country may have a comparative advantage in a product, but producers in the country may not be able to turn it into a competitive advantage either in export markets or in their domestic market. This situation often results when the governments in other countries are heavily subsidizing or protecting their own producers. Exports of palm-oil-based products in Southeast Asia are impeded by subsidies and barriers to trade in the United States and Europe designed to protect domestic producers of vegetable oils; sugar producers in the Philippines have often faced world prices below their production costs, even though the Philippines has a comparative advantage in sugar; U.S. exports of computers, telecommunications equipment, and aircraft are impeded by national programs in Europe, Brazil, Japan, and elsewhere.

Market Identification

For a firm with both a comparative and competitive advantage that give it the potential to undertake ongoing exports, the next step in the analysis is to identify markets abroad to which it can export its product. This step entails analysis of trends in demand arising from changes in population, income levels, and consumer preferences in potential export markets. If there is a demand for the firm's products in a market, the supply capabilities of domestic firms and other exporters worldwide to meet this demand at lower prices or higher quality must be assessed. For example, paper consumption in Japan has risen rapidly with the rise in Japan's GNP and consumer incomes. Concerns with environmental pollution have placed restrictions on the ability of its pulp manufacturers to increase output to meet this demand. This trend toward an imbalance between demand and supply has created the potential for increased exports to Japan for both pulp and paper products. Japanese pulp and paper firms have also responded to this trend by locating production facilities abroad to produce pulp for their downstream paper production facilities. For a pulp and paper producer in North America, the analysis would then revolve around the issue of whether these developments present an opportunity to increase exports to Japan. The analysis of export markets forms the second block in the framework.

Impediments to Trade

The third block of analysis concerns the impediments to trade flows, both natural ones, such as transportation costs, and measures governments have taken to impede or to facilitate the linking of producers and buyers through international trade. Government policies to restrict and to promote trade can have a decisive influence on (1) trade flows, (2) the competitive position of firms in export markets, (3) the availability and price of imports, and (4) the ability of firms to compete with imports. Hence, an analysis of the level and trends in tariff and nontariff barriers to trade is an essential component of the international trade framework. Governments can also facilitate exports directly by such measures as concessional export financing, export subsidies, differential taxation of export earnings, and financing for export market development.

Trade Intermediaries

If the firm has a competitive advantage *and* if there is demand for its product in an export market *and* if government intervention in the international trade system (or through movements in real exchange rates) does not prevent the producer from accessing buyers in the export market, the final area of analysis concerns the linkages of producers in one country to buyers in the export market. A competitive product and a receptive market are not enough; the product must somehow be transported from the factory to the point of shipment (port or airport) to export market, be received in the export market, clear customs, move through distribution channels to the point of sale, be sold to the customer, and be serviced after sale. International channels of distribution are often long, multilayered, complex, difficult to analyze and understand, and expensive to access or to develop. Channel costs may represent three times the production cost of a product.

Marketing in a country with which a producer is not familiar can present substantial problems as well. The success or failure of a firm's export initiative may stand or fall on the pricing, promotion, advertising, and distribution policies it follows in export markets. These subjects are examined in more detail in the next chapter.

The framework presented above may seem quite complicated at first, but it represents the bare bones of the international trading system in which exporters and importers must manage their trade operations. Each block in this analytical framework is examined in more detail in the next sections of this chapter and in the following chapter.

Comparative and Competitive Advantage

It is important for managers of firms engaged in international trade to understand the driving forces behind the international flow of goods and services. As with any form of voluntary exchange between independent, value-maximizing agents, international trade takes place when value is created for the participants in the transaction above the value they can receive through alternative uses of their resources. Put more bluntly, trade must be profitable for both the seller and the buyer or it will not continue—at least over the long run.

For the exporter, the value of international trade comes from some combination of higher prices, increased volume, decreased costs (through economies of scale and learning by doing), and the effects of international trade on product quality and design. For the importer, value may be created through lower prices, greater variety, increased quality, and diversification of sources of supply. International trade operations may also affect the risks faced by importers and exporters alike: risks may be decreased by diversifying sales among several markets and sources among several producers; risks may be increased through greater exposure to the effects of trade restrictions, exchange-rate movements, and demand, supply, and price fluctuations in foreign markets. Managers of international trade operations must balance the effects of international trade on both profits and risks in order to maximize the value of the firm through its international trade operations.

Managers must bear in mind that the goal of international trade operations is to increase the value of the firm; exports for exports' sake (except in the short run to gain market share) are not the goal. Similarly, for countries, the goal of international trade is not to increase exports (and to decrease imports), but rather to increase national income through international trade. Exports in general and of a specific product are *not* "good" in and of themselves, and imports in general or of specific products are *not* "bad." Yet this view often seems to be the presumption behind the policies of governments around the world as they try to promote exports and to impede imports in general and of specific products.

In fact, exports might be considered "bad." A nation's resources—labor, capital, technology, natural resources—are used to produce exports, but consumers abroad receive the benefits of consuming them and they reduce the supply of goods available for domestic consumption. Imports could be considered "good." They are produced using the resources of other countries, but are consumed domestically and they increase the goods and services available for domestic use. Exports are only "good" to the extent that the receipts from export sales allow a country to finance imports or to service its accumulated international debt. Similarly, accumulating foreign exchange reserves is beneficial only to the extent that these reserves may allow a country to smooth out the effects of short-term fluctuations in export receipts and import payments and to import products in the future. These facts are difficult for individuals and governments to accept.

This view of value creation as the driving force behind international trade raises the question of what factors lead a firm (or a country) to produce a product for export or to import a product from abroad. How and why is value created when some products are exported and others imported? To understand the answer to this most fundamental question of international trade requires a (short) digression into the theory of international trade. Understanding this theory is important to managers. International trade theory can be thought of as the fundamental tides beneath the turbulent waves of day-to-day international trade activity. Understanding both the tides and the waves of international trade is important for managers engaged in international trade operations.

Absolute and Comparative Advantage

Consider the two countries, *A* and *B,* which produce two products, *X* and *Y,* with labor as the only input to the production process. Before trade, country *A* produces and consumes 16 units of product *X,* using 8 hours of labor, and produces and consumes 4 units of product *Y* using 4 hours of labor. Country *B* produces and consumes

EXHIBIT 3–2   Absolute Advantage

	Output		Output/Hour			
	X	Y	X	Y	Labor Hours	Py/Px
Country A	16	4	2	1	12	2
Country B	4	4	1	2	6	½
Total output (no trade)	20	8				
Total output (trade)	24	12				

4 units of X using 4 hours of labor, and produces and consumes 4 units of Y using 2 hours of labor (Exhibit 3–2). In country A, the price of Y relative to X would be 2 (since it takes twice as long to produce a unit of Y as it does to produce a unit of X); in country B the price ratio is ½ (since it takes half as long to produce a unit of Y as it does to produce a unit of X). Country A has an *absolute* advantage in product X; country B has an absolute advantage in product Y. If the two countries are opened to trade, country A will tend to specialize in product X and country B will tend to specialize in product Y. If there is total specialization, country A could produce 24 units of X (12 hours times 2 units per hour) and country B could produce 12 units of Y (6 hours times 2 units per hour), compared to total production of 20 units of X and 8 units of Y with no trade. With international trade, both more X and more Y are produced and consumed and both countries are better off. Under trade, the price of Y relative to X will fall somewhere between 2 and ½.

The gains from trade may not be shared equally, however. For country A, producers and workers in the Y industry and heavy consumers of product X have lost; the Y producers have gone out of business, the Y workers have had to shift to the production of X, and X consumers are facing higher prices for X. Producers and workers in the X industry and heavy consumers of Y have won. The same applies to country B; producers and workers in the X industry and heavy consumers of X have won. Overall, however, both countries have gained, since there is more output to be consumed in both countries. The distribution of the gains among the two countries is also uncertain. In general, the smaller the country and the greater its absolute advantage in one product relative to the absolute advantage of the other country, the greater its share of the gains. A small, natural-resource-intensive country like New Zealand has more to gain from trade than a large country with a more balanced economy such as the United States.

Now consider two other countries, C and D, producing X and Y (Exhibit 3–3). Country C produces 12 units of X in 3 hours and four units of Y in 2 hours; country D produces 7 units of X in 7 hours and 7 units of Y in 7 hours. Notice that country D is less efficient in producing *both* products. But trade is still possible and yields gains. With trade, country C will specialize in X, while country D will specialize in Y, since the ratio of C's efficiency in X relative to Y is higher than that in D. If there is total specialization, then country C could produce 20 units of X and country D

EXHIBIT 3–3   Comparative Advantage

	Output		Output/Hour			
	X	Y	X	Y	*Labor Hours*	*Py/I*
Country *C*	12	4	4	2	5	2
Country *D*	7	7	1	1	14	1
Total output (no trade)	19	11				
Total output (trade)	20	14				

---

could produce 14 units of *Y*. Before trade, total production was just 19 units of *X* and 11 units of *Y*. The important point here is: Even if one country is more efficient in *both* products, there are still gains for each country through trade. In this example, since country *D* is less efficient than country *C* in both products, with trade, although both countries have gained, incomes will still be higher in *D* than in *C*. To be more concrete, even if both steel producers and garment producers in the United States were more productive than steel and garment producers in India, there would still be gains for both countries if the United States produced steel and India produced garments. This is the theory of *comparative* advantage.

For managers, there are two lessons to be learned from this analysis. It is important to understand what factors contribute to the comparative advantage of both country *C* in product *X* and country *D* in product *Y*. The reason is *not* that producers in country *C* are more or less efficient than those in country *D*. The important factor is the *ratio* of the efficiency in the two industries in country *C* *compared* to their *ratio* in country *D*. If, through technology generation or transfer, education programs, and so on, producers of product *X* in country *D* improve their efficiency to above 2 units per hour (and assuming that all other producers do not increase their efficiencies), then country *D* would become a net exporter of *X*, *even though* there had been no changes in the relative efficiency of producers in country *C and* even through producers of *X* in country *C* were still more efficient than those in country *D*. Such a situation has occurred in such products as orange and apple juices, canned pineapples, tomatoes, and cut flowers. Producers in developing countries have increased their efficiencies through transfer of agricultural technology and reduced transportation costs over the past decade to the point where they have a comparative advantage in these products. In analyzing the effects of trade on an industry, the important factor is the comparison of these two ratios among trading partners and how they change over time.

Pineapple producers and canners in Hawaii are the most efficient in the world. Yet over time, the efficiency of producers in other countries has increased rapidly, and first Taiwan, then Thailand, and more recently Indonesia have displaced Hawaiian producers from the market and forced them to close. A similar situation has occurred for garment producers in North America. They are highly efficient and their efficiency has increased over time relative to many other manufacturing industries. Yet the efficiency of garment manufacturers in low-wage countries has increased even more rapidly compared to the efficiency of other producers in these countries. The result has been the gradual decline of garment manufacturers in North America and the rise of exports from first Japan, then from Korea, Taiwan, and Hong Kong, and more recently from Thailand, India, China, Turkey, and Indonesia.

Although the theories of absolute and comparative advantage as presented above involve only two countries producing two products and using one factor of production with a constant return-to-scale production function, they can be generalized to many countries, many products, many factors' inputs, and diminishing returns to scale. The conclusions of this more complicated analysis generally are the same as those for the simple analysis presented above: Trade enhances the welfare of both countries, but the distribution of these gains among participants within each country and among the countries is not uniform. The more complicated theories also show that:

1. Trade improves the relative welfare of the factors of production that are used intensively in the exported product. For example, if a country exports steel (a capital-intensive product), the welfare of those who have capital will be improved relative to those who supply labor.

2. If labor and capital are immobile among sectors, then the returns to the factors of production (labor and capital) in the exporting industry will improve relative to those in the importing sector.

3. The welfare of consumers of the exported products will decline relative to consumers of imported products (since prices of the exported product will rise relative to the imported product). For example, if a country exports food and imports consumer durables, the welfare of the poor, whose budgets contain a relatively high proportion for food, will decline relative to the rich, who can afford consumer durables.

4. Countries will tend to export products that use their relatively inexpensive and abundant factors of production intensively. For example, a country in which labor is relatively inexpensive compared to capital will export labor-intensive products and import capital-intensive ones.

5. Trade brings about an equalization of the returns to factors of production; that is, trade tends to equalize capital costs and wage rates among countries over time.

The overriding conclusion of this analysis is that a country will *always* have a comparative advantage in some product groups. The product groups may change over time, however. A situation will never arise in which a country will lose comparative advantage in almost all product groups and not gain it in others. High wages do not make a country noncompetitive on export markets. They make it uncompetitive in labor-intensive products. A deteriorating trade deficit is not a sign of a loss of comparative advantage. As discussed below, it is a sign that the country's real exchange rate has risen to an inappropriate level. The U.S. trade deficit in the 1980s was not due to the loss of its comparative advantage. The United States still had a comparative advantage in some products (although the products in which it had a comparative advantage might have changed). The U.S. trade problems came largely from an appreciation of its real exchange rate over the 1977–85 period. Over this period the real exchange rate of the U.S. dollar rose by almost 50 percent against the currencies of its trading partners. The exchange-rate appreciation had the effect of pricing products in which the United States had a comparative advantage out of world markets.

New Theories of International Trade

The theories of absolute and comparative advantage are most easily used to explain interindustry trade, that is, trade in which one country exports a product of industry *X* and imports a product of industry *Y*. But much of international trade is composed of *intra*industry trade, that is, trade among countries in products in the same industry. France both exports and imports garments; the United States both exports and imports steel; England both exports and imports consumer electronics, and so on. In fact, a majority of the trade in manufactured products among high-income countries is comprised of intraindustry trade.[4]

There are basically two explanations for intraindustry trade. The first is well within the framework of comparative advantage as presented above. France exports high-quality, high-fashion garments and imports low-quality, standard ones; the United States imports standard steels and exports specialized steels; England imports mass-market consumer electronics and exports state-of-the-art ones, and so on. Each country, then, is exporting the products that make intensive use of its relatively abundant factors of production (fashion designers, steel technologists, and sound engineers).

This is only part of the explanation, however. In industries in which there are economies of scale in production, R&D, distribution, advertising, and sales operations, a firm may be able to establish a *competitive* advantage in the domestic and international market. Duralex glasses, Bally shoes, YKK zippers, and Heineken beer are examples of products that have successfully established a sustainable competitive advantage based on economies of scale and product differentiation.

Once a firm has achieved a competitive advantage based on scale economies or product differentiation (through branding, R&D, or design), it may be able to use its current competitive position to erect barriers to entry for other, later entrants. One way to do this is to signal implicit or explicit threats to potential competitors that the firm will lower prices or increase volumes if entry does occur. If incumbent firms were to follow through with this threat, new entrants might find themselves in an untenable position. To gain market share they would have to price below established producers (due to brand loyalty), yet, initially, their costs would be high due to their initial small market share (and hence pro-duction volumes) and their limited experience. Barriers to entry are especially high in industries in which there are large economies of scale (implying high up-front capital investments), large initial R&D expenditures, and high cost to establishing a brand name. In such industries, if incumbent firms are far

---

[4]The percentage of intraindustry trade in international trade depends on the definition used for "industry": the broader the definition, the greater the percentage. For example, the percentage of intraindustry trade in "textiles and garments" is higher than it would be for "men's T-shirts."

down on the learning curve, operating at efficient scale, or have a considerable degree of brand loyalty, these threats may be sufficiently "credible" to dissuade potential entrants from starting production.

There is another set of conditions that some groups of firms and whole industries in some countries have been able to develop, which has allowed them to achieve and sustain a competitive advantage in world trade. Rarely is a firm a freestanding entity that can produce all the necessary inputs for production, perform all the design and R&D for product development, and provide all the marketing and after-sales services by itself. Firms most often rely on a wide variety of suppliers for inputs, outside design and R&D firms for design and product development, and a wide range of sales and after-sales support firms. In some regions and some countries, industry clusters have developed over time. Ideas are exchanged among personnel of these firms. A trade infrastructure is built up to support them, with elements internal to the firms, in separate support firms, and in transportation and communications systems. The demand by this cluster of firms for specific job skills is met in part by in-house training and in part by government programs that set up an education system to provide workers with those skills. This view of how international competitive advantage can be created and sustained has been most forcefully presented by Michael Porter in *The Competitive Advantage of Nations*. In the first chapter of this book a list of 100 industry clusters is presented for 10 countries. To pick a few examples: food additives and furniture in Denmark; cutlery and printing presses in Germany; ceramic tiles, footwear, and wool fabrics in Italy; air-conditioning machinery, musical instruments, and forklift trucks in Japan; pianos, travel goods, and wigs in Korea; ship repair and apparel in Singapore; mining equipment, environment control equipment, and refrigerated shipping in Sweden; dyestuffs, heating controls, and survey equipment in Switzerland; confectionary, auctioneering, and electrical generation equipment in the United Kingdom; and detergents, agricultural chemicals, and motion pictures in the United States. In Canada (not covered in Porter's book), a similar situation exists for packaging equipment. Often these industries are clustered geographically as well as nationally.

Porter concludes that among the firms and supporting infrastructure in these clusters there are substantial economies of scale, positive spillover effects (externalities), and interlinkages that cannot be replicated in another country or region unless a similar cluster is developed. Such development can be extremely difficult, since the whole of the cluster is greater than the sum of its parts. Hence, substantial parts of the cluster must exist before the individual firms can compete internationally. Porter also concludes that it is possible for countries to foster the development of clusters through government action to influence de-mand patterns, education and training programs, industry protection, and trade promotion. For example, at one time the United States, the United Kingdom, and Sweden had clusters in shipbuilding. But first Japan and more recently Korea have been able to develop clusters in these industries and out-compete them internationally. Similar shifts in the location of clusters have occurred in cars, semiconductors, apparel, and footwear.

In other instances, even a concerted attempt to develop a cluster has not been successful. For example, in the late 1970s and early 1980s as wages rose in Japan, the apparel industry there tried to develop a sustainable competitive advantage in high-fashion clothing. The design schools of Europe were flooded with students from Japan and Japanese high-fashion houses were developed. Despite the success of some firms, such as Hanae Mori and Isye Myake, the clothing industry in Japan has continued to decline.

"First-mover advantages" and the presence of industry clusters can be overcome by new entrants with sufficient resources to bear the initial losses entry entails.[5] Such strategic moves by individual firms can be assisted by government policy, which can give a firm a "deep pocket" to finance its initial losses on entry or that can give it a protected domestic market for initial sales. This situation may have occurred for firms in Japan and some of the newly industrializing countries. This view of the driving force behind international trade in these types of products gives credence, at least in theory, to government intervention in international trade both to protect existing national firms in such industries from attack by new entrants and to assist new national firms as they break into the market.

Two trends have reinforced the ability of firms and industrial clusters to establish a sustainable competitive advantage based on economies of scale and product differentiation, and two trends have lessened their ability. National incomes per capita, wages, and capital costs among countries in the upper third of the world income distribution have tended to become more homogeneous over time and the importance of endowments of many natural resources has declined. Among these countries, competitive advantage has become based less on relative factor endowments and costs and more on firm-specific ownership advantages—such as economies of scale, management, technology, brand names—as well as on highly developed support industries, education, worker skills, and trade infrastructure. As incomes have risen, buyers have become more discriminating in their purchases as to style, quality, fashion, design, and performance. Consumers have also come to value a wider range of products with a wider range of product attributes. These trends have increased the ability of producers to differentiate their products entering international trade. In the United States, shoes made by Bally (produced in Italy and Switzerland) compete with shoes from Gucci (Italy), Church (England), and Alden (United States) at the top end of the market in the $200 plus range. But shoes from Indonesia, Taiwan, China, and South Korea are demanded in the $10 to $20 price range.

The increasingly rapid pace of technology transfer and diffusion has led to a growing number of firms (in a growing number of countries) possessing or having access to more or less the same product and process technology. In industries in which technological ability (including design and quality control) has become more widely diffused, competition may once again become based on relative factor costs. Falling transportation costs and trade barriers have also accentuated the force behind comparative advantage. Many firms have become multinational enterprises. These

---

[5]This may have been the case of Great Giant Pineapple (GGP), a subsidiary of Genung Sewu, a large conglomerate in Indonesia. Initially GGP priced 15 percent below the producer in Thailand with the worst reputation for quality *and* graded all its pineapple rings as "Grade C" to ensure that, in delivering at least the quality described in the contract (and usually higher quality), it could keep its name among buyers as living up to its contract. By 1989, with its reputation established and with 8 percent of the world market, GGP was pricing above the Thai producer with the best reputation and was selling grades A and B slices. By 1996, GGP had 15 percent of the world market for canned pineapple.

firms, to the extent that relative factor costs are still important, can rationalize production and sales on a global basis.

The overwhelming conclusion of all the theories of international trade is that trade creates value for *all* the participants. The more open a country is to trade, the better off it will be in the long run. In the short run, there may be adjustment problems for some sectors and some firms within these sectors, but, overall, all countries win. In Chapter 2, "world competitiveness rankings" were given for a number of countries. This should *not* be interpreted to mean that, as in a sports contest, some countries will win and others lose in international competition through trade and foreign investment. Individual companies may win or lose, but at the national level, countries all win by opening up to trade (and foreign investment). A more apt comparison is with dancing rather than a sports contest. The closer we dance together, the greater the benefits will be for both partners (although there may be some stumbling and hurt toes as we learn to dance together).

These newer theories of the driving forces behind international trade have several implications for managers. It is necessary to analyze which of the forces will predominate in the industry in which the firm operates, that is, can the firm establish a sustainable competitive advantage based on some proprietary ownership advantage that will allow it to operate internationally, or will the forces of comparative advantage predominate? Governments may intervene in the market to assist firms in some industries to "create" their own comparative and competitive advantage. In theory, governments can increase national welfare by protecting firms in this type of industry from trade competition while they are still struggling to gain scale efficiency, undertake R&D, differentiate their products, and promote exports. Many governments around the world have "targeted" manufacturers of products in industries such as computers, biotechnology, aircraft, telecommunications, robotics, ceramics, and fiber optics, for protection and incentives during their developmental stages. For firms in these industries, government policies at home and in competing countries may be the key to competitive success in export as well as in domestic markets.

A word of warning is needed, however. Often, management and governments have focused their attention on the "hot" industries on the cutting edge of technology when they have tried to identify the "winners of tomorrow" in export markets. For many, even most, of the industries in which firms have achieved a sustainable competitive advantage, technology of the bubbling test tube and whizzing computer variety is *not* the norm. German firms export knives and garden equipment; English firms export razors, combs, cookies, and candy; Swiss firms export shoes, textiles, and cereals; American firms export textiles and clothing and processed food products; Canadian firms export packaging machinery, feed mixers, dental drills, and garbage cans; Japanese firms export zippers, disposable lighters, and books; and Swedish firms export saws and scissors. These firms have all achieved a sustainable competitive advantage in export markets, based not on "high" technology but on design, quality, and marketing expertise.[6]

---

[6]See Porter, *The Competitive Advantage of Nations,* Chapter 1, Table 1.2, pp. 27–28, for a complete list of the 100 industries that he and his coauthors studied. In particular note that many of the firms and the industries that have been able to establish a competitive advantage are not particularly high-tech. Rather, their competitive advantage is based on quality, design, innovation, and so on.

Firms that enter the hot industries based on government incentives may find themselves caught in a worldwide subsidy war in which competitive advantage is based more on which governments are willing to subsidize the most and which governments ultimately flinch from the mounting costs of these subsidies. If several governments continue to subsidize their "national champions," worldwide overcapacity may exist in the long run, prices will remain below costs, and the ultimate winners will be consumers in importing countries.

Real Exchange Rates

Beyond comparative and competitive advantage, there are two important factors that influence trade flows: the real exchange rate and demand conditions over the business cycle. The concept of the "real exchange rate" is a difficult one to master and to use. But the influence of real exchange rates on trade flows is so great that it should be mastered. Everyone is familiar with exchange rates in general. If we travel abroad we change our domestic currencies into the currencies of the countries that we visit at the prevailing exchange rate. For example, in mid-1996, one U.S. dollar could be changed into 105 yen or into 1.33 Canadian dollars. This is the nominal exchange rate. The *nominal* exchange rate is important for international business. A Canadian importer receives a shipment from the United States with payment in dollars. Canadian dollars must then be converted into U.S. dollars at the prevailing exchange rate and sent to the United States. In mid-1996, the Canadian importer would have to pay $1.33 to buy one U.S. dollar. This is a straightforward transaction and easy to understand. If the nominal exchange rate between the U.S. dollar and the Canadian dollar falls to $1.40, the importer will have to pay $1.40 Canadian to buy one U.S. dollar. Such a fall of the Canadian dollar can have important implications for the prices the importer must charge when the product is sold or on its profit margins if prices cannot be changed.

The "real" exchange rate is more difficult to understand, but it is of even greater importance in many instances. The concept of the real exchange rate can be illustrated with a stylized example. In year one, assume that U.S. and Japanese producers of machine tools are making normal economic profits; the landed, duty-paid price of a U.S. machine tool in Japan is $100,000; the nominal exchange rate is 100 yen = $1; and the price of comparable machine tools *in yen* is 10,000,000. The U.S.-produced machine tool is then competitive in Japan (since $100,000 = 10,000,000 yen) and exports take place. Over the next year, inflation in the United States is 10 percent and in Japan it is only 3 percent, *and* the *nominal* exchange rate remains at 100 yen = $1. What has happened to the ability of the U.S. producer to export to Japan? If the total costs of the U.S. producer (including a normal profit) have risen by the average rate of U.S. inflation, its costs would be $100,000 × 1.10 = $110,000 = 11,000,000 yen. The price of Japanese competitors *in yen* has risen by the Japanese rate of inflation to 10,000,000 × 1.03 = 10,300,000. Hence, the U.S. producer must either cut prices in dollars to $103,000 and severely reduce its profit margins or the Japanese importer will not be able to sell the product in competition with Japanese-made products.

In this example, although the *nominal* exchange rate has remained constant, the ability of the U.S. producer to export to Japan has declined due to differing inflation rates between Japan and the United States. The real exchange rate is a measure of this loss of competitive ability due to differing inflation rates (and hence changing relative costs). In this example, the *real* exchange rate has *risen* by about 7 percent. The real exchange rate can be thought of as an index number. In the example, if it were 100 in year one, it would have risen to 106.8 (1.10/1.03 × 100) in year two. (For small percentage inflation rates, the calculation can be simplified to: the real exchange rate in year two = 100 + U.S. inflation − Japanese inflation rate = 100 + 10 − 3 = 107.) In order for the U.S. producer to remain competitive, the *nominal* exchange rate in this example would have had to fall by 6.36 percent to 93.6 (1.03/1.10 − 1 = 0.0636), more or less the inflation rate differential. If this had occurred, then the *real* exchange rate would have remained constant.

Just as a rise in the real exchange rate reduces the competitive ability of national producers in export markets, it also increases the competitive ability of producers abroad to export to the domestic market. Hence, all else equal, a rise in the real exchange rate leads to reduced export growth rates and increased import growth rates. Conversely, a fall in the real exchange rate leads to increased export growth rates and reduced import growth rates. Notice that this effect is *independent* of either comparative or competitive advantage of the nation or of its firms.

For managers engaged in international trade operations, an analysis of movements of the real exchange rates is crucial for determining success in export markets and success in competing with imports. In the mid-1980s, the United States had a comparative advantage in sophisticated machine tools, but its currency was overvalued by almost 50 percent (i.e., its real exchange rate has moved from 108 in to 154). U.S. producers found themselves priced out of export markets on the one hand and under threat of import competition on the other.

Estimates of the real exchange rate of major trading countries are available on a monthly basis from many sources, most notably the *International Financial Statistics Yearbook* (published by the International Monetary Fund).[7] For example, over the 1978 to 1993 period (with 1990 indexed as 100), the real exchange rate of the U.S. dollar rose from 108.1 in 1978 to as high as 154.3, fell to 96.5 in 1992, and only rose marginally through late 1995. The effects of these movements in the U.S. real exchange rate on U.S. exporters and firms that compete with imports were dramatic—and completely swamped out any effects of relative competitive ability due to "Japanese management," technological superiority, product quality differentials, or national trade strategies, factors which have figured prominently in the press as causes of the U.S. trade deficit.

Exhibit 3–4 displays the real exchange rate of the U.S. dollar from 1970 to 1993 and the U.S. trade deficit *lagged by two years* (i.e., from 1972 to 1995). The lag was included since imports and exports respond to changes in the real exchange rate with a lag. Firms take time to switch among sources of supply on the international market and to fill export and import orders. With the fall of the dollar in 1985, U.S. exports began to expand rapidly and import growth was reduced. From 1985 to 1991, U.S. export volume increased by 68 percent and import volume increased by 26 percent.

---

[7]See the technical notes in the IMF publication for a description of how the various measures of real exchange rates have been calculated.

EXHIBIT 3–4 **U.S. Real Exchange Rates, 1975–1993, and Balance of Trade, 1977–1995**

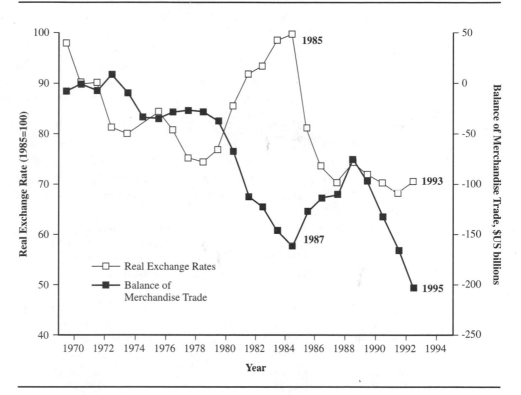

Note: The trade balance in billions of dollars (right-hand scale) is lagged behind the real exchange rate (left-hand scale, with 1985 = 100).

Source: IMF, *International Financial Statistics Yearbook,* 1995.

Over the same period, export and import volumes in Japan increased 65 and 17 percent, respectively; for Germany the figures were 24 and 61 percent.[8] This dramatic reversal of the fortunes of U.S., Japanese, and German exporters was largely the result of the changes in the real exchange rates of these countries.[9] In Japan, the situation was roughly the reverse of that in the United States. From an index of 85.8 in 1985, its real exchange rate rose to 119.1 in 1988, declined to 100 in 1990, rose continuously to a high of 166.7 in mid-1995, and then fell dramatically to 124 in mid-1996. These real-exchange-rate movements have had a dramatic effect on Japanese

---

[8]These figures are for the overall exchange rates, not the bilateral ones between the U.S. and Japan or Germany. The fluctuations of these rates were higher still. Similarly, the trade statistics are for total, not bilateral, trade. If the bilateral trade figures had been given, both the change in real exchange rates and the change in export growth rates would have been substantially greater.

[9]Demand conditions also influence international trade and are an important factor in explaining post-1991 changes in the U.S. balance of trade. This point is discussed at the end of this chapter.

firms and the economy as a whole. Major Japanese firms have had to downsize and lay off workers, relocate production abroad, and increase productivity substantially. This restructuring and redeployment of resources was one of the major factors that contributed to the slow growth of the Japanese economy in the mid-1990s.

As part of this block of the analysis, the key role of the level and potential movements of the real exchange rate between the two countries must be assessed. The IMF publishes real exchange rates for many countries in the *International Financial Statistics Yearbook.* For those countries for which data are not available, a rough approximation of the movement of the real exchange rate can easily be made. Essentially, if the inflation rate in one country exceeds that of another, in order for its real exchange rate to remain constant, its nominal exchange rate must devalue by the inflation rate differential. In the example above, the U.S. inflation rate was 7 percent higher than that in Japan. So, for the real exchange rate to remain constant, the yen would have to appreciate against the dollar by about 7 percent. If it did not, but rather appreciated by only 2 percent, then the real value of the dollar would have risen by about 5 percent.

An increase in a country's real exchange rate has many of the same effects as a reduction in its tariff rate: it makes market access easier as the prices of imports relative to domestic production fall. A fall in the real exchange rate has the opposite effect. It is difficult to overemphasize the importance of movements of the real exchange rate of the home country and potential destination countries for international trade flows and for the success of import and export operations.

The importance of the real exchange rate holds for large and small countries and for high-income and developing countries alike.[10] In the early 1990s, foreign investors perceived that the Philippines had a relatively stable government. Foreign direct and portfolio investment began to pour into the Philippines. At the same time, transfers from abroad (largely by Filipino overseas workers) accelerated. The consequent 25 percent rise in the real exchange rate of the Philippines from 1991 to 1995 led to a reduction in export growth, an increase in import growth, and a reduction in manufacturing employment of 16 percent, despite a surge of foreign investment.

Real exchange rates may change for several reasons. If there is a gap between investment demand and domestic savings, real interest rates will rise and capital will flow in from abroad, thereby driving up the real exchange rate. The inevitable imbalances that this appreciation of the real exchange rate will cause will lead to mounting external debt and eventually to an unwillingness of investors abroad to hold more debt. Capital inflows will decline and the real exchange rate will fall. For the United States, high investment demand (due to an expanding economy) and a low savings rate (due to low personal savings and large government deficits) led to high real interest rates, capital inflows, a rise in the real exchange rate, and a deterioration of U.S. trade accounts from 1977 to 1985. Over the 1985 to 1988 period, private investors outside the United States became increasingly reluctant to hold more U.S.-

---

[10]The exception to this generalization is when a country counteracts movements in its real exchange rate by additional offsetting export promotional measures and import impeding measures. Korea is one example of a country which through 1985 was able to follow such a policy.

dollar-denominated debt, capital inflows from these sources declined, and the real exchange rate declined.

Similarly, short-term government macroeconomic policy (to reduce inflation, for example) may lead to relatively high interest rates and an appreciation of the real exchange rate. Over the 1986 to 1991 period, Canada's real exchange rate rose by 27 percent in response to a government policy of halting inflation by setting high interest rates. The policies worked, but at the expense of the trade sector. Once inflation was reduced and the government relaxed its monetary policies in 1991, the real exchange rate fell by 23 percent.

Real exchange rates may also increase (decrease) if a country's terms of trade (the ratio of unit export prices to unit import prices) move in its favor (against it). If this change is permanent, then the real exchange rate will remain at this higher level. For example, if the decline in oil prices over the 1981–88 period were permanent, the real exchange rates of oil-exporting countries would have to fall permanently in order for them to maintain their trade accounts at a sustainable level. In fact, the real exchange rates of oil exporters, such as Saudi Arabia and Bahrain, did fall from 40 to 50 percent with the decline in oil prices in the mid-1980s through the early 1990s.

A country's real exchange rate can also appreciate if some valuable natural resource is discovered within the country. For example, when natural gas was discovered in Holland's offshore waters, its real exchange rate rose as this gas was exported. The rise in Holland's real exchange rate caused manufacturers in Holland to be priced out of export markets for manufacturing products and led to a decline in its manufacturing sector, the so-called Dutch disease. If a country's productivity increases relative to that of its trading partners, its real exchange rate will rise, unless the government acts to hold it down by accumulating foreign exchange reserves and investing abroad. In this case, the country will generate ever increasing trade surpluses until the time when it lets its exchange rate rise to an appropriate level. This phenomenon occurred in such countries as Japan, South Korea, and Taiwan over the 1985 to 1988 period. Singapore is an interesting example of a country that has resisted this pressure to revalue its currency. From 1985 to 1995, it maintained the real exchange rate of the Singapore dollar while at the same time accumulating $69 billion in foreign exchange reserves ($23,000 per capita, by far the largest per capita foreign exchange reserves in the world outside the oil-exporting countries). In the future, despite the unwillingness of the Singapore government to revalue its currency, its real value will have to rise.

The examples given above should not lead to a conclusion that real exchange rates are highly volatile. The real exchange rates of Switzerland, Austria, and Thailand have not changed by more than 10 percent over the past decade. Real exchange rates move dramatically only in response to strong economic forces. It is, however, important to identify those times when real exchange rates move away from their long-run equilibrium position and to make appropriate decisions regarding trade and investment.

The theory and evidence from international finance show that over the short run the foreign exchange market is "perfect," i.e., that investors on average cannot make economic profits in speculating in foreign exchange. Over the longer term, however, it is possible to forecast movements in the real exchange rate (and hence the nominal exchange rate) when the real exchange rate is significantly above or below its long-run equilibrium value. The long run is the appropriate time frame for those engaged in international trade (a long-term investment in export markets) and foreign direct investment. Although it is impossible to "beat" the foreign exchange market consistently over the short term, from time to time it is both possible and necessary to predict the direction of real and nominal exchange-rate movements accurately over the longer term. This task is part of an international manager's job.

For managers, there are several implications of this analysis of the effects of movements in real exchange rates on the competitive advantage of their firms. First, they must try to determine if changes in real exchange rates are short- or long-term. The effects of short-term movements in real exchange rates on their competitive ability should be taken into account when making such decisions as whether to change the volume and prices of their exports in response to exchange-rate movements or to absorb the impact of these changes on the profitability of export operations.

In the early 1980s, with the rise of the real value of the U.S. dollar, Japanese car producers increased their market penetration by pricing aggressively in dollars (while still maintaining their profit levels in yen). When the combination of increased imports and the recession led to layoffs and losses in the U.S. car industry, the U.S. government was induced to negotiate restraint agreements on cars from Japan. Japanese car manufacturers responded to volume restrictions by raising prices on existing models and by introducing new models at even higher prices (to clear the market) and made enormous profits in the U.S. market. With the fall of the dollar in 1985, the Japanese were faced with a dilemma: either raise U.S. prices dramatically and lose market share or have profit levels decline. A similar dilemma was faced by Japanese consumer electronics firms. Both groups of firms did raise prices, but not to the extent of the decline of the dollar against the yen. The result was that by the early 1990s most Japanese car and consumer electronics firms were running operating losses (partially offset by nonoperating profits on their portfolio investments of their previous profits). Over the longer term, when the Japanese saw that the real value of the yen would remain high, they upgraded product quality, increased efficiency, laid off workers, and invested heavily abroad.

The second implication for managers is that identification of times when their home country's real exchange rate is above its long-run equilibrium level and when a destination country's real exchange rate is below this level can assist in identifying export market opportunities, since, unless the change in permanent, ultimately overvalued and undervalued exchange rates will move back to their equilibrium levels.

Third, identification of short- and long-run movements of real exchange rates in the future can assist in identification of threats and opportunities arising from international markets.

Another implication of real-exchange-rate movements goes beyond international trade into both portfolio and direct investment management. As mentioned above, the rise of the U.S. dollar through 1985 was largely fueled by huge inflows of investment in U.S. financial instruments: short- and long-term bonds and stock purchases. Investors used their relatively cheap foreign currencies to buy relatively expensive dollars to make these investments. When the dollar fell, the value of these investments in terms of foreign currencies fell as well. For these investors, the good news was that they earned relatively high returns (interest and stock appreciation and dividends) in dollars; the bad news was that they lost substantial capital when they converted their depreciated U.S. dollars into their national currencies. Japanese financial institutions were reported to have lost upward of $40 billion (in terms of yen).

For direct investors in plant and equipment, the situation was somewhat different. They too converted relatively cheap foreign currencies to buy relatively expensive dollars. And they were hurt when the dollar declined. On the other hand, as the dollar fell, the cost competitiveness of their investments increased (just as it did for U.S. manufacturers) and hence profits rose above projections. However, these profits were in dollars. Similarly, in the Philippines, as of 1996, most analysts agree that the real value of the peso is too high; eventually it will fall. When it does fall, the fall may be dramatic as portfolio investors take their profits and pull their money out of the stock market. This fall in the peso will make Philippine exports more competitive and spur economic growth. The question facing direct investors is whether to invest now and face a loss in the value of their Philippine investment, but be well-positioned to take part in the coming boom, or to wait for the fall of the peso.

For all these reasons, a close watch should be kept on movements of real exchange rates. Further, forecasts of real-exchange-rate movements should be made. Although this forecasting exercise is difficult, it can be extremely useful. And not to forecast is to miss opportunities and to court trouble. All else equal, for real exchange rates, what goes up must come down, and vice versa.

One of the problems in this analysis, however, is to decide whether a rise in the real exchange rate is a movement back toward equilibrium or away from equilibrium. A good starting point can be found by determining a time period when the country's trade is roughly balanced, then counting back two years (to account for lag effects) and defining this level as 100. Movements away from 100 in the real exchange rate will tend to be movements away from equilibrium, which eventually will be reversed. Other indications of an *overvalued* real exchange rate are persistent and worsening trade deficits, high real interest rates, unusual capital inflows, and chronic international debt problems. For countries with a high concentration of exports in a particular natural resource product, such as oil or natural gas, a long-term shift (up or down) will put pressure on the real exchange rate (up or down). Conversely, for countries with persistent trade surpluses, mounting foreign exchange reserves, and burgeoning international investments, there will be pressures for the real exchange rate to rise.

Demand

The final factors influencing international trade (both imports and exports) are demand conditions over the business cycles in the domestic market and in export markets, and source countries for imports. If the domestic economy is expanding relative to the economies of other countries, exporters will tend to divert production to the domestic market, where demand and prices are rising. Producers abroad, faced with slack demand at home, will tend to try to push excess production onto export markets. For example, the record Japanese trade surplus in 1992 was in part due to the *fall* of the yen (from an index of 112 in 1989 to 100 in 1990). But also it was influenced by the deceleration of the growth rate of the Japanese economy and import demand there and the increase in import demand in the United States as the U.S. economy began to expand.

Summary

The *first* step in a firm's analysis of its international trade position is to analyze the forces in the national economy that give rise to some form of comparative advantage or disadvantage. The exporter must also analyze what competitive advantage the firm has or can develop, based either on the country's comparative advantage or on "ownership advantages"—such as economies of scale, marketing, management, and R&D—which cannot easily be duplicated by other competitors worldwide. In general, the more closely a firm's competitive advantage is aligned with the country's comparative advantage, the more easily it can develop, maintain, and increase its competitive advantage. In Thailand there is a saying, "It's easier to help an elephant get up when it's getting up than it is to hold it up when it wants to lie down." Our youth culture phrases this as "Go with the flow." These sayings apply to international trade.

Supplementary Reading

Cline, William R. *American Trade Adjustment: The Global Impact.* Policy Analysis in International Economics Series No. 26. Washington, D.C.: Institute for International Economics, 1989.

Jackson, John. *The World Trading System.* Cambridge, MA: MIT Press, 1992.

Kennen, Peter B. *The International Economy.* 3rd ed. New York: Prentice-Hall, 1993.

Krugman, Paul, and Maurice Obstfeld. *International Economics: Theory and Practice.* 2nd ed. New York: HarperCollins, 1991.

Porter, Michael. *The Competitive Advantage of Nations.* New York: Free Press, 1990.

Thurow, Lester. *Head to Head: The Coming Economic Battle Among Japan, Europe, and America.* New York: William Morrow and Company, 1992.

Scherer, F.M., and Richard S. Belous. *Unfinished Tasks: The New International Trade Theory.* New York, Ottawa, and London: The British-North American Committee, 1995.

Vernon, Raymond, and Debora Spar. *Beyond Globalism: Remaking American Foreign Economic Policy.* New York: Macmillan, Free Press, 1989.

World Economic Forum. *World Competitiveness Report.* Lausanne, Switzerland: IMD, 1996.

4   MANAGING EXPORT OPERATIONS

In Chapter 3, the STEP framework was introduced. This framework can be used by managers to analyze a firm's comparative and competitive advantage in export markets. A firm's competitive advantage can be moderated by movements in the real exchange rate and in demand conditions abroad. The second block of analysis centers on the analysis of export markets to assess their potential demand for the firm's products. The firm may have a product with a competitive advantage, but it also needs to identify a market in which users value its product above the products that are currently available in the market from domestic producers and exporters from other countries. One procedure for accomplishing this analysis involves three steps. Initially, the analysis will focus on single-country markets, but later on in the chapter regional and global markets will be brought into the analysis.

Step 1: Segment World Markets

Market segmentation lies at the heart of marketing for many products, especially the differentiated products that have become increasingly important in international trade. This chapter, however, is not the place for an elaborate description of market segmentation techniques; this can be found in introductory marketing textbooks.

In segmenting markets in countries abroad, several fundamental questions must be addressed: Is there a market segment in the potential export market that will value the product characteristics of the exporter's product? Is this segment large enough to justify the costs of exporting? Is this segment adequately served by existing domestic producers or other exporters? Can it be accessed by the exporter?

Markets can be segmented in a number of ways. The two most important are product quality and product features. Both of these two segmentation techniques have implications for product price. Typically, the higher the quality and the greater

---

This chapter was prepared by Donald J. Lecraw.

the number of distinctive product features, the higher the costs of production and marketing and the higher the price. One of the characteristics of international markets is the wide range of quality and product characteristics that are in demand by some groups of potential buyers. As examples, sweaters sell for $8 at a discount store, while across town at a fashionable store sweaters are sold for over $1,000, name-brand ballpoint pens, such as Cross or Mount Blanc, sell for $70 to $200, while Bic pens are sold for 50 cents—sometimes in the same store.

Initially, in the 1960s, Japanese automobile firms entered the U.S. market by following a niche strategy aimed at the low end of the market. They targeted buyers with low incomes, buyers who wanted a second car, and buyers who were more interested in basic transportation than in quality or features. Over time, these Japanese producers have upgraded their products to compete in ever higher priced segments of the market. On the other hand, in the 1980s, when Honda entered the U.S. market for products using small, gas-powered engines—such as lawn mowers, outboard motors, and generators—it chose the very high end of the market to cater to high-income consumers who wanted dependability, quality, unique design, and high performance and had the money to pay for these features.

Market segments often differ between countries in the number, size, and characteristics by which they are segmented. In the United States, markets may be segmented regionally, whereas in Japan there may be few regional differences. Markets in a large-population country, such as the United States, may have more segments (with enough demand in each segment to make the segmentation effort pay off) than in less populous countries, such as Canada. The proportion of the market in each segment often differs among countries. For consumer products, differences in the age distribution of the population, income level and growth, and the distribution of income may affect segment size and relative importance.

If, for example, the exporter's product is of high quality or has unique design features, one starting point would be to segment countries by GNP per capita (as a proxy for personal disposable income) and then to focus on countries with high GNP per capita. This crude segmentation could be refined, however, by examining the income distributions of both the initial target group and lower-income countries (that had been left out of the group) to identify countries with a disproportionately high percentage of high-income or high-wealth residents, such as many of the countries in South America and some of the countries in the Asia-Pacific region. If the exporter's product were most appropriate for one age group, trends in these countries in the age distribution of the population could then be examined. For products appropriate for older people, Japan and some European countries would stand out; for the youth market, Indonesia, the Philippines, and certain South American countries; for infants, certain African countries, Canada, and the United States. For example, in Canada and the United States, there has been a boom in high-quality children's books for the yuppie generation's children.

Consumer tastes also influence segment size. Consumers in Japan, for example, place considerable value on product quality and design features and often prefer to buy a limited number of high-quality, high-priced products, rather than a large number of low-quality, low-priced products. Countries could also be grouped by weather conditions—average temperature and range, and amount of rainfall—for products whose performance and appropriateness are dependent on these conditions. For tropical countries, both packaging and product may have to be changed to be more resistant to humidity and high temperatures. As an example, Tetra packs for juices and milk are more prevalent in tropical countries, particularly lower-income ones where refrigeration is not in widespread use.

For industrial machinery and inputs, the level and dispersion of wages and technical skills and the composition of industrial output affect the size and importance of market segments. Very high-technology, highly automated, but flexible machinery might be targeted at northern Europe, Japan, and Canada; somewhat more standardized, mass-production machinery might be directed at the newly industrializing countries; and older, standardized machinery targeted at the developing countries. For example, a Canadian company, Husky Injection Moulding, has been able to extend the life of its product line by selling its highest-priced, most-advanced, high-speed equipment to the United States, Europe, and Japan, while at the same time selling its older, much cheaper, slower equipment to countries in which demand is lower. Similarly, countries could be segmented based on their natural resource and agricultural bases by exporters of production equipment for mining and agriculture or for processing of these products.

Fast growth often leads to strains on infrastructure. In Indonesia, for example, the demand for electricity has grown by 9 percent a year for the last decade, leading to a huge demand for electrical generating equipment and services. Similar demand growth can be found in fast-growing countries for construction and earth-moving equipment, water distribution and treatment facilities, telecommunications equipment, sewage treatment equipment, pollution control equipment, and garbage handling and processing equipment. In many developing countries privatization of many basic infrastructure operations has led to a burgeoning demand for investment in these services.

Once the potential export destinations have been placed in groups with higher and lower priorities, the market potential in each country needs to be examined in more detail. Part of this analysis has already been accomplished in the analysis of the previous block, when the firm's sustainable competitive advantage was identified. The consumers and industrial buyers that value the firm's product in the home country and give it a competitive advantage there are often similar to the ones that will value it in export markets. The consumer segment that values a firm's high-quality pots and pans in the home market may be the same as the consumer segment in export markets. As well, in many cases firms with export potential will have received (and sometimes filled) unsolicited orders from customers or importers abroad. The problem, then, is to discover if there is sufficient demand in these export markets to justify a more concerted export marketing effort. After paying for transportation costs, agents' fees, and tariffs, the price the firm must charge to be profitable in an export market may have risen several-fold above the price that its normal target segment is willing to pay. Then the problem is to determine if there are sufficient potential purchasers in the segment who can and are willing to buy in this price range and if the firm's product will have a competitive advantage in this segment. For example, a pots and pans manufacturer in the United States may have a competitive advantage in the large middle segment of the U.S. market, but in Japan it will have to aim at the top end of the market, a smaller segment. Yogurt sells for 50 cents a container in Australia, but yogurt exported from Australia to Indonesia sells there for $2 a container while Häagen-Dazs ice cream sells for $10 a pint.

Three conditions may be particularly important in this type of analysis: (1) emerging demand met by innovations in product technology in one country that are mirrored in other countries, (2) the deregulation and restructuring of markets, and (3) government policies and programs. As examples, changing energy prices have led to emerging demand for vehicles powered by natural gas in many countries. Compressed natural gas units to power vehicles developed in response to demand conditions in one country may face the same demand conditions in other countries. The deregulation of the telecommunications industry in the United States has opened up markets there for equipment developed in other countries for digital switching and fiber optics. The restructuring of markets in Japan in response to rising incomes and efforts by the Japanese government to open up the country to international trade has presented opportunities for many exporters to penetrate channels of distribution (such as door-to-door sales, large discount stores, and catalog sales), and to increase sales of heavily branded luxury products.

Identification of emerging product and segment demand is a prime tool of export marketing. It is often easier to penetrate a rapidly growing market or segment of the market than to penetrate markets and segments in which demand is stagnant. In these more dynamic markets and segments, existing suppliers may be experiencing problems with expanding capacity, or they may have grown complacent as their sales have boomed. At least part of the success of the Airbus during the 1980s stemmed from the capacity problems experienced by Boeing in the face of escalating demand for civilian aircraft. In buoyant markets and segments, existing suppliers may be less prone to retaliate against a new exporter. Although existing suppliers may lose market share to the newcomer, their sales levels will continue to increase. In emerging markets and segments, the distribution system may also be in a state of flux, and traditional buyer-seller relationships may be weaker than in slower-growing markets and segments.

Step 2: Select an Entry Strategy to Promote Sustainable Competitive Advantage

Once a viable segment of the market has been selected, the next step is to determine the best strategy by which to penetrate this segment. Strategy formulation does not end with matching product characteristics to market segments. It should include channels of distribution, sales and advertising techniques, service before and after sales, and so on. Japanese producers give substantial support to wholesalers and retailers. They provide fast delivery, inventory support, and technical assistance and training before the sale—and repair and maintenance support after the sale. This support has been a powerful weapon in their export expansion and in defending their positions at home. On the other hand, some firms have been successful in export markets, including Japan, by providing a lower level of these services to their distribution networks and to consumers and, instead, competing more on the basis of price.

Having a different strategy than the major competitors in the market also has advantages. Large entrenched producers with strong brand images may find it difficult to respond to exporters following a strategy that differs from their own. For example, producers of audiophile sound systems have been very successful in Japan. The large Japanese producers have not been able to respond to entry by these firms, since to develop audiophile lines of their own would cast a shadow on the quality of their mainline products. A similar situation exists in many markets for entrants at the bottom end of the market. The branded major producers may not be able to respond without damaging their brand images.

The final, and arguably the most important, decision in a firm's export strategy is whether to sell a standardized product worldwide or whether to tailor products and the entire marketing mix to meet individual country requirements. There is no one right or wrong answer to this problem. The correct answer depends on a host of considerations, such as the ability and capacity of the firm to modify products, the R&D and design costs of modifications, and the effects on production, inventory, and distribution costs of producing and marketing a more diverse set of products.

In the past, exporters in different countries tended to follow one of three different strategies. In general, firms in Japan tended to export one standardized product to all markets; firms in the United States tended to follow a product life-cycle strategy by first introducing a new product in the U.S. market and later exporting it as demand by other countries became more similar to U.S. demand; and firms in Europe tended to be more responsive to local market conditions and to view each market as a separate entity.[1] These generic strategies tended to converge and overlap during the 1980s, as firms tried to incorporate all the strengths of flexibility to respond to individual market needs, global marketing to gain economies of scale, and international learning to access and supply worldwide product and process innovations. As examples, Toyota, after initially selling the same car in Canada as it did worldwide, now tailors its cars sold in Canada to better withstand diverse weather conditions: extremes of heat and cold and prolonged exposure to salt. In 1989, Kodak introduced a new line of film—first in Japan, then in Europe, and only a year later in the United States.

Export strategies can be changed over time in response to changing conditions. Initially, Japanese car firms exported inexpensive standard cars that competed on price, not quality, design, or features. Over time, they broadened their product line to access consumers with different preferences to increase market share. The high value of the dollar during the mid-1980s gave them the opportunity both to introduce cars at the high end of the market at relatively low prices and to offer a wide range of features in their cars for each segment. The fall of the dollar placed huge cost and profit

---

[1]See Christopher Bartlett and Sumantra Ghoshal. *Managing across Borders: The Transnational Solution* (Boston: Harvard Business School Press, 1989) for an analysis of these three strategies and how they are evolving into a "transnational strategy" that combines elements of all three. The implications of this are not only for exporters but also for broader international business strategy.

pressure on these firms. By 1993, their profits had shrunk to virtually zero. Some Japanese manufacturers withdrew from the U.S. market. Others have had to cut back the range of options available on each model to reduce logistics, production, and inventory costs. Nissan, for example, had options for 86 different steering wheels, and Toyota had 30 different sound systems on the cars it exported to America. Nissan reduced the number of parts in its cars by 40 percent and the number of variations of models by 50 percent; Toyota and Mazda cut 40 percent in both areas.

In general, most exporters would prefer to follow a standard product and marketing-mix strategy worldwide. Such a strategy reduces production, logistics, and inventory costs, complexity, market and product research and development, and managerial time. Such a strategy is obviously more appropriate for some products than for others. If demand characteristics are similar in many potential export markets, then a standardized product approach is often most appropriate, and vice versa. The same Pringles potato chips are exported all over the world. On the other hand, U.S. cookie manufacturers have had to reduce the sugar content of their product for export to Europe. The key question to be addressed is the extent to which demand will be increased through product and marketing-mix changes (at constant prices) and to what extent differentiation will lead to higher costs, higher prices, and decreased demand. Usually, tailoring a product for individual markets through product modification will increase market share. Unless the full costs of this tailoring can be recouped in higher prices or increased demand, however, following this strategy will not be successful, where success is defined in terms of profits on export markets.[2] Even for the same product, different companies can successfully follow different strategies. In personal health care products, for example, Ponds sells the same face cream worldwide, while other producers tailor their products to individual markets, based on such characteristics as skin color, texture, and weather conditions. P&G sells Tide laundry detergent in bars in many developing countries, where most washing is done by hand. But it also sells its standard powdered detergent. Philips sells the same lighting products worldwide. But firms from Taiwan sell lower-quality lighting products at lower prices to developing countries.[3]

A company may follow a combination of both strategies for one product. It can sell a standard product in markets of one group of countries and tailor its product for another group of countries. Similarly, a company may follow a standard product strategy for one product and a tailored product strategy for another. Coca-Cola, for example, follows a standard product strategy for Coke, but a tailored product strategy for Fanta by which it sells a wide range of flavors in some countries.

---

[2]See Adrian Ryans, "Strategic Market Entry Factors and Market Share Achievement in Japan," *Journal of International Business Studies,* Fall 1988.

[3]Ironically, Philips's expensive, but long-life, energy-efficient "new lighting" fluorescent lamps (which it developed for high-income markets) face severe problems in some developing countries. The problem is not competition with lower-priced products; the problem is that to achieve energy efficiency and long life, the necessary voltage tolerances on these products make them inappropriate for countries with problems in voltage swings and low voltage.

Step 3: Take a Long-Run Perspective

Rome was not built in a day; neither are export markets. Building and maintaining a sustainable competitive advantage in any one export market, let alone worldwide, is an *investment* (although for accounting purposes it must unfortunately be treated as a current cost). The initial R&D, channel development, and advertising (all necessary to launch a product) are best viewed as investments, not current costs. So, too, should the costs of entering export markets be viewed as investments. They are investments whose payoffs come only over time. A firm must invest the time and the money in export markets. It must gain expertise in export operations and in identifying export markets; identify, select, and manage channels of distribution into those markets; gain the technical expertise to modify products for export markets; and develop on-the-ground experience in an export market. As well, often initial losses are incurred to penetrate markets through low prices. All these costs are *investments* in export markets, not expenses.

This characterization of the initial stages of export marketing as an investment strengthens the value of the systematic approach to export operations outlined in this framework. The costs of undertaking the research involved in using this framework to analyze export opportunities are low, compared to the costs of investment in product and process R&D, channels of distribution, and market development that often follow a decision to enter an export market.

The "overnight" success of Japanese firms in export markets was not simply based on delivering products that offered good value for the money; it was also based on thorough market research on evolving demand patterns, market segments, how value was created for buyers within those segments, and on the selection of appropriate channels of distribution and selling techniques. Many managers are weary of being told to emulate the Japanese, especially when Japanese-style management may not be appropriate for managers and firms in other countries. Investment in export research and analysis, however, is one area in which lessons from the Japanese can be learned and applied by managers in other countries. When Mitsubishi decided to launch a major drive to penetrate the Malaysian market, it sent a team of four people to study the market and distribution system for one year. At the end of the year they had a short list of 20 potential distributors. Year 2 was spent selecting and negotiating with distributors. Year 3 was spent in training. In year 4, Mitsubishi began exporting.

Factors That Impede and Facilitate Trade

If a firm's product has a competitive advantage in export markets and if there is a country market or a segment within that market that values the product sufficiently above the products of competing suppliers to offset the costs of exporting, attention can be turned to the factors that may impede or facilitate access to this demand. These factors can be divided into natural and government-imposed ones. Natural factors include transportation costs and the cost of doing business in a different country.

Government-imposed factors include impediments such as tariff and nontariff barriers to trade and undervalued exchange rates. On the other hand, governments of the exporting country can also facilitate trade through export incentives, concessional financing for exports, information services, sponsored trade fairs, and export missions.

Over the decades, transportation, communications, and travel costs have fallen, thereby reducing some of the natural impediments to trade and world competition. National differences have also decreased due to the convergence of income levels in many countries, mass media, and travel (and arguably the spread of English as the language of international business). National differences in language, culture, social values, and political systems, however, can still represent major barriers to trade, especially for a new exporter. Many Canadian firms have experienced difficulty in operating in the United States—even though the two countries seem to be quite similar. The Japanese language is a major barrier to exporting to and operating in Japan. People differ among countries in how they relate to each other and in how they do business. These differences act as impediments to trade. Lack of knowledge and expertise in doing business abroad in general and in specific export markets is a key barrier to trade. It is a key impediment for firms in their efforts to realize the potential competitive advantage of their products. Conversely, having this knowledge and expertise is a key competitive strength, but one that can be developed only at considerable cost. The manager of a large Japanese trading company in Singapore has stated that the company is not much interested in its operations in Singapore. The Singapore economy and government regulations are too open, transparent, and straightforward. This company largely left Singapore to new, smaller firms who competed fiercely with each other—and made small profits. The manager preferred operations in Indonesia, where markets and government regulation were complex and filled with "anomalies," which, once understood, led to substantial profits.

Trade Regulation

The GATT and the WTO.   Many of the means that governments use to impede trade historically have fallen under the purview of the General Agreement on Tariffs and Trade (GATT). As World War II drew to a close, the Allies decided to set up three organizations to improve the performance of the world economy: the International Monetary Fund to regulate exchange rates and international capital movements, the World Bank to assist developing countries, and the International Trade Organization to regulate world trade. However, the U.S. Congress did not support the creation of the International Trade Organization, since the Congress felt that its authority would extend too far into domestic economic affairs. As a second best alternative, the General Agreement on Tariffs and Trade was negotiated to deal with two aspects of international trade: tariffs and nontariff barriers to trade.

From the end of World War II through the early 1980s, trade negotiations under the auspices of the GATT succeeded in reducing barriers to trade, particularly tariff barriers, significantly. During the Tokyo round of trade negotiations in the mid-1970s, attention was turned toward reducing nontariff barriers to trade as well. By the end of negotiations in 1979, only partial success had been achieved. In part, this result was due to the number, the complexity, and the sensitivity of nontariff barriers. A study conducted by the GATT Secretariat identified over 600 nontariff barriers to trade. These ranged from quotas and antidumping and countervailing duty laws to labeling, product standards, customs inspection procedures, and government procurement regulations.

In part, the relative lack of success was due to the subtle nature of the motivations for, and the administration of, many nontariff barriers to trade. For example, a country's health and safety standards could be formulated in response to legitimate concerns on these issues or they could be designed to block trade. Requirements for periodic on-site plant inspections by nationals of the importing country legitimately could be a means of ensuring quality control to meet these standards. Alternatively, these inspections could be required to impose costs on potential exporters. In spite of these problems, the Tokyo round did achieve further tariff reductions among member countries and undertakings to reduce some of the more obvious and disruptive nontariff barriers to trade, such as those arising from government procurement practices and unique national standards and systems for administering standards.

The most recent round of the GATT negotiations, the Uruguay round, was started in 1986 and completed in December 1993. It addressed even more challenging problems. These problems were also addressed in an environment that was less hospitable to trade liberalization. A wide variety of issues have been placed on the table: again standards, also known as technical barriers to trade; trade in agricultural products, a most politically charged issue; trade in services, such as banking and insurance, advertising, media, and tourism; intellectual property rights protection of patents, trademarks, copyrights, and brand names; barriers to trade in technology, such as regulations on mandatory licensing or maximum licensing fees; and trade-related investment measures (TRIMs) that link investment incentives to exports, the Multifiber Agreement (MFA), the "safeguard measures" (often called the "escape clause") used to deal with import surges, and "voluntary export restraints" (VERs).

The number of countries involved in the negotiations had also expanded from 100 (with 70 contracting parties) in the Tokyo round to 117 (with 113 contracting countries). These negotiations took place in a more difficult environment than was the case in previous rounds. The United States was running a large and unsustainable trade deficit. Europe was struggling with the integration of the former Eastern Bloc countries into a more unified trading area. At the same time, economic growth in many European countries had stagnated and unemployment was over 10 percent. The electorate in many countries was increasingly restive.

Many developing countries needed to achieve, maintain, and increase their trade surpluses if they were to have any chance of servicing their external debts. Expanding exports was also the only alternative open to them if they were to achieve even some modest economic growth. The political stability of many developing countries is directly linked to export expansion. These developing countries were not particularly interested in, and were often antagonistic to, the goals of high-income countries for liberalization of trade in services, agricultural products, protection of intellectual property rights, and technology transfer. They saw these initiatives as leading to domination by foreign financial and media firms; higher prices for imported food and loss of food self-sufficiency; higher prices for products with patents, brand names, and trademarks; and higher prices for and reduced volumes of technology transfer. Their interests lay in regaining the market access they had lost over the past decade to protectionist measures implemented by high-income countries, and in enhanced access in the future. In particular, they wanted the removal of the MFA, which reduced their ability to increase exports of textiles and garments, and the "escape clause," which could be invoked to limit export growth in other products.

The contentious nature of many of the issues under negotiation, the diversity of the interests involved, the greater number of countries taking part in the negotiations, and the hostility toward freer trade in many countries combined to increase the difficulty of achieving meaningful results under the Uruguay round of trade negotiations. The target date for the finalization of the negotiations was extended several times. In the United States, the Congress extended the "fast-track" status of the GATT agreement. Under the fast-track provisions, the U.S. president is empowered to present whatever agreement is reached on a "take it or leave it basis" to the Congress. Without the fast track, the Congress could modify the agreement item-by-item before ratifying it. Such a modified agreement would certainly not be acceptable to the other member countries of the GATT.

Given this uncertain, even hostile, environment, the Uruguay round was completed in December 1993, and came into full effect on January 1, 1995. By and large it was a success, although a qualified one. Many issues were agreed to in principle, but the crucial details were left for future negotiations. High-income countries agreed to reduce their tariffs over time from an average of 6.4 to 4 percent. Of special interest to developing countries, the proportion of imports from developing countries allowed duty-free access will increase from 20 to 43 percent and tariffs on agricultural products from these countries will be reduced by 34 percent over time. The MFA will be phased out through the year 2005 and the use of VERs was further circumscribed.

High-income countries, especially the United States, also made substantial progress toward achieving their negotiating goals. Trade in services was brought within rules and disciplines of the organization with the creation of a General Agreement on Trade in Services. This agreement relates to trade in financial services, telecommunications, air transport, and the movement of labor. In agriculture, nontariff barriers to trade are to be replaced with their tariff equivalents and these tariffs reduced over time by 36 percent for high-income countries and 24 percent for developing countries. A number of export subsidy schemes were prohibited and others reduced. As well, intellectual property rights were placed within the MFN (Most Favored Nation) framework. This means that if two countries have MFN status in trade, they must also extend reciprocal protection of intellectual property rights.

Over the 12-year period from 1993 to 2005, the reduction of trade barriers under the Uruguay round is expected to lead to a 1 percent per year increase in the growth rate of trade volume (from 3 to 4 percent per year) such that trade will be $745 billion 1992 dollars higher in 2005. World income will be $230 billion higher in 2005 (in 1992 dollars), about 1 percent of world income. Of this amount, about $80 billion (about one-third) will accrue to developing countries, although the total of their GDPs is only about one-fifth world GDP.

Perhaps most importantly, a World Trade Organization was formed. The WTO includes the GATT, the newly negotiated GATS, a Dispute Settlement Board (DSB), a Trade Policy Review Board, and a Ministerial Conference, which will meet every two years. The formation of the WTO represents a major achievement for advocates of freer trade. It represents a move toward the model of an International Trade Organization, proposed after World War II, with broad powers over all forms of trade. It can also serve as an ongoing forum for further trade negotiations and dispute settlement. For example, the United States has committed to bringing its disagreements with individual countries on protection of intellectual property rights to the DSB before proceeding with invoking Section 301 of the Trade Act unilaterally against countries that it deems to be offenders.

There remains much to do on the WTO's agenda for the future. First and foremost is to finalize the details of the issues that were left unresolved at the end of the Uruguay round. The provisions on trade in services for telecommunications, finance, audiovisual products, commercial aircraft, and steel need to be extended further. The issues of trade and the environment and trade and labor standards, two contentious issues of particular interest to high-income countries, need to be addressed. On the one hand, to do this will require formulation of worldwide environmental codes and labor codes. On the other hand, it will require formulation of rules under which countries can block trade in products that were not produced according to these codes. This will be a formidable task. Another important area to be included within the WTO is foreign investment. Trade and foreign investment are closely linked, with about one-third of world trade undertaken by MNEs. As yet, however, country-level investment regulations are not governed by any global agreements. Finally, China and Russia will have to be brought within the WTO. At present, it is ironic that two of the five permanent members of the United Nations Security Council are not members of the WTO.

In addition to the multilateral trade agreements under the WTO, a growing number of regional trade groups have been formed. These have had a major impact on world trade and investment. For example, in 1996, General Motors announced that it would invest over one billion dollars in a manufacturing facility in Thailand. This investment was not made in relationship to the Thai market, but in relationship to the total market of the ASEAN countries—Thailand, Singapore, Indonesia, Brunei, Vietnam, and the Philippines. Under the ASEAN Free Trade Area (AFTA), tariffs among these countries have been reduced substantially and are scheduled to be reduced even further. GM was then investing to enable it to trade and sell its cars throughout the ASEAN countries.

The U.S.-Canada Free Trade Agreement.   On October 3, 1987, the United States and Canada agreed in principle to enter into a free trade agreement, thus creating the world's largest free trade area. This agreement became law in both nations on January 2, 1988. The agreement culminated what had been an almost century-long process of formalizing and securing trade between Canada and the United States. Since the two nations enjoy the world's largest bilateral trade, with each country being the other's largest trading partner, the FTA was expected to be of considerable benefit to both nations. Of particular importance, the agreement did not set up a customs union or trading bloc. It is fully consistent with the letter and intent of the GATT; each country remains free to pursue independently its trade policy with other nations.

With a general liberalization of trade, involving reduced duties across almost every sector of the economy, the FTA is in the long-run interests of both nations. What is particularly significant, especially for the Canadians, is the dispute resolution mechanisms. In the past, whenever the United States passed a trade bill, Canadian lobbyists would have to pressure for Canadian exemption based on the "special relationship" between the United States and Canada. This moral suasion was not always successful and was understandably unreliable. The FTA established a panel of judges with an equal number of American and Canadian representatives. After a number of disputes on, among other things, forest and agricultural products, both nations appear to have been willing to abide by the panel's rulings, although some individual companies and industries on both sides of the border are not happy with it.

The North American Free Trade Agreement (NAFTA).   Building on the momentum of the FTA, Canadian and American trade negotiators opened talks in June 1991 with Mexican representatives to establish a continent-wide free trade agreement. NAFTA created the largest trading area in the world, surpassing the trade area created by the FTA. In fact, NAFTA was a logical extension of the FTA. Although the trilateral negotiations on NAFTA were set within a rhetoric of free trade, NAFTA was largely the result of uniquely U.S. and Mexican initiatives. Canada, sensing that an U.S.-Mexican agreement was virtually a certainty, became a party to the agreement in order not to be frozen out.

Concerns about the agreement generally centered on differential labor rates and working conditions and environmental issues. The claim was that companies in Mexico, especially foreign multinational enterprises, would have access to a considerably cheaper labor pool, and lower safety standards would not be subject to the more rigorous and expensive environmental regulations in place in the United States and Canada.

With the successful negotiation of NAFTA, other countries in Latin America, such as Chile, Costa Rica, Venezuela, and Ecuador, have approached the United States with proposals to join. In 1992, U.S. president George Bush promised Chile that it would be the next member. In the mid-1990s, however, these initiatives may have lost momentum and NAFTA itself has come under attack by some politicians in the United States. Yet at the same time, negotiations are underway for a Free Trade in the Americas Agreement (FTAA). FTAA negotiators are working to bring together interhemispherical trading agreements such as NAFTA (between Mexico, the U.S., and Canada) and Mercosur (which links the economies of countries in the southern half of the hemisphere). Currently NAFTA and Mercosur are fundamentally different arrangements. NAFTA is an advanced model of free trade, while Mercosur is an attempt to achieve a common market in the southern half of the hemisphere. FTAA negotiations are scheduled to be completed well before 2005, and the successful completion of FTAA would liberalize trade in the hemisphere beyond that stipulated by the WTO.

The European Union and the Single European Market (SEM).   The integration of Europe has been a slow and at times tortuous process. However, in the almost 40 years since efforts at increased European integration were begun, what is now the European Union has grown to include 16 nations from Denmark to the United Kingdom to Spain to Greece.[4] As a political body, the EU is the result of the amalgamation of three component communities: the European Coal and Steel Community, founded in 1952 under the Treaty of Paris (1951); the European Economic Community, founded in 1958 under the Treaty of Rome (1957); and the European Atomic Energy Community (EURATOM), founded in 1958 under a separate Treaty of Rome (1957). The amalgamation of these three bodies was formalized by the Treaty of Brussels in 1965, which established a common council, commission, court of justice, and parliament.

What is most distinctive about the EU is that it is founded on the principle of supranationality (i.e., the EU councils and commissions are intended to be paramount over national laws and legislatures). For trading purposes, this means that member nations cannot enter into any trade agreements that are inconsistent with EU regulations. Within EU itself, the elimination of tariffs was achieved in 1961, with the establishment of a common external commercial policy and a common agricultural policy. With the passing of the Single Market Act in 1985, all member nations committed themselves to realizing the single market by the end of 1992. This act removed all barriers to trade in goods and services; barriers to mobility for the citizens of EU member countries; and all national regulations that might discriminate against a product, business, or individual from a member country.

The net impact of the SEM on trade and investment is still uncertain. Already it has induced multinational enterprises based in countries outside Europe to invest there to have free access to this huge market. What is less certain is whether the new economic system will turn these countries into "Fortress Europe" or whether it will promote multilateral freer trade. In trade negotiations, the EU must negotiate as a unified bloc with a uniform position. Individual countries within the EU can try to influence its position on various trade issues, but they cannot "go it alone" and maintain their own position.

For managers of international trade operations, the results of all these sets of negotiations are of prime importance. Expansion of international trade operations is often a long-term investment. To make the correct decision, and to implement it effectively, will require ever increasing levels of knowledge, expertise, and sophistication in assessing the environment for international trade and in engaging in international trade operations. The difficulty of predicting the future direction of trade regulations, much less formulating an effective trade strategy, can be illustrated with an example.

Under the FTA, the 22 percent duty on exports of Canadian wool outerwear was to be phased out over 10 years. In response, some Canadian producers began to

---

[4]EU membership consists of the original members of Belgium, France, Germany, Italy, Luxembourg, and the Netherlands (1965), plus the United Kingdom (1993), Ireland (1973), Denmark (1973), Greece (1981), Spain (1986), Portugal (1986), Sweden (1995) Austria (1995), and Finland (1995). Several other countries have applied for membership, but consideration and approval of their applications will take many years.

increase exports to the United States. In particular, Peerless Clothing increased sales from about $10 million to over $70 million in just three years. In response, when the NAFTA was being negotiated, U.S. clothing producers used Peerless as an example of the damage they had sustained under the FTA. They induced the U.S. government to establish North American content requirements for wool-based garments that would enter the United States. Almost no Canadian-made wool-based products could meet these requirements. For these products, a quota of a 5 million square meter equivalent was allowed. By 1993, Canadian exports were running about a 3.5 million square meter equivalent (up from 1.5 million in 1988), and the Canadian government announced that it would have to hold back a portion of the remaining quota for potential new entrants in the future. The end result has been that existing exporters were not able to increase exports to the United States beyond their 1994 levels.

Channels of Distribution and Export Marketing

The last block of analysis involves identifying the means by which the product can be moved from the producer to the ultimate buyer.

Four characteristics of the channels of distribution that link producers in one country with buyers in another are especially important:

1. International channels of distribution are usually more complex and have more layers than do channels in the national market. A typical channel for the domestic market would be: producer-wholesaler-retailer. For export it might be: producer-export agent-import agent-major wholesaler-small wholesaler-retailer.

2. The costs of international channels are usually higher than those of domestic channels, so a higher percentage of the final price to the buyer comes from the costs of building, accessing, and operating through international channels of distribution.

3. An exporter may have to operate through different types of channels of distribution on export markets than it uses in its domestic market. For example, in the domestic market, its scale of operations or the value of close customer contact may argue for an in-house distribution and sales system all the way to the ultimate purchaser. To set up such a system in an export market might be prohibitively expensive, given planned export volumes. Conditions in export markets might be such that expertise in local marketing techniques (which the firm does not possess) may be more important than product knowledge. Regulations in the export market may hinder or even prohibit a firm from entering into distribution and sales operations. Conversely, in a firm's domestic market, there may be a well-developed system of independent distributors for the firm's product, whereas in the export market such a distribution system may not exist or company personnel may not have the skills required to distribute and sell the firm's product effectively.

4. International channels of distribution are often also the source of information to the firm about conditions in its export markets, and how and why its product is succeeding or falling in these markets. In such a situation, a firm must either integrate forward into distribution and sales, place some of its personnel in the export market, or develop close ties and good information flows between itself and its distributors abroad.

For these four reasons, a firm's strategy toward, and management of, its international channels of distribution are usually relatively more important, more costly, and more difficult for export marketing than are its channels for marketing in the domestic market. A firm can have a competitive product, but if it chooses the wrong channel of distribution or mismanages its relationships with the channel, its export performance will be reduced below potential. As well, exporters, particularly new exporters, have less expertise with international channels of distribution than they have with the channels in their national markets.

Firms entering export operations are often caught in a bind when they select their channels of distribution. The more closely the channel matches the one they use in their domestic market, the greater their expertise at managing the channel, and the higher the probability of success. On the other hand, the more appropriate the channel is for the export market, the higher the probability of export success. The implications of these two generalizations on the factors influencing export success for channel selection may differ, however. A firm may use an in-house wholesale and retail system in the domestic economy, but access to a similar system in an export market may not be available, purchasing one may be too expensive, or the firm may not want to risk investing so much capital outside its home country. In this situation, it must turn to independent agents or distributors to gain access to the export market. Similarly, a firm may use direct selling in the domestic market, but such an approach may be inappropriate in the export market.

There is a wide variety of possible channels of distribution from which an exporter may choose: brokers, factors, manufacturer's representatives, export agents, wholesalers, retailers, import jobbers, trading houses, and so on. These trade intermediaries can be characterized in two dimensions. The first dimension is ownership of the goods: agents who act on the firm's behalf for a fee versus distributors who pay for, take title to, and sell the goods on their own behalf. The second dimension is channel control: a direct approach (in which the firm owns and operates the channels) versus an indirect approach (in which the channels are independent of the firm).

Selection between these four basic alternative combinations (and the many different types of organizations within each type) is a difficult but important task. The decision will rest on such criteria as the size, capabilities, and resources of the exporter; its strategy in the export market; the degree of risk it is willing to undertake; the extent of its current and future export sales; the importance of coverage, penetration, control, and information feedback; and the differences between the export market and the domestic market.

Conflicts can easily arise between exporters and independent (indirect) channels over many issues. Often importers desire sole import rights for the product in the country. Exporters want sole product rights—that is, for the importer to carry no competing products. There can be conflicts over pricing, cost sharing for advertising and service, margins, new product introduction, and so on. The benefits of using indirect channels are that typically resource costs are lower and the independent channels may have superior first-hand knowledge of, and access to, customers in the export market. The major costs are in loss of control, less ability to push goods through the channels by discounts, promotions, and direct selling or to pull goods through the channels through control of advertising. Use of indirect channels usually reduces information flows and reduces knowledge acquisition of market information when compared to direct channels. The costs and benefits of using direct (company-owned) channels tend to be the reverse of the costs and benefits of indirect channels: initially less first-hand knowledge of, and expertise in, the market; less access to customers, greater up-front costs on the one hand, but fewer conflicts, increased control, and greater information flows on the other.

Often an exporter's success with using indirect (independent) channels of distribution rests on whether its bargaining power is greater or less than that of its independent agent/distributor. Superior bargaining power can rest with either side and largely depends on which side provides the most value, which side faces the greatest range of alternatives, and which side needs the other the most. The importance of channels of distribution and the difficulty in accessing them in Japan often tip the balance of bargaining power in favor of independent agents and distributors in Japan. Yet American firms have been able to access these channels or to develop their own through direct selling and in-house distribution and sales networks. Whatever channels are chosen and whatever the relative bargaining power, the complexity and the length of international channels of distribution add to their cost.

Trade Intermediaries

Import Traders

The topic of importing has received relatively little attention in books on international marketing or international business. Yet for every export, there is an import. And arm's-length importing still represents the majority of imports. This section focuses on "pure" importers, i.e., importers who purchase products abroad for resale. The important topic of sourcing imports for use as inputs in the production process is the subject of the next chapter.

This section is quite brief, since much of the framework of analysis has already been presented. From the perspective of the importer, the export framework presented above needs only to be turned inside out. An importer assesses the comparative and competitive advantages of producers outside the home market; assesses the evolving demand and supply characteristics of the home market to look for gaps in markets or segments of markets that these producers' products could fill; assesses the impediments to connecting producers abroad with buyers in the home market and the factors that might facilitate this linkage; and assesses the channels of distribution that might be used to link producers abroad with buyers in the home market. An importer could either have the objective to resell the imported products (an import marketer) to other buyers or to use these products as raw or semifinished materials, or as components in its own final products (an import purchasing manager).

Pure importers usually have an "ownership advantage" related to the domestic market in which they operate, such as knowledge of the domestic market, ownership of or access to the channels of distribution, or expertise in evaluating government regulation of imports or business practices in the domestic market. Importers typically possess one of two other ownership advantages: knowledge and expertise in operations in one or more foreign countries or knowledge and expertise of the production capabilities of some product or range of products worldwide. The knowledge of domestic conditions allows importers to create value for producers abroad relative to the value they could access by exporting directly to buyers in the domestic economy. Knowledge of production capabilities worldwide allows them to create value for domestic producers (for imported inputs) and domestic retailers relative to the value they would receive if they tried to search out these products for themselves.

Pure importers are market connectors; they create value through linking producers abroad to buyers in the domestic market. If they do not continue to create value after the initial link has been made, producers abroad may begin to sell directly to the buyers in the domestic market. Similarly, purchasers in their domestic market will make direct connections with producers abroad.

Export Traders

In the section on export operations, the viewpoint of an export producer, rather than a pure export trader, was taken. This was done since in most respects the analysis of the international trade environment is the same from both perspectives. The major difference between the producer-exporter and the export trader is that the latter has the opportunity to buy products from (or act as an agent for) different producers in the same or different industries. In this respect, an export trader shares many of the same characteristics as an import trader. The "ownership advantages" of export traders typically lie in knowledge of markets in particular countries or in knowledge of worldwide markets for particular products. They are also market connectors and face the same problems as pure importers once they have linked domestic producers with buyers in export markets.

Trading Houses

In some cases, pure import operations and pure export operations may be joined together within the same firm: the trading house. Typically, however, a trading house will specialize in either exports or imports. The exception to this generalization is found in the large trading houses in Japan, Hong Kong, and Korea and to some extent in Europe, and in firms that specialize in trading such commodities as energy products, minerals, and agricultural products.

Import and export operations also exist together in some export producers. These firms may need to source inputs for their production operations and to fill out their product lines from abroad and to export their output as well. As discussed below, some export sales are contingent on reciprocal imports under various forms of countertrade. These operations can be handled by this type of department as well.

In summary, managers of export operations or those about to engage in export operations need to address five questions:

1. Does our product and firm have a sustainable competitive advantage in export markets and, if so, why?
2. What are the export markets and the segments of those markets that will value our product sufficiently (relative to other competing products) to offset our costs of production and distribution?
3. Should the firm export a standard product with a standard marketing mix worldwide or should it tailor its products and marketing mix to individual export markets?
4. What natural and government-imposed trade barriers impede linking production in one country to purchase in another, and what factors might facilitate this linkage?
5. What are the most appropriate channels of distribution for our product to achieve our goals in export markets?

Pricing in Export Markets

Product pricing is an important and difficult decision in any market. Four pricing strategies can be identified that are unique to export markets: (1) requiring prices in export markets that yield higher returns than are available in domestic markets; (2) pricing to yield similar returns in domestic and export markets; (3) pricing to yield lower returns, or even losses, in export markets—at least in the short run; (4) and pricing to sell production in excess of the needs of the domestic market so long as these sales make a contribution to fixed overhead and profit.

The first pricing strategy is often based on the belief that export operations are more risky relative to domestic sales, and they often entail hidden costs that are not picked up by standard accounting systems. Under this viewpoint, the prices and profits recorded on export sales must be higher than those for domestic markets if exports are to be undertaken.

The second strategy is based on the viewpoint that export markets do not differ from domestic markets. This strategy is often taken by experienced exporters, for whom there is little differentiation between export and domestic sales. It is also taken by new and inexperienced exporters, who take an "if they order it, we'll ship it" attitude toward export markets.

The third strategy reflects an approach that views export markets as the potential growth markets of the future. These are the markets in which the firm must operate if it is to survive in the long run. These aggressive exporters are willing to take short-term losses to buy market share, to develop products that are appropriate for export markets, and to achieve economies of scale. They believe that, in the long run, once their position in export markets has been established, their costs will be lowered and they will be able to earn satisfactory returns. This strategy, however, may make the firm vulnerable to antidumping action by domestic competitors in the export market and subject to antidumping duties.

The final strategy reflects a view of export markets as a dumping ground for production in times of excess capacity. Although this type of export does make a contribution to profits, firms that view export markets in this way cannot be regarded as true export marketers.

Whatever pricing strategy is chosen, the relatively high fixed costs per unit that are typical of international distribution channels have a significant effect on the ability of the firm to use price as a competitive weapon. To take an extreme case, often the costs of international distribution are a fixed amount *per unit* (due to transportation costs based on weight or volume, tariffs levied on a per unit basis, and channel costs/fees on a per unit basis). They do not vary with cost or price. Then a change in 10 percent at the producer price level may only change the price faced by the buyer by 2 percent. Yet a 10 percent reduction in price may reduce the producer's margins over direct costs by 50 percent. Buyer response to such a price cut would have to be enormous for this price cut to be worthwhile.

At least some of the costs of distribution are indeed set with respect to the producer's selling price, such as inventory costs, some agents' fees, and some components of tariff charges. Sales taxes are usually based on the landed, duty-paid price of the product. They vary with price. But there is also a fixed component due to the fixed transportation costs per unit. Most of the fees charged by independent agents are usually based on producer prices, as are the markups taken through the channels of distribution. Despite these portions of the price paid by purchasers that vary with the producer prices, in export marketing there is usually a higher component in final prices that vary with the number of units sold than for domestic marketing. This characteristic of export marketing must be taken into consideration by firms in their export marketing pricing strategies.

Stages of Export Market Involvement

For firms operating solely in the domestic market, starting a new business or introducing a new product are major strategic moves and are undertaken only after careful research, analysis, and consideration. The decision to enter export operations at all or in a particular export market is more often quite haphazard and made by chance, or the decision itself may go unnoticed. Most frequently, a firm will enter export operations based on an unsolicited order from abroad, or an offer from an agent or importer abroad to represent the firm or sell its products. Other unplanned entries into export marketing may come from internal factors, such as overproduction, declining domestic sales, and excess capacity. Such external events as competitive pressures, "follow the leader" behavior, government-sponsored trade fairs, and funded export missions may also lead to unplanned entry into export markets.

Most firms initially develop, produce, and market products for their domestic markets without regard for export markets. They may even turn down orders from abroad. If a firm continues to receive unsolicited orders, it may move toward filling orders as they are received, despite the problems of documentation and payment that may arise. Gradually, the firm may develop management expertise in the basic mechanics of exporting and these orders begin to become a significant part of sales. In this situation, a firm may begin to explore why these orders have been received. It may try to determine if there is a potential to increase sales to the firms that have already placed orders and to other firms in the same export market.

In the next stage of export involvement, the firm begins to evaluate the impact of export sales on its performance in a more systematic way. If it finds this impact to be positive, it may begin to change its export operations to increase their effectiveness. It is at this stage when a systematic analysis of exporting, as described in these chapters, can be of value. In the final stage, exports become a major, even the deciding, factor in the firm's strategy and operations. For firms at this stage, products are often developed and introduced in relationship to export markets as well as the domestic market.

This process of internationalization may be short-circuited at any stage if the results of export operations are not seen as favorable. Such a decision may be incorrect if the firm has not really given export operations the same attention that it has given domestic markets. Conversely, a firm may have no choice but to start at some more advanced stage. The domestic market may be too small to support any operations at all, much less a scale-efficient one. Increasingly, however, the evolution of the international trading environment has forced more and more firms at a faster and faster pace through these stages of internationalization to become full-fledged export marketers.

Global Trade and Investment

So far, the viewpoint of exporting has been one of a producer-exporter or importer or a trade intermediary exporting products to one country market. This viewpoint, although useful to present the basics of international trade, is highly simplistic and may give a false impression of international trade in the late 1990s. This basic model can be extended to encompass a more realistic view of world trade. The model of international trade presented so far can be extended to make it more realistic in three ways.

First, as tariff and nontariff barriers to trade have fallen globally and as free trade areas have developed, firms often now analyze trade opportunities on a regional, even global basis; Exports to Belgium may not be of interest, but exports to Belgium as a gateway to Europe as a whole make a much more interesting proposition.

Second, exports are often not sent directly from one home production site to an export market abroad. Rather, inputs are sourced in a number of countries and assembled in other countries, and the final product is sold in yet other countries. Japanese car producers manufacture parts in Japan and ship them for assembly in

Europe, in North America, and in developing countries. In turn they source some parts in these countries for use in Japan and in their assembly operations abroad.

Third, trade has become intricately linked with foreign investment, joint ventures, licensing, franchising, contract production, and component sourcing. These topics are described in later chapters. In particular there is a strong link between trade and foreign investment. A large component of international trade is carried out by multinational enterprises (MNEs). About a third of all world trade in manufactured products is through MNEs. In the late 1980s, almost 80 percent of U.S. merchandise exports were undertaken by U.S. MNEs or affiliates of foreign-owned MNEs operating in the United States. A similar situation prevailed in the United Kingdom. Japanese MNEs accounted for over 40 percent of exports from and 60 percent of imports to Japan. A considerable proportion of the trade conducted by MNEs is within the firm (i.e., between units of the MNE located in different countries).

Is the analytical framework developed so far useful for analyzing trade by MNEs? What then are the differences between trade via or within MNEs and arm's-length trade? The answer to the first question is yes, but with some modifications. By definition, an MNE has investments and (usually) production operations in more than one country. At the headquarters level of the MNE, basic decisions are made about where different activities along the value-added chain are located geographically. For example, one U.S. manufacturer of scientific instruments performs R&D and product design in the United States and produces the key high-quality, low-tolerance components there. It exports raw materials to its subsidiary in Puerto Rico for production of lower-tolerance, labor-intensive standard components. Components from its U.S. and Puerto Rican facilities are exported to Malaysia for assembly. The finished instruments are then exported to Singapore for inspection and then to Ireland for final testing. The final products are then re-exported all over the world at the direction of the head office. Managers in the head office then balance production costs and capabilities with transportation costs in an effort to minimize the costs of production, transportation, and inventories. They also search out markets for the firm's products worldwide. At the conceptual level, their analysis and activities are similar to the ones described in the framework for export operations, but on a larger and more complex scale. For managers at the subsidiary level, however, trade is performed at the direction of the head-office staff. At the subsidiary level, although managers are engaged in export and import operations, the volume, type, and destination of the subsidiary's exports are controlled from the head office.

As international business has evolved over the decades, the forms of international involvements have increased in number and complexity. Beside exports, a firm utilizes its core skills to service markets abroad via investment in production facilities in another country, by licensing its product or process technology, or by contract production. In the early 1990s, IKEA, the Swedish household products company, decided to move some of its product sourcing to Southeast Asia. To accomplish this move, it tried to avoid equity participation in production facilities. Rather, it formed long-term relationships with producers who it determined had the basic production and management capabilities to produce to its design and quality specifications. It now distributes and sells these products worldwide. IKEA, however, engages in extensive training with its suppliers. It also will supply equipment and train producers in its use. In exchange, it receives price concessions on its future purchases. IKEA supplies these producers with the designs and needed imported inputs. Although IKEA's contract suppliers both import inputs and export their output, for all intents and purposes they are not engaged in international trade.

Special Topics

Countertrade

From the mid-1970s to the mid-1980s, countertrade, the linked exchange of goods for goods in international trade, expanded rapidly. In the latter part of the 1980s, however, the growth of countertrade slowed. Indonesia, for example, stopped mandating countertrade purchases for its government purchases from abroad. Nonetheless, countertrade still remains an important feature of international trade.

The term *countertrade* covers eight types of trade operation:

1. Barter: The simultaneous exchange of goods without money.
2. Counterpurchase: The assumption by the exporter through a separate but linked contract, of an obligation to import some percentage of the price of the goods exported in the form of goods purchased in the importing country.
3. Compensation or buyback: The agreement by an exporter of plant and equipment to buy back some portion of output of the goods produced by the equipment it exports from the importing firms.
4. Production sharing: Similar to buyback, but used in mining and energy projects, where the developer is paid out of a share of the production of the mine or well.
5. Industrial offsets: An obligation undertaken by the exporter to produce or assemble part of the product and source parts in the importing country. Exporting from the importing country may also be undertaken as part of an industrial offset arrangement.
6. Switches: An undertaking by the exporter to import goods from a third country with whom the importing country has developed a trade surplus in its "clearing account" under a bilateral trade agreement.
7. Unblocking funds: The use of suppliers' credits that cannot be repatriated due to foreign exchange controls (blocked funds) in the importing country to purchase goods there for export.
8. Debt for equity swaps: The conversion of international debts owed by the importing country to equity in some operation there.

Countertrade contracts can be very complicated and costly to negotiate and to execute. They are filled with pitfalls for the unwary exporter. Only 1 in 10 countertrade arrangements is ever finalized. For an inexperienced exporter or an exporter who is not familiar with countertrade, the best course of action is to seek the advice and support of an experienced countertrader. Many exporters have been caught unaware when countertrade demands are introduced in the negotiation process of a trade arrangement.

Countertrade contracts have nine important characteristics:

1. The timing of the flow of goods. (Will the export precede, be simultaneous with, or follow the countertraded import?)
2. The duration of the contracts. (Within what time period must the matching import be made?)
3. The countertrade percent. (What percent of the export price must be taken back in countertraded products?)
4. Voluntary or mandatory countertrade.
5. The penalties for noncompliance with the countertrade contract.
6. The product requirements for the linked imports. (Is the exporter free to choose any goods to fulfill the countertrade obligation or must the exporter source from an approved list?)
7. Whether the countertraded goods must be incremental to the exporter's previous purchases in the importing country.
8. Country destination of the linked imports. (Can they be sold to any country or must their final destination be the exporter's home country?)
9. Whether the exporting firm itself must fulfill the countertrade obligation or whether it can transfer it to another party.

Each of these provisions is subject to negotiations between the exporter and the importer or the importing country's government. As can be appreciated from the preceding description of countertrade operations, they require exporters to develop a new set of skills—often at great cost in terms of management time, risks, and failed and unprofitable countertrade arrangements. Essentially, countertrade requires a "double coincidence of needs": the importer needs the exporter's product and the exporter either needs products from the importer of the importing country or can identify buyers who do. In general, countertrade is an inefficient form of trade. It creates costs and risks for both importers and exporters and reduces the value created by international trade. In general, using money to facilitate trade is much more efficient than countertrade.

Major Project Development

The importance of major project development in international trade and investment has increased during the 1990s and there is every prospect that it will continue to increase into the future. These projects are often for infrastructure development such as electricity generation, telecommunications, water and sewage treatment facilities, and even roads and ports. These major projects are of three types: turnkey projects; build, operate, and transfer projects; and build, operate, and own projects.

In a turnkey project, the project manager undertakes to construct a major project, such as a smelter or electrical generating plant, and then turn it over to its owners when it is in full operation. Turnkey projects offer exporters a means of increasing their exports dramatically by one sale. Turnkey projects differ on two dimensions: self-engineered versus construction to specification; fixed price versus cost-plus. In the self-engineered project, the exporter undertakes to meet certain performance requirements set by the importer, but the actual equipment and plant design is left up to the exporter. For example, the exporter might undertake to construct a pipeline with the capacity to pump a specified quantity of natural gas per day from one location to another. The size and thickness of the pipe and the power and number of the pumping stations are left to the discretion of the exporter; the exporter bears the risk of not meeting the performance requirements. In construction to specification, the exporter undertakes to construct the project to the importer's specifications. As long as these are met, the risk of performance failure rests with the importer.

Both self-engineered and construction to specification contracts can be undertaken on a fixed-price or a cost-plus basis. On a cost-plus contract, the risk of cost overruns lies with the purchaser. With a fixed-price contract, the risk lies with the exporter. Usually the purchaser specifies in the bid documents the types of contract to be undertaken. An inexperienced, risk-averse purchaser may choose a fixed-price, self-engineered contract to shift the risk to the exporter. This type of contract usually leads to a higher bid price, since the exporter must be compensated for the increased risk it undertakes.

For turnkey projects, bids are usually submitted by a small number of exporters or groups of exporters. The importer typically screens the bidders prior to the actual bid to eliminate bidders who lack the required technical skills to undertake the contract. In this situation, with only a few bidders, the higher an exporter bids, the greater the expected profits, but the lower the probability of winning the bid. Assessing the trade-off between higher profits and decreased probability of winning the bid is one of the key factors in turnkey operations. Often, after the bids have been opened, the importer will go back to the exporters and try to negotiate with those with the lowest bids to get them to reduce their bids by playing one against the other.

Build, operate, and transfer (BOT) and build, operate, and own (BOO) projects have many of the same features as turnkey projects. Firms bid for the right to construct the project. BOT and BOO projects of course differ from turnkey projects in that the winning firm also operates the facility after it is completed, hence there is an element of foreign direct investment in these types of projects. For BOT projects, ownership is limited to a certain time period, at which time the project is to be transferred to another organization, usually the host country government. For both BOT and BOO projects, output prices and volume over time are often specified.

Exports, Imports, and International Finance

Three important aspects of international finance need to be understood by every exporter and importer: the effect of the real exchange rate on competitive advantage, the effect of variations in the nominal exchange rate on export and import profitability, and the effect of trade on financing needs and sources.

Movements in the nominal exchange rate can have a dramatic impact on the profitability of international trading operations. Take the case of an importer in Canada sourcing from the United States. The importer buys a machine worth $100,000 for sale to a Canadian company with a 10 percent markup over landed cost with delivery six months later. If, over this six-month period, the U.S. dollar appreciates against the Canadian dollar by 2 percent, the importer's gross profit margin is reduced by 20 percent.

An importer has several options through which to handle this risk. It can insist that the U.S. exporter price the machine in Canadian dollars and set its markup based on this price. This alternative simply shifts the exchange rate risk back onto the U.S. exporter and may result in a higher purchase price. The importer may decide to bear the risk and hope that the Canadian dollar does not fall, or even that it may rise. In this case, the importer may try to shift the cost of this risk onto the ultimate customer by increasing its selling price. This action, however, may result in the loss of the sale.

Alternatively, the importer may use some type of currency hedge to eliminate the exchange-rate risk. At the time of the sale, the importer can exchange the Canadian dollar equivalent of $100,000 U.S. (minus the six-month interest rate) into U.S. dollars and place them in a six-month financial asset. When the machine is shipped, the importer can then cash in the U.S.-dollar-denominated financial asset and pay for the purchase. Alternatively, the importer could also enter the foreign exchange market and buy $100,000 U.S. six months forward at the six-month forward rate prevailing at the time. When the machine is shipped in six months, it can exercise its forward contract for U.S. dollars at the exchange rate that was set six months before. The forward market for currencies (in this example U.S. and Canadian dollars) is exactly the same as the spot market for foreign exchange. The rate is set by the supply and demand for U.S. and Canadian dollars six months forward. Buying dollars forward obligates the purchaser to exercise the contract in six months at the rate set at the time of the purchase in the forward market for foreign exchange.

By either of these two methods, the importer can be certain of the Canadian dollar cost of the U.S. import. The importer can then price to the ultimate purchaser in terms of this Canadian dollar price. A Canadian producer that sources inputs in the U.S. could follow the same procedure before making a purchase in order to be able to compare the Canadian dollar price of the import with the prices of other inputs in the Canadian market.

There is another aspect of international trade that has important implications for corporate finance: the effect of international trade on working capital requirements. For international trade, in most cases there is a longer time period between when a product is produced and the time the ultimate purchaser receives it. Someone must finance the capital requirements and pay the capital costs of these larger inventories of final products: the producer, the exporter, the importer, or some financial intermediary. Who finances these inventory costs depends on the financial strength of the importer and the exporter. For example, the exporter can demand payment when the goods are shipped through an irrevocable letter of credit that is discharged when the goods are loaded on the international carrier. In this case, the importer must arrange the financing for the period from the time the goods are exported until they are sold and the importer receives payment. Similarly, the importer could demand that payment be made only when the goods arrive in the destination country. Whichever party finally agrees to finance this inventory, arranging the financing often proves to be difficult and costly.

The problem lies with the valuation and security of the goods from the viewpoint of whoever is going to finance them. If, for example, the importer rejects the goods when they arrive as being not to specification or damaged, what is their value and how can it be recovered? As an extreme example, an American producer of customized vehicles received an order from Libya for ambulances that were to be specially modified for desert conditions. The size of the order was several times the net worth of the company. Who would finance such a specialized product by such a country? The sale fell through for lack of financing.

An alternative approach is to require that the importer open an irrevocable letter of credit for the amount of the purchase. The exporter is then paid via this letter when the goods are shipped. This shifts the financing costs onto the importer. It also shifts other problems onto the importer, since the importer has already paid for the products. The products may be of unacceptable quality, or not to specification, or the order may not be complete, or the product may be damaged during shipping. These problems can be addressed through the use of inspection and certification firms that act on behalf of the importer and through buying insurance.

The importance of export financing as an export tool has grown over the years as more and more importers and importing countries have experienced problems in accessing foreign exchange to pay for imports. The debt situation in many developing countries and in some of the eastern European countries has further increased the importance of export financing in export marketing. A firm may have a competitive product, there may be demand for the product in an export market, but trade may be blocked unless some means is found to finance the sale.

The governments of most European countries and the United States, Japan, and Canada have set up government-owned and funded institutions to provide export financing. The interest rates and the terms and conditions on the loans provided by these institutions are designed to promote exports from their countries. When firms from different countries bid on an export contract, there is a tendency for these government-backed banks to make the terms of the loans more and more favorable in order to win the contract for the exporter they are supporting. Interest rate wars can easily break out. To prevent this situation from occurring, an informal agreement has been reached among them that they will not provide funds at rates below their own cost of capital. This agreement has proven impossible to enforce, however. The cost of capital of these banks is difficult to calculate and varies over time and among countries. Exporters often exert pressure through the government for these banks to make their terms more favorable so that they can win the export contract. Governments themselves often have an interest in promoting exports of certain products or exports to certain countries.

Summary

In the previous chapter, a framework was developed to analyze international trade operations. In that chapter, the factors that influence comparative and competitive advantage and the effect of real exchange rates on export performance were described. This chapter started off where the previous chapter ended. It described how to analyze export markets and various strategies for entering those markets. It then described the factors that can impede or facilitate trade. As the final block in the analysis, it described how the producer itself might enter export markets and use various pricing strategies in export markets. Beyond direct exports by the firm, there are also several types of trade intermediaries through which a firm can export, such as importers and exporters and trading houses. The basic model was then extended to the more complex forms of trade that are currently prevalent today: the linkages between trade, joint ventures, foreign direct investment, licensing, and contract production. The model was also extended to regional trade and trade, investment, production, and sales in several countries along the value-added chain.

The last section of the chapter dealt with several special topics, such as countertrade, turnkey, BOT, and BOO projects, and trade finance. These two chapters cover the basics of international trade operations.

In the future, there is every prospect that a higher and higher percentage of world output will be traded internationally. For firms in many industries, the question is not, "Should we trade internationally?" They have no choice if they are to maintain and enhance their competitive position. Rather, the question is, "How can we trade more effectively?" Expertise in international trade will become an increasingly important skill for managers to acquire.

Supplementary Reading

Buzzell, Robert D., John A. Quelch, and Christopher A. Bartlett. *Global Marketing Management.* 2nd ed. New York: Addison-Wesley Publishing, 1992.

Czinkota, Michael R. *International Marketing.* 2nd ed. Hinsdale, IL: Dryden Press. 1990.

Harper, Timothy. *Cracking the New European Markets.* NewYork: John Wiley &,Sons, 1990.

JETRO. *Selling in Japan. The World's Second Largest Market.* Tokyo: JETRO, 1985.

Preeg, Ernest. *Traders in a Brave New World: The Uruguay Round and the Future of the International Trading System.* Chicago: University of Chicago Press, 1995.

Renner, Sandra L., and W. Gary Winget. *Fast-Track Exporting.* New York: AMACOM, 1991.

Ricks, David. *Blunders in International Business.* Cambridge, MA: Basil Blackwell, 1993.

Schaffer, Matt. *Winning the Countertrade War: New Export Strategies for America.* New York: John Wiley & Sons, 1989.

Thorelli, Hans B., and S. Tamer Cavusgil, eds. *International Marketing Strategy.* 3rd ed. Elmsford, N.Y.: Pergamon Press, 1995.

Triller, Lawrence W., *Going Global: New Opportunities for Growing Companies to Compete in World Markets.* Homewood, IL: Business One Irwin, 1991.

Weiss, Kenneth D. *Building an Export/Import Business.* New York: John Wiley & Sons, 1991.

5   GLOBAL SOURCING STRATEGY: R&D, MANUFACTURING, AND MARKETING INTERFACES

International business has experienced a major metamorphosis of an irreversible kind. Today, executives have come to accept a new reality of global competition and global competitors. An increasing number of companies—particularly from the United States, western Europe, and Japan—are competing head-on for global dominance. Global competition suggests a drastically shortened life cycle for most products, and no longer permits companies a polycentric, country-by-country approach to international business. If companies that have developed a new product do follow a country-by-country approach to foreign market entry over time, a globally oriented competitor will likely overcome their initial competitive advantages by blanketing world markets with similar products in a shorter period of time.

A framework that is frequently used to describe cross-national business practices is the international product cycle theory. The theory has provided a compelling description of dynamic patterns of international trade of manufactured products and direct investment as a product advances through its life cycle. According to the theory, changes in inputs and product characteristics toward standardization over *time* determine an optimal production location at any particular phase of the product's life cycle.

However, three major limitations of the international product cycle theory have to be borne in mind:

1. **Increased pace of new product introduction and reduction in innovational lead time,** which deprive companies of the age-old polycentric approach to global markets.
2. **Predictable sourcing development during the product cycle,** which permits a shrewd company to outmaneuver competition.
3. **More active management of locational and corporate resources on a global basis,** which gives a company a preemptive first-mover advantage over competition.

This chapter was prepared by Masaaki Kotabe, The University of Texas at Austin. Copyright © Masaaki Kotabe, 1996.

One successful example of such globally oriented strategy is Sony Corporation. Sony developed transistorized solid-state color TVs in Japan in the 1960s and marketed them initially in the United States before they were introduced in the rest of the world, including the Japanese market. Mass marketing initially in the United States and then throughout the world in a short period of time had given this Japanese company a first-mover advantage as well as economies of scale advantages. In contrast, EMI provides an example of the failure to take advantage of global opportunities that existed. This British company developed and began marketing CAT (computerized axial tomography) scanners in 1972. Inventors Godfrey Houndsfield and Allan Cormack, won a Nobel Prize for developing CAT technology. Despite an enormous demand for CAT scanners in the United States, the largest market for state-of-the-art medical equipment, EMI failed to export them to the United States immediately and in sufficient numbers. Instead, the British company slowly, and probably belatedly, began exporting them to the United States in the mid-1970s, as if to follow the evolutionary pattern suggested by the international product cycle model. Some years later, the British company established a production facility in the United States, only to be slowed down by technical problems. By then, EMI was already facing stiff competition from global electronics giants, including Philips, Siemens, General Electric, and Toshiba. Indeed, it was General Electric that in a short period of time blanketed the U.S. market and subsequently the rest of the world with its own version of CAT scanners, which were technologically inferior to the British model.

In both cases, technology diffused quickly. Today, quick technological diffusion has virtually become a matter of fact. Without established sourcing plans and distribution and service networks, it is extremely difficult to exploit both emerging technology and potential markets around the world simultaneously. General Electric's swift global reach could not have been possible without its ability to procure crucial components internally and on a global basis. As a result, the increased pace of new product introduction and reduction in innovational lead time calls for more proactive management of locational and corporate resources on a global basis. In this chapter, we emphasize logistical management of the **interfaces** of R&D, manufacturing, and marketing activities on a global basis—which we call **global sourcing strategy**—and also the importance of the ability to procure major components of the product in-house such that companies can proactively standardize either components or products. Global sourcing strategy requires a close coordination among R&D, manufacturing, and marketing activities across national boundaries.[1]

There always exist conflicts in the "tug-of-war" of differing objectives among R&D, manufacturing, and marketing. Excessive product modification and proliferation for the sake of satisfying ever-changing customer needs will undermine manufacturing efficiency and have negative cost consequences, barring a perfectly flexible computer-aided design (CAD) and computer-aided manufacturing (CAM) facility. CAD/CAM technology has improved tremendously in recent years, but the full benefit of flexible manufacturing is still many years away.[2] In contrast, excessive

---

[1]Kotabe, 1992.

[2]"A Survey of Manufacturing Technology," *Economist,* March 5, 1994, pp. 3–18.

product standardization for the sake of lowering manufacturing costs will also be likely to result in unsatisfied or undersatisfied customers. Similarly, innovative product designs and features as desired by customers may indeed be a technological feat but might not be conducive to manufacturing. Therefore, topics such as product design for manufacturability and components/product standardization have become increasingly important strategic issues today. It has become imperative for many companies to develop a sound sourcing strategy in order to exploit R&D, manufacturing, and marketing most efficiently on a global basis.

Extent and Complexity of Global Sourcing Strategy

In this chapter, we introduce international subject matters not ordinarily covered in an international management textbook. It is our strong belief that managers should understand and appreciate the important roles that product designers, engineers, production managers, and purchasing managers, among others, play in corporate strategy development. Strategy decisions cannot be made in the absence of these people. The overriding theme throughout this chapter is that successful management of the interfaces of R&D, manufacturing, and marketing activities determines a firm's competitive strengths and consequently its market performance. Now we will look at logistical implications of this interface management.

One successful interface management is illustrated by Toyota's global operations. The Japanese carmaker is equipping its operations in the United States, Europe, and Southeast Asia with integrated capabilities for creating and marketing automobiles. The company gives the managers at those operations ample authority to accommodate local circumstances and values without diluting the benefit of integrated global operations. Thus, in the United States, Calty Design Research, a Toyota subsidiary in California, designs the bodies and interiors of new Toyota models, including Previa and Lexus, for production in the United States. Toyota has technical centers in the United States and in Belgium to adapt engine and vehicle specifications to local needs. Toyota operations that make automobiles in Southeast Asia supply each other with key components to foster increased economies of scale and standardization in those components—gasoline engines in Indonesia, steering components in Malaysia, transmissions in the Philippines, and diesel engines in Thailand.

Undoubtedly, those multinational companies, including Toyota, not only facilitate the flow of capital among various countries through direct investment abroad, but also significantly contribute to the world trade flow of goods and services as well. Multinational companies combine this production and distribution to supply those local markets hosting their foreign subsidiaries, and then export what remains to other foreign markets or back to their parent's home market.

Let us revisit the significance of multinational companies' foreign production relative to their exports from their home base. U.S. multinational companies sell over three times as much overseas through their subsidiaries as they export to the world. For U.S. multinationals, the 3:1 ratio of foreign sales to exports has remained largely unchanged since the mid-1960s. This ratio for European multinationals grew from

3:1 in the 1970s to 5:1 by 1990. Similarly, the ratio for Japanese multinationals increased from 1:1 in the mid-1970s to 2.5:1 by 1990. Also, both American and Japanese subsidiaries make over 20 percent of their foreign sales in third-country markets (including their home markets), while European subsidiaries in the United States and Japan sell approximately 10 percent in third-country markets.[3] As a result, the total volume of international trade among the Triad regions (i.e., the United States, European Community, and Japan) alone increased more than tenfold in 20 years to well over $500 billion in 1995 from $44.4 billion in 1970, or approximately by 4 times in real terms. This phenomenal increase in international trade is attributed largely to foreign production and trade *managed* by multinational companies.

Two notable changes have occurred in international trade. First, in the last 25 years we have observed a decline in the proportion of trade between the European Union and the United States, and conversely an increase in trade between the United States and Japan, and in particular, between the European Union and Japan. It strongly indicates that European countries and Japan have found each other to be increasingly important markets. Second, newly industrialized countries (NICs) in Asia—including South Korea, Taiwan, Hong Kong, and Singapore—have dramatically increased their trading positions vis-à-vis the rest of the world. Not only have these NICs become prosperous marketplaces, but more significantly they have become important manufacturing and sourcing locations for many multinational companies.

From the sourcing perspective, U.S. companies were procuring a less expensive supply of components and finished products in NICs for sale in the United States. As a result, U.S. bilateral trade with NICs increased sixtyfold to $130 billion in 1995 from $1.8 billion in 1970, of which the United States accounts for more than 90 percent. Trade statistics, however, do not reveal much beyond the amount of bilateral trade flows between countries. It is false to assume that trade is always a business transaction between independent buyers and sellers across national boundaries. It is equally false to assume that a country's trade deficit in a certain *industry* equates with the decline in the competitiveness of *companies* in that industry. As evidenced above, an increasing segment of international trade of components and finished products is strongly influenced by multinational companies' foreign direct investment activities.

Trends in Global Sourcing Strategy

Over the last 20 years, gradual yet significant changes have taken place in global sourcing strategy. Most of the changes are in the way business executives think of the scope of global sourcing for their companies and exploit various opportunities available from it as a source of competitive advantage. Management guru and business historian Peter Drucker once said that sourcing and logistics would remain the

---

[3]Dennis J. Encarnation, "Transforming Trade and Investment, American, European, and Japanese Multinationals across the Triad," Paper presented at the Academy of International Business Annual Meetings, November 22, 1992.

darkest continent of business—the least exploited area of business for competitive advantage. Naturally, many companies that have a limited scope of global sourcing are at a disadvantage compared with those that exploit it to their fullest extent. Five trends are identified.[4]

Trend 1: The Decline of the Exchange Rate Determinism of Sourcing

Since the early 1970s, exchange rates have fluctuated rather erratically. If the U.S. dollar appreciates, U.S. companies find it easy to procure components and products from abroad. Such was the case in the first half of the 1980s when the U.S. dollar appreciated precipitously. The appreciation of the dollar was reflected in the surge of U.S. imports. Contrarily, if the U.S. dollar depreciates, U.S. companies find it increasingly difficult to depend on foreign supplies, as they have to pay higher dollar prices for every item sourced from abroad. In these scenarios, companies consider the exchange rate in determining the extent to which they can engage in foreign sourcing.

However, this exchange-rate determinism of sourcing is based on price factors alone. Foreign sourcing also occurs for noncost reasons such as quality, technology, and so on. First of all, since it takes time to develop overseas suppliers for noncost purposes, purchasing managers cannot easily drop a foreign supplier when exchange-rate changes have an adverse effect on the cost of imported components and products. Second, domestic suppliers are known to increase prices to match rising import prices following exchange-rate changes. As a result, switching to a domestic supplier may not ensure cost advantages. Third, many companies are developing long-term relationships with international suppliers—whether those suppliers are their subsidiaries or independent contractors. In a long-term supply relationship, exchange rate fluctuations may be viewed as a temporary problem by the parties involved. Finally, some companies with global operations are able to shift supply locations from one country to another to overcome the adverse effects of exchange rate fluctuations.

Trend 2: New Competitive Environment Caused by Excess Worldwide Capacity

The worldwide growth in the number of manufacturers has added excess production capacity in most industries. The proliferation of manufacturers around the world in less sophisticated, less capital-intensive manufactured products is much greater than in more complex, knowledge-intensive products such as computers. Thus, there has been a tremendous downward pressure on prices of many components and products around the world. Although the ability to deliver a high volume of products of satisfactory quality at a reasonable price was once the hallmark of many successful companies, an increasing number of global suppliers have rendered the delivery of volume in an acceptable time no longer a competitive weapon. There has since occurred a strategic shift from *price* and *quantity* to *quality* and *reliability* of products as a determinant of competitive strength.[5] According to a recent survey (See Table 5–1),

---

[4]See Swamidass, 1993.

[5]Martin K. Starr and John E. Ullman, "The Myth of Industrial Supremacy," in Martin K. Starr, ed., *Global Competitiveness,* New York: W. W. Norton and Co., 1988.

TABLE 5–1   **Key Factors for Sourcing from Abroad**

	Factor
Very Important	1. Better quality
	2. Lower price
	3. Unavailability of items in the U.S.
Important	4. More advanced technology abroad
	5. Willingness to solve problems
	6. More on-time delivery
	7. Negotiability
	8. Association with foreign subsidiary
Neutral	9. Geographical location
	10. Countertrade requirements
	11. Government assistance

Source: Adapted from Hokey Min and William P. Galle, "International Purchasing Strategies of Multinational U.S. Firms," *International Journal of Purchasing and Materials Management,* Summer 1991, p. 14.

better product and component quality, lower price, unavailability of item locally, and more advanced technology abroad are among the most important reasons for increased sourcing from abroad.

Trend 3: Innovations in and Restructuring of International Trade Infrastructure

Advances in structural elements of international trade have made it easier for companies to employ sourcing for strategic purposes. The innovations and structural changes that have important influences on sourcing strategy include (1) the increased number of purchasing managers experienced in sourcing, (2) improvements made in transportation and communication (e.g., fax), (3) new financing options, including countertrade, offering new incentives and opportunities for exports from countries without hard currency, and (4) manufacturing facilities diffused throughout the world by globally minded companies.

Trend 4: Enhanced Role of Purchasing Managers

During the last 15 years, many manufacturers were under pressure to compete on the basis of improved cost and quality as just-in-time (JIT) production was adopted by a growing number of companies. JIT production requires close working relationships with component suppliers and places an enormous amount of responsibility on purchasing managers. Furthermore, sourcing directly from foreign suppliers requires greater purchasing know-how and is riskier than other alternatives that use locally based intermediaries. However, now that purchasing managers are increasingly making long-term commitments to foreign suppliers, direct dealing with suppliers is justified. According to one major survey, the dominant form of purchasing from abroad was to buy directly from foreign sources.[6] The finding suggests that purchasing managers are increasingly confident about their international know-how and that they may be seeking long-term sourcing arrangements.

Trend 5: Trend toward Global Manufacturing

As a global company adds another international plant to its network of existing plants, it creates the need for sourcing of components and other semiprocessed goods to and from the new plant to existing plants. Global manufacturing adds enormously to global sourcing activities either within the same company across national boundaries or between independent suppliers and new plants.

In the late 1980s, U.S. companies increased sourcing from abroad despite the depreciation of the U.S. dollar. In response to slow productivity growth in the United States relative to other major trading nations in the 1980s, U.S. parent companies' technology was increasingly transferred directly to their foreign affiliates for production. Mature companies are increasingly assigning independent design and other R&D responsibilities to satellite foreign units so as to design a regional or world product. As a result, foreign affiliates have also developed more independent R&D activities to manufacture products for the parent markets in addition to expanding local sales.

Potential Pitfalls in Global Sourcing

A global sourcing strategy requires close coordination of R&D, manufacturing, and marketing activities, among others, on a global basis. However, while national boundaries have begun losing their significance both as a psychological and as a physical barrier to international business, the diversity of local environments still plays an important role not as a facilitator, but rather as an inhibitor, of optimal global strategy development. Now the question is to what extent successful multinational companies can circumvent the impact of local environmental diversity.

Indeed, we still debate the very issue raised more than 20 years ago: counteracting forces of "unification vs. fragmentation" in developing operational strategies, as John Fayerweather[7] wrote. The same counteracting forces have since been revisited in such terms as "standardization vs. adaptation" (1960s), "globalization vs. localization" (1970s), "global integration vs. local responsiveness" (1980s), and most recently, "scale vs. sensitivity" (1990s). Terms have changed, but the quintessence of the strategic dilemma that multinational companies face today has not changed and will probably remain unchanged for many years to come.

One thing that has changed, however, is the *ability* and *willingness* of these companies to integrate various activities on a global basis in an attempt either to circumvent or to nullify the impact of differences in local markets to the extent possible. It

---

[6]Somerby Dowst, "International Buying: The Facts and Foolishments," *Purchasing,* June 25, 1987.

[7]John Fayerweather, *International Business Management: Conceptual Framework,* New York: McGraw-Hill, 1969.

may be *more* correct to say that these companies have been increasingly compelled to take a global view of their businesses, due primarily to increased competition, particularly among the Triad regions of the world.

The last 25 years have seen a tremendous growth and expansion of European and Japanese multinational companies encroaching on the competitive strengths of U.S. multinational companies in almost all the markets around the world. While U.S. multinational companies have subsidiaries all over the world, they have been somewhat reluctant to develop an integrated and well-coordinated global strategy such as successful European and Japanese multinational companies have managed to establish. At the core of an integrated global strategy lies the companies' ability to coordinate manufacturing activities with R&D, engineering, and marketing on a global basis. Indeed, European and Japanese multinational companies have invested heavily in, and improved upon, their strengths in manufacturing, which many U.S. multinational companies have ignored. As a result, U.S. companies tend to have ill-coordinated manufacturing strategies that result in a poor match between their manufacturing system capability and markets.

This functional mismatch has been traced to U.S. management's strategic emphasis having drifted away from manufacturing to marketing and to finance over the years. U.S. management's attention was focused on marketing in the 1960s, followed by a preoccupation with finance in the 1970s, culminating in the merger and acquisition craze of the 1980s—aptly called "paper entrepreneurship."[8]

As a result, manufacturing management gradually lost its influence in the business organization. Production managers' decision-making authority was reduced such that R&D personnel prepared specifications with which production complied, and marketing imposed its own delivery, inventory, and quality conditions, but not productivity considerations. In a sense, production managers gradually took on the role of outside suppliers within their own companies. Production managers' reduced influence in the organization led to a belief that manufacturing functions could be transferred easily to independent operators and subcontractors, depending on the cost differential between in-house and contracted-out production. Thus, in order to lower production costs under competitive pressure, U.S. multinational companies turned increasingly to *outsourcing* of components and finished products from newly industrializing countries such as South Korea, Taiwan, Singapore, Hong Kong, Brazil, and Mexico. Akio Morita, a co-founder of Sony, chided such U.S. multinational companies as "hollow corporations" that simply put their well-known brand names on foreign-made products and sell them as if the products were their own.[9]

However, we should not rush to a hasty conclusion that outsourcing certain components and/or finished products from foreign countries will diminish a company's competitiveness. Many multinational companies with plants in various parts of the world are exploiting not only their own competitive advantages (e.g., R&D, manufacturing, and marketing skills) but also the locational advantages (e.g., inexpensive labor cost, certain skills, mineral resources, government subsidies, and tax

---

[8]Robert Reich, *The Next American Frontier,* New York: Times Books, 1983.
[9]"Special Report: The Hollow Corporation," *Business Week,* March 3, 1986, pp. 56–59.

advantages) of various countries. Thus, it is also plausible to argue that these multi-national companies are in a more advantageous competitive position than are domestic-bound companies.

Then isn't the "hollowing-out" phenomenon indicative of superior management of both corporate and locational resources on a global basis? What is wrong, if anything, with Caterpillar Tractor Company procuring more than 15 percent of components for its tractors from foreign suppliers? How about Honeywell marketing in the United States the products manufactured in its European plants? Answers to these questions hinge on a company's ability and willingness to integrate and coordinate various activities.

Value Chain and Functional Interfaces

The design of global sourcing strategy is based on the interplay between a company's competitive advantages and the comparative advantages of various countries. **Competitive advantage** influences the decision on *what* activities and technologies a company should concentrate its investment and managerial resources in, relative to its competitors in the industry. **Comparative advantage** affects the company's decision on *where* to source and market, based on the lower cost of labor and other resources in one country relative to another. The **value chain concept** offers a general framework for understanding what it takes to manage the interrelated value-adding activities of a company on a global basis.[10] A company is essentially made up of a collection of activities that are performed to design, manufacture, market, deliver, and support its product. This set of interrelated corporate activities is called the value chain. Therefore, to gain competitive advantage over its rivals in the marketplace, a company must perform these activities either at a lower cost or in such a way as to offer differentiated products and services, or accomplish both.

The value chain can be divided into two major activities performed by a company: (1) *primary activities,* consisting of inbound logistics (procurement of raw materials and components), manufacturing operations, outbound logistics (distribution), sales, and after-sale service; and (2) *support activities,* consisting of human resource management, technology development, and other activities that help promote primary activities. Competing companies constantly strive to create value across various activities in the value chain. Of course, the value that a company creates is measured ultimately by the price buyers are willing to pay for its products. Therefore, the value chain is a useful concept that provides an assessment of the activities that a company performs to design, manufacture, market, deliver, and support its products in the marketplace.

Five continuous and interactive steps are involved in developing such a global sourcing strategy along the value chain.[11]

---

[10]Michael E. Porter, *Competition in Global Industries,* Cambridge, MA: Harvard Business School Press, 1986.

[11]Richard D. Robinson (ed), *Direct Foreign Investment: Costs and Benefits,* New York: Praeger, 1987.

1. Identify the separable links (R&D, manufacturing, and marketing) in the company's value chain.
2. In the context of those links, determine the location of the company's competitive advantages, considering both economies of scale and scope.
3. Ascertain the level of transaction costs (e.g., cost of negotiation, cost of monitoring activities, and uncertainty resulting from contracts) between links in the value chain, both internal and external, and then select the lowest-cost mode.
4. Determine the comparative advantages of countries (including the company's home country) relative to each link in the value chain and to the relevant transaction costs.
5. Develop adequate flexibility in corporate decision making and organizational design so as to permit the company to respond to changes in both its competitive advantages and the comparative advantages of countries.

In this chapter, we focus on the three most important interrelated activities in the value chain: namely, R&D (i.e., technology development, product design, and engineering), manufacturing, and marketing activities. Management of the interfaces, or linkages, among these value-adding activities is a crucial determinant of a company's competitive advantage. A basic framework of management of R&D, manufacturing, and marketing interfaces is outlined in Exhibit 5–1. Undoubtedly, these value-adding activities should be examined as holistically as possible, by linking the boundaries of these primary activities. Thus, global sourcing strategy encompasses management of (1) the interfaces among R&D, manufacturing, and marketing on a global basis, and (2) logistics identifying which production units will serve which particular markets and how components will be supplied for production.

EXHIBIT 5–1   R&D, Manufacturing, and Market Interfaces

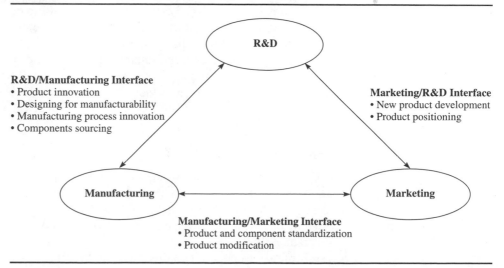

R&D/Manufacturing Interface

Technology is broadly defined as know-how composed of product technology (the set of ideas embodied in the product) and process technology (the set of ideas involved in the manufacture of the product or the steps necessary to combine new materials to produce a finished product). However, executives tend to focus solely on product-related technology as the driving force of the company's competitiveness. Product technology alone may not provide the company a long-term competitive edge over competition unless it is matched with sufficient manufacturing capabilities.

For example, the British discovered and developed penicillin, but it was a small U.S. company, Pfizer, which improved on the fermentation (i.e., manufacturing) process and, as a result, became the world's foremost manufacturer of penicillin. The first jet engine was developed in Britain and Germany, but it was again U.S. companies, Boeing and Douglas, that improved on the technology and eventually dominated the jet plane market.

Ignoring manufacturing as a strategic weapon, many U.S. companies have historically placed emphasis on product innovations (i.e., product proliferation and modifications). However, as the U.S. technological lead over foreign competition has virtually evaporated in some sectors, there will be fewer products that U.S. companies can export simply because no one else has the technology to manufacture the products. Stressing the historical linkage of imitation and product innovations, it is contended that imitation (manufacturing process learning), followed by more innovative adaptation, leading to pioneering product design and innovation, forms the natural sequence of industrial development. In other words, product innovation and manufacturing activities are intertwined such that continual improvement in manufacturing processes can enable the company not only to maintain product-innovation-based competitiveness, but also to improve its product innovative abilities in the future.

These examples amply suggest that manufacturing processes should also be innovative. To facilitate the transferability of new product innovations to manufacturing, a team of product designers and engineers should strive to design components so that they are conducive to manufacturing without undue retooling required and that components may be used interchangeably for different models of the product. Low levels of retooling requirements and interchangeability of components are necessary conditions for efficient sourcing strategy on a global scale. If different equipment and components are used in various manufacturing plants, it is extremely difficult to establish a highly coordinated sourcing plan on a global basis.

Manufacturing/Marketing Interface

There exists a continual conflict between manufacturing and marketing divisions. It is to the manufacturing division's advantage if all the products and components are standardized to facilitate low-cost production. The marketing division, however, is more interested in satisfying the diverse needs of consumers, requiring broad product lines and frequent product modifications, adding cost to manufacturing. How have successful companies coped with this dilemma?

Recently, there has been an increasing amount of interest in the strategic linkages between product policy and manufacturing—long ignored in traditional considerations of global strategy development. With aggressive competition emphasizing corporate product policy and concomitant manufacturing, many companies have realized that product innovations alone cannot sustain their long-term competitive position without an effective product policy linking product and manufacturing process innovations.

Four different ways of developing a global product policy are generally considered an effective means to streamline manufacturing, thus lowering manufacturing cost, without sacrificing marketing flexibility: (1) core components standardization, (2) product design families, (3) universal product with all features, and (4) universal product with different positioning.[12]

Core Components Standardization.   Successful global product policy mandates the development of universal products or products that require no more than a cosmetic change for adaptation to differing local needs and use conditions. A few examples illustrate the point. Seiko, a Japanese watchmaker, offers a wide range of designs and models, but based only on a handful of different operating mechanisms. Similarly, the best-performing German machine-tool-making companies have a narrower range of products, use up to 50 percent fewer parts than their less successful rivals, and make continual, incremental product and design improvements, with new developments passed rapidly on to customers.

Product Design Families.   This is a variant of core component standardization. For companies marketing an extremely wide range of products due to cultural differences in product-use patterns around the world, it is also possible to reap economies-of-scale benefits. For example, Toyota offers several car models based on a similar family design concept, ranging from Lexus models to Toyota Avalons, Camrys, and Corollas. Many of the Lexus features that were well-received by customers have been adopted into the Toyota lines with just a few minor modifications (mostly downsizing). In the process, Toyota has been able to cut product development costs and meet the needs of different market segments. Similarly, Electrolux, a Swedish appliance manufacturer, has adopted the concept of "design families," offering different products under four different brand names, but using the same basic designs. A key to such product design standardization lies in standardization of components, including motors, pumps, and compressors. Thus, White Consolidated in the United States and Zanussi in Italy, Electrolux's subsidiaries, have the main responsibility for components production within the group for worldwide application.

Universal Product with All Features.   As noted above, competitive advantage can result from standardization of core components and/or product design families. One

---

[12]Hirotaka Takeuchi and Michael E. Porter, "Three Roles of International Marketing in Global Strategy," *Competition in Global Industries,* Michael E. Porter, ed., Boston: Harvard Business School Press, 1986, pp. 111–146.

variant of components and product standardization is to develop a universal product with all the features demanded anywhere in the world. Japan's Canon has done so successfully with its AE-1 cameras and newer models. After extensive market analyses around the world, Canon identified a set of common features customers wanted in a camera, including good picture quality, ease of operation with automatic features, technical sophistication, professional looks, and reasonable price. To develop such cameras, the company introduced a few breakthroughs in camera design and manufacturing, such as use of an electronic integrated circuitry brain to control camera operations, modularized production, and standardization and reduction of parts.

Universal Product with Different Positioning.   Alternatively, a universal product can be developed with different market segments in mind. Thus, a universal product may be positioned differently in different markets. This is where marketing promotion plays a major role. Product and/or components standardization, however, does not necessarily imply either production standardization or a narrow product line. For example, Japanese automobile manufacturers have gradually stretched out their product line offerings while marketing them with little adaptation in many parts of the world. This strategy requires manufacturing flexibility. The crux of global product or component standardization calls for proactive identification of homogeneous segments around the world, and is different from the concept of marketing abroad a product originally developed for the home market. A proactive approach to product policy has gained momentum in recent years as it is made possible by intermarket segmentation. In addition to clustering of countries and identification of homogeneous segments in different countries, targeting different segments in different countries with the same products is another way to maintain a product policy of standardization.

For example, Honda has marketed almost identical Accord cars around the world by positioning them differently from country to country. Accord has been promoted as a family sedan in Japan, a relatively inexpensive sports car in Germany, and a reliable commuter car in the United States. In recent years, however, Honda has begun developing some regional variations of the Accord for the United States, European, and Japanese markets. Nonetheless, Honda adheres to a policy of *core component standardization* such that at least 50 percent of the components, including the chassis and transmission, are shared across the variations of the Accord.

Marketing/R&D Interface

Both R&D and manufacturing activities are technically outside marketing managers' responsibility. However, marketing managers' knowledge of the consumers' needs is indispensable in product development. Without a good understanding of the consumers' needs, product designers and engineers are prone to impose their technical specifications on the product rather than fitting them to what consumers want. After all, consumers, not product designers or engineers, have the final say in deciding whether or not to buy the product.

Japanese companies, in particular, excel in management of the marketing/R&D interface. Indeed, their source of competitive advantage often lies in marketing and R&D divisions' willingness to coordinate their respective activities concurrently. In a traditional product development, *either* a new product was developed and pushed down from the R&D division to the manufacturing and to the marketing division for sales *or* a new product idea was pushed up from the marketing division to the R&D division for development. This top-down or bottom-up new product development takes too much time in an era of global competition in which a short product development cycle is crucial to meet constant competitive pressure from new products introduced by rival companies around the world.

R&D and marketing divisions of Japanese companies are always on the lookout for emerging technologies to use initially in existing products, in order to satisfy customer needs better than their existing products and their competitors'. This affords them an opportunity to gain experience, debug technological glitches, reduce costs, boost performance, and adapt designs for worldwide customer use. As a result, they have been able to increase the speed of new product introductions, meet the competitive demands of a rapidly changing marketplace, and capture market share.

In other words, *the marketplace becomes a virtual R&D laboratory for Japanese companies to gain production and marketing experience as well as to perfect technology.* This requires close contact with customers, whose inputs help Japanese companies improve upon their products on an ongoing basis.

In the process, they introduce new products one after another. Year after year, Japanese companies unveil not-entirely-new products that keep getting better in design and are more reliable and less expensive. For example, Philips marketed the first practical VCR in 1972, three years before Japanese competitors entered the market. However, Philips took 7 years to replace the first-generation VCR with the all-new V2000, while the late-coming Japanese manufacturers launched an onslaught of no fewer than three generations of improved VCRs in a five-year period.

Another recent example worth noting is the exploitation of so-called "fuzzy" logic by Hitachi and others. Ever since fuzzy logic was conceived in the mid-1960s at the University of California at Berkeley, nobody other than several Japanese companies has paid serious heed to it for its potential application in ordinary products. Fuzzy logic allows computers to deal with shades of gray or something vague between 0 and 1—no small feat in a world of the binary computers that exist today. Today, Hitachi, Matsushita, Mitsubishi, Sony, and Nissan Motors, among others, use fuzzy logic in their products. For example, Hitachi introduced a "fuzzy" train that automatically accelerates and brakes so smoothly that no one uses the hanging straps. Matsushita, maker of Panasonic products, began marketing a "fuzzy" washing machine with only one start button that automatically judges the size and dirtiness of the load and decides the optimum cycle times, amount of detergent needed, and water level. Sony introduced a palm-size computer capable of recognizing written Japanese, with a fuzzy circuit to iron out the inconsistencies in different writing styles. Now fuzzy circuits are put into the autofocus mechanisms of video cameras to get constantly clear pictures. By the beginning of 1990, fuzzy chips were appearing at a fast pace in a wide range of consumer products.

The continual introduction of *newer* and *better designed* products also brings a greater likelihood of market success. Ideal products often require a giant leap in technology and product development, and naturally are subject to a much higher risk of consumer rejection. Not only does the Japanese approach of incrementalism allow for continual improvement and a stream of new products, but it also permits quicker consumer adoption. Consumers are likely to accept improved products more quickly than very different products, since the former are more compatible with the existing patterns of product use and lifestyles.

Logistics of Sourcing Strategy

Sourcing strategy includes a number of basic choices companies make in deciding how to serve foreign markets. One choice relates to the use of imports, assembly, or production within the country to serve a foreign market. Another decision involves the use of internal or external supplies of components or finished goods. Therefore, the term "sourcing" is used to describe management by multinational companies of the flow of components and finished products in serving foreign markets.

Sourcing decision making is multifaceted and entails both contractual and locational implications. From a contractual point of view, the sourcing of major components and products by multinational companies takes place in two ways: (1) from the parents or their foreign subsidiaries on an "intrafirm" basis, and (2) from independent suppliers on a "contractual" basis. The first type of sourcing is known as **intrafirm sourcing.** The second type of sourcing is referred to commonly as **outsourcing.** Similarly, from a locational point of view, multinational companies can procure components and products either (1) domestically (i.e., *domestic sourcing*) or (2) from abroad (i.e., *offshore sourcing*). Therefore, as shown in Exhibit 5–2, four possible types of sourcing strategy can be identified.

In developing viable sourcing strategies on a global scale, companies must consider not only manufacturing costs, the costs of various resources, and exchange-rate fluctuations, but also availability of infrastructure (including transportation, communications, and energy), industrial and cultural environments, the ease of working with foreign host governments, and so on. Furthermore, the complex nature of sourcing strategy on a global scale spawns many barriers to its successful execution. In particular, logistics, inventory management, distance, nationalism, and lack of working knowledge about foreign business practices, among others, are major operational problems identified by multinational companies engaging in international sourcing.

Many studies have shown, however, that despite (or maybe as a result of) those operational problems, *where* to source major components seems much less important than *how* to source them. Thus, when examining the relationship between sourcing and competitiveness of multinational companies, it is crucial to distinguish between sourcing on a "contractual" basis and sourcing on an "intrafirm" basis, for these two types of sourcing will have a different impact on a firm's long-run competitiveness.

Intrafirm Sourcing.   Multinational companies can procure their components in-house within their corporate system around the world. They produce major components at their respective home base and/or at their affiliates overseas to be incorporated in their products marketed in various parts of the world. Thus, trade does take place between a parent company and its subsidiaries abroad, and also between foreign subsidiaries across national boundaries. This is often referred to as *intrafirm*

Exhibit 5–2   Types of Sourcing Strategy

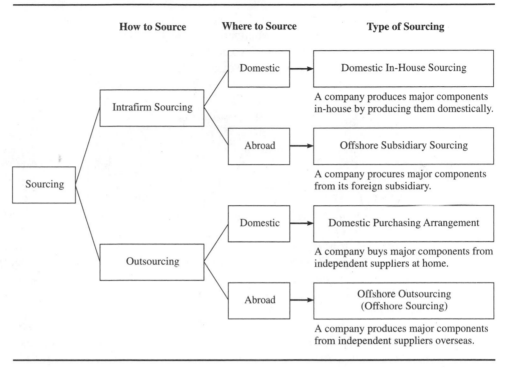

sourcing. If such in-house component procurement takes place at home, it is essentially *domestic in-house sourcing.* If it takes place at a company's foreign subsidiary, it is called *offshore subsidiary sourcing.* Intrafirm sourcing makes trade statistics more complex to interpret, since part of the international flow of products and components is taking place between affiliated companies within the same multinational corporate system, which transcends national boundaries. According to a study conducted by the United Nations Center on Transnational Corporations, about 30 percent of U.S. exports is attributed to U.S. parent companies transferring products and components to their affiliates overseas, and about 40 percent of U.S. imports is accounted for by foreign affiliates exporting to their U.S. parent companies. For both Japan and Britain, intrafirm transactions account for approximately 30 percent of their total trade flows (exports and imports combined), respectively.

Outsourcing.   In the 1970s, foreign competitors gradually caught up in a productivity race with U.S. companies, which had once commanded a dominant position in international trade. It coincided with U.S. corporate strategic emphasis drifting from manufacturing to finance and marketing. As a result, manufacturing management gradually lost its organizational influence. Production managers' decision-making authority was reduced when R&D personnel prepared specifications with which production complied and marketing imposed delivery, inventory, and quality conditions.

Productivity considerations were ignored. In a sense, production managers gradually took on the role of outside suppliers within their own companies.

Production managers' reduced influence in the organization further led to an erroneous belief that manufacturing functions could, and should, be transferred easily to independent operators and subcontractors, depending upon the cost differential between in-house and contracted-out production. A company's reliance on domestic suppliers for major components is basically a *domestic purchase arrangement.* Furthermore, in order to lower production costs under competitive pressure, U.S. companies turned increasingly to *outsourcing* of components and finished products from abroad, particularly from newly industrialized countries, including Singapore, South Korea, Taiwan, Hong Kong, Brazil, and Mexico. Initially, subsidiaries were set up for production purposes (i.e., *offshore subsidiary sourcing*), but gradually, independent foreign suppliers took over component production for U.S. companies. This latter phenomenon is usually called *offshore outsourcing* (or *offshore sourcing,* for short).

Component procurement from overseas (i.e., *offshore subsidiary sourcing* and *offshore outsourcing*) is receiving an increasing amount of attention, as it affects domestic employment and economic structure. As stated earlier, U.S. companies using this strategy have been described pejoratively as hollow corporations. It is occasionally argued that U.S. companies are increasingly adopting a "designer role" in global competition—offering innovations in product design without investing in manufacturing process technology.

This widespread international sourcing practice could have a deleterious impact on the ability of U.S. companies to maintain their initial competitive advantage based on product innovations. Indeed, keeping abreast of emerging technology through continual improvement in R&D and manufacturing is the *sine qua non* for a company's continued competitiveness.

Long-Term Consequences

There are two opposing views of the long-term implications of offshore sourcing. One school of thought argues that many successful companies have developed a dynamic organizational network through increased use of joint ventures, subcontracting, and licensing activities across international borders. This flexible network system is broadly called *strategic alliances.* Strategic alliances allow each participant to pursue its particular competence. Therefore, each network participant can be seen as complementing rather than competing with the other participants for the common goals. Strategic alliances may even be formed by competing companies in the same industry in pursuit of complementary abilities (new technologies or skills) from each other. The other school of thought argues, however, that while the above argument may be true in the short run, there could also be negative long-term consequences resulting from a company's dependence on independent suppliers and subsequently the inherent difficulty for the company to keep abreast of constantly evolving design and engineering technologies without engaging in those developmental activities. These two opposing arguments will be elaborated below.

Strategic Alliances

The advantage of forming a strategic alliance is claimed to be its structural flexibility. Strategic alliances can accommodate a vast amount of complexity while maximizing the specialized competence of each member, and provide much more effective use of human resources that would otherwise have to be accumulated, allocated, and maintained by a single organization. In other words, a company can concentrate on performing the task at which it is most efficient. This approach is increasingly applied on a global basis, with countries participating in a dynamic network as multinational companies configure and coordinate product development, manufacturing, and sourcing activities around the world.

First, due to the need for fast internationalization and related diversification, strategic alliances provide a relatively easy option to access the world markets and to combine complementary technologies. Thus, AT&T needed Olivetti's established European network to enter the European market for telephone switchboard equipment. Similarly, Toyota established a joint venture with General Motors so that the Japanese carmaker could learn to work with UAW union members while General Motors could learn just-in-time inventory management from Toyota.

Second, and more relevant to sourcing issues, an increasing number of companies have funneled out manufacturing functions to independent partners. In 1989, for example, Apple Computer enlisted Sony to design and manufacture a new notebook-size Macintosh computer called the PowerBook 100. In this arrangement, Apple gave Sony the basic blueprint, and Sony engineers, who had little experience building personal computers, developed Apple's smallest and lightest machine from drawing board to factory floor in less than 13 months. This is a strategic alliance in which Apple's basic design ability was complemented by Sony's miniaturization technology. The result has been a spectacular success for Apple that could not have materialized without Sony's participation.

However, it has also become immediately apparent that Apple could no longer manufacture the next generations of notebook-size computers without Sony's participation. On the other hand, Sony, having mastered engineering and manufacturing of Apple's notebook computers, has gradually increased its role upstream to assisting Apple in product designing. Such a relationship could prove to be detrimental to Apple's competitiveness if Sony is able to take over most of what it needs to develop a notebook computer.

Dependence

Companies that rely on independent external sources of supply of major components tend to forsake part of the most important value-creating activities to, and also become dependent on, independent operators for assurance of component quality. Furthermore, those multinational companies tend to promote competition among independent suppliers, ensure continuing availability of materials in the future, and exploit full benefits of changing market conditions. However, individual suppliers are forced to operate in an uncertain business environment, which inherently necessitates a shorter planning horizon. The uncertainty about the potential loss of orders to competitors often forces individual suppliers to make operating decisions that will likely increase their own long-term production and materials costs. In the process, this uncertain business environment tends to adversely affect the multinational companies sourcing components and/or finished products from independent suppliers.

The rapid decline of IBM in recent years offers the most vivid example of the problems caused by its dependence on independent suppliers for crucial components in the personal computer market. As a relatively late entrant into the burgeoning personal computer market in the early 1980s, IBM decided, contrary to its long-held policy of developing proprietary technology in-house, to rely on microprocessors from Intel and operating software from Microsoft. Given its massive size and marketing abilities, IBM was able to become a market leader in the personal computer business in a short period of time. However, Intel and Microsoft were also free to market their wares to any other companies. As a result, many small and nimble personal computer companies rushed into the personal computer market and began marketing IBM-compatible personal computers at the cost of IBM's market share position. Yet, being slow to respond to this competition, IBM has already lost its dominant position and subsequently control of the industry that it had helped create a decade ago.

Gradual Loss of Design and Manufacturing Abilities

Those multinational companies that depend heavily on independent suppliers also tend in the long run to lose sight of emerging technologies and expertise, which could be incorporated into the development of new manufacturing processes as well as new products. Apple-Sony and IBM-Intel-Microsoft alliances may be illustrative of such possibilities. Thus, continual sourcing from independent suppliers is likely to forebode those companies' long-term loss of the ability to manufacture at competitive cost and, as a result, loss of their global competitiveness. However, if technology and expertise developed by a multinational company are exploited within its multinational corporate system (i.e., by its foreign affiliates and by the parent company itself), the company can retain its technological base to itself without unduly disseminating its technological knowledge to competitors. The benefit of such internalization is likely to be great, particularly when technology is highly idiosyncratic or specific, with limited alternative uses, or when it is novel in the marketplace. For such a technology, the market price mechanism is known to break down as a seller and potential buyers of the technology tend to see its value very differently. Potential buyers, who do not have perfect knowledge of how useful the technology will be, tend to underrate its true market value. As a result, the seller of the technology is not likely to get the full economic benefit of the technology by selling it in the open market.

In addition, by getting involved in design and production on its own, the multinational company can keep abreast of emerging technologies and innovations originating anywhere in the world for potential use in the future. Furthermore, management of the quality of major components is required to retain the goodwill and confidence of consumers in the products. As a result, "intrafirm" sourcing of major components and finished products between the parent company and its affiliates abroad and between its foreign affiliates themselves would more likely enable the company to retain a long-term competitive edge in the world market.

Summary

The scope of global sourcing has expanded over time. Whether or not to procure components or products from abroad was once determined strictly on price and thus strongly influenced by the fluctuating exchange rate. Thus a currency appreciation prompted companies to increase offshore sourcing, while a depreciation encouraged domestic sourcing. Today many companies consider not simply price but also quality, reliability, and technology of components and products to be procured. Those companies design their sourcing decision based on the interplay between their competitive advantages and the comparative advantages of various sourcing locations for long-term gains.

Trade and foreign production managed by multinational companies are very complex. In growing global competition, sourcing of components and finished products around the world within the multinational company has increased. The development of global sourcing and marketing strategies across different foreign markets has become a central issue for many multinational companies. Traditionally, a polycentric approach to organizing operations on a country-by-country basis allowed each country manager to tailor marketing strategy to the peculiarities of local markets. As such, product adaptations were considered a necessary strategy to better cater to the different needs and wants of customers in various countries. Product adaptation tends to be a reactive, rather than a proactive, strategic response to the market. A high level of product adaptation may make it difficult for multinational companies to reap economies of scale in production and marketing and to coordinate their networks of activities on a global scale.

Global sourcing strategy requires close coordination of R&D, manufacturing, and marketing activities on a global basis. Managing geographically separated R&D, manufacturing, and marketing activities, those companies face difficult coordination problems of integrating their operations and adapting them to different legal, political, and cultural environments in different countries. Furthermore, separation of manufacturing activities involves an inherent risk that manufacturing in the value chain will gradually become neglected. Such neglect can be costly, as continued involvement in manufacturing leads to pioneering product design and innovation over time. An effective global sourcing strategy calls for continual efforts to streamline manufacturing without sacrificing marketing flexibility. To accomplish this, a conscious effort either to develop core components in-house or to develop product design families or universal products is called for.

A caveat should be also noted. While a company's ability to develop core components and products and market them in the world markets on its own is preferred, the enormousness of such a task should be examined in light of rapid changes in both technology and customer needs around the world. Those changes make the product life cycle extremely short, sometimes too short for many multinational companies to pursue product development, manufacturing, and marketing on a global basis without strategic alliance partners. Benefits of maintaining an independent proprietary position should always be weighed against the time cost of delayed market entry.

Supplementary Reading

Cohen, Stephen S., and John Zysman. "Why Manufacturing Matters: The Myth of the Post-Industrial Economy." *California Management Review,* 29, Spring 1987, pp. 9–26.

Czinkota, Michael R., and Masaaki Kotabe, "Product Development the Japanese Way." *Journal of Business Strategy,* 11, November/December 1990, pp. 31–36.

Guile, Bruce R., and Harvey Brooks, eds. *Technology and Global Industry: Companies and Nations in the World Economy.* Washington, D.C.: National Academy Press, 1987.

Kotabe, Masaaki. *Global Sourcing Strategy: R&D, Manufacturing, and Marketing Interfaces.* New York: Quorum Books, 1992.

Kotabe, Masaaki, and K. Scott Swan. "Offshore Sourcing: Reaction, Maturation, and Consolidation of U.S. Multinationals." *Journal of International Business Studies,* 25, First Quarter, 1994, pp. 115–40.

Markides, Constantinos, and Norman Berg. "Manufacturing Offshore Is Bad Business." *Harvard Business Review,* 66, September-October 1988, pp. 113–20.

Monczka, Robert M., and Robert J. Trent. "Global Sourcing: A Development Approach." *International Journal of Purchasing and Materials Management,* 27, Spring 1991, pp. 2–8.

Porter, Michael E. *Competition in Global Industries.* Boston: Harvard Business School Press, 1986.

Reich, Robert. *The Next American Frontier.* New York: Times Books, 1983.

Starr, Martin K., and John E. Ullman. "The Myth of Industrial Supremacy," in Martin K. Starr, ed. *Global Competitiveness.* New York: W. W. Norton and Co., 1988.

Swamidass, Paul M., "Import Sourcing Dynamics: An Integrative Perspective." *Journal of International Business Studies,* 24, Fourth Quarter 1993, pp. 671–91.

6 LICENSING

Licensing is a contractual arrangement whereby the licensor (selling firm) allows its technology, patents, trademarks, designs, processes, know-how, intellectual property, or other proprietary advantages to be used for a fee by the licensee (buying firm). Licensing is a strategy for technology transfer. It is also an approach to internationalization that requires less time or depth of involvement in foreign markets, compared to export strategies, joint ventures, and foreign direct investment (FDI).

Most international licensing agreements are between firms from industrialized countries. As well, licensing occurs most frequently in technology-intensive industries. It is not surprising, then, that the overall use of licensing varies greatly from country to country. For example, licensing of foreign technology by Korean firms exceeded $4 billion in 1995, with 75 percent of that going to U.S. or Japanese licensors.

A great deal of international licensing also occurs in industries that are not technology-intensive. These industries range from food to sports teams to publishing. The popular press is replete with announcements regarding international licensing (see box for examples).

Much of the licensing discussion that follows assumes a technology transfer. This would generally constitute a more complex form of licensing than that involving trademarks, for example.

The term "licensing" is also frequently used internationally in reference to national governments, which provide licenses for foreign banks or insurance companies to operate in their market, for resource companies to undertake exploration, and so forth. This is a different form of permission than the focus of this chapter.

When Is Licensing Employed?

The strategic advantages to be gained by licensing depend on the technology, firm size, product maturity, and extent of the firm's experience. A number of internal and external circumstances may lead a firm to employ a licensing strategy. From the perspective of the licensor these would include:

This chapter was prepared by Paul W. Beamish.

Recent International Licensing Announcements

Marvel Entertainment Group, the world's biggest comic book publishers, generated $20 million in revenue from licensing in 1995.

Beer manufacturers have turned to licensing their brand names overseas as an alternative to exporting.

Jurassic Park, one of the biggest-grossing movies of all time, is also a "global brand" made possible through licensing agreements with such organizations as McDonald's, Kmart, toy companies, and so forth.

Most major multinational food manufacturing firms are involved in some form of international product licensing. This might take place through outbound licensing, or through the production of goods under names licensed from foreign firms.

The licensing fees from more than 2,500 hours of television programming are expected to produce a stable annuity stream for MGM/United Artists Entertainment Company.

The Licensing Division at Converse Shoes has been expanded to put the marketable Converse name on items such as sport bags and watches.

National Hockey League Enterprises, in a bid for more centralized control of its overseas efforts, allowed its agreement with six European licensing agents to expire in August 1995.

Chiquita Brands International is licensing its brand to Connor Foods for a new food line.

---

1. A firm lacks the capital, managerial resources, or knowledge of foreign markets required for exporting or FDI, but it wants to earn additional profits with minimal commitment.
2. Licensing is a way of testing and proactively developing a market that can later be exploited by direct investment.
3. The technology involved is not central to the licensor's core business. Not surprisingly, single- or dominant-product firms are very reluctant to license their core technology, whereas diversified firms are much more willing to license peripheral technologies.
4. Prospects of "technology feedback" are high (i.e., the licensor has been contractually ensured of access to new developments generated by the licensee and based on licensed knowledge).
5. The licensor wishes to exploit its technology in secondary markets that may be too small to justify larger investments; the required economies of scale may not be attainable.
6. Host-country governments restrict imports or FDI, or both; or the risk of nationalization or foreign control is too great.
7. The licensee is unlikely to become a future competitor.
8. The pace of technological change is sufficiently rapid that the licensor can remain technologically superior and ahead of the licensee, who is a potential competitor. As well, if the technology may become obsolete quickly, there is pressure to exploit it fully while the opportunity exists.

From the perspective of the licensee, the main advantage of licensing is that the licensee's existing products or technology can be acquired more cheaply, faster, and with less risk from third parties (licensors) than by internal R&D. Another advantage is that the licensee can gain product designs for a desired diversification, to complement other assets it possesses such as production or marketing capability.

Risks Associated with Licensing

The most important risk associated with licensing is that the licensor risks the dissipation of its proprietary advantage, since the licensee acquires at least a portion of that advantage via licensing. Thus, any licensor should try to ensure that its licensee will not be a future competitor. Not surprisingly, many license agreements are made between firms from different countries so as to reduce the likelihood of creating a competitor in the domestic market. Other approaches include limiting the licensee's market and insisting on technology feedback or flowback clauses.

Licensed trademarks remain the licensor's property in perpetuity, whereas licenses normally have a finite lifetime. A licensor may retain considerable bargaining power in proportion to the perishability of the licensed technology and the licensor's ability to provide a continuing supply of new technology in the future.

A second risk with licensing is that the licensor jeopardizes its worldwide reputation if the licensee cannot maintain the desired product standards and quality or if it engages in questionable practices. Because the licensor will typically become aware of licensee questionable practices only after the fact, this suggests the need to devote more time during the original negotiations to understanding the character of the licensee.

Another consideration with licensing is that profits to the licensor may not be maximized. This is because (a) their involvement in the licensed markets is indirect, (b) exchange rates change, (c) some countries limit the amount of outward payments for licenses, and so forth.

Some of the standard elements of a license agreement are more difficult than others for the licensor to enforce. These would include (a) guaranteeing flowback of actual improvements, (b) sublicensing, (c) diligence, and (d) quality control. As a result, sometimes licensing may not provide even the minimum expected benefits.

Intellectual Property Rights

In many countries intellectual property legislation either does not exist or is not enforced. Not surprisingly, in the latter half of the 1990s, a major issue for many companies is infringement of their intellectual property rights. With billions of dollars at stake, this issue has become a key element in trade negotiations.

Some companies have deemed it necessary to enter into license agreements as a means of offsetting trademark piracy. The logic behind such "reluctant licensing" is that by licensing a local firm the local firm will, in turn, take the necessary steps to stop unlicensed domestic competitors from using the intellectual property.

There are numerous implications with such a scenario. For example, many organizations are feeling pressure to internationalize their operations sooner than they were expecting. As a consequence, they view licensing as a defensive solution, rather than an opportunity.

Costs of Licensing

Licensing is sometimes incorrectly viewed as a one-time transaction involving little in the way of costs for the licensor. In reality, there are costs associated with (a) the protection of industrial property, (b) establishing the license agreement, and (c) maintaining the license agreement.

Establishment costs would include expenses for searching for suitable licensees, communication, training, equipment testing, and so forth. Some products/technologies lend themselves to licensing, while others do not. The greater the cost and complexity of modifying the underlying intellectual property, the more difficult it is to effectively employ a licensing strategy.

Maintenance costs might include backup services for licensees, audit, ongoing market research, and so forth. These are not trivial expenses.

To all of these out-of-pocket expenses must be added opportunity costs. Opportunity costs are made up of the loss of current or prospective revenues from exports or other sources.

Unattractive Markets for Licensing

A number of conditions directly impact "real" licensing returns and make a particular country an unattractive market for licensing. The first of these conditions occurs where there is a regulatory scheme governing licensing. In some countries—such as France, Ireland, and Spain—licenses are not valid until government approval or registration is completed.

A second condition occurs when licenses granting exclusive rights to certain products or territories are not allowed. In some cases, governments may prohibit them because competition will be substantially lessened. Also, some countries place limits on the allowable duration of agreements.

Another condition occurs when there are foreign exchange controls or other restrictions on royalty payments (license fees). Frequently, a withholding tax on royalty payments to nonresident licensors may be applied. In Europe, the combined withholding tax and VAT (value-added tax) can range from 15 percent to as much as 52 percent.

Finally, some countries impose royalty and fee limits. Some use a 10 percent limit, while others employ a more stringent 3 percent limit. Any of these government-set rates can, and frequently do, change over time.

Overall, licensing tends to be more attractive when agreements formed in the country enjoy the benefit of freedom of contract. Here the parties may, for the most part, create their own legal framework by the manner in which the contract is written.

Major Elements of the License Agreement

The license agreement is the essential commercial contract between licensee and licensor, which specifies the rights to be granted, the consideration payable, and the duration of the terms. The licensed rights usually take the form of patents, registered trademarks, registered industrial designs, unpatented technology, trade secrets, know-how, or copyrights. The license agreement should make explicit reference to the product as well as to the underlying "intangible" or "intellectual" property rights.

Although no definitive standard form exists for license agreements, certain points are typically covered. In many cases, licensors will have developed standard forms for these contracts, based on their past experiences in licensing. Typically, a license agreement will include the following:

1. A clear and correct description of the parties to the agreement, identifying the corporate names of each party, its incorporating jurisdiction, and its principal place of business.

2. A preamble or recitals describing the parties, their reasons for entering into the arrangement, and their respective roles.

3. A list of defined terms for the purposes of the particular contract to simplify this complex document and to eliminate ambiguity or vagueness (e.g., definitions of the terms *licensed, product, net profit, territory,* and so forth).

4. A set of schedules, in an exhibit or appendix, where necessary, to segregate lengthy detailed descriptions of any kind.

5. The grant that is fundamental to the agreement and explicitly describes the nature of the rights being granted to the licensee. This grant may be based on promotion methods, trade secrets, list of customers, drawings and photographs, models, tools, and parts; or know-how. Know-how, in turn, may be based on invention records, laboratory records, research reports, development reports, engineering reports, pilot plant design, production plant design, production specifications, raw material specifications, quality controls, economic surveys, market surveys, etc.

6. A description of any geographical limitations to be imposed on the licensee's manufacturing, selling, or sublicensing activities.

7. A description of any exclusive rights to manufacture and sell that may be granted.

8. A discussion of any rights to sublicense.

9. The terms relating to the duration of the agreement, including the initial term and any necessary provisions for the automatic extension or review of the agreement.

10. Provisions for the granting of rights to downstream refinements or improvements made by the licensor in the future.

11. Provisions for "technological flowback" agreements where some benefit of improvements made by the licensee revert to the licensor. The rights to the future improvements by either the licensor or licensee are often used as bargaining chips in negotiations.

12. Details regarding the royalties or periodic payments based on the use of licensed rights. The percentage rate of the royalty may be fixed or variable (based on time, production level, sales level, and so forth), but the "royalty

base" for this rate must be explicitly defined. Some methods of calculating royalties include percentage of sales, royalties based on production, percentage of net profit, lump-sum payments, or payment-free licenses in cross-licensing arrangements.

There are no hard and fast rules for establishing royalty rates. One arbitrary rule (see Contractor in Supplementary Reading) is the "25 percent rule of thumb," which suggests that the licensor aim for a 25 percent share of the licensee's related profits and then convert this profit level to a certain royalty rate. Others suggest that licensors will often specify a minimum or target absolute compensation. This can be derived from technology transfer cost considerations or a judgment of how much it may cost the prospective licensee to acquire the technology by other means or from an "industry norm." Royalty escalation clauses and the currency of payment should also be specified.

It is often quite difficult for the licensor to accurately estimate the market potential for its property. As a consequence, the licensee, with its greater knowledge of local conditions, is often in a stronger position when the royalty rate terms are being negotiated.

13. Specification of minimum performance requirements (e.g., minimum royalty payments, unit sales volumes, employment of personnel, minimum promotion expenditures, and so forth) to ensure the "best efforts" of the licensee so that the license potential is fully exploited. For example, most license agreements that confer exclusive selling rights in a given area to the licensee also require either a sizable down payment or a minimum annual royalty payment. Otherwise, the licensee may "sit on" the license and block the licensor from entering the market in question.

14. Other clauses common to most license agreements include those to protect the licensed rights against licensees and third parties and those regarding title retention by the licensor, confidentiality of know-how, quality control, most-favored-licensee status, the applicable language of the contract, and any provisions with respect to the assignability of rights by the licensee.

The above list of elements common to most license agreements is by no means exhaustive. For a more detailed checklist for license agreements, see Stitt and Baker in Supplementary Reading. Any potential license agreement should be reviewed by company counsel. It must be noted that every license agreement is unique in some way and, therefore, great care should be taken in its negotiation and formal documentation.

Supplementary Reading

Atuahene-Gima, Kwaku. "International Licensing of Technology: An Empirical Study of the Differences between Licensee and Non-Licensee Firms." *Journal of International Marketing,* 1(2), pp. 71–87, 1993.

Buckley, Peter J. "New Forms of International Industrial Co-operation." In *The Economic Theory of the Multinational Enterprise,* ed. P.J. Buckley and M. Casson. London: Macmillan, 1985.

Business International Corporation. *International Licensing Management.* New York: Business International Corporation, 1988.

Caves, Richard E. *Multinational Enterprise and Economic Analysis,* 2nd ed. Cambridge, MA: Cambridge University Press, 1996.

Caves, Richard E., Harold Crookell, and J. Peter Killing. "The Imperfect Market for Technology Licenses." *Oxford Bulletin of Economics and Statistics,* August 1983, pp. 249–67.

Clegg, Jeremy. "The Determinants of Aggregate International Licensing Behavior: Evidence from Five Countries." *Management International Review* 30 (1990/3), pp. 231–51.

Contractor, Farok J. "A Generalized Theorem for Joint-Venture and Licensing Negotiations." *Journal of International Business Studies,* Summer 1985, pp. 25–47.

Ehrbar, Thomas J. *Business International's Guide to International Licensing: Building a Licensing Strategy for 14 Key Markets Around the World.* New York: McGraw-Hill, Inc.

Hill, Charles W.L. "Strategies for Exploiting Technological Innovations: When and When Not to License." *Organization Science,* 3(3), 1992, pp. 428–41.

Horstmann, Ignatius, and James R. Markusen. "Licensing Versus Direct Investment: A Model of Internalization by the Multinational Enterprise." *Canadian Journal of Economics,* 20(3), pp. 464–81, 1987.

Pfaff, John F. "Changes in the EC Licensing Environment and Their Effect on Licensing as a Strategy for Europe 1992." *The International Executive* 34(5), pp. 415–39.

Root, Franklin, R. *Entry Strategies for International Markets.* Lexington, MA: Lexington Books, 1987.

Stitt, Hubert J., and Samuel R. Baker. *The Licensing and Joint Venture Guide,* 3rd ed. Toronto: Ontario Ministry of Industry, Trade, and Technology, 1985.

7 THE DESIGN AND MANAGEMENT OF INTERNATIONAL JOINT VENTURES

An international joint venture is a company that is owned by two or more firms of different nationality. International joint ventures may be formed "from scratch" or may be the result of several established companies deciding to merge existing divisions. However they are formed, the purpose of most international joint ventures is to allow partners to pool resources and coordinate their efforts to achieve results that neither could obtain acting alone.

In recent years, international joint ventures and other forms of corporate alliances have become increasingly popular. For example, in 1995 the number of airline alliances alone rose from 324 to 389. Joint ventures have moved from being a way to enter foreign markets of peripheral interest to become a part of the mainstream of corporate activity. Such firms as the Ford Motor Company, AT&T, and General Electric are using international joint ventures as a key element of their corporate strategies. Even firms that have traditionally operated independently around the world, such as General Motors and IBM, are increasingly turning to joint ventures.

The increase in the popularity and use of international joint ventures and cooperative alliances is occuring during a time of rapid growth in international business. Throughout the 1980s and into the 1990s, exports, foreign direct investment, and the number of alliances formed all grew rapidly. The growth in foreign direct investment has been particularly strong. In the international environment, at least, alliances are being formed more often because of the growth in international business. But the rate of joint venture use does not change much from year to year. In general, joint ventures are the mode of choice about 35 percent of the time by U.S. multinationals and in 40 to 45 percent of foreign subsidiaries formed by Japanese multinationals.

The popularity of alliances has continued despite their reputation for being difficult to manage. Failures are common and usually widely publicized. Dow Chemical, for example, reportedly lost more than $100 million after a dispute with its Korean

---

This chapter was prepared by Peter Killing and Paul Beamish.

joint venture partners caused the firm to sell its 50 percent interest in its Korean venture at a loss, and to sell below cost its nearby wholly owned chemical plant.

Other cautionary tales include a French multinational firm that lost a substantial sum when it bailed out of its two-year-old venture in Japan, after having transferred much of its world-leading technology to the Japanese partner. Whether the French have created a new competitor remains to be seen, but it seems likely. The dispute that led to the breakup of the venture centered on the issue of who was going to manage the venture. Both firms wanted to be dominant.

Surveys suggest that as many as half the companies with international joint ventures in developed countries are dissatisfied with their ventures' performance, and that the dissatisfaction rate for ventures in developing countries is even higher. Why do managers keep creating new joint ventures in the face of such widespread dissatisfaction and the potentially high costs of failure? The reasons are presented in the remainder of this chapter, as are some guidelines for international joint venture success.

Why Companies Create International Joint Ventures

International joint ventures can be used to achieve one of four basic purposes. As shown in Exhibit 7–1, these are: to *strengthen the firm's existing business,* to take the firm's existing products into *new markets,* to obtain *new products* that can be sold in the firm's existing markets, and to *diversify* into a new business.

Companies using joint ventures for each of these purposes will have different concerns and will be looking for partners with different characteristics. Firms wanting

EXHIBIT 7–1   Motives for International Joint Venture Formation

	Existing Products	New Products
New Markets	To take existing products to foreign markets	To diversify into a new business
Existing Markets	To strengthen the existing business	To bring foreign products to local markets

to strengthen their existing business, for example, will most likely be looking for partners among their current competitors, while those wanting to enter new geographic markets will be looking for overseas firms in related businesses with good local market knowledge. Although often treated as a single category of business activity, international joint ventures are remarkably diverse, as the following descriptions indicate.

Strengthening the Existing Business

International joint ventures are used in a variety of ways by firms wishing to strengthen or protect their existing businesses. Among the most important are joint ventures formed to achieve economies of scale, joint ventures that allow the firm to acquire needed technology and know-how, and ventures that reduce the financial risk of major projects. Joint ventures formed for the latter two reasons may have the added benefit of eliminating a potential competitor from a particular product or market area.

Achieving Economies of Scale.   Small and medium-sized firms often use joint ventures to attempt to match the economics of scale achieved by their larger competitors. Joint ventures have been used to give their parents economies of scale in raw material and component supply, in research and development, and in marketing and distribution. Joint ventures have also been used as vehicles for carrying out divisional mergers, which yield economies across the full spectrum of business activity.

Raw Material and Component Supply.   In many industries the smaller firms create joint ventures to obtain raw materials or jointly manufacture components (see Exhibit 7–2). Renault, Volvo, and Peugeot, for instance, developed a jointly owned engine plant to supply certain low-volume engines to all three companies. Producing engines for all three parents provides economies of scale, with each company receiving engines at a lower cost than it could obtain if it were to produce them itself.

EXHIBIT 7–2   Raw Material/Component Supply Joint Venture

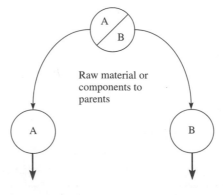

Parents are likely to compete in end markets

The managers involved in such ventures are quick to point out that these financial savings do not come without a cost. Design changes in jointly produced engines, for example, tend to be slow because all partners have to agree on them. In fact, one joint venture that produced computer printers fell seriously behind the state of the art in printer design because the parents could not agree on the features they wanted in the jointly designed printer. Because all of the venture's output was sold to the parents, the joint venture personnel had no direct contact with end customers and could not resolve the dispute.

Transfer pricing is another headache that arises in joint ventures that supply their parents. A low transfer price on products shipped from the venture to the parents, for instance, means that whichever parent buys the most product obtains the most benefit. Many higher-volume-taking parents claim that this is fair, as it is their volume that plays an important role in making the joint venture viable. On the other hand, some parents argue for a higher transfer price, which means that the economic benefits are captured in the venture, and will flow, most likely via dividends, to the parents in proportion to their shareholdings in the venture. As the shareholdings generally reflect the original asset contributions to the venture and not the volumes taken out every year, this means that different parents will do well under this arrangement. Clearly, the potential for transfer price disputes is significant.

Research and Development.   Shared research and development efforts (see Exhibit 7–3) are common in Japan and Europe but have only recently begun to be allowed in the United States, under its relatively strict antitrust laws. The rationale for such programs is that participating firms can save both time and money by collaborating, and may, by combining the efforts of the participating companies' scientists, come up with results that would otherwise have been impossible.

The choice facing firms wishing to carry out collaborative research is whether to simply coordinate their efforts and share costs or to actually set up a jointly owned company. Hundreds of multi-company research programs in Europe are not joint ventures. Typically, scientists from the participating companies agree on the research objectives and the most likely avenues of exploration to achieve those objectives. If

EXHIBIT 7–3   Research and Development Joint Venture

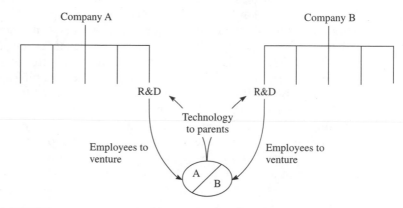

there are, say, four promising ways to attack a particular problem, each of four participating companies would be assigned one route and told to pursue it. Meetings would be held, perhaps quarterly, to share results and approaches taken and when (hopefully) one route proved to be successful, all firms would be fully informed on the new techniques and technology.

The alternative way to carry out collaborative research is to establish a jointly owned company and to provide it with staff, budget, and a physical location. In 1984, for example, three European computer firms established a joint research company in Munich, known as the European Computer Research Center (ECRC). This company, funded at a level of approximately $10 million per year, comprised a staff of 50 researchers working on artificial intelligence projects. Using a joint venture for such work offered the advantage that all the staff were in the same place, making it easier to discuss ideas and results and to alter research priorities. The disadvantage of the common site, however, may be that many researchers will not want to move there. In the case of ECRC, only one-third of the research staff in Munich came from the parent companies, which were located in France, Britain, and Germany.

In the United States, a somewhat different problem arose when the president of a joint research company established by a dozen U.S. computer firms discovered that the participating companies were not sending their best people to the new company. He ended up hiring more than 200 of the firm's 330 scientists from the outside.

A sensitive issue for firms engaging in collaborative research, whether through joint ventures or not, is how far the collaboration should extend. Because the partners are usually competitors, the often expressed ideal is that the joint effort will focus only on "precompetitive" basic research and not, for example, on product development work. This is often a difficult line to draw. In the case of ECRC, the decision was made to license any technology developed by the venture on a royalty-free basis to the parents, who then adapted it for their own purposes.

Marketing and Distribution.   Many international joint ventures involve shared research, development, and production but stop short of joint marketing. The vehicles coming out of the widely publicized joint venture between Toyota and General Motors in California, for instance, are clearly branded as GM or Toyota products and are sold competitively through each parent's distribution network. The same is true of the Fords and Mazdas rolling off an assembly line in Michigan. Antitrust plays a role in the decision to keep marketing activities separate, but so does the partners' intrinsic desire to maintain separate brand identities and increase their own market share. These cooperating firms have not forgotten that they are competitors.

There are, nevertheless, some ventures formed for the express purpose of achieving economies in marketing and distribution (see Exhibit 7–4). A three-way venture formed between Bacardi International of the United States, Martini and Rossi of Italy, and Bass, Britain's largest brewer, to sell a combined portfolio of the brands of all three companies in England and Wales is a typical example of what can be done. Each firm is hoping for wider market coverage at a lower cost. The trade-off is a loss of direct control over the sales force, potentially slower decision making, and a possible loss of direct contact with the customer.

EXHIBIT 7–4   Marketing and Distribution Joint Venture

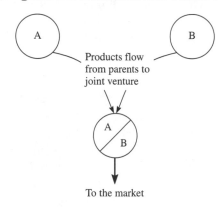

Somewhat similar in intent are cooperative marketing agreements, which are not joint ventures but agreements by two firms with related product lines to sell one another's products. When Control Data pulled out of the supercomputer business in 1989, for example, it established an agreement with Cray Research, the world's leading supercomputer manufacturer, that allowed Control Data to sell Cray supercomputers, while Cray would sell Control Data's mainframes and workstations. Both companies ended up with a more complete line to sell, without the managerial complications of a joint venture.

Divisional Mergers.   Multinational companies with subsidiaries that they have concluded are too small to be economic have sometimes chosen to create a joint venture by combining their "too small" operations with those of a competitor. Fiat and Peugeot, for example, merged their automobile operations in Argentina, where both companies were doing poorly. The new joint venture started life with a market share of 35 percent and a chance for greatly improved economies in design, production, and marketing. Faced with similar pressures, Ford and Volkswagen have done the same thing in Brazil, creating a jointly owned company called Auto Latina.

Similarly, Dresser Industries of Illinois and Komatsu of Japan combined existing businesses in 1988 to create an equally owned joint venture to compete in the construction and mining equipment business in the Western Hemisphere. Komatsu's motivation for entering the venture was to establish a manufacturing source for its products in North America, as a rapidly rising yen made sourcing from Japan ever more expensive. Explaining Dresser's desire for the joint venture, a vice president stated that the equipment business was becoming ever more capital-intensive, and the only routes to success were to be a very narrow niche player or a major full-line producer. The Komatsu deal created the latter—a strong full-line company with first-year sales in excess of $1.5 billion, ranked number two in the Americas.

A divisional merger can also allow a firm a graceful exit from a business in which it is no longer interested. General Motors appeared to be taking this route when it merged its heavy truck business with that of Volvo, forming a new company in which GM maintained only a 24 percent interest. In a similar move, Honeywell gave up trying to continue alone in the computer industry when it folded its business into a venture with Machines Bull of France and NEC of Japan. Honeywell held a 40 percent stake in the resulting joint venture.

Acquiring Technology in the Core Business

Firms that have wanted to acquire technology in their core business area have traditionally done so through license agreements or by developing the technology themselves. Increasingly, however, companies are turning to joint ventures for this purpose, because developing technology in-house is seen as taking too long, and license agreements, while giving the firm access to patent rights and engineers' ideas, may not provide much in the way of shop floor know-how. The power of a joint venture is that a firm may be able to have its employees working shoulder to shoulder with those of its partner, trying to solve the same problems. This is where real learning can take place.

The General Motors joint venture with Toyota provided an opportunity for GM to obtain a source of low-cost small cars, and to watch firsthand how Toyota managers, who were in operational control of the venture, were able to produce high-quality automobiles at low cost. Most observers have concluded that the opportunity for General Motors to learn new production techniques was more significant than the supply of cars coming from the venture. Some have even suggested that, if GM can apply the lessons of the joint venture to its other American plants, the venture will have been worthwhile—even if every car the venture produced was driven into the Pacific Ocean!

Reducing Financial Risk

Some projects are too big or too risky for firms to tackle alone. This is why oil companies use joint ventures to split the costs of searching for new oil fields, and why the aircraft industry is increasingly using joint ventures and "risk-sharing subcontractors" to put up some of the funds required to develop new aircraft and engines. A group of Japanese firms, for example, have developed and built approximately 15 percent of the total airframe of the Boeing 767, under an arrangement that allows the Japanese firms to benefit if the plane sells well—and suffer if it does not. On the newer Boeing 777 project, the Japanese share has increased to 21 percent.

Do such joint ventures make sense? For the oil companies the answer is a clear yes. In these ventures, one partner takes a lead role and manages the venture on a day-to-day basis. Management complexity, one of the major potential drawbacks of joint ventures, is kept to a minimum. If the venture finds oil, transfer prices are not a problem—the rewards of the venture are easy to divide between the partners. In situations like this, forming a joint venture is an efficient and sensible way of sharing risk.

It is not as obvious that the aircraft industry ventures are a good idea. At least not for such industry leaders as Boeing. The Japanese are not entering these ventures simply in the hopes of earning an attractive return on their investment. They are gearing

Exhibit 7–5   Foreign Technology/Local Market Knowledge Joint Venture

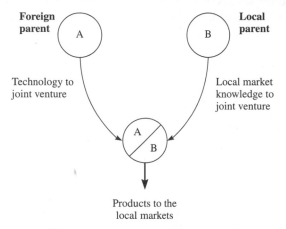

up to produce, sooner or later, their own aircraft. When asked why Boeing was willing to train potential competitors in aircraft design and manufacture, the president replied that he would rather have the Japanese in a venture with him than in one with his competitors.

Taking Products to Foreign Markets

Firms with domestic products that they believe will be successful in foreign markets face a choice. As discussed in Chapter 1, they can produce the product at home and export it, license the technology to local firms around the world, establish wholly owned subsidiaries in foreign countries, or form joint ventures with local partners. Many firms conclude that exporting is unlikely to lead to significant market penetration, building wholly owned subsidiaries is too slow and requires too many resources, and licensing does not offer an adequate financial return. The result is that an international joint venture, while seldom seen as an ideal choice, is often the most attractive compromise (see Exhibit 7–5).

Moving into foreign markets entails a degree of risk, and most firms that decide to form a joint venture with a local firm are doing so to reduce the risk associated with their new market entry. Very often, they look for a partner that deals with a related product line and, thus, has a good feel for the local market. As a further risk-reducing measure, the joint venture may begin life as simply a sales and marketing operation, until the product begins to sell well and volumes rise. Then a "screwdriver" assembly plant may be set up to assemble components shipped from the foreign parent. Eventually, the venture may modify or redesign the product to better suit the local market and may establish complete local manufacturing, sourcing raw material and components locally. The objective is to withhold major investment until the market uncertainty is reduced.

Following Customers to Foreign Markets. Another way to reduce the risk of a foreign market entry is to follow firms that are already customers at home. Thus, in recent years, many Japanese automobile suppliers have followed Honda, Toyota, and Nissan as they set up new plants in North America and Europe. Very often these suppliers, uncertain of their ability to operate in a foreign environment, decide to form a joint venture with a local partner. There are, for example, a great many automobile supplier joint ventures in the United States formed between Japanese and American auto suppliers to supply the Japanese "transplant" automobile manufacturers. For the Americans, such ventures provide a way to learn Japanese manufacturing techniques and to tap into a growing market. Such ventures are often not very satisfactory for the American partners, for reasons to be discussed subsequently.

Investing in "Markets of the Future." Some of the riskiest joint ventures are those established by firms taking an early position in what they see as their "markets of the future." Attracting the most attention in recent years have been ventures in China, eastern Europe, and Russia. Each of these areas offers a very large untapped market, as well as a possible source of low-cost raw materials and labor. The major problems faced by Western firms in penetrating such markets are their unfamiliarity with the local culture, establishing Western attitudes toward quality, and, in some areas, repatriating earnings in hard currency. The solution (sometimes imposed by local government) has often been the creation of joint ventures with local partners who "know the ropes" and can deal with the local bureaucracy.

Even a local partner, however, is no guarantee of success, as the rules of the game can change overnight in such regions. Xerox Shanghai is a good example of a joint venture that has had to adapt to major changes. Formed in 1987 with Shanghai Moving Photo Industry Corp. after four years of negotiation, Xerox Shanghai's first shock came in 1988, when the government introduced purchase controls, stating that before purchasing a copier a potential customer must obtain permission from several government agencies. The net result, in Xerox's estimation, was that the market was only 20 percent of what it would be in the absence of such controls. The joint venture's other problem stemmed from a devaluation of the local currency, which dramatically raised the cost of imported components. However, by 1994 Xerox had 700 employees and produced six profitable models. The company obtained tax concessions, and with its excellent *guanxi* (connections) the company continued to adapt and was able to collect $US10 million in profits from exports in 1994.

Bringing Foreign Products to Local Markets

For every firm that uses an international joint venture to take its product to a foreign market, a local company sees the joint venture as an attractive way to bring a foreign product to its existing market. It is, of course, this complementarity of interest that makes the joint venture possible.

Local partners enter joint ventures to get better utilization of existing plants or distribution channels, to protect themselves against threatening new technology, or simply as an impetus for new growth. Typically, the financial rewards that the local partner receives from a venture are different from those accruing to the foreign partner. For example:

- Many foreign partners make a profit shipping finished products and components to their joint ventures. These profits are particularly attractive because they are in hard currency (which may not be true of the venture's profits) and because the foreign partner captures 100 percent of them, not just a share.
- Many foreign partners receive a technology fee, which is a fixed percentage of the sales volume of the joint venture. The local partner may or may not receive a management fee of like amount.
- Foreign partners typically pay a withholding tax on dividends remitted to them from the venture. Local firms do not.

As a result of these differences, the local partner is often far more concerned with the venture's bottom-line earnings and dividend payout than the foreign partner. This means the foreign partner is likely to be happier to keep the venture as simply a marketing operation or a screwdriver assembly operation, as previously described, than to develop it to the point where it buys less imported material.

Although this logic is understandable, such thinking can be shortsighted. The best example of the benefits that can come back to a parent from a powerful joint venture is Fuji Xerox, a venture begun in Japan in the early 1960s between Xerox and Fuji Photo. This is probably the most successful American-Japanese joint venture in Japan.

Fuji Xerox was, for the first 10 years of its life, strictly a marketing organization. It did its best to sell Xerox copiers in the Japanese market, even though it was painfully obvious that the U.S. company had done nothing to adapt the machine to the Japanese market. For example, to reach the print button on one model, Japanese secretaries had to stand on a box. After 10 years of operation, Fuji Xerox began to manufacture its own machines, and by 1975 it was redesigning U.S. equipment for the Japanese market. Soon thereafter, with the encouragement of Fuji Photo, and in spite of the resistance of Xerox engineers in the United States, the firm began to design its own copier equipment. Its goal was to design and build a copier in half the time and at half the cost of previous machines. When this was accomplished, the firm set its sights on winning the Deming award, a highly coveted Japanese prize for excellence in total quality control. Fuji Xerox won the award in 1980.[1]

It was also in 1980 that Xerox, reeling under the impact of intense competition from Japanese copier companies, finally began to pay attention to the lessons that it could learn from Fuji Xerox. Adopting the Japanese joint venture's manufacturing techniques and quality programs, the parent company fought its way back to health in the mid-1980s. Without the lessons learned from Fuji Xerox, it is unlikely that Xerox, whose world market share had fallen from 82 percent to 41 percent, would have survived as an independent company.

---

[1]The Xerox story is well told by Gary Jacobsen and John Hillkirk in *Xerox: American Samurai* (New York: Collier Books, MacMillan Publishing, 1986).

Using Joint Ventures for Diversification

As the previous examples illustrate, many joint ventures take products that one parent knows well into a market that the other knows well. However, some break new ground and move one or both parents into products and markets that are new to them.

Learning from Your Partner

One of the most interesting stories about the rise of Japanese companies since the Second World War is that of their attempt to move into the commercial aircraft market. In 1962, with the backing of the Japanese government, Mitsubishi, Fuji, and Kawasaki Heavy Industries introduced a medium-sized short-haul aircraft called the YX-11. It was a commercial disaster because, according to a later government study, the participants lacked basic knowledge and experience in design, production, and marketing of aircraft. The best solution, it was decided, was to form alliances with firms in the industry that knew what they were doing.[2]

Since then, these three Japanese companies have joined with Boeing in the manufacture of the 767 and, with a number of major engine manufacturers, to develop a new jet engine. As mentioned earlier, the most recent step has been their shouldering of a 21 percent share of the production and development costs for the Boeing 777. This was a very significant move for the Japanese, as they placed 50 technicians at Boeing's operations in Seattle to be involved in design, testing, and development work. Production and assembly of the aircraft will be carried out at Mitsubishi's, Kawasaki's, and Fuji's plants.

Using such arrangements to acquire the skills necessary to compete in a new business is a long-term proposition, but clearly one that the Japanese are willing to live with. Given the fact that most acquisitions of unrelated businesses do not succeed, and that trying to enter a new business without help is extremely difficult, choosing partners who will help you learn the business does not look like a bad strategy.

Learning with Your Partner

Very occasionally, two firms form a joint venture to take them into a business that is new to both of them. Usually the new business is somewhat related to an existing business of one partner or the other, but the joint venture is nevertheless a significant step into the unknown. One such venture was formed in 1982 between John Labatt, a Canadian brewing company, and the Canada Development Corporation, to enter the biotechnology field. The venture was funded from the outset for a 10-year period, at an estimated total cost of $90 million. With most of its staff being scientists and engineers, this joint venture looked in its early years exactly like the research and development ventures described earlier. The difference, however, is that Allelix, as

---

[2]A good account of the learning taking place by the Japanese firms in the aircraft industry is provided by Mike Yoshino, in M. Porter (ed.) *Competition in Global Industries* (Boston: Harvard Business School Press, 1986).

the venture is called, will eventually produce and sell its own products, rather than supplying its technology to its parents.

When moving into a new field, such as biotechnology, in which the payoff is seen as being a long way in the future, a joint venture offers several advantages. The most obvious is that costs are shared. The other important factor is that it may be more difficult for a firm to drop the project because of commitments made to its partner. An in-house project can be quietly folded up, but a decision to pull out of a joint venture is more public—and generally more difficult. Thus, if perseverance is a key to success, the extra staying power that a joint venture can provide may be crucial.

Requirements for International Joint Venture Success

The checklist in Exhibit 7–6 presents many of the items that a manager should consider when establishing an international joint venture. Each of these is discussed in the following sections.

Understanding Your Capabilities and Needs

The decision to enter a joint venture should not be taken lightly. As mentioned earlier, joint ventures require a great deal of management attention and, in spite of the care and attention they receive, many prove unsatisfactory to their parents.

EXHIBIT 7–6   Joint Venture Checklist

1. Understanding your capabilities and needs.
   - Do you really need a partner? For how long?
   - How big is the payoff? How likely is success?
   - Is a joint venture the best option?
2. Choosing an appropriate partner.
   - Does the partner share your objectives for the venture?
   - Does the partner have the necessary skills and resources? Will you get access to them?
   - Will you be compatible?
   - Can you arrange an "engagement period"?
3. Designing the joint venture.
   - Define the venture's scope of activity, and its strategic freedom vis-à-vis its parents.
   - Lay out each parent's duties and payoffs to create a win-win situation.
   - Establish the managerial role of each partner.
4. Doing the deal.
   - How much paperwork is enough? Trust versus legal considerations?
   - Agree on an endgame.
5. Making the venture work.
   - Give the venture continuing top management attention.
   - Manage cultural differences.
   - Watch out for inequities.
   - Be flexible.

Firms considering entering a joint venture should satisfy themselves that there is not a simpler way, such as a nonequity alliance of the type referred to in Chapter 1, to get what they need. They should also carefully consider the time period for which they are likely to need help. Joint ventures have been labeled "permanent solutions to temporary problems" by firms that entered a venture to get help on some aspect of their business; then, when they no longer needed the help, they were still stuck with the joint venture.

Choosing an Appropriate Partner

Joint ventures are sometimes formed to satisfy complementary needs. But when one partner acquires (learns) another's capabilities, the joint venture becomes unstable. The acquisition of a partner's capabilities means that the partner is no longer needed. If capabilities are only accessed, the joint venture is more stable. It is not easy, before a venture begins, to determine many of the things a manager would most like to know about a potential partner, like the true extent of its capabilities, what its objectives are in forming the venture, and whether it will be easy to work with. A hasty answer to such questions may lead a firm into a bad relationship or cause it to pass up a good opportunity.

For these reasons, it is often best if companies begin a relationship in a small way, with a simple agreement that is important but not a matter of life and death to either parent. As confidence between the firms grows, the scope of the business activities can broaden. The Ford-Mazda relationship, which is probably the largest and most complex corporate alliance in existence, began in the 1970s as a simple buy-sell agreement under which Mazda would sell light pickup trucks to Ford. Gradually, more and more deals were made between the companies and, by the late 1980s, more than 50 separate agreements were in place, ranging from relatively simple sourcing agreements to joint car design and production, to manufacturing joint ventures established in countries such as Thailand. This joint venture, called Auto Alliance Thailand, will produce up to 135,000 small pickups a year under both the Ford and Mazda names.

Another good example is provided by Corning Glass, which in 1970 made a major breakthrough in the development of optical fibers that could be used for telecommunication applications, replacing traditional copper wire or coaxial cable. The most likely customers of this fiber outside the United States were the European national telecoms, which were well-known to be very nationalistic purchasers. To gain access to these customers, Corning set up development agreements in 1973 and 1974 with companies in England, France, Germany, and Italy that were already suppliers to the telecoms. These agreements called for the European firms to develop the technology necessary to combine the fibers into cables, while Corning itself continued to develop the optical fibers. Soon the partners began to import fiber from Corning and cable it locally. Then, when the partners were comfortable with each other and each market was ready, Corning and the partners set up joint ventures to produce optical fiber locally. These ventures have worked extremely well, and their continuing success became particularly important in the late 1980s, as growth in the U.S.

market leveled off. Corning is widely acknowledged as one of the world's most successful users of joint ventures.

Managers are constantly told that they should choose a joint venture partner they trust. As these examples suggest, however, trust between partners is something that can only be developed over time, as a result of shared experiences. You can't start with trust.

Designing the Joint Venture

In the excitement of setting up a new operation in a foreign country, or getting access to technology provided by an overseas partner, it is important not to lose sight of the basic strategic requirements that must be met if a joint venture is to be successful. The questions that must be addressed are the same when any new business is proposed: Is the market attractive? How strong is the competition? How will the new company compete? Will it have the required resources? And so on.

In addition to these concerns, three others are particularly relevant to joint venture design. One is the question of *strategic freedom,* which has to do with the relationship between the venture and its parents. How much freedom will the venture be given to do as it wishes with respect to choosing a product line, suppliers, and customers? In the Dow Chemical venture referred to earlier, the dispute between the partners centered on the requirement that the venture buy materials, at what the Koreans believed to be an inflated price, from Dow's new wholly owned Korean plant. Clearly, the American and Korean vision of the amount of strategic freedom open to the venture was rather different.

The second issue of importance is that the joint venture be a *win-win* situation. This means that the payoff to each parent if the venture is successful should be a big one, because this will keep both parents working for the success of the venture when times are tough. If the strategic analysis suggests that the return to either parent will be marginal, the venture should be restructured or abandoned.

Finally, it is critical to decide on the *management roles* that each parent company will play. The venture will be easier to manage if one parent plays a *dominant* role and has a lot of influence over both the strategic and the day-to-day operations of the venture, or if one parent plays a *lead role* in the day-to-day operations of the joint venture. Most difficult to manage are *shared management* ventures, in which both parents have a significant input into both strategic decisions and the everyday operations of the venture. The possibilities are shown in Exhibit 7–7.

In spite of the fact that dominant-parent ventures are easier to manage than shared-management ventures, they are not always the appropriate type of venture to establish. Dominant-parent ventures are most likely to be effective when one partner has the knowledge and skill to make the venture a success and the other party is contributing simply money, a trademark, or perhaps a one-time transfer of technology. Research has indicated, for instance, that ventures in developing countries in which the foreign parent is dominant do not tend to be successful. Shared-management ventures are necessary when the venture needs active consultation between members of each parent company, as when deciding how to modify a product supplied by one

EXHIBIT 7–7   Joint Venture Management Roles

Operating Decisions	Dominated by Parent A	Unlikely	**Parent A Lead partner**	**Parent A Dominant**
	Shared	Unlikely	**Shared-management Joint venture**	Unlikely
	Dominated by Parent B	**Parent B Dominant**	**Parent B Lead partner**	Unlikely
		Dominated by Parent B	Shared	Dominated by Parent A
		Strategic Decisions		

parent for the local market that is well known by the other, or how to modify a production process designed by one parent to be suitable for a workforce and working conditions well known by the other.

A joint venture is headed for trouble when a parent tries to take a larger role in its management than makes sense. An American company with a joint venture in Japan, for instance, insisted that one of its people be the executive vice president of the venture. This was not reasonable, because the man had nothing to bring to the management of the venture. He simply served as a constant reminder to the Japanese that the American partner did not trust them. The Americans were pushing for a shared-management venture, when it was more logical to allow the Japanese, who certainly had all the necessary skills, to be the dominant or at least the leading firm. The major American contribution to the venture was to allow it to use its world-famous trademarks and brand names.

A second example, also in Japan, involves the French firm referred to at the start of this chapter. This company was bringing complex technology to the venture that needed to be modified for the Japanese market. It was clear that the French firm required a significant say in the management of the venture. On the other hand, the French had no knowledge of the Japanese market and, thus, the Japanese also needed a significant role in the venture. The logical solution would have been a shared-management venture and equal influence in decisions made at the board level. Unfortunately, both companies wanted to play a dominant role, and the venture collapsed in a decision-making stalemate.

Doing the Deal

Experienced managers argue that it is the relationship between the partners that is of key importance in a joint venture, not the legal agreement that binds them together. Nevertheless, most are careful to ensure that they have a good agreement in place—one that they understand and are comfortable with.

The principal elements of a joint venture agreement are listed in Exhibit 7–8. Most of these are straightforward and relate to topics discussed in this chapter. One item on the list that has not been discussed is the termination of the venture.

Although some managers balk at discussing divorce during the marriage ceremony, it is important to work out a method of terminating the venture in the event of a serious disagreement, and to do this at a time when heads are cool and goodwill abounds. The usual technique is to use a *shotgun clause,* which allows either party to name a price at which it will buy the other's shares in the venture. However, once this provision is activated and the first company has named a price, the second firm has the option of selling at this price or buying the first company's shares at the same price. This ensures that only fair offers are made, at least as long as both parents are large enough to be capable of buying each other out.

Making the Venture Work

Joint ventures need close and continuing attention, particularly in their early months. In addition to establishing a healthy working relationship between the parents and the venture general manager, managers should be on the lookout for the impact that cultural differences may be having on the venture and for the emergence of unforeseen inequities.

International joint ventures, like any type of international activity, require that managers of different national cultures work together. Unless managers have been

---

EXHIBIT 7–8   Principal Elements of a Joint Venture Agreement

- Definitions
- Scope of operations
- Management:
  1. Shareholders and supervisory roles regarding board
  2. Executive board
  3. Arrangements in the event of deadlock
  4. Operating management
- Arbitration
- Representations and warranties of each partner
- Organization and capitalization
- Financial arrangements
- Contractual links with parents
- Rights and obligations and intellectual property
- Termination agreements
- Force majeure
- Covenants

Source: "Teaming Up for the Nineties—Can You Survive without a Partner?" Deloitte, Haskins & Sells International, undated.

sensitized to the characteristics of the culture that they are dealing with, this can lead to misunderstandings and serious problems. Many Western managers, for instance, are frustrated by the slow, consensus-oriented decision-making style of the Japanese. Equally, the Japanese find American individualistic decision making to be surprising, as the decisions are made so quickly, but the implementation is often so slow. Firms that are sophisticated in the use of international joint ventures are well aware of such problems and have taken action to minimize them. Ford, for example, has put more than 1,500 managers through courses to improve their ability to work with Japanese and Korean managers.

It is important to remember that cultural differences do not just arise from differences in nationality. For example:

- Small firms working with large partners are often surprised and dismayed by the fact that it can take months, rather than days, to get approval of a new project. In some cases the cultural differences appear to be greater between small and large firms of the same nationality than, say, between multinationals of different nationality, particularly if the multinationals are in the same industry.
- Firms working with two partners from the same country have been surprised to find how different the companies are in cultural habits. A Japanese automobile firm headquartered in rural Japan is a very different company from one run from Tokyo.
- Cultural differences between managers working in different functional areas may be greater than those between managers in the same function in different firms. European engineers, for example, discovered when discussing a potential joint venture with an American partner that they had more in common with the American engineers than with the marketing people in their own company.

A very common joint venture problem is that the objectives of the parents, which coincided when the venture was formed, diverge over time. Such divergences can be brought on by changes in the fortunes of the partners. This was the case in the breakup of the General Motors–Daewoo joint venture in Korea in 1992. Relations between the partners were already strained due to GM's unwillingness to put further equity into the venture, in spite of a debt to equity ratio of more than 8 to 1, when, in 1991, faced with rapidly declining market share, the Korean parent decided that the venture should go for growth and maximize market share, whereas General Motors, itself in a poor financial position, insisted that the emphasis be on current profitability. When Daewoo, without telling General Motors, introduced a concessionary financing program for the joint venture's customers, the relationship was on the rocks, never to recover.

A final note concerns the unintended inequities that may arise during the life of a venture. Due to an unforeseen circumstance, one parent may be winning from the venture while the other is losing. A venture established in the mid-1980s between Japanese and American parents, for instance, was buying components from the Japanese parent at prices based in dollars. As the yen rose in value, the Japanese partner was receiving fewer and fewer yen for each shipment. The advice of many experienced venture managers is that, in such a situation, a change in the original agreement should be made, so the hardship is shared between the parents. That was done in this case, and the venture is performing extremely well, although it is not as profitable as originally anticipated.

Summary

For the reasons outlined in this chapter, international joint ventures are an increasingly important part of the strategy of many firms. They are, however, difficult to design and manage well, and so far, many ventures are performing below their management's expectations. This should not, however, be an excuse for firms to avoid such ventures. In many industries, the winners are going to be the companies that most quickly learn to manage international ventures effectively. The losers will be the managers who throw up their hands and say that joint ventures are too difficult, so we had better go it alone.

Supplementary Reading

Joint Venture Strategy and Objectives

Datta, Deepak K. "International Joint Ventures: A Framework for Analysis." *Journal of General Management* 14, No. 2 (Winter 1988).
Hamel, Gary, Yves Doz, and C. K. Prahalad. "Collaborate with Your Competitors—and Win." *Harvard Business Review,* January-February 1989.
Harrigan, Kathryn R. *Strategies for Joint Ventures.* Lexington, Mass.: Lexington Books, 1985.
Inkpen, Andrew C., and Paul W. Beamish. "Knowledge, Bargaining Power and International Joint Venture Stability." *Academy of Management Review*, Vol. 22, No. 1, 1997.

Managing the Venture

Janger, A. R. "Organization of International Joint Ventures." The Conference Board, Inc., Report No. 787. New York, 1980.
Killing, Peter. "How to Make a Global Joint Venture Work." *Harvard Business Review*, May-June, 1982, pp. 120–27.
Schaan, Jean-Louis. "How to Control a Joint Venture Even as a Minority Partner." *Journal of General Management* 14, No. 1 (Autumn 1988).

Managing Cultural Differences

Lane, Henry W., and Paul W. Beamish. "Cross-Cultural Cooperative Behavior in Joint Ventures in LDCs." *Management International Review*, Special Issue 1990, pp. 87–102.
Lane, Henry W., and Joseph DiStefano. *International Management Behavior: From Policy to Practice.* 2nd ed. Boston: PWS-Kent Publishing, 1992.

Joint Ventures in Developing Countries

Beamish, Paul W. "The Characteristics of Joint Ventures in The People's Republic of China." *Journal of International Marketing*, 1, No. 2 (1993), pp. 29–48.

Fey, Carl F. "Important Design Characteristics for Russian-Foreign Joint Ventures," *European Management Journal*, 13, 1995, pp. 405–15.

Schaan, Jean-Louis, and Paul W. Beamish. "Joint Venture General Managers in Developing Countries." In *Cooperative Strategies in International Business*, eds. F. Contractor and P. Lorange. Lexington, MA: Lexington Books, 1988, pp. 279–99.

Collections

Beamish, Paul W., and J. Peter Killing (eds.). *Cooperative Strategies: European Perspectives.* San Francisco, The New Lexington Press, 1997.

Beamish, Paul W., and J. Peter Killing (eds.). *Cooperative Strategies: North American Perspectives.* San Francisco, The New Lexington Press, 1997.

Beamish, Paul W. and J. Peter Killing (eds.). *Cooperative Strategies: Asian Perspectives.* San Francisco, The New Lexington Press, 1997.

Beamish, Paul W., and J. Peter Killing (eds.). Special Issue on Cooperative Strategies. *Journal of International Business Studies,* Vol. 27, No. 5, 1996.

8   INTERNATIONAL STRATEGY FORMULATION

This chapter focuses on the formulation of strategies to maximize the international competitiveness of the firm. Implicit in the discussion is the notion that international strategy evolves with changes in the competitive environment. As barriers to market penetration have been dismantled and as technologies have emerged that facilitate international organizational control, businesses have worked hard to expand their scope to include new international markets. Globalization—a term used somewhat loosely to describe an interdependent, borderless world—has became a common objective for many businesses. As a result of a broad movement toward more global competition, businesses have increasingly abandoned traditional approaches to international competition in favor of new, more innovative strategies.

Changes in the Global Competitive Environment

During the late 1980s and early 1990s a series of dramatic events transformed the business environment. The Soviet Union, burdened by inefficient industries at home and witnessing rapid expansion of Pacific Rim economies, embraced *perestroika* and later, as a splintered association of quasi-independent republics, free-market reform. Multinational companies poured in. In Moscow alone, an estimated 80,000 foreigners had set up residence by 1994. In China, market reforms unleashed by Deng Xiaoping continued to gather steam. Annual GNP growth rates hovered around 10 percent for China throughout the first half of the 1990s. In India, reforms begun in 1991 by Prime Minister P.V. Narasimha Rao pushed economic growth from only 0.6 percent in the early 1990s to an estimated 6 percent in 1995. In Europe, the move toward greater economic integration continued despite lingering concerns over the desirability of monetary union. Eastern European countries—including Poland,

This chapter was prepared by Allen Morrison and Harold Crookell.

Hungary, and the Czech Republic—have pushed for full membership in the European Union. During the early 1990s, the Canada–U.S. Free Trade Agreement was expanded to include Mexico. Although Chile was lobbying hard to be included in an expanded North American Free Trade area, resistance from the United States pushed Chile in 1995 to pursue a bilateral free trade agreement with Canada. Throughout Latin America, the replacement of military-led governments with populist regimes has led to reduced inflation, greater economic openness, reduced nationalist tendencies, and rapid economic growth. In Brazil, annual GNP growth averaged 8 percent throughout the first half of the 1990s; it was expected to stay at this level through the turn of the century.

In the background, unparalleled technological changes in developing, storing, and communicating information have made the world seem much smaller. Advances in telecommunications, satellite television, and the Internet all moved to link people together irrespective of country location. In the foreground, Japan demonstrated that the rapid commercial application of new technology could produce rising global market share. Notwithstanding a recession that slowed Japan in mid-decade, other Asia-Pacific nations were following Japan's lead. South Korea, Singapore, Malaysia, Indonesia, and Thailand have all embraced technology-led industrial development. China, with its low-cost labor and huge domestic market, has begun to assert itself as a major economic force. At 1995 growth rates, China was slated to become the world's largest market by 2010. The impact this will have on world political and economic relations is anything but certain.

In response to the accelerating changes around them, MNCs have developed new criteria for determining both where and how they compete. By the mid-1990s, most MNCs were finding that to remain competitive at home they had to significantly increase the number of countries where they conducted business. In determining where to compete, MNCs needed to assess countries according to their strategic importance. A country's strategic importance is a function of both overall market size and its ability to provide easy access to high-value inputs such as labor, energy, or capital. For most MNCs, globalization has significantly increased the number of strategically important countries. Countries such as China, India, Russia, Indonesia, South Korea, Malaysia, and Brazil are being actively targeted by many MNCs.

It is in determining how to compete that most MNCs have run into problems. MNCs in the late 1990s are confronted with a bewildering array of strategy options. Most MNCs conceptualize strategy as a hierarchy that includes both corporate-level strategies and business-unit-level strategies. Corporate strategies typically focus on two things: (1) determining the industries in which the MNC will compete, and (2) determining how the various businesses within the MNC will coordinate activities. Business-unit strategies focus on market share battles through competitive and international positioning. Business-unit managers rather than corporate executives have become the primary drivers of international strategy.

MNCs typically have multiple international strategies. Each of these strategies will be driven by different business units within the corporation as they strive to match their unique skills with pressures and opportunities to be globally integrated. IBM, for example, designs and manufactures microprocessors, which have become a globally demanded product. Competing in this industry requires IBM to construct world-scale fabrication facilities that produce globally standardized semiconductor products. IBM also competes in service industries where customers require enormous care and localized attention. A strategy based on maximizing local responsiveness seems most appropriate for much of IBM's service activities. To maximize its overall competitiveness, IBM encourages each business to approach international markets in a way that is most consistent with industry pressures. As a result, understanding MNC strategy means focusing on businesses and the industry pressures they confront.

Understanding Industry Pressures

An appropriate starting point for understanding international strategy is analyzing the industry pressures confronting each business within the MNC. Every industry—whether high-tech or low-tech, service or manufacturing—is confronted by two sets of competing imperatives: pressures to be globally integrated and pressures to be locally responsive. These pressures drive business strategy and cannot be overlooked in formulating an appropriate international strategy.

Pressures Toward Globalization

Pressures that encourage businesses to adopt global integration strategies include both broad facilitating factors and imperatives that vary by industry. Broad facilitating factors include three developments:

- Freer trade
- Global financial services and capital markets
- Advances in communications technology

Together, these facilitating factors have made global competition possible but not necessarily desirable for all businesses. To determine whether global integration is advisable, businesses are encouraged to examine pressures that are specific to their particular industry. These industry-specific imperatives include:

- Universal customer needs
- Global customers
- Global competitors
- High investment intensity
- Pressures for cost reduction

Broad Facilitating Factors

Freer Trade.   For the past 50 years, declining tariffs and the emergence of regional trading blocs have had an enormous impact on world trade and investment. Data from the General Agreement on Tariffs and Trade (GATT) indicated that the

Uruguay round of trade negotiations resulted in the adoption of new commercial liberalization policies by 72 governments.[1] Since then, regional trading blocks have moved to strengthen ties in North America, Europe, Southeast Asia, Africa, and Latin America. The removal of tariffs and nontariff barriers signals a weakening of the economic role of nation states and an invitation to "think global." It should be pointed out, however, that the objectives of the European Union and free trade agreements established by ASEAN countries or Canada, the United States, and Mexico are quite different instruments. The European Union is designed to limit national sovereignty by creating supranational political and administrative bodies. In contrast, free trade agreements attempt to achieve the economic benefits of tariff removal without so much loss of national sovereignty. While Europe is harmonizing its regulatory affairs, Canada, the United States, and Mexico are not.

Global Financial Services and Capital Markets.   The globalization of financial services and capital markets have facilitated the efforts of many businesses to globally integrate their activities. Capital can now be sourced through transnational banks (for example, Citibank), overseas venture capitalists (for example, Investcorp, a Saudi-owned firm) and soon, sources such as the Internet. Recent trends in financial technology allow the trading of financial instruments 24 hours per day, 365 days per year, irrespective of national location. In addition, the ability of MNCs to manage interest rate risk and currency exchange rates through hedging and computerized market trading have reduced the importance of placing investment capital under one national umbrella.

Advances in Communications Technology.   Managing a far-flung international business requires extensive communication in order to maintain organizational control. Advances in computer and fax technology have made such communication easier and less costly. The availability of huge on-line databases and E-mail systems have greatly increased the ability of companies to manage international operations. Direct electronic links, for example, have enabled Boeing and a consortium of Japanese partners to design aircraft together. Advances in information technology have also made it possible for the financial services industry in New York to export thousands of backroom data processing jobs to lower-cost labor in Ireland.

Industry-Specific Pressures

Universal Customer Needs.   While advances in telecommunications have enabled companies to better control global activities, television, movies, radio, the print media, and telephones have dramatically increased the information available to consumers around the world. By seeing what other people have or enjoy doing, consumers can put enormous pressure on businesses to globalize. Successful world products like watches, cameras, fast food, blue jeans, luxury writing instruments,

---

[1]See "GATT Effort Must Not Be Wasted," *The Financial Times*, July 17, 1993, p. 19.

personal computers, and cellular telephones are welcomed in more and more national markets. Many sports have also become globalized. The popularity of U.S. sports has led to sell-out crowds for American football and basketball games in Europe and Japan and a surging public interest in sports celebrities, whose names are used to sell everything from perfume to pizza. Depending on the industry, people increasingly want the same products and services irrespective of home country.

Global Customers.   Many MNCs do not sell directly to consumers but focus instead on other MNCs as customers. When these customers are themselves globalized, they demand standardized inputs around the world. General Motors, for example, has made major progress in globalizing its purchasing activities. To GM this means that it searches the world for the best products at the lowest prices. An automotive components company must be able to meet GM's global standards for quality, features, and pricing. As GM moves into new markets, these suppliers are expected to respond. Take Prince Corp., for example. Prince is a $350 million Holland, Michigan-based manufacturer of dashboard components and interior paneling for the automotive industry. One of Prince's biggest customers is GM. In order to streamline design, keep costs low, and maximize production efficiencies, Prince and GM have developed a very close working relationship. As GM expands its presence in Latin America, it has encouraged Prince to establish a major production facility near its manufacturing complex in Brazil. Prince must respond in a positive way or risk jeopardizing its core North American partnership with GM.

Global Competitors.   No pressure is quite so strong as an international competitor taking your market share. Some industries are dominated by global businesses that establish competitive norms. Once competitive norms have been set in an industry, businesses can choose either to follow the pack and adhere to the norms or pursue much narrower niche strategies.

High Investment Intensity.   Investment intensity includes costs for developing products and gearing up for production. In general, the higher the investment intensity the greater the pressure on businesses to globally standardize output. Boeing, for example, spent nearly $6 billion bringing its new 777 aircraft to market. The investment included money for new computer systems, research and design activities, assembly operations, tooling, testing, certification, and so forth. While Boeing clearly wants to recoup this investment, it must do so in a very competitive marketplace. The key for Boeing will be to maximize the number of planes sold and thereby reduce the per-unit development costs. In order to effectively amortize development costs over a huge base, Boeing faces enormous pressures to standardize production. Other industries—including civil aircraft, microprocessors, boats, locomotives, computer software, telecommunications equipment, and automobiles—face similar pressures.

Pressures for Cost Reduction.   In industries where price is the key purchase criterion, producers have a great incentive to find new ways to lower costs to maintain profits. Economies of scale and learning both have enormous impacts on operational efficiency. The greater the impact of learning and volume, the greater the incentive to maximize output. The issue in terms of globalization is a determination of the volume where minimum per unit costs can be achieved. If minimum per unit costs can be achieved at an output of 200,000 units per year, and if domestic demand is only 50,000 units per year, businesses will have an incentive to standardize output and get into the export business for the remaining 75 percent of output. Whether the business does or not will depend in part on the importance the customer places on price. In the petroleum industry price is critical and so producers push production volumes out as far as possible. In the newspaper industry, local content and responsiveness is far more important than production efficiencies.

Pressures Toward Localization

Although the pendulum swung decisively in the direction of globalization during the 1990s, industries have been affected in different ways. The transition to globalization is not complete and may well pass numerous industries by. Localization pressures include both country-specific factors and MNC-specific factors. Country-specific factors include three primary pressures:

- Trade barriers
- Cultural differences
- Nationalism

MNC-specific factors include four principal pressures that either limit an MNC's ability to respond to globalization pressures or facilitate its ability to be locally responsive:

- Organizational resistance to change
- Transportation limitations
- New production technologies
- Just-in-time manufacturing

Country-Specific Pressures

Trade Barriers. Tariff barriers encourage businesses to compete internationally through foreign direct investment rather than trade. Servicing a local market through a dedicated manufacturing facility enables businesses to maximize local responsiveness, which is typically an objective of government-imposed barriers. With tariffs in place, competitors are encouraged to establish operations in a host country, thereby preserving national culture and sovereignty. When tariffs decline, the international competitiveness of a country's industries becomes more vital. Serious loss of market share to imports often triggers nontariff barriers in nations concerned over the short-term loss of jobs. Subsidies directed at domestic producers represent a common nontariff barrier. Perhaps the best example of government subsidies can be found in agriculture. In 1990, it was estimated that the first-world countries were spending approximately $275 billion per year on agricultural subsidies.[2] Virtually every country in the world maintains some form of agricultural subsidies, including supply management schemes, import restrictions, and direct financial support to farmers.

Voluntary export restrictions represent another common nontariff barrier to trade. In the early 1980s, Japanese automobile manufacturers agreed to limit exports of automobiles to the United States. One study found that as a result of the export restrictions, Japanese automobile manufacturers began shifting production to the United States, creating an estimated 55,000 jobs by the middle of the decade.[3] However, the study also found that both U.S. and Japanese automobile manufacturers raised prices substantially as a result of the export restrictions. It was estimated that Japanese manufacturers captured an additional $2.2 billion in cash flow by using increases in prices to limit volume; U.S. producers captured an additional $2.6 billion by matching Japanese price increases. In all, the study estimated that the same reduction in Japanese automobile exports could have been achieved with an imposition of an 11 percent tariff. In the final analysis, export restrictions may have helped Japanese manufacturers more than they hurt.

Government regulations are a third important means of restricting trade. A clear example of the limits of globalization is the international television industry. The international television industry remains dominated by three global broadcast standards: one for North America, one for Europe, and one for Japan/Asia Pacific. While the emergence of high-definition TV has promoted a convergence in broadcast standards, political pressures have put these efforts on hold. Imbedded in each of the broad regional standards are intraregional standards. In Europe, for example, technical standards differ across countries in seven different areas of technical design. European integration has had only a modest impact on these standards. Beyond standards, duties on imported televisions remain at approximately 10 percent, despite initiatives undertaken in 1992 to lower tariffs. Similar barriers are in place in North America, Japan, and many newly industrialized countries.

Cultural Differences. While satellite television and the international media are shrinking the world and homogenizing consumer tastes, national culture continues to pull in the opposite direction. Traditions and religious beliefs run deep and often conflict with international media messages. Although individuals may display an initial interest in a product because it is "foreign," they may also shun the same product over time because of the changes in lifestyles it promotes. For example, Kellogg set up a manufacturing plant in India in 1994 but has an uphill battle convincing Indians of the merits of cold breakfast cereal. To the extent different cultures lead to divergent consumer preferences, global product strategies can miss the mark, or can require major adaptation from market to market.

---

[2]GATT Brief: The American Connection, *The Economist*, April 21, 1990, pp. 85–86.

[3]See G. Hufbauer, D. Berliner, and K. Elliot. *Trade Protection in the United States: 31 Case Studies*. Washington, DC: Institute for International Economics, 1986.

Nationalism. From the republics of former Yugoslavia, to the Basque region of Spain, to the Canadian province of Quebec, to the now-dissolved Czechoslovakia, nationalism enjoyed a significant resurgence in the early 1990s. The combination of new political freedoms and the backlash against the forces of globalization have merged to create aspirations for national autonomy around the world. Nationalism is often symbolic and almost always powerfully emotional. By representing common values and attitudes, nationalism provides the basis for social cohesion and is often used to justify obstructions in the international movement of goods and services. In countries where national institutions and power systems have been fractured, tribalism has seen a renaissance. Tribal loyalties, often born of common language and history, are fast replacing national allegiances in countries torn by civil war or economic strife. By focusing attention inward, both nationalism and tribalism foster values that deter globalization.

MNC-Specific Pressures

Organizational Resistance to Change. Globalization for MNCs means imposing central control on country managers, who in many cases have been functioning with substantial autonomy. This imposition of corporate control often means the redesign of an affiliate's product to meet global specifications or the rationalization of operations for the good of the overall corporation. In either case, the "not invented here" syndrome may intervene. For MNCs with histories of autonomous affiliates—companies like General Motors, Ford, IBM, Philips, and Nestlé—organizational resistance to global integration has become a major obstacle. A case in point is Warner Lambert's pharmaceutical operations in Europe. In 1970 Warner Lambert acquired Parke-Davis in an effort to expand its international position in pharmaceuticals. With decades of experience in Europe, Parke-Davis had established manufacturing operations in France, the U.K., Italy, Spain, Germany, Belgium, and Ireland. Affiliates in these countries were given considerable autonomy and developed substantial competencies. Beginning in the mid-1980s, Warner Lambert began a major initiative to reduce the number of pharmaceutical manufacturing units in Europe while concurrently specializing production in the units that remained. Fearful of losing power and convinced that the parent was overestimating the impact of globalization, affiliate managers fought back. Working together, the major affiliates were able to convince the parent to proceed much more cautiously than planned. Decisions that were expected to have been made in weeks or a few months ended up being moved to committees that took over three years to process. While the parent has now made a number of rationalization decisions, the major European affiliates have been successful in retaining much of their original powers. Other companies have experienced similar resistance to change. In Europe, powerful unions have opposed Europe-wide reengineering. At IBM, for example, French unions filed suit in 1994 to stop the company from cutting 1,300 jobs. In September 1994, IBM Europe's chairman, Hans-Olaf Henkel, resigned after IBM Chairman Lou Gerstner forced a reorganization of the European sales force that augmented the role of corporate head office decision makers over regional chiefs.[4]

Transportation Difficulties.   Businesses with products that are highly susceptible to spoilage or that have high weight-to-value ratios are not typically good candidates for globalization. The dairy and bread industries, for example, tend to be some of the most locally responsive, in part because of short shelf lives. Other industries such as fresh seafood and cut flowers have largely overcome spoilage problems by developing special packaging and efficient transportation procedures. However, these actions add substantial costs to the consumer and are only justifiable to the degree premium prices can be passed on. In industries with high weight-to-value, transportation costs may outweigh any benefits of global integration. Sand, gravel and coal, potted plants, diapers, and paint are examples of products whose high weight-to-value ratio or high volume-to-value ratio discourages global integration.

New Production Technologies.   New computer-assisted design and manufacturing technologies have allowed an increasing number of industries to maximize efficiencies at relatively small production volumes. Making multiple products in a single factory is more practical because machine changeover time has been reduced dramatically. In the U.S. steel industry, for example, Nucor Corporation and Chaparral Steel, through their development of minimill and micromill technologies, emerged in the mid-1980s as fast-growing international success stories. The result of short-production-run technologies is that products can be adapted, if necessary, for different markets at a more reasonable cost than used to be possible. New technologies have also made it possible to introduce new products in record time, making speed a new source of competitive advantage. Whistler, one of the largest manufacturers of radar detectors in the United States, introduced leading-edge technology in product design and manufacturing configuration and raised its pass rate on its assembly line from 75 percent to over 99 percent. In doing so, it cut production delays and reduced overall costs, saving hundreds of U.S.-based jobs that were slated for transfer to South Korea.

Just-in-Time Manufacturing.   Heavy equipment manufacturers and automotive assemblers have led the way in pursuing just-in-time manufacturing strategies. In many cases suppliers to these industries are required to ship an agreed-upon quantity of components so that they arrive at the customer's plant within hours of assembly. By adopting just-in-time manufacturing, the assemblers are able to pass inventory costs as well as other risks on to suppliers. In many cases these savings more than offset the potential production economies that may result from global component manufacturing. Businesses that supply inputs to just-in-time customers may face serious limitations insofar as globalization is concerned.

---

[4]W. Echikson, "IBM's European Travail." *Fortune*, October 3, 1994, p. 88.

Globalization Impacts Industries

In assessing the net impact of globalization and localization pressures, it is essential to recognize that globalization pressures vary from industry to industry. For example, while a reduction in trade barriers may have a dramatic impact on the computer industry, it may be of little consequence to the cement industry. Similarly, while advances in telecommunications may make it easier to develop standardized advertising programs, the demand for a wide variety of products remains deeply imbedded in local cultures. Within industries, globalization and localization pressures vary in intensity. Relatively few industries emphasize all globalization or localization pressures to the maximum degree. Many segments of the food processing industry, for example, could achieve considerable cost savings through global production; however, the industry's globalization potential is limited by spoilage problems and low value-to-weight ratios, which make shipping prohibitively expensive.

Before further exploring MNC strategies, it is useful to determine which industries or products require local adaptation and therefore strong local responsiveness strategies and which face strong globalization pressures (i.e., major scale economies in production, R&D, or marketing) and therefore strong central control. The following two-by-two matrix attempts to do this by contrasting the pressures toward globalization with the pressures toward localization (Exhibit 8–1).

In the two right quadrants, local adaptation is important. In the two top quadrants, the pressures toward globalization are significant. The top left quadrant identifies industries where local differences are minor and the benefits to global integration are significant. The bottom right quadrant represents the opposite extreme, where local differences are significant and there are few advantages to globalization. The bottom left quadrant represents industries where local differences are minor but globalization is limited by other factors (e.g., transportation in the case of cement). The types of organization strategy best suited to the key quadrants are shown in the diagram and are discussed below. It is important to repeat, however, that when we talk of globalization pressures increasing, what we mean is that more and more products and industries are moving up from the bottom quadrants to the top quadrants.

Globalization Impacts Business Strategy

Historically, U.S. and European MNCs have approached international competition by pursuing multidomestic strategies. Multidomestic strategies are designed to maximize the local responsiveness of businesses. Encouraged by historically fragmented European markets, and cultures that readily accommodated the delegation of decision making to overseas managers, U.S. and European MNCs achieved major successes in international markets in the 1960s and 1970s by emphasizing multidomestic strategies. From 1950 to 1975, for example, U.S. FDI in Europe increased by over 500 percent to almost $125 billion. From 1975 to 1987, FDI increased another 350

EXHIBIT 8–1   Organization Consequences of Internationalization

---

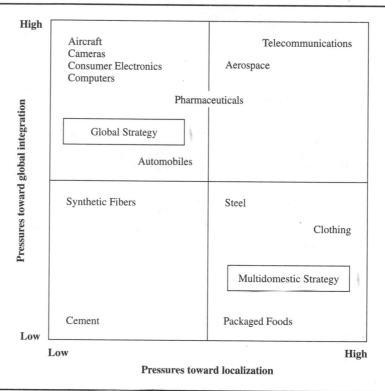

percent to almost $428 billion.[5] By 1990, U.S. companies employed more than 2 million people in Europe and produced about 85 percent of all U.S.-branded goods and services marketed in the European Union in facilities located in Europe (the remaining 15 percent were generated from exports from the United States).[6] A similar pattern was also evident in Canada, which has become the largest host country to U.S. investment; by the early 1990s, fully one-quarter of Canada's largest 500 corporations were affiliates of U.S. parent corporations.[7]

During the mid-1990s the pace of FDI increased. Total FDI flows into developed countries reached an estimated $325 billion in 1995, up from $216 billion in 1994

---

[5]Figures are for all of Europe. United States Department of Commerce, "U.S. Multinational Companies: Operations in 1987." *Survey of Current Business*, 69 (June 1989).

[6]United Nations Centre on Transnational Corporations, "Regional Economic Integration and Transnational Corporations in the 1990s: Europe 1992, North America, and Developing Countries." ST/CTC/SER.A/15, July 1990.

[7]According to the *Financial Post 500,* in 1989, 123 of Canada's largest firms were controlled by U.S.-based companies (block foreign ownership or wholly foreign-owned).

and $130 billion in 1993.[8] Of the European economies, the U.K. received the highest volume of FDI. In 1994, FDI flows to the U.K. were $10.1 billion; by 1995, they had risen almost threefold to $29.9 billion. In contrast, Germany in 1994 had net negative FDI flows; by 1995, the deficit had switched to a positive FDI flow of $9 billion.[9]

In 1995, the United States was the largest host country for FDI. Total flows of FDI to the United States reached $74.7 billion in 1995, up from $49.4 billion in 1994.[10] One study reported that net FDI stocks in the United States increased by an average 17.1 percent per year from 1980 to 1992.[11] Much of this new FDI could be traced to major acquisitions of U.S.-based MNCs. In 1995, for example, Swiss-based Hoechst paid $7.1 billion for Marion Merrell Dow; U.K.-based Cadbury Schweppes purchased Dr. Pepper/Seven-Up. Cos. for $2.6 billion.[12]

During the same period, MNCs from the European Union (E.U.) also increased the number of multidomestic affiliates substantially. During the 1980s, for example, outward flows of FDI by MNCs in the E.U. averaged about twice the amount directed to the E.U. itself. Most of these flows were designed to establish locally responsive U.S. affiliates. Within the E.U., most intra-regional FDI flowed among the large economies of France, the U.K., Germany, and the Netherlands. The elimination of many tariff barriers among European Union countries, as well as greater currency stability, facilitated the regionalization of FDI. Still, rising unemployment, generous welfare systems, and rising trade tensions threatened to derail economic integration in the mid-1990s. Government resistance to integration was increasing. Despite the promises of economic union, the national legislatures of member countries have proven far less eager to implement European Union laws.

Multidomestic Strategies

The establishment of stand-alone overseas affiliates is consistent with the adoption of multi-domestic strategies. Businesses pursuing multidomestic strategies first develop products for their home market and then offer them for sale or adaptation by their overseas affiliates. Affiliates are developed with the capacity to absorb parent company technology and adapt the resulting products to local conditions and tastes. Traditionally, multidomestic affiliates manufacture products for their own national markets, adapting the parent company product line as required. If specialization is at the heart of global strategies, duplication and autonomy are at the heart of multidomestic strategies. In the pure multidomestic model, it is technology and skills that cross national boundaries, not products.

---

[8]United Nations Conference on Trade and Development, *World Investment Report, 1995.*

[9]Ibid.

[10]Ibid.

[11]See R. Grosse, and L. Trevino, (1996). "Foreign Direct Investment in the United States: An Analysis of Country of Origin," *Journal of International Business Studies*, 27 (1), 139–55.

[12]For a more complete discussion of 1995 FDI patterns, see "Multinational Firms Spent $325 Billion in 1995 on Foreign Direct Investment," *The Wall Street Journal*, June 5, 1996, pp. A2, A4.

During the high-tariff decades of the 1950s, 1960s, and 1970s, multidomestic strategies appeared appropriate. However, with the emergence of the first strains of globalization pressures in the 1970s, multidomestic strategies began to falter in many industries. As industry pressures began to take on more global dimensions, it became possible for business to gain a competitive advantage by pursuing global strategies.

Global Strategies

Under a global strategy, businesses focus on maximizing international efficiency by locating activities in low-cost countries, producing standardized products from world-scale facilities, globally integrating operations, and subsidizing intracountry market share battles. Global businesses conceive and design products for world markets from the outset. Frequently, affiliates in key markets have input into product design, but once the parent organization launches a new product, the affiliate's role reverts to that of implementer.

Global products are usually marketed to international similarities rather than to cultural differences, and marketing strategies are therefore established as a rule in the parent organization. Products are manufactured wherever in the world the necessary quality standards can be achieved at the lowest cost, including transportation to key markets. As a practical matter, large markets attract production because market share is often enhanced by the presence of a production facility. Also host country governments sometimes induce local production through nontariff barriers to trade, but the classic global strategy is conceived without artificial impediments to the movement of goods.

Globalization Impacts Host Governments

Increasing demands by governments for investment capital, for economic and trade diversification, and for increasingly sophisticated product and process technologies have shifted the bargaining power in favor of multinational companies (MNCs). While these needs augment the bargaining power of all MNCs, MNCs pursuing globally integrated strategies further strengthen their relative bargaining power positions vis-à-vis governments. In developing policies to respond to global MNCs, a critical issue facing governments is the degree to which MNCs have adopted truly global strategies.

MNCs pursuing global strategies gain additional bargaining power over governments as a result of their abilities to control both how, and where, activities are geographically positioned and how they are coordinated. These abilities are manifest in two broad areas.[13] First, globally integrated MNCs have the ability to bias the financial results of affiliates and thereby shift profits from high- to low-tax jurisdictions.

---

[13]For a more complete discussion of the concerns of host countries regarding integrated MNCs, see Y. Doz, "Government Policies and Global Industries," in M. Porter (ed.), *Competition in Global Industries*. Boston: Harvard Business School Press, 1986, pp. 225–66.

EXHIBIT 8–2   The Impact of Economies of Scale on Transfer Pricing

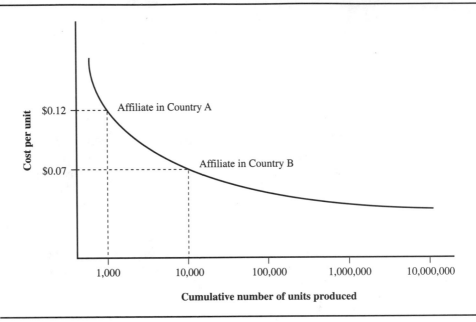

The manipulation of financial results can be achieved through transfer pricing and favorable remittance policies. Exhibit 8–2 presents the hypothetical example of a company with two affiliates. Under this example, the affiliate in country A produces only 1,000 units of output per month at a unit cost of $0.12. The affiliate in country B produces 10,000 units per month at a per unit cost of $0.07. If the affiliate in country A shuts down its factory and sources from country B, its costs will go down to just below $0.07 per unit. If, however, country A's marginal tax rate is higher than that of country B, the company may want to charge the affiliate in country A the old rate of $0.12 per unit. In this way, profits are shifted from country A to country B and taxes are minimized.

A second way globally integrated MNCs exert power over host governments is through their ability to control the direction and location of technology and skills. MNCs often have the capability to rapidly reconfigure value adding activities. By constantly focusing on shifting patterns of comparative advantage, MNCs can move operations from one country to another as factor costs shift. This mobility, combined with the ownership of technology, skills, and jobs and the ability of MNCs to generate tax revenues, results in countries competing against each other for new investment as well as the retention of existing MNC activities. Even subnational governments are into the bidding game. In Phoenix, Arizona, for example, the city council in 1995 voted to approve major tax breaks and infrastructure investments to encourage Sitix, a division of Japanese giant Sumitomo Corporation, to invest almost $500 million in a silicon wafer manufacturing plant. The Phoenix area was already home to major microprocessor fabrication plants of Intel, Motorola, and SGS-Thomson and was concerned about maintaining its global position as a center of high-tech excellence.

Key Considerations in Adopting a Global Strategy

Although global strategy has been viewed as ideal in global industries, not all businesses are capable of pursuing a global strategy. Resource constraints, bureaucratic obstacles, and histories of affiliate autonomy have forced a large number of businesses to pursue a variety of nonglobal options. Some have viewed country-based, multidomestic strategies as ultimately untenable in global industries. Others have argued that multidomestic strategies are appropriate as a long-term niche approach to international competition.

Although pure global strategies may not always be appropriate, heightened international competition is forcing almost every business to globalize at least some activities. In considering how and where to proceed, the following steps should be considered.

1. Determine Where the Critical Scale Economies and Other Benefits of Globalization Lie

Offshore production is often the first thought of North American or European firms threatened by heightened international competition. Many managers may feel that the perfect solution is to shift the labor-intensive production processes to low-wage countries and otherwise continue business as usual. A globalization strategy, however, implies much more than this. Products need to be designed for key world markets; furthermore, designs need to be sensitive to production processes and to global standards of product reliability, technology, and quality. Under globalization, the issue is not where a business can make it cheaper, but where a business can achieve the best combination of technology, quality, and cost.

On this basis, different products end up being manufactured in different countries. Some factories concentrate on component parts; others on assembly. In both cases, factories are set up to serve the business's worldwide needs, or at least a major portion of them. Many large businesses are nervous about having single sources of supply of key products or components. Although they often develop multiple sources, they normally designate one factory as the prime source and assign to it the ongoing related product development responsibility. Other competing units within the corporation may over time try to displace it as the prime source of products based on superior cost and quality performance.

While production scale economies are an important benefit of globalization, they are not the only benefit. Advertising and promotion can in some cases be globalized too. It is just as possible to advertise to global similarities as to national differences, but to do it successfully requires a lot of understanding of the mood and mind-set of different regions. There is an enormous difference between successful global advertising and the view that what's good for Iowa or Ontario is good for India or Malaysia. The same is true for global design.

Just as the globalization benefits are not the same for all industries, they differ significantly from product to product and from activity to activity. Key questions include: How homogeneous are customer needs from one country to another? What savings are possible from designing the product for global markets and manufacturing it to global capacity? What technology does large-scale specialized production make possible? Can the company benefit by adopting a common approach to marketing the product around the world? What problems might arise in particular countries or regions from such an approach? As questions like these are answered, product line by product line and activity by activity, it is possible to identify where globalization fits best and where localization is more important.

2. Rotate Country Managers More Frequently to Help Them Develop a Global Vision

Country managers with long-term appointments do not easily develop global perspectives, and it is difficult to globalize an organization successfully without those perspectives in place. One way to accelerate globalization is to move senior people from one international affiliate to another, or from the affiliate to head office and back. Of course, this means sending in nonnationals to run affiliates, but if the rotation is understood as global management training, resentment of the nonnational boss will be minimized. There are other benefits to rotation too. The corporation is able to utilize managers from all over the world in whatever positions they best fit. Furthermore, morale in the affiliates is sometimes higher because managers there see opportunities beyond their own borders.

A wide variety of corporations—including Ford, 3M, ABB, and Dow Chemical—use management rotation regularly to build up a core of international managers. Not everyone likes to be moved around the world, however. Some managers like the opportunity early in their careers, but not when they have to worry about their children's schooling and other family matters. It is also expensive. Expatriate managers usually get paid a premium for living abroad or get their living accommodations paid. Family trips back home and private schooling for dependent children are also often part of the package. Building a global management team leads to some expensive traditions in corporate culture. These benefits are also often very visible to host country nationals, who often view them as excessive.

3. Change the Performance Measurement System to Fit the Mandate

Under traditional multidomestic strategies, country managers have broad strategic autonomy over corporate activities in the country and should therefore reasonably be evaluated on the basis of country-specific results. Broad measures of growth and return on invested capital are commonly used criteria. However, to hold a manager responsible for results after his or her autonomy is reduced under globalization is more problematic. The company, of course, is more interested in its overall global results than in the results of any one affiliate, but if results are to be used to measure a manager's performance, they must somehow fit the mandate assigned to the manager. While normal growth and return on investment criteria might apply to products made for the domestic market only, imported products may be better evaluated with a system that measures sales growth by market segment. And products made for world markets may require a system that evaluates cost of production only. On the other hand, if the affiliate has the marketing assignment for its global products, the measurement system might include growth of export sales.

Clearly, globalization leads to more complex measurement systems. That is because responsibility is divided in different ways. This is evidenced in Exhibit 8–2, where the affiliate manager in country A may be responsible for perpetually subsidizing the profits of another affiliate. Being responsible for selling a product designed for the global market at a price set by a head office is quite different from selling a domestically designed product at a price set at home. Measurement systems have to reflect these changes in responsibility. They are complicated further by transfer prices on intercorporate trade, and intercorporate trade increases significantly under globalization.

Globalization has ultimately promoted interdependence rather than independence, and cooperation rather than confrontation. With such changes, globalization is an important development for countries, industries, and MNCs. For MNCs, globalization means significant changes in strategies. These changes are followed by more flexible ways of organizing activities for the 1990s. This is the focus of Chapter 9.

Supplementary Reading

Birkinshaw, Julian, and Warren Richie. "Balancing the Global Portfolio." *Business Quarterly*, Summer 1993, pp. 40–49.

Hamel, Gary, and C. K. Prahalad "Do You Really Have a Global Strategy?" *Harvard Business Review*, July-August 1985, pp. 139–48.

Hedlund, Gunnar. "The Hypermodern MNC—A Heterarchy?" *Human Resource Management*, Spring 1986.

Henzler, Herbert, and Wilhelm Rall, "Facing Up to the Globalization Challenge." *The McKinsey Quarterly*, Fall 1986.

Kim, W. Chan, and Renee Mauborgne. "Effectively Conceiving and Executing Multinationals' World Wide Strategies." *Journal of International Business Studies*, Vol. 24, No. 3, 1993, pp. 419–48.

Morrison, Allen. *Strategies in Global Industries: How U.S. Businesses Compete*. Westport, CT: Quorum Books, 1990.

Morrison, Allen, and Kendall Roth. "A Taxonomy of Business-Level Strategies in Global Industries." *Strategic Management Journal*, Vol. 13, 1992, pp. 399–417.

Ohmae, Kenichi. "Planting for a Global Harvest," *Harvard Business Review*, July-August 1989.

Porter, Michael. "Changing Patterns of International Competition." *California Management Review*, Vol. 28, 1986, pp. 9–40.

Prahalad, C. K., and Yves Doz. *The Multinational Mission: Balancing Local Demands and Global Vision*. New York: The Free Press, 1987.

Yip, George. *Total Global Strategy: Managing for Worldwide Competitive Advantage*. Englewood Cliffs, N.J.: Prentice Hall, 1992.

9 THE IMPACT OF GLOBALIZATION ON THE ORGANIZATION OF ACTIVITIES

This chapter focuses on the organization of business activities in the face of rising globalization. How companies organize activities—research and development, production, marketing, and service, among others—often means the difference between failure and success. Organization decisions ultimately focus on how activities are *configured* and *coordinated*.[1] Configuration pertains to the geographic positioning of activities and is driven by a company's interest in accessing markets and sources of comparative advantage. Activities range from being "concentrated" (i.e., each activity is located in a single country from which the world is served), or "dispersed" (i.e., all activities are located in each host country). In contrast, coordination pertains to the integration or interdependence of activities, and is driven by a company's interest in exploiting competitive advantages across countries. Coordination ranges from very low—where each activity of a business is performed independently—to very high, where the same activities are tightly coordinated or linked across geographical locations. How a company configures and coordinates its activities directly impacts its ability to exploit country-specific comparative advantages as well as company-specific competencies.

This chapter examines how rising globalization pressures have forced managers to re-examine every aspect of how activities are configured and coordinated. Particularly, it is about the organization structures through which MNCs carry out their activities, and the interplay between international strategy and structure. Inasmuch as the 1990s have emerged as the decade of globalization, this chapter assesses the scope and limits of globalization and examines its impact on the interplay between evolving international strategy and structure.

This chapter was prepared by Allen Morrison and Harold Crookell.

[1]For a more complete discussion of the concepts of configuration and coordination in international organizations, see M. Porter, "Changing Patterns of International Competition," *California Management Review*, 28, 1986, pp. 9–40.

Common International Organization Structures

International Division Structure

Much of the early work on international organization structures took the logical approach of relating the structure to the growth of a company's international activity. A company, for example, might begin with an export department to handle the technical requirements of shipping products across national borders. With success in export markets would come a greater awareness of international opportunities, and the next organizational stage might be the establishment of an international division to look after both exports and foreign investments. The organization structure of a company with an international division might appear as shown in Exhibit 9–1.

Under an international division structure, all functional activities—with the possible exception of sales—are maintained at home. When international sales and profits are a minor percentage of a division's overall activity, it is difficult to get a busy division manager to spend time cultivating and building international activity. Time tends to get spent where the big sales and profits are. Building and cultivating are best done by a division devoted exclusively to that task—hence the international division. One clear advantage of an international division structure is that it allows a company to give international sales much greater support and attention. As a result, the manager of the international division has to understand the product-market strategies of each product division and adapt them to international markets.

Area Division Structure

As international sales grow as a percentage of total company sales, many successful companies evolve out of an international division structure and create an area division structure (Exhibit 9–2). While an area division will often continue to report to a corporate vice president international, strategic decision making is shifted to regional and/or country managers. As a result, the position of vice president international is one of the few positions in business where success can bring declining influence.

Exhibit 9–1   The International Division Structure

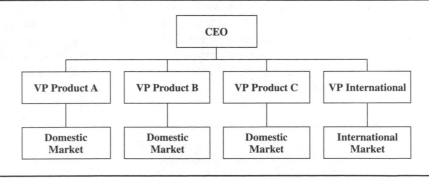

EXHIBIT 9–2   **The Area Division Structure**

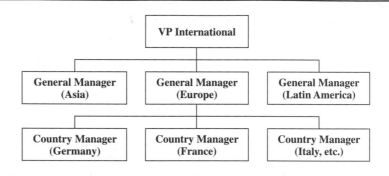

For many companies, area division structures capture the majority of efficiency advantages that result from globalization. Relatively few activities actually require global volumes to reach maximum levels of economic efficiency.[2] Furthermore, area organizations may be more efficient and effective than global structures because of increased responsiveness, reduced bureaucracy, communication efficiencies, and improved employee morale. In many cases area structures can facilitate faster delivery, allow greater customization, and require smaller inventories than would be possible under more complex organization forms.

Characteristics.   Under an area division structure, regional and country managers have a high degree of autonomy in how they adapt the strategies of the home country product divisions to meet the particular circumstances of their regions and countries. The Kellogg Company of Battle Creek, Michigan, has made a major commitment to its area division structure. Kellogg has 12 of the world's 15 best-selling brands of ready-to-eat cereal. However, the company decides on an area basis which brands to sell, manufacture, and market. The company's four area presidents (Europe, Asia-Pacific, North America, and Latin America) have been given wide discretionary power over marketing, production, and sourcing (they both support and help identify global brands). Ford, IBM, General Motors, and Philips Electronics are examples of other MNCs widely known for powerful area headquarters.

The more local conditions influence consumer demand, the more autonomy country managers usually get. Local responsiveness is its main achievement. As a result, an area division structure is most appropriate for companies pursuing multidomestic strategies. Take, for example, the Kenny Rogers Roasters in China case. The key decision in the case centers on whether the company should make a substantial investment in time and resources to secure market access in China via the

---

[2]For a more complete discussion of regional organizations, see A. J. Morrison, D. Ricks, and K. Roth. "Globalization versus Regionalization: Which Way for the Multinational?" *Organizational Dynamics*, Winter 1991, pp. 17–29.

FIGURE 9–3   Multidomestic Affiliate Structure

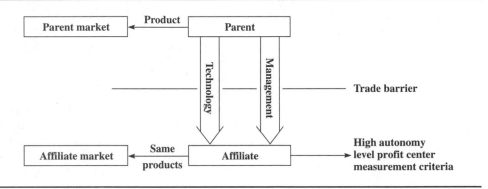

city of Beijing. Investments to secure market position are invariably based on an appraisal of the size and growth potential of the market in question. The local market is important, and therefore the local manager is going to be important. For Kenny Rogers Roasters in China, the issue of how or if local management should be controlled is an essential aspect of any investment decision.

Under an area division structure, the majority of activities are "dispersed," or located in each country where the company competes. At Shell Oil, for example, major refineries are located throughout almost all of the major markets of the world; crude oil purchasing activities are dispersed; and marketing and sales activities are also positioned around the world. Under an area division structure, these dispersed activities are loosely coordinated. This means that each activity is performed independently. For Shell Oil, purchasing decisions made in the United States are not coordinated with purchasing decisions made in France or Indonesia.

Multidomestic Affiliates.   Area structures are most often adopted by companies that pursue multidomestic strategies. Host countries have long used the term *miniature replica* to describe the traditional multidomestic affiliate. The term arises because the affiliate is like a scaled-down version of the parent, in that it produces the same products but in lower volume for a smaller "domestic" market. In many cases, trade barriers keep international markets separated and permit the affiliate to operate profitably, even though its production costs are often higher than the parent company's because of the need to produce multiple products in relatively small volume. The diagram in Exhibit 9–3 tries to capture the features of a traditional multidomestic affiliate.

Multidomestic affiliates are typically evaluated by profit center criteria keyed to results rather than obedience to head-office policies. Usually, local nationals are appointed as country managers and management turnover is relatively slow. Each affiliate takes on a character and personality of its own, and formulates its own internal strategy. The role of country manager is similar to the role of the parent CEO, except for the more limited geographical sphere of activity.

Given the high levels of affiliate autonomy and the results-oriented performance measurement systems, one might suppose that host governments would be relatively pleased with the multidomestic structure. Complaints against it, however, have been numerous. One of the most frequent has been that "miniature replica" affiliates do not do R&D; they simply bring in parent technology and adapt it where necessary. Most studies confirm that this complaint is fairly accurate. Many affiliates cannot afford to pay for their own R&D and still make a profit on the sales generated in the host market alone. They tend to manufacture many products for a relatively small market—a strategy that can succeed only with imported technology and tariff protection. Another complaint has been that "miniature replica" affiliates do not export. Again, this complaint has, with notable exceptions, proven to be fairly accurate. The reason for it has not been parent unwillingness as much as the affiliate's inability to export competitively. That inability is due largely to the affiliates' lack of cost-competitiveness—they are typically high-cost producers relative to their parents; and to the affiliates' lack of product differentiation—they typically use parent technology.

The fundamental concerns in host governments have been that tariff protection generally leads to an inefficient industrial structure. There is a growing realization among developing countries that multidomestic affiliates cannot play an effective role in the emerging globalization of business. Hence, many countries are lowering tariffs in an effort to transform their industrial structures and make them more competitive. But if host countries complained about foreign ownership under the miniature replica structure, they are likely to continue to do so under a global structure. The complaints, however, will have a different ring to them.

From a home country, head-office perspective, an area-centered structure is ideal as long as it is advantageous to disperse key activities and control them with local decision makers. However, high local autonomy often results in three problems:

1. Communications between home country product divisions and distant overseas affiliates are often more complex and break down. Corporate policies and standards may not be effectively communicated to or adopted by the affiliates. In many cases important product-market information also fails to reach the field abroad. This is a particularly difficult problem when products have a high globalization potential.

2. Affiliate autonomy is not conducive to MNC learning. Excellent practices and products can typically be found in each affiliate. To maximize learning, each affiliate must promote its products and practices within the MNC as well as embrace appropriate new practices and products generated by other affiliates. The greater the affiliate autonomy, the lower the likelihood that excellent practices and products will either be communicated or adopted.

3. Rising international sales and profits heighten the interest of home country product managers. As affiliates develop self-sufficiency, the power of home country managers is challenged. For products that are viewed as strategically important, home country managers may try to disrupt moves by affiliates to achieve greater autonomy.

Global Product Divisions

As a general rule, the relative importance of product managers increases with the number of products being offered by a company. As the diversity of foreign products increases, many successful companies have adopted global product division structures. Du Pont became the first major U.S. company to adopt a modern divisionalized structure not long after the turn of the century. By 1970, as many as 90 percent of *Fortune* 500 companies had adopted product divisional structures.

Divisions are usually organized to correspond to particular industries, or industry segments. U.K.-based Hanson PLC has 12 major divisions, each confronting substantially different industry pressures: Jacuzzi, Smith Corona, Imperial Tobacco, Farberware, Ames, Grove Crane, London Brick, Kaiser, SCM Chemicals, Universal Gym, British Ever Ready, and Ground Round. Other MNCs—including ITT, Bayer, General Electric, Sandoz, Grand Metropolitan, Philip Morris, and Eastman Kodak—have highly diversified operations that lend themselves to distinct industry analyses and diverse business unit strategies. Under a divisionalized structure, all functional activities (for example, R&D, production, marketing) are controlled by a product group. An example of a global product divisional structure is included in Exhibit 9–4.

Characteristics.   When global product divisions take over, they tend to achieve direct lines of communication into key markets and can therefore get their product and market know-how through to the field unimpeded. Because activities are tightly coordinated by the head office, country managers are often involved only in the local administrative, legal, and financial affairs of the company. Product decisions are made by home country managers and input from overseas affiliates is often discouraged. What is lost in terms of local responsiveness is gained in terms of global efficiencies.

Global product division structures represent a chain of vertically integrated activities. Product division managers can configure activities according to variances in costs or skills across countries. This makes the product divisions ideal for global strategies. Under a global product division structure, some activities may be dispersed—for example, component manufacturing and assembly—while others may be centrally located—for example, research and development. For U.S. and European companies, the advantages of global structural flexibility have became increasingly apparent through the growing international success of Japanese MNCs. In an

---

EXHIBIT 9–4   The International Division Structure

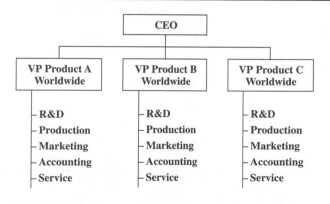

attempt to drive costs down, a frequent reaction for U.S. and European companies has been to move labor-intensive upstream activities to low-wage countries with highly skilled workers and duty-free zones. Many of these factories ended up in the Far East and, for American companies, in Mexico.

One of the reasons that many large companies have shifted to global product division structures is because it helps managers focus more easily on maximizing competitiveness. When the competitive domain is set by industry boundaries, competitors can be clearly identified and decisions focused on upgrading functional skills. With rising globalization, plants can be more easily focused in terms of product, robotized in terms of technology, and diversified in terms of markets served. Country managers whose chief expertise is a knowledge of their domestic markets cannot expect to survive globalization with their autonomy intact.

Global Affiliates.   Under a global product division structure, affiliates around the world do not operate with a great deal of autonomy. They become an integrated part of a global organization and often play no independent strategic role at all. If production does take place in a particular affiliate, it will often be specialized production of a single model or component for use throughout the corporation. Hence the design and specification of what is produced is seldom handled by the affiliate because it is not aimed primarily at the affiliate's market. In these conditions, coordination between parent and affiliates is critical, and is often achieved by sending parent executives to run affiliate operations for three- to five-year terms. Because specialization is at the heart of global company strategies, affiliates are expected to be obedient and are evaluated as cost centers. The profit-center concept just does not fit the strategy. Global affiliates have little strategic autonomy and take few if any initiatives.

Affiliates that operate under a global product division structure are largely treated as a source of supply. Inputs—technology and components—are provided by either the parent or other affiliates within the vertically controlled structure, the inputs are further processed—components are refined or assembled—and then re-exported back to the parent or sister affiliates within the division. While affiliate exports may or may not return to the home country of the parent, divisional managers control the destination and sales price for each input. Once final assembly has occurred, the parent generally supervises international marketing; while the affiliate may employ its own marketing staff, they are typically accountable to divisional marketing managers. The diagram in Exhibit 9–5 tries to capture the features of a global affiliate structure.

Contrasting Area and Global Product Division Structures

Area and global product division structures can both be appropriate, depending on the objectives a company is trying to achieve. Area structures work best when international sales represent an important percentage of total sales and when the requirements for local responsiveness are high. Global product division structures work best when the number of products the company produces has proliferated and when

EXHIBIT 9–5   Global Affiliate Structure

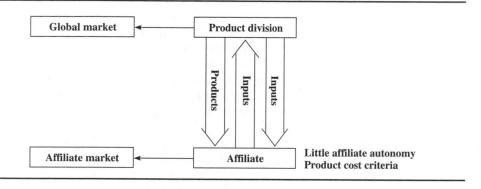

EXHIBIT 9–6   Contrasting Global Product and Multidomestic Area Structures

	Global Product Structure	*Multidomestic Area Structure*
Product line	Specialized	Duplicated
Market emphasis	International	National
Transfers	Product/Technology	Technology/Skills
Affiliate evaluation	Cost center	Profit center
Affiliate role	Implement strategy	Develop & implement strategy
Affiliate autonomy	Low	High
Affiliate management	Foreign, short-term	Local, long-term

globalization requirements are high. To establish the contrast more clearly, Exhibit 9–6 summarizes the essential differences between multidomestic area and global product division structures.

Under the global product division structure, efficient communication of product know-how is maximized. The country manager under a global structure plays more of an administrative-legal role than a strategic one. Not surprisingly, the global product structure works best in conditions where product knowledge is more vital than market knowledge. While outputs are tightly controlled, specific operations in any given country may not be well coordinated and there may be some duplication of selling effort. However, each product line gets someone's maximum attention.

Under the area division structure, region and country managers are ultimately responsible for corporate strategy in their regions or countries. They have to become familiar with the products and markets of each division. Their task is to adapt corporate strategy to local conditions. Knowledge of local politics, markets, suppliers and channels constitutes their distinctive competence. They may not give each product the same degree of effort, but will seek out first their strongest competitive opportunities, i.e., where market demand is highest or competition weakest.

The biggest weaknesses in the global product structure are the growing dependence over time of the affiliates on the parent, and the lack of substantive ideas or initiatives arising from the affiliates. As a result, global product structures are notoriously inflexible. A case in point is Matsushita Electric Industrial, which first introduced a product division structure in 1933. Matsushita's tightly controlled structure was designed to build managerial talent, promote internal competition, and maximize international growth by treating each product division as an independent small business. Overseas marketing affiliates were established, international sales soared, and profits were consolidated on a global basis. By the mid-1980s, Matsushita had emerged as the world's largest producer of consumer electronics. Despite this success, Matsushita has faced serious challenges in the 1990s. Demand for its mainstream color television and VCR products has flattened and profit margins have slipped substantially. Many observers blame Matsushita's once successful product division structure for much of the company's woes. By locating most R&D activities in Japan, Matsushita has missed out on a stream of critical innovations taking place in the United States and Europe. The company has also faced growing demands by host governments for local production and innovation. As technologies such as semiconductors, computers, and robots have blurred, Matsushita's reliance on strictly defined product divisions has only compounded the problems associated with product division inflexibility.

While global product structures have serious shortcomings, area structures may not be the perfect solution. The biggest weakness in the area structure is the difficulty the parent has imposing an overarching strategy on its autonomous affiliates, and hence obtaining some of the benefits of specialization. As a result, area structures are notoriously inefficient. Rather than produce standardized products in world-scale production facilities, area structures mandate smaller plants that are less scale-efficient. Because research and development, purchasing, marketing, and distribution are also duplicated across geographic territories, cumulative overhead costs can be much higher than with most product structures. In an increasingly competitive world, these added costs are often difficult to sustain. Take, for example, the case of General Electric Canada, which since the mid-1970s has manufactured a wide line of home appliances through its Camco affiliate. Camco has had a history of relative independence. Unfortunately, this independence combined with low scale efficiencies resulted in refrigerators that cost 20 percent more to build in Canada than in General Electric facilities in the United States. In 1987 and 1988, General Electric invested nearly $1 billion retooling and expanding its U.S.-based refrigerator operations, resulting in a widening of the cost differential between the Canadian affiliate and the parent. As a result, Camco has increasingly shifted away from a broad portfolio of activities (R&D, procurement, manufacturing, marketing, sales, and service) to relatively few (marketing, sales and service of home appliances imported from the parent). Unless the host market is protected or customers are prepared to pay extra for unique local features or services, companies will have a hard time justifying the added costs associated with area structures.

The weaknesses in both the area and product structures are enhanced when a company adopts a structure inconsistent with its international strategy. In other words, if a company has a strategy that emphasizes affiliate input about local markets and yet adopts a global product structure, then lack of affiliate initiative becomes a serious impediment. On the other hand, if a company can increase its efficiency by rearranging its production and standardizing needless differences, but has adopted an area structure, then the autonomy of affiliate managers becomes a serious impediment.

The Transnational Option

What should be clear by now is that there can be serious potential problems with both the global product and multidomestic area structures. With one you get greater global efficiencies and the other, greater local responsiveness. Since there is really no such thing as a perfect organization anyway, one is tempted to suggest simply picking the one closest to the company's product-market thrust and learning to live with the organizational deficiencies. For many companies, that is sound advice. There are, however, a number of companies for which these deficiencies are too costly. Telecommunications is a good illustration. Telecommunications companies face powerful pressures toward globalization from high R&D costs and available scale economies, and also powerful pressures toward localization from differences in the systems in place in each country and in the politicization of the industry. Firms facing such challenges sometimes try to capture the benefits of both the global and the multidomestic structures by developing hybrid structures.

When companies ask, "Isn't there some way to have it all?" the transnational organization and the matrix system have been suggested by some as the solution.[3] The key elements of the transnational structure include a two-way flow of ideas and resources, frequent movement of people between units, extensive use of local boards of directors, and a global perspective on the part of both parent and affiliate. The affiliates of transnational corporations have a good deal more autonomy than those in global corporations, but still they are an integrated part of a global strategy. In the transnational corporation, initiatives arise in affiliates as well as parents, and interaffiliate linkages are encouraged. Rather than function as a hierarchy, transnational organizations function as a *network* of horizontal decision making. The trade-offs between globalization and localization are made in the field by managers committed to the corporation and its competitive objectives, and aware of local market anomalies and differences. The organizational challenge is to ensure a continuous supply of such managers over time.

A transnational structure attempts to capture concurrently all of the advantages of area and global product division structures. In order to achieve these dual sets of

---

[3]For further information about transnational structures see Bartlett and Ghoshal, *Managing Across Borders—The Transnational Solution*, Harvard Business School Press, 1989. It is important to point out that Bartlett and Ghoshal present the transnational structure as an idealized form rather than a reality in business. At the same time, they hold it out as a structure toward which many international businesses are moving because of the deficiencies of alternative approaches.

benefits, the configuration and coordination of activities are mixed; affiliates play leadership roles for some activities and supporting roles for others. Decisions are based on maximizing company skills and competencies, irrespective of activity location or affiliate nationality. To be both efficient and effective, linkages between the company's headquarters and affiliates, as well as across affiliates, are subject to rapid change.[4] As a result, a company with a transnational structure acts essentially as a network of activities with multiple headquarters spread across different countries. Affiliates are given complete control over local products, provide support roles for some global products, and control other global products. Affiliate roles shift over time, and learning and sharing are emphasized. To work effectively, transnational structures emphasize extensive horizontal linkages, effective communication, and extreme flexibility so that companies are able to develop competitive responses not only at head office but in the periphery as well.[5]

A good example of a company with a transnational organization structure is ABB.[6] In 1995, ABB had sales that approached US $34 billion and employed almost 210,000 people in over 140 countries around the world. ABB is organized into four different business segments, 36 business areas, and 1,000 companies. With country units in place, ABB is essentially organized as a matrix. Business area managers are given the power to set global strategies for each of the 36 businesses; country managers, however, maintain effective control over profit centers and incorporated companies within their geographic jurisdiction. As a result, business managers need the cooperation of country managers to rationalize operations internationally. When there is a conflict, business managers and country managers can bring the dispute to the corporate executive committee for adjudication. Such appeals are, however, discouraged. Structural fluidity and quick decision making based on the good of the global organization are constantly stressed.

What makes a transnational structure ideal from ABB's perspective is that it provides direct access to world markets in each area of specialization. Without first-hand knowledge of global customer needs, there is only limited value in conducting R&D and product renewal activities at the affiliate level. As an increasing number of key customers have established global purchasing criteria, ABB affiliate country and business area managers can work together to maximize customer responsiveness. From the executive committee's perspective, a transnational structure provides global economies of scale while recognizing that considerable skills and resources reside in an affiliate. A transnational organization also allows affiliates to respond to local demand by developing or importing products at their own initiative.

---

[4]A discussion of "speed" advantages of transnationals is found in C. Bartlett, "Building and Managing the Transnational: The New Organizational Challenge." In M. Porter (ed.), *Competition in Global Industries.* Boston: Harvard Business School Press, 1986.

[5]G. Hedlund, "The Hypermodern MNC: A Heterarchy?" *Human Resource Management*, 25 (1), (1986), pp. 9–35.

[6]For further information on Asea Brown Boveri's structure, see Tom Peters, *Liberation Management: Necessary Disorganization for the Nanosecond Nineties.* New York: Alfred A. Knopf, 1992.

The reason so many companies are experimenting with network organizations of this kind is more than just the desire to have the coordination benefits. Other factors are at play. The rise of international alliances is more manageable for firms with strong "global" affiliates. The supply of global managers is not so dependent on head office. Good people join the affiliates—because they have interesting enough mandates to attract good people—and end up in other parts of the corporation, including head office. Quality global managers are in short supply and limiting that supply to head office, or to the "home" country, exacerbates the shortage.

Transnational Affiliates and the Development of Mandates.   Transnational organizations are designed to concurrently maximize efficiency, local responsiveness, and organizational learning. Affiliates may still manufacture one or two products for world markets, but instead of functioning largely as a factory, they handle worldwide responsibilities for other products. In other words, the affiliate functions like a domestic product division in some areas while assuming world product mandates in others. The diagram in Exhibit 9–7 tries to capture these features of a transnational structure.

What keeps the affiliate alive as an organism under the transnational structure is direct access to world markets through the development of world product mandates in its area of specialization. World product mandates represent global strategies controlled by the affiliate as opposed to the parent. Exhibit 9–8 provides examples of affiliates that have developed global product mandates. In each of these examples, world product headquarters are located in key affiliate countries. Technically, the parent's home country is treated as a foreign market for these products.

Despite these high-profile examples, most parent companies remain reluctant to give up control of R&D and product renewal for products that they themselves developed. Sometimes the key professionals involved do not want to be transferred, and do not see any reason why they should be. As a result, most world product mandate

EXHIBIT 9–7   Transnational Affiliate Structure

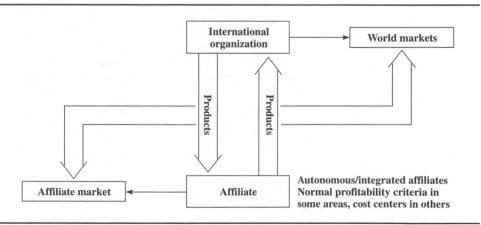

EXHIBIT 9–8   Examples of Affiliates with Global Product Responsibilities

Company	Home Country	Host Country	Product Mandate
AT&T	U.S.A.	France	Corded telephones
Hyundai Electronics Industries	South Korea	U.S.A.	Personal computers
Motorola	U.S.A.	Canada	Two-way radios
Siemens	Germany	U.K.	Air-traffic management
Siemens	Germany	Japan	Compact magnetic resonance imaging machines
Du Pont	U.S.A.	Switzerland	Lycra business
Nestlé	Switzerland	U.K.	Confectionery
Akzo	Netherlands	Germany	Fibers
Rhone Poulenc	France	Canada	Vaccines
Pechiney	France	U.S.A.	Beverage cans
Sony	Japan	U.S.A.	Motion pictures/television programs
Philips	Netherlands	U.K.	Teletexts-TV sets
Ericsson	Sweden	U.S.A	Fiber optic communications systems

Source: Company documents, interviews. Also, see *The Wall Street Journal*, December 9, 1992, p. B1.

---

arrangements that do exist arose from affiliate initiative in companies whose cultures reward innovative effort. In many cases, large companies acquire firms with existing global products and then turn these firms into affiliates.

In order for a transnational structure to work effectively, affiliates need strong senior managers able to function well among parent company senior managers. If an affiliate becomes a sole or major source of supply and marketing of a specified product area worldwide, its managers soon find themselves operating in the top management committees of the parent organization. The parent has to have confidence in the affiliate's ability to manage its product market and to function effectively within the overall corporate system. As a rule, this means a network of affiliates interchanging sales forces and cross-linking R&D and production facilities.

Interest in affiliate mandates has increased as the number of affiliates has grown around the world. In 1991, foreign affiliates generated an estimated $4.8 trillion in sales.[7] By 1994, there were an estimated 37,000 MNCs with more than 200,000 foreign affiliates operating around the world.[8] In the early 1990s, the United States was home to approximately 3,000 parent MNCs; it also hosted approximately 15,300 affiliates.[9] (In contrast, China was home to less than 400 parent MNCs but hosted

---

[7]*World Investment Report, 1994: Transnational Corporations, Employment and the Workplace*. New York: United Nations, 1994, p. *xxi*.

[8]Ibid.

[9]Ibid., p. 4.

EXHIBIT 9–9   Affiliate Competence and Affiliate Initiative*

	Low Affiliate Capability	*High Affiliate Capability*
High localization pressures	Form alliances or make acquisitions	Take strategic initiatives
High globalization pressures	Follow parent instructions	Influence parent strategies

---

*This diagram is adapted from a diagram in Bartlett and Ghoshal's "Tap Your Affiliates for Global Reach."

about 45,000 foreign-owned affiliates.) Entire sectors of the U.S. economy are dominated by foreign companies. As a result of globalization, managers may find themselves increasingly searching for international opportunities within foreign companies. The mandates they are able to successfully pursue will depend in large part on the level of skills and competencies they display.

The Importance of Affiliate Depth and Competence.   There is always a danger when recommending strategic initiatives to affiliates. If handled badly they can seriously undermine the affiliate's performance and can easily cause a quick exit for both the affiliate and the affiliate general manager. For example, no affiliate is going to be successful in making a major acquisition without its parent's approval. The reality is that in some areas of activity, affiliate initiative is more acceptable than in others. Every company is different, of course, but if an affiliate wants to understand when to take strategic initiatives and when to take orders, the diagram in Exhibit 9–9 may help.

What the diagram suggests is that affiliates should be careful about taking initiatives. First they should assess their own capability in the area in question; then they should assess the parent's capability. As a rule, the parent's competence to act in the affiliate's market will depend on whether the affiliate's market is significantly different from what the parent is used to (i.e., high localization pressures). If it is, and if the affiliate has a good depth of knowledge in the area, it should provide strategic leadership. If neither the parent nor the affiliate has the necessary competence, the company should either get out of the segment or the affiliate should try to build capability, perhaps by alliance or acquisition. In product areas where globalization potential prevails, parent company expertise will be relevant in the affiliate's market. When the affiliate's technological and market knowledge is low relative to the parent's—i.e., in conditions of rationalization—the affiliate should simply follow parent company direction. However, when the affiliate's competence is also high—i.e., in conditions of product mandate—the affiliate should try to influence parent strategy.

Affiliate managers, whether taking strategic initiative or following parent instructions, absolutely have to be well plugged-in at headquarters. It is not a good idea to presume the competence level of the parent in a given product area. One has to know. At the same time, it is not a good idea to make an acquisition or take a strategic initiative without prior parent approval. Taking initiative is not the same as declaring independence. It is interdependence that is needed, and interdependence requires a measure of integration and working together. Taking the initiative in an interdependent relationship means bringing ideas and plans to the key management committees and championing them. Success is achieved through the quality of the ideas and through the competence with which they are expressed, but also through the preconditioning of other executives present. That is why it is essential for affiliate managers to be well plugged-in at headquarters. They need to understand the mind-set of the other executives and they need opportunities to influence it.

Challenges with Developing Transnational Structures.   Managing under multiple mandates is difficult. Most managers want clarity and exactness in roles and measurements. In ABB's case, for example, each of its 36 business area managers acts in many ways like an air traffic controller. They know where they want the businesses to go and they can set the flight plans, but the country managers ultimately act as pilots. Some may deviate from the plan; some may not be listening. It is not a job for the faint-hearted. To run smoothly, the transnational organization requires managers to work toward the benefit of the corporation as a whole. At a time when many companies are shedding employees, it is often difficult to ask employees to think first of the corporation. Transnational companies that concurrently pursue global efficiencies and local responsiveness risk crossing signals and doing neither well. Affiliates remain suspicious of each other, and many product managers, despite pleas to think globally, continue to favor home country employees and markets. As a result, the transition to a transnational organization is inherently bumpy.

Because of the difficulties of effective implementation, the transnational structure has been proposed as more of an idealized form than a reality. The problem is ultimately one of definition. The transnational structure theoretically achieves the optimal blend of global efficiency and local responsiveness. But these descriptive statements do not constitute a definition of the transnational structure. How does a firm know when it has one? For some, the presence of a shared responsibility matrix structure is the best evidence. In such a structure, geographic areas and product divisions share responsibility for affiliate decisions. The idea is that by sharing the responsibility one forces a constructive dialogue through which the best decision emerges. In this sense, the best decision is one that balances the need for local adaptation with the need for global efficiency. Since the optimal balance is subjective and is constantly shifting, it is difficult for a firm to know whether it has achieved it regardless of the structure it follows. Furthermore, people's egos sometimes get in the way, and the matrix structure often fails to achieve its purpose. It is entirely possible to have a transnational perspective without a matrix structure. One simply finds a way to put the matrix mentality into the heads of country managers, or of product division managers, as the case may be. This may ultimately be the managerial challenge of the last half of the 1990s.

What is clear from these characteristics is that they are more about managerial attitude than about organization structure. That is why the transnational organization is an idealized form. However, what it stands for is important to companies anxious to hold on to good people throughout the world. Without good people, it is difficult for any organization to learn about critical commercial information elsewhere in the world and remain competitive. Without an interesting role or mandate for the affiliate, it is difficult to hold on to good talent there, and the company grows increasingly dependent on culturally bound head-office management. When this occurs, the ability of the company to learn and adapt is impaired. In some industries this is a dangerous state of affairs, given that technology generation has become a truly global phenomenon. The transnational approach is really about learning. It is about raising the awareness level of key executives worldwide about the corporate mission, and providing them an ongoing opportunity to influence it. It is much more about style, attitude, and mind-set than it is about formal organization structure.

The Seamless Organization

A driving goal of an increasing number of companies is the development of a seamless organization. Formal structures are the antithesis of seamlessness. Seamlessness is built on the notion of destroying barriers inside and outside the organization. Formal structures acknowledge and promote barriers between affiliates and headquarters, between affiliates and affiliates, and between the company and suppliers and customers. These barriers prevent learning, produce inefficiencies, and blunt responsiveness. Increasingly, companies are struggling to tear down these barriers to maximize ultimate value for the customer while at the same time promoting an organizational context that engenders commitment and hard work among employees.[10]

The primary unit of analysis in the seamless organization is a team. Teams involve groups of individuals who are brought together to achieve a common objective. Teams that blur the boundaries of the company typically include a variety of alliances across suppliers and buyers. Boeing, for example, spent several years working with a consortium of its largest airline customers in designing its new 777 aircraft. Airline personnel became fully involved in developing the final configuration of the aircraft. At one point, United Airlines had upwards of 500 people working with Boeing on 777 design issues. This involvement improved the overall quality of the final aircraft and engendered a much greater commitment of the airline companies to the 777 specifically and Boeing more generally. Other companies that have exerted enormous efforts in developing seamless interactions with customers include FedEx (through global tracking), EDS (through on-site management of computer systems), and Brunswick Corporation. Brunswick's Sea Ray boats division will fly new owners of boats (which cost more than $1 million) to the company's factory at Merritt Island, Florida, to select every imaginable piece of hardware for the boat and determine the internal configuration of the craft.

Erasing vertical boundaries also involves working more closely with suppliers. Virtually every major automobile assembler has identified a set of key suppliers that are included in design, scheduling, and quality decisions. Wal-Mart, the world's largest retailer, uses its own satellite system to provide key suppliers around the world with sales and inventory information for each Wal-Mart distribution center and store. The system has shifted inventory management (and costs) to suppliers

---

[10]The notion of ultimate value was championed by Richard D'Aveni, *Hyper-Competition: Managing the Dynamics of Strategic Maneuvering.* New York: The Free Press, 1994.

while eliminating the need for expensive sales representatives. In China, ARCO and its joint venture partner Nan Hai West have worked closely with a huge consortium of engineering companies, steel mills, transportation and shipping companies, and marine construction companies (including 30 support boats) to lay an 880-km underwater natural gas pipeline from a field in the South China Sea to Hong Kong. The $560 million pipeline was finished ahead of schedule (mid-1995) and on budget because the companies were able to erase barriers and work as a seamless team toward a common goal.

Seamless organizations are also preoccupied with erasing boundaries inside the company. Much of the reengineering and downsizing efforts of the 1990s have been devoted to delayering the management structure, cutting bureaucracy, and getting the people who need to talk to each other together. Teams have become a common mechanism used by companies to link people from different divisions, functions, and geographies. As such, internal teams represent a type of organizational structure that may replace the more rigid boxes and lines in standard organization charts. In an era of globalization and accelerating technological change, teams can help speed organizational adaptation and improve the overall quality of decisions. Linking people with multiple backgrounds promotes an atmosphere where new ideas can emerge and where arrogance is reduced.

Technologies such as Lotus Notes, E-mail, and video conferencing enable global teams to keep in close contact. Teams may stay intact for weeks or years. Members may come and go and the team's objectives may evolve. While the fluidity and flexibility of teams may be a great strength in terms of responsiveness, they are also troubling to some individuals who crave structure and clarity. Seamless organizations draw heavily on personal relationships and the desire and ability of individuals to work effectively together. The human element of effective teamwork is discussed in greater detail in Chapter 10.

Summary

This chapter has focused on the challenges and opportunities associated with the international organization of activities. Given the preponderance of globalization pressures, the traditional area division structure with its high autonomy and multidomestic focus is not likely to endure unscathed. MNCs will increasingly abandon country-focused structures in favor of either the global product or transnational structures. The transition is not likely to be without pain. Moving to a more global product structure means imposing corporate will on hitherto autonomous affiliates. It means changing affiliate mandates and reducing strategic independence. There are going to be a lot of organizational wrecks on the shoals of globalization.

The reality is that almost every company customizes its structure in some way by using a combination of tools to organize and control activities. Few companies are identical to the structures described in this chapter. Most rely on mixed structures that are influenced by idiosyncratic histories and the personalities of key decision makers. Despite these differences, however, competitive advantage may well be achieved by those companies that can reinvent themselves by empowering those who need power and by rationalizing those who do not. Appropriate structures are ultimately determined by understanding the tasks that need to be done both today and tomorrow. As environmental change accelerates, speed and flexibility will undoubtedly be more valuable over the next decade than size and past successes.

Supplementary Reading

Bartlett, Christopher A., and Sumantra Ghoshal. "Tap Your Subsidiaries for Global Reach." *Harvard Business Review*, November-December 1986.

Bartlett, Christopher A., and Sumantra Ghoshal. *Managing Across Borders—The Transnational Solution*. Boston: Harvard Business School Press, 1989.

Crookell, Harold. "Managing Canadian Affiliates in a Free Trade Environment." *Sloan Management Review*, Fall 1987.

D'Aveni, Richard. *Hyper-Competition: Managing the Dynamics of Strategic Maneuvering*. New York: The Free Press, 1994.

Egelhoff, William G. "Strategy and Structure in Multinational Corporations: A Revision of the Stopford and Wells Model." *Strategic Management Journal*, January-February 1988.

Hamel, Gary, and C. K. Prahalad, *Competing for the Future*. Boston: Harvard Business School Press, 1994.

Hedlund, Gunnar. "The Hypermodern MNC—A Heterarchy?" *Human Resource Management*, Spring 1986 (Vol. 25, No. 1).

Malnight, Thomas W. "The Transition from Decentralized to Network-Based MNC Structures: An Evolutionary Perspective." *Journal of International Business Studies*, Vol. 27, No.1, 1996, pp. 43–65.

Morrison, A. J., D. Ricks, and K. Roth. "Globalization versus Regionalization: Which Way for the Multinational?" *Organizational Dynamics*, Winter 1991.

Porter, Michael. "Changing Patterns of International Competition." *California Management Review*, 1986 (Vol. 28, pp. 9–40).

Prahalad, C. K., and Yves Doz. *The Multinational Mission: Balancing Local Demands and Global Vision*. New York: The Free Press, 1987.

Roth, K., and A. J. Morrison. "Implementing Global Strategy: Global Affiliate Mandates." *Journal of International Business Studies*, 1992 (Vol. 23, No. 4).

10   THE EVOLVING MULTINATIONAL

Introduction

A number of chapters in this book have discussed specific forms of foreign market entry, such as managing exports and imports, licensing, and joint ventures. Each of these may be the best way to enter a given foreign market, yet it is important to remember that most multinational firms do not make just *one* foreign entry, but typically a *series* of foreign market entries over the course of years. While we should have a clear understanding of the motivations and challenges of any one entry, we should also bear in mind the overall development of the multinational firm.

The previous chapter identified some of the challenges of organizing and managing the MNC. In particular, the transnational model was suggested as a way for MNCs to seek the benefits of both global integration and local responsiveness. This model argued that multinational firms should be thought of as multicentered organizational forms, with foreign subsidiaries playing different roles within a larger network structure. By adopting an internally differentiated form, rather than insisting on identical roles for each foreign subsidiary, the MNC can tap the distinctive capabilities of each subsidiary and optimize its worldwide operations. Such MNCs are also better positioned to benefit from network flexibility, as they can shift production and sourcing among subsidiaries as various external conditions—competitive, financial, or regulatory—change.

Although many management experts agree on the desirability of the transnational model, there is much less agreement about how MNCs can achieve this multicentered and differentiated form. After all, very few MNCs begin as complex, internally differentiated organizations. Most begin in a single country, and establish subsidiaries in foreign countries over many years. Once established, these foreign subsidiaries may initially begin operation in a subset of the parent's lines of business, and over time

---

This chapter was prepared by Philip Rosenzweig.

take on more lines of business. Furthermore, each line of business may begin by performing a restricted set of functions, such as sales or final assembly, and take on added responsibilities over time. It is by evolving along each of these three dimensions—a *geographic dimension*, a *line of business dimension,* and a *functional dimension*—that MNCs achieve a complex and internally differentiated form. The result may be an MNC with subsidiaries in a number of foreign markets, each of which is active in a somewhat different mix of businesses, and each of which plays a somewhat different role, ranging from a minor one to a role of worldwide strategic leadership.

This chapter focuses on the evolution of MNCs. Rather than looking at a single foreign market entry, we take a broader look at the firm's trajectory, examining not only entry into new geographic markets but also into new lines of business and functions performed by each line of business. The first part of the chapter examines evolution along these three dimensions, offering insights into some of the factors that facilitate or impede evolution. The second part discusses the ways in which evolution along these dimensions is integrated, with knowledge leveraged so that the MNC can evolve in an efficient manner, minimizing duplication and performing activities in an optimal manner. We take the view that the ability to leverage knowledge among MNC dimensions is central to their effective management.

Dimensions of Evolution

Geographic Expansion

In recent years we have begun to see examples of firms that are "born multinational"—that from their birth have productive operations in more than one country. Yet these firms remain a distinct minority. The great majority of MNCs begin in a home country and expand abroad through foreign market entry. The sequence by which firms expand from their home country into foreign markets is influenced by several factors, including *geographic proximity, cultural similarity*, and *similarity in economic development.*

Geographic proximity.   The first location for foreign direct investment is often a neighboring country. Entering a neighbor country is a natural first step, as the firm can more easily identify market opportunities and gather vital information about competitive reactions and government policies in a nearby country than in a distant one. Firms may also prefer to enter neighboring countries first, as the cost of communicating with the foreign subsidiary is lower. Once the firm has expanded into nearby countries it may then move sequentially into countries that are farther away, minimizing the incremental distance of each move. Over time, through this process of entry based on geographic proximity, the firm can achieve a broad international position.

Cultural similarity.   The sequence of geographic expansion may also reflect cultural similarity between the MNC's home country and the host country. Success in a foreign country requires an understanding of local customs and consumer habits;

effective communication with customers, suppliers, and employees; and good relations with governmental bodies. For all these reasons, firms often prefer to enter countries that are relatively similar in culture, i.e., where the "psychic distance" is low. As they gain experience in countries that are relatively similar to their own, MNCs learn how to manage outside their home country and may subsequently enter countries that are progressively less similar. Eventually they may be able to enter countries that are at a considerable "psychic distance" from their country of origin.

Similarity in economic development.   The level of host country economic development also affects the choice of which markets to enter. MNCs are often attracted to foreign markets where consumer buying habits and levels of disposable income are similar to those of home market consumers. In such markets, the MNC's product formulation and its marketing approach may require only modest adaptation. As the MNC learns how to compete effectively in foreign markets of similar economic standing, it develops capabilities that may allow it to enter increasingly different foreign markets.

Although they have been studied separately, *geographic proximity*, *cultural similarity*, and *similarity in economic development* can all be understood in terms of organizational learning and capability development. In each instance, firms first expand into countries where the capabilities developed in their home market are most likely to be successful, and defer entry into countries where success is less likely. Accumulating experience in initial foreign markets enables the firm to develop new capabilities, which allow it to expand into countries that are more distant and less similar. MNC geographic expansion is not merely the sequential exploitation of *existing* capabilities in markets that are progressively farther from home, but the development of *new* capabilities as well.

An example of geographic expansion through capability development is provided by Colgate-Palmolive, the American consumer products firm, which was founded in the nineteenth century and slowly developed into a far-flung MNC. Colgate-Palmolive's first foreign market entry was to Canada, a neighboring country that was similar to the United States both culturally and in economic development. By the 1940s, Colgate-Palmolive had established subsidiaries in 20 countries, virtually all of which were either geographically close to the United States (Canada and Mexico), shared an Anglo-Saxon culture and English language (Canada, United Kingdom, Australia, and New Zealand), or were similar to the United States in economic development (Canada, several countries in western Europe, Scandinavia, Australia, and New Zealand). By restricting itself to these countries, Colgate-Palmolive needed to make only modest adaptations in product formulation and in its marketing approach; it refrained from entering countries where it would have faced sharp differences in culture and economic development.

Based on its experiences in these initial 20 countries, Colgate-Palmolive was later able to enter more-distant markets. In the 1950s and 1960s it expanded into Central America, which was geographically close to the United States but less similar in culture or economic development. More recently, the firm expanded to several Asian and African nations, as well as to newly opened markets in eastern Europe—

countries that were far from the United States, culturally dissimilar, and often sharply different in economic development. By the mid-1990s, Colgate-Palmolive managed subsidiaries in 75 countries on six continents, and ranked among the world's leading MNCs. Its broad geographic position had not been achieved in one or even a few steps, but was the result of a gradual process of geographic expansion.

Colgate-Palmolive's pattern of incremental geographic expansion is typical of older MNCs, which evolved over the course of many years. Today's younger MNCs, including firms such as Finland's Nokia and Germany's SAP, cannot afford to evolve over decades but must establish a presence in multiple countries in a short period of time. Even so, the *sequence* of geographic expansion is similar: from closer and more similar to farther away and less similar. Of course, there has also been a shift in the relative importance of the three factors. As the challenge of managing across long distances has declined given the enormous improvements in communication and transportation, it has become less critical for firms to follow strictly a pattern of geographic proximity. Moreover, the need to minimize "psychic distance" may also be lower than in decades past, as business practices continue to converge and as more people around the world can communicate in a common business language—English. As a consequence, firms expanding abroad in the 1990s may be less concerned with minimizing geographic distance and "psychic distance," and may more readily enter foreign markets based on economic criteria such as similar levels of economic development.

Line of Business Diversification

Whereas some MNCs are single-business firms, most compete in more than one line of business. Foreign subsidiaries for such firms often begin by competing in one or a few of the parent's lines of business, over time adding more lines of business, and eventually operating in many or all of the parent's businesses. For many MNCs, then, *line of business diversification* represents a second dimension of evolution. Interestingly, there has been relatively little research into line of business diversification within foreign subsidiaries. It has been more common to speak of "the country subsidiary" as if it were monolithic, yet it is clear that most MNCs ramp up their activities over time, rather than entering in all lines of business at once.

In what sequence do foreign subsidiaries add lines of business? A recent study of Japanese electronics firms in the United States from 1976 to 1989 showed a sequential pattern of entry, beginning with lines of business that enjoyed the greatest advantage over local firms. By choosing their strongest line of business, these firms could offset the disadvantages they faced due to lack of familiarity with the local market and its competitive environment. As the subsidiary gained experience in doing business locally, it could add lines of business that enjoyed lower competitive advantage. Finally, when the MNC learned to compete effectively in the local environment, it could add lines of business that offered little or no competitive advantage, but that sought to learn from technologically superior U.S. firms. Several subsidiaries of Japanese electronics firms added lines of business in precisely this fashion, adding new lines of business only when confident of success. This sequence is illustrated in Exhibit 10–1.

EXHIBIT 10–1   Typical Pattern of Line of Business Diversification

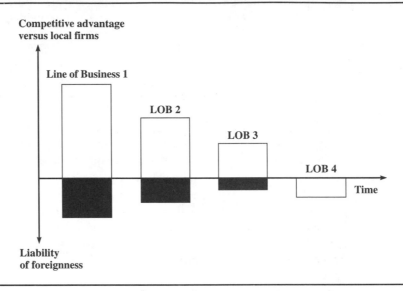

A good example of sequential line of business entry by a Japanese electronics firm is provided by Sony Corporation. Sony first entered the United States in 1972 with a television assembly plant in San Diego, California. For Sony, televisions represented a core line of business, which enjoyed a strong competitive advantage over local firms. Two years later it entered a second line of business, audio equipment, and shortly thereafter in a third, magnetic tape. Sony's diversification resumed in the mid-1980s when a shift in the yen-dollar exchange rate stimulated further foreign investment. At that time, with a strong U.S. country organization and substantial experience, Sony entered lines of business where it sought to tap U.S. technological leadership, such as data storage systems and personal telecommunications. Related to entry by line of business is the choice of entry mode, where once again Sony's experience was consistent with existing theory. At first Sony relied on small-scale greenfield investments as a way to ensure careful replication of its home country advantage; later, as it gained confidence in its ability to manage in the United States and as it sought to capture host country capabilities, it began to make acquisitions.

This pattern of incremental evolution may appear typical of Japanese firms, which are often thought to take a gradual and long-term perspective. Recent evidence, however, has shown that an evolutionary approach to the addition of lines of business describes the behavior of many MNCs, not just Japanese MNCs. Data from European electronics firms entering the United States show largely the same pattern. Some European chemicals firms also exhibit a sequential approach to line of business entry, as exemplified by the French firm Rhone-Poulenc, which first entered the United States in areas of traditional strength such as agrochemicals and basic chemicals, and later acquired positions in surfactants and pharmaceuticals in order to tap local expertise and leverage it around the world.

Of course, a line of business diversification does not happen automatically, but is driven by an intrafirm decision process of evaluation, action, monitoring, and further action. At each step, the firm must determine if the benefits of adding new lines of business are sufficient to offset disadvantages faced in the local market. Over time, as local expertise is accumulated and the subsidiary offers a strong infrastructure for country management, the firm may become increasingly confident of its ability to add new lines of business. With each successive entry the firm adds to its resources: it develops a reputation as a good employer and as a good customer for local suppliers, it learns about local regulations, and in general it accumulates capabilities that make it possible for the firm to enter additional lines of business. Entry into these later lines of business might only be possible because of a strong country organization, which can provide management support, financial infrastructure, and technical expertise to new lines of business.

Functional Migration

A third dimension of evolution, called *functional migration,* takes place within each line of business. Functional migration speaks to the development of activities performed by lines of business within a country. The seminal work on internationalization by Johanson and Vahlne showed that Swedish MNCs tended first to export to foreign markets, then to set up foreign sales subsidiaries to manage these imports, and eventually to establish wholly owned subsidiaries. Once established, lines of business typically continued to perform functions in their home country that lent themselves to economies of scale, such as R&D, product design, and strategic leadership. They performed in the host country only those functions that called for local knowledge, typically marketing and distribution. Over time, however, the subsidiary may take on additional functions, including assembly, local design, and procurement. In some instances, when the subsidiary develops worldwide expertise in the line of business, it may take on the role of business planning and even strategic leadership. In other instances, subsidiaries establish particular functions that serve as "centers of excellence" for the MNC. This common sequence of functional migration is depicted in Exhibit 10–2.

The process of functional migration is seen most clearly in greenfield investments, where subsidiaries begin with a limited number of functions and add new ones incrementally. Entry through acquisition quite naturally exhibits a different pattern. If the MNC acquires a local firm that is vertically integrated, it effectively bypasses the process of functional migration and gains all functions in a single step. Very often, however, MNCs enter a foreign market by acquiring a local company that performs some but not all functions. For example, some MNCs acquire local firms in order to gain an established distribution network through which they can sell imported products. Initial functions are acquired rather than set up from scratch, but subsequent functions—including assembly and product design—are added over time. The subsidiary still migrates from left to right in Exhibit 10–2, but begins somewhere along the continuum rather than at the extreme left. In other instances, firms may enter a foreign market with a greenfield investment, then add functions through the acquisition of local firms. Examples include the acquisition of manufacturing

---

EXHIBIT 10–2   Typical Pattern of Functional Migration

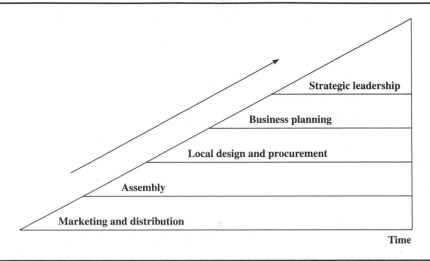

capacity (especially attractive when the industry has considerable excess capacity and building a new plant makes little sense) or the acquisition of a local R&D lab. Thus, acquisitions may differ from greenfield investments in that they accelerate functional migration, yet they typically do not alter the basic sequence.

As with line of business diversification, functional migration depends on an intrafirm decision process. To illustrate, consider the functional migration of Sony's television line of business in the United States. Until 1972, Sony managers maintained that all manufacturing should take place in Japan; no functions were performed in the United States aside from sales and marketing. What triggered a change was the charge of dumping, which led Sony's CEO, Akio Morita, to consider direct investment in the United States. The combination of internal assessments and external forces led to the decision to invest in the United States initially at a low level of functionality, performing only final assembly. Technical knowledge, including both process know-how and product know-how, was transferred by expatriates from Sony's television division in Japan to San Diego, where an identical assembly process was built. In addition to receiving financial resources and technical and managerial know-how from its Japanese parent, the new subsidiary secured resources locally, leasing factory space, hiring local employees, and purchasing some inputs and equipment locally. By combining resources from its parent with resources secured locally, the San Diego plant began to perform its initial functions, assembling kits into working televisions. The plant was carefully monitored by managers in Japan, who wanted to know whether American workers could achieve satisfactory performance. Once Sony management was satisfied with the quality of final assembly in its U.S. plant, it began to add more functions. Soon CRT manufacturing was shifted to the U.S. in light of the expense and breakage associated with transpacific shipment of glass tubes. In time, additional functions were performed, including local sourcing of inputs, additional product design, and finally, some 20 years after first entry, strategic leadership for the television line of business in North America.

Migrating to higher levels of functionality faces a shifting set of impediments. At early steps, which usually involve the location of assembly or manufacturing activities in the new subsidiary, the most important impediments frequently involve the effective transfer of technical know-how and the ability to secure resources locally. Later stages encounter very different—and sometimes more severe—obstacles, as the objective is not merely to *replicate* existing functions in a foreign market, but actually to *shift* functions from the home country to a foreign subsidiary. Such a shift may trigger resistance from home country managers, making evolution to higher functions a very difficult matter.

MNC Evolution as an Integrated Process

So far we have examined each dimension of evolution separately. We described the typical progression of an MNC from a home-based firm into one that enters multiple countries, in each country sequentially adds lines of business, and within each line of business begins with limited functions and over time migrates to higher levels of functionality. We also noted that acquisitions may compress the process of evolution, but typically do not change the basic pattern.

Of course, the hallmark of an MNC is that its dimensions are *not* separate and unrelated, but that they are *interconnected*. As noted by Yves Doz and C. K. Prahalad, the ability to leverage knowledge across and among dimensions is precisely what gives MNCs their most compelling advantage. Accordingly, evolution along one dimension should not disregard evolution along other dimensions, but should affect, and be affected by, changing activities elsewhere in the firm. Without such integration, the MNC may exhibit substantial duplication, both among lines of business and also of functions within lines of business. In the following sections, we identify three different ways that MNC evolution is integrated across dimensions.

Accelerated Evolution

We noted above that the acculumation of knowledge allows MNCs to evolve along each of three dimensions. Learning about doing business in foreign countries helps further geographic expansion, learning about a given host country enables a sequential line of business addition in that country, and so forth. Of course, experience gained by a line of business in one country not only leads to greater knowledge of *that* country, it can also lead to greater knowledge of the line of business, which can be leveraged *across* countries to speed up the entry of that business in other countries. In this way, leveraging knowledge across dimensions results in evolution that is faster and more extensive at any point in time than it would otherwise have been.

Again Sony provides an example. As we described above, Sony first set up a television assembly plant in the United States in 1972, then entered into additional lines of business over the next few years. In 1974, Sony set up a television assembly plant in Europe, and soon thereafter entered into audio equipment. Entry in Europe in audio equipment was facilitated by two kinds of knowledge accumulation: greater expertise about Europe gained through the initial entry to Europe in televisions, and also knowledge about audio products that was transferred from the U.S. operation to the new plant in Europe. By leveraging lines of business knowledge across countries, Sony was able more efficiently and more successfully to add a new line of business in Europe.

Functional migration can also be accelerated by knowledge of particular functions accumulated across lines of business in the same country. For instance, it may be difficult for the first line of business in a country to undertake a new function, such as local parts procurement, product design, or strategic planning. Once the first line of business has successfully added that function, its experience can be leveraged to other lines of business in the same country, helping speed up their migration to the same level of functionality. Similarly, functional knowledge can be leveraged across countries to accelerate functional migration elsewhere in the world.

Punctuated Evolution

Leveraging knowledge among dimensions of an MNC can also lead to evolution that is discontinuous, or that skips steps, which we call *punctuated evolution*. Punctuated evolution can take place along each of the three dimensions. Along each dimension the notion is the same: By identifying and taking advantage of economies of scale and scope, firms may be able to share capabilities across dimensions, obviating the need to perform every step. The result is a more efficient evolution, as the firm maximizes the salutary effects of scale and scope economies.

Assume that a line of business within a subsidiary performs a variety of functions. If a new line of business is added, that line of business may perform its own functions or it may make use of functions already performed by existing lines of business. For example, if the first line of business develops an effective procurement system, or establishes a strong treasury and legal department, and if these functions offer economies of scope, lines of businesses added subsequently may avail themselves of these functions and avoid having to perform them. These lines of business may still add functions in the sequence shown in Exhibit 10–2, but may be able to skip certain ones.

MNCs may also be able to share functions across countries within a single line of business. For instance, if one line of business performs manufacturing at a sufficient capacity to serve a neighboring country as well, the line of business in the neighboring country may not need to perform any manufacturing. Similarly, the presence of a strong R&D lab in one country may obviate the need for a subsidiary in another country to perform its own R&D. In each instance, scale economies associated with the function in one country may render unnecessary the performance of that function in another country. These latter lines of business may well exhibit a sequence of functional migration similar to that shown in Exhibit 10–2, but will skip functions where they are more efficiently performed elsewhere. As an example, consider Bank of Boston, whose long-standing Argentine subsidiary performed all banking functions.

Recently Bank of Boston set up new subsidiaries in other Latin American countries, but has made use of the economies of scale in back-room processing in Argentina to obviate performing similar functions in new subsidiaries such as Mexico.

If *all* functions in a given line of business offer economies of scale, it might be unnecessary to perform *any* functions of that line of business in a second country. In that event, there would be no need to add that line of business in a second country, since the second country could be served by the first for that line of business. If we extend this logic one step further, it could be that *all* lines of business can serve a neighboring country, making it unnecessary to establish a subsidiary in that country at all. Examples of this kind are increasingly common in the European Union, where the establishment of a subsidiary in one EU country may enable a firm to operate in other EU countries without setting up separate subsidiaries. For instance, the Turkish bank, Finansbank, needed to enter only one EU country—the Netherlands—to be able to conduct banking in all EU countries. Other examples are found in Latin America or in Asia, where a mature subsidiary in one country is considered adequate to handle all or virtually all activities in an adjacent market.

By identifying and taking advantage of economies of scale and scope, MNCs may evolve in a discontinuous manner, skipping functions in given lines of business, skipping lines of business in some countries, or even deciding not to enter particular countries at all. MNCs that evolve in a punctuated manner will exhibit a pattern of development that is irregular and asymmetrical, but that achieves a minimum of duplication and therefore secures a greater level of efficiency.

Reverse Evolution

In recent years, as global competition has intensified due to a convergence of consumer demand, increasing opportunities for economies of scale and scope, and rising levels of industrialization around the world, many MNCs have begun to restructure their worldwide operations. In some instances they have consolidated existing functions and lines of business, and in other instances have shut down entire subsidiaries. The effect has been *reverse evolution.*

When might reverse evolution be most common? Firm factors and industry factors are both likely to be important. Regarding firm factors, the potential for efficiencies through global restructuring might be most common in MNCs that expanded many years ago. Because close coordination of foreign subsidiaries was relatively difficult, older MNCs were frequently organized on a country-by-country basis and pursued a multidomestic strategy. These MNCs often performed *all* functions in each line of business, resulting in a high level of duplication among countries. Recently, because of enhanced global communications and transportation, opportunities have arisen to capture greater scale and scope economies, leading to a consolidation of functions among lines of business, as well as a consolidation of lines of business among country subsidiaries. The pressure for restructuring is also likely to be greater in global industries, where competition on a global scale imposes an imperative for worldwide efficiency. As firms in an industry begin to manage their activities on a worldwide basis, other firms will face an imperative to do likewise.

Taking these points together, MNCs that are most likely to restructure their activities are those that expanded abroad long ago and now find themselves in highly global industries. As an example consider IBM, the computer giant that expanded abroad long ago. When IBM set up foreign subsidiaries in many South American countries, these subsidiaries performed a full set of functions. Recently, in response to intense pressures to improve efficiency and cut costs, IBM consolidated its South American activities into three regions—Brazil; the Andean region (Venezuela, Colombia, Ecuador, Peru, and Bolivia); and southern cone (Argentina, Paraguay, Uruguay, and Chile). In the latter two regions, where several country subsidiaries were consolidated into a single entity and managed jointly, a number of functions were located in a single country and discontinued in the others. In the Andean region, for instance, human resource management was centralized in Peru; the HR function in other Andean countries was eliminated. The subsidiaries in the other Andean nations, which had performed all functions, now experienced the elimination of several functions.

The process of reverse evolution is difficult, as there is natural resistance within the firm to restructuring and consolidation, yet the end result is similar to that of punctuated evolution: an asymmetrical mix of functions in each line of business, a varying set of lines of business in each country, and even an irregular set of subsidiaries around the world. The exact profile of an MNC's activities will, of course, be shaped by the most efficient use of scale and scope economies. Further, as with accelerated evolution and punctuated evolution, there are clear performance implications of reverse evolution: MNCs that can identify potential economies of scale and scope, and that can restructure their activities swiftly and efficiently, will be in a better position to compete on a global basis than those that evolved in a graduated fashion but now fail to undertake such restructuring.

Summary

Multinational firms are increasingly viewed as multicentered and internally differentiated firms, yet the process by which firms achieve this complex form has not received much attention. This chapter has viewed MNC evolution as consisting of three separate dimensions: *geographic expansion*, *line of business diversification*, and *functional migration*. Evolution along each dimension takes place through a process of knowledge development. We have also maintained that these three dimensions are not separate and independent, but can affect each other. In fact, it is by leveraging knowledge among dimensions that MNCs avoid unnecessary duplication and achieve a profile of internal differentiation and asymmetry. By identifying opportunities for scale and scope economies, and by actively leveraging knowledge across dimensions, MNCs can evolve toward an optimal configuration. While it is important to understand the nuances of particular approaches to market entry, it is also vital that we take a holistic perspective and seek to manage the entire worldwide network, sharing functions among some lines of business, or serving some national markets from adjacent countries.

The importance of these topics is likely to grow given the ongoing globalization of economic activity. Firms that expanded abroad early in the century could afford to evolve incrementally over several decades. Competitive pressures did not compel them to accelerate their evolution; rather, they could watch the progress of overseas subsidiaries and undertake further evolution when they were ready. By contrast, firms that have expanded abroad in recent decades have had to move more aggressively to build a differentiated network, seeking the benefits of scale and global integration in years rather than decades. Today the pressure is greater than ever for firms to achieve a differentiated and mature global position in a short time. Examples include Thomson, the French consumer electronics firm, which in the 1980s found itself without a strong global position in an industry where worldwide scale was an imperative. In just a few years, Thomson transformed itself from a national player into a truly global firm by accelerating its evolution along all three dimensions—by entering many new countries, by shifting functions and rationalizing activities among its foreign subsidiaries, and by expanding into new lines of business, including digital satellite systems and high-definition television (HDTV). Another example is Intel, the U.S. leader in microprocessors, which announced in October 1995 plans to invest $3 billion simultaneously in new semiconductor labs in Malaysia, Israel, and Ireland. Stiff competition and rapid technological change make it impossible for firms like Intel to evolve in a slow or incremental manner; they must now take a concerted approach to at once sharing expertise across countries, across functions, and across lines of business, so as to move efficiently and swiftly on a large scale. As Thomson, Intel, and many other firms find themselves in intensely competitive global industries, their ability to accelerate evolution—to derive the full benefits of scale and scope economies in punctuated evolution, and to swiftly and fully restructure worldwide activities—is critical. Understanding MNC evolution in an integrated way, and emphasizing the importance of knowledge development and leveraging knowledge, is an important step forward.

Supplementary Reading

Bartlett, Christopher A., and Sumantra Ghoshal. *Managing Across Borders: The Transnational Solution.* Boston: Harvard Business School Press, 1989.

Birkenshaw, Julian. "Approaching Heterarchy: A Review of the Literature on Multinational Strategy and Structure." *Advances in International Comparative Management*, 9, 1994, pp. 111–44.

Chang, Sea-Jin. "International Expansion Strategy of Japanese Firms: Capability Building Through Sequential Entry." *Academy of Management Journal*, 1995, pp. 383–407.

Doz, Yvez L., and C. K. Prahalad. "Managing DMNCs: A Search for a New Paradigm." *Strategic Management Journal*, 12, 1991, pp. 145–64.

Johanson, Jan, and Jan-Erik Vahlne, "The Internationalization Process of the Firm: A Model of Knowledge Development and Increasing Foreign Market Commitments." *Journal of International Business Studies*, 8, 1997, pp. 23–32.

Kogut, Bruce, and Sea-Jin Chang. "Technological Capabilities and Japanese Foreign Direct Investment in the United States." *Review of Economics and Statistics*, 73, 1991, pp. 401–13.

Kogut, Bruce, and Udo Zander. "Knowledge of the Firm and the Evolutionary Theory of the Multi-national Corporation." *Journal of International Business Studies*, 24, 4, 1993, pp. 625–45.

Malnight, Thomas W. "Globalization of an Ethnocentric Firm: An Evolutionary Perspective." *Strategic Management Journal*, 16, 1995, pp. 119–41.

Nelson, Richard R., and Sidney G. Winter. *An Evolutionary Theory of Economic Change.* Cambridge: The Belknap Press of Harvard University Press, 1982.

11   THE GLOBAL MANAGER

This book is about how firms become and remain international in scope and how they come to grips with an increasingly competitive global environment. Firms often fail abroad, however, not because their strategy or structures necessarily were wrong, but because the operating plan may have been incomplete, or executives were not well prepared for their assignments. Failure may come when executives are sent overseas and are not able to understand the new culture or to function in their new environment. Someone has to implement, or oversee the implementation of, a strategy or plan. To do this means leaving headquarters and traveling to another country where it is necessary to work with people from another culture. In our experience, companies *and managers* often fail not because they had the wrong strategy, but because they were not capable of implementing it successfully. Preparation for these cross-cultural encounters is important, since the costs of failure can be high, either in terms of lost contracts and sales, or in out-of-pocket costs like premature returns from long-term assignments.

International business and management are not impersonal, conceptual activities. People are required to put understanding into practice. For example, licensing agreements do not materialize from thin air and joint ventures do not spring into being unaided—managers make these arrangements happen. These agreements become reality because managers go to other countries to work out deals. The globalization phenomenon is not limited in impact to some impersonal entity called a corporation. It has an impact on managers—real people—in their daily lives. Expatriates employed in a foreign subsidiary will be working with host country nationals at many levels in the organization and, most likely, with people from government. Headquarters personnel will interact with local country managers and staff members

This chapter was prepared by Henry W. Lane and Joseph J. DiStefano. It was adapted from Henry W. Lane, Joseph J. DiStefano, and Martha Maznevski, *International Management Behavior,* 3rd ed. Blackwell Publishers, 1996. It is published with permission of the authors. © 1996 Henry W. Lane, Joseph J. DiStefano, and Martha Maznevski. All rights reserved.

from other cultures as headquarters and regional offices become more "international." They require new skills to cope with the demands globalization brings in order to be successful in their roles and careers.

Some of the substantive issues facing managers in a diversified multinational corporation (DMNC) include:[1]

- Integrating large international acquisitions
- Understanding the meaning of performance and accountability in a globally integrated system of product flows
- Building and managing a worldwide logistics capability
- Developing country-specific corporate strategies that take into account the political as well as economic imperatives
- Forming and benefiting from collaborative arrangements around the world
- Balancing the pressures for global integration and local demands

Managers of the future will require knowledge of the type suggested but also an ability to take action. Although this was true in the past also, the knowledge base is now different and the skills required are dramatically different. What has changed? One of the most dramatic changes has been that now implementation takes place in many different cultures, often simultaneously. In these days of increased globalization even if one does not leave one's own country, it still will be highly likely that it will be necessary to work with someone from another culture.

The global manager will have to master more than concepts and theories; he or she will also have to command new skills. If one looks at the requirements for success in the global economy, it seems pretty clear that a global manager is going to have to have a repertoire comprising a comprehensive knowledge base and a well-developed set of relational and cross-cultural skills. It will include knowledge about business and technical matters, social, political and economic systems, and culture; an ability to define and solve problems in the face of uncertainty; implementation skills; and a keen sense of how and when previous experience is relevant in new cultural settings.

The purpose of this chapter is to identify and describe the skill set of the global manager. These include those skills necessary for possible international assignments. We realize that it is not possible to develop those skills by reading a chapter in a book, but we can challenge the readers to start thinking about where and how they will start acquiring these skills.

Skills of the Global Manager

What does the emergence of the term "global manager" really imply? In the broadest terms, it means reorganizing the way one thinks as a manager and as a student of

---

[1]C. K. Prahalad, "Globalization: The Intellectual and Managerial Challenges," *Human Resource Management,* Spring 1990, Vol. 29, No. 1, p. 29.

EXHIBIT 11–1   Executive Traits Now and in the Future[2]

Now	*The Future*
All knowing	Leader as learner
Domestic vision	Global vision
Predicts future from past	Intuits the future
Caring for individuals	Caring for institutions and individuals
Owns the vision	Facilitates vision of others
Uses power	Uses power and facilitation
Dictates goals and methods	Specifies processes
Alone at the top	Part of an executive team
Values order	Accepts paradox of order amidst chaos
Monolingual	Multicultural
Inspires the trust of boards, shareholders	Inspires the trust of owners, customers, and employees

---

management. As one executive put it, "To think globally really requires an alteration of our mind-set."[3] Thinking globally means *extending* concepts and models from one-to-one relationships (we to them) to holding multiple realities and relationships in one's head simultaneously, and *acting* skillfully on this more complex reality. The shift means that even if one has a regional responsibility, say as marketing manager for Central and South America, it is likely that more will be required than an understanding of Latin cultures and a capacity to speak Spanish and Portuguese. One also may have to deal with R&D labs in Japan, Europe, and North America to provide them with customer information and to get updates on emerging new products. Similarly, the regional marketing manager may have to discuss product problems with manufacturers in Southeast Asia late at night, North American time, and then send a fax about the potential solution to an alternative supplier in eastern Europe.

Many of the requirements of a global manager were articulated at a symposium organized by the Board of Governors of the American Society for Training and Development. (See Exhibit 11–1).

This list encompasses many of the particular skills required by global managers.[4] Reviewing a wide range of literature dealing with global strategy, global marketing, global operations management, and global human resource management, the authors identified a profile of effective global executives.[5]

---

[2]Patricia A. Galagan, "Executive Development in a Changing World," *Training and Development Journal* (June 1990), pp. 23–41.

[3]Personal communication from Mr. Bernard Daniel, Secretary-General, Nestlé Vevey, Switzerland.

[4]Brenda McMillan, Joseph J. DiStefano, and James C. Rush, "Requisite Skills and Characteristics of Global Managers," Working Paper, National Centre for Management Research and Development, Western Business School, The University of Western Ontario, London, Canada N6A 3K7, 1991.

[5]Subsequent to our literature review and the publication of an earlier version of this chapter in *International Management Behavior,* 2nd ed. (PWS-Kent, 1992), Stephen Rhinesmith published a book, *A Manager's Guide to Globalization,* in which the chapter headings closely parallel the set of skills we elaborate below, giving further crédence to their emerging importance.

1. Ability to develop and use global strategic skills
2. Ability to manage change and transition
3. Ability to manage cultural diversity
4. Ability to design and function in flexible organization structures
5. Ability to work with others and in teams
6. Ability to communicate
7. Ability to learn and transfer knowledge in an organization.

To assist the reader in advancing his or her understanding of what the emerging world requires of global managers, each of these abilities are explored in the following sections. The development of these skills is a lifelong process and it is unlikely that a single executive will master all of them.

Ability to Develop and Use Global Strategic Skills

Earlier chapters discussed the emergence of a new global economy. The result is a shift in the worldwide business base that is forcing managers and corporations to adjust and to shed their parochial views. Players in this new global environment will have a fast response capability, will be comfortable with cross-cultural influences, and will be entrepreneurial and flexible. Global managers will require a working knowledge of international relationships and foreign affairs, including global financial markets and exchange-rate movements.[6] These expanded business management skills will need to be coupled with global responsibilities to take advantage of manufacturing rationalization, "mass customization" of products, and low-cost, global sourcing.[7]

The global mind-set required by these new economic and competitive realities will be needed at all levels in the firm. Managers with this global perspective will need to strike a balance between national responsiveness and exploitation of global economies of scale. This is the vaunted ability to "think globally, but act locally."

Although the trend is toward standardization with some products and services, for others, managers must be sensitive to both local idiosyncrasies and global imperatives in reaching strategic decisions. A few examples illustrate the need to think globally, but to adapt to local conditions to avoid the pitfalls of inappropriate standardization.

• Procter and Gamble's liquid detergent failed in Europe when it was introduced in the early 1980s because European washing machines were not equipped for liquid detergent. Modifications to the detergent were made and sales subsequently improved.

• McDonald's sells beer in Germany and tropical shakes in Hong Kong, while Dunkin' Donuts sells cake donuts in the United States but yeast donuts in Brazil. Marketing strategies for global recognition were successfully implemented by adapting to local preferences.

---

[6]Stephen H. Rhinesmith, John N. Williamson, David M. Ehlen, and Denise S. Maxwell, "Developing Leaders for the Global Enterprise," *Training and Development Journal* (April 1989), pp. 25–34.

[7]Masaaki Kotabe, *Global Sourcing Strtategy: R&D, Manufacturing, and Marketing Interfaces,* New York: Quorum Books, 1992.

• Kellogg's Corn Flakes were (mis)used as a snack when first introduced in Brazil. With educational advertising, corn flakes gained in acceptance as a breakfast food.

These examples suggest that global success is contingent on striking a balance between capitalizing on resources and needs within national boundaries, and the ability to capture a vision of a world without boundaries. One aspect of managing this balance will likely include moving decision-making authority as close to the customer as possible to ensure that local requirements are satisfied. But local managers will need to know and understand the global strategy, yet enact it within the context of their local environment.

Ability to Manage Change and Transition

Managing change in the unstable environment described earlier will be an unending challenge. Constantly fine-tuning the balance between global and local pressures under changing competitive conditions will contribute to the need for frequent reorganization of resources, human networks, technology, and marketing and distribution systems. The shortening of product life cycles, driven by technological change in the products and how they are manufactured and delivered, contributes to the acceleration of change.

As difficult as these constant changes are to manage, the *overall* transition to global operations represents a formidable challenge in itself. Existing international operations, often marked by standardization of products and uniformity of procedures, may be a barrier to effective globalization. For example, a long history of mass-producing standard products may make it especially difficult to invest in and effectively operate flexible factories, one way that firms may offer differentiated products to different markets on a global scale.[8]

For a successful transition to global operations, it is also important that country managers are in agreement with the strategy. If poorly implemented, the move to globalization can pit headquarters managers against country or field managers. There is a tendency for autonomous units in a firm to protect their own turf. If global strategy is perceived as a move toward a centralization of responsibility, a local manager's role may become less strategic. Subsidiary managers who joined a company because of its commitment to local autonomy and adapting products to local environments may become disenchanted or even leave the organization.[9]

In terms of organization structure, effective global managers will need the skills to manage the transition from independence/dependence to interdependence, from control to coordination and cooperation, and from symmetry to differentiation.

Another method of making the transition to global operations is through the formation of a strategic alliance, or the formation of a network to reduce, for example,

---

[8]Sandra M. Huszagh, Richard J. Fox, and Ellen Day, "Global Marketing: An Empirical Investigation," *Columbia Journal of World Business* 20, Issue 4 (1986), pp. 31–43.

[9]John A. Quelch and Edward J. Hoff, "Customizing Global Marketing," *Harvard Business Review* (May-June 1986), pp. 59–68.

the high cost of R&D. As noted in Chapter 7, managing within international alliances or joint ventures is not the same as managing within a wholly owned subsidiary. Managing change within an alliance requires particular attention to the needs of the different partners, and an ability to enter into multiple trusting relationships.

Ability To Manage Cultural Diversity[10]

As one starts to function internationally, an understanding of culture and its impact on behavior, particularly management behavior and practices, becomes essential. Very often, people experience difficulties when they have to work in another culture because peoples' world views and mental programs are different in different cultures. Culture has been called "the collective programming of the mind which distinguishes one human group from another."[11] As a result of having different mental programs, people often see situations differently and have different approaches and solutions to problems. Each tends to believe that his or her way is the right way and makes the most sense. The result can be frustration, conflict, and an inability to successfully carry out strategy or plans. Understanding has two parts: *cultural awareness* or how another person's culture affects his or her behavior; and *self-awareness* or understanding how our own culture affects our behavior. It is not sufficient to understand how others differ, if we do not understand how we also differ.

The first imperative for effectively managing cultural diversity is cultural sensitivity. The marketers of Coca-Cola, the world's most recognized brand, attribute their success to the ability of their people to hold and to understand the following perspectives simultaneously:

- Their corporate culture
- The culture of their brand
- The culture of the people to whom they market the brand[12]

Sometimes cultural sensitivity leads to marketing one's products to a particular market segment *across* cultural boundaries, basically finding common subcultures within otherwise diverse cultures. In a classic study of international marketing practices of several bed linen companies headquartered in the United Kingdom, findings stressed the ability to develop a high level of cultural awareness in order to:

---

[10]This is a skill set that shows the potential transfer of learning between domestic and international or global activities. The recent explosion of books on managing diversity in North America demonstrates this point. Books such as Sondra Thiederman's *Profiting in America's Multicultural Marketplace* (Lexington: Lexington Books, 1991); Roosevelt Thomas's *Beyond Race and Gender: Unleashing the Power of Your Total Workforce by Managing Diversity* (New York: AMACOM, 1991); John Fernandez's *Managing a Diverse Work Force: Regaining the Competitive Edge* (Lexington: Lexington Books, 1991); and Ann Morrison's *The New Leaders: Guidelines on Leadership Diversity in America* (San Francisco: Jossey-Bass, 1992) include concepts and approaches similar to those written about international activities.

[11]Geert Hofstede, *Culture's Consequences: International Differences in Work-Related Values,* Beverly Hills, CA: Sage Publications, 1980.

[12]Harold F. Clarke, Jr., "Consumer and Corporate Values: Yet Another View on Global Marketing," *International Journal of Advertising* 6 (1987), pp. 29–42.

- Obtain high product acceptance in light of the fact that culturally rooted differences have a significant impact on a product's success in a global market.
- Understand that the older the consumption pattern, the less likely a global product will be a success.
- Recognize universal themes by segmenting according to similarities instead of geographical differences.[13]

Lack of cultural awareness can be devastating to organizations competing globally. An organization not managed according to values felt by its members is likely to experience conflict. Hidden values and beliefs must be recognized and understood in order to manage effectively. In the 1970s, in the Republic of Panama, there were more than 20 serious disputes between MNCs and local labor that were related to popular culture. Also during that period, all six Central American republics imposed restrictions on expatriate managers that resulted in their replacement by nationals.[14]

Global managers must have the ability to recognize that cultural differences operate internally and externally. It is important to understand the influence of the home office's own cultural filters when dealing with foreign affiliates and to accept that the home office way of doing things will not be appropriate in all instances. In today's global environment, a firm's home culture must no longer dominate the entire organization's culture.[15] Instilling such an attitude, a global mind-set, is not as simple as sending a memo announcing the change. Attitudes are notoriously resistant to change.

There are four distinct attitude clusters that are useful in thinking about, and characterizing, corporate worldviews or mind-sets: ethnocentric, polycentric, regiocentric, and geocentric.[16] These attitudes may be reflected in a firm's structure; authority and decision-making processes; selection, development, evaluation, control, and reward systems; information flows; and geographical identification.[17] In short, these attitudes permeate the strategy and operations of a company and its managers. A brief description of these attitudes follows.

Ethnocentrism (home-country orientation).   This is a preference for using home-country personnel in key positions around the world and rewarding them better than the locals. As with an ethnocentric attitude there is also a belief in the inherent superiority of the home-country personnel, systems, and ways of operating:

---

[13]Jeryl M. Whitelock, "Global Marketing and the Case for International Product Standardization," *European Journal of Marketing* (UK) 21, Issue 9 (1987), pp. 32–44.

[14]Antonio Grimaldi, "Interpreting Popular Culture: The Missing Link Between Local Labor and International Management," *Columbia Journal of World Business* 21, Issue 4 (Winter 1986), pp. 67–72.

[15]Nancy J. Adler and Fariborz Ghadar, "International Strategy from the Perspective of People and Culture: The North American Context," *Research in Global Business Management,* Vol. 1, Greenwich, CT: JAI Press Inc., 1990.

[16]Howard V. Perlmutter, "The Tortuous Evolution of the Multinational Corporation," *The Columbia Journal of World Business,* January 1969. pp. 9–18.

[17]David A. Heenan and Howard V. Perlmutter, *Multinational Organizational Development: A Social Architectural Perspective.* Reading, MA: Addison-Wesley, 1979.

. . . This group is more intelligent, more capable, or more reliable . . . ethnocentrism is often not attributable to prejudice as much as to inexperience or lack of knowledge about foreign persons and situations.[17] (p. 17)

Polycentrism (host-country orientation).   This attitude sees and focuses on the differences among cultures and finds foreigners difficult to understand. It also tends to be a low-involvement attitude, since everything in the other country is believed to be so difficult to understand:

> In justifying a decision, headquarters executives of such a company might say: "Let the Romans do it their way. We really don't understand what's going on there, but we have to have confidence in them. As long as our foreign managers earn a profit, we want to remain in the background." Local nationals in polycentric organizations occupy virtually all the key positions in their respective local subsidiaries and appoint and develop their own people . . . Headquarters with its holding company attitude is manned by home-country nationals who try not to interfere in the territory of each local manager. This low profile approach of headquarters is justified on managerial and political grounds.[17] (p. 20)

Regiocentrism (regional orientation).   Corporations with this attitude see

> . . . advantages in recruiting, developing, appraising and assigning managers on a regional basis. Such a personnel policy is viewed as supportive of functional rationalization . . . Such an approach has the merit of anticipating emerging politico-economic communities. (p. 20)

Geocentrism (world orientation).   This attitude

> . . . is evidenced in the attempt to integrate diverse regions through a global systems approach to decision-making. Headquarters and subsidiaries see themselves as parts of an organic world-wide entity. Superiority is not equated with nationality. Executives convey in their key decisions the attitude that the distinctive competence of the truly multinational firm is its capacity to optimize resource allocation on a global basis. Good ideas come from any country and go to any country within the firm.[17] (pp. 20–21)

Recent research[18] has found support for a link between a firm's mind-set or orientation and its mode of international operations. In a study of small and medium-sized Canadian companies, it was found that ethnocentric firms favored less-risky and higher control modes such as exporting and sales subsidiaries; firms with the other sets of attitudes were more likely to use a wider range of modes (with their associated risks) up to, and including, local production. A relationship was also found between international performance and attitude. Geocentric firms had the highest level of performance; poly/regiocentric were in the middle; and ethnocentric firms had the lowest performance.

Even though there may be real economic benefits to expanding the world view of executives and corporations, developing recognition of the existence and benefits

---

[18]Jonathan L. Calof, *The Internationalization Process: An Examination of Mode Change, Mode Choice, and Performance;* unpublished Ph.D. dissertation, The University of Western Ontario, London, Canada, 1991.

of diversity in global management does not come easily to North American executives, who often have less exposure to multicultural realities in their workplace than, for instance, their European counterparts. For example, Nestlé has a long history of having many nationalities among its top 100 executives (one count had it over 40), while, in one survey, IBM had the largest number among U.S. large companies—only 11! Although these types of anecdotal reports may be misleading, the limited language ability of many North American managers makes the same point another way. Language training, cross-cultural and expatriate experiences early in careers, membership on international task forces, and global content in all management training programs are among a few ways to counter the ethnocentricity of domestic managers, regardless of their country of origin. Using the case exercise presented later in this text entitled "Where Have You Been?" we have found a correlation between high mobility and exposure to other countries with a geocentric mind-set.

Learning to manage global cultural diversity effectively can start with the recognition of cultural diversity at home. The requirement to hire African Americans, Hispanics, and Native Americans in the U.S. is forcing many firms to come to grips with new mixes of employees. Demographic projections, which suggest that early in the next century, white males will represent only one in five of the workforce in the United States, also mean cultural diversity will be a domestic reality. There are large minorities of people newly arrived from India, Pakistan, Vietnam, Hong Kong, Central America, and eastern Europe. The opportunities to gain insight and experience in managing cultural diversity are local as well as global.

To manage diversity, domestically or globally, a modern human resource strategy requires some minimal orientations:

- An explicit recognition by headquarters that its own way of managing reflects the home culture values and assumptions.
- An explicit recognition by headquarters that foreign subsidiaries may have different ways of managing people, which may be more effective.
- A willingness to acknowledge cultural differences, and to take steps to make them discussible and, thus, usable.
- A commitment to the belief that more creative and effective ways of managing people can be developed as a result of cross-cultural learning.[19]

Ability to Design and to Function in Flexible Organizations

Given the complexities of the global economy and its attendant demands on managers, it is unlikely that any single organizational form will be adequate to the tasks. Global managers will surely need significantly increased creativity in organizational design, but limited organizational capability may represent the most critical constraint in responding to the new strategic demands.

---

[19]Andre Laurent, "The Cross-Cultural Puzzle of International Human Resource Management," *Human Resource Management* 25, Issue 1 (Spring 1986), pp. 91–102.

As mentioned earlier, an individual manager cannot be expected to develop and use all the diverse skills required for successful global management. It is essential then that the organization support global managers. Global managers will, therefore, be called on to design and operate the very organizations that will help them to be more effective.

The best managers are already creating borderless organizations where the ability to learn, to be responsive, and to be efficient occurs within the firm's administrative heritage.[20] This suggests that a wide range of people in such firms must demonstrate the capacity for strategic thinking and action, assisted by open communication of plans, decentralization of strategic tasks, early opportunities for development of top management capabilities, and control systems measuring performance across many dimensions.[21] These new organizations will have multiple centers of influence and managers will move between jobs at these centers. This lateral movement between centers and jobs will be common and will displace hierarchy and promotion "up the ladder."

To ensure that the potential cultural diversity in such situations is taken advantage of, managers will need the ability to create an alignment of authority and responsibility between home office and field offices that moves decision making as close as possible to the customer. Balance is required though and, as noted earlier, the ability to coordinate manufacturing interdependencies to maximize economies of production will be a key task of the global manager.

To operate effectively in these radically different, global organizations will take new skills and old skills honed to a new sharpness. Some of the abilities and characteristics needed by the global manager to function in flexible organizations will be:

- High tolerance for ambiguity
- New levels of creativity and inventiveness in organizational design
- The ability to learn, be responsive, and be efficient, all simultaneously
- The ability to identify and implement diverse managerial behaviors and ideas for ongoing renewal of the organization
- The ability to coordinate complicated financial, human resource, marketing and manufacturing interdependencies, not only across functions, but also within each business activity
- The ability to recognize different manufacturing, marketing, and organizational problems and priorities across different locations and to accommodate these with new structures and processes.[22]

Ability to Work with Others and in Teams

Even before the advent of global companies, effective teamwork was becoming essential for managerial success. As specialization of people and differentiation in

---

[20]C. A. Bartlett and S. Ghoshal, *Managing Across Borders,* Boston: Harvard Business School Press, 1989.

[21]For an article describing these and other organizational innovations, see Gunnar Hedlund, "The Hypermodern MNC—A Heterarchy?" *Human Resource Management* 25, No. 1 (Spring 1986), pp. 9–35.

[22]K. Ferdows, J. G. Miller, J. Nakane, and T. E. Vollmann, "Evolving Global Manufacturing Strategies: Projections into the 1990s, *International Journal of Operations and Production Management* 6, No. 4 (1986), pp. 6–16.

organizations increased (often driven by technological improvements, fragmentation of markets, explosions in product variations, etc.), there was a concomitant increased need for integration—for putting the specialized units back together in the service of the organization's objectives. Teams, committees, and task forces were among the devices used to accomplish the desired integration.

With the increased complexity of global operations, the ability to function in work teams—especially in culturally diverse groups—is even more important. A Conference Board Report on the experiences of 30 major MNCs in building teams to further their global interests showed the following:

- Teams used solely for communication or to provide advice and counsel still exist, but more and more firms are also using teams in different and more participative and powerful ways.

- Global teamwork can do more than provide improved market and technological intelligence. It can yield more flexible business planning, stronger commitment to achieving worldwide goals, and closer collaboration in carrying out strategic change.

- Teams that span internal organization boundaries or that span the company's outside boundary (joint venture partners, suppliers, customers) are often required.[23]

The need for transnational teamwork shows up in different ways in different functions. Consider the different assumptions about the nature and purpose of accounting and auditing in various parts of the world, for example. In one country financial statements are meant to reflect fundamental economic reality and the audit function is to ensure that this is so. In another country the audit is to check the accuracy of the statements vis-à-vis the economic records. In still another country it is only to make sure legal requirements have been met.[24] Imagine, then, the need for cross-cultural understanding and sensitivity in auditing an international subsidiary or the teamwork needed to develop international audit standards.[25]

Other functions pick up the teamwork theme differently. In operations management, the literature emphasizes the need to develop system-sensitive outlooks and processes that will develop personal relationships across subsidiaries.[26] The human resource literature emphasizes the need to develop capabilities for leading multinational teams in flexible and responsible ways. The global marketing literature discusses the ability to take advantage of a local execution strategy where "not invented

---

[23]Ruth G. Shaeffer, "Building Global Teamwork for Growth and Survival," *The Conference Board Research Bulletin,* No. 228.

[24] Leslie G. Campbell, *International Auditing* (New York: St. Martin's Press, 1985), p. 141.

[25]William S. Albrecht, Hugh L. Marsh Jr., and Frederick H. Bentzel Jr, "Auditing an International Subsidiary," *Internal Auditor* 45, Issue 5 (October 1988), pp. 22–26; Joseph Soeters and Hein Schreuder, "The Interactions Between National and Organizational Cultures in Accounting Firms," *Accounting, Organizations and Society* 13, No. 1 (1988), pp. 75–85; and Nicholas M. Zacchea "The Multinational Auditor: Overcoming Cultural Differences to Apply Audit Standards," *Internal Auditor* 45, Issue 5 (1988), pp. 16–21.

[26]Briance Mascarenhas, "The Coordination of Manufacturing Interdependencies in Multinational Companies," *Journal of International Business Studies* (Winter 1984), pp. 91–106.

here" becomes "now improved here."[27] Using this strategy, an international core team is formed to gather ideas and to pass them to local levels where the final marketing decisions are made and implemented.

The ability to work effectively with other people and in teams will be critical to the successful implementation of a global strategy. Participation in global teams should, therefore, occur early in the careers of managers in order to transform these developing people into globally effective managers.

Ability to Communicate

It is obvious that in a global environment managers will need to be able to communicate with diverse groups of people. To do so effectively will require multilingual skills and high levels of cross-cultural awareness and sensitivity. In addition to the positive effects of good communication skills among colleagues and with customers, there is another advantage of particular importance to geographically dispersed and culturally diverse organizations. Sensitive communications will also build trust, and a common message can help build a strong corporate culture emphasizing shared, global value systems.

In addition to the skills necessary for effective interpersonal communication, managers will need to be able to take advantage of increasingly global communications systems resulting from broadcast deregulation and growth in global media firms such as Sky Channel and Pan European Press. Data gathered in 1987 indicates that the market for Pan European advertising campaigns has been growing at a rate of more than 25 percent per year, in spite of the many technological difficulties encountered by the new satellite technology. As always, the need to be sensitive to local requirements is evidenced by several lawsuits launched against the global media by local advertisers wishing to retain advertising revenue and by regulatory bodies seeking to retain control over advertising content.[28]

The advent of global communications exposes managers to new risks as well as new advantages. Recently, CNN aired an interview with a U.S. senator from the steps of the Capitol in Washington on their European broadcasts. Apparently directing his comments to his constituents in his home state, the senator was engaging in Europe-bashing in defense of local industries. At the same time U.S. trade representatives were trying to negotiate sensitive issues with their European Community counterparts in Brussels. The senator was probably unaware that this interview would be aired the same day throughout Europe. Global communications provide as great an opportunity to offend as they do to please.

Ability to Learn and to Transfer Knowledge in an Organization

Given the diversity of market requirements and needs, the dispersion of manufacturing and sourcing, the rise of R&D leadership in Europe and Japan, and the importance of

---

[27]Teresa J. Domzel and Lynette S. Unger, "Emerging Positioning Strategies in Global Marketing," *Journal of Consumer Marketing* 4, Issue 4 (Fall 1987), pp. 23–40.

[28]Laurel Wentz, "Global Marketing and Media: TV Nationalism Clouds Sky Gains," *Advertising Age* 58, Issue 53 (December 14, 1987), p. 56.

technological advances for product and process innovations, learning and transfer of knowledge are key to global success. Managers who are globally competent will be deeply curious; organizations that are successful will be able to coordinate, transfer, and use the knowledge gained by curious executives rapidly and effectively.

At the individual level, broad interests, an openness to a variety of experiences, and a willingness to experiment and to take risks are all ingredients of success. A visiting scholar from the People's Republic of China typified these characteristics for the authors. Soon after her arrival she knew more people than several others who had been at our institution for many months. Although her specialty was finance, she audited classes across all functions. She interviewed the "old-timers," secretaries, researchers, students, and seasoned teachers. Nor were her interactions confined to work. She learned humor; visited churches; traveled across the country by air, bus, train, and boat; went to country fairs; and even insisted on trying golf! By the end of her year, she understood the institution better than most who had been in it for several years; she understood the country almost as well as any native. Then, she transferred her knowledge to her colleagues in China and abroad through an extraordinary report[29] and through a series of lectures and seminars.

At an organizational level even more can be done. For example, at Citicorp, operating managers are encouraged to look for opportunities in one country that can be transferred elsewhere. These opportunities, or experiments, are the responsibility of national managers, while their transfer is the responsibility of corporate management.[30] The use of cross-national task forces for problems of corporate-level concern (or for problems that reoccur in various parts of the world) is also a feature of that company.

The transfer of technology is also important. Global MIS systems are now required and a manager must have the skills necessary to access and interpret worldwide information. One way to transfer technology is through the development of strong functional management to allow the building and transference of core competencies.

Yet there are indications that too often companies neglect the rich information made available to them by expatriates in other countries, especially when they return to their home country. These organizations not only lose out on a valuable opportunity to transfer some cross-cultural managerial knowledge, but also cause the expatriate to experience some potentially serious reentry difficulties.[31]

The ability of organizations to learn and to transfer knowledge will only increase in importance as markets continue to globalize. In a global environment, the ability of people to learn from diverse sources and to transfer knowledge within their organization is essential for success.

---

[29]Jiping Zhang, *The Building and Operation of a North American Business School* (in Chinese), Tsinghua University Press (Beijing, 1990) (English version published March 1987 by the Western Business School, The University of Western Ontario, London, Ontario N6A 3K7.)

[30]Alan J. Zakon, "Globalization Is More Than Imports and Exports," *Management Review* 77, Issue 7 (July 1988), pp. 56–57.

[31]Robert T. Moran, "Corporations Tragically Waste Overseas Experience," *International Management* (UK) 43, Issue 1 (January 1988), p. 74.

Summary Profile

This review might lead the reader to conclude that an effective global manager is superhuman. But keeping in mind the necessity of teamwork and the potential support to the managers through effective organizational design, systems, and processes, the prospect of developing global skills might be seen as an exciting challenge rather than an impossible task. To develop skills to the level necessary will be a lifelong process because the demands will likely expand along with the global economy. Each of us needs to continue to improve in the aforementioned areas as we move toward the new century.

Developing Global Managers

American companies went through a period of reducing the number of expatriates they sent overseas for many reasons.[32] One major reason was the expense associated with relocating them and their families. Their salaries were usually higher than those of local managers, and they usually received benefits to make an overseas move attractive. Many of these benefits were not usually provided to local employees. Benefits often included items like housing or housing allowance, moving expenses, tax equalization, home leave, overseas premiums, cost of living allowances, and schooling for children. The incremental costs to the MNE of using expatriates can be shockingly high, particularly in some locales. A high-quality apartment rental accommodation for a senior manager posted to Hong Kong can run US$100,000/year. North American managers transferred to Switzerland claim that "everything" is more expensive than what they are accustomed to paying at home for a comparable material living standard.

In addition to lowering costs, having fewer expatriates has resulted in reduced conflict between employees and groups in the local environment. As well, it has increased the development of host country managerial and technical capabilities.

Although this trend could be seen as a positive step in the globalization process of American companies, there is a question about whether the real reason for the reduction was Americans' inability to function abroad successfully. Estimates of expatriate failure rate run between 20 percent and 50 percent, and the average cost per failure to the parent company ranges from $55,000 to $150,000.[33] There are studies claiming the failure rate is between 30 and 70 percent. The accurate identification of the actual rate of failure is less important than how high the range is. The fact that this range represents a large number of managers who cannot function successfully in other cultures is disturbing. The reduction in expatriate personnel also has ramifications for strategic management and control, such as less identification with, and knowledge about, the global operations and organization, and less control by headquarters over local subsidiaries. Thus:

---

[32]Stephen J. Kobrin, "Expatriate Reduction and Strategic Control in American Multinational Corporations." *Human Resource Management,* Vol. 27, No. 1, 1988. See also Michael Harvey, "Empirical Evidence of Recurring International Compensation Problems," *Journal of International Business Studies,* Vol. 24, No. 4, 1993.
[33]Ibid.

... There is increasing value to expatriate assignment as firms become global competitors . . . A means must be found to provide this experience to as many managers as possible. That would probably involve shorter-term expatriate assignments whose purpose is avowedly developmental—for both the individual and the organization.[34]

A more recent phenomenon affecting the mobility of many (especially North American and European) managers is the dual-career reality of their family unit. As the Colgate-Palmolive case suggests, dual careers have introduced new complexities for MNEs wishing to develop global managers.

Careful selection and preparation of expatriates—and their families—for their foreign assignments should be high-priority issues for multinationals. Unfortunately, this has not generally been the case. Now, corporations must reconsider their human resource management policies, including expatriation, in light of globalization. Cross-cultural understanding and experience are essential in today's business environment, and foreign assignments can be a critical part of a manager's development. However, experience in a job in another country does not automatically ensure a manager's increased sensitivity to cultural issues or an ability to transfer whatever has been learned to other managers. Cross-cultural training, even for experienced people, can add significantly to their understanding of their past experiences and to their skill in future assignments.

International experience is an important consideration in firms' recruiting and hiring practices. A study of 122 major Canadian corporations found a preference for hiring people with international experience for international positions.[35] The respondents to the survey also stated that expertise in international business was among the important skills that executives needed. Although corporations will have to spend more time, effort, and money in providing international experiences to their managers in order to help develop the global skills required for the future, individuals can take responsibility for their own development by seeking out international opportunities such as teaching language courses in other countries or working for agencies such as the U.S. Peace Corps or Canadian University Students Overseas (CUSO). In addition, acquiring fluency in a second or third language would be helpful.

Managing International Assignments

As was mentioned earlier, there are strategic implications to the use of expatriate personnel. MNCs must think about expatriation as a strategic tool that is used to develop managers with a global orientation, but also that is used to manage key organizational and country relationships.[36] Although organizational and management development are important, the emphasis should be:

34Ibid., p. 74.

35Paul W. Beamish and Jonathan L. Calof, "International Business Education: A Corporate View," *Journal of International Business Studies,* Vol. 20, No. 3, 1989.

36Nakiye A. Boyacigiller, "The International Assignment Reconsidered," in *International Human Resource Management,* Mark Mendenhall and Gary Oddou, eds., Boston: PWS-Kent, 1991, p. 154.

. . . on long-term commitment to learning about international markets. If high-potential individuals are carefully selected and trained for overseas positions, they will not only facilitate the maintenance of an international network of operations in the short term but should be allowed to continue providing informational support upon their return.[36]

Although it might sound pretty straightforward, the process of developing globally minded managers with the requisite skills is more difficult that it appears. The quote contains the conditions that most often are not met—*if high-potential individuals are carefully selected and trained*—and which are crucial to the successful use of expatriation for development and strategic purposes.

Selection: In 1973, published research[37] showed that people were selected for international assignments based on their proven performance in a similar job, usually domestically. The ability to work with foreign employees was at, or near, the bottom of the list of important qualifications. Unfortunately, 20 years later the situation has not changed dramatically for the better.[38] Very often technical expertise and knowledge are used as the most important selection criteria. Although these are important considerations, they should not be given undue weighting relative to a person's ability to adapt to, and function in, another culture. It does no good to send the most technically qualified engineer or finance manager to a foreign location if he or she cannot function there and has to be brought home prematurely. As noted earlier, the cost of bad selection decisions is high to the corporation as well as to the individual and to his or her family.

In a very useful model of overseas effectiveness, which focuses on adaptation, expertise, and interaction,[39] for a person to be effective, he or she:

> must adapt—both personally and with his/her family—to the overseas environment, have the expertise to carry out the assignment, and interact with the new culture and its people.[40]

Training. The training that a person undergoes before expatriation should be a function of the degree of cultural exposure to which he or she will be subjected.[41] Two dimensions of cultural exposure are the degree of integration and the duration of stay. The integration dimension represents the intensity of the exposure. A person could be sent to a foreign country on a short-term, technical, trouble-shooting matter and experience little significant contact with the local culture. On the other hand, a

---

[37]E. L. Miller, "The International Selection Decision: A Study of Some Dimensions of Managerial Behavior in the Selection Decision Process," *Academy of Management Journal,* Vol. 16, No. 2, 1973, pp. 239–52.

[38]Mark E. Mendenhall, Edward Dunbar, and Gary R. Oddou, "Expatriate Selection, Training and Career Pathing: A Review and Critique," *Human Resource Management,* Vol. 26, No. 3, 1987.

[39]Daniel J. Kealey, *Cross-cultural Effectiveness: A Study of Canadian Technical Advisors Overseas,* Ottawa: Canadian International Development Agency, 1990. This study was based on a sample of over 1,300 people, including technical advisors, their spouses, and host-country counterparts.

[40]Ibid., p. 8.

[41]Mendenhall et al., op. cit.

person could be in Japan for only a brief visit to negotiate a contract, but the cultural interaction could be very intense and may require a great deal of cultural fluency to be successful. Similarly, an expatriate assigned abroad for a period of years is likely to experience a high degree of interaction with the local culture from living there.

One set of guidelines[42] suggests that for short stays (less than a month) and a low level of integration, an "information-giving approach" would suffice. This includes area and cultural briefings, and survival-level language training, for example. For longer stays (2–12 months) and a moderate level of integration, language training, role-plays, critical incidents, case studies, and stress reduction training are suggested. For people who will be living abroad for one to three years and/or will have to experience a high level of integration into the culture, extensive language training, sensitivity training, field experiences, and simulations are the training techniques recommended.

Effective preparation would also stress the realities and difficulties of working in another culture and the importance of establishing good working relationships with the local people.

Repatriation.   Selecting the right people, training them properly, and sending them and their families to their foreign posting is not the end of the exercise. Getting these people back and integrated into the company so that the company can continue to benefit from their experience and expertise has been shown to be a problem. Research suggests that the average repatriation failure rate—those people who return from an overseas assignment and then leave their companies within one year—is about 25 percent.[43] If companies want to retain their internationally experienced managers, they are going to have to do a better job managing the repatriation process. See the Yutaka Nakamura case for a detailed elaboration of this point.

The international assignment may be an important vehicle for developing global managers; achieving strategic management control; coordinating and integrating the global organization; and learning about international markets and competitors, as well as foreign social, political, and economic situations. However, this idealized goal of becoming a global, learning organization will be reached only if the right people are selected for foreign assignments, trained properly, repatriated with care, valued for their experience, and are used in a way that takes advantage of their unique background.

---

[42]Ibid.

[43]Meg G. Birdseye and John S. Hill, "Individual, Organizational/Work and Environmental Influences on Expatriate Turnover Tendencies: An Empirical Study," *Journal of International Business Studies,* Vol. 26, No. 4, 1995. J. Stewart Black and Hal R. Gregersen, "When Yankee Comes Home: Factors Related to Expatriate and Spouse Repatriation Adjustment," *Journal of International Business Studies,* Vol. 22, No. 4, 1991; J. Stewart Black, Hal R. Gregersen, and Mark E. Mendenhall, "Toward a Theoretical Framework of Repatriation Adjustment," *Journal of International Business Studies,* Vol. 23, No. 4, 1992.

Supplementary Reading

Adler. Nancy *International Dimensions of Organization Behavior,* 2nd ed. Boston: PWS-Kent, 1991.

Beamish, Paul W., and Jonathan L. Calof. "International Business Education: A Corporate View." *Journal of International Business Studies,* Fall 1989.

Black, J. Stewart, and Hal B. Gregersen, "Serving Two Masters: Managing the Dual Allegiance of Expatriate Employees." *Sloan Management Review,* Summer 1992.

Black, J. Stewart, Hal B. Gregersen, and Mark E. Mendenhall. *Global Assignments: Successfully Expatriating and Repatriating International Managers.* San Francisco: Jossey-Bass, 1992.

Cascio, Wayne F., and Manuel G. Serapio, Jr. "Human Resources Systems in an International Alliance: The Undoing of a Done Deal." *Organizational Dynamics,* Winter 1991.

Dowling, Peter, and Randall Schuler. *International Dimensions of Human Resource Management,* Boston: PWS-Kent, 1990.

Lane, Henry W., Joseph J. DiStefano, and Martha Maznevski. *International Management Behavior,* 3rd ed., Cambridge, MA: Blackwell Publishers, 1996.

Maisonrouge, Jacques G. "The Education of a Modern International Manager." *Journal of International Business Studies,* Spring/Summer 1983.

Mendenhall, Mark, and Gary Oddou. *Readings and Cases in International Human Resource Management,* Boston: PWS-Kent, 1991.

O'Grady, Shawna, and Henry W. Lane. "The Psychic Distance Paradox," *Journal of International Business Studies,* Vol. 27, No. 2, 1996.

Pucik, Vladimir, Noel M. Tichy, and Carole K. Barnett, eds., *Globalizing Management: Creating and Leading the Competitive Organization.* New York: John Wiley & Sons, 1992.

Rhinesmith, Stephen H. *A Manager's Guide to Globalization: Six Keys to Success in a Changing World.* Burr Ridge, IL: Business One Irwin, in cooperation with The American Society for Training and Development,1992.

Rosenzweig, Philip M., and Nitin Nohria. "Influences on Human Resource Management Practices in Multinational Corporations." *Journal of International Business Studies,* Vol. 25, No.2, 1994.

12   POLITICAL RISK: MANAGING GOVERNMENT INTERVENTION

- Unstable political governments (Rwanda, Zaire)

- Organized crime (Russia)

Managers in multinational enterprises are concerned and frustrated by governments that force unwanted changes in their preferred method of operations. While intervention forms such as expropriation have declined, host governments intervene in subsidiaries of multinational enterprises (MNEs) by restricting foreign ownership and control; regulating financial flows, foreign management, and technical fees; and instituting requirements for local content and minimum export levels. Historically, MNEs have responded by trying to negotiate changes in either the intervention laws or their implementation, by attempting to bypass the laws, or by reducing their exposure in nations with a record of frequent interventions.

Academics and consultants have been examining the intervention experiences of MNEs. This effort has produced several ideas and approaches for improving the MNE's management of intervention. The purpose of this chapter is to summarize these findings and examine how they can be incorporated into a strategy for defending the MNE from unwanted intervention.

While parent companies are usually the focus of attention in such discussions, the focus here is on the subsidiary/affiliate. This is not only for the obvious reason that subsidiaries are more exposed to the policies of host governments. It is because intervention policies are sometimes determined less by ideology, politics, and economics and more by the character of the subsidiary itself. While ideology, political stability, and the supply of hard currency reserves set the stage, the foreign subsidiary is the actor.

Given the crucial role of the subsidiary, managers should refocus their attention on subsidiary strategies. This chapter proposes a general strategy for defending the subsidiary, concentrating on a strategy that can be implemented by most manufacturing multinationals without dramatic changes in their existing organization and operation.

This chapter was originally prepared by Thomas A. Poynter and adapted from his article "Managing Government Intervention," *Columbia Journal of World Business,* Winter 1986. Revised and updated by Paul Beamish.

Intervention Management: A Shift

Traditional political risk analysis no longer meets the needs of MNEs. Historically, political risk analysis focused on assessing political instability. While international banks may find this analysis still appropriate to their needs, multinational manufacturing firms know this kind of information is not particularly useful in managing their political risks. Political instability forms only a small portion of all the risks faced by multinational enterprises.[1] Instead, MNEs find that actions like forced joint ventures, unilateral contract renegotiations, and regulations calling for increased local value-added, top their list of concerns. Even when revolutions and similar shocks occur, they do not necessarily affect all firms equally.

While some nations intervene more than others, avoiding intervention by predicting a nation's intervention behavior is ineffective. "Safe" countries sometimes turn into hot-beds of intervention, while host countries led by unrepentant Marxists provide profitable opportunities. It appears that almost all countries intervene in the operations of foreign-owned firms.

How, then, does the foreign-owned firm defend itself? One dominant characteristic of host government intervention behavior leads the way toward a solution: governments discriminate. They force some subsidiaries into unwanted joint ventures, and impose taxes and limit prices, while allowing others 100 percent foreign ownership and financially supporting them. Even when legislation calls for the equal treatment of all foreign firms, discriminatory enforcement is often the norm.

The basis of this discrimination lies in the differing characteristics of subsidiaries. Case studies, casual observation, and large-scale empirical investigations conducted by several observers lead to substantial agreement on this issue.[2] A key element is the bargaining power associated with each subsidiary. In this context, bargaining power refers to the control the *MNE parent* has over those resources necessary to operate the *subsidiary* successfully. Intervention occurs when domestic firms, entrepreneurs, or government officials feel they have sufficient resources (e.g., technology, export markets, raw materials, or components, and so on) to operate part or

---

[1]See Theodore H. Moran, "International Political Risk Assessment, Corporate Planning and Strategies to Offset Political Risk," in *Managing International Political Risk: Strategies and Techniques*, eds. F. Ghadar, S. J. Kobrin, and T. H. Moran (Washington, D.C.: The Landegger Program in International Business Diplomacy, Georgetown University, 1983), pp. 158–66.

[2]The concept of "bargaining power" finds its roots in the work of Raymond Vernon, *Sovereignty at Bay: The Multinational Spread of U.S. Enterprises* (New York: Basic Books, 1971) and was further developed using natural resource firms by T. H. Moran, *Multinational Corporations and the Politics of Dependence: Copper in Chile* (Princeton, N.J.: Princeton University Press, 1974). The comments in this chapter are based on the substantially similar findings of four independent projects examining the causes of intervention: D. G. Bradley, "Managing Against Expropriation," *Harvard University Review*, July-August 1977; T. A. Poynter, "Government Intervention in Less Developed Countries: The Experience of Multinational Companies," *Journal of International Business Studies*, Spring-Summer 1982; N. Fagre and L. T. Wells, Jr., "The Bargaining Power of Multinationals and Host Government," *Journal of International Business Studies*, Fall 1982; Donald J. Lecraw, "Bargaining Power, Ownership and Profitability of Subsidiaries of Transnational Corporations in Developing Countries," *Journal of International Business Studies*, Spring-Summer 1984.

all of the activities of the subsidiary without assistance from the MNE. In other words, local groups will press the government to intervene on their behalf when continued MNE support is no longer required to keep the subsidiaries profitable. At that point, the MNE's bargaining power is low. Negotiations usually occur no matter what the bargaining power of the subsidiary, but the level of bargaining power is a good predictor of the outcome of the negotiations.

The bargaining power of the host nation comes from two sources. One source directly counters the power of the MNE, namely the host nation's ability to replace the business resources normally supplied by the MNE. The nation's stock of managerial, technical, and similar resources is either internally generated, or, is obtained through consultants, license agreements, and the like. The capabilities of host nations are growing.

The second source of host nation bargaining power comes from its control over the subsidiary's access to the host nation's market, raw materials, labor, and capital.[3] As these factors grow in importance, more MNEs compete to locate there, thus maximizing the bargaining power of the host nation. Hence, the larger and more attractive the local market becomes, the more intervention the firm will experience, all things being equal.

Summarizing the bargaining power (BP) model, intervention will not occur when the subsidiary's bargaining power is greater than the nation's business resources plus the attractiveness of the local market. In this model, bargaining power is derived from two sources: the availability of business resources needed to operate the subsidiary and, for the host nation only, the attractiveness of its market.

It is important here to reiterate the source and applicability of this model. It is based on the intervention experiences of many individual subsidiaries. The model shows what circumstances are typically found when intervention occurs. In practice, low subsidiary bargaining power sets into motion actions by domestic entrepreneurs, government officials, and the like, who actually bring about intervention. One must also note that this model does not examine why one nation would intervene on average more than another. For example, one of the reasons Nigeria intervenes more than the Ivory Coast may have to do with the latter's more open market, which is less distorted by government intervention. But this chapter is about reducing the level of intervention relative to all other firms in a nation. Given that one must choose to operate in a particular nation, defending the subsidiary against high levels of intervention is a key managerial activity.

The subsidiary's defense strategy is based on the bargaining model presented above, coupled with other subsidiary characteristics that also affect the level of intervention. Because the firm's bargaining power can usually be changed, firms can now manage intervention.

---

[3]For a detailed discussion of sources of a nation's bargaining power see T. A. Poynter, *Multinational Enterprises and Government Intervention* (New York: St. Martin's Press; and London: Croom Helm, 1985), pp. 57–68.

Applicability of the Strategy

Not all kinds of intervention, nor all kinds of MNEs, are covered here. The proposed strategy is only applicable to unwanted interventions and not interventions represented by such inducements as tax holidays, subsidies, and so forth. Interventions that take place before the investment is made, such as lists of businesses restricted to local ownership, are not included either. On the corporate side, the strategy is restricted to manufacturing MNEs and not to those in the service sector or those involved in activities of a project nature. This chapter is also not concerned directly with organizational and integration issues within the MNE, which were considered in Chapters 8 and 9.[4]

The strategy applies to a wide selection of nations, developed and less-developed alike. Only in those select nations where discriminatory legislation against foreign firms is nonexistent, either because of judicial restraints or because the presence of overwhelming bilateral exchanges mitigates against intervention, does this strategy not apply.

Defense Strategies

Successful strategies are based on two separate activities: profitably increasing the subsidiary's bargaining power, and adapting its political behavior to its political profile. In addition, several ineffective yet popular strategies are also discussed. Finally, modifications to the basic defense strategy are described.

Maximizing Subsidiary Bargaining Power

The most frequently used method of increasing the bargaining power of the subsidiary is to stay ahead of the technical and managerial capabilities of the host nation. Over time this is operationalized by *significant technological upgrades* within the existing product line. Alternatively, if the speed of technological change is not rapid enough to outrun the domestic learning rate, or if the level of technology is not sufficiently complex, then staying ahead will require the *introduction of new products*.

The purpose of these upgrades is to keep bargaining power high by maintaining the gap between the capabilities of local entrepreneurs and businesspeople, and the capabilities needed to operate the subsidiary. While this gap is maintained, the subsidiary is still dependent on the MNE, creating a bargaining disadvantage for local interventionists.

Another means of increasing bargaining power is through *significant exports*. To be effective these must either be to a market where the MNE has a strong competitive advantage, or they must be so price-sensitive that continued MNE manufacturing support is a prerequisite. While providing rapid and visible bargaining

---

[4]For a discussion of some of the implementation and integration difficulties encountered by this kind of activity, see S. J. Kobrin, *Managing Political Risk Assessment* (Berkeley: University of California Press, 1982).

power, the successful implementation of this strategy is also the most demanding of the defense strategies.

The final major source of bargaining power stems from MNE *sourcing* or *vertical integration,* as discussed in Chapter 5. Obviously, there are strong disincentives for local business or government to intervene in a firm that, say, imports a proprietary one-third-completed product for further assembly, with sales locally and to other parts of the MNE. While obvious examples occur in the auto industry, manufacturers of industrial tools, of some specialized chemicals, and of electronics can implement this strategy as well. Japanese MNEs are frequent users of this strategy, using world-scale plants and trading houses. To guarantee effectiveness, multiple sourcing of the same components or products within the MNE system is necessary to ensure that the subsidiary will not be held hostage by a government taking advantage of its role as a sole supplier within the multinational system.

Threats to the Strategy.   The effectiveness of these strategies for increasing the subsidiary's bargaining power can be reduced in two ways. The first comes from the existence of significant foreign competition either within the host nation or outside that is wishing to enter the host nation. Such competition reduces the nation's dependence on one MNE to supply the resources needed to operate the subsidiary. In effect, such competition forces individual MNEs to build a stronger bargaining position than would otherwise be necessary.

An even greater and more recent threat to these strategies comes from the growth of alternative suppliers of complete technology. These firms supply host nation companies, eroding the role of the MNE as the exclusive supplier of such resources, and reducing the bargaining position of the foreign direct investor. These suppliers arc usually small firms from developed nations, and tend to specialize in a complex product that they sell worldwide.

Implementing the Strategy.   Successful implementation revolves around two management issues: knowing *when* to upgrade or increase the subsidiary's bargaining power, and successfully *installing* the upgrade (new process, a profitable export market, and the like) in both the subsidiary and the MNE's worldwide organization.

Basic to the successful management of costly intervention is the determination of the subsidiary's bargaining position vis-à-vis any potential interventionist. In other words, to what extent can the MNE contribution be replaced, in whole or in part, by domestic firms? Knowing one's bargaining position helps one assess the probability of intervention and the need for a bargaining power upgrade.

Exhibit 12–1 illustrates in a conceptual sense the subsidiary's intervention management problem. Upon entry into the host nation, the subsidiary's bargaining position is usually high ("A"). The subsidiary's level of technology and management skill is generally higher than the capabilities resident in the host country. Over time this gap decreases, as host nationals learn directly from the subsidiary or from other foreign firms, training, overseas education, and so forth. This learning reduces the dependence on the MNE as the supplier of these resources, that ensure the continued success of the subsidiary. In other words, the relative bargaining power of the MNE dissipates over time as the skills are learned by host nationals.

Conceptually, the ideal time to upgrade, or increase one's bargaining power, is just before the host nation's bargaining power is "equal" to the firm's (point "B" in Exhibit 12–1). At this point, the host nation government or interest groups begin to believe that they can replace the MNE contribution with domestic technology, management, sourcing, and so on, without too great a loss. By this time, MNE threats to withdraw services or skills in the hope of preventing intervention are less of a deterrent to domestic entrepreneurs and others who have been pushing for government intervention.

A bargaining power upgrade at point "B" would include any of the items noted earlier in this chapter. To illustrate this point, for a subsidiary importing electronic components for assembly into a mature electromechanical device, an upgrade could involve the domestic manufacture of the more sophisticated electronic components not easily available in the host country. This tactic could raise the subsidiary's position to point "C." Failure to upgrade one's bargaining position will eventually result in some form of costly intervention (point "D"), such as a forced joint venture or a forced local sourcing of components.

Operationally, to determine each subsidiary's bargaining power requires a measurement of the local firm's ability to provide the following resources:

EXHIBIT 12–1   Relative Bargaining Power over Time

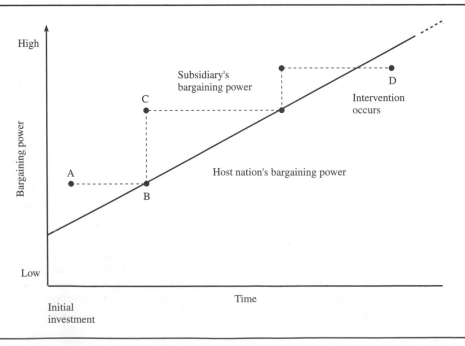

- Technology (process/product)
- Management skill
- Ability to replace MNE sourcing (inputs-outputs)

Collecting these data requires specific management resources. Executives capable of monitoring the activities, growth, and capability of existing or potential interventionists are required. Not only does this monitoring require considerable senior management time, but these executives must be familiar with and be able to obtain intelligence on local competitors. Most U.S. MNEs are particularly hard hit by the latter requirement, given their personnel strategy of frequently relocating executives.

MNEs have developed various mechanisms to collect these data. Some use staff specialized in competitor analysis, while others have the subsidiary general manager develop appropriate procedures. Generally, it appears to require a couple of years before the mechanism works well, but there are some tangible short-term benefits. The approach immediately focuses management attention—albeit without precision—on the single most important aspect of their intervention environment: existing or potential domestic competitors.

The second management issue associated with implementing the defense strategy involves the successful installation of the bargaining power upgrade. On one level, upgrading the technological and managerial complexity of the subsidiary by introducing new processes or products is strategically straightforward. Managerially, to extract a profitable return from the upgrade, the challenge is to find and train staff to handle the new activities. MNEs already accustomed to rapid technical change have a special advantage here. The container manufacturer who can progress from cork-lined to plastic-lined bottle caps, to three-seam cans, seamless cans, pressurized cans, all the way up to the sale and maintenance of complex bottling equipment, is a classic example of a firm in which one product line allows for a natural progression up the scale of technological complexity. Preparing managers and technical staff to handle those upgrades is much easier than preparing staff to handle brand new products or highly complex technologies.

Exporting as a defense mechanism is often noted by executives and observers, but very difficult to implement successfully. To be successful, production must be at world prices, with the attendant world-scale plant. While these stringent demands can be partially allayed by generous host government capital, operating subsidies, and export assistance, often the success of this strategy is mitigated by the unavailability of competitively priced inputs, uncompetitive wage and productivity rates, and managers more accustomed to operating behind tariff walls than over them.

Such an export strategy can be successful if one constructs a portfolio of different businesses with high *average* bargaining power. Multiproduct firms can establish a single export plant in a host country, providing both high bargaining power and foreign exchange. Other operations, such as the local manufacture—or even importation—of a mature product can be grouped with the export plant and, hence, be protected. Viewed in this manner, the lower intervention risk—but often lower profits—offered by the export operation when matched with the high profits obtained from imported or protected products provides an acceptable overall strategy.

The implementation problems associated with intra-MNE component and product sourcing are not unlike those associated with exporting. While the need to match the world price is slightly relaxed when sales are to associate firms, additional resources are spent ensuring that product specifications, supply, and so forth, are accepted worldwide. As with exports, the ability to append products with less bargaining power but more profit makes this strategy more attractive.

Reducing Barriers to Successful Implementation.   Several multinationals have had problems successfully implementing some of the strategies recommended in this chapter. The difficulties appear to be of two different kinds: first, a scarcity of personnel appropriate to the new strategy; and second, the fact that this strategy runs completely counter to the MNE's traditional response to intervention.

The defense strategies call for more managerial and technical capabilities to be located in subsidiaries. Not only do export strategies, technology upgrades, and intra-MNE sourcing call for more technical skills, but—as all observers of the international scene suggest—increased numbers of politically attuned executives can be profitably used in subsidiaries, too. The high cost of the former, and the scarcity of the latter, deter some MNEs.

These implementation difficulties are not found in all MNEs, however. Some MNEs appear to have far fewer problems in obtaining executives willing to spend most of their careers in subsidiaries. The sources of their success include differences in control systems, executive recruitment policies, promotion and compensation patterns, and perceived subsidiary autonomy. In addition, there is a strong suggestion that most MNEs have great difficulties managing both technologically adept executives and politically adept executives in the same organization. It appears that organizational structures, as well as promotion and reporting relationships, cannot easily adjust to dealing with such diametrically opposed executives. In a technology-driven MNE, executives with considerable political or country-based skills often find themselves in ineffectual staff positions. Such executives seem to be more active and to hold line positions in MNEs where knowledge of domestic markets, distribution channels, and so forth is the driving force behind the company, as in the consumer packaged-foods industry, for example.

While consumer-driven firms seem to be the main benefactors of the politically adept executive, the technology-driven MNEs do not automatically suffer from increased intervention as a result of their absence. The reason, of course, lies in the latters' use of changing technology as a source of bargaining power, a defense infrequently available to consumer-driven firms.

Successful MNEs are able either to accommodate both kinds of executives in the same organization, or recognize clearly their intolerance for such accommodation and behave accordingly. These latter firms decide which kind of executive their firm needs and then organize to keep a steady supply available. Consumer-driven MNEs hire, train, and promote politically skilled executives with local market knowledge who defend the subsidiary primarily through the addition of new products and adroit intervention forecasting. These executives tend to remain in particular subsidiaries for long periods. Technology-driven firms concentrate on executives who are good "transporters of technology," as one MNE called them, and who tend to treat the world as one market. These MNEs tend to develop subsidiaries with export markets, complex technologies, and proprietary sourcing.

The second problem that makes MNEs hesitate to implement the defensive strategy is the complete reversal it represents from the traditional MNE response to intervention. For much of their history most MNEs responded to threats by *reducing* their asset exposure and speeding up profit repatriation. They justified this response by referring to the highly unpredictable nature of government intervention. This response also paralleled the behavior—and won the approval—of international bankers. In contrast, new subsidiary defense strategies call for *increased* investment when intervention threatens.

Many MNEs also find the decision to increase the managerial and technical capabilities of subsidiary personnel to have a double edge. Because these capabilities can be partially acquired by potential interventionists by hiring away personnel, MNEs sometimes see the training of subsidiary personnel as a threat to their bargaining power. Some MNEs think it is best to withhold training. In reality, though, such "leakage" of capabilities and technology from the subsidiary to potential interventionists will always occur without regard to the level of capabilities. Unfortunately, the MNE does not have an option, because withholding training and new equipment only serves to reduce the MNE's bargaining power even further.

Optimum Political Strategy

The choice of political strategy is determined by the political profile the subsidiary exhibits. This political profile seems to be determined by the size of the firm and the firm's strategic importance to the host country. Action against a large employer provides greater publicity impact, allows greater opportunities for implementing political directives and, in some nations, satisfies trade unions. For similar reasons, firms in strategically important industries—such as natural resources, banking, insurance, and public utilities—also have a high political profile.

The political strategy for very-high-profile firms tries to affect the political as well as the economic costs of intervention. Political involvement is necessary because raising the *economic* costs of intervention alone is frequently not sufficient to offset the high *political* benefits that accrue to interventionists. Under this strategy, some MNEs establish joint ventures involving firms from several nations, and use similarly syndicated project finance. This transnational web of MNEs and financial institutions, which raises the political as well as the economic cost of intervention, is common.[5] The object of such equity and financial participation is to involve nations that are the export markets, suppliers, bankers, political supporters, and aid donors of the host

---

[5]For further discussion of this role of project finance, see T. H. Moran with Debbie Havens Maddox, *Transnational Corporations in the Copper Industry* (New York: UN Center on Transnational Corporations, 1981); and Moran's outline of possible complications facing U.S. MNEs in F. Ghadar, S. J. Kobrin, and T. H. Moran, eds., Managing International Risk (Washington, D.C.: The Landegger Program, Georgetown University, 1983), p. 164.

government. This type of deterrent is subject to much criticism from host governments, but it appears to be an effective defense for firms with a high political profile.

Most subsidiaries, however, do not have a high political profile and, hence, do not automatically provide large political benefits to interventionists. Unlike the high-profile ones, these subsidiaries have a whole range of political strategies available to them. They may remain uninvolved, initiating no contacts with the host government and, when interaction is necessary, use the local board of trade instead of direct interaction. The more active alternative involves the maintenance of working relationships with several ministers and senior civil servants.

The optimum political behavior strategy is, again, determined by company characteristics. Research in several nations suggests that only small, nondescript subsidiaries should be politically noninvolved. Here the ability of the firm to remain anonymous is *enhanced* by its lack of political involvement. But all others, it is suggested, will benefit from political involvement. Politicians and civil servants can be briefed on the MNE's contribution to the subsidiary's success—its bargaining power. More importantly, such relationships can help the subsidiary identify proponents of intervention, providing the opportunity to offer arrangements satisfactory to the interventionist but less costly to the subsidiary.[6]

Ineffective Strategies

The rhetorical preoccupations of politicians, civil servants, and most critics of MNEs are not useful guides to the formulation of successful strategies. Cries for appropriate technology, for the creation of foreign exchange, for an often-cited but undefined good corporate citizenship, for licensing (as discussed in Chapter 6), and for joint partnerships do not lead to a parallel reduction in the intervention experiences of MNEs that so accommodate their hosts.

While some of these recommended strategies are harmless, others have the opposite effect and cause governments to intervene at an accelerated rate. Some MNEs respond to requests for "appropriate technology" only to find that their labor-intensive, low-to-moderate technology facility has been taken over, or duplicated, by a domestic firm. Voluntary joint ventures, while providing several advantages to both partners, also provide an ideal opportunity for an active domestic partner to learn the latest technology and management skills, hence reducing the MNE's bargaining power (as discussed in Chapter 7). Some domestic partners go on to compete with their MNE partners. Italian scooter manufacturers are facing competition from their Indian ex-partners, as are U.S. petrochemical firms from South Korean ex-partners.

To offset this leakage of technology in joint ventures, the defensive strategies are usually restricted to intra-MNE sourcing and, to a lesser extent, exporting to protected markets. However, some firms have maintained complete control over subsidiary joint ventures by continually changing the production processes—reducing

---

[6]For a more general discussion of the organizational issues involved when MNEs deal with host governments, see Amir Mahini, "The Management of Government Relations in U.S. Multinationals," D.B.A. dissertation, Harvard Business School, 1982.

the ability of local personnel to gain experience by restricting participation in local research activities to expatriates.

Modifications to the Basic Strategy

While the basic defense strategy is similar for most manufacturing MNEs, modifications are required, depending on the host country. The main source of the variation is the difference in bargaining power of each host nation. For many reasons, individual nations are at different positions on the bargaining power ladder. One could also postulate that nations move up the bargaining power ladder at different rates, as we have observed with the development of some of the newly industrialized countries.

Other modifications to the basic strategy are possible if MNEs have unique skills or business strategies. MNEs without access to more-complex technology, export markets, or proprietary intrafirm sourcing resort to innovative techniques for increasing their bargaining power. This might include, for example, always linking up with an aggressive domestic entrepreneur.

Implications for MNE Parents

The proposed strategy for defending the subsidiary affects the MNE's allocation of human, technical, and capital resources and introduces new managerial activities to the parent's organization.[7] The new strategy must also be institutionalized, or integrated into the MNE's organization.

The greatest implication of this strategy is that each subsidiary will require a greater amount of capital (machinery, working capital, and the like) and a larger number of better-trained technicians and managers. For the majority of MNEs, such increased subsidiary needs can be so high as to be unaffordable. They face a choice of retaining either the existing number of intervention-prone subsidiaries around the world or of supporting fewer subsidiaries but with an effective defense strategy. The trade-off is difficult for many MNEs and, again, runs counter to the intuitively appealing strategy of a larger diversified portfolio of subsidiaries. The subsidiary defense strategy, on the other hand, calls for a smaller portfolio containing less risky subsidiaries.

New activities, such as intervention management, have to fit into existing organizational and decision-making structures of the MNE to be effective. While the existing organizational structures may not be optimal, organizations do not easily change structures to accommodate new activities. Those MNEs implementing this strategy find that requests for bargaining power upgrades are presented in much the same way as capital budget requests. However, the similarities end there. The staff in most MNEs have little experience in evaluating such bargaining upgrade requests;

---

[7]For a description of how MNE parents vary in their management of intervention, see Y. L. Doz and C. K. Prahalad, "How MNEs Cope with Host Government Intervention," *Harvard Business Review,* March-April 1980.

moreover, most upgrades will affect other subsidiaries as well. Export and sourcing strategics, for example, can affect the product offering of the whole MNE system.

Multinational enterprises that trade in machinery, products, processes, and managers will experience a significant increase in intracompany trade under the defense strategy. Consequently, another managerial activity is the coordination of subsidiaries that now trade with each other. Agreements must be made on product characteristics, price, and quantity, and when problems arise they must be perceived as being equitably resolved.

Several MNEs have centered many of the management activities in newly revived area headquarters. This is the point in the organization where there appears to be the best supply of pertinent product and country information, all of which is necessary to perform the allocation and integration activities required of the defense strategy.

While MNEs vary in how they defend their subsidiaries from intervention, some patterns are emerging. The patterns can be observed in Exhibit 12–2, which divides MNEs into those that follow a global strategy and those that follow a multinational strategy.

Summary

A better understanding of the changing world of government-MNE relations has prompted a shift in political risk analysis. For the multinational manufacturing firms, assessing the vulnerability of each subsidiary to intervention is now far more important than assessing broad political shocks. While very few nations offer a safe haven from intervention, certain kinds of subsidiaries do. This chapter suggests that MNEs should decrease their emphasis on choosing the right country and, instead, develop strategies to defend individual subsidiaries from intervention.

There are several strategies that constitute a successful defense. Strategies calling for manufacturing activities requiring continued MNE technological or managerial input, intra-MNE sourcing of proprietary components and end products, and exporting are the more successful ones. The success of these strategies is facilitated as new processes and products are introduced, technological upgrades take place, and scale efficiencies allow for intra-MNE sourcing and exporting. These strategies increase the cost to interventionists of unilaterally increasing their share of a foreign-owned operation.

They have their roots in a defense system, and they do not always produce short-term financial or technical benefits. One may have to say no to the engineers and the finance department and, instead, structure the subsidiary's activities in a way that always leaves the MNE with something to offer either when the technology matures or after a coup, when vulnerability is inevitable.

Another requirement of a successful defense is to adapt the subsidiary's political behavior to its political profile. Only extremely strong or small subsidiaries without any strategic importance can afford the luxury of avoiding political interaction.

Like most strategies, implementation is a difficult phase. Capital, machinery, technicians, and managers who are well trained and politically adept; export markets; and area coordinators are the scarce resources necessary to make the defense

EXHIBIT 12–2   **Kind of Multinational Enterprise**

	Global	*Multinational*
Defense strategy	State-of-the-art technology Exports Intra-MNE sourcing	Introducing new products Better intervention forecasting
Political strategy	Lower priority	High local political knowledge and interaction
Staffing	Short-term, technologically oriented	Long-term, politically oriented

strategy work. While the scarcity of resources poses surmountable obstacles for most MNEs, the bigger obstacle is the psychological turnaround this defense mechanism represents. While traditional strategies call for asset reduction and country diversification, this new strategy usually demands an increase in the assets at stake in each country, often necessitating a commensurate decrease in the number of countries served. MNEs, for good business reasons, have difficulty accommodating dramatically different strategic responses. Change will be slow.

MNEs that compete globally will find this defense strategy relatively easy to accommodate and implement. Three popular means of defense—intra-MNE sourcing, exports, and state-of-the-art technology—are characteristic of such MNEs. MNEs that compete on a country-by-country basis tend to rely on introducing new products, building alliances with domestic firms, and better forecasting of when upgrades are necessary.

The importance of proper management of intervention is emphasized when one considers that the same qualities that make some nations attractive to MNEs also increase those nations' bargaining power and, hence, their tendency to intervene. If MNEs react to intervention by withdrawing or reducing their exposure, or by trying to confront and obstruct host government policies, they may foreclose potentially attractive investment opportunities.

The results of such a strategy for the host nation are higher average levels of technology transfer and more foreign direct investment. For the MNE, the results include lower level of intervention, stable profits, and less-frustrated executives. Upon closer examination, for MNEs accustomed to serious competition in their home market, this is a more familiar strategy than the traditional one of forecasting political stability and ideology.

Conclusion

With this chapter, we have come full circle. From our introductory chapters on the global environment and internationalization, through the entire process of multinational management, our constant emphasis has been on ways of understanding and improving the practice of international management. As this chapter has demonstrated, even political risk, viewed by so many as totally beyond the control of the MNE, can in part be managed.

Our desire to see improved international management practice is motivated by much more than the needs of the existing or potential individual manager or firm. Well-managed international businesses can be an engine of international development, a means of responsibly improving the standard of living around the world.

Supplementary Reading

Boddewyn, Jean J. "Political Aspects of MNE Theory." *Journal of International Business Studies* 19, No. 3, 1988.

Brewer, Thomas L. "An Issue-Area Approach to the Analysis of MNE-Government Relations." *Journal of International Business Studies* 23, No. 2, 1992.

Harvey, Michael G. "A Survey of Corporate Programs for Managing Terrorist Threats." *Journal of International Business Studies* 24, No. 3, 1993.

Makhija, Mona. "Government Intervention in the Venezuelan Petroleum Industry: An Empirical Investigation of Political Risk." *Journal of International Business Studies* 24, No. 3, 1993.

Miller, Kent D. "A Framework for Integrated Risk Management in International Business." *Journal of International Business Studies* 23, No. 2, 1992.

Minor, Michael S. "The Demise of Expropriation as an Instrument of LDC Policy, 1980–92." *Journal of International Business Studies* 25, No. 1, 1994, pp. 177–88.

II CASES ON INTERNATIONALIZATION

1   DIALOGUE: RUSSIA

In November 1987, Joe Ritchie was in Russia meeting with Pyotr and Tanya Zrelov to discuss the creation of a joint venture to produce and distribute computer equipment and computer software in Russia and abroad. Ritchie, an American, had no previous business experience in the computer industry or the Soviet Union, but was keen to create a venture with the Zrelovs, whom Ritchie judged to be extremely bright, hardworking, and trustworthy. The Zrelovs' plan called for Ritchie to contribute up to US$5 million for a minority (perhaps 25 percent) share in the joint venture.

The Situation in the USSR in 1987

Mikhail Gorbachev became General Secretary of the Communist Party in 1985 and was handed a country rapidly approaching an economic crisis. The USSR's Net Material Product[1] had decreased from 4.3% in 1976-1980 to 1.6% in 1987. External debt had increased in the USSR from US$28.9 billion dollars in 1985 to US$39.2 billion dollars in 1987. To try to prevent the USSR from entering into an economic crisis, Gorbachev started a program of wide-sweeping economic reforms called *Perestroika*. This was accompanied by *Glasnost*, a program of increased political freedom for the Russian people. As part of *Perestroika*, in 1987 the Soviet Union passed a new law on foreign investment that allowed Western firms to form joint ventures in

Carl Fey prepared this case under the supervision of Professor Peter Killing solely to provide material for class discussion. The case is not intended to illustrate either effective or ineffective handling of a managerial situation. Certain names and other identifying information may have been disguised to protect confidentiality. The authors would like to thank Tanya Zrelova and Joe Ritchie for their help with this case. Copyright © 1995, The University of Western Ontario.

[1]Net material product is a measure commonly used in Eastern Block countries to measure output from the "productive sphere." The measure is based on the Marxian distinction between productive and unproductive work. All manufacturing and a few services (e.g., tourism) are considered part of the "productive sphere."

all of its republics. The law provided joint ventures with several advantages over other types of business, the most important of which was a two-year tax holiday which began the first year the joint venture made a profit. Russia, which had a population of over 140 million, was the largest of the Soviet republics and was judged by most people to be the most attractive to foreign investment. The largest cities in Russia were Moscow and St. Petersburg, with over 8.5 and 4.5 million people respectively. Russia had a Gross National Product (GNP) of US$1,268 billion in 1987. GNP per capita was US$8,556. Inflation was 5.6% and unemployment was 0%. Russia covered 6.6 million square miles of land which is almost twice the size of the United States. However, investing in the Soviet Union was clearly risky and presented many problems because the Soviet Union did not possess a market economy.

Joe Ritchie

A philosophy major in college, Joe Ritchie's first jobs after graduation were as a bus driver and a policeman. Then in 1977, at the age of 30, Ritchie and three friends decided to start a small commodities-trading firm named Chicago Research and Trading (CRT). He had so little money when he started the company that he had to wear a borrowed suit to business meetings. Ten years later, CRT had become the world's largest options-trading company and the envy of the rest of the industry due to its fast growth and consistent excellent performance. There were two apparent keys to CRT's success. First, the company's trading was based on mathematical models which had been developed by Ritchie, who was described as a "natural math genius" despite never having taken an advanced math course. Second, Ritchie created a unique atmosphere at CRT which made people feel relaxed, empowered, and part of a team. By 1987, Ritchie had accumulated substantial personal wealth.[2]

In the mid 1980s, Ritchie was taken with the idea of starting a joint venture in a country emerging from communism. In 1985, he made three trips to China, but in spite of many meetings with potential partners, he did not find anyone whom he thought appropriate. In July, 1987, Ritchie took a trip to Russia, primarily as a vacation, but also out of interest to see how Russia was changing. In the back of his mind he was still searching for an appropriate partner for a joint venture. Ritchie recalled:

> I wanted to start a joint venture with Russia, not solely to make money, but because I was intrigued by the chance to show that business can work well without people pursuing their own unbridled self-interest. I wanted to demonstrate another way of organizing people, which I have found works very well in the U.S., but which is quite different from the way most U.S. companies work. I wanted to show that you can follow the golden rule, treat people well, and think about what is good for society, and still do well in business.

---

[2]Much of the information for this paragraph was obtained from "Money Machine", *The Wall Street Journal*, February 8, 1988.

Ritchie did not actively pursue finding a joint venture partner, and he did not meet anyone by chance who would make a good partner. He did, however, find Russia interesting and decided to return in September 1987. This time John Nikolopolus, a friend of Ritchie's who was an American journalist currently living in Russia, told Ritchie that he thought he knew a couple who would be ideal for Ritchie to start a joint venture with. On September 10, Nikolopolus arranged for Ritchie and Tanya and Pyotr Zrelov to meet. From the very beginning Joe Ritchie and the Zrelovs got along well, and Ritchie thought he might have found the partners he was looking for. The Zrelovs intrigued Ritchie because they looked like young lovers, despite being in their early 40s. Ritchie was impressed by the way this couple worked side by side very peacefully with each other. They appeared to be excited about discovering their new world, and they seemed to be the type of people who would rather lose money than let down a friend or participate in an unethical act. These were exactly the type of people Ritchie had been seeking.

Ritchie, believing that people are what make a business work, considered that finding the correct people to run the joint venture was his most important task and that deciding what the joint venture would do was secondary. As a result, Ritchie was willing to start a joint venture in whatever field these "ideal people" thought made sense, as long as it seemed to have some promise for the future. Ritchie explained his focus on trust as follows:

> If you are going to start a joint venture with someone in a country that is as physically and culturally distanced from the U.S. as Russia is and you think that you are going to successfully exercise much control over the business, you are dreaming. That is why I knew that if I were going to make a venture with Russia work, I had to find a partner that I implicitly trusted, so that trust became a non-issue. This was the case for the Zrelovs.

Thus, once Ritchie had found the correct people to work with he gave them trust and autonomy. Ritchie believed that if employees want to cheat you, they will find a way, and therefore there is no point in trying to make many complicated agreements and exert tight control over employees. Such tactics, according to Ritchie, made people less productive. Further, he believed that empowering employees could often act as a stronger control mechanism than exerting tight control over them, because they would feel that they did not want to let down the owner who he had placed so much trust in them.

Pyotr and Tanya Zrelov

Because the Zrelovs were well connected, Nikolopolus was confident that they would be able to find good organizations to serve as the Russian partners for the joint venture. Pyotr Zrelov was the designer and director of information systems at Kamaz, Russia's largest truck manufacturer. Tanya Zrelov was a computer scientist at the Russian Academy of Sciences. They both had Ph.D.'s in computer science and were in their mid 40s. Pyotr and Tanya Zrelov, both friendly and outgoing, were hard workers who were willing to take risks. They also appeared to be natural leaders.

Developing the Relationship

Nikolopolus had arranged for Ritchie and the Zrelovs to meet at a telecommunications company where Pyotr Zrelov had some negotiations dealing with the purchase of new telecommunications systems for Kamaz. They did not know that this meeting was set up or that Ritchie was interested in their running his joint venture. To the Zrelovs, it simply appeared as if Ritchie and his colleagues were waiting in the telecommunications firm for a later appointment. After Ritchie had observed the Zrelovs in negotiations, he decided he liked what he saw. When the Zrelovs were finished, Ritchie introduced himself, explained that he was interested in starting a joint venture, and stated that he would like to get to know the Zrelovs better, as he thought they might be good people to run this joint venture.

The Zrelovs and Ritchie talked for two hours at the telecommunications company. From the very first meeting, the Zrelovs and Ritchie got along very well. They discovered that they all not only wanted to be in business, but that they wanted to help make the world a better place to live as well. At the end of their discussion, they agreed to meet for dinner two days later. At Ritchie's request, John Nikolopolus accompanied him to this meeting and many of Ritchie's future meetings in Russia. Nikolopolus served not only as a language translator, but more importantly, as a cultural translator, explaining to Ritchie what different Russian actions really meant. At dinner the Zrelovs persuaded Ritchie to extend his trip to Russia and come to visit the Kamaz factory, 1000 km from Moscow. Ritchie accepted this offer. At the time, Ritchie thought that the Zrelovs would propose a joint venture for manufacturing trucks. Certainly, this was not an area that Ritchie knew anything about and it was not the first field in which he would have chosen to start a joint venture. However, Ritchie was primarily concerned about finding the correct partners for his joint venture, and not about what the joint venture would do.

Pyotr Zrelov had recently been assigned the large task of implementing from the start an information system at Kamaz. He thought it would make sense to develop this project on a larger scale by participating in a joint venture, which could bring in additional expertise to assist with the project and also provide a similar service for other companies.

When Ritchie arrived at Kamaz, Ritchie was pleasantly surprised that the Zrelovs wanted to start a joint venture that would produce computer equipment and computer software rather than trucks. Fortunately, Ritchie knew much more about computers than trucks. In addition to starting the joint venture to serve the needs of Kamaz, the Zrelovs argued that there were other good reasons to start a joint venture to produce and distribute computer software and computer equipment. Russia had many highly skilled computer programmers who would be willing to work for very low salaries by Western standards. Further, the Zrelovs argued that these computer programmers currently did not have access to adequate computing equipment or an environment with enough freedom to reach their creative potential. The Zrelovs also recognized the vast need for personal computer equipment in Russia. They expected the market for personal computer equipment in Russia to expand rapidly in the next few years. Ritchie thought that the Zrelovs' ideas and logic sounded good.

After spending three days at Kamaz, Ritchie had to return to the United States, but he told the Zrelovs to develop their ideas about the joint venture, and promised to return to Russia in two months.

The November Visit

On November 5, 1987, Ritchie returned to Russia, and the Zrelovs further explained their ideas for the joint venture including who the Russian partners would be. The Zrelovs proposed that the Russian partners would be Kamaz, Vneshtechnika, Moscow State University, Central Institute for the Study of the Economy and Mathematics, General Demonstration Computer Center of the Central Exhibition Center of the USSR, and the Space Research Institute. Ritchie was impressed that the Zrelovs had found such well-known and influential partners for the joint venture; but as far as he was concerned, his real partner was the Zrelovs, and it would be up to them to manage the others. Ritchie commented:

> If we go ahead with this, our joint venture will be one of the first, in fact maybe *the* first, U.S./Soviet joint venture in existence. Time is of the essence. There are *four* personal computers in Moscow State University right now. Four! If Pyotr walks in there in three months with 100 personal computers that we have shipped in from the U.S., he can completely captivate the best computer people in the place, and have them all working for him.

At the end of the visit, the Zrelovs asked Ritchie if he would sign the statement of intent shown in Exhibit 1.

EXHIBIT 1   Protocol of Intentions between Kamaz (USSR) and CRT (USA) on the Subject of Forming the Joint Stock Company Dialogue

---

Moscow, 27 October 1987

Taking into consideration the importance of forming a joint venture on the territory of the USSR and trying to promote further cooperation and mutual understanding between USA and USSR, Kamaz and CRT are establishing the following intentions:

1. Object
The main item of cooperation is to form on the territory of the USSR the joint venture company and for it to produce personal computers and different software and to sell these products in the USSR, USA, and in markets in third world countries.

2. The Main Product
The main products of the joint stock company are personal computers and different software for them (made to order or worked out by Soviet participants for their own aims).

3. Organization of the Joint Venture
The starting capital is needed for us to form a joint venture. The amount of starting capital would be discussed on the next negotiations taking into considerations the necessity of providing the main activities of the joint venture.

The stock of the partners should be not less than 51% and the stock of the firm should be not more than 49% of the starting capital. (Joe *Ritchie interpreted this to mean that firm employees could never own more than 49% of the firm.*)

3.1 From the side of USSR the following organizations are shareholders of the joint venture: Kamaz, Moscow State University, Space Research Institute, Central Institute for the Study of Economy and Mathematics, All Union Foreign Trade Organization

---

EXHIBIT 1   (CONCLUDED)

"Vneshtechnika", and the General Demonstration and Testing Computer Center of the Exhibition of Economic Achievements of the USSR. The participation of these organizations is determined by the charter of the joint stock company. The number of these organizations is determined in the charter of the joint venture. The number of shareholders could be increased.

3.2 The Soviet side would offer the following as stock:

- People for producing software
- Capacity for producing personal computers
- Office for the representatives of CRT during the time of their stay in Moscow

3.3 CRT would offer the following as stock:

- Starting capital
- The delivery of the first lot of personal computers (300)
- Organization of the trade
- Teaching and consulting in the field of trade
- Equipping the office in Moscow

4. The Planning of the Amount of Production

Year	Personal Computers	Software (in Mil. Rubles)	Others
1988	3000	.5	1.4
1989	5000	1.0	3.0
1990	5000	3.0	5.7
1991	10000	10.0	10.0

5. Organization of the Main Activities of the Joint Venture

The following items would be used during the preparation of the charter of the joint venture:

- The property of the joint venture will be estimated in rubles at agreed prices taking into consideration the prices of the world market.
- The joint venture will be planning its activities proceeding from the demand on the trading markets and currency resources of the partners.
- Foreign trade operations will be done by the joint venture itself or with the help of the Soviet foreign-trade organizations. The realization of the products to the Soviet consumers will be done with the help of the Soviet trade organizations and will be estimated at rubles in agreed prices taking into consideration the prices on the world market.
- In general the personnel of the joint venture will be formed from the Soviet citizens. Management of the joint venture will be done by the administration board and the board of directors.
- The setting of the personnel will be done by mutual consent of the both sides.
- The administration board is the leading authority of the joint venture. The economic operation of the joint venture will be controlled by the board of directors. Only the citizens of the USSR could be either head of the administration board or board of directors.
- Conditions of paying salary, work, and rest are regulated according to Soviet laws.
- The application of the same laws is extended to the foreign citizens except in the question of paying the salary. This items would be specially discussed.
- While signing the contract the list of positions and quantity of the foreign specialists to be involved in the work of the joint venture will be also specially discussed.
- The responsibility of the joint venture is limited with all of its property. The work of the joint venture will be organized according to the laws of the USSR, according to the charter of the contract about forming the joint venture.

2   KENNY ROGERS ROASTERS IN CHINA (A)

Situation

It was mid-October 1995 and Tony Wang, President of Franchise Investment Corporation of Asia (FICA), had just returned to Hong Kong from a one week visit to Beijing. FICA had earlier in the year been granted the franchise rights for Kenny Rogers Roasters (KRR), a rotisserie chicken restaurant concept, for both Beijing and Shanghai. While Wang was eager to move forward, serious concerns had emerged over the challenges of doing business in China. Just as most foreign companies had looked to local partners to help ameliorate some of these concerns, Wang had begun joint venture discussions with three companies. Although each potential partner appeared eager to work with FICA, Wang was wondering whether the time was right to proceed and if so, with which company.

KRR Overview

The driving force behind KRR was John Y. Brown, an entrepreneur with a long history in the food service industry. In 1964, Brown, who at the time was a 29-year-old Kentucky lawyer, and his partner, 60-year-old Jack Massey, purchased *Kentucky Fried Chicken* from 74-year-old Harland Sanders for $U.S. 2 million. Over the next 5 years the partners added 1,000 new stores and grew sales by an average of 96 percent per year. Observers attributed this growth to two main factors: (1) the company's reliance on less costly franchise expansion over company-owned stores, and (2) Brown's ability to select hard charging and entrepreneurial franchisees. KFC was sold to Heublen Inc. in 1971 for $U.S. 275 million, making both partners wealthy men.

This case was prepared by Professor Allen J. Morrison in collaboration with Professor J. Stewart Black and Tanya Spyridakis. Additional assistance was provided by Jan Visser. The case study is not intended to illustrate either effective or ineffective handling of a managerial situation. Copyright © 1996, Thunderbird-The American Graduate School of International Management.

During the 1970s Brown went on to become Governor of the State of Kentucky and owner of three professional basketball teams including the *Boston Celtics*. In 1979 he married 1971 Miss America, Phyllis George. During the early 1980s Brown helped launch *Miami Subs* and *Roadhouse Grill* franchises and bankrolled his wife's *Chicken by George* line of prepared chicken sold in grocery stores.

By the late 1980s, Brown was becoming increasingly convinced of the enormous market potential for roasted chicken. The health craze that swept the United States in the 1980s significantly increased the demand for lighter, nonfried food options. This affected many segments of the food industry, and the poultry industry was no exception. Many restaurant owners began investing in rotisserie ovens and introducing more healthy menus.

In looking for a new way to grab the customer's attention, Brown thought it a natural to team with long-time friend Kenny Rogers. Kenny Rogers, once described as "the most popular singer in America," had a career that spanned more than three decades, half of which as a solo artist. Rogers's popularity manifested itself in the many awards and honors that he had received over the years: three Grammies, 11 People's Choice Awards, 18 American Music Awards, five Country Music Association Awards, eight Academy of Country Music Awards, four platinum albums, five multi-platinum albums, one platinum single, and numerous gold albums and singles. Rogers also dabbled in several businesses including a partnership in Silver Dollar City, in Branson, Missouri considered country music's capital. When Brown came up with the concept of a rotisserie chicken restaurant chain, Rogers was very enthusiastic.

> When I saw this concept, I thought it was so outstanding I was willing to put my reputation on the line, not just as an endorser, but as an owner and partner. . . I believe nonfried chicken is the wave of the 90s, and working with folks who made fried chicken a billion dollar business gives me the confidence we are doing it right.

Kenny Rogers Roasters (KRR) began operations on January 17, 1991, in Louisville, Kentucky, and opened its first restaurant in August of that year in Coral Gables, Florida. The menu: citrus and herb-marinated wood roasted chicken and about a dozen side dishes such as mashed potatoes and gravy, corn-on-the-cob, baked beans, and pasta salad. Growth was rapid. From an original group of five people, the company grew to include a corporate staff of more than 100. By late 1995, the company had moved headquarters to Ft. Lauderdale, Florida, and had over 310 stores. KRR operated in approximately 35 U.S. states, had more than a dozen stores in Canada and had at least one store in Greece, Cyprus, Israel, Malaysia, Korea, the Philippines, Japan, Jordan, and Singapore. Company plans called for the addition of almost 1,200 new stores in the United States and 240 stores internationally by 2002.

The Rotisserie Chicken Business

The market's switch to rotisserie chicken did not escape the competition. In 1993, KFC spent $100 million to roll out its Colonel's Rotisserie Gold in all 5,100 of its stores in the United States. Rotisserie chicken constituted about 25 percent of KFC sales in company-owned stores by the end of 1995. In all, KFC enjoyed a 58 percent share of the retail chicken industry, and gross sales of over $3.5 billion. Other fast-food restaurants, noting the trend, also attempted to expand into the nonfried market. For example, Popeye's Famous Chicken entered the nonfried market despite its lack of capital; it featured a roasted chicken that could be cooked in the same ovens as its biscuits. Boston Market (formerly known as Boston Chicken) was another up-and-coming competitor in the rotisserie chicken segment. Opening its first store in 1985, by 1993 the company had 166 stores in approximately 25 states, and sales of $154 million (more than triple its 1992 sales). By the end of 1995, Boston Market had become a public company with over 825 stores operating (none outside the U.S.) and was opening a new store each business day.

While sales of rotisserie chicken were still considerably smaller ($700 million vs. $6 billion for fried chicken in 1993), advocates of nonfried chicken firmly believed that the gap would close within ten years. Statistics confirmed the growing popularity of nonfried chicken in the United States: sales of fried chicken consumed outside the home grew an average of 3.5 percent from 1989 to 1995, while sales of nonfried chicken grew an average of 10.75 percent in the same period. Annual growth in per capita chicken consumption between 1984 and 1994 was 38.5 percent.

Despite its rapid growth, rotisserie chicken had several drawbacks. Uncooked rotisserie chicken had a shorter shelf life than fried chicken. Rotisserie chicken took 75 to 90 minutes to cook compared to 30 minutes for fried chicken. Additionally, a cooked rotisserie chicken needed moisture and would spoil if kept under a heat lamp for too long; this, however, posed no problem for fried chicken. Finally, customer demand would often be greater than supply in peak hours which was difficult for rotisserie chicken vendors due to the longer cooking times.

Kenny Rogers Roasters

By 1995 KRR was still a privately held company, with no immediate plans to go public. The equity breakdown was approximately John Y. Brown, Jr. 28 percent; Kenny Rogers 14.5 percent; and a group of Malaysian investors 35 percent; various friends of Brown and Rogers held the remaining 22.5 percent. Brown served as the company's CEO and Chairman of the Board. Rogers sat on the board of directors and, though he was not directly involved in running the company, attended many meetings and assisted in promoting the company. In building his management team, Brown recruited several people with whom he had worked in his days at KFC. Other management talent was recruited from fast-food chains such as Wendy's, Burger King, Pizza Hut, Arby's, and McDonald's.

In the United States, KRR's restaurants averaged 2800 square feet in size, with seating capacity for 80 to 100 people. The stores had a country-western motif and were decorated with memorabilia from Rogers's career. Television monitors were also located throughout the restaurant showing customized music videos featuring performances by Rogers and other country and western entertainers. Advertising and promotional messages were interspersed with the music videos. A signature wood-fire rotisserie with surrounding wood piles were placed in full view of the customer. The serving counter was buffet-like in style, with a wide range of side dishes kept warm in a glass display case. Servers on the other side of the counter put together plates for customers based on their choice of entree and side dishes.

All menu items at KRR restaurants were prepared on-site. The chicken was marinated overnight and roasted the next day over a hard-wood fire to an internal temperature of about 180°. Most side dishes were made from scratch, though a few items were prepared from mixes developed at the company's training and development center near the corporate headquarters. The labor-intensive nature of KRR was not without its downside; labor costs averaged between 26 and 27 percent of sales, food costs ran just under 30 percent.

A free-standing Kenny Rogers restaurant with a drive-through window generally went through 1,800 chickens a week and generated approximately $1 million in annual sales. By 1995, take-out orders comprised about 45 to 50 percent of sales; the company's goal was to increase this to around 60. Total KRR revenues in 1995 were estimated at $321 million, up from $68.7 million in 1993 and $150 million in 1994.

KRR Franchises

From the very beginning, franchising played a big part of the company's expansion. By 1995, franchise stores accounted for about 85 percent of KRR's 310 stores. All of KRR's international stores were owned by franchisees. Though the company had solicited a few of its franchisees, most franchisees had approached KRR. The company carefully screened all franchisees for previous restaurant experience, especially multi-unit operations experience, references, credit rating, and net worth. KRR wanted franchisees who knew and liked the restaurant business, who were or had been in it, and who appreciated the difference the company was trying to make with customer service and product quality.

KRR set up *franchise* and *development* contracts. Both typically had a duration of twenty years. A franchise agreement was for a single store; a development agreement was for a specified number of restaurants, within a set time frame, in a designated area. When signing development agreements, KRR typically awarded territories in small clusters of five to 50 restaurants. The boundaries of the territory varied depending on the size and experience of the group or individual involved, as well as availability within the region requested.[1]

The costs involved in a franchise agreement included the initial franchise payment of $29,500; a royalty fee of 4.5 percent of gross sales; and contributions to the company advertising production fund, the national advertising fund, as well as a local or regional advertising fund of 0.75 percent, 2 percent, and (a minimum of) 3 percent of gross sales, respectively. The initial franchise fee was due upon signing the franchise agreement; all other fees were due monthly once the store was in operation. Fees related to a development agreement were similar to those of a franchise

---

[1]The franchising scheme of KRR's principal rival, Boston Market, differed considerably. Boston Market sold whole regions and provided up to 75 percent of its franchisees' financing. Boston Market did have an unusual caveat that accompanied the financing plan: After two years, Boston Market had the right to convert the unpaid debt into an ownership share in the franchise.

agreement. In addition to normal franchise fees, a developer was typically required to pay a development fee of $10,000 for each restaurant covered under the agreement. This fee was nonrefundable and was due (along with the full $29,500 for the first store to be built) upon signing the development agreement. The development fee was to be applied in equal portions as a credit against the initial franchise fee for each restaurant to be developed under the development agreement. The balance of each additional store's (within a development area) franchise fee was due as each store went into construction, according to the development schedule.

Company research showed that the average costs to build a new restaurant in the United States ranged from $560,000 to $672,000; the costs to convert an existing site ranged from $405,000 to $545,000. These costs included such expenses as property rental or payments, architectural and engineering fees, insurance, business licenses, equipment, furniture, signs, office supplies, opening inventory, and so forth.

Training and Development

KRR put great emphasis on training and provided franchisees and operators with three training courses. These courses took place at the company's training and development center located near corporate headquarters in Ft. Lauderdale, Florida. All expenses (travel, living, etc.) incurred in the training process were the responsibility of the franchisee. The first course was an optional three-day executive orientation program for all first-time franchisees and partners. The remaining two courses were not optional. All franchisees were required to certify and maintain a minimum of two managers for each store. The company's level one course for all managers was an intense four-week program held four to six weeks prior to the store's opening. Dubbed as KRR's version of boot camp, management trainees essentially lived with their trainer, learning all aspects of daily operations. Once a developer had opened a substantial number of stores within the designated territory, it was possible to apply for accreditation, that is, to set up its own level-one management training program. The second level of management training was required for any manager before being promoted to a general store manager. Held either before or after a store opening, this six-day program focused not so much on operational procedures, but rather on how to deal with the more sensitive issues of management, i.e., how to deal with staff members and customers, especially when there were problems.

In addition, for each new store opening, franchisees were provided an opening team to assist in the initial training of hourly employees. The size of the team and the duration of its stay depended on the number of stores the franchisee already had in operation. The opening team would be sent once KRR had received a "Certificate of Occupancy" and a completed "Pre-Opening Checklist" from the franchisee. The franchisee was responsible for making sure that the store was ready for pre-opening training, though the opening date of the store could be pushed back if the store was not ready.

In the United States, typically 60 to 65 hourly employees were hired for each new store. Of those initially hired, approximately 60 percent would quit within the first few months. KRR's training and development center designed a 12-part video training program which demonstrated proper operating procedures for equipment and preparation of food items. These videos were used to train new employees in all stores, both domestic and international.

Control Issues

Menu adjustments were a particular concern for international stores. Some side dishes did not go over well in various parts of the world. For example, baked beans with bacon was not served in Jordan and other Muslim countries. Franchisees were encouraged to offer alternative side dishes that would be better received in their country or region of the world, while still meeting the company's quality standards. Sometimes recipes of existing dishes had to be altered for regional tastes. Most notably sugar content had to be reduced for dishes served in the Asia–Pacific region where people had less of a "sweet tooth" than Americans. All new menu items or variations in recipes had to pre-approved by corporate headquarters.

In addition to approving menus, KRR developed standards and specifications for most of its food products and equipment. To ensure consistency, KRR approved suppliers of chickens, breads, spices, mixes, marinades, plastic products, packaging, and so forth, in each territory or country where the company operated. Generally, finding approved local suppliers for chickens and other major food products was not a problem. However, many overseas franchisees ordered such specialized products as marinades and packaging materials from KRR's contracted U.S. distributor.

In order to maintain constant communication between KRR's corporate office and any given store, franchisees were required to install computer systems in each store. This system allowed KRR to instantly receive information concerning sales of each restaurant, and, in turn, to provide franchisees with information necessary to prepare financial statements and better manage the restaurant. Also, the company had standard forms for use in such areas as inventory control, profit-and-loss control, and monitoring daily and weekly sales.

Tony Wang and KRR in China

KRR's efforts in China were spearheaded by Ta-Tung (Tony) Wang, a former KFC executive with considerable experience in the Far East. Wang was born in Sichuan province in the People's Republic of China in 1944 and raised in Taiwan. In the late 1960s he moved to the United States to complete graduate work. Upon graduation he took a management position with KFC in Louisville, Kentucky. A series of promotions culminated with Wang's appointment as KFC Vice President for Southeast Asia in 1986. The position, based in Singapore, charged Wang with aggressively expanding KFC throughout the Asia–Pacific region. Wang focused his efforts primarily on China, a country of 1.2 billion people with an undeveloped food service industry. In 1987, he gained considerable international notoriety by operating the first Western style fast food restaurant in China. The store was KFC's largest in the world and was located just opposite Mao's mausoleum off Tiananmen Square.

Wang credited the careful selection of joint venture partners as key in securing the store's prime location and in expediting the opening of the store. Three Chinese partners were selected and each played a different role in the start-up and ongoing operation of the store: Beijing Animal Production Bureau (which owned 10 percent of the joint venture) accessed locally grown chickens; Beijing Tourist Bureau (which had a 14 percent ownership position) helped with site selection, permits, lease issues and hiring; and the Bank of China (which had a 25 percent ownership position) assisted in converting soft currency renminbi profits to hard currency. Despite high chicken prices (KFC-approved chicken in China cost over $1 per pound, well over twice U.S. levels), the operation was a major success. In reflecting back on that time Wang noted: "We were the first Western quick service restaurant in any communist country. It was very exciting. There were crowds lining up outside the store in the morning even before we opened. It was not unusual for us to have to call the police to control the crowds."

After opening additional restaurants in China, in September, 1989, Tony Wang left KFC to become president of CP Food Services Co., a subsidiary of the Charoen Pokphand Group, the largest agri-business company in Asia. In September 1991, Wang moved back to the United States to become president of Grace Food Services, a subsidiary of W.R. Grace & Co. A year later Tony Wang left Grace to become president of Foodmaker International, the $1.2 billion parent company of Jack-in-the-Box and Chi-Chi's restaurants. Wang had a mandate to open 800 new restaurants over an 8-year period, primarily in the Pacific Rim. In January 1993, catastrophe struck when contaminated hamburgers were served at a Seattle Jack-in-the-Box restaurant. Although the tainted hamburger was traced to a California-based supplier, Foodmaker was hit with a series of costly lawsuits and devastating publicity. Sales nose-dived and, in order to conserve finances, the company's international expansion plan was shelved.

Wang sensed an important win-win opportunity for all and offered to continue the company's expansion using his own money. An agreement was struck whereby Wang's own company, QSR (Quick Service Restaurant), became a Jack-in-the-Box Master Licensee with franchise and development rights for 20 countries in the Middle East and Asia (including China but not Japan). The agreement with Foodmaker, which came into effect on January 1, 1994 and lasted 10 years, gave QSR complete control over the selection and development of all franchises within these 20 countries. QSR had the right to select stand alone franchisees, establish joint ventures with franchisees, or set itself up as a franchisee within any or all of the designated countries. Under the Master License agreement, Foodmaker and QSR split all franchise fees for Jack-in-the-Box restaurants. In assessing Foodmaker's rationale in setting up the Master License agreement, Wang commented: "this is a mutually beneficial concept for both parties. If they have the know-how but not the money, what have they got? They have a great concept but are not able to implement it internationally."

FICA (Franchise Investment Corporation of Asia)

Once Wang left Foodmaker, he began to explore other franchise investment opportunities in Asia. For assistance, Wang turned to American International Group, Inc.

(AIG), one of the largest U.S.-based insurance companies.[2] Wang had been discussing franchise investment concepts with several senior AIG (Asia) managers since the late 1980s. In 1990, AIG (Asia) formed FICA as a subsidiary company designed to pursue multiple franchise options and invited Wang to serve as its first president. Wang declined, saying that he thought it was premature at the time. Consequently, FICA was put on hold.

In early 1994, Wang reopened discussions with AIG and in January 1995 joined FICA as its president and co-owner. FICA's ownership was split between AIG (60 percent) and QSR (40 percent). Wang served as president and primary decision maker in an office which was established by FICA in Hong Kong. Wang commented on the ownership structure: "as president of FICA, I am also an employee of FICA. I am president because of my skills and contacts. But my 40 percent ownership is based on financial contribution."

FICA had a threefold mandate: (1) to develop and invest in franchise concepts in Asia, (2) to act as a consultant to franchisees in the region, and (3) to establish food processing and other franchise support/commissary functions. Primary emphasis focused on investing in established franchise concepts. The philosophy was explained by Wang:

> Every franchiser has a very strict non-compete clause for products in the same category. Our strategic plan was for FICA to become a multi-concept regional franchise investment and development company. We began to look at categories of products that did not compete.

After considerable effort, FICA signed far-reaching franchise agreements with Circle-K for both the Philippines and Thailand and with Carvel Ice Cream for China. By the fall of 1995, the company was continuing negotiations with these companies for additional franchise territories within Asia Pacific. In 1994, FICA also began investigating KRR in the context of a broader China strategy. (Economic and social trends for China are shown in Exhibit 1.) Wang explained why KRR seemed natural for China:

> We identified various franchise categories and one of those was chicken. I knew a lot of people at KRR who used to work for KFC. I knew John Brown and Loy Weston [former General Manager of KFC in Japan and for 18 months President of KRR Pacific]. Some of the best people who worked for KFC now work for KRR. I also knew Lenny Abelman, [KRR's newly appointed vice-president in charge of International Development] who I had used as a consultant while I was at Foodmaker. But beyond having a lot of contacts, KRR made good business sense for China. It represents American life style. It is not fast food like KFC or McDonald's. It is an entirely new category. Also, young people in China really like Kenny Rogers as a singer.

Wang's negotiations focused on gaining the franchise rights for KRR for both Shanghai and Beijing.

> I didn't need the rights to the whole country. Beijing and Shanghai are on the leading edge of China. I am sure that KRR will not partner with anyone else until they see what happens in Beijing and Shanghai. If they can get someone else to do it better, fine. But if I do a good job, why would John Brown want someone else to do it? In any case, Beijing and Shanghai are both huge.

---

[2]In 1994, AIG had net profits in excess of $4 billion on revenues in excess of $24 billion and assets of approximately $130 billion.

Exhibit 1 Economic and Social Trends in China

Economic Indicators	1989	1990	1991	1992	1993	1994	1995*	1996*	1997*	1998*	1999*
GNP at current market prices ($ bn)	424.8	369.9	380.1	435.9	544.6	477.2	525.9	569.6	616.7	670.4	730.2
Real GNP growth (%)	4.4	4.1	8.2	13.0	13.4	11.8	9.8	8.6	8.3	8.4	8.5
GNP, per capita ($)	380.0	324.0	330.0	374.0	462.0	399.0	434.0	463.0	494.0	530.0	569.0
Consumer price inflation (%)	17.5	1.6	3.0	5.4	13.0	25.0	18.0	12.0	11.5	11.5	11.0
Exchange rate (av.) Rmb: $ (official rate)	3.8	4.8	5.3	5.5	5.8	8.6	8.6	9.5	10.0	10.5	11.0
Av. growth rate in wages; urban workers (%)[a]	10.8	10.5	9.4	15.8	19.6	18.0	15.0	13.0	12.5	13.0	12.5

Demographics	1989	1990	1991	1992	1993	1994[b]
Urban population (billion)	295.4	301.9	305.4	323.7	333.5	
Rural population (billion)	831.6	841.4	852.8	848.0	851.7	
Total population (billion)	**1,127.0**	**1,143.3**	**1,158.2**	**1,171.7**	**1,185.2**	

[a]State enterprises only.
[b]Data not yet available.

Demographic and Social Trends	1991	1996*	2001*	Annual average % change 1991–2001*
Total population (billion)	1.15	1.13	1.31	1.3
Population growth rate (% per year)				1.3
Age profile (% of population)				
0–14	27.5	26.9	26.4	0.9
15–64	66.5	66.9	67.2	1.4
65+	6.2	6.4	6.4	2.0
Life expectancy (years)				
Male	66	67	68	N/A
Female	69			N/A
Literacy rate (% of population)				
10 years and over	80	82	84	N/A
Labor force (million)	584	645	712	2.0

*EIU estimates.

Source: These tables were compiled from China: *Country Report* and *Country Forecast*. Economist Intelligence Unit, 1995.

EXHIBIT 2   **FICA (Franchise Investment Corporation of Asia), 1995**

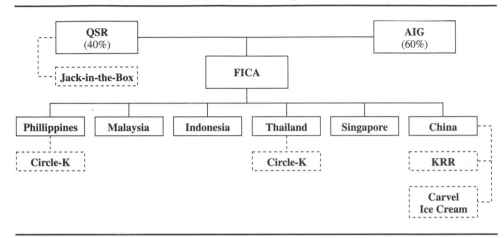

In the spring of 1995, FICA was granted the KRR rights for both Beijing and Shanghai. While FICA did not pay a fee for the KRR rights to these two cities, it did agree to pay an upfront franchise fee for each store based on opening 15 stores in total. According to Wang, the upfront franchise fees "were consistent with U.S. per-store fees discounted by an allowance for new market development." FICA's 1995 structure is presented in Exhibit 2.

Beyond franchise fees, Wang recognized that considerable money would be required to build the first KRR store. Costs were not directly comparable with U.S. levels. The location of the store, terms and conditions of the lease and size of the store all affected costs. To Wang, "I didn't even ask what a U.S. store cost. I knew it would be irrelevant. U.S. stores are 90 percent free standing. They also involve a lot of real estate. None in China are or will be free standing. Also you can't buy real estate in China."

In deciding on a Beijing or Shanghai location for the first store, Wang commented:

> I didn't make the decision of predetermining where the first store would be located. I looked at the opportunities and at supporting functions. The first concern was where we could get good employees and managers. We settled on Beijing.

Finding a Partner

Once the decision had been made to focus on Beijing, Wang began the process of finding an appropriate local partner. Despite years of open door economic policies, Chinese investment regulations remained complex and cumbersome. There were also legal issues to be considered. Wang explained:

> The law in China is both clear and uncertain in the area of ownership. The regulations state that you cannot have 100 percent foreign ownership in food services. Beyond that it is not clear. So

we had to think about a partner or several partners. . . I wanted to find a partner who could bring me some skills and organizational strength. The organizational strength might be an understanding of retailing in Beijing or an understanding of real estate or something else valuable.

Wang initially thought of contacting his old KFC partners. However, this was ruled out because of strict noncompete agreements that Wang had forced upon each partner when the original KFC joint venture was established in 1987. Wang then turned to East City Food Services and Distribution Co., a firm with which he had some familiarity. East City was a city government owned enterprise with 30 different Chinese style sit-down restaurants and over 100 retail food outlets in the greater Beijing area. Preliminary discussions with East City's management indicated considerable excitement at partnering with KRR. East City promised access to its extensive labor pool that could either be transferred to KRR or hired through the company's normal channels. East City also had extensive local market knowledge and could be useful in marketing efforts and pricing issues. Finally, through their upstream contacts, the company promised to assist in accessing chickens and various food ingredients that would be essential in the smooth running of KRR restaurants. In assessing their potential contributions, Wang commented:

We would save some starting legwork by partnering with them. They could represent a smart option given my other FICA commitments. I think they are seriously worth considering. One drawback, however, is that they couldn't provide much in the way of finances.

A second option Wang was considering was the Beijing Branch of the China Great Wall Trading Co., a major investor-owned international trading company. China Great Wall had extensive international contacts and was very familiar with Western business practices. They were also very entrepreneurial and were seeking new investment opportunities with multinational corporations in Beijing. Wang sized up this option:

China Great Wall has a lot of appeal because it can provide a bridge between the Chinese and American ways of doing business. Mr. Lu Hong Jun, the General Manager, was someone I have known for some time. He seems quite easy to work with. I admire his entrepreneurial spirit. China Great Wall also seems to have plenty of money, including access to hard currency.

As a third option, Wang considered D&D Realty Co. D&D was a Hong Kong-based real estate development and leasing company with revenues in excess of $U.S. 1.8 billion. In 1993 it began a major push in to China and in 1994 opened its first office in Beijing. In early 1995 it signed a contract as leasing agent for a new 14-story office complex being built by Hong Kong investors in a commercial area in central Beijing. It was interested in filling ground floor space with a signature store and in September 1995 approached FICA with an offer to form a partnership with KRR. D&D communicated its plans for aggressive expansion in Beijing and promised Wang that as a partner it could provide relatively easy access to prime retail space within the city. Wang was clearly intrigued by the potential. "It is a very interesting concept. My worry is that they are still new and don't have mature contacts. Still, they deserve careful consideration."

Future Direction

Wang was clearly committed to moving KRR forward in Beijing in as expeditious a manner as possible. While he clearly had other responsibilities as President of FICA, Wang realized KRR's approach to the Beijing market would set a clear precedent for the expansion of other FICA retailing concepts in China. He was also aware that the competition was not standing still. By the fall of 1995, McDonald's had 17 restaurants running in Beijing; KFC was operating 10. Other restaurant companies including Hard Rock Café, Pizza Hut, and TGI Friday's, had either established operations or had broken ground for new stores in the Beijing area.

Despite the obvious popularity of Western food and the enormous potential of the Chinese market, the Chinese food service industry remained poorly developed and at risk. McDonald's and KFC were both involved in difficult lease negotiations. In February 1995, McDonald's managers were informed that its flagship restaurant in Beijing (and McDonald's largest in the world) would be raised to accommodate the construction of an enormous shopping, office, and residential complex being developed by Hong Kong billionaire Li Ka-Shing. McDonald's refused to vacate its building arguing that it had a valid long-term lease. Demolition of the surrounding area continued and by October 1995 the restaurant was still operating, but in what appeared to be a war zone. A spokesperson for the developer asserted that McDonald's never had a clean lease on the property. Rumors that McDonald's had cut a special deal with Li Ka-Shing's group were circulating among Western business people in Beijing. One other rumor circulating was that KFC would not renew its 10-year lease on its flagship Tiananmen Square store because of soaring rent costs.

The problems of doing business in China did not stop with leasing issues. Wang learned that import duties for equipment and materials would average 50 to 100 percent. It was estimated that each KRR store would require a minimum of $U.S. 150,000 in imported equipment (not including lease-hold improvements). While import permits were relatively straightforward, Wang lacked the staff to manage the development of 15 new stores in a short period of time. Another concern was hiring and training the new workers. With 15 restaurants, over 1,000 new employees would be required over the next few years. Who would interview them, hire them and train them? No one in KRR's training group spoke Mandarin nor were Chinese language training materials available.

Wang also learned that wage rates had climbed substantially over the past decade. Multinational companies were paying from a low 1,500 RMB per month for office clerks who spoke some English to as high as 10,000 RMB per month for senior managers who spoke fluent English.[3] Over 95 percent of employees in Beijing worked for state-owned enterprises where salaries averaged between 500 to 700 RMB per month. In Beijing, anyone—including those who worked for multinational companies—making less than 2,000 RMB per month was entitled to subsidized housing. Government subsidies reduced rent costs to less than 80 RMB per month.

---

[3]In October 1995, the Chinese renminbi (RMB) had an exchange rate of 1 $U.S. = 8.11 RMB.

The cheapest unsubsidized apartments started at over 1,000 RMB per month and increased sharply according to location, size and quality.

Wang was also acutely aware that by October 1995 none of the local food suppliers had been either identified or approved by KRR's head office. Related to this was a real concern over the menu. KRR's menu had never been tested in Beijing. While chicken was commonly eaten in China, would the Chinese be attracted to a premium product that was promoted in the U. S. as a healthy alternative to fried chicken? Furthermore, should KRR develop new menu items for China and if so, who would actually develop the concepts? Even if tasty new concepts could be developed, how long would they take to get corporate approval and could they be produced economically without costly new equipment?

These were all questions that were weighing heavily on Wang's mind. One thing that was clear was that whoever was selected as FICA's local partner would have a major impact on the success or failure of KRR in China. With so many unresolved issues, Wang was wondering whether the time was right to formalize a partnership.

3   STERLING MARKING PRODUCTS, INC.

Situation

On November 27, 1988, Jan d'Ailly, the 29-year-old international marketing manager for Sterling Marking Products of London, Ontario, was reviewing his options with regard to selling the Mark Maker embosser in the United Kingdom. He had identified possibilities for licensing, exporting, joint venture, and acquisition. Jan was expected to make his recommendations at tomorrow's International Marketing Committee meeting.

In addition to the U.K. market, a larger question loomed. The Mark Maker, which had captured over 60 percent of the Canadian embosser market in just two years, was starting to attract attention from dealers around the world. Jan had received inquiries from firms in Australia, Japan, Sweden, Italy, France, Barbados, Spain, and Indonesia. These firms were interested in selling and in some cases manufacturing the Mark Maker. How, thought Jan, should Sterling move on these worldwide opportunities?

Embossers and the Embosser Market

Used to imprint seals on corporate, legal, and certain government documents (Exhibit 1), embossers had been around for hundreds of years. Since that time, the only significant innovations were the development of a pocket seal and the Mark Maker. Throughout the world, lawyers, corporations, and consumers had purchased seals for either legal requirements or personal reasons, such as embossing their names on books and documents to show ownership or make them look more official. In countries where the legal system was based on English common law, an embosser was frequently a legal requirement for notary publics (lawyers who authenticated

Case material of The Western Business School is prepared as a basis for classroom discussion. This case was prepared by Jonathan Calof, under the direction of Professor Paul Beamish. Copyright © 1989, The University of Western Ontario.

EXHIBIT 1   Examples of Seals and Seal Impressions

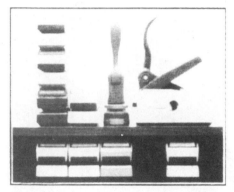

Illustration from an advertisement comparing the Mark Maker to traditional desk seals

MARK MAKER™

NEW

---

documents). Currently 90 percent of Mark Makers were purchased by lawyers and corporations. The fact that embossers appealed to business and nonbusiness consumers alike made any country in the world a potential market for embossers. Exhibit 2 outlines per capita GNP, population, basis of law (common, civil, and so forth), and, where available, statistics on lawyers and incorporations for 31 countries.

In 1986, the Canadian legal embosser market was estimated to be $1.5 million per year. While an embosser was not a legal requirement for companies, almost all the 70,000 incorporations and 20,000 corporate name changes per year resulted in embosser sales, with the remaining sales accounted for by those new lawyers who decided to become notary publics. Most embosser sales were accounted for by the traditional desk seal.

Throughout most of the world, the process of producing and selling embossers was similar (Exhibit 3). The embosser was composed of two parts: a subassembly, which was the actual body, and a die, which contained the text and graphic to be imprinted on documents. The die was then placed in the subassembly. Subassemblies were typically manufactured by national firms with metalworking expertise. Within

EXHIBIT 2   **International Markets—Selected Information**

Country	Population (in millions)	Per Capita GNP 1987	Notary	Number of Lawyers	Yearly Increase Lawyers and Incorporations	Basis of Law
Argentina	30	2,130	Yes			Civil
Australia	16	10,840	Yes	16,077		Common
Bangladesh	101	150	Yes			Common
Brazil	135	1,640	Yes			Civil
Canada	25	13,670	Yes		82,000	Both
China	1,041	310		12,000		Other
Colombia	28	1,320	Yes			Civil
Egypt	47	680	State*			Civil
France	55	9,550	Yes			Civil
Germany, Fed	61	10,940	Yes	30,510		Civil
India	765	110	Yes	200,000		Common
Indonesia	162	530	Yes			Civil
Iran	45	NA	Yes			Other
Italy	57	6,520				Civil
Japan	121	11,330	Yes	82,042		Both
Kuwait	1	14,270				Other
Mexico	79	2,080	Yes			Civil
Nigeria	100	760	Yes			Both
Norway	4	13,890	State*	2,000		Civil
Pakistan	95	380	Yes			Common
Philippines	55	600	Yes			Both
Poland	37	2,120	State*			Other
South Africa	32	2,010	Yes			Common
Spain	39	4,366	Yes			Civil
Sweden	8	16,421		2,000		Common
Switzerland	10	16,380	Yes			Both
Thailand	51	830				Both
Turkey	49	1,130	Yes			Civil
U.K.	56	8,390	Yes		200,000	Common
U.S.A.	239	16,400	Yes		820,000	Common
U.S.S.R.	277	NA	Yes	127,000		Other

*In these countries, notarization of documents is the responsibility of state bureaucratic officials and not lawyers.

Canada, five firms produced most embosser bodies. Embosser die production was more diffused, with a proliferation of small, regional dies manufacturers.

The actual sale of a complete embosser (subassembly and die) occurred through either product suppliers or service firms. Product suppliers (e.g., legal stationery suppliers) stocked products, such as incorporation kits, and other supplies required by lawyers. Service firms, such as name search houses, were usually employed by lawyers to assist in the incorporation process. Typically, these firms, as part of their service, provided an embosser.

An embosser sale resulted for one of two reasons: (1) a firm approached a lawyer to help them incorporate or (2) a lawyer became a notary public and required a seal. In both cases, the lawyer would then approach either a product supplier or a service firm (if the lawyer was using the particular service), and request an embosser. Product

---

EXHIBIT 3   The Process of Embosser Manufacturing and Sales in the Legal Market

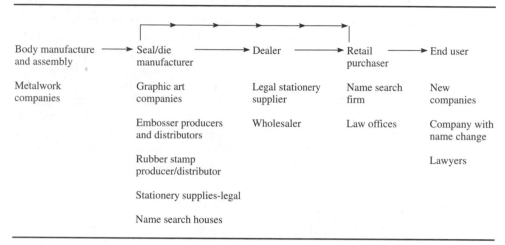

Body manufacture and assembly	→	Seal/die manufacturer	→	Dealer	→	Retail purchaser	→	End user
Metalwork companies		Graphic art companies		Legal stationery supplier		Name search firm		New companies
		Embosser producers and distributors		Wholesaler		Law offices		Company with name change
		Rubber stamp producer/distributor						Lawyers
		Stationery supplies-legal						
		Name search houses						

---

and service firms had two avenues for supplying embossers: they could purchase the subassembly, contract out the die manufacturing to one of the regional die suppliers, assemble the complete unit, and then sell it to the lawyer; or they could purchase the subassembly, produce the die internally, and then assemble the embosser.

Throughout the world, the legal seal industry had remained stagnant. While the number of models had grown, there had been very little innovation for 50 years. Three factors had contributed to this: the legal profession had accepted the problems associated with the seal; most of the die manufacturers were small, without funds for product development; and, for the larger firms, embosser sales were typically not the dominant product, thus there was little incentive for them to undertake embosser research and development. The combination of these factors resulted in such a deterioration in the function of embossers that it ceased to be an image product. The once proud seal became a commodity purchased on the basis of price alone.

In many cases, medium and large manufacturers in the embosser industry also produced rubber stamp products. The rubber stamp industry had higher margins and was more competitive than was the embosser industry. Much innovative product and process R&D had occurred for rubber stamps. While rubber stamps and embossers were both used for marking purposes, until recently the products were complements and not competitors. However, in some countries where corporations did not require an embossing seal, firms were starting to purchase rubber stamps to stamp their corporate seal on documents, rather than the harder-to-use embosser.

The Mark Maker

The Mark Maker Sterling Marking Products, Inc., was founded in 1945 by Warren R. Schram, initially as a one-man rubber stamp company in London, Ontario. Under Warren Schram's leadership and focus on customer service, Sterling developed a committed dealer network almost 1,000 strong. In 1976, Mr. Schram's son, Bob, a University of Western Ontario MBA, who had worked at Sterling for 11 years (since he was 19), acquired the business. At that time, Sterling's primary focus was still on the production and sale of rubber stamp products. In 1981, Bob Schram, Sam Hassan (controller), and Cam Fink (general manager) decided that the time was right to strike out into a new area. In the past, Sterling's embosser involvement consisted of supplying customers with assembled embossers. Since the subassembly was not manufactured by Sterling, their only value-adding activity was the actual assembly of the embosser and the manufacturing of the die. In management's view, all Sterling offered was an easily copied service. They decided that getting into embosser production and supply made strategic sense, as it increased Sterling's independence. Bob, Sam, and Cam discussed many times whether the new embosser should be a bold, innovative design or the old, traditional desk seal but with some of its flaws corrected.

Bob wanted his firm to bring back prestige to the embosser. The suppliers believed that lawyers wanted to buy the lowest cost items, regardless of utility or prestige. Bob felt that this assumption was inappropriate. "Lawyers buy BMWs and have large offices—prestige must be important to them." However, to try to develop a new, more functional, and prestigious embosser could be dangerous. Failure on an innovative design could damage their credibility with the employees, which the new management team was trying to establish. There were some significant benefits: They would learn about plastic molding and how to manage new-product development. Further, if they succeeded, the nature of competition could shift from a commodity-like product dominated by small firms to a differentiated product market dominated by one large firm, Sterling.

As a first step, Sterling applied for and received a $30,000 grant from the Ontario provincial government to underwrite the Mark Maker's industrial design. To help in the design, Bob conducted interviews with lawyers in which they were asked what they would like in a seal. From these discussions, and an analysis of other problems which he had identified with desk and pocket seals, Bob obtained an idea of the product features required in the new seal (Exhibit 4). Sterling then turned the design over to an industrial design consultant.

By the end of 1981, after extensive meetings with Bob and Cam, the consultant returned with the completed design, molds, and tooling required to produce the Mark Maker. A meeting was subsequently held in which the product was shown to Sterling management. Bob assembled the Mark Maker, and to his horror discovered that "it would not even emboss toilet paper."

Employees were already questioning the young management team's initial decision to develop the Mark Maker. At the same time a poor economic climate was affecting Sterling's profits. Bob felt that attention was better spent focusing on Sterling's current problems, rather than on developing the Mark Maker. For the next 30 days, management discussed possible modifications for the Mark Maker; subsequently the project was shelved.

By the end of 1982, attention started to shift back to the Mark Maker. Management felt that perhaps they were too hasty in their abandonment of the project. Since

EXHIBIT 4   Features of the Mark Maker and Competing Products (all prices are in $U.S. from Blumberg catalog)

Mark Maker: $29.95

Advantages	*Disadvantages*
On-line ordering systems:	Nonchangeable dies
• ease of ordering	Nonreversible dies
• accuracy	Die size limitation
• speed of delivery	
Plastic impression quality	High subassembly cost
Modern appearance	Will not fit in corporate registration binder
Ease of use	
Durability	
Easy-to-read index system	
Nonskid/nonmark pads	
Easy-to-use handle mechanism	

Pocket Seal: $19-$30

Advantages	*Disadvantages*
Compact—fits in corporate registration binder	Poor impression quality
Lightweight	Hard to use
Inexpensive	Looks cheap
Proven market acceptance (80% of the U.S. market)	No indexing possible
Rotating die set	Short throat
Various die sizes available	

Traditional Desk Seal: $25-$35

Advantages	*Disadvantages*
Various die size available	Impression is inconsistent
Good quality impression	Heavy
Recognized as the classic	Awkward
Special intricate logo capability	Awkward to use
	Noninterchangeable
	Nonreversible
	Frames crack
	Not easily stored
	Hard to transport
	Sharp metal edges

Source: Advantages and disadvantages from Sterling records.

they already had the basic design and the tooling for the Mark Maker, they could develop the product internally. Cam Fink hired Anthony Gentelle (a Fanshawe College industrial design student). Willy Brandt, an independent mold maker, was contracted to help in the mold design, and Du Pont Canada, Inc., was brought in to help select the appropriate materials for the Mark Maker. Cam and Anthony met after work for over a year, attempting to correct the flaws in the initial Mark Maker. By October 1984, the project which had taken five years and $400,000 to develop was completed. All that was left was to apply for a patent and then enter the new product on the market.

Sterling was proud of the Mark Maker (Exhibit 1). It weighed less than one pound and was trim. The weight and durability arose from using Du Pont Delrin acetal resin and glass reinforced Zytel nylon resin. It had a collapsible handle in nylon, which could lie flat at the push of a button, making the unit 13.5 centimeters long, 7 centimeters high, and 5.4 centimeters wide (small enough to fit into a briefcase). Its impression quality was tested to 25,000 embossing operations and, with the handle serving as a lever, the manual force needed to exert pressure on the die and achieve a clear impression was reduced. The parts were injection molded so the assembly could be quickly snapped together. While Sterling would own the molds and tooling, subassembly production was contracted out to Willy Brandt's firm, Exacu Mould, Inc., in London.

In December 1984, Sterling entered the product on the market. The subassembly was priced at $8.05, allowing Sterling a 50 percent profit. Competitor products were sold for $6.50; but Sterling felt that, if they met this price, the ensuing 25 percent profit was insufficient to justify the investment. Further, it was felt that the Mark Maker's superior features should allow for a price premium.

Mark Maker orders were encouraging. In the first year (1985), 40,793 Mark Maker subassemblies were sold. Unfortunately, Sterling learned that many Mark Makers were gathering dust on the shelves of the legal stationers and name search houses. Sterling identified two primary reasons for the poor results: changing the image of the embosser from a commodity-like product to a differentiated one required more direct sales than dealers had used in the past; and, as Sterling only sold the subassemblies, they had no control over die production, and unfortunately, most of the dies were not manufactured to the rigorous specifications set out by Sterling. The inferior dies were damaging Mark Maker's credibility in the market.

As dealers were unwilling to change their die production processes, Sterling realized that they had to somehow convince their customers to exit the lucrative seal production aspect of their business and allow Sterling to sell them both the Mark Maker subassembly and the die.

At the same time that this problem was developing, Sterling's computer systems/services division was implementing a program which interfaced the computer with the typesetter. This initiative, started around 1981, was not related to Mark Maker. Rather, it was an attempt to increase the efficiency of stamp making operations by standardizing activities and automating production. Cam, Sam, and Bob realized that with some modifications the program could be used for on-line ordering and production of the Mark Maker. Customers would be supplied with terminals and modems (approximate cost $1,000) which would be used to dial into Sterling's computers in London using telephone lines and enter the text for their embosser. The host computer could then communicate with the production computer engraving systems, which would then output the text for the die. Getting the client to enter the text directly into the system virtually assured error free final text. In the past, some errors had occurred as a result of operators entering the client's text from the order form incorrectly. The on-line text outputting processes would also result in improved quality and lowered production costs. A by-product of the automated text processes could be that, as part of the same run, text could be output, which could be used to manufacture a brass identification plate. Previously, customers used a piece of paper placed in a plastic window on top of the Mark Maker for identification purposes.

Management felt that increased quality and service would help convince the majority of their customers who manufactured the dies to relinquish die production and make the customer captive to the Sterling system. However, Sterling realized that the major hurdle for getting dealers to relinquish production of the die was the price and speed of delivery. Die production, though only a small part of most of Sterling's customers' business, was none the less extremely profitable with margins of 50 percent. Sterling found a price which maintained most of their customers' old profit. In addition, Sterling endeavored to provide dealers with sales support (marketing literature and sales incentives). The new Mark Maker, which cost Sterling $6.64 in labor and materials ($5.01 for the subassembly and $1.63 for the die), $1.75 for shipping, and $2.00 for selling and computer allocation, was retailed at $34.95 with wholesale volume discounts of up to 55 percent. Direct sales could be made to lawyers at the full list price of $34.95; however, this was not encouraged, as it would put Sterling in competition with the primary customers (legal stationers and name search houses). To ensure that dealers did not produce their own dies for the Mark Maker, Sterling limited subassembly sales to 20 percent of a customer's order. Sam Hassan felt that this was a necessary but high-risk decision, as it precluded Sterling from selling only subassemblies as they had in the past.

In 1986, 22,948 assembled Mark Makers had been sold ($424,359) and five of Sterling's largest customers were using the on-line ordering system. In 1987, 41,287 units were sold ($712,332). Sales for 1988 were forecasted to be 58,705 ($1,004,415) —67 percent of all Canadian embosser sales. And with its gross margin of $8.63 per unit and a forecasted $6.63 per unit contribution after allocated expenses, Mark Maker was the number one product for Sterling. Mark Maker had become so entrenched in the Canadian market that it was becoming more difficult to find the old metal desk seal subassemblies in Canada. Few sales went to the traditional stationer houses (the bulk of the 1,000 dealer network developed by Warren Schram). Ninety percent of sales went to a new type of customer: the legal stationer and law firm.

True to their initial objectives, Sterling had managed to change the competitive dynamic of the Canadian embosser market. Smaller, regional die manufacturing firms were being pushed out of the business, the product was losing its commodity-like status, and metal subassembly manufacturing (which was dominated by American firms) was dying out. The only competitive reaction had been by Marque D'Or, a rival of Sterling's in Quebec. In response to the introduction of the Mark Maker, Marque D'Or had lowered its price for the old metal seal. However, in the past month, Marque D'Or had begun to place more orders with Sterling because its largest customer had requested the Mark Maker. Sterling management felt that, with this latest development in Quebec and recent inroads in western Canada, it was conceivable that Mark Maker would have a 90 percent market share within the next few years.

The innovativeness of the Mark Maker was widely recognized. In 1986, the Mark Maker received two awards: a design Engineering Achievement Award at the Plast-ex show in Toronto, and the federal government's Award for Excellence in industrial design.

Despite this success, and lack of competitor reaction, management decided to continually innovate Mark Maker's product and service to discourage competitors. While the product and its design was patented for the next 15 years in Canada, the United States, and the European Economic Community, any modification (such as a different handle mechanism) would allow a competitor to legally duplicate the Mark Maker concept. However, the on-line ordering system could be difficult to replicate.

Sterling Marking Products, Inc.—1988

Sterling operated its production facility and head office in London, Ontario, with sales offices in London, Toronto, and Windsor. Directly employing 141 people, Sterling offered a variety of products and services (Exhibit 5), which were divided into four operating segments: (1) stationer items—rubber stamps, signs, and markers; (2) industrial marking systems—code dating; (3) graphics—artwork, commercial printing, and typesetting; and (4) data management and printing real estate books.

Many of these products were developed by Sterling. However, most of the industrial sales products, such as high-speed label makers and line-coding machines, had been developed by other firms with Sterling holding the Canadian distribution rights.

This diversified product line arose from the visions of Bob Schram (42), Cam Fink (32), and Sam Hassan (42). Bob Schram's commitment to customer service and desire for innovation led him to seek ways to increase the utility of products. He often discussed new-product ideas with customers, suppliers, and employees. Sam's main interests were in computer technology. When he joined Sterling in 1978 he had a vision of a firm with unique computer capabilities. To help realize this, he formed a relationship with Ultimate Computers, a value-added resaler of computer hardware. Cam joined Sterling in 1981 after working for a firm which supplied automotive products to General Motors. Cam brought with him a focus on production efficiency. He saw Sterling making thousands of "somethings" efficiently, thereby reaping the benefits of economies of scale.

One of the by-products of these visions was the development of Sterling's computer skill advantage. The original purpose of the computer technology was to assist in processing and storing transactions. The custom nature of Sterling's marking products activity (e.g., stamps are personalized) created a tremendous paper burden in the organization as each sale generated its own order form. As Sterling grew, so did the number of individual orders. By 1980, it had reached the stage that the processing of transactions had become a costly and time-consuming part of the production process. Sterling realized that, without an efficient method of processing transactions, future growth would be limited; thus, they looked toward computers.

In 1980, Sterling bought their computer system. As they spent time developing administrative applications for the system and learned more about the computer's

EXHIBIT 5   **Product Overview**

Products	Distribution	Strengths

Marking device and stationery products:
  Legal and consumer Mark Maker
    Embosser®
  Rubber and perma stamps
  Dating and numbering devices
  Signage systems
  Desk plates (badges)
	Large consumer customer base
	Direct-mail programs
	Major national accounts
		Loyal customers
		Strong customer service
		Unique on-line computer
		Integrated manufacturing system

Industrial products group:
  Date coding application (mechanical
    and computer spray-jet machines)
  Shipping supplies
  Steel type and punches
Mechanical presses
	Large consumer customer base
	Regional sales force based in Toronto,
	  London, Windsor, and Niagara
	  Peninsula
	Dealers
		Application-responsive sales and
		  manufacturing group
		Worldwide product sourcing

Graphics product group:
  Commercial artwork and typesetting
  Printing plates
    Corrugated cartons
    Type and label
    Flexo for poly bags
  Bingo plates and computer programs
  Printing
    MLS directories
    Direct-mail brochures
	National sales effort
	Large consumer customer base
	Major national accounts (Labatts)
		Outstanding responsive sales and
		  manufacturing capability to satisfy
		  customer requests
		Superior technical capability

Computer systems/services:
  Hardware selected from a wide range
    of vendors which support ultimate
    operating system
  Specialty software
  Bingo programs
  MLS on-line system
  Dealer on-line system incorporating
    proprietary computer-integrated
    manufacturing software driving
    typesetting and N/C computerized
    engraving output
  Real estate broker systems for
    administration function and on-line
    inquiries
	Companywide sales and marketing effort
	Satisfied customers including 11 real
	  estate boards
	On-line sales through consumer customer
	  and dealers
		Superior operating system offering
		  excellent migration flexibility of
		  software
		Creative, responsive sales and
		  programming staff
		Unique programs for typesetting output
		  and data manipulation

capabilities, they started to realize that the computer could also be used for production and product development purposes. For example, the data manipulation routines used for order information coupled with the typesetting expertise garnished from the production of stamps could also be used to produce database systems for real estate agents. All that was needed was some efficient searching routines. As well, the on-line production system would, if interfaced with the real estate database, result in a cost-effective method for printing the real estate books. In 1986, MLS database products and real estate book production were added to Sterling's business lines. In September 1988, this lucrative area had attracted contracts from 14 real estate boards in Canada. Other products and services arose from this technological edge, such as on-line ordering and production. Another innovative extension was the production of Bingo cards. A program was developed which would design Bingo cards. The program determined the number of cards to produce based on hall sizes, output the printing plates, and designed the Bingo cards such that no card had a higher probability of hitting "BINGO" than any other.

The company also focused attention on improving production processes. Sterling's quality standards were fast being adopted by the larger firms in the industry. However, most firms could not keep up with Sterling's process innovations. Without Sterling's level of expertise, most were unable to progress much beyond the technology and processes of the 1960s.

Product and process innovation were viewed as a principal task for Sterling. The impetus behind this was a desire for growth. Sterling viewed themselves as a potential future IBM in terms of size. But the focus on growth, innovation, and service had to be balanced with management's deep concern for employee well-being. Schram felt that employees were the key to Sterling's success.

One of the primary objectives for the organization was to increase the satisfaction of employees and managers. Consideration of these and other intangible benefits was so important that Sam Hassan's job was not to merely look at return on investment but to rationalize investment on the basis of its long-term benefit to the company. Sterling's investment decision criteria focused on the investment's effect in terms of the learning benefits of the investment, the impact of investment failure on both the employees' respect for management and overall operations, and what the employees would think of management for undertaking the investment. Financial considerations (e.g., ROI), while being important, were usually of secondary status.

The focus on innovation, service, and employee well-being led to an adaptable, flexible organization, the result of which was dramatic increases in sales and profits. Between 1983 and 1987, sales increased 73 percent going from $4.6 million to $8 million, with 1988 sales estimated to be $10 million (Exhibit 6).

Managing Growth

Management's primary concern was the management of growth. The managers felt that what had "made" Sterling was its identity—a focus on innovation and a 40-year-old service ethic. Maintaining the sense of commitment and an environment where "it was fun to come up with something that benefits the customer" would be difficult. In recruiting they sought individuals like themselves. They looked for people who could "share the vision." Salaries were low but Sterling offered would-be employees opportunities for growth. An apprenticeship period was served by most new management employees (with the exception of marketing) where the individual was expected to develop informal leadership in the organization. Titles were meaningless

EXHIBIT 6   Selected Financial and Corporate Information

	1983	1984	1985	1986	1987	1988*
Mark Maker sales:			*(Subassemblies)*		*(Complete units)*	
Units			40,793	22,948	41,287	58,705
$000s			343	424	712	1,004
Gross margin ($000s)					428	615
Contribution ($000s)					224	402
Employees:						
Full-time	106	103	120	122	130	
Part-time		9	11	6	11	
Sales ($000s)	4,598	5,369	6,536	7,285	7,971	
Debt/equity	2.13	1.57	1.24	1.16	1.06	

*Estimate.

and new hires were expected to work their way slowly into management, gaining respect from other employees and distinguishing themselves as leaders. New hires who were not able to earn the respect of employees would not last long. Management personnel were seldom given a clear role, direction, or authority.

Organizational Structure

While Sterling had explored the possibility of many different structures, they maintained the simple structure of the past, with most major decisions being made by Bob Schram after receiving input from various employees. Recently, the three senior managers had begun a process of adding more management employees, thereby removing themselves strictly from day-to-day operations and, instead, allowing themselves to focus on longer-range strategic issues. Despite this, the three senior managers continued to work six to seven days a week.

The structure was undergoing other transformations. Attempts were being made to divisionalize Sterling's product groups. For example, Jan d'Ailly was put in charge of marketing for all marking devices. However, as one employee stated: "We see ourselves in the longer run going toward a divisional structure; but given the current dynamic of Sterling and its success, it is hard to get any sort of structure, functional or divisional."

Sterling's international activities were coordinated by the international marketing department and the international marketing committee. The international marketing committee consisted of Jan, Sam, Cam, Bob, Rick Verette (operations manager), Vince Lebano (a representative of the Ontario Provincial government), and was chaired by Mel Dear, an ex-3M sales executive who was now a private consultant. The committee met every two to four weeks to discuss all aspects of international operations. The committee used a broad definition of international which included any sales outside of Ontario.

Jan d'Ailly was hired as the one-man international marketing department in 1986, shortly after completing his MBA at the University of Western Ontario. Jan had worked in France, Taiwan, Australia, and South Africa and spoke English, Dutch, French, and Mandarin. Consistent with Sterling's focus on customer service, Jan was hired more to provide customer support than to make sales. In fact, Jan did not have previous sales experience prior to joining Sterling. It was Jan's job to identify foreign markets for Sterling's products and to help foreign customers. Since joining Sterling, Jan's time had been devoted to the Mark Maker. He had personally conducted market research trips to the United States and the United Kingdom and was also involved in selecting Julius Blumberg Inc. to introduce the Mark Maker into the United States.

The United Kingdom Trips

Three market research trips had been made to the United Kingdom. These trips yielded information on the U.K. embosser market as well as information on labor availability, and information pertinent to Sterling's other products. Exhibit 7 presents a portion of Sterling's market study. The last trip was in November 1988. Jan, together with Cam, Warren Schram, and a consultant, went to the United Kingdom for one week. The purpose of this trip was to confirm Sterling's perceptions of the U.K. market and to investigate alternative modes for competing in the United Kingdom. The information in this section is based on the results of these research trips.

The United Kingdom was the only European country where seals were a legal requirement for corporations. Thus, all of the 172,000–120,000 incorporations, 50,000 corporate name changes, and 12,000 new lawyers per year required embossers. This provided a fertile ground for embosser sales. However, the U.K. government had recently indicated that an embossed seal might not be legally required in the future. Similar to Canada, sales were dominated by the traditional desk seal (approximately 50 percent of all sales). The major buyers of seals were lawyers and accountants who purchased some 70 percent of all seals, primarily for their incorporation clients.

Unlike Canada, the major embosser manufacturers were fully integrated. The largest manufacturers of both dies and embosser subassemblies were Jordan and Bolson. Much of Jordan's sales were to their own name search houses. In recent years, some of these were expressing displeasure at this arrangement as they wanted the flexibility to select embossers. The largest market shares of the seal production market were held by Bolson (50 percent) and Jordan and Sons (28 percent).

Eighty-five percent of legal seals were handled through company formation agents. Similar to the service firms in Canada, formation agents were hired by lawyers to assist in incorporations. These agents also provided an embosser as part of their service; thus, if Sterling was to seriously compete in the U.K. market, they would have to either usurp Jordan's production or supply Bolson's customers. The major agents were Jordan and Sons (26 percent share of seal sales), Stanley Davis (13 percent), and London Law (10 percent).

EXHIBIT 7 Sterling Marking Products, Inc.

Market Size

Company registrations	100,000} Range to 170,000
Name changes	50,000}
Vehicle testing stations	10,000 best guess
Personnel embossers	12,000 Jones Clifton
Total market	172,000 seals per year
	Work with 680 per day

Rubber Stamp Market

MacFarlane—$22,000,000	35%-50%
Mark C. Brown	? 10%
William James Clifton	? 5%-10%
40-60 smaller firms	
Said no one is making any money	

Structure of the Legal Seal Market

Seal Production

Jordans	48,000	28%
Bolsoms	84,000	49%
Western Pro Marketing		
City Seals	21,000	12%
	153,000	89%
Jones Clifton	18,000	10%
Totals	**172,000**	**100%**

Price competitive.

Generally very low quality seals.

Seals delivered to name search houses or mailed direct to end users.

Name Search Houses

Jordans (A group of small houses)	45,000	26%
Stanley Davis	22,500	13%
London Law	17,200	10%
Smaller houses	65,300	38%
(All less than Stanley Davis)		
Rubber stamp companies		
	150,000	87%
Retailers, wholesalers, Direct mail		
Rubber Stamp Man.	22,000	12%
MBF Clansman	?	
Totals	**172,000**	**100%**

As a whole, a very fragmented market.

Heavy price competition "Cheaper is Better."

Jordans seen as a leader in the industry, higher priced, and maintains a whole database and reporting business.

Stanley Davis determined to catch Jordans.

End Users

Lawyers	60,000	35%
Accountants	60,000	35%
Private legal	30,000	17%
Vehicle testing stations	10,000	6%
Consumers	12,000	7%
Totals	**172,000**	**100%**

Source: Company report on the U.K. market.

The relationship between the seal producers and formation agents was one of great loyalty. Jordan and Sons purchased their seals from Jordan, while Stanley Davis purchased from Bolson.

Pocket seals were priced at 5.50 and desk seals at 7.50 (prices in pounds sterling—1 pound sterling = $2.10 Canadian, $1 U.S. = $1.22 Canadian). Similar to the Canadian product, the quality of the seals was poor.

The Current Situation

Jan looked again at his notes on the United Kingdom. Several possibilities existed. They could continue exporting subassemblies to Jordan. In 1984–85 Sterling had sold 5,000 Mark Maker subassemblies to Jordan. They were originally to be a distributor for Mark Maker; however, due to problems in die manufacturing and weak sales efforts, not only were sales low but there was some concern that the Mark Maker was developing a bad reputation. Jordan had recently improved the quality, developed an effective on-line production system, and was manufacturing high-quality dies. This, coupled with placing the Mark Maker prominently in their brochure, resulted in 3,000 Mark Makers being sold in the past year. Jordan was interested in continuing their relationship with Sterling, but they wanted to produce the dies themselves.

Perhaps, thought Jan, Sterling could export the finished product. Duty was only 4.6 percent, the value-added tax (a tax levied at each stage of production) was 15 percent, and overnight courier costs were $7.50 per Mark Maker (the minimum courier charge was $60). Meeting U.K. demands would be no problem. Sterling could produce 168,000 Mark Makers with seals per year out of its London, Ontario, plant, 250,000 if they added a third shift.

Alternatively, Sterling could use licensing. MBF McFarlane, a U.K.-based rubber stamp manufacturer, had expressed an interest in this possibility. Maybe, thought Jan, all MBF wants is Sterling's computer technology and to keep Sterling from marketing other products there. In fact, MBF had visited Sterling in the spring of 1988 and in their recent catalogue claimed to have computer ordering capability.

Perhaps, Sterling could purchase one of the seal producers or construct their own branch. Labor availability was not a problem. Martyn Wright, a director of production with Jordan, had expressed a strong interest in leaving Jordan and heading a Sterling operation in the United Kingdom. Martyn felt that Sterling could purchase Jordan's seal operations and tie the computer typesetting business into Jordan's production facility. Alternatively, Sterling could build their own branch. A 60,000 per year Mark Maker plant required two employees and $50,000 in equipment. This included the on-line ordering and production systems, and the software. Administrative support, rent, and the employees' salaries were estimated at $5,000 per month.

Jan tried to elicit management opinion on the various entry mode options. They saw Mark Maker as a product which could open foreign market doors for Sterling, thereby paving the way for the introduction of Sterling's other products. Unfortunately, senior management was not in total agreement on the appropriate entry modes required to attain these objectives. One of the managers believed that greater profits could be attained by licensing the product to a U.K. manufacturer. He felt that Sterling should be focusing its attention on developing new products and a stronger sales organization, not spreading resources thinner by getting involved in an overseas branch. Another senior manager felt that, providing there was a reasonable chance of success in the United Kingdom, it would be in Sterling's best interest to have a branch there. This manager envisioned creating five branch plants with sales offices each year over the next five years. Each branch would control $1 million in yearly sales. Branch plants in the United States and United Kingdom were essential for the realization of this plan. He also felt that Sterling had developed a culture of innovation and risk taking. Accepting a licensing agreement would send the wrong message to employees.

Management was unsure of Sterling's ability to manage a foreign branch. They had experienced difficulties in managing the Windsor and Toronto offices and thought a branch overseas would pose even greater difficulties. They were considering putting a production and sales branch in Montreal within the next few years as a test of Sterling's ability to manage a foreign operation.

Another more recent experience was Sterling's foray into the United States. On May 1, 1988, Julius Blumberg, Inc., (a U.S. legal stationery supplier) was made Sterling's exclusive sales agent for the United States for a seven-month period, after which, Sterling would have the option of appointing other agents. Under this arrangement, Blumberg would not produce the seal; rather, they would send their customers' orders to Sterling who would produce the seal and then ship both the seal and subassembly to the appropriate Blumberg office. It was felt that the market presence of Blumberg and a guarantee of featuring the Mark Maker in their catalogue would result in substantial U.S. sales. Jan looked back over the past five months. Overall sales had been disappointing (under 100 units per week). However, Sterling had learned much about the U.S. market from this experience. Jan felt that the low sales could have resulted from using the traditional passive approach to selling embossers. A catalogue could not impress upon customers the advantages of the Mark Maker over other embossers. Jan suspected that some direct promotion was required. During the past year, he had traveled to Blumberg offices in Albany, New York, and Texas. During these visits, he had tried to convince the salespeople to use a more direct sales approach. As an incentive, he offered them one dollar for each Mark Maker sold. The results of these visits were impressive. For example, in Albany, prior to Jan's visit, Mark Maker sales averaged five per week; shortly after his visit, sales increased to 70 per week. Blumberg felt that the direct approach was inappropriate and instructed their sales force to tone down the sales approach. Subsequently, sales dropped to their old levels.

The same problem had occurred in Canada. However, when the legal stationers started using more aggressive sales techniques and Sterling started dropping into legal offices to show them the Mark Maker, sales increased dramatically.

Jan looked over the U.K. market report again. How to decide? And how fast to move? More fundamentally, should they do anything with respect to the United Kingdom without first developing a broad approach to international markets?

4   INDIA GOLD FISH LEATHER, LTD.

"You're writing cases about India? Well, have I got one for you! A classic, for sure! Here's my card; let me buy you a beer. Hey, give us two beers here." With this introduction, Mr. Bob Roberts, president director of India Gold Fish Leather, Ltd., settled in to tell his story one night in late October 1992 in Goa.

"Well my company is in the fish skin leather business. You know what that is, I suppose?"

"No, not only do I not know about the fish skin leather business, I've never even heard about it, and frankly, I don't see why I should want to know. How can you make leather out of fish skins?" replied the casewriter, somewhat taken aback.

"Here. Let me show you. Look at these. Beautiful aren't they? We've got them in all sizes and shapes, all colors and designs. They almost have the tensile strength of rawhide and their deformation is much lower. Nike here tested this one last week. They were amazed. They couldn't believe their own instruments. Look, this one is carp; this one is perch; this one is grouper. Terrific aren't they? Don't sniff them like that; you can't smell fish on them."

"We've shown them in fashion shows all over the world. Look at these pictures: Rome, New Zealand—that dress won first prize with those fish leather insets—Tokyo, Hong Kong, everywhere. That's all our stuff. Soon we'll be exporting all over. That's what the case is all about."

"Wait a minute," interjected the suddenly enthusiastic casewriter. "Fish skins are an agricultural product—well kind of, anyway—and you're upgrading them and plan to export them. Right? I'm supposed to be writing a case about upgrading agricultural products for export. Maybe I'd better hear your story. How about over there, out of the crowd?"

"That's what I've been trying to tell you," said Bob. And off he went with his story:

This case was prepared by Professor Donald J. Lecraw. The country and the financial and cost figures have been disguised.

After I graduated from the University of Nebraska in business administration, I went into finance and banking. About 15 years ago I joined up with the North American Bank—a good bank then, lots of training; that's where I had a lot of cases, in their training courses. So I know about cases.

Anyway, in '86/87 the bank sent me over to India as vice president, commercial lending. Good job; lots of responsibility; met a lot of important people; became familiar with how business is done here. Well, I liked it here: nice people, warm climate, good beaches, and good business opportunities. So, when the bank got into a lot of trouble in 1989, they wanted me to come home. But for what? People were getting fired all over the place. So I stayed on here. Did a little bit of this, a little bit of that—mostly financial consulting for the people I'd met through the bank. I bought a house on the beach here in Goa, not much of a house, but comfortable. Good life, but not too much money.

So a year or so ago, I got talking with an Australian friend of mine named John on the beach. I'd known John around town—nice guy and very concerned about the environment. Well, he was all excited about fish skins and making them into leather. All I knew about fish was you ate them—and the fish cannery across the bay from my house made an awful smell. Well, it was that factory that had gotten John all excited. It was just throwing its fish skins away with all the rest of the junk inside the fish or grinding them up into fish meal. That's why the place smelled so bad. John wanted to take the skins and make them into leather. He was wild about the idea; he said it was a natural; everyone would love it: save endangered species, reduce pollution, promote exports. How could it miss? At least that's what John was thinking.

Now they've been making fish skin leather for a long time—centuries really. But it's all been from exotic fish: shark skin, eel skin, sting ray skin. Ever seen a briefcase made from a sting ray? Prettiest thing you ever saw and very expensive. The Japanese are crazy about them—lasts forever. They use sting ray skin for samurai vests that can even stop a bullet—so they say; never tried it myself, you know.

Anyway, about five years ago they figured out how to make leather out of regular fish, fishy fish, like what you eat. Call them table fish. See, look at all those kinds of fish in the picture. We can make leather from them all.

Anyway, I thought, why not give it a try? What's a year here or there if the opportunity seems worth it? So John and I formed a partnership. Then I asked an Indian friend, Anil, he's very wealthy, to register a company for us in his name. Since it was 100 percent domestically owned, there were no problems from the board of investment. My friend Anil didn't put any money into it. Not much to put in, anyway. We rent or contract out almost everything. I know Anil won't try to cheat me. He borrowed millions of dollars at the bank when I was there—that's how I met him—and always paid it back. On time, too. And John and I didn't put big money into the company, about $50,000 or so in total—and that's all we've got in the company so far—plus one year of my life; John's life, too. We have a few chemicals and some tanned fish skins lying around; that's about it.

So we went to this company in New Zealand to get the technology. "No way! For what?" That's what they told us. We worked with some chemical companies and figured out how to do it in about three months. We buy the fish skins from the processing plant for almost nothing. The only expensive part is the presser and we contract that out to a tannery. See, that's a picture of our office. That's me, my friend, my secretary, and the billing clerk. See that name on the building? I consult for them, so we get the office free. That's the factory there in that building. We arranged another deal on that. There's a leather bag and belt company next door and they do any finished goods we need, like wallets, executive diaries, that sort of thing.

Well, we've had a lot of interest lately. All those trade fairs we've shown our products at, you know. The Australians are interested. They want to take our fish leather and produce shoes and stuff like that in Australia. But when they saw our labor costs, they changed their minds. Now maybe they'll invest here to produce shoes and buy our leather. Same thing with the Japanese.

We've sent samples all over the world—200 square feet here; 400 square feet there. All in all, maybe 8,000 square feet. How much do we sell it for? An average of $4.50 a square foot. Beautiful isn't it? Look at these pictures. Would you believe it?

So our biggest customer is this German company. First class. Top of the line. Look at these pictures. That's our leather. Look, here's a purse; here's a wallet; here's some shoes—we didn't make the shoes. Beautiful aren't they? This German company wants to ship our leather to its plant in Spain. But when the Germans saw our costs, well, they think maybe they'll move here. We're so sure about how good our skins are we made this company pay 50 percent up front when it placed the order. How much? Four thousand square feet. If the Germans like it, they'll order all we can produce, full capacity, maybe 5,000 square feet a month. How's that for one customer? See what I mean—great business. Can't lose.

The problem is—and it's the same problem for any company here—we're OK for the small volume runs when we can watch everything. We're contracting out the processes that require the big investment in machinery. And that's OK so long as we can watch them all the time. Now, looks like we're about to be really successful and we can go to big volumes pretty easy. But if we contract it out in big volumes, the quality will go down, sure as sure. We have to do it ourselves.

But where do we get the money? My partner John and I have, maybe, $50,000 in net worth between the two of us. My Indian friend, Anil, isn't interested in investing in fish skins. He likes wood. In fact, he loves wood. He says to me, "I can go out and count my trees. See, there they are: one, two, three—all those are my trees. How am I going to count fish? They're in the ocean under all that water. Trees are better." He ought to know. He's got 20,000 hectares [50,000 acres] of them.

I've got a house and a car and some furniture and something in the bank. Enough to live on for a few months. We can forget about borrowing locally from a bank. My Indian friend won't guarantee a loan, either.

But if we're going to really do this the right way, we'll have to do it ourselves—with our own equipment, our own production workers and supervisors, everything ourselves. Have to keep the quality up. That's the problem in India: getting high and consistent quality. Without it, we just can't compete on export markets. The good news is we've got the lowest costs of fish skins on this planet—*on this planet*—bar none. But low input and labor costs without quality is nothing. Right now they're maybe 15/20 companies in the world making fish skin leather. Last year there were maybe 10. Next year maybe there will be 100. I don't care; it doesn't matter. We can be competitive. Our costs are the lowest and always will be. Too many people—look at this place, will you? Too many people looking for jobs. And we can provide them with jobs. And make profits, too. Would you believe a 70 percent profit margin, price over total cost (excluding my partner's and my time), even when we contract our work out? I figure that if we did everything ourselves, our total costs would go down to less than $1 per square foot.

The government will love us: upgrading, value added, labor intensive, 100 percent exports. We'll get all the incentives. What incentives? Well, maybe they'll permit majority foreign ownership, maybe a promotional fair someplace. We had a booth at the Delhi Fair for free. No export taxes. What else? Not much, come to think of it. At least they aren't against us. Neutrality is about as much as you can expect here. That'll sure be enough for us. But what's going to happen in a few years is they'll ban leather exports to force companies to add additional value in India. Look at what they already did for leather "crust" [leather after the first stage of processing]. Now that's leather from cows; that law doesn't apply to us. But fish leather will come, maybe soon. I don't know. So we'll have to go for finished products sometime—and that's way bigger money than I've got.

What about the board of investment? Yes, that's a problem. Right now we're registered as a private firm with the Ministry of Industry under my friend's name. What's that kind of company called again? I forget. Anyway, if we get bigger than we are now, that may be a problem. But we'll still be too small for the board of investment to allow us to register as a foreign joint venture. We'll need more than $100,000 just as a start. Lots of workers lots of exports, not much capital. The board of investment is not receptive to foreign joint ventures in small companies like us. You got to have big bucks if you're a foreigner before they'll look at you, much less let you in. Why? I don't know why.

We've got all kinds of offers to form joint ventures. Just had one today. We talked all day. They want to invest $100,000 for half the ownership, 50-50. Well, it's not bad; but it's not good, either. We've started this thing, stuck our necks out, spent our time, and now they want to come in and get half for $100,000. With this amount of investment, we'd only be able to produce maybe 100,000 square feet a year. Enough as a start, but not for the long run. Everyone likes our product. Can we borrow from a bank? Try selling a bank on the idea of loaning money to produce fish leather. They just turned up their noses at us. And anyway, interest rates for a small business like ours are over 20 percent—even though the inflation rates is only 12 percent. Interest payments would kill us.

So what arc we going to do? You're the case expert. You tell me! Give me a call on Monday.

5   NEILSON INTERNATIONAL IN MEXICO

In January, 1993, Howard Bateman, Vice President of International Operations for Neilson International, a division of William Neilson Limited, was assessing a recent proposal from Sabritas, a division of Pepsico Foods in Mexico, to launch Neilson's brands in the Mexican market. Neilson, a leading producer of high quality confectionery products, had grown to achieve a leadership position in the Canadian market and was currently producing Canada's top selling chocolate bar, "Crispy Crunch". In the world chocolate bar market, however, Neilson was dwarfed by major players such as M&M/Mars, Hershey/Lowney, and Nestlé-Rowntree. Recognizing their position as a smaller player with fewer resources in a stagnant domestic market, Neilson in 1990 formed its International Division to develop competitive strategies for their exporting efforts.

Recent attempts to expand into several foreign markets, including the United States, had taught them some valuable lessons. Although it was now evident that they had world class products to offer to global markets, their competitive performance was being constrained by limited resources. Pepsico's joint branding proposal would allow greater market penetration than Neilson could afford. But, at what cost?

Given the decision to pursue international opportunities more aggressively, Bateman's biggest challenge was to determine the distributor relationships Neilson should pursue in order to become a global competitor.

This case was prepared under the supervision of Professors P. W. Beamish and C. B. Johnston by Gayle Duncan and Shari Ann Wortel solely to provide material for class discussion. The case is not intended to illustrate either effective or ineffective handling of a managerial situation. Certain names and other identifying information may have been disguised to protect confidentiality. Copyright © 1995, The University of Western Ontario.

EXHIBIT 1   **World Chocolate Exports (Value as Percent of Total)–1990**

	1987	1988	1989	1990
Africa	x1.5	x1.0	x1.1	x0.7
Americas	8.1	9.1	9.2	x9.1
LAIC[1]	2.1	1.9	1.4	x1.4
CACM[2]	0.1	x0.1	x0.1	x0.1
Asia	2.5	3.2	3.4	2.9
Middle East	x0.5	x0.5	x0.7	x0.4
Europe	86.4	85.0	84.2	85.4
EED (12)[3]	73.3	71.8	71.3	73.5
EFTA[4]	12.5	12.7	12.1	11.5
Oceania	x1.5	1.8	x2.1	x1.8

Figures denoted with an "x" are provisional or estimated.

[1]LAIC = Latin American Industrialists Association.

[2]CACM = Central American Common Market

[3]EEC (12) = The twelve nations of the European Economic Community.

[4]EFTA = European Free Trade Association.

Source: Adapted from The United Nations, *International Trade Statistics Yearbook,* Vol. II, 1990.

The Chocolate Confectionery Industry[1]

The "confectionery" industry consisted of the "sugar" segment, including all types of sugar confectionery, chewing gum, and the "chocolate" segment which included chocolates and other cocoa-based products. Most large chocolate operations were dedicated to two major products: boxed chocolates and bar chocolates which represented nearly 50 percent of the confectionery industry by volume.

Competition from imports was significant with the majority of products coming from the United States (39%). European countries such as Switzerland, Germany, the United Kingdom and Belgium were also major sources of confectionery, especially for premium products such as boxed chocolates. (See Exhibit 1 for a profile of chocolate exporting countries.) In order to maintain production volumes and to relieve the burden of fixed costs on operations, Canadian manufacturers used excess capacity to produce goods for exporting. Although nearly all of these products were traditionally exported to the United States, in the early nineties the world market had become increasingly more attractive.

Firms in the confectionery industry competed on the basis of brand name products, product quality and cost of production. Although Canadian producers had the advantage of being able to purchase sugar at the usually lower world price, savings

[1]Some information is this section was derived from: J. C. Ellert, J. Peter Killing and Dana Hyde, "Nestlé-Rowntree (A)", in *Business Policy, A Canadian Casebook,* Joseph N. Fry et al. (Eds.), Prentice Hall Canada Inc., 1992, pp. 655-667.

were offset by the higher prices for dairy ingredients used in products manufactured for domestic consumption. Other commodity ingredients, often experiencing widely fluctuating prices, caused significant variations in manufacturing costs. Producers were reluctant to raise their prices due to the highly elastic demand for chocolate. Consequently, they sometimes reformatted or reformulated their products through size or ingredient changes to sustain margins. Three major product types were manufactured for domestic and export sales:

Blocks.   These products are molded blocks of chocolate that are sold by weight and manufactured in a variety of flavours, with or without additional ingredients such as fruit or nuts. Block chocolate was sold primarily in grocery outlets or directly to confectionery manufacturers. (Examples: baking chocolate, Hershey's Chocolate Bar, Suchard's Toblerone).

Boxed Chocolates.   These products included a variety of bite-sized sweets and were generally regarded as "gift" or "occasion" purchases. Sales in grocery outlets tended to be more seasonal than for other chocolate products, with 80 percent sold at Christmas and Easter. Sales in other outlets remained steady year round. (Examples: Cadbury's Milk Tray, Rowntree's Black Magic and After Eights).

Countlines.   These were chocolate covered products sold by count rather than by weight, and were generally referred to by consumers as "chocolate bars". The products varied widely in size, shape, weight, and composition, and had a wider distribution than the other two product types. Most countlines were sold through nongrocery outlets such as convenience and drug stores. (Examples: Neilson's Crispy Crunch, Nestlé-Rowntree's Coffee Crisp, M&M/Mars' Snickers, and Hershey/Lowney's Oh Henry!)

Sweet chocolate was the basic semi-finished product used in the manufacture of block, countline, and boxed chocolate products. Average costs of sweet chocolate for a representative portfolio of all three product types could be broken down as follows:

Raw material	35%
Packaging	10
Production	20
Distribution	5
Marketing/sales	20
Trading profit	10
Total	100% (of manufacturer's selling price)

For countline products, raw material costs were proportionately lower because a smaller amount of cocoa was used.

In value terms, more chocolate was consumed than any other manufactured food product in the world. In the late eighties, the world's eight major markets (representing over 60 percent of the total world chocolate market) consumed nearly three million tonnes with a retail value close to $20 billion. During the 1980s countline was the fastest growing segment with close to 50 percent of the world chocolate market by volume and an average annual rate of growth of 7 percent. An increasing trend towards indulgence in snack and "comfort" foods strongly suggested that future growth would remain strong.

Competitive Environment

In 1993, chocolate producers in the world included: M&M/Mars, Hershey Foods, Cadbury-Schweppes, Jacobs Suchard, Nestlé-Rowntree, United Biscuits, Ferrero, Nabisco, and George Weston Ltd. (Neilson). Chocolate represented varying proportions of these manufacturers' total sales.

For the most part, it was difficult to sustain competitive advantages in manufacturing or product features due to a lack of proprietary technology. There was also limited potential for new product development since the basic ingredients in countline product manufacturing could only be blended in a limited variety of combinations. This forced an emphasis on competition through distribution and advertising.

Product promotion played a critical role in establishing brand name recognition. Demand was typified by high-impulse and discretionary purchasing behaviour. Since consumers, generally, had a selection of at least three or four favourite brands from which to choose, the biggest challenge facing producers was to create the brand awareness necessary to break into these menus. In recognition of the wide selection of competing brands and the broad range of snack food substitutes available, expenditures for media and trade promotions were considerable. For example, Canadian chocolate bar makers spent more than $30 million for advertising in Canada, in 1992, mostly on television. This was often a barrier to entry for smaller producers.

Major Competitors

M&M/Mars

As the world leader in chocolate confectionery, M&M/Mars dominated the countline sector, particularly in North America and Europe, with such famous global brands as Snickers, M&Ms and Milky Way. However, in Canada, in 1992, M&M/Mars held fourth place with an 18.7 percent market share of single bars. (Exhibits 2 and 3 compare Canadian market positions for major competitors).

M&M/Mars' strategy was to produce high quality products which were simple to manufacture and which allowed for high volume, and automated production processes. They supported their products with heavy advertising and aggressive sales, focusing marketing efforts on strengthening their global brands.

Hershey/Lowney

Hershey's strength in North America was in the block chocolate category in which it held the leading market position. Hershey also supplied export markets in Asia, Australia, Sweden, and Mexico from their chocolate production facilities in Pennsylvania.

EXHIBIT 2   Single Bars Canadian Market Share: 1991–1992

Manufacturer	1992	1991
Neilson	28.1%	29.4%
Nestlé/Rowntree	26.9	26.2
Hershey/Lowney	21.6	21.9
M&M/Mars	18.7	19.0
Others	4.7	3.5

Source: *Neilson News.* Issue #1, 1993.

In Canada, in 1992, Hershey held third place in the countline segment with a 21.6 percent share of the market.

Hershey's strategy was to reduce exposure to volatile cocoa prices by diversifying within the confectionery and snack businesses. By 1987, only 45 percent of Hershey's sales came from products with 70 percent or more chocolate content. This was down from 80 percent in 1963.

Cadbury Schweppes

Cadbury was a major world name in chocolate, with a portfolio of brands such as Dairy Milk, Creme Eggs, and Crunchie. Although its main business was in the United Kingdom, it was also a strong competitor in major markets such as Australia and South Africa.

Cadbury Schweppes diversified its product line and expanded into new geographic markets throughout the 1980s. In 1987, Cadbury International sold the Canadian distribution rights for their chocolate products to William Neilson Ltd. Only in Canada were the Cadbury brands incorporated into the Neilson confectionery division under the name Neilson/Cadbury. In 1988, Cadbury sold its U.S. operations to Hershey.

Nestlé/Rowntree

In 1991, chocolate and confectionery comprised 16 percent of Nestlé's SFr 50.5 billion revenue, up sharply from only 8 percent in 1987. (In January 1993, 1SFr = $0.88 CAD = $0.69 U.S.) This was largely a result of their move into the countline sector through the acquisition in 1988 of Rowntree PLC, a leading British manufacturer with strong global brands such as Kit Kat, After Eights and Smarties. In 1990, they also added Baby Ruth and Butterfinger to their portfolio, both "Top 20" brands in the United States. Considering these recent heavy investments to acquire global brands and expertise, it was clear that Nestlé/Rowntree intended to remain a significant player in growing global markets.

EXHIBIT 3   Top Single Candy Bars in Canada: 1991–1992

Top Single Bars	Manufacturer	1992	1991
Crispy Crunch	Neilson	1	1
Coffee Crisp	Nestlé/Rowntree	2	3
Kit Kat	Nestlé/Rowntree	3	2
Mars Bar	M&M/Mars	4	4
Caramilk	Cadbury Schweppes	5	6
Oh Henry!	Hershey/Lowney	6	5
Smarties	Nestlé/Rowntree	7	7
Peanut Butter Cups	Hershey/Lowney	8	8
Mr. Big	Neilson	9	11
Aero	Hershey/Lowney	10	10
Snickers	M&M/Mars	11	9
Crunchie	Cadbury Schweppes	12	12

Source: *Neilson News.* Issue #1, 1993.

Neilson

Company History

William Neilson Ltd. was founded in 1893, when the Neilson family began selling milk and homemade ice cream to the Toronto market. By 1905 they had erected a house and factory at 277 Gladstone Ave., from which they shipped ice cream as far west as Winnipeg and as far east as Quebec City. Chocolate bar production was initiated to offset the decreased demand for ice cream during the colder winter months and as a way of retaining the skilled labour pool. By 1914, the company was producing one million pounds of ice cream and 500,000 pounds of chocolate per year.

William Neilson died in 1915, and the business was handed down to his son Morden, who had been involved since its inception. Between 1924 and 1934, the "Jersey Milk", "Crispy Crunch" and "Malted Milk" bars were introduced. Upon the death of Morden Neilson in 1947, the company was sold to George Weston Foods for $4.5 million.

By 1974, "Crispy Crunch" was the number one selling bar in Canada. In 1977, "Mr. Big" was introduced and became the number one teen bar by 1986. By 1991, the Neilson dairy operations had been moved to a separate location and the ice cream division had been sold to Ault Foods. The Gladstone location continued to be used to manufacture Neilson chocolate and confectionery.

Bateman explained that Neilson's efforts under the direction of the new president, Arthur Soler, had become more competitive in the domestic market over the past three years, through improved customer service and retail merchandising. Significant improvements had already been made in Administration and Operations. All of these initiatives had assisted in reversing decades of consumer share erosion. As a

EXHIBIT 4   Canadian Confectionery Market–1993

	Dollars (millions)	%
Total Confectionery Category	**$1,301.4**	**100.0**
Gum	296.5	22.8
Boxed Chocolates	159.7	12.3
Cough Drops	77.0	5.9
Rolled Candy	61.3	4.7
Bagged Chocolates	30.3	2.3
Easter Eggs	22.0	1.7
Valentines	9.4	0.7
Lunch Pack	3.6	0.3
Countline Chocolate Bars	641.6	49.3
Total Chocolate Bar Market Growth	**+8%**	

Source: Neilson Marketing Department estimates.

result, Neilson was now in a position to defend its share of the domestic market and to develop an international business that would enhance shareholder value. (Exhibit 4 outlines the Canadian chocolate confectionery market.)

Neilson's Exporting Efforts

Initial export efforts prior to 1990 were contracted to a local export broker—Grenadier International. The original company objective was to determine "what could be done in foreign markets" using only working capital resources and avoiding capital investments in equipment or new markets.

Through careful selection of markets on the basis of distributor interest, Grenadier's export manager, Scott Begg, had begun the slow process of introducing Neilson brands into the Far East. The results were impressive. Orders were secured for containers of "Mr. Big" and "Crispy Crunch" countlines from local distributors in Korea, Taiwan, and Japan. "Canadian Classics" boxed chocolates were developed for the vast Japanese gift ("Omiyagi") market. Total 1993 sales to these markets were projected to be $1.6 million.

For each of these markets, Neilson retained the responsibility for packaging design and product formulation. While distributors offered suggestions as to how products could be improved to suit local tastes, they were not formally obliged to do so. To secure distribution in Taiwan, Neilson had agreed to launch the "Mr. Big" bar under the distributor's private brand name "Bàng Bang," which was expected to generate a favourable impression with consumers. Although sales were strong, Bateman realized that since consumer loyalty was linked to brand names, the brand equity being generated for "Bang Bang," ultimately, would belong to the distributor. This put the distributor in a powerful position from which they were able to place significant downward pressure on operating margins.

EXHIBIT 5   World Chocolate Imports (Value as Percent of Total)–1990

	1987	*1988*	*1989*	*1990*
Africa	x0.7	x0.7	x0.7	x0.7
Americas	x15.6	x15.0	x13.9	x13.2
LAIC[1]	0.2	0.4	1.1	x1.3
CACM[2]	x0.1	x0.1	x0.1	x0.1
Asia	11.7	x13.9	x15.6	x12.9
Middle East	x3.5	x3.3	x3.9	x2.8
Europe	70.8	68.9	67.7	71.4
EEC (12)[3]	61.1	59.5	57.7	59.3
EFTA[4]	9.3	9.0	8.9	8.4
Oceania	x1.3	x1.7	x2.1	x1.8

Figures denoted with an "x" are provisional or estimated.

[1]LAIC = Latin American Industrialists Association.

[2]CACM = Central American Common Market

[3]EEC (12) = The twelve nations of the European Economic Community.

[4]EFTA = European Free Trade Association.

Source: Adapted from the United Nations, *International Trade Statistics Yearbook,* Vol. II, 1990.

Market Evaluation Study

In response to these successful early exporting efforts Bateman began exploring the possible launch of Neilson brands into the United States (discussed later). With limited working capital and numerous export opportunities, it became obvious to the International Division that some kind of formal strategy was required to evaluate and to compare these new markets.

Accordingly, a set of weighted criteria was developed during the summer of 1992 to evaluate countries that were being considered by the International Division. (See Exhibit 5 for a profile of the world's major chocolate importers.) The study was intended to provide a standard means of evaluating potential markets. Resources could then be allocated among those markets that promised long-term incremental growth and those which were strictly opportunistic. While the revenues from opportunistic markets would contribute to the fixed costs of domestic production, the long-term efforts could be pursued for more strategic reasons. By the end of the summer, the study had been applied to 13 international markets, including the United States. (See Exhibit 6 for a summary of this study.)

Meanwhile, Grenadier had added Hong Kong/China, Singapore, and New Zealand to Neilson's portfolio of export markets, and Bateman had contracted a second local broker, CANCON Corp. Ltd, to initiate sales to the Middle East. By the end of 1992, the International Division comprised 9 people who had achieved penetration of 11 countries for export sales. (See Exhibit 7 for a description of these markets.) As of January 1993, market shares in these countries was very small.

EXHIBIT 6   Summary of Criteria for Market Study (1992)

Criteria	Weight	Australia	China	Hong Kong	Indonesia	Japan	Korea	Malaysia	New Zealand	Singapore	Taiwan	Mexico	EEC	USA
* U.S. countline	—	4	4	4	4	4	4	4	4	4	4	4	4	4
1 Candy bar economics	30	20	20	30	20	20	28	20	15	25	15	20	10	10
2 Target market	22	12.5	14	13	15.5	19	15	10	7	9.5	12.5	21	22	22
3 Competitor dynamics	20	12	15	8	7.5	11	13.5	10	12	14.5	12	**11**	20	6.5
4 Distribution access	10	9	4	4	3.5	5	6	6.5	9	3.5	7.5	9.5	9	9
5 Industry economics	9	2.5	3.5	6	5.5	2	5	2.5	7	4.5	3	3.5	3.5	4.5
6 Product fit	8	7	6	6	6	3	7.5	7.5	7.5	8	4	8	5	8
7 Payback	5	4	4	1	2.5	4	5	2.5	4	2	2	5	2	1
8 Country dynamics	5	5	1	4	3	5	3.5	4.5	4.5	5	4	3	2	4
Total	109	72	67.5	72	63.5	69	83.5	63.5	66	72	60	81	73.5	65

Competitor Dynamics	Score	Mexico
Financial success of other exporters	0-8	5
Nature (passivity) of competition	0-6	2.5
Brand image (vs price) positioning	0-6	3.5
Score/20	/20	11

Due to Neilson/Cadbury's limited resources, it was not feasible to launch the first western-style brands into new markets. The basic minimum criteria for a given market, therefore, was the presence of major western industry players (ie: Mars or Hershey). Countries were then measured on the basis of 8 criteria which were weighted by the International Group according to their perceived importance as determinants of a successful market entry. (See above table.) Each criterion was then subdivided into several elements as defined by the International Group, which allocated the total weighted score accordingly. (See table, right.)

This illustration depicts a single criteria, subdivided and scored for Mexico.

Source: Company records.

The U.S. Experience

In 1991, the American chocolate confectionery market was worth U.S.$5.1 billion wholesale. Neilson had wanted to sneak into this vast market with the intention of quietly selling off excess capacity. However, as Bateman explained, the quiet U.S. launch became a Canadian celebration:

> Next thing we knew, there were bands in the streets, Neilson t-shirts and baseball caps, and newspaper articles and T.V. specials describing our big U.S. launch!

The publicity greatly increased the pressure to succeed. After careful consideration, Pro Set, a collectible trading card manufacturer and marketer, was selected as a distributor. This relationship developed into a joint venture by which the Neilson

---
EXHIBIT 7   Neilson Export Markets–1993

Agent (Commission)	Country	Brands
Grenadier International	Taiwan	Bang Bang
	Japan	Mr. Big, Crispy Crunch, Canadian Classics
	Korea	Mr. Big, Crispy Crunch
	Hong Kong/China	Mr. Big, Crispy Crunch, Canadian Classics
	Singapore	Mr. Big, Crispy Crunch
CANCON Corp. Ltd.	Saudi Arabia	Mr. Big, Crispy Crunch, Malted Milk
	Bahrain	Mr. Big, Crispy Crunch, Malted Milk
	United Arab Emirates	Mr. Big, Crispy Crunch, Malted Milk
	Kuwait	Mr. Big, Crispy Crunch, Malted Milk
Neilson International	Mexico	Mr. Big, Crispy Crunch, Malted Milk
	United States	Mr. Big, Crispy Crunch, Malted Milk

Source: Company records.

Import Division was later appointed distributor of the Pro Set cards in Canada. With an internal sales management team, full distribution and invoicing infrastructures and a 45-broker national sales network, Pro Set seemed ideally suited to diversify into confectionery products.

Unfortunately, Pro Set quickly proved to be an inadequate partner in this venture. Although they had access to the right outlets, the confectionery selling task differed significantly from card sales. Confectionery items demanded more sensitive product handling and a greater amount of sales effort by the Pro Set representatives who were used to carrying a self-promoting line.

To compound these difficulties, Pro Set sales plummeted as the trading-card market became over-saturated. Trapped by intense cashflow problems and increasing fixed costs, Pro Set filed for Chapter 11 bankruptcy, leaving Neilson with huge inventory losses and a customer base that associated them with their defunct distributor. Although it was tempting to attribute the United States failure to inappropriate partner selection, the United States had also ranked poorly relative to other markets in the criteria study that had just been completed that summer. In addition to their distribution problems, Neilson was at a serious disadvantage due to intense competition from the major industry players in the form of advertising expenditures, trade promotions and brand proliferation. Faced with duties and a higher cost of production, Neilson was unable to maintain price competitiveness.

The International Division was now faced with the task of internalizing distribution in the United States, including sales management, broker contact, warehousing, shipping and collections. Neilson managed to reestablish a limited presence in the American market using several local brokers to target profitable niches. For example, they placed strong emphasis on vending-machine sales to increase product trial with minimal advertising. Since consumer purchasing patterns demanded product variety in vending machines, Neilson's presence in this segment was not considered threatening by major competitors.

In the autumn of 1992, as the International Division made the changes necessary to salvage past efforts in the United States; several options for entering the Mexican confectionery market were also being considered.

Mexico

Neilson made the decision to enter the Mexican market late in 1992, prompted by its parent company's, Weston Foods Ltd., own investigations into possible market opportunities which would emerge as a result of the North American Free Trade Agreement (NAFTA). Mexico was an attractive market which scored very highly in the market evaluation study. Due to their favourable demographics (50 percent of the population was within the target age group), Mexico offered huge potential for countline sales. The rapid adoption of American tastes resulted in an increasing demand for U.S. snack foods. With only a limited number of competitors, the untapped demand afforded a window of opportunity for smaller players to enter the market.

Working through the Ontario Ministry of Agriculture and Food (OMAF), Neilson found two potential independent distributors:

> *Grupo Corvi.*   A Mexican food manufacturer, operated seven plants and had an extensive sales force reaching local wholesalers. They also had access to a convoluted infrastructure which indirectly supplied an estimated 100,000 street vendor stands or kiosks (known as "tiendas") representing nearly 70 percent of the Mexican confectionery market. (This informal segment was usually overlooked by marketing research services and competitors alike.) Grupo Corvi currently had no American or European style countline products.
>
> *Grupo Hajj.*   A Mexican distributor with some experience in confectionery, offered access to only a small number of retail stores. This limited network made Grupo Hajj relatively unattractive when compared to other distributors. Like Grupo Corvi, this local firm dealt exclusively in Mexican pesos, historically, a volatile currency. (In January 1993, 1 peso = $0.41 CAD.)

While considering these distributors, Neilson was approached by Sabritas, the snack food division of Pepsico Foods in Mexico, who felt that there was a strategic fit between their organizations. Although Sabritas had no previous experience handling chocolate confectionery, they had for six years been seeking a product line to round out their portfolio. They were currently each week supplying Frito-Lay type snacks directly to 450,000 retail stores and tiendas. (The trade referred to such extensive customer networks as "numeric distribution.") After listening to the initial proposal, Neilson agreed to give Sabritas three months to conduct research into the Mexican market.

Although the research revealed strong market potential for the Neilson products, Bateman felt that pricing at 2 pesos (at parity with other American style brands) would not provide any competitive advantage. Sabritas agreed that a one peso product, downsized to 40 grams (from a Canadian-U.S. standard of 43–65 grams), would provide an attractive strategy to offer "imported chocolate at Mexican prices."

Proposing a deal significantly different from the relationships offered by the two Mexican distributors, Sabritas intended to market the "Mr. Big", "Crispy Crunch" and "Malted Milk" bars as the first brands in the "Milch" product line. "Milch" was a fictitious word in Spanish, created and owned by Sabritas, and thought to denote goodness and health due to its similarity to the word "milk." Sabritas would offer Neilson 50 percent ownership of the Milch name, in exchange for 50 percent of Neilson's brand names, both of which would appear on each bar. As part of the joint branding agreement, Sabritas would assume all responsibility for advertising, promotion, distribution and merchandising.

The joint ownership of the brand names would provide Sabritas with brand equity in exchange for building brand awareness through heavy investments in marketing. By delegating responsibility for all marketing efforts to Sabritas, Neilson would be able to compete on a scale not affordable by Canadian standards.

Under the proposal, all "Milch" chocolate bars would be produced in Canada by Neilson. Neilson would be the exclusive supplier. Ownership of the bars would pass to Sabritas once the finished goods had been shipped. Sabritas in turn would be responsible for all sales to final consumers. Sabritas would be the exclusive distributor. Consumer prices could not be changed without the mutual agreement of Neilson and Sabritas.

Issues

Bateman reflected upon the decision he now faced for the Mexican market. The speed with which Sabritas could help them gain market penetration, their competitive advertising budget, and their "store door access" to nearly a half million retailers were attractive advantages offered by this joint venture proposal. But what were the implications of omitting the Neilson name from their popular chocolate bars? Would they be exposed to problems like those encountered in Taiwan with the "Bang Bang" launch, especially considering the strength and size of Pepsico Foods?

The alternative was to keep the Neilson name and to launch their brands independently, using one of the national distributors. Unfortunately, limited resources meant that Neilson would develop its presence much more slowly. With countline demand in Mexico growing at 30% per year, could they afford to delay? Scott Begg had indicated that early entry was critical in burgeoning markets, since establishing market presence and gaining share were less difficult when undertaken before the major players had dominated the market and "defined the rules of play."

Bateman also questioned their traditional means of evaluating potential markets. Were the criteria considered in the market evaluation study really the key success factors, or were the competitive advantages offered through ventures with distributors more important? If partnerships were necessary, should Neilson continue to rely on independent, national distributors who were interested in adding Neilson brands to their portfolio, or should they pursue strategic partnerships similar to the Sabritas opportunity instead? No matter which distributor was chosen, product quality and handling were of paramount importance. Every chocolate bar reaching consumers, especially first time buyers, must be of the same freshness and quality as those distributed to Canadian consumers. How could this type of control best be achieved?

6   CAMBRIDGE PRODUCTS, INC. (A)

Seated in his Cambridge, Massachusetts, office one morning in June 1982, Bill Spencer picked up one of his recently printed business cards. On one side, above his name, address, title (Vice President, Corporate Relations) and the "Cambridge Products, Inc." logo, an American flag stood out prominently against a silver background; on the other side the same information was printed in Japanese characters. The cards and the company brochures printed in Japanese were just the latest (and relatively minor) expense items in CPI's bid to export its conventional, top-of-the-line cookware products to Japan.

A week earlier, in Tokyo, Spencer had met with Jiro Hattori, president of the Kuwahara Company, one of the largest manufacturers of cookware in Japan. Hattori had proposed that Kuwahara would distribute 1,500 sets of CPI cookware a month in the Japanese market starting in October, if CPI could produce an exclusive cookware product, with whistling knobs and specially designed handles. In a few hours' time, Bill would be meeting with Jack Nolin, executive vice president, to discuss whether CPI should begin a crash development program to modify CPI's existing product at an anticipated cost of over $140,000, and place orders for steel and other raw materials worth over $100,000 by the end of the week, to prepare for the expected October delivery. For CPI, with 1981 sales of $6.3 million and net profits of $500,000, this represented a substantial investment.

As he gazed at the Japanese print on his business card, Bill Spencer wondered what he should recommend to Jack Nolin. Should CPI make the investment? There appeared to be considerable potential in the Japanese market but the risks were enormous. Would CPI be better off concentrating on familiar markets in which it was

Case material of the Richard Ivey School of Business is prepared as a basis for classroom discussion. This case was prepared by Ken Coelho under the direction of Professor Donald J. Lecraw. The case was prepared with the cooperations of a company that prefers to remain anonymous. Names, locations, and figures have been disguised, but essential relationships have been preserved. Copyright © 1990, The University of Western Ontario.

already quite successful, rather than attempting to penetrate that notoriously difficult market in a far corner of the world?

The Company

CPI's origins can be traced back to 1944, when Brian Wilson, a young entrepreneur, started up a small metal finishing plant that polished "anything in metal." Sales in that first year were $4,000. The company specialized in custom metal-working jobs that included polishing of cookware for other manufacturers. In 1952, Wear Ever, one of CPI's customers, went bankrupt and left CPI holding a substantial quantity of cookware. CPI inadvertently entered the cookware business.

Initially, CPI marketed aluminum cookware manufactured for them by others. By the early 1960s, the company brought in new equipment and began to manufacture their own cookware products. Cookware sales in the early 1960s reached $1 million. CPI, which until then sold only aluminum cookware, began to experiment with stainless steel, and discovered that stainless steel cookware was "a market whose time had come." By 1967, CPI was completely out of aluminum and sold only stainless steel cookware.

By the late 1960s, CPI had acquired major department store accounts and sales had risen to $200,000 a month. Throughout this period the company maintained its original industrial sales business, which provided a fall-back position when problems arose in the cookware industry. In the 1970s, the American market for cookware declined. Competition was strong and included both foreign and domestic companies, such as Supreme Aluminum, Ltd., Soren, Paderno, Regal, Culinaire, Westbend, Ekco, and Lagostina.

Yet CPI performed well in this market, managing to capture a market share of approximately 20 percent in the segments in which it competed. It had managed to accomplish this by constant product innovation and efficient, low cost production. In fact, CPI had, at one time or another, supplied parts directly to its competitors at prices lower than the competitors could produce for themselves, while still making a profit. In 1981, CPI operated an 80,000-square-foot manufacturing facility in Cambridge, Massachusetts (where it also conducted its R&D activities), and a sales office in Toronto, Canada.

Product Development

In the late 1960s, CPI was the first developer (at a cost of $1 million) of five-ply cookware, which it marketed under the brand name "Ultraware." Five-ply construction bonded a three-layer aluminum core between two layers of stainless steel. Because of aluminum's exceptionally good capacity to store and conduct heat, the multi-layered construction resulted in quick and even heat distribution across the bottom and sides of the utensil, reducing cooking time and saving energy. CPI also experimented and designed specially weighted covers, knobs, and handles—innovations that paid off well in terms of sales.

In the early 1980s, CPI began experimenting with seven-ply cookware and magnetic steel which, in the future, could be used with magnetic stoves then being developed in Japan. The use of magnetic stoves and utensils would result in energy savings of up to 30 percent, which was of far greater significance in energy-poor Japan than in North America (three-ply cookware sold better in the United States and Canada than the five-ply variety, which, although more expensive, was more energy efficient).

Exports

When CPI first started in the cookware business in the early 1950s, it realized that the regional market was not large enough to support an efficient scale operation. CPI found it convenient to do business through Wear Ever distributors in the United States and Everglo in eastern Canada. It promoted products through trade shows both in the United States and abroad. CPI's industrial sales division also sold its products in Canada.

By 1979, exports constituted $2 million of $4.8 million in total sales. Canadian exports made up 70 percent of total exports. The other countries to which CPI exported included Italy, Australia, and South Africa. Exports to EEC countries were especially difficult, since the EEC had imposed tariffs of up to 22.5 percent on cookware. In the 1980s, CPI put sales to Canada "on the back burner," while it concentrated on markets in Japan, Australia, and Europe.

In 1981, CPI exports were $3.5 million of total company sales of $6.3 million (Exhibit 1). Of total exports, $2 million were to Canada, $800,000 to Australia, and the remainder ($700,000) to Europe, Hong Kong, Singapore, and Japan. Sales to Japan, however, were very small and sporadic. Every once in a while CPI received an order, but there was little ongoing business.

Exhibit 1   1981 Financial Summary

Total sales	$6.3 million	
Total exports	$3.5 million	
Profit before taxes	$800,000	
Net profit	$500,000	

Assets (as of 1982)	Net Book Value	Realizable Value
Inventory	$3 million	$3 million
Building	$500,000	$2.0 million
Machinery and equipment (10 percent straight-line depreciation)	$800,000	$2.5 million
Dies, tools	0	$500,000
Equity and Retained earnings	$1.4 million	

Entry into the Japanese Market

CPI's entry into the Japanese market was almost accidental. An earlier routine introductory letter to the U.S. embassy in Japan had elicited the reply that the Japanese market was too difficult for CPI to successfully penetrate—they should not even try. CPI did have one customer in Japan prior to 1981, who had seen CPI cookware at a trade show and ordered about 100 sets (worth approximately $16,500) sporadically (every two or three months).

In early 1982, David Taylor, vice president of CPI's Canadian subsidiary, showed samples of CPI cookware to an acquaintance, Izu Tsukamoto. Tsukamoto, born of Japanese parents in China, had moved to Japan with his parents as a child. Shortly after World War II, the Tsukamotos migrated to Canada. Izu spoke Japanese and was familiar with Japanese customs. In 1982, Izu Tsukamoto worked as a Vancouver-based distributor of cookware on a 5 percent commission basis. Tsukamoto felt that CPI's product would sell well in Japan and sent samples (by Federal Express) to distributors in Japan.

Tsukamoto's first contact was Jiro Hattori, president of Kuwahara Company, a Japanese import-export firm specializing in cookware and related items, such as china and cutlery. Kuwahara was 50 percent owned by Hattori and 50 percent by Ohto Overseas Corporation, one of the largest pen manufacturers in the world, with assets of over 2 billion yen ($100 million U.S.). Kuwahara in 1981 distributed approximately 100,000 sets of Regal and Westbend cookware (imported from the United States) and one product line of Japanese make, to six or seven direct sales organizations.

CPI's five-ply cookware, relatively new to Japan, was so well received by Jiro Hattori that Tsukamoto decided to travel personally to Japan. Thus began a series of trips by Tsukamoto, Taylor, Nolin, and Spencer, which culminated in Jiro Hattori's proposal to CPI in June 1982.

Hattori's Proposal

Jiro Hattori expressed an interest in distributing 3 of CPI's 20 styles of cookware. However, he wanted exclusive products and two major modifications—a whistling knob and specially designed wraparound flameguards. These flameguards around the handles were desirable, said Hattori, because most Japanese customers used liquid propane gas (LPG) for cooking (even though the existing cookware did have heat resistant phenolic handles). If CPI could have satisfactory samples of the redesigned cookware ready by the end of August, Hattori would accept deliveries of 1,500 sets a month for four months and more thereafter. The exact price would be negotiated later, but Spencer had tentatively suggested a price of $130 a set, cif.

Bill Spencer gathered all the notes on the Japanese market that he had made during his trips—the useful information provided by the Massachusetts government trade office in Japan (the U.S. government office in Japan, in contrast, was useless, Bill felt), and his analysis of the development costs. There were several factors he would have to consider before making his recommendations to Jack Nolin.

The Market

The Japanese purchased more cookware per capita than any other country in the world. The market for cookware in Japan was estimated to be about $100 million. It was (as the market for most consumer goods in Japan appeared to be) very competitive. The high end in which CPI would be competing was approximately $60 million and was dominated by imports (97 percent).

Regal, which had just introduced five-ply cookware and had developed a whistle knob (which was probably the reason for Hattori's haste, Bill thought), Westbend, and Ekco, which produced bonded bottom cookware, were already well entrenched in the market. Two local Japanese manufacturers served the low end of the market.

The Japanese Consumer

The clichés about a Japanese consumer—"very knowledgeable, extremely quality conscious, and willing to pay high prices for exclusive, prestigious products"—appeared to be quite true, Bill Spencer reflected. He recalled conversations with the CPI and other executives doing business in Japan:

> The Japanese market is the toughest in the world. I would prefer to deal in Taiwan or South Korea.
>
> The Japanese customer is very knowledgeable, very demanding, and the market is extremely competitive. Understanding Japanese customs and preferences is a necessary prerequisite for doing business in Japan.
>
> The Japanese are very thrifty—as individuals they are among the highest savers in the world. They arc willing to spend money only on high quality goods. In the United States there are three criteria by which consumers select cookware: (1) Price, (2) Quality, and (3) Appearance. In Japan they are: (1) Quality, (2) Quality, and (3) Quality! The Japanese are so quality conscious, it is almost revolting; there are customers who check cookware handles using a screwdriver! It is not unusual to see a car buyer *underneath* a car in a showroom, checking it out.
>
> Japanese consumers are very knowledgeable. They read every word in a brochure (you must have literature in Japanese) and ask pointed questions. The distributors are also extremely knowledgeable—the typical distributor knows as much about a product's characteristics as a manufacturer in North America.
>
> The Japanese are also very fond of exclusivity and designer names—this appears to be the only exception to the Quality rule. We know this from experience. A line of cheap yellow-colored pans sold a million sets in a very short time because they bore the designer name Pierre Cardin!
>
> It is important to understand Japanese customs. Because the islands are so crowded and houses are so small, it is common for a family of four to occupy a one-bedroom apartment. Cookware is hung on the wall so it is important for the cookware to look good (and to be exclusive).
>
> Understanding Japanese customs is also important when negotiating. They use a lot of euphemisms—if they say they will "think about it" more than three times, most likely they are politely saying no. If they do say no, directly—you had better leave quickly.
>
> They may take very long to make decisions. When negotiating with a team, it is difficult to identify the decision maker—he is usually silent. The person you do most of your talking to is not usually the decision maker. When negotiating with the Japanese, you have to be very well prepared—know precisely what your costs are, and what potential modifications will cost you.

Method of Entry

Given the potential in the Japanese market, there were other possible means of entry besides sales through the Kuwahara company. CPI had ruled out a wholly owned subsidiary or a joint venture in Japan since CPI did not have the necessary resources. Even a sales office would be too expensive to maintain for a company with sales of $6 million and net profits of $500,000. Bill estimated that it would cost $50,000 in salary and $150,000 in expenses for a one-man operation. Licensing was a poor option—patents were, for all practical purposes, ineffective in protecting cookware design and, in addition, the prestige associated with "imported" goods was an important buying criterion for the Japanese customer.

The choice of the appropriate distribution system in Japan often posed a serious problem to many companies trying to penetrate the Japanese market. There were three broad patterns of distribution for consumer goods (Exhibit 2). Distribution varied depending on the type of product. (The distinction between the three routes are for illustrative purposes only. In actual fact, the distribution routes could be very complex.)

The Open Distribution Route was used for distributing merchandise over extremely broad areas and involved many intermediate distributors, such as primary and secondary wholesalers. Manufacturers who sold products through this route usually entrusted ensuing sales to the wholesaler, not knowing clearly where or how their merchandise would be sold from then on. They had little direct contact with the secondary wholesalers or retailers. This form of distribution was adopted primarily for basic essential products with a wide demand, such as fresh and processed foods.

The Restricted Distribution Route was restricted to certain licensed retail stores, with the products going through specialized distribution channels. This form of distribution was common for specialty items, such as pharmaceuticals and cosmetics.

The Direct Distribution Route involved direct transactions between the producer and retailer, or the producer and consumers via door-to-door salespersons. The Kuwahara Company employed a form of this method of direct sales, which was common for imported products in the cookware category, where the originality and specific features of the foreign merchandise had to be directly conveyed to consumers.

While in Japan, the CPI executives had contacted several distributors besides Kuwahara: Basic Japan, Silverware, Noah, Zeny, Prima, Magry Systems, Royal Cookware, and Sunware. These were operations similar to the Kuwahara Company, one of the largest and better established firms (distributing 8,000 cookware sets a month, as well as other kitchenware products).

The direct sales organizations that Kuwahara had connections with comprised several hundred door-to-door salespersons who underwent a six to eight weeks' training program organized by Kuwahara. Each sales organization serviced a certain region (such as Osaka). The selling techniques emphasized getting in the door —once that was accomplished, there was usually an 80 percent chance of getting a sale. Part of the selling job included lessons on how to use the cookware. Some distributors had even set up test kitchens to teach women how to cook and to display cookware. This tactic proved very effective. It was estimated that approximately 80

EXHIBIT 2   Examples of Distribution Routes for Consumer Goods in Japan

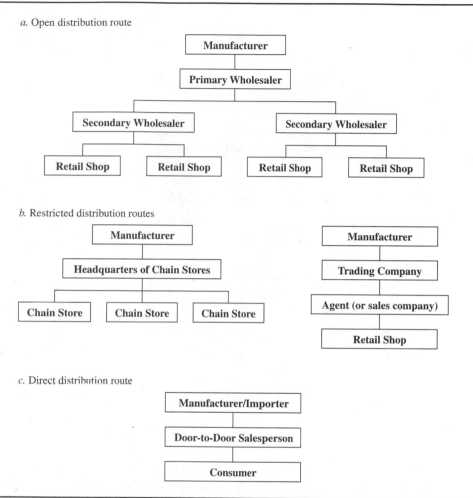

a. Open distribution route

b. Restricted distribution routes

c. Direct distribution route

---

percent of Japanese women learned to cook outside their homes. The average salesperson sold two to three cookware sets a week, in addition to such related items as china and cutlery.

Pricing

The tentative sales price that CPI and Hattori agreed on ($125 per set) would enable CPI to earn a margin of 15 percent, which was normal for a volume of 1,500 to 2,000 sets a month. CPI would charge up to 35 percent for smaller volumes. Izu Tsukamoto would earn a 5 percent commission and David Taylor would get 5 percent after

Tsukamoto's commission. The cookware would be subjected to a 20 percent tariff, and Kuwahara would usually sell at a 30 percent markup over landed costs. The door-to-door salesperson would sell at a 75 percent markup over the Kuwahara price. Payment would be made by letters of credit.

An illustration of the margins involved is seen in Exhibit 3.

Development Costs

The modifications that Jiro Hattori requested would, under normal circumstances, take CPI about five months to develop; but Hattori wanted samples by the end of August and that left CPI only 10 weeks in which to redesign the handles and knobs. Bill was confident it could be done. The costs involved would be as follows:

Whistle knob development	$100,000
Two molds for new handles @ $20,000 each	40,000
Total	$140,000

In addition, at $5,000 per trip to Japan for travel and the traditional Japanese after-hours business entertainment, CPI had already spent $25,000 on exploring the market; and travel costs could be expected to total at least $50,000 more if the decision to begin product development was made.

Capacity

The cookware industry enjoyed boom years in 1980–81. Manufacturers in the industry were usually affected by downturns in the economy with a six-month lag, being cushioned by retailers' preplanned orders. In late 1981, however, the U.S. and Canadian economies had turned sharply downward, and demand for cookware was expected to decrease in the second half of 1982. CPI was working at full normal capacity, which involved 10-hour shifts, four days a week, producing approximately 4,125 sets a month. The machines could be worked up to 18 hours a day (one 8-hour shift five days per week and one 10-hour shift four days per week) or the work week extended to accommodate extra sales to Japan if necessary; but such a pace could not be maintained in the long run (over one year) without adversely affecting machine maintenance. Also, CPI's planned four-year, $2 million machine-upgrading program might have to be speeded up should capacity utilization be increased.

CPI currently employed approximately 60 production workers, and an increase in capacity utilization would necessitate hiring about 30 to 40 new employees. To begin deliveries in October, CPI would have to begin hiring and training workers by July. In addition, because of the long lead times involved, steel and other raw materials worth over $100,000 would have to be ordered by the end of the week. By the end of August, orders for a further $200,000 in steel (which constituted 50 percent of

---

EXHIBIT 3   CPI Margins

CPI direct cost	$70.00
CPI total cost	100.00
CPI price (ex factory)	115.00
Freight and insurance	15.00
	$130.00
Tsukamoto's commission	5.75
Taylor's commission	5.45
CPI's price to Kuwahara (C.I.F.)	141.20
Tariffs	28.24
Kuwahara's landed costs	169.44
Kuwahara's price to sales organization	220.27
Price to final customer	$385.50

---

the direct costs of sales) would have to be placed, for a total investment of $300,000 in raw materials, $140,000 in product development, and $75,000 in travel costs before a firm order could be obtained. Because of CPI's good relationship with its banks, Bill foresaw no problem in obtaining an extension in its line of credit to cover the increased working capital.

As he reviewed his notes, Bill Spencer wondered what recommendations he should make to Jack. Could CPI compete in the Japanese market? The risks were enormous. As yet, CPI had no written contract with Jiro Hattori, and, once product development was started and the steel was ordered, these costs were sunk. The decision that the CPI managers would make that day would indeed be critical to CPI's future operations.

7   RUSSKI ADVENTURES

On July 15, 1991, Guy Crevasse and Andrei Kakov, the two major partners in Russki Adventures (Russki), contemplated their next move. They had spent the last year and a half exploring the possibility of starting a helicopter skiing operation in the USSR. Their plan was to bring clients from Europe, North America, and Japan to a remote location in the USSR to ski the vast areas of secluded mountain terrain made accessible by the use of helicopters and the recent business opportunities offered by glasnost.

During the exploration process, Crevasse and Kakov had visited a number of potential locations in the USSR, including the Caucasus Mountains near the Black Sea, and the Tien Shen and Pamir ranges north of Pakistan in the republics of Kazakistan and Tadzhikistan, respectively. After close inspection of the three areas, and consideration of many issues, the partners had decided upon the Caucasus region.

After almost two years of planning and research, the thought of making a solid commitment weighed heavily on their minds. Their first option was to accept the partnership offer with Extreme Dreams, a French company that had started a small ski operation in the Caucasus Mountains during the 1991 season. Their second option was to enter a partnership with the USSR's Trade Union DFSO and a Russian mountaineer, and establish their own venture in a Caucasus Mountains area made available to them by a Soviet government agency. Their final option was to wait, save their money, and not proceed with the venture at this time.

This case was prepared by Ian Sullivan under the supervision of Professor Paul Beamish for the sole purpose of providing material for class discussion at the Richard Ivey School of Business. Certain names and other identifying information may have been disguised to protect confidentiality. It is not intended to illustrate either effective or ineffective handling of a managerial situation. Any reproduction, in any form, of the material in this case is prohibited except with the written consent of the School. Copyright © 1992, The University of Western Ontario.

The Partners

Andrei Kakov, 27, was born in Russia. His family emigrated to Italy and then to Canada when he was 17 years old. After completing an undergraduate degree in economics at the University of Toronto, he worked with Sebaco for two years, before enrolling in 1989 in the masters of business administration (MBA) program at the University of Western Ontario (Western). Sebaco was a Canadian–Soviet joint venture that, since 1980, had been facilitating business ventures in the Soviet Union by acting as a liaison between the foreign firms and the different levels of Soviet government and industry. This job gave Kakov extensive contacts in the Soviet Union and in many of the firms, such as McDonald's and PepsiCo, which were doing business in the Soviet Union. Kakov was fluent in Russian, Italian, English, and Japanese.

Guy Crevasse, 28, had an extensive ski racing career, which began at a young age and culminated with participating in the World Cup with the Canadian National Ski Team. His skiing career took him to many countries in Europe, North America, and South America. During his travels he learned to speak French, Italian, and some German. After retiring from competitive ski racing in 1984, Crevasse remained active in the ski industry as a member of the Canadian Ski Coaches Federation. He led the University of Western Ontario varsity ski team to four consecutive Can–Am titles as a racer/coach while pursuing an undergraduate degree at Western. Before returning to Western to complete an MBA, Crevasse worked for Motorola, Inc., in its sales and marketing departments, where he worked on key accounts, set up product distribution channels, and developed product programs with original equipment manufacturers in the automobile industry. Crevasse had also worked with a ski resort planning and development firm on a number of different projects.

Overview of the Skiing and Helicopter Skiing Industries

Development of the Ski Resort Industry

In 1990, the worldwide ski market was estimated at 40 million skiers. The great boom period was in the 1960s and 1970s when growth ran between 10–20 percent annually. However, the growth stagnation which began during the 1980s was expected to continue during the 1990s. Some of this decline was attributable to increased competition for vacationers' time, the rapidly rising real costs of skiing, and baby boom effects. The only growth segment was female skiers, who represented 65 percent of all new skiers. The total revenue generated by ski resorts in the United States for 1990 was estimated at $1.5 billion. This figure did not include any hotel or accommodation figures.

Prior to World War II, most skiing took place in Europe. Since there were no ski lifts, most skiing was essentially unmarked wilderness skiing, requiring participants who enjoyed the thrill of a downhill run to spend most of their time climbing. There were no slope grooming machines and few slopes cut especially for skiing.

The development of ski lifts revolutionized the sport, increased the accessibility to many previously unaccessible areas, and led to the development of ski resorts. After the skiing market matured, competition for skiers intensified and resort operators shifted their efforts away from the risk sport focus toward vacation and entertainment. In order to service this new market and to recover their large capital investments, the large resorts had developed mass market strategies and modified the runs and the facilities to make them safer and easier to ski in order to serve a greater number of customers.

Introduction of Helicopter Skiing

This change in focus left the more adventurous skiing segments unsatisfied. For many, the search for new slopes and virgin snow was always a goal. The rapid rise in the popularity of skiing after World War II increased demand on existing ski facilities and, thus, competition for the best snow and hills became more intense. Those who wanted to experience the joys of powder skiing in virgin areas were forced to either get up earlier to ski the good snow before the masses got to it, or hike for hours from the top of ski areas to find new areas close to existing cut ski runs. Hiking to unmarked areas was tiring, time consuming, and more dangerous because of the exposure to crevasses and avalanches.

This desire to ski in unlimited powder snow and new terrain away from the crowds eventually led to the development of the helicopter skiing industry. The commonly held perception was that powder skiing was the champagne of all skiing, and helicopter skiing was the Dom Perignon. The first helicopter operations began in Canada. From the beginning of the industry in 1961, Canadian operations have been typically regarded as the premium product in the helicopter skiing industry for many reasons, including the wild, untamed mountains in the western regions. For many skiers worldwide, a trip to a western Canadian heliski operation is their "mecca."

Operators used helicopters as a means of accessing vast tracts of wilderness areas, which were used solely by one operator through a lease arrangement with the governments, forest services, or regional authorities. The average area leased for skiing was 2,000–3,000-square kilometers in size, with 100–150 runs. Due to the high costs in buying, operating, maintaining, and insuring a helicopter, the vast majority of operators leased their machines on an as-needed basis with rates based on hours of flight time.

In the 1970s and early 1980s, the helicopter skiing industry was concentrated among a few players. During 1990–91, the number of adventure/wilderness skiing operators increased from 41 to over 77. The industry could be divided between those operations that provided day trips from existing alpine resorts (day-trippers) and those operations that offered week-long trips (destination-location).

By 1991, the entire global market for both day-trippers and destination-location was estimated to be just over 23,000 skiers per year, with the latter group representing roughly 12,000–15,000 skiers. Wilderness skiing represented the largest area of growth within the ski industry in the 1970s and 1980s. Market growth in the 1980s was 15 percent per year. Only capacity limitations had restrained growth. The addictive nature of helicopter skiing was illustrated by the fact that repeat customers accounted for over 75 percent of clients annually. The conservative estimate of total

---

TABLE 1   Helicopter Skiing Margin per Skier Week (North America)

Price	$3,500	100%
Costs:		
Helicopter*	1,260	36
Food and lodging	900	26
Guides	100	3
Total operating costs	2,260	65
Total margin	$1,240	35

---

*Note: Helicopter costs were semivariable, but were based largely on a variable basis (in-flight hours). The fixed nature of helicopter costs arose through minimum flying hours requirements and the rate negotiation (better rates were charged to customers with higher usage). On average, a helicopter skier used seven hours of helicopter time during a one-week trip. A typical all-in rate for a 12-person helicopter was $1,800 per flying hour. Hence, the above figure of $1,240 was calculated assuming full capacity of the helicopter using the following: $1,800 per hour for seven hours for 10 skiers + pilot + guide.

margin available to the destination-location skiing industry (before selling and administration costs) was US$12.4 million in 1990. Table 1 gives typical industry margin figures per skier for heliskiing.

From a cost standpoint, efficient management of the helicopter operations was essential. Table 2 provides a larger list of industry key success factors.

Combination of Resort and Helicopter Skiing

The number of resorts operating day facilities doubled in 1990. Competition in the industry increased for a number of reasons. Many new competitors entered because of the low cost of entry (about $250,000), low exit barriers, the significant market growth, and the rewarding margin in the industry. The major growth worldwide came mainly from the day operations at existing areas, as they attempted to meet the needs for adventure and skiing from their clientele. The major concentration of helicopter operators was in Canada; however, competition was increasing internationally. Industry representatives thought that such growth was good, because it would help increase the popularity of helicopter skiing and introduce more people to the sport.

In Canada, where helicopter skiing originated, the situation was somewhat different. Out of the 20 wilderness skiing operations in Canada in 1991, only 2 were tied to resorts. However, for the rest of the world, roughly 80 percent of all the operations were located and tied closely to existing ski operations. Both Crevasse and Kakov realized that there were opportunities to create partnerships or agreements with existing resorts to serve as an outlet for their helicopter skiing demand.

Russki's Research of the Heliski Industry

Profile of the Skier

The research that the Russki group had completed revealed some important facts. Most helicopter skiers were wealthy, independent, professional males of North American or European origin. Increasingly, the Japanese skiers were joining the

---
TABLE 2   Helicopter Skiing Industry Key Success Factors

Factors within management control:

• Establishing a safe operation and a reliable reputation.
• Developing great skiing operations.
• Attracting and keeping customers with minimal marketing costs.
• Obtaining repeat business through operation's excellence.
• Providing professional and sociable guides.
• Obtaining operating permits from government.
• Managing relationships with environmentalists.

Location factors:

• Accessible destinations by air travel.
• Available emergency and medical support.
• Favorable weather conditions (i.e., annual snowfall, humidity, altitude).
• Appropriate daily temperature, sunshine, daylight time.
• Suitable terrain.
• Quality food and lodging.

---

ranks. The vast majority of the skiers were in their late 30s to mid-60s in age. For them, helicopter skiing provided an escape from the high pace of their professional lives. These people, who were financially secure with lots of disposable income, were well educated and had done a great many things. Helicopter skiing was a good fit with their calculated risk-taker image. Exhibit 1 describes a typical customer. It was not unusual for the skiing "addict" to exceed 100,000 vertical feet of skiing in a week. A premium was then charged to the skier.

Buyers tended to buy in groups, rather than as individuals. They typically had some form of close association, such as membership in a common profession or club. In most cases, trips were planned a year in advance.

Geographically, helicopter skiers could be grouped into three segments: Japan, North America (USA and Canada), and Europe; in 1991, they represented 10 percent, 40 percent (30 percent and 10 percent), and 50 percent of the market, respectively. There were unique features associated with each segment and Crevasse and Kakov knew that all marketing plans would need to be tailored specifically to each segment. In general, they felt that the European and North American customers placed more emphasis on the adventure, were less risk-averse, and had a propensity to try new things.

Analysis of the Competition

Crevasse and Kakov had thought that more detailed information on their competitors would help answer some of their questions. During the winter of 1991, they conducted a complete physical inspection of skiing and business facilities of many helicopter skiing operations. As a result of the research, Russki determined that the following companies were very significant: Rocky Mountain Helisports (RMH),

EXHIBIT 1   Description of a Typical Helicopter Skiing Addict

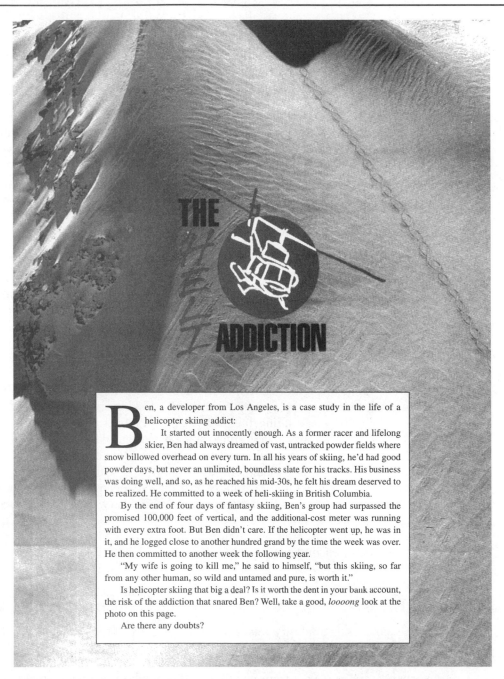

en, a developer from Los Angeles, is a case study in the life of a helicopter skiing addict:

It started out innocently enough. As a former racer and lifelong skier, Ben had always dreamed of vast, untracked powder fields where snow billowed overhead on every turn. In all his years of skiing, he'd had good powder days, but never an unlimited, boundless slate for his tracks. His business was doing well, and so, as he reached his mid-30s, he felt his dream deserved to be realized. He committed to a week of heli-skiing in British Columbia.

By the end of four days of fantasy skiing, Ben's group had surpassed the promised 100,000 feet of vertical, and the additional-cost meter was running with every extra foot. But Ben didn't care. If the helicopter went up, he was in it, and he logged close to another hundred grand by the time the week was over. He then committed to another week the following year.

"My wife is going to kill me," he said to himself, "but this skiing, so far from any other human, so wild and untamed and pure, is worth it."

Is helicopter skiing that big a deal? Is it worth the dent in your bank account, the risk of the addiction that snared Ben? Well, take a good, *loooong* look at the photo on this page.

Are there any doubts?

Source: *Powder: The Skier's Magazine,* November 1990.

Cariboo Snowtours, and Heliski India. RMH and Cariboo Snowtours were industry leaders and Heliski India was another new entrant trying to establish itself in the market. A close analysis had provided Crevasse and Kakov with some encouraging information.

Rocky Mountain Helisports, the first operation to offer helicopter skiing, was started in 1965 in Canada by Gunther Pistler, a German immigrant and the "inventor" of helicopter skiing. In 1991, his operation, servicing 6,000 skiers, represented roughly 40–50 percent of the worldwide destination-location market. He followed a strategy which cloned small operating units at seven different sites in the interior of British Columbia. RMH's strategy was designed to offer a product that catered to a variety of different skier abilities and skiing experiences. The company serviced all segments that could afford the $4,000 price of admission, including introducing less able skiers to the experience of helicopter skiing. Compared with the revenue of traditional Canadian ski resorts, such as Whistler Resorts in British Columbia, RMH's gross revenue for the 1990 season was larger than any resort in Canada at over $21 million. RMH, which had developed a loyal following of customers in North America and Europe, enjoyed significant competitive advantage because of proprietary client lists, a loyal consumer base, and economies of scale due to its large size.

Cariboo Snowtours, the second-largest operation in the world, was established by another German immigrant, Fritz Mogler, at Blue River, British Columbia. In 1991, Cariboo Snowtours served over 2,000 skiers, a number which represented roughly 18 percent of the market. Mogler developed a strategy of one mega-operation and enjoyed economies of scale in the operations area. Similar to RMH, Cariboo Snowtours had a loyal following from North America and Europe and catered to a variety of skiing abilities and price levels.

Heliski India was a new entrant to the helicopter skiing business. In 1990, the first year of operation, the company serviced 30 skiers in a three-week period, increasing to 120 skiers during the 1991 season. Heliski India followed a more exclusive and adventurous strategy aimed at the experienced helicopter skiing enthusiast. To cover the high costs and low volume the operation charged $5,500.

Russki estimated margins and profit dynamics for these three operations. Exhibit 2 contains the projection for RMH. These projected statements were best-guess estimates, based on discussions with a wide range of industry experts, managers, and investors. Cariboo Snowtour's total profit was estimated as slightly over $2 million, while Heliski India was projected to turn a small profit. Crevasse and Kakov found these figures very encouraging.

Land Usage and Environmental Concerns in the Industry

The helicopter skiing industry was facing some land use issues which were tough on many operators, but which also created new opportunities on which Russki wanted to capitalize. Of particular concern to many helicopter skiing operations, especially European, were pressures from environmentalists who were concerned that noise from helicopters could adversely affect wildlife habitats and start avalanches.

EXHIBIT 2   Russki's 1991 Projections
Profit Dynamics of Typical RMH Operation

Revenues

Ski season duration—peak	20 wks		
—regular	0 wks		
Total season duration	20 wks		
Revenue per skier—peak		$3,500	
Weekly group size: (10 skiers + 1 guide × 4) 44 people			
Total season regular revenue (3,500 × 40 skiers × 20 wks)			$2,800,000
Revenue from skiers exceeding 100,000 vertical feet (10%)			280,000

Total Revenue			$3,080,000
Expenses			
Variable:			
9 nights lodging/person/night		$80	$ 720
9 days meals/person/day		50	450
Total variable cost/person/week			$ 1,170
Total annual variable costs (20 wks × 44 × $1,170)			$1,029,600
Contribution margin			$2,050,400
Fixed:			
Helicopter cost/weekly basis (20-week season)		$50,000	$1,000,000
Guides—1 guide per 10 skiers @ $50,000 per guide/year	4 guides		$200,000
Support staff—5 employees @ $20,000 per employee			$100,000
Promotional			$250,000
Total direct fixed costs			$1,550,000
Total margin (Revenue – Dir. variable costs – Dir. fixed costs)			$500,400
Annual overhead—communication		$20,000	
—staff travel		50,000	
—office branch		20,000	
—office North America		100,000	
—insurance @ $5/day/person		50,000	
Total overhead			$ 240,000
Operating profit			$249,600
Number of operations	7		
Total operating profit			$1,747,200

As a result, severe downsizing or complete shutdown of existing European operations had recently occurred, leaving only eight helicopter skiing operations in continental Europe in 1991. The one Swiss and one Austrian operation were under pressure to close, and a 1992 season for the latter was already doubtful. The six small operations in Italy, which worked in conjunction with existing ski areas, were basically the only helicopter skiing available in Western Europe. Flying for skiing in France was illegal due to environmentalists' concerns about a negative impact on the limited areas in the Alps. In Sweden, a few companies operated with a shorter season, due to the high latitude, and provided less expensive daily services for visitors who skied within the existing lift systems, but week-long packages were not part of their program.

The North American industry had not been exposed to the same environmental and limited area constraints as the European, mainly because of the vast size of the mountain ranges and good relationships with all interested parties. The American operators, who were associated mostly with the large ski areas, had good working relationships with the forest services, which controlled the areas and issued the working permits.

Canadian operators received their permits from the Ministry of Lands and Forests and the provincial governments. Helicopter skiing had been encouraged because of its ability to bring money into the regions. Due to the vast size of the Canadian mountain ranges and the limited competition for the land use, pressure on the operators in any form had been minimal or nonexistent.

Crevasse and Kakov realized that the environmental and capacity constraints in Europe provided helicopter skiing operators worldwide with significant opportunities. Thus far, it had been mainly the North American operators who had capitalized on this situation, and Russki wanted to find a way to capture unsatisfied demand.

Russian Environment

The Political Environment

Crevasse and Kakov knew that starting a venture in the Soviet Union at this time would be complex. The political situation was very unstable in July 1991, and most expert predictions were not encouraging, including the possibility that the Soviet Union might not exist in the near future. There was a major power struggle going on: the hardliners, most of whom were from the old guard of the Communist Party, were trying to hang on to power; and others, such as Russian President Boris Yeltsin, wanted sweeping democratic changes. The new buzzword on the streets was not "glasnost" or "peristroika" but "razgosudarstvo," which refers to the breakup of the Soviet state. Secession pressures from many of the republics such as the Baltics tested the mettle of the political leaders, peristroika, and the strength of the union itself.

On a regional basis, the future status of some of the regions and republics where the physical conditions met the requirements for helicopter skiing, such as Georgia and Kazakhstan, was unknown. However, Crevasse and Kakov were encouraged by the fact that experts predicted that, no matter what the state of the whole union, Russia would remain intact and continue to function as a unit. This was one of the many reasons why the Russian Republic was selected for the potential initial location.

The Economic Environment

The economy of the Soviet Union was in dire straits. Confusion, lack of focus, and compromise were crippling the process of change from a government controlled economy to a market-based one. Real gross domestic product was projected to drop anywhere from 3 to 11 percent or more in 1991. Soviet President Mikhail Gorbachev had been given authority to overhaul the economy. However, what changes he would initiate, and whether he still had the support and power to see the process through to completion, were questionable.

Therefore, developing a helicopter skiing operation in the Soviet Union presented Russki with a difficult business environment. Marshall Goldman, director of Harvard's Russian Research Center, summed up part of the dilemma facing any new venture in the Soviet Union at this time:

> For those entrepreneurs who think chaos is an ideal environment, this is a perfect time, but for others it is a scary time. The society is collapsing. The economy—both the marketing portion and the planning and administrative sector—is a shambles.

Russki's research indicated that only 20 percent of the 1,300 joint ventures signed since 1987 were operational, because of currency exchange problems, bureaucratic delays, and lack of legal framework to make agreements. Also, it had been very hard for the few operational ventures to realize a return on their investments. In 1991, any business in the Soviet Union had to be viewed with a long-term bias in mind. The big question for many businesses was getting hard currency out of Soviet ventures, because there was no international market for the Soviet currency, the ruble. Those who were operating business ventures in the Soviet Union suggested to Russki that it was not an area for the fainthearted to tread. PlanEcon's Keith Crane advised that, "Even after the agreement has been signed it can be very difficult to get down to specifics and venture into working entities. It took McDonald's 14 years to do it." Due to the political and economic realities of the Soviet environment, firms were making deals with republics, with city agencies, directly with Soviet firms or factories, and sometimes with all of them. More and more frequently, firms had to go to the enterprise level to find the right people and partners. Additionally, foreign firms found the business environment difficult, because the concept of business that Westerners had was very different from the one that the Soviets had after 70 years of a controlled Marxist economy. The addition of cultural differences made for a demanding business climate. Russki thought long and hard about the fact that doing business in the Soviet Union had never been easy. In 1991, as the nation wrestled with the gargantuan task of restructuring the country, most firms were finding it more confusing than ever. No road map or blueprint for business development existed.

In addition, without the significant financial resources of a highly capitalized firm that could overlook short-term profits for long-term gains, Crevasse and Kakov realized they would be in a more exposed position if they decided to go ahead with the venture. Political unrest or civil war in the Soviet Union, especially in Russia, could destroy their business and investment. Without a steady supply of repeat and new customers, the venture would be finished as an ongoing concern. They knew that credibility from an existing operation or established name would make the task of attracting customers to an uncertain environment easier but, in a time of crisis, would guarantee nothing.

The Opportunities

Despite all the negatives, Crevasse and Kakov thought that helicopter skiing in the Soviet Union would be developed on a large scale in the next few years for a number of reasons. The sport was experiencing tremendous growth, environmental pressures were great in Europe, and capacity at all of the good locations was already stretched.

Therefore, a current opportunity existed in the industry. The partners speculated about how fast they could proceed with their business plan and whether they were exposing themselves to too much risk for the return. Would the opportunity still exist in a couple of years? Could a business of this nature function with the future of the Soviet Union being so unstable? The complete answer to these questions was unknown. Crevasse and Kakov felt as if they were doing a case back at business school where someone had left out half the case facts. Regardless, this was a real-life situation, and a decision had to be made on the knowledge available.

After looking closely at their competition and the general environment, they concluded that, despite the instability in the Soviet environment, there were a number of strong points that suggested they might be able to make a venture of this nature work. On a positive note, the Canadian prime minister, Brian Mulroney, had recently signed the Foreign Investment Protection agreement to ensure stability of Canadian ventures in the USSR. Also encouraging to entrepreneurs wanting to enter the Soviet Union was the new law that allowed for full ownership of Soviet subsidiaries by foreign firms. Experts suggested that these agreements would be honored by whatever form of government was in place.

The critical factor in the minds of the Russki partners was the fact that they would be taking in all revenue in hard currency. Thus, the absence of profit repatriation risk decreased this business exposure dramatically. Russki would operate all of the sales and administrative tasks outside of the Soviet Union and, as a result, all of its revenues would be collected in the West in hard currency, thereby eliminating the currency risk completely. This was a position that would be envied by any firm attempting to do business in the Soviet Union. Also, Russki was attractive to all levels of government, because the venture would bring desperately needed hard currency into the country.

Mt. Elbrus, the highest peak in Europe and the Caucasus mountain region, was where Russki had options to locate. It was well known throughout Europe, and its high altitudes and warm climate offered ideal skiing conditions. Because a strong allegiance already existed between the European customers and the Canadian operators, Russki's Canadian background would sit well with customers. In addition, Russki would deliver comparative cost advantage for the Europeans in a Soviet operation, as shown in Exhibit 5 on page 290 even if Russki charged similar costs for a week of skiing.

The uniqueness of the region and mystique of Russia offered an interesting alternative for tourism. Russia had a 2,000-year history and a rich culture, which was reflected in the traditions of the local people and the architecture. Furthermore, the Black Sea area close to the Caucasus Mountains had been used as a resort area for centuries. The dramatic changes during the early 1990s in the Soviet Union and Eastern Europe had resulted in tremendous interest in these areas.

Since Russki already had the money required for startup, the company could move quickly without having to take time to raise the capital. The low cost of leasing Soviet helicopters, pilot salaries, service, and fuel as compared with North America was a distinct advantage, and one of the original attractions of Russia. Negotiations with the Russians had shown that this cost advantage was obtainable. The high costs of helicopter operations represented the largest part of the operating costs in helicopter skiing. Lower helicopter costs in Russia would result in cost savings in the range of 50 percent or more in this expense relative to North American competitors.

The Russki management team was strong. Both men were business school trained individuals with international work experience, language skills, and ski industry backgrounds. Additional hard-to-copy assets, including access to the "Crazy Canucks" (a World Cup ski team) and European ski stars as guest guides, and Soviet knowledge, would be tough for anyone to match in the short term.

Positioning and Marketing of Russki Adventures

Positioning and Pricing

The Russki team had considered two positioning strategies, a high and low pricing strategy. A premium pricing and service strategy like that of Heliski India at around US$6,000 would require superior service in every aspect of the operation. The lower priced strategy at $3,500 to $4,000 was $500 below the US$4,000 to US$4,500 pricing of Canadian operators like RMH for the initial season. The second positioning strategy would be designed to target a larger market and concentrate on building market share during the first few years, allowing more time and flexibility to move down the learning curve.

Even with parallel pricing of US$4,000, the all-in costs would give an advantage to the European and Japanese customers (see Exhibit 5). Crevasse and Kakov knew that this situation would help challenge customers' traditional allegiance to the Canadian operators.

Based on a "best guess scenario," profit models for the two pricing strategies using conservative sales levels are shown in Exhibits 3 and 4. Though the higher priced strategy was more lucrative, Crevasse and Kakov felt that they had a higher capacity to execute the lower price strategy during the first few years of operations regardless of which partner they chose. They were not sure that they could meet the sales volume for the premium strategy as shown in Exhibit 4, regardless of the realization of savings from use of Russian helicopters. (In the unlikely event that the projected helicopter savings could not be realized the discounted cash flow in Exhibit 3 dropped from $526,613 to $293, and in Exhibit 4 from $597,926 to $194,484.)

These estimates were extremely conservative. One helicopter could service 44 people per week (four groups of 10 skiers and one guide). All projections for the profit dynamics were made with the number of skiers per week below capacity. In addition, the first two years were estimated, using 10 and 15 skiers, respectively. In subsequent years, the number of skiers was increased, but never to full capacity, to keep estimates conservative. Russki realized that operating at or close to capacity on a weekly basis would increase its efficiency and returns dramatically.

Russki also built in an additional $250 in the variable costs per skier per week for contingent expenses, such as the cost of importing all food stuffs.

EXHIBIT 3   Profit Dynamics Low Price Strategy with Low Helicopter Costs

	Year 1	Year 2	Year 3	Year 4	Year 5
Revenues					
Total season duration	10 weeks	15 weeks	15 weeks	20 weeks	20 weeks
Revenue per skier—peak	$4,000	$4,000	$4,000	$4,000	$4,000
Weekly group size	10	15	20	25	25
Total season revenue	$400,000	$900,000	$1,200,000	$2,000,000	$2,000,000
Expenses					
Total variable cost (variable cost/skiers @ $1,000)	$100,000	$225,000	$300,000	$500,000	$500,000
Contribution margin	$300,000	$675,000	$900,000	$1,500,000	$1,500,000
Fixed					
Helicopter cost (assumes Soviet costs of $10,000/week)	$100,000	$150,000	$150,000	$200,000	$200,000
Guides—1 guide per 10 skiers @ $50,000 per guide/year	$50,000	$75,000	$100,000	$125,000	$125,000
Soviet staff—3 employees @ $5,000 per employee	$15,000	$15,000	$15,000	$15,000	$15,000
Promotional	$100,000	$100,000	$100,000	$100,000	$100,000
Total direct fixed costs	$265,000	$340,000	$365,000	$440,000	$440,000
Total Margin					
(Revenues - Direct variable costs – Direct fixed costs)	$35,000	$335,000	$535,000	$1,060,000	$1,060,000
Total overhead	$35,000	$115,000	$115,000	$115,000	$115,000
Operating profit	0	$220,000	$420,000	$945,000	$945,000

	Year 0	Year 1	Year 2	Year 3	Year 4	Year 5
Investment	−$230,000					
Operating profit		0	$220,000	$420,000	$945,000	$945,000
N/A partner's share: 100%		0	$220,000	$420,000	$945,000	$945,000
Taxes @ 30%		0	$ 66,000	$126,000	$283,500	$283,500
Profit	−$230,000	0	$154,000	$294,000	$661,500	$661,500
DCF year 1–5 PV @ 20.00%		$526,613				
IRR	71.86%					

If Russki proceeded with the lower priced approach, it would position its product just below the industry standard at US$4,000 initially. The intent would be to attack the market as the Japanese automobile manufacturers had done when entering into the North American luxury car market.

Crevasse and Kakov were encouraged by the numbers, because the conservative sales estimates using the low price positioning strategy would allow them to generate a profit in the second year of operations if they could realize the projected savings with Russian helicopters. However, if they didn't, the strategy would still show a profit in the third year. They thought that the return on their investment would be sufficient as far as the internal rate of return was concerned, but they wondered whether the risk of the Soviet environment should increase their demands even more.

EXHIBIT 4   **Profit Dynamics Premium Price Strategy with Low Helicopter Costs**

	Year 1	Year 2	Year 3	Year 4	Year 5
Revenues					
Total season duration	5 weeks	10 weeks	10 weeks	20 weeks	20 weeks
Revenue per skier—peak	$6,000	$6,000	$6,000	$6,000	$6,000
Weekly group size	10	10	15	15	20
Total season revenue	$300,000	$600,000	$900,000	$1,800,000	$2,400,000
Expenses					
Total variable cost (variable cost/skier @ $1,000)	50,000	$100,000	$150,000	$300,000	$400,000
Contribution margin	$250,000	$500,000	$750,000	$1,500,000	$2,000,000
Fixed					
Helicopter cost (assumes Soviet costs of $10,000/week)	$50,000	$100,000	$100,000	$200,000	$200,000
Guides—1 guide per 10 skiers @ $50,000 per guide/year	$50,000	$50,000	$75,000	$75,000	$100,000
Soviet staff—3 employees @ $5,000 per employee	$15,000	$15,000	$15,000	$15,000	$15,000
Promotional	$100,000	$100,000	$100,000	$100,000	$100,000
Total direct fixed costs	$215,000	$265,000	$290,000	$390,000	$415,000
Total Margin					
(Revenues - Direct variable costs – Direct fixed costs)	$35,000	$235,000	$460,000	$1,110,000	$1,585,000
Total overhead	$35,000	$115,000	$115,000	$115,000	$115,000
Operating profit	0	$120,000	$345,000	$995,000	$1,470,000

	Year 0	Year 1	Year 2	Year 3	Year 4	Year 5
Investment	-$230,000					
Operating profit		0	$120,000	$345,000	$995,000	$1,470,000
N.A. partner's share: 100%		0	$120,000	$345,000	$995,000	$1,470,000
Taxes @ 30%	0	0	$ 36,000	$103,500	$298,500	$ 441,000
Profit	-$230,000	0	$ 84,000	$241,000	$696,500	$1,029,500
DCF year 1–5 PV @ 20.00%		$597,926				
IRR	70.78%					

Product

Crevasse and Kakov planned to model the Russski product after the RMH operation, which was the best in the industry, by evaluating what RMH had built and improving on its processes. Although Russski wanted very much to differentiate itself from the rest of the industry, the partners were not sure how far they could go within the constraints of the Soviet environment.

Geographical Distribution

Although Russski would focus on the European and North American markets, the former segment was most important. Both Crevasse and Kakov realized that they would need a strong European operation in marketing and sales if they were going to capitalize on the opportunity available. Developing these functions quickly, especially in

---

EXHIBIT 5   Cost Comparison by Geographic Location

North America
Costs for customer to go heliskiing in North America from different geographic locations.

Origin of Skier	Trip	Transportation	Total
Japan	$4,000	$2,500	$6,500
Europe	$4,000	$2,000	$6,000
North America	$4,000	$ 750	$4,750

Russia
Cost for customer to go heliskiing in Russia from different geographic locations.

Origin of Skier	Trip	Transportation	Total
Japan	$4,000	$2,000	$6,000
Europe	$4,000	$1,000	$5,000
North America	$4,000	$2,500	$6,500

Conclusion: This comparative analysis of all-in costs to the consumer shows that the Russian operation offers a 20 percent cost advantage to the European and Japanese customers.

Europe, which was not their home turf, was a major concern. They had to decide on the best sales and marketing channels immediately and set them up as soon as possible if they decided to go ahead with the venture.

Promotion

Due to the small size of the target market and promotion budgets, the new company would have to make sure that the promotional dollars spent were directed effectively. Russki would do this by direct mail, personal selling by the owners, travel agents, and free tour incentives to trip organizers and guides. Long-term word of mouth would be the best promotional tool, but it had to be supplemented especially in the startup phase of the business.

Additionally, Crevasse and Kakov planned to increase the value to customers by inviting business and political speakers to participate in the skiing activities with the groups in return for their speaking services. Celebrity skiers, such as Canadian Olympic bronze medalist and World Cup champion Steve Podborski, would be used as customer attractions. As outlined in Table 3, they budgeted $100,000 for promotional expenses.

Labour

Where possible, Russki planned to employ Russians and make sure that they received excellent training and compensation, thereby adding authenticity to the customers' experience. Providing local employment would also ensure the Canadian company's existence and create positive relations with the authorities.

TABLE 3   Marketing Promotion Budget—Year 1

Information nights with cocktails @ $1,000/night @ 20 cities	$20,000
Travel expenses	10,000
Trip discounts (1 free trip in 10 to groups)	25,000
Direct mail	5,000
Brochures	5,000
Commissions	15,000
Celebrity	20,000
Total	$100,000

Currency

Through Kakov's contacts, Russki had worked out a deal to purchase excess rubles from a couple of foreign firms, which were already operating in the Soviet Union but which were experiencing profit repatriation problems. Russki would pay for as many things as possible with soft currency.

The Partnership Dilemma

During the exploration period, Crevasse and Kakov had well over a dozen offers from groups and individuals to either form partnerships or provide services and access to facilities and natural resources. They even had offers from people who wanted them to invest millions to build full-scale alpine resorts. Many of the offers were easy to dismiss, because these groups did not have the ability to deliver what they promised or their skill sets did not meet the needs of Russki. Crevasse and Kakov's inspection and site evaluation helped them to determine further the best opportunities and to evaluate firsthand whether the site and potential partner were realistic. This research gave Russki a couple of excellent but very distinct partnership possibilities. They knew that both options had trade-offs.

Extreme Dreams

A partnership with the Extreme Dream group had some definite strengths. This French company, located in Chamonix, an alpine town in the French Alps, had been running the premier guiding service in and around Mont Blanc, the highest peak in the Alps, for 11 years. Chamonix was the avant garde for alpinists in Europe and one of the top alpine centres in the world. Extreme Dreams had a 5,000-person client list, mostly European but with some North American names.

What Extreme Dreams had was the operational expertise Russki needed to acquire in order to run the helicopter skiing and guiding side of the business. However, it lacked experience in the key functional areas of business. During the 1991 winter season, it had run a three-week operation servicing 50 skiers in the Elbrus region in the Caucasus Mountains. The Soviet partner facilitated an arrangement with a small resort villa in the area. The facilities, which had just been upgraded during the summer, now met Western standards.

The French company had invested roughly US$100,000 and, although it did not have a capital shortage, the partnership agreement that was outlined would require Russki to inject the same amount of capital into the business. The firm would be incorporated in the United States and the share split would be equal amounts of 45 percent of the stock with 10 percent left over for future employee purchase. The Soviet partner, a government organization that helped facilitate the land use agreements and permits, would be paid a set fee for yearly exclusive use of the land.

However, Extreme Dreams lacked experience in the key functional areas. Possibly, this situation could be rectified by the partnership agreement, whereby the management team would consist of three members. Marc Testut, president of Extreme Dreams, would be in charge of all operations. Guy Crevasse would act as president for the first two years and his areas of expertise would be sales and marketing. Andrei Kakov would be chief financial officer and responsible for Soviet relations.

Extreme Dreams had overcome the lack of some foodstuffs by importing on a weekly basis products not securely attainable in Russia. These additional costs were built into the variable cost in projected financial statements. Russki would do the same if it did not choose Extreme Dreams as a partner.

Trade Union DFSO

The other potential partnership had its strengths as well. The partnership would be with the All-Union Council of Trade Union DFSO, and with a mountaineer named Yuri Golodov, one of the USSR's best-known mountaineers, who had agreed to be part of the management team. Golodov, who had been bringing mountaineers from all over the world to parts of the Soviet Union for many years, possessed valuable expertise and knowledge of the Caucasus area. One of his tasks would be coordination of travel logistics for Soviet clientele. Sergei Oganezovich, chief of the mountaineering department, had made available to Russki the exclusive rights to over 4,000 square kilometers in the Caucasus Mountain Range about 50 kilometres from the area awarded to Extreme Dreams. A small user fee per skier would be paid to the trade organization in return for exclusive helicopter access to the area.

A profit-sharing agreement with Golodov, which would allow him to purchase shares in Russki and share in the profits, was agreed to in principle by Russki, the trade union DFSO, and Golodov. Under this agreement, Crevasse and Kakov would remain in control of the major portion of the shares. Capital requirements for this option would be in the $230,000 range over the first two years. The two Canadians would perform essentially the same roles as those proposed in the Extreme Dreams agreement. If Crevasse and Kakov selected this option, they would need to bring in a head guide, preferably European, to run the skiing operations. On a positive note, a small resort centre that met the standards required by Western travelers had been selected for accommodations in the area.

As far as medical care in case of accidents, both locations were within an hour of a major city and hospital. Less than an hour was well under the industry norm. In addition, all staff were required to take a comprehensive first aid course.

After discussions with many business ventures in the Soviet Union and with Extreme Dreams, Russki concluded that having the ability to pay for goods and services with hard currency would be a real asset if the situation were critical. Russki would use hard currency, where necessary, to ensure that the level of service was up to the standard required by an operation of this nature.

Crevasse and Kakov knew that selecting a compatible and productive partner would be a great benefit in this tough environment. Yet, they had to remember that a partnership would not guarantee customer support for this venture in the Soviet environment or that the USSR would remain stable enough to function as an ongoing concern.

The Decision

Crevasse and Kakov knew that it would take some time for the business to grow to the level of full capacity. They were willing to do whatever it took to make ends meet during the early years of the business. Because helicopter skiing was a seasonal business, they realized that they would need to find a supplementary source of income during the off-season, especially in the startup phase.

However, they also were confident that, if they could find a way to make their plan work, they could be the ones to capitalize on the growing market. The Soviet Union had the right physical conditions for helicopter skiing, but the business environment would present difficulties. Moreover, the two partners were aware that starting a venture of this nature at any time was not an easy task. Starting it in the present state of the Soviet Union during a recession would only complicate their task further. Yet the timing was right for a new venture in the industry and, in general, they were encouraged by the potential of the business.

Crevasse and Kakov had to let all parties involved know of their decision by the end of the week. If they decided to go ahead with the venture, they had to move quickly if they wanted to be operational in the 1992 season. That night they had to decide if they would proceed, who they would select as partners if they went ahead, and how they would go. It was going to be a late night.

8   CAMERON AUTO PARTS (A) – REVISED

Alex Cameron's first years in business were unusually harsh and turbulent. He graduated from a leading Michigan business school in 1991 when the American economy was just edging out of recession. It was not that Alex had difficulty finding a job, however; it was that he took over the reins of the family business. His father timed his retirement to coincide with Alex's graduation and left him with the unenviable task of cutting back the workforce to match the severe sales declines the company was experiencing.

History

Cameron Auto Parts was founded in 1965 by Alex's father to seize opportunities created by the signing of the Auto Pact between Canada and the United States. The Auto Pact permitted the Big Three automotive manufacturers to ship cars, trucks, and original equipment (OEM) parts between Canada and the United States tariff free, as long as they maintained auto assembly facilities on both sides of the border. The Pact had been very successful with the result that a lot of auto parts firms sprang up in Canada to supply the Big Three. Cameron Auto Parts prospered in this environment until, by 1989, sales had reached $60 million with profits of $1.75 million. The product focus was largely on small engine parts and auto accessories such as oil and air filters, fan belts and wiper blades, all sold as original equipment under the Auto Pact.

Professor Harold Crookell prepared this case solely to provide material for class discussion. The case is not intended to illustrate either effective or ineffective handling of a managerial situation. Certain names and other identifying information may have been disguised to protect confidentiality. Revised by Professor Paul Beamish. Copyright © 1996, The University of Western Ontario.

When Alex took over in 1991, the company's financial position was precarious. Sales in 1990 dropped to $48 million and for the first six months of 1991 to $18 million. Not only were car sales declining in North America, but the Japanese were taking an increasing share of the market. As a result, the major North American auto producers were frantically trying to advance their technology and to lower their prices at the same time. It was not a good year to be one of their suppliers. In 1990, Cameron Auto Parts lost $2.5 million, and had lost the same amount again in the first six months of 1991. Pressure for modernization and cost reduction had required close to $4 million in new investments in equipment and computer-assisted design and manufacturing systems. As a result, the company had taken up over $10 million of its $12 million line of bank credit at an interest rate which stood at 9.5 percent in 1991.

Alex's first six months in the business were spent in what he later referred to as "operation survival". There was not much he could do about working capital management as both inventory and receivables were kept relatively low via contract arrangements with the Big Three. Marketing costs were negligible. Where costs had to be cut were in production and, specifically, in people, many of whom had been with the company for over fifteen years and were personal friends of Alex's father. Nevertheless, by the end of 1991, the workforce had been cut from 720 to 470, the losses had been stemmed and the company saved from almost certain bankruptcy. Having to be the hatchet man, however, left an indelible impression on Alex. As things began to pick up during 1992 and 1993, he added as few permanent workers as possible, relying instead on overtime, part-timers, or subcontracting.

Recovery and Diversification

For Cameron Auto Parts, the year 1991 ended with sales of $38 million and losses of $3.5 million (see Exhibit 1). Sales began to pick up in 1992 reaching $45 million by year-end with a small profit. By mid-1993, it was clear that the recovery was well underway. Alex, however, while welcoming the turnaround, was suspicious of the basis for it. Cameron's own sales hit $27 million in the first six months of 1993 and company profits were over $2 million. The Canadian dollar had dropped as low as 73 cents in terms of U.S. currency and Cameron was faced with more aggressive competition from Canadian parts manufacturers. The short-term future for Cameron however, seemed distinctly positive, but the popularity of Japanese cars left Alex feeling vulnerable to continued total dependence on the volatile automotive industry. Diversification was on his mind as early as 1991. He had an ambition to take the company public by 1997 and diversification was an important part of that ambition.

Unfortunately, working as an OEM parts supplier to the automotive industry did little to prepare Cameron to become more innovative. The auto industry tended to standardize its parts requirements to the point that Cameron's products were made to precise industry specifications and consequently, did not find a ready market outside the industry. Without a major product innovation it appeared that Cameron's dependence on the Big Three was likely to continue. Furthermore, the company had developed no "in-house" design and engineering strength from which to launch an attempt

---

EXHIBIT 1   Income Statements For Years Ended December 31, 1991, 1992, 1993 ($000s)

	1991	1992	1993
Net Sales	$38,150	$45,200	$67,875
Cost of goods sold:			
Direct materials	6,750	8,050	12,400
Direct labor	12,900	10,550	12,875
Overheads (including depreciation)	16,450	19,650	27,600
Total	36,100	38,250	52,875
Gross Profit	2,050	6,950	15,000
Expenses			
Selling and administration			
(includes design team)	3,150	3,800	6,200
Other (includes interest)	2,400	2,900	3,000
Total	5,500	6,700	9,200
Net Profit before Tax	(3,500)	250	5,800
Income Tax	(500)	0	200
Net Profit after Tax	$(3,000)	$ 250	$5,600

Note: Alex expected total sales to reach $85 million in 1994 with profits before tax of $10 million. Flexible couplings were expected to contribute sales of $30 million and profits of $5 million on assets of $12 million.

---

at new product development. Because product specifications had always come down in detail from the Big Three, Cameron had never needed to design and develop its own products and had never hired any design engineers.

In the midst of "operation survival" in mid-1991, Alex boldly decided to do something about diversification. He personally brought in a team of four design engineers and instructed them to concentrate on developing products related to the existing line but with a wider "non-automotive" market appeal. Their first year together showed little positive progress, and the question of whether to fund the team for another year (estimated budget $425,000) came to the management group:

Alex: Maybe we just expected too much in the first year. They did come up with the flexible coupling idea, but you didn't seem to encourage them, Andy (production manager).

Andy McIntyre: That's right! They had no idea at all how to produce such a thingin our facilities. Just a lot of ideas about how it could be used. When I told them a Canadian outfit was already producing them, the team sort of lost interest.

John Ellis: (Finance) We might as well face the fact that we made a mistake, and cut it off before we sink any more money into it. This is hardly the time for unnecessary risks.

Alex: Why don't we shorten the whole process by getting a production licence from the Canadian firm? We could start out that way and then build up our own technology over time.

Andy: The team looked into that, but it turned out the Canadians already have a subsidiary operating in United States —not too well from what I can gather—and they are not anxious to licence anyone to compete with it.

Alex: Is the product patented?

Andy: Yes, but apparently it doesn't have long to run.

At this point a set of ideas began to form in Alex's mind, and in a matter of months he had lured away a key engineer from the Canadian firm with an $110,000 salary offer and put him in charge of the product development team. By mid-1993, the company had developed its own line of flexible couplings with an advanced design and an efficient production process using the latest in production equipment. Looking back, in retrospect, Alex commented:

> We were very fortunate in the speed with which we got things done. Even then the project as a whole had cost us close to $1 million in salaries and related costs.

Marketing the New Product

Alex continued:

> We then faced a very difficult set of problems, because of uncertainties in the market place. We knew there was a good market for the flexible type of coupling because of its wide application across so many different industries. But, we didn't know how big the market was nor how much of it we could secure. This meant we weren't sure what volume to tool up for, what kind or size of equipment to purchase, or how to go about the marketing job. We were tempted to start small and grow as our share of market grew, but this could be costly too and could allow too much time for competitive response. Our Canadian engineer was very helpful here. He had a lot of confidence in our product and had seen it marketed in both Canada and the United States. At his suggestion we tooled up for a sales estimate of $30 million - which was pretty daring. In addition, we hired eight field sales representatives to back up the nationwide distributor and soon afterwards hired several Canadian-based sales representatives to cover major markets. We found that our key Canadian competitor was pricing rather high and had not cultivated very friendly customer relations. We were able to pay the modest (and declining) Canadian tariffs and still come in at, or slightly below, his prices. We were surprised how quickly we were able to secure significant penetration into the Canadian market. It just wasn't being well-serviced.

During 1993, the company actually spent a total of $2.5 million on equipment for flexible coupling production. In addition, a fixed commitment of $1.5 million a year in marketing expenditures on flexible couplings arose from the hiring of sales representatives. A small amount of trade advertising was included in this sum. The total commitment represented a significant part of the company's resources and threatened serious damage to the company's financial position if the sales failed to materialize.

"It was quite a gamble at the time," Alex added. "By the end of 1993, it was clear that the gamble was going to pay off." (See below)

Sales by Market Sector ($millions)

	OEM Parts Sales	Flexible Couplings Sales	Total Sales	After Tax Profits
1989	60	Nil	60	1.75
1990	48	Nil	48	(2.50)
1991	38	Nil	38	(3.50)
1992	45	Nil	45	.25
1993	58	10 (six months)	68	5.80

Cameron's approach to competition in flexible couplings was to stress product quality, service and speed of delivery, but not price. Certain sizes of couplings were priced slightly below the competition but others were not. In the words of one Cameron sales representative:

> Our job is really a technical function. Certainly, we help predispose the customer to buy and we'll even take orders, but we put them through our distributors. Flexible couplings can be used in almost all areas of secondary industry, by both large and small firms. This is why we need a large distributor with wide reach in the market. What we do is give our product the kind of emphasis a distributor can't give. We develop relationships with key buyers in most major industries, and we work with them to keep abreast of new potential uses for our product, or of changes in size requirements or other performance characteristics. Then we feed this kind of information back to our design group. We meet with the design group quite often to find out what new types of couplings are being developed and what the intended uses are, etc. Sometimes they help us solve a customer's problem. Of course, these 'solutions' are usually built around the use of one of our products.

Financing Plant Capacity

When Alex first set his diversification plans in motion in 1991, the company's plant in suburban Detroit was operating at 50 percent capacity. However, by early 1994, sales of auto parts had recovered almost to 1989 levels and the flexible coupling line was squeezed for space. Andy McIntyre put the problem this way:

> I don't see how we can get sales of more than $85 million out of this plant without going to a permanent two-shift system, which Alex doesn't want to do. With two full shifts we could probably reach sales of $125 million. The problem is that both our product lines are growing very quickly. Auto parts could easily hit $80 million on their own this year, and flexible couplings! Well, who would have thought we'd sell $10 million in the first six months? Our salespeople are looking for $35–40 million during 1994. It's wild! We just have to have more capacity.
>
> There are two problems pressing us to consider putting flexible couplings under a different roof. The first is internal: we are making more and more types and sizes, and sales are growing to such a point that we may be able to produce more efficiently in a separate facility. The second is external: The Big Three like to tour our plant regularly and tell us how to make auto parts cheaper. Having these flexible couplings all over the place seems to upset them, because they have trouble determining how much of our costs belong to Auto Parts. If it were left to me I'd

EXHIBIT 2   Balance Sheets for Years Ended December 31, 1991, 1992, 1993 ($000's)

	1991	1992	1993
Assets			
Cash	$ 615	$ 430	$ 400
Accounts Receivable	5,850	6,850	10,400
Inventories	4,995	4,920	7,500
Total Current Assets	11,460	12,200	18,300
Property, Plant and Equipment (net)	10,790	11,800	13,000
Total Assets	22,250	24,000	31,300
Liabilities			
Accounts Payable	4,850	5,900	9,500
Bank Loan	11,500	12,000	10,000
Accrued Items (including taxes)	450	400	500
Total Current Liabilities	16,800	18,300	20,000
Common Stock (Held by Cameron family)	500	500	500
Retained Earnings	4,950	5,200	10,800
Total Equity	5,450	5,700	11,300
Total Liabilities	$22,250	$24,000	$31,000

just let them be upset, but Alex feels differently. He's afraid of losing orders. Sometimes I wonder if he's right. Maybe we should lose a few orders to the Big Three and fill up the plant with our own product instead of expanding.

Flexible couplings were produced on a batch basis and there were considerable savings involved as batches got larger. Thus as sales grew, and inventory requirements made large batches possible, unit production costs decreased, sometimes substantially. Mr. McIntyre estimated that unit production costs would decline by some 20 percent as annual sales climbed from $20 million to $100 million, and by a further 10 percent at $250 million. Scale economies beyond sales of $250 million were not expected to be significant.

John Ellis, the company's financial manager, expressed his own reservations about new plant expansion from a cash flow perspective:

We really don't have the balance sheet (Exhibit 2) ready for major plant expansion yet. I think we should grow more slowly and safely for two more years and pay off our debts. If we could hold sales at $75 million for 1994 and $85 million for 1995, we would be able to put ourselves in a much stronger financial position. The problem is that people only look at the profits. They don't realize that every dollar of flexible coupling sales requires an investment in inventory and receivables of about 30 cents. It's not like selling to the Big Three. You have to manufacture to inventory and then wait for payment from a variety of sources.

As it is, Alex wants to invest $10 million in new plant and equipment right away to allow flexible coupling sales to grow as fast as the market will allow. We have the space on our existing site to add a separate plant for flexible couplings. It's the money I worry about.

Foreign Markets

As the company's market position in North America began to improve, Alex began to wonder about foreign markets. The company had always been a major exporter to Canada, but it had never had to market there. The Big Three placed their orders often a year or two in advance, and Cameron just supplied them. As Alex put it:

> It was different with the flexible coupling. We had to find our own way into the market. We did, however, start getting orders from Europe and South America, at first from the subsidiaries of our U.S. customers and then from a few other firms as word got around. We got $40,000 in orders during 1993 and the same amount during the first four months of 1994. This was a time when we were frantically busy and hopelessly understaffed in the management area, so all we did was fill the orders on an FOB, Detroit basis. The customers had to pay import duties of 5 percent into most European countries (and a value-added tax of about 20 percent) and 20–50 percent into South America, on top of the freight and insurance, and still orders came in.

Seeing the potential in Europe, Alex promptly took an European Patent from the European Patent Office in the U.K. The cost of the whole process was $30,000. The European Patent Office (EPO) headquartered in Munich, Germany, received more than 50,000 patent applications each year. Since the EPO opened in 1978, additional countries had joined the EPO, often in step with joining the European Economic Community, now known as the European Union (EU). However, the EPO was not part of the EU, rather it was an autonomous organization. The current sixteen member states of the EPO are Austria, Belgium, Denmark, Finland, France, Germany, Greece, Ireland, Italy, Luxembourg, Monaco, Netherlands, Portugal, Spain, Sweden, Switzerland (including Liechtenstein), and United Kingdom. The official filing fees, although high, were much less than the fees which would be encountered by filing separate patent applications before the individual national patent offices.

A Licensing Opportunity

In the spring of 1994, Alex made a vacation trip to Scotland and decided while he was there to drop in on one of the company's new foreign customers, McTaggart Supplies Ltd. Cameron Auto Parts had received unsolicited orders from overseas amounting to $40,000 in the first four months of 1994, and over 10 percent of these had come from McTaggart. Alex was pleasantly surprised at the reception given to him by Sandy McTaggart, the 60-year-old head of the company.

Sandy: Come in! Talk of the devil. We were just saying what a shame it is you don't make those flexible couplings in this part of the world. There's a very good market for them. Why my men can even sell them to the English!

Alex: Well, we're delighted to supply your needs. I think we've always shipped your orders promptly, and I don't see why we can't continue... .

Sandy: That's not the point, laddie! That's not the point! Those orders are already sold before we place them. The point is we can't really build the market here on the basis of shipments from America. There's a 5 percent tariff

---

Exhibit 3   Data on McTaggart Supplies Ltd.

1993 Sales – £35 million (down from £44 million in 1991).

Total assets – £11 million: Equity £6.5 million.

Net profit after tax – ±£1.5 million.

Control – McTaggart Family.

Market coverage – 15 sales representatives in U.K., 2 in Europe, 1 in Australia, 1 in New Zealand, 1 in India.

Average factory wage rate – £5.00 per hour (which is below the UK mean of £6.70 due to the factory being located in a depressed area (versus $11.70 in America).

Factory – Old and larger than necessary. Some very imaginative manufacturing know-how in evidence.

Reputation – Excellent credit record, business now 130 years old, good market contacts
  (high calibre sales force).

Other – Company sales took a beating during 1991-92 as one of the company's staple products was badly hurt by a U.S. product of superior technology. Company filled out its line by distributing products obtained from other manufacturers. Currently about one-half of company sales are purchased from others. Company has capacity to increase production substantially.

Pricing	Index
Cameron's price to McTaggart	100
(same as net price to distributor in America)	
+ Import duty	4
+ Freight and insurance	11
Importer's Cost	115
+ Distributor's (McTaggart's) margin (30%)	35
+ Value-added tax (17.5% on cost plus margin)	26
= Price charged by McTaggart	176
versus Price charged by American distributor in U.S.	120

Note: Under the European Union agreement, all imports from non-EU countries were subject to common external tariffs (CET). In 1994, the CET for the flexible coupling had an import duty of 4 percent. (It was expected that with the GATT agreement, CET would be totally abolished by 2000 AD.) In addition to the import duty, all imported items were subjected to the value-added tax (VAT) which was applied on all manufactured goods—for both imported as well as locally made. The VAT was going through a harmonization process but it was expected to take some years before a common VAT system was in place. As of 1994, the VAT for United Kingdom was 17.5 percent, and France 20.6 percent. Sweden had the highest VAT at 25 percent.

coming in, freight and insurance cost us another 10 percent on top of your price, then there's the matter of currency values. I get my orders in pounds (£)[1] but I have to pay you in dollars. And on top of all that, I never know how long the goods will take to get here, especially with all the dock strikes we have to put up with. Listen, why don't you license us to produce flexible couplings here?

After a lengthy bargaining session, during which Alex secured the information shown in Exhibit 3, he came round to the view that a license agreement with McTaggart might be a good way of achieving swift penetration of the U.K. market via McTaggart's sales force. McTaggart's production skills were not as up-to-date as

---

[1]One pound was equivalent to U.S. $1.50 in 1994.

Cameron's, but his plant showed evidence of a lot of original ideas to keep man-ufacturing costs down. Furthermore, the firm seemed committed enough to invest in some new equipment and to put a major effort into developing the U.K. market. At this point the two executives began to discuss specific terms of the license arrangements:

> *Alex:* Let's talk about price. I think a figure around 3 percent of your sales of flexible couplings would be about right.
>
> *Sandy:* That's a bit high for an industrial license of this kind. I think 1½ percent is more normal.
>
> *Alex:* That may be, but we're going to be providing more than just blueprints. We'll have to help you choose equipment and train your operators as well.
>
> *Sandy:* Aye, so you will. But we'll pay you for that separately. It's going to cost us £500,000 in special equipment as it is, plus, let's say, a $100,000 fee to you to help set things up. Now you have to give us a chance to price competitively in the market, or neither of us will benefit. With a royalty of 1½ percent I reckon we could reach sales of £500,000 in our first year and £1 million in our second.
>
> *Alex:* The equipment will let you produce up to £4 million of annual output. Surely you can sell more than a million. We're getting unsolicited orders without even trying.
>
> *Sandy:* With the right kind of incentive, we might do a lot better. Why don't we agree to a royalty of 2½ percent on the first million in sales and 1½ percent after that. Now mind you, we're to become exclusive agents for the U.K. market. We'll supply your present customers from our own plant.
>
> *Alex:* But just in the U.K.! Now 2 percent is as low as I'm prepared to go. You make those figures 3 percent and 2 percent and you have a deal. But it has to include a free technology flow-back clause in the event you make any improvements or adaptations to our manufacturing process.
>
> *Sandy:* You drive a hard bargain! But it's your product, and we do want it. I'll have our lawyers draw up a contract accordingly. What do you say to a five-year deal, renewable for another five if we are both happy?
>
> *Alex:* Sounds good. Let's do it.

Alex signed the contract the same week and then headed back to America to break the news. He travelled with mixed feelings, however. On the one hand, he felt he had got the better of Sandy McTaggart in the bargaining, while on the other, he felt he had no objective yardstick against which to evaluate the royalty rate he had agreed on. This was pretty much the way he presented the situation to his executive group when he got home.

> *Alex:* … so I think it's a good contract, and I have a cheque here for $100,000 to cover our costs in helping McTaggart get set up.
>
> *John (Finance):* We can certainly use the cash right now. And there doesn't seem to be any risk involved. I like the idea, Alex.

Andy (Production): Well, I don't. And Chuck (head of the Cameron design team) won't either when he hears about it. I think you've sold out the whole U.K. market for a pittance. I thought you wanted to capture foreign markets directly.

Alex: But Andy, we just don't have the resources to capture foreign markets ourselves. We might as well get what we can through licensing, now that we've patented our process.

Andy: Well, maybe. But I don't like it. It's the thin edge of the wedge if you ask me. Our know-how on the production of this product is pretty special, and it's getting better all the time. I hate to hand it over to old McTaggart on a silver platter. I reckon we're going to sell over $20 million in flexible couplings in the United States alone during 1994.

9   HUSH PUPPIES CHILE

In July 1992, Ricardo Swett, age 50, could look back on a decade of exceptional growth of his family owned Hush Puppies line of casual shoes and retail outlets in Chile. Unlike the parent company, which had experienced serious difficulties in the 1980s, Hush Puppies in Chile had seen profits climb and sales explode by an average of 30 percent per year since 1985. By emphasizing excellence in design and by developing a chain of up-scale retail shoe stores as well as an efficient factory, Hush Puppies had become the favorite brand of upper-class Chilean men. Expansion into women's and children's shoes during the last three years had also been successfully implemented.

As the company's market position in Chile soared, Ricardo Swett, who served as general manager of Hush Puppies in Chile, began to contemplate further expansion in other Latin American markets. The company had recently established a limited presence in Uruguay, Bolivia, and Paraguay and was beginning to enter Argentina with its line of Brooks athletic shoes. Ricardo was uncertain how fast the company should expand in these countries or whether efforts should be focused instead on promoting exports to North America or on consolidating the company's market position in Chile. Ricardo was also wondering about expanding into other retailing concepts in Chile, including athletics and outdoor clothing stores as well as children's shoes and apparel. In contemplating how and when to proceed, Ricardo recognized that key family members were waiting for a recommendation.

This case was prepared by Professor Allen J. Morrison at The American Graduate School of International Management and Professor James Bowey at Bishop's University for the sole purpose of providing material for classroom discussion. Certain identifying information may have been disguised to protect confidentiality. It is not intended to illustrate either effective or ineffective handling of a managerial situation. Copyright © 1993 by The American Graduate School of International Management—Thunderbird and Bishop's University.

Company Background

Hush Puppies Chile began operations in 1980 through the concerted efforts of three brothers, Alfonso, Ricardo, and Juan Pablo Swett. In the early 1960s, the three brothers formed NORSEG, a start-up company that supplied safety equipment to industrial and mining sites throughout Chile. With rising sales and a healthy cash flow, the brothers gradually expanded operations to include real estate development, several agricultural projects, and a 10 percent equity position in Elecmetal S.A., one of the largest industrial companies in Chile. Over time, these operations were organized as separate companies under the family owned Costanera S.A.C.I. Holding Co.

Wolverine World Wide

In the spring of 1979, the three Swett brothers were informed by their advertising agency, Veritas, Ltd., that Wolverine World Wide was interested in expanding into Chile. Wolverine, based in Rockford, Michigan, controlled a portfolio of footwear brands including Hush Puppies casual shoes, Wolverine work and outdoor boots, Bates uniform shoes, and Brooks athletic shoes. Incorporated in 1954, Wolverine traced much of its initial success in footwear markets to its reliance on the production of casual pigskin shoes. In the mid-1950s, Wolverine developed a new elaborate pigskin tannage technology to take advantage of the characteristics of fine grain pigskin and in 1958 introduced Hush Puppies casual pigskin shoes.

During the 1960s and 1970s, Hush Puppies emerged as a major brand with particular strength in the men's segment. The infamous basset hound became a widely recognized symbol for quality and comfort. Success in the United States was followed by international expansion, initially in Canada and Europe. In the early 1980s, spurred by fears that the U.S. government might lift import quotas on low cost shoes from the Far East and Latin America, Wolverine moved to accelerate its international expansion. By 1992, Wolverine World Wide had established joint ventures or licensing agreements in over 40 countries, including most of Europe, Japan, and South America.

In Chile, Wolverine was looking for an agent to import or manufacture Hush Puppies branded shoes under license. In response to Wolverine's initiatives, the Swett brothers commissioned market research studies, which revealed that the Chilean shoe market was dominated by formal, dressy products and that no companies effectively met the demand for casual shoes. The market research also indicated that Bata, a large Canadian-owned shoe company with worldwide operations, controlled an estimated 60 percent share of the market in Chile. Bata Chile operated primarily as a manufacturing company, which sold the bulk of its output to small independent stores throughout the country. Independent retailers had considerable power over manufacturers in controlling which brands to promote and which styles to display. Bata also operated several dozen of its own retail stores throughout Chile and was rumored to be considering further expansion.

Like most Chileans, Ricardo, Alfonso, and Juan Pablo believed that the open market of 1980 provided an ideal opportunity to start a new business. The brothers were particularly interested in the upper-class market in Chile which, by exposure through international travel, was positively familiar with the Hush Puppies' brand, quality, and unique designs. Wolverine World Wide also appeared to be an open company; its managers were supportive and personable. The brothers agreed that any venture with Wolverine would succeed.

A Move to Retailing

In working with Wolverine, the brothers decided early on that retailing provided the best option for getting Hush Puppies into Chile. According to Renato Figueroa, commercial manager of Hush Puppies Chile in 1980:

> Manufacturers risked their efforts, their capital, and their futures, while the retailers had control of the market. . . . Retailers treated all brands alike, not giving special treatment to any brand in particular. [We came to the conclusion that] the best way was to build our own store chain. . . . Our decision was based on the notion that we would be able to influence and handle the market. We would know our consumers. This would enable us to place Hush Puppies in a different position from the rest of the competition in Chile.

After negotiations with Wolverine, Hush Puppies Chile was given exclusive rights to import Hush Puppies shoes and develop retail outlets in Chile. Although no up-front fees were paid to Wolverine, the brothers committed to open as many as 25 retail stores within three years. Expectations were that the costs for the first five stores, including leasehold improvements, training, inventories, and so on, would total about $2 million. Of this amount, about $1 million would be borrowed. The remaining $1 million represented a substantial risk to the brothers.

As agreed, stores were designed as family concept outlets in which both parents and children could find comfortable, casual shoes. The best Hush Puppies shoes would be imported from around the world, with about 80 percent coming from United States. The target market was identified as high-income consumers representing the "ABC" market, or top 10 percent of wage earners in Chile. Given the stratification of wealth in Chile, these consumers compared favorably with upper-middle and upper-income U.S. consumers, making the target market in Chile substantially different than that in the United States.

Stores were situated in large, convenient locations primarily in the Santiago metropolitan area. The sales staff was extensively trained to better relate to the up-scale customers and were well compensated, reflecting the desire for continuity and professionalism. Shoe prices were set at a 10 percent premium over average shoe prices and were the same in every store. In distant locations in Chile, the plan was for Hush Puppies Chile to grant franchises to independent retailers. As agreed upon by the brothers, Ricardo assumed responsibility as the general manager of Hush Puppies Chile. Juan Pablo Swett assumed responsibility as the general manager of NORSEG Chile. Alfonso was involved in major investment decisions and strategic planning for all family owned businesses as well as some day-to-day decision making at Hush Puppies Chile. By early 1982, Hush Puppies Chile had established seven shoe stores in the greater Santiago area.

A Move into Manufacturing

After several years of promising economic growth, the bottom fell out of Latin American economies in 1982. Hit by slumping commodity prices, massive national debt, soaring interest rates, and worldwide recession, the Chilean economy, like every other in Latin America, plunged into a state of depression. In Chile, the GNP fell by 14 percent in 1982 alone. Between 1982 and 1985, unemployment officially hovered around 14 percent; unofficially, it surpassed 30 percent. During the same period, the Chilean peso lost two-thirds of its value against the U.S. dollar, leading to a commensurate rise in import costs.

With Hush Puppies Chile totally reliant on imported shoes, the company was devastated by the economic downturn. Only two options appeared possible: shut down in the face of massive losses or move into manufacturing. According to Alfonso and Ricardo:

> We believed in the brand. The consumer liked it. As a result, we had no choice but to get into manufacturing. All our businesses have always been very conservative with low debt load. So we weren't at real risk in the downturn. We saw the business in the long term. Besides, we could get into manufacturing inexpensively as everyone else was getting out, so real estate was cheap.

In April 1982, the decision was made to move Hush Puppies Chile into shoe manufacturing. In November 1982, a partnership was formed between Wolverine World Wide and Hush Puppies Chile with 70 percent of the manufacturing joint venture owned by Hush Puppies Chile and 30 percent owned by Wolverine. Both partners agreed to contribute representative amounts of capital to ensure that manufacturing output met growth targets.

From Wolverine's perspective, a manufacturing facility in Chile made sense for a number of reasons. In 1981, import quotas ended in the United States and Wolverine moved aggressively to shift production overseas. Under the joint venture agreement with Hush Puppies Chile, Wolverine would have access to a new source of shoes made with low cost Chilean labor. The U.S. company would also receive royalties on Hush Puppy sales as well as benefit from profit sharing from the Chilean production facility. Finally, Wolverine's wholly owned Puerto Rican affiliate would become an ongoing supplier of some selected components for the Chilean operation.

In February 1983, a small new manufacturing facility was opened in suburban Santiago, which included approximately 10,000 square meters of manufacturing capacity, a two-story executive office complex, and a factory retail outlet. Manufacturing, imports, and export sales were handled by Hush Puppies Chile, Ltd. Retail operations were organized under the separate company name of Commercial Puppies, Ltd.

Hush Puppies Chile and Commercial Puppies were both organized with their own boards of directors, which included the three Swett brothers as well as a small group of trusted Western-educated managers from the operating companies. Most directors served on two or three boards. Strategic decisions were made at the board level and passed down to the operating company general managers. While both Hush Puppies Chile and Commercial Puppies were recognized as separate companies with their own functional structures, managers worked closely together to coordinate activities.

Rapid Growth

By 1985, the Chilean economy started to turn around and from 1985 to 1990 the company enjoyed rapid growth. In 1985, Hush Puppies Chile added Brooks athletic shoes to fill out its product line. Brooks athletic shoes were owned by Wolverine and had benefited in the United States by the upsurge in interest in physical fitness. While some of the Brooks shoes were to be manufactured in Santiago, most were to be imported from the Far East. It was anticipated that about 70 percent of the Brooks shoes distributed in Chile would be sold to outside retailers; the remaining 30 percent would be sold in Hush Puppies shoe stores.

As overall sales picked up, Hush Puppies Chile and Commercial Puppies focused more on building and maintaining key brands. The objective was to develop a reputation for excellence in marketing by emphasizing advertising, service, and style. Feedback from retail stores proved a major strength in focusing design and manufacturing on consumer needs. Hush Puppies Chile managers regarded the company as market oriented, as opposed to manufacturing oriented, thus differentiating the company from many Far East suppliers. By the end of 1985, Commercial Puppies was managing 22 company owned stores and Hush Puppies Chile was supervising four franchise stores.

To strengthen marketing efforts, advertising budgets were expanded, reaching 5 percent of sales in 1987. In 1987, the company started a major advertising program entitled "the pleasure of walking," which was particularly appealing to increasingly health conscious upper- and upper-middle-class Chileans. Follow-up multicolor ads promoting Hush Puppies' line of outdoor casual and hiking boots were placed in major newspapers and top magazines throughout the country (see Exhibit 1). Television advertisements were also developed, which focused on Hush Puppies as statements of quality and style. During the late 1980s and early 1990s, Hush Puppies Chile won three annual Wolverine World Wide awards for the quality of its advertising campaign and marketing strategy.

The company's strategy to strengthen the Hush Puppies brand succeeded. By the end of 1987, the production of shoes reached 265,000 pairs, an increase of 18 percent over 1986. In 1988, production increased an additional 15 percent to 305,000 pairs; in 1989, shoe production was up 29 percent to 392,000 pairs. Despite these impressive gains, the company remained relatively weak in two important categories: women's shoes and children's shoes. In an effort to reposition itself in these fast-growing segments, several bold initiatives were undertaken in the late 1980s.

A Move into Women's and Children's Shoes

To strengthen the company's position in the women's shoe market, more effort was devoted to product design and marketing. The women's product manager, Cardina Schmidt, believed that prior to 1990 the women's product line had not adequately satisfied the style and fashion demands of Chilean women. Good design was particularly important in the women's segment, in which styles changed nearly every six

EXHIBIT 1   Sample Advertisement Placed by Hush Puppies Chile in Major National Magazines

months. Women in the target segment were particularly fashion conscious and were generally familiar with the newest fashions in Europe and North America.

In order to make Hush Puppies more appealing to women, high-fashion shoes were imported from Italy, France, and Argentina. Hush Puppies Chile also hired exclusive designers to develop its own collection of women's shoes. Designers and managers regularly visited Hush Puppies stores to question women on desired design features like colors and styles. New window displays were designed to establish a more stylish image, and a major television advertising campaign was launched. As a result of these efforts, sales growth in the women's segment increased dramatically.

During this same period, the company also undertook a major initiative in children's shoes. The history of the company's efforts with children's shoes was reported by Sebastian Swett, a second-generation Swett and a product manager for kids' shoes:

> Surveys detected great opportunities for us in the children's market. The market was very traditional. It offered old models in brown or white. . . . The market seemed willing to pay a higher price for shoes with aggressive colors and concepts, such as comfort and security. . . . We had a few advantages, such as the excellent Hush Puppies' image, which was attractive for children

and easily identified. . . . We also had several disadvantages. Our stores were not appropriate for selling kids' shoes; other competitors had years in the market; [and finally] we didn't have the machinery to develop a great collection for kids up until 12 years in age.

In early 1990, Hush Puppies for Kids was launched, consisting of four different categories that varied according to the age of the child. *Soft Puppies* shoes were introduced for infants; *Little Puppies* were designed for children age 1 to 3 years; *Young Puppies* were introduced for children aged 4 to 8 years; and finally, *Junior Puppies* were designed for children age 9 to 14 years. The introduction was accompanied by extensive television advertising. Hush Puppies for Kids was an immediate success.

Strengthening the Athletic Position

By the summer of 1989, Brooks was positioned as the number three brand in the Chilean athletic shoe market after Diadora and Adidas. In the United States, however, Brooks was a relatively weak brand, a fact not altogether lost on fashion-conscious Chilean adolescents, and L.A. Gear was emerging as the top trendy shoe for adolescents. L.A. Gear was a relative newcomer in the athletic shoe industry and, to capitalize on its increasingly popularity, had begun to search for international distributors. The opportunity to market a more fashionable brand in L.A. Gear was clear and Alfonso approached the company in the summer of 1990.

After considerable discussion, L.A. Gear agreed in the fall of 1990 to work with Hush Puppies Chile to bring the L.A. Gear brand to Chile. L.A. Gear shoes would be imported from U.S. inventories or directly from the manufacturers in Korea and China, thus sparing Hush Puppies any manufacturing risks. Hush Puppies Chile's intention was to consolidate the L.A. Gear operations with those of Brooks; however, L.A. Gear insisted that Hush Puppies Chile create a distinct sales company to maximize the brand's potential. Wolverine World Wide was also very concerned about the impact that the L.A. Gear initiative would have on Brooks in Chile. In response, Costanera created Top Sport to manage the sale of L.A. Gear. A separate company, Coast Sport, was organized to manage all Brooks sales. It was hoped that creating separate companies for athletic shoes would allow greater focus for Hush Puppies brands as well as encourage new sales initiatives for athletic shoes.

Wolverine's Manufacturing Position Is Purchased

In December 1991, Costanera acquired the 30 percent of Hush Puppies Chile operations owned by Wolverine World Wide. The buyout was prompted by Wolverine's failure to support Hush Puppies Chile's ambitious expansion plans. During late 1989 and 1990, manufacturing facilities were increased over 30 percent in Chile to keep pace with booming demand. Plans called for production capacity to be increased by another 20 percent in 1991. New investment requirements in Chile as well as other countries, combined with the need to reinvest profits, translated into a negative cash flow for Wolverine. At the same time, Wolverine was facing changes in the business

EXHIBIT 2   Costanera Holding: Organization Chart

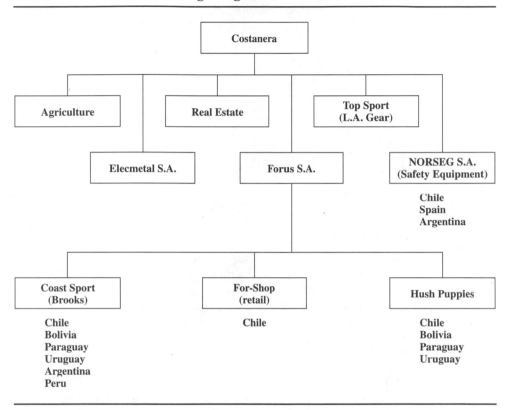

in the United States and was struggling to conserve capital. As a result, a buyout became an attractive option for both parties. The purchase of Wolverine's 30 percent share of manufacturing was estimated to have cost Costanera approximately $3.6 million. With the buyout complete, Hush Puppies Chile changed its name to Forus, S.A. In January 1992, the name of Commercial Puppies was changed to For-Shop, Ltd. Exhibit 2 provides a full organization chart for Costanera Holding.

Under the terms of the acquisition, Wolverine extended its licensing agreement to Forus for 20 years. In addition, Forus pushed for and received the rights to manufacture and sell Hush Puppies brands in Bolivia, Paraguay, and Uruguay. Forus was also licensed to sell—but not manufacture—Brooks athletic shoes in Bolivia, Paraguay, Uruguay, Argentina, and Peru. Outside these countries, sales of Hush Puppies or Brooks branded products could only be made to other Wolverine licensees. For Wolverine, Costanera's program for growth, endorsed by the success obtained in Chile, made it the best company to build sales in Latin America. Increased sales in the region would mean higher royalties to Wolverine as well as an increase in the export of raw materials.

EXHIBIT 3   **Business Relations with Wolverine World Wide (thousands of U.S. dollars)**

	Total 1987–91	Projected 1992
Purchases		
Leather and raw material	$ 6,302	$2,000
Hush Puppies finished shoes	557	640
Brooks shoes	3,960	1,400
Total	$10,819	$4,040
Royalties		
Hush Puppies	$ 1,032	$ 500
Brooks	441	120
Total	$ 1,473	$ 620

After the buyout, the relationship between Costanera and Wolverine remained strong. Both companies continued to share designs and coordinate product introductions. Forus also remained a major purchaser of leather and leather products as well as Brooks shoes. Exhibit 3 reports the extent of business relations between Forus and Wolverine World Wide over a six-year period.

Broad Market Appeal

By the end of 1991, Forus had succeeded in significantly broadening the market appeal of its Hush Puppies brands. In the ABC1 men's market, Hush Puppies was number one in market share; in the ABC1 women's market, Hush Puppies was number five in terms of market share; and in the ABC1 children's market, Hush Puppies was number four in market share. Market mix for the ABC1 segment and Hush Puppy branded sales ratios on a unit volume basis are included in Figure 1.

Growth in Retail Operations

By the end of 1991, total annual retail sales of Hush Puppy, Brooks, and L.A. Gear shoes amounted to 328,000 pairs. About 74 percent of these shoes were sold in 25 company owned stores. An additional 9 percent of sales was generated through "Hush Puppies Corners," which had been established in shoe departments of 14 major retail department stores. In promoting Hush Puppies Corners, For-Shop agreed to train sales employees and assist in designing and setting up displays. About 10 percent of the company's sales was also generated through small independent retail outlets. Franchise sales represented approximately 7 percent of total retail sales. In 1991, the company had five franchise stores located in isolated cities in Chile. By the summer of 1992, the number of company owned retail stores in Chile had increased to 26, with 4 more planned by year end. Exhibit 4 presents retail sales data for 1990 and 1991, as well as projections for 1992.

FIGURE 1   ABC1 Segment Mix and Hush Puppy Sales Mix (year end, 1991)

ABC1 Market Mix (%)		Hush Puppies Sales Mix (%)		Hush Puppies Market Share (%)	
Men	24%	Men	46%	Men	30%
Women	47	Women	30	Women	8
Children	29	Children	24	Children	11

EXHIBIT 4   For-Shop: Retail Sales, 1990–1992

	1990	*1991*	*1992**
Number of stores	25	25	26
Sales (pairs 000s):			
H.P. men's	152	164	188
H.P. women's	69	74	125
H.P. children's	37	49	61
Sports shoes	31	41	44
Total pairs	289	328	418
Sales (US$000s):			
Total shoes	$8,575	$12,163	$17,260
Total accessories	519	841	1,226
Total	$9,094	$13,004	$18,486
Avg. US$ retail price (pair)	$29.67	$37.08	$41.29
Avg. monthly inventory (pairs 000s)	122	129	158
Annual inventory turnover	2.4	2.5	2.7
Number of employees	154	177	203

*1992 sales are estimates.

Note: These figures do not include franchises, department stores, or export sales.

International Expansion

Although the Swett brothers were pleased with Hush Puppies overall growth in Chile, they were constantly reminded of the vulnerability lessons of 1982. Certainly Costanera was a much more balanced company by mid-1992 than it was 10 years earlier. It had a healthy balance sheet, a portfolio of popular American brand names, improving manufacturing capabilities, world-class design skills, and substantial marketing expertise. Despite these advantages, Ricardo and several managers began to realize that the depth of Hush Puppies Chile's market penetration, particularly in the ABC1 men's casuals, would lead to increased competition from new European and American brands.

With these concerns in mind, Ricardo began considering other alternatives for growth. A move into men's dress shoes was rejected, because the segment was already highly competitive and because managers at Hush Puppies Chile did not believe that their skill base would provide the company with a significant competitive advantage. However, other opportunities for growth were being seriously studied. These included growth by expanding exports to North America and Europe and growth through product and market diversification in South America.

Export Opportunities—North America

Since it began manufacturing almost 10 years earlier, Hush Puppies Chile had always hoped to develop a strong export business, particularly to North America and Europe. Success in exports seemed likely, given Chile's comparative advantage of low-cost labor and Hush Puppies Chile's excellent styling and product-development skills. Hush Puppies Chile's manufacturing labor costs in 1991 averaged $2.00 per hour, including all benefits; in neighboring Argentina, wages in the shoe industry averaged from $2.25 to $2.50 per hour. In addition to being at least comparable in terms of costs, the quality and consistency of Chilean labor was generally regarded as superior to that available in neighboring countries.

From a company perspective, an emphasis on exporting seemed to make sense for two reasons. First, sales to the Northern Hemisphere could potentially offset cyclical sales in the Southern Hemisphere. Forus was typically over capacity in the period leading up to fall/winter (February through July) and under capacity in spring/summer (August through January). Any additional export sales during the off-season would provide a better utilization of plant and equipment while minimizing fluctuations in employment levels. Second, the additional export sales volume would allow the ever increasing manufacturing and new product development overheads to be spread over a larger volume, thereby boosting overall profits.

Despite the appeal, exports to North America and Europe remained relatively modest. One problem was that exports from Chile were expected to compete with much lower cost footwear from China, India, and the Philippines. Hush Puppies' domestic target market was also the high-end segment, which added design and service costs that negated many of Chile's labor cost advantages. Also, Hush Puppies Chile's very diversified product line increased per-unit production costs through short production runs while at the same time removing opportunities for high-volume exports. A final problem was that direct and indirect labor costs represented only about 25 percent of total manufacturing costs, thus limiting the company's ability to pursue a low-cost exporting strategy. Because of these difficulties, several managers in the company believed that an export strategy built on superior design and marketing had the most chance to succeed. Others disagreed, arguing that if Hush Puppies Chile were serious about substantially increasing exports to North America and Europe it would have to develop lower priced shoes. Such a move would also open additional mass market opportunities for the company in Chile.

The company had never seriously considered shifting manufacturing to lower cost Asian countries. Difficulties in controlling overseas production and the need to respond to rather fickle customer needs undermined the potential savings of overseas manufacturing. Managers at Hush Puppies Chile also believed the company had no competitive advantage in importing. Estimates for 1992 were that the company would import about US$3.0 million in raw materials (mostly soles and leathers) and about US$1.7 million in finished shoes. The United States would supply approximately 25 percent of these imports, with the rest coming from the Far East, Argentina, Brazil, Italy, Spain, Germany, Mexico, and the United Kingdom.

Opportunities in Latin America

From 1987 to 1991, the average annual sales growth for Forus, For-Shop, and Coast Sport was 20 percent per year. From 1990 to 1991, sales growth accelerated to a staggering 35 percent, encouraged in part by the rapid growth of the Chilean economy. Strict adherence to free markets and free trade had led to booming economic growth in Chile, with the economy expanding an average of 6 percent per year from 1987 to 1992. Many economists were predicting GDP growth of 10 percent per annum throughout the remainder of 1992, making Chile one of the fastest-growing economies in the world and an engine of economic growth in the region. (For a brief overview of Chile's economic development over the last two decades, see Exhibit 5.)

The company's initiative in Latin America began in earnest in May 1989, when Hush Puppies Chile began exporting Hush Puppies shoes to Uruguay. With air freight to Uruguay averaging about US$0.55 per kg., transportation costs appeared favorable for exports. By the end of 1989, the company had sold more than 19,000 pairs of shoes in a country with a total population of just 3 million. In 1990, Hush Puppies Chile granted exclusive franchise rights to the Moliterno family, a diversified industrial company based in the capital city of Montevideo. Moliterno quickly established Hush Puppies Uruguay as a wholly owned subsidiary. During 1990, three Hush Puppies retail outlets were opened, two in Montevideo and one in Maldonado.

Despite high ambitions, sales remained weak. Ricardo was convinced that Moliterno, with little experience in retailing, had chosen less than optimal retail locations. Stores were poorly maintained, and Moliterno spent essentially nothing on Hush Puppies advertising and promotion. Sales were also hurt by competition from low priced footwear exported by financially strapped manufacturers in Argentina and Brazil.

In the spring of 1991, Forus purchased 55 percent of Hush Puppies Uruguay. According to Ricardo, Hush Puppies Chile had always wanted to be a partner with Moliterno. The original agreement included an option to buy a majority stake in Hush Puppies Uruguay that Forus decided to exercise. Under the terms of the investment, Forus and Moliterno contributed US$400,000 to create a new company called Hush Puppies Uruguay S.A., which in turn purchased the Hush Puppies related assets of Moliterno. After gaining effective control over retailing, Hush Puppies Chile moved to strengthen operations. Sales employees received additional training, and new store locations were sought. By the end of 1991, three more Hush Puppies Uruguay stores were opened, bringing to six the total number of Hush Puppies', locations in that country.

EXHIBIT 5   The Chilean Economy: A Brief Overview

Political polarization under the left-wing government of President Salvador Allende (1970–73) brought the country close to a civil war and ended in September 1973 with a coup d'etat led by General Augusto Pinochet. During his 17-year rule, Pinochet turned to the writings of free market advocate and Nobel Prize-winning economist Milton Friedman to guide national industrial policy. Immediately after seizing power, martial law was imposed, the economy was liberalized, and foreign corporations were invited to return to Chile. Pinochet's 1980 blueprint for political democratization was completed on December 14, 1989, when a national plebescite was held and Patricio Alwin, the Christian Democratic leader of a center-left coalition, was elected president. He took office on Market 11, 1990. While in mid-1992 Augusto Pinochet remained commander of the nation's armed forces, the emerging democracy seemed stable and strong to most observers.

The success of Chile's free market reforms after a decade of stagflation and debt crisis amazed many observers. Most economists attributed Chile's enviable economic growth to its unrelenting dedication to free markets. By mid-1992, the bulk of the Chilean left was no longer anticapitalist, and a remarkable degree of consensus existed in the country about the need to maintain a liberal market economy and prudent fiscal policies. The main dividing issues related to a new labor code granting more rights to unions, and the questions of what to do about serious human rights violations that occurred under the Pinochet regime.

Economic Data—Chile: 1983–1991

	1983	1985	1987	1989	1991
GDP ($ billions)	19.8	15.6	18.9	25.4	30.0
Population (millions)	11.7	12.1	12.5	13.0	13.1
GDP per head ($)	1,692	1,289	1,512	1,954	2,239
Inflation (%)	23.1	26.4	21.5	21.4	18.7
Unemployment	17.4	10.9	8.0	4.8	5.2
Total debt/GDP (%)	91.9	130.7	109.3	68.4	63.1

Despite its interest in open markets, Chile has shunned involvement in Mercosur or the free trade zone that neighboring Paraguay, Uruguay, Argentina, and Brazil hoped to have running by 1994. Confident after nine years of stability and growth, Chile in 1992 was aspiring to become the first Latin American country to join the NAFTA. If NAFTA membership were to prove elusive, the government intended to pursue a free trade agreement with Japan, Chile's top export market after the United States.

Essentially no Hush Puppies shoes were exported to Paraguay in 1991, and no changes were planned for 1992. Customs duties on shoes averaged 70 percent in Paraguay but were being slowly cut under pressure from the GATT, as well as broader initiatives undertaken in creating the Southern Cone Economic Market. Ricardo believed that as the economy opened up in 1993, Forus would begin some modest exports.

In Bolivia, a country of 7 million, Forus established a licensing agreement with Global Trading Company of La Paz. Although the agreement had been in place for less than a year, two stores had been opened and Hush Puppies Corners had been set up in two department stores. Ricardo estimated that exports for 1992 would amount to about 15,000 pairs, or about US$525,000. Because of prevailing import tariffs, retail prices in Bolivia were set at a 10 percent premium over Chilean net prices. Although it was too early for managers at Forus to evaluate the long-term effectiveness of Global Trading Company in Bolivia, Forus had an option to buy up to a 50 percent equity position in the company at a time of its choosing.

In 1992, the company's efforts in Argentina were focused exclusively on promoting its Brooks line of athletic shoes. Coast Sport Argentina was established in 1991 and acted exclusively as a wholesaler for a variety of independent retail outlets in the country. Eighty percent of the new company was owned by Coast Sport Chile and 20 percent by NORSEG Argentina, which had, as a majority owner, NORSEG Chile. Brooks shoes were imported directly from factories in the Far East, or from Coast Sport inventories in Chile. Ricardo estimated that in 1992 in Argentina the company would sell about 32,500 pairs of Brooks shoes, worth approximately US$1 million.

Recent Developments

After witnessing almost a decade of accelerating growth and profits, Ricardo was reflective. Projections indicated that 1992 would be the best year ever for the company, with after-tax profits at over 15 percent of sales and return on equity surpassing 35 percent. (Financial statements for 1990 and 1991 are reported in Exhibit 6.) With such growth and profitability, it was easy to feel confident.

By the summer of 1992, Ricardo was weighing a number of options to recommend to Alfonso and Juan Pablo for consideration. One major thrust under consideration was to move aggressively into the retailing of apparel. Although Costanera had little experience with clothing, apparel seemed to fit well with the company's other retail operations. It was thought that the best way to proceed would be to open a chain of stores, combining both Brooks and L.A. Gear athletic shoes with branded sports clothing. While the combination of athletic shoe and clothing stores had proved a major hit in Europe, Japan, and North America, it had yet to be effectively pursued in Chile. A combination outlet would have the advantage of allowing the company to move incrementally into apparel while concurrently expanding athletic shoe sales. Costs for a retail space in a typical up-scale Santiago shopping mall were estimated at 7 percent of net sales with leasehold improvements averaging about US$30,000. Unfortunately, the company did not have a brand under consideration and was wondering how to aggressively proceed.

A second option being considered was to open a chain of outdoor clothing stores. The outdoor clothing and accessory market was particularly attractive, because it was a segment that appeared to have been neglected in Chile. Through visits to the United States, all three Swett brothers had become familiar with a variety of fast-growing outdoor clothing stores, such as Timberland, Eddie Bauer, and North-by-Northwest. Market research in Chile indicated that outdoor clothing sales could grow rapidly, and Ricardo wondered if he should recommend a major move into this segment. What was uncertain was the extent to which the skills learned in marketing shoes could be transferred to outdoor clothing.

EXHIBIT 6   Financial Statements for Forus, S.A. (for the years ended December 31, 1990 and 1991)

	Income Statements	
	1990 (Ch. $)	*1991 (Ch. $)*
Operating revenues	$3,917,656,542	$5,092,329,385
Operating costs	(2,874,204,603)	(3,507,627,947)
Gross margin	1,043,451,939	1,584,701,438
Administrative and sales expenses	(534,015,090)	(666,112,679)
Operating results	509,436,849	918,588,759
Nonoperating expenses	(113,686,107)	110,645,279
Income before tax	395,750,742	1,029,234,038
Income tax	16,273,224	49,547,770
Net income	$ 379,477,518	$ 979,686,268
US $1 = $ Chilean	337.09	374.09

	Balance Sheet	
	1990(Ch. $)	*1991 (Ch. $)*
Assets		
Total current assets	$1,678,518,025	$2,561,279,678
Total fixed assets	2,084,031,742	2,387,101,951
Less accumulated depreciation	(544,166,086)	(699,091,557)
Net fixed assets	1,539,865,656	1,688,010,394
Investment in related companies plus other assets	1,632,891,422	1,966,126,263
Total assets	$4,851,275,163	$6,215,416,335
Liabilities and Stockholders' Equity		
Total current liabilities	$1,530,707,772	$1,756,973,367
Long-term liabilities:		
Bank debt	377,752,696	608,837,630
Other accounts payable	130,702,501	152,427,111
Total long-term liabilities	508,455,197	761,264,741
Total stockholders' equity	2,812,112,194	3,697,178,227
Total liabilities and equity	$4,851,275,163	$6,215,416,335

A third option for the company was the introduction of a new retailing concept for children's shoes and apparel. While first Hush Puppies Chile and then Forus had been selling children's shoes for the past 10 years, the introduction of Hush Puppies for Kids had been a major hit in the marketplace. In July 1992, managers at Hush Puppies Chile were debating whether to extend the Kids line to include branded children's clothing and accessories. A full line of merchandise would accompany a full move into children's retailing by filling out stores and providing an added draw for consumers. Wolverine had been trying for years to introduce Hush Puppies branded clothes for children in the United States, but the efforts had not gone well. To better develop a recognizable brand in the United States, Wolverine had just recently adopted the Hush Puppies for Kids logo that had been developed in Chile. While Ricardo realized the potential for new retail concepts, he was also fully aware that a movement into retailing would have serious consequences for the company.

Behind the increasing interest in diversifying the retail base of the company was the recognition that retailing was becoming more specialized. The need for even greater specialization was articulated by Renato Figueroa, general manager of For-Shop's retail operations: "As the market becomes more globalized, our next move must be to specialize in our stores. Where we have family stores, we must in the future have men's stores, kids' stores, women's stores, and lifestyle stores."

Ricardo was also faced with the decision of focusing management efforts on increasing sales in Chile or on expanding sales in other Latin American countries. Some in the company argued that Costanera could do both at the same time. Others disagreed by highlighting the risk that foreign operations would increasingly siphon critical resources away from core Chilean operations.

For Ricardo Swett, the critical issue was management:

> Our big problem with growth is people. How can the management of the company keep up with such rapid growth? We need good middle managers. . . . On average, about 60 percent of our senior managers have had formal university training in management. When we exclude manufacturing managers, this number climbs to about 80 percent. Still, we spend a lot of effort training our managers. On average, each of our managers receives about two and a half weeks of training per year.
>
> Sometimes I feel that we are moving too slowly. The world is changing so fast that it is increasingly difficult to stay abreast of what is going on internationally. What worries me is that our managers might not be reacting fast enough. There needs to be a daily commitment to learning.

Clearly, Ricardo had much to consider. While any major decision would require the support of both Alfonso and Juan Pablo, Ricardo realized that they would be relying on him for direction. Ricardo seemed to have more questions than answers. How fast should they move and where should they target expansion? Despite enormous success in the past, it was uncertain in which direction to turn.

10   TECHNOPHAR IN VIET NAM

As Gary Dube, vice president of Technophar Equipment & Service Ltd .(Technophar), a leading manufacturer of hard and soft gelatin capsule machines, proceeded to his meeting with Mark Habuda, vice president of marketing, and Herman Victorov, president, he reviewed the history of their recent venture in Viet Nam. Negotiations had proceeded smoothly since the initial contact 18 months ago, and an agreement had been reached with the Vietnamese partner, Cuulong Pharmaceutical Import and Export Company (Cuulong). However, the initial deposit, due on December 15, 1994, had not arrived, and now, on January 15, 1995, concern about the Viet Nam contract had intensified. Dube wondered if Technophar should renegotiate the contract, cancel the contract, or continue to wait patiently for a payment that might not ever arrive. In the back of his mind, Dube re-evaluated their approach to securing foreign contracts.

The Gelatin Capsule Industry

Hard gelatin capsules were invented in 1833 by the French pharmacist A. Mathes. Originally produced in a hand process by Parke Davis (Capsugel), they were first machine-processed by Eli-Lilly (Elanco) in the late 19th century. The first semiautomatic machine was developed in 1909 by Arthur Colton who continued to innovate and improve the capsule manufacture process through the first half of the 20th century. He introduced the first fully automatic machine in the 1930s and eventually sold his company and machine design patents to Snyder Co. of Detroit, Michigan. In 1963, Snyder Co. was purchased by Cherry-Burrell Corporation, the company from which Technophar was spun-off. Technophar's position in the gelatin capsule industry was

Andrew Delios prepared this case under the supervision of Professor Paul Beamish, solely to provide material for class discussion. The case is not intended to illustrate either effective or ineffective handling of a managerial situation. Certain names and other identifying information may have been disguised to protect confidentiality. Copyright © 1995, The University of Western Ontario.

EXHIBIT 1   The Gelatin Capsule Industry

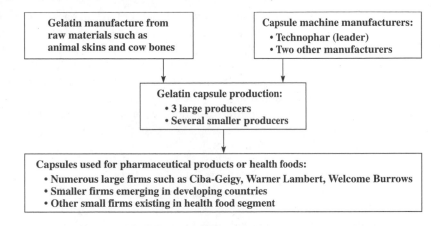

that of a supplier of machines and turnkey plants for the manufacture of hard and soft gelatin capsules (see Exhibit 1). Two other firms, one in Canada and the other in the United States, competed directly with Technophar. Technophar manufactured machines that were widely considered technologically superior in design and operating performance. In 1995 it was the industry leader with an 80 percent share of the growing worldwide market for capsule machines. However, high price sensitivity among machine purchasers required Technophar to price their machines on par with competitors' machines.

Capsule machine manufacture and gelatin capsule production existed as niche businesses within the larger pharmaceutical industry. Large pharmaceutical firms, with the exception of Shinogi and Capsugel, were not involved in gelatin capsule production. Pharmaceutical firms were reluctant to integrate backwards for three reasons: (1) pharmaceutical firms preferred to concentrate on the production of fine chemicals used in pharmacological products, (2) a small capsule factory produced 1.5 billion capsules per year and most pharmaceutical firms filled fewer than a billion capsules annually, and (3) gelatin capsule production was a notoriously difficult and finicky process. Capsules were easier to buy than produce; as a result, the gelatin capsule industry was initially a duopoly.

In the early 1970s, the U.S.-based R. P. Scherer Co. (Scherer) entered into capsule production, joining the first two producers of hard gelatin capsules: Capsugel and Elanco. By the 1990s, these three producers had secured an 80 to 85 percent share of the worldwide gelatin capsule market and were protective of their processes and technology. Dube commented on the impression these capsule producers had created:

> For many years Capsugel and Elanco portrayed the technology of making capsules as an exclusive, painstaking craft which few people had the God-given ability to do well, and these few were employed by Capsugel and Elanco. Consequently these two companies put factories in a few key countries around the world, and really controlled the market until the early 1970s. Then

R. P. Scherer came in and took a little bite out of it. Finally we started to sell the technology which opened up the industry.

Capsugel was the largest producer of hard capsules with 140 hard capsule machines located in eight countries around the world (see Exhibit 2). Shinogi, a Japanese pharmaceutical firm and previously Elanco's joint venture partner in Japan, purchased Elanco's capsule production business in the 1990s. Shinogi operated 80 hard capsule machines and had centralized capsule production to facilities in the United States, Spain, and Japan. Scherer, the third largest producer of hard capsules with 40 machines in three different countries, was the dominant firm in the soft capsule market. Scherer had a 60 to 65 percent world share in this rapidly growing segment of the capsule market.

The hard capsule factory location decision was driven mainly by transportation cost considerations. Gelatin capsules, a light, voluminous product consisting mostly of air, were expensive to transport because of their low value per unit volume. Accordingly, to minimize transportation costs, capsule factories had been located close to pharmaceutical firms' manufacturing facilities in Europe and North America. However, in recent years, pharmaceutical firms had been shifting production to developing countries to take advantage of lower labour costs and tax incentives, and to be closer to the source of fine chemicals used as fillers in encapsulated products. Indonesia, Puerto Rico, and China had emerged as popular host sites for manufacturing investments by pharmaceutical firms.

The relocation of pharmaceutical facilities created new opportunities for capsule producers. Capsule factories placed in developing countries had a transportation cost advantage in supplying these new pharmaceutical plants. Also, pharmaceutical firms from developing countries were entering the worldwide market for pharmacological products and, for similar reasons, these firms required nearby capsule factories.

Market Development

Capsule production technology became available to firms around the globe through Technophar's innovative efforts. Technophar simplified and standardized capsule production enabling the process to be transferred with relative ease. Dube stated, "We took the production process and broke it down so that you could teach it to a ten year old." The company developed procedures and manuals to support its simplified process. These manuals detailed the intricacies of the production process and explained machine operations, maintenance and repair.

Technophar's innovations led to demand growth in less-developed regions of the world such as Eastern Europe, Africa, Latin America, and regions of Asia. For example, prior to Technophar's technology transfer to China, the market for hard capsules had been small because capsules were expensive to produce. Capsules were produced in a labour-intensive, hand-dipping process which had a very low productivity. As automated capsule production technology became available to producers in China through Technophar's efforts, the market for hard capsules began to grow. Hard capsules produced with Technophar's technology became inexpensive to produce (US$3

EXHIBIT 2   Location of Hard Capsule Factories and Machines (as of 1995)

Manufacturer	Country	No. of Machines
Capsugel	Belgium Brazil China France Japan Mexico Thailand United States	Total: 140 machines
Shinogi	Japan Spain United States	Total: 80 machines
Scherer	Brazil Canada Germany	Total: 40 machines

Source: Company records.

per thousand) or purchase. As a result, developing countries could produce their own capsules which facilitated upstream entry into the pharmaceutical industry.

Company History

Herman Victorov, president and founder of Technophar, had been a plant engineer for Scherer. During his tenure there, he developed a process modification which nearly doubled the hourly yield of capsule production from 28,000 to 48,000. In 1983, a subsequent process improvement increased output another 4,000 capsules per hour. In 1984, he left Scherer and established Multi-Motion Engineering Inc. in Windsor, Ontario, which was purchased by Cherry Burrell in 1985.

Technophar, a spin-off of the Canadian division of Cherry Burrell, came into existence as a private company in 1988. Technophar, was in the words of Dube, "a company of machine builders led by Victorov's desire to be an engineer and machine designer." Technophar employed 50 people, many of them highly-skilled technicians who had worked with Victorov at Cherry Burrell's Canadian division.

Technophar, building on Victorov's experience in Bulgaria, Germany, China and Romania, quickly emerged as an international supplier of hard capsule machines. Sales, while initially slow at seven machines for the 1988–1990 period, increased dramatically in 1992 when eight machines were sold. This rapid growth rate continued, and 20 machines were sold in 1994. Revenues in 1994 were US$12 million and the company was moderately profitable.

Technophar's customers were primarily in developing countries. The company's management team, experienced in the pharmaceutical industry and in international markets, was well-suited to dealing with the uncertainty and risk in these emerging markets. Dube commented on the nature of Technophar's business:

> When you are doing business internationally, quite often you are dealing with countries that are relying on aid money and it tends to be a feast or famine business. Our employees were either working 60 hours a week building machines, or they were painting doorknobs.

Technophar was accustomed to a high variability in orders. When the order book was empty, management was more willing to accommodate riskier contracts. Four or five contracts represented the company's annual business and Dube was well aware of the cost of a lost contract.

> If you are planning on two or three projects and a major one crumples on you, it can be devastating to a small company like ours. With our uneven stream of revenues, we have to be a private company. We could not be a public company with quarterly reporting requirements.

Technophar manufactured hard capsule machines in its Oldcastle, Ontario location for distribution and re-assembly in a variety of countries around the world. New capsule machines were list priced for US$535,000 to US$635,000. The company designed and constructed a number of different models for different needs, though components were readily interchangeable between models. Hence, machines tailored to specific customer needs were essentially identical across customers. The Oldcastle facility could produce 20 capsule machines annually with a single shift.

Technophar's Activities

International Operations

Technophar participated in several international alliances. Most alliances were manufacturing joint ventures and three of these were located in Romania, Victorov's country of birth. In Bucharest, Technophar had established a model turnkey plant for prospective clients. While this plant vertically integrated the firm forward, it was not an entry into the hard capsule market. Technophar did not want to compete with its own customers in the hard capsule market. Output from this plant was used to demonstrate the quality of Technophar's machinery and hard capsule product. A second joint venture in Bucharest operated as an engineering and trading company. The third joint venture, located in Odorheiu, was a manufacturing facility which produced components used in the assembly of capsule machines.

To date, China was Technophar's largest purchaser of hard capsule machines and factories (see Exhibit 3). For that reason Technophar had devoted considerable resources to serving the Chinese market and was positioned to exploit the huge untapped potential (see Exhibit 4). Mark Habuda was stationed in Guangzhou, Guangdong and two joint ventures had been established: The one in Qingdao, Shandong assisted with Technophar's projects in China; the other located in Guangzhou, Guangdong was a complete manufacturing facility which employed both local personnel and Canadian technicians. It produced capsule machines and support equipment for turnkey plants in China.

Exhibit 3   Technophar's Worldwide Market (as of 1995)

Country	No. of Machines Sold
Brazil	1
Bulgaria	4
Canada	2
China	31
Colombia	1
France	5
Germany	4
Indonesia	1
Israel	2
Korea	1
Romania	4
Taiwan	3
United States	1
Venezuela	1

Source: Company records.

Turnkey Plants

Technophar's main business was turnkey projects in developing countries. The sale of a turnkey plant was a complicated and time-consuming process: contracts were often courted for several years. Once the contract had been negotiated, a 10 to 15 percent deposit and a letter of credit for the balance was sent to Technophar. Because Technophar did not stock inventory, it would not begin capsule machine manufacture until these two items had been received. Technophar shipped the completed machines when it received the remaining portion of the contracted amount, less 10%. When the turnkey plant had been certified as fully operational, it was turned over to the purchaser in exchange for the 10% holdback amount.

The technology transfer consisted of four major components: preliminary building designs, the equipment necessary for the production of hard capsules, auxiliary equipment, and training in plant operations. Under the terms of the technology transfer agreement, the purchaser was responsible for the construction and cost of the Technophar-designed facility. Technophar used a standardized design which was adapted to local operating criteria. Once the facility had been constructed, a team of Technophar's technicians accompanied the machinery and equipment to the purchaser's facility.

The machines and auxiliary equipment were manufactured in one of Technophar's three manufacturing facilities. The auxiliary equipment included items such as dehumidifiers, air conditioners, and operational controls. Half of the turnkey contract's value was in this auxiliary equipment and the other half in the hard and soft capsule machines. The machines and auxiliary equipment once manufactured and tested, were disassembled and shipped to the purchaser's facility, where they were reassembled by the plant set-up team.

EXHIBIT 4   Market Penetration in China (No. of Machines as of 1995)

Province or Major Municipality	1994 Est. Population (million)	1993 GDP (US$ billion)	Per Capita GDP (US$)	GDP Annual Growth Rate (%)	Known No. of Hard Capsule Machines*
Anhui	60	28	469	17	
Beijing	11	20	1,806	0	
Fujian	31	23	744	10	
Gansu	23	10	426	18	
Guangdong	71	91	1,277	21	7
Guangxi	44	19	434	21	
Guizhou	34	9	262	8	
Hebei	64	37	577	−1	
Heilongjiang	39	26	673	11	2
Henan	89	37	417	−2	4
Hubei	57	37	649	19	
Hunan	65	29	442	13	
Inner Mongolia	23	11	492	22	
Jiangsu	73	102	1,398	10	
Jiangxi	40	18	249	11	
Jilin	27	19	720	18	
Liaoning	43	54	1,251	16	
Ningxia	5	2	516	17	
Qinghai	5	2	443	33	
Shaanxi	35	15	442	11	
Shandong	89	76	853	1	12
Shanghai	14	52	3,683	21	2
Shanxi	30	15	506	2	
Sichuan	120	52	432	15	
Tianjin	9	18	1,962	0	
Tibet	2	1	182	0	
Xinjiang	16	11	692	29	
Yunnan	39	15	393	22	
Zhejiang	47	53	1,127	5	4
Total for China	**1,205**	**882**	**743**	**11**	**31**

*Technophar machines only.

Sources: Department of Population Statistics, State Statistical Bureau, People's Republic of China, Beijing, July 1985, Table 34; *World Bank Atlas* 1995; company records.

The plant set-up team comprised five technicians. The first technician, who arrived in the purchaser's country toward the end of facility construction, inspected the new building and supervised installation of the climate control equipment. The next crew was responsible for auxiliary equipment set-up and capsule machinery installation. The final crew made the plant operational and subjected the plant to a 72-hour test run, termed the production test protocol (PTP). If the plant operated well under the PTP, Technophar completed their instruction about machine operations, formulations, and gelatin preparations. Technophar's contractual obligations ended when it formally turned the plant over to the purchaser.

Service Business

Throughout the facility construction process, Technophar's technicians had the opportunity to interact with people who would be operating the plant. They emphasized to the purchaser's staff the importance of following Technophar's well-documented operating procedures. Despite this stress on conformity with procedures, factories often "went to hell in a handbasket. After the keys had been handed over, the purchaser would take shortcuts and forget about the operating rules."

Although Technophar's guarantee did not cover operational difficulties arising from equipment misuse, company technicians were available to help repair machines. This form of after-sale service was offered for a fee, but purchasers seldom took advantage of it. Plants located in developing countries typically did not have discretionary funds for maintenance and repairs. Also, the efficiency imperative found in private companies was not present in many of these state-supported plants. Thus, machines capable of operating 24 hours per day and producing 65,000 capsules per hour, were operated for 13 or 14 hours each day, and when operated, the machines ran at 60 percent efficiency.

Technophar was also engaged in the service, repair, and upgrading of existing capsule machines, a number of which had been operating for many years. These machines were much slower and produced lower quality capsules than the newer machines. Technophar had refurbished a few machines, but managers were uncertain of the size of the existing market for machine upgrades.

Auxiliary Businesses

Technophar's expertise in machine manufacture and design facilitated the company's entry into other related businesses. The company had designed and manufactured various mechanical systems and machinery for firms in the metallurgical, chemical, and automotive industries. A major food processing company in North America had purchased original machines and prototypes for use in packaging. Technophar was also engaged in the manufacture of machinery for the small but rapidly expanding soft capsule industry.

Markets

Hard Gelatin Capsule

Estimates of annual worldwide capsule consumption ranged between 100 and 200 billion capsules: North America, the largest market for capsules, consumed 50 to 55 billion; Western Europe, the second largest market, consumed 40 billion. The size of other large regional markets was uncertain. Technophar's management estimated worldwide market growth to be 3 to 5 percent per annum (see Exhibit 5).

Gelatin Capsule Machine

Firms in developing countries and newly industrializing countries formed the large majority of Technophar's customers. One gelatin capsule plant was often sufficient

---

EXHIBIT 5   Worldwide Capsule Consumption (as of 1995)

Region	1995 Est. Population (million)	Estimated GDP in each Region (US$ billion)	Average GDP per person (US$)	Capsule Consumption (Est.)
North America	300	7,350	24,500	55 billion
Western Europe	465	8,439	18,148	40 billion
Eastern Europe	447	1,879	4,203	Not known
Asia/Pacific	3,294	6,670	2,025	Not known
Latin America*	494	1,416	2,866	Not known
Africa	683	463	678	Not known
Middle East	212	1,007	4,750	Not known
World	**5,895**	**27,224**	**4,618**	**100–200 billion**

*Includes the countries of South and Central America.

Note: The worldwide market for capsules was estimated by Dube to be growing at 3 to 5 percent per year.

Source: *World Bank Atlas* 1995; company records.

to satisfy domestic demand in these countries and Technophar was continually challenged to find new market opportunities. However, Technophar lacked formal marketing procedures and did not employ a sales force or agents dedicated to seeking and developing opportunities.[1] Trade shows, in which Technophar could display its product and meet potential customers, were deemed of little value because the North American market for gelatin capsule machines was saturated.

Technophar relied on two processes for accessing opportunities. The first was internal: managers were experienced both internationally and in the pharmaceutical industry. Dube, Victorov and Habuda had, respectively, 30, 17, and 13 years of experience in this industry and direct experience in the countries of Asia, Latin America and Eastern Europe. Dube expanded on the importance of experience and industry contacts:

> Over a period of time we had learned who was buying capsules. When I worked at R. P. Scherer I knew who was buying capsules because we had agents in 13 or 14 countries. We also knew where our competitors had factories.
>
> In determining opportunities for Technophar, we used our industry experience and went either through the gelatin end or through the pharmaceutical industry. We asked ourselves, "Is a pharmaceutical company interested in making capsules?" Or a group of people may leave these companies and become entrepreneurs. They would want to start a capsule-making business and would be natural customers for our product.

In determining opportunities, these managers operated a lot on 'gut feel', and each brought a unique perspective to their joint evaluation of a country. Entering into their intuitive assessment were a number of factors, one of which was the type of capsule

---

[1]An agent would travel extensively, incurring expenses of US$400 per day, and would receive salary and benefits of approximately US$60,000 per year. A secretary for this agent could be employed at an annual cost of US$30,000. (Source: John W. Wright, *The American Almanac of Jobs and Salaries,* 1995.)

consumption. Capsules were used for some ethical pharmaceutical products (prescription drugs and over-the-counter drugs), and for health food products, a rapidly growing market segment in North America and Europe. Ethical pharmaceutical consumption was multiplying in developing countries, particularly with the increased emphasis on health care.

The managers also considered the location of existing hard capsule factories. The Middle East, for example, was a promising region because only one small company produced capsules there. Other factors included the type of government in a country, its emphasis on health care (and by association, hard capsule consumption), and the openness of the country to international trade.

The second process for finding markets was also informal. Technophar gathered market information through a network of non-company agents and contacts. For example, it had an arrangement with Marubeni, a large Japanese trading company with offices around the world, to use its agents for information about potential markets. Canadian embassies and consulates had also been helpful by providing leads and by disseminating Technophar's promotional literature within their regional spheres of responsibility. American embassies, host country nationals residing in Canada, and agents within China, provided an informal source of information and often approached Technophar with unsolicited orders. An agent whose efforts resulted in an actual delivery, received a commission of 3–8% of the value of the contract. Contract values for a four-machine turnkey plant averaged US$3–4 million.

Developing Opportunities

Technophar's unblemished reputation for honesty, integrity and reliability was instrumental in securing new contracts. The company had gone to considerable lengths in the past to protect its highly valued reputation. In 1992 for example, it had received a deposit of US$1.3 million from Saudi Arabia for a turnkey plant. Technophar had begun machine manufacture and had invested a considerable amount of time and money in bringing the deal to fruition. However, a change in priority in Saudi Arabia led to the cancellation of the contract. Technophar was under no obligation to return the deposit; nevertheless, to protect its reputation and to promote the likelihood of future business in the region, it refunded all but accrued out-of-pocket expenses. From the goodwill created by this gesture, Technophar had secured contracts with other countries in the Middle East (e.g., Jordan) and was presently speaking with representatives from the United Arab Emirates, Qatar, and a new Saudi group about capsule machine sales.

Technophar continually cultivated new clients, as winning contracts often required an extended period of negotiations. It was not unusual for managers to spend US$10,000 on travel plus weeks of management time exploring an opportunity which might not ever result in a contract. Dube and Habuda, for example, traveled more than 140 days in 1994.

During the early stages of negotiation, Technophar assisted the purchaser with market and feasibility studies for the proposed plant. Technophar had a series of standard schedules for assessing manufacturing costs which were adaptable to factor

---

EXHIBIT 6   Market Penetration in Asia (as of 1995)

Country	Hard Capsule Machine
Bangladesh	No
Burma	No
Cambodia	No
China	Yes
Hong Kong	No
India	Yes (old, inferior quality)
Indonesia	Yes
Japan	Yes
Laos	No
Malaysia	No
Nepal	No
North Korea	??
Pakistan	No ?
Philippines	No
Singapore	Yes
South Korea	Yes
Taiwan	No ?
Thailand	Yes
Viet Nam	Contracted

Source: Company records.

conditions in the purchaser's country. Using these schedules, the purchaser plugged in the relevant figures to make projections of its production costs and profitability.

The Viet Nam Opportunity

Technophar received an unsolicited order for the Viet Nam contract. The deal had a *Viet Kieu* connection, as Mr. Ly Van Phi, the owner of an import-export business in Montreal, originally approached Technophar with officials of Cuulong about supplying hard-capsule-making equipment to Viet Nam.[2] The proposed project was valued at US$4 million and the agreement to provide the plant and equipment was signed on November 15, 1994, during Canadian Prime Minister Chretien's two-day visit to Viet Nam.

Though Technophar had been handed this opportunity, management had to evaluate the viability of the Viet Nam technology transfer as compared with other potential projects. The company, which normally had seven or eight projects in the process

---

[2]*Viet Kieu* refers to members of the 1975 exodus from Viet Nam to countries such as Canada, the United States, and Australia after the collapse of South Viet Nam. The 180,000 Canadians of Vietnamese origin were, with their valuable ties and business connections, becoming increasingly important for doing business in Viet Nam. While it had been stated that *Viet Kieu* were welcome to assist in rebuilding Viet Nam, their exact status under Vietnamese law was still uncertain.

EXHIBIT 7   Characteristics of Countries in Southeast Asia and South Asia

	1994 GNP/ Capita (US $)	GNP: Growth Rate (%)	Inflation Rate, 1993 (%)	1993 Population (000)	Political Risk*	Life Expectancy (years)	Mftg. Wages (US$/hr.)
Viet Nam	170	4.8	5.2	73,103	C	67	0.24
China	743	6.5	18	1,164,908	D	69	0.37
Malaysia	3,160	5.7	3.6	19,032	B	71	1.90
Singapore	19,310	6.1	2.4	2,867	A	75	NA
Thailand	2,040	8.4	4.1	58,824	B	69	0.92
Indonesia	730	4.8	10	187,151	B	60	0.17
Philippines	830	1.6	7.6	65,775	C	65	0.67
Burma	950	5.0	30	44,277	NA	60	NA
Cambodia	600	7.5	60	10,265	NA	49	NA
Hong Kong	17,860	5.3	9.5	5,865	B	78	NA
India	290	3.0	8.0	900,543	D	61	NA

* A = Low; D = High.

Sources: *World Bank Atlas* 1995; *The Vietnam Business Journal,* 1(3), 1993; Economist Intelligence Unit; *Business Asia,* January 16, 1995.

of negotiation, was also developing opportunities in Russia, France, Thailand, Malaysia, India, China, and in three other countries of the former Soviet Union. An issue was: Why enter Viet Nam when other opportunities existed in China and Southeast Asia? (See Exhibits 6 and 7.)

Technophar had a number of reasons for entering Viet Nam. The central government's support was a major consideration because it was an active participant in larger projects. It supported this technology transfer because of its favourable balance of payments effects. Imports of gelatin capsules would be reduced, and exports would be upgraded in the forward integration of Viet Nam's pharmaceutical industry. Also, the government's position on health care implicitly supported the deal. A state-supported health industry was thought to lead to increased encapsulated drug consumption.

A second set of reasons for entering Viet Nam entailed a longer term perspective. Although Technophar did not perceive a market there for more than one or two capsule plants, opportunities existed for the company's related, but as yet, undeveloped businesses. Victorov, an entrepreneur and inventor, had a patent on a sugar extraction process which greatly increased the yield of sugar from sugar cane. Viet Nam had a sizable sugar cane industry but the country's poor infrastructure hampered processing. Victorov's process was uniquely suited to the country's needs as sugar processing units could be built individually and located close to the supply of sugar cane. A second opportunity existed in the development of processing machinery for the extraction of gelatin from pig skins, beef skins and cow bones, which were usually discarded by the Vietnamese. The introduction of this technology would enable Viet Nam's pharmaceutical industry to further integrate backwards. However, the two projects involved a much greater financial commitment and would not likely materialize in the next three to four years.

Offsetting these reasons for entering the Viet Nam market was Technophar's limited experience in the country. Previously, sales in developing markets had been to those countries in which managers had prior experience—Victorov in Romania and Bulgaria, and Habuda in China. Technophar's managers were inexperienced in Viet Nam and needed to know more about the basic characteristics of the country to which they were actually committed.

Viet Nam—Country Study[3]

Market Promise   Viet Nam was positioned in the heart of the dynamic countries of the Pacific Rim (see Exhibit 8). While slow to reach the economic growth levels of other countries in the region and saddled with a turbulent past, recent reforms had positioned Viet Nam to become the next tiger in the region (see Exhibit 7).

The package of economic renovations (*Doi Moi*) instituted in 1986, had been a turning point for the country's economy. Viet Nam had made significant progress in recent years moving away from the planned economic model toward a more effective, market-based economic system. Most prices were now fully decontrolled, and the Vietnamese currency had been devalued and floated at world market rates. In addition, the scope for private sector activity had been expanded, primarily through decollectivization of the agricultural sector and the introduction of laws giving legal recognition to private business.

Sectorally, economic growth was not evenly dispersed as industries in the economy were treated differently under the guidelines of *Doi Moi*. Land reforms had created more autonomy. Light industries, such as textiles and food manufacture, had been emphasized, as export promotion and diversification were seen to be key variables in Viet Nam's future economic success. In 1994, nearly three-quarters of export earnings were generated by only two commodities, rice, and crude oil. Led by industry and construction, the economy did well in 1994 with GNP rising 4.8 percent.

In response to *Doi Moi,* foreign direct investment (FDI) in Viet Nam had surged dramatically in recent years. From US$ 360 million in 1988, FDI approvals had grown tenfold to US$ 4 billion in 1994. FDI was dominated by firms from Asian countries; European and North American firms had been slow to invest in the region (see Exhibit 9). Firms from the United States had not been permitted to invest in Viet Nam prior to February 3, 1994, though only hours after President Clinton announced the lifting of the U.S. embargo against Viet Nam, both PepsiCo and Coca-Cola made commitments to begin bottling and distributing in Viet Nam.

Foreign investors were attracted to Viet Nam for a number of reasons. Investors were permitted to have 100 percent equity ownership in their ventures, unlike in some countries in the Asia-Pacific region. Low corporate tax rates, tax holidays, potential waivers on import and export duties, and full profit repatriation were other

---

[3]Sources: Joseph P. Quinlan, *Vietnam: Business Opportunities and Risks,* Pacific View Press: Berkeley, CA, 1995; The Economist Intelligence Unit reports; The Central Intelligence Agency, *The World Factbook 1995,* Internet location: www.ic.gov:80/94fact/fb94toc/fb94toc.html.

EXHIBIT 8   **Map of Asia**

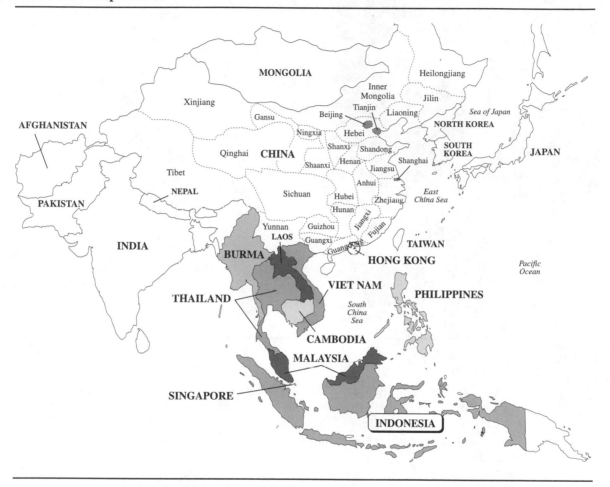

government-centred investment incentives. Investors were also encouraged by market conditions. Wage rates were low; Viet Nam was considerably well-endowed with
natural resources such as forests, marine life, minerals, crude oil, and a workforce of
32 million people. Infrastructure was poor which hampered economic development,
but created considerable opportunity for companies in this sector.

Risks

Social.   Other factors mitigated these attractions. Viet Nam was classified as a 'least
developed nation' by the United Nations. Malnutrition was high, double that in
China, and diseases not prevalent in other countries in Southeast Asia were found in
Viet Nam. Infant mortality (45.5 deaths/1000 live births) was high and literacy rates
(88 percent) comparatively low. A significant proportion of children did not complete

EXHIBIT 9   FDI in Viet Nam by Country (as of 1995)

	Country	No. of Projects	Total Capital Committed (US$ million)
1	Taiwan	179	1,964
2	Hong Kong	171	1,788
3	Singapore	76	1,070
4	South Korea	97	884
5	Japan	73	783
6	Australia	42	655
7	Malaysia	31	581
8	France	58	534
9	Switzerland	14	463
10	Britain	15	376
11	Netherlands	16	348
12	United States	28	270
13	Thailand	43	236
14	Indonesia	11	160
15	Russia	34	125
16	Ireland	13	81
17	Sweden	7	78
18	Canada	9	66
19	Philippines	12	58
20	Ukraine	6	45

Source: *Vietnam Business Journal,* III(1), 1995.

secondary (high school level) schooling. Improved living standards had been given priority, though little attention had been paid to human rights and basic freedoms. Viet Nam's natural resource advantages were suffering from environmental degradation. Deforestation, water pollution, overfishing, and soil degradation were issues of concern.

Economic.   While wealthy in natural resources and people, Viet Nam was still one of the poorest countries in the Southeast Asia region. The industrial sector remained burdened by uncompetitive state-owned enterprises that the government was unwilling or unable to privatize. The economy was primarily agrarian, with 40 percent of GDP accounted for by agricultural products, and 65 percent of employment in agriculture. Eighty percent of Viet Nam's 70 million people lived as peasant farmers without the income to spend on items other than necessities such as food and shelter.

Unemployment loomed as a serious problem. Roughly 25 percent of the workforce was without work and population growth swelled the ranks of the unemployed yearly. The government ran a 5 percent budget deficit in 1993, and imports at US$3.1 billion exceeded exports (US$2.6 billion). Moreover, the government would issue no information on foreign currency reserves. Doubts existed as to the ability of the central government to exhibit sound fiscal management, and inflation had reached 14.4 percent by 1995.

Political.   The political risk in Viet Nam was still considerable (see Exhibit 7). Viet Nam was a one-party state in which political power came from the Communist party and its politburo. Although the Communist party enjoyed little support from the populace and was widely disliked in the south, there was no real challenge to the government's authority. However, as a vocal generation of Vietnamese emerged in the thrills and throes of economic freedom, the potential for conflict between political authoritarianism and growing market freedoms was increasing.

The central government, despite its free-market preaching, often participated overtly in markets by restricting competition and by acting as a partner in the majority of foreign ventures. Its market participation was not always valued because Vietnamese government officials had little experience in dealing with multinational agencies and corporations or in formulating and implementing projects. Also, Vietnamese security officials were suspicious of foreigners to the point of paranoia which created apprehension in many foreign investors.

Conflict still remained between central and regional governments. Similar to the situation in China, economic power was fragmented and economic policies varied by province in their internal competition for foreign investment. Laws and regulations were interpreted differently in each region and, in some cases, were disregarded. For example, officials in Ho Chi Minh City had developed their own income tax laws and had threatened to prevent foreigners from leaving the country until all personal taxes had been reconciled.

Corruption, bribery, and copyright and patent infringement were not uncommon for want of effective legal enforcement. Institutions supporting free enterprise were absent. Without a legal framework, a viable banking system or private land ownership (all land was the property of the state), business in Viet Nam involved considerable risk. Thus, the raw potential and attractiveness of the country was countervailed by these social, economic, and political risk factors. Consequently, only one-third of the US$12 billion in FDI committed to Viet Nam since 1988 had been implemented and US$1 billion of projects had been cancelled.

The Viet Nam Contract

Negotiations for the Viet Nam contract transpired smoothly and quickly. The initial discussions went well when Habuda visited the Vietnamese purchasers during one of his trips to China. He returned for a second set of meetings, during which he assisted with local market and feasibility studies. Cuulong completed these evaluations and recognized the large domestic market for pharmaceuticals as well as the export potential of hard capsules. After his transfer to China, Habuda visited Viet Nam for a third time and completed the technology transfer package. The final task was to get all of the political players in place, and the contract was signed when Prime Minister Chretien's Asian trade mission arrived in Viet Nam.

The deal, though quickly negotiated, had been dragging on for a number of months. Internal changes on the Vietnamese side had caused some delays and Technophar's costs had changed considerably since the contract had been negotiated. For example, stainless steel, a large component of the auxiliary equipment, had increased in price by 30 to 35 percent in the last six months. Technophar's management recognized the difficulties faced by Cuulong because of the poor infrastructure in the country, but concern about the contract became acute when the December 15 deposit did not arrive.

Management at Technophar communicated weekly with Pharmexco, the official importer of the equipment, and Cuulong. In these communications, a great deal of uncertainty began to develop about the project and the partners. Technophar's managers, who were having difficulty sorting fact from fiction in their dealings with Pharmexco and Cuulong, had no way of judging the validity of the many reasons given for the delays. Much of what was said had to be taken on faith.

Despite the increased uncertainty, Technophar's managers were reluctant to cancel the contract outright. Doing so would tarnish the company's reputation, and the contract, even with the cost increases, was still profitable. However, with additional orders coming onto the books, Technophar could keep its plant producing for at least the next six months. Thus, Technophar could legally cut the order off and renegotiate at a later date.

A more fundamental issue was Technophar's presence in Viet Nam. Largely, the company's growth had been in developing countries in markets where the managers had previous experience. Otherwise, large sales had been to developed countries such as Germany and France. The few sales that had been to riskier, developing countries involved a smaller stake: One machine had been sold to each of Brazil, Columbia, Venezuela, and Indonesia. The sale of a plant, complete with four machines and auxiliary equipment, to Viet Nam, one of the least developed countries, was a considerable departure from Technophar's established practices. Dube wondered whether Technophar should even be in Viet Nam.

Technophar's entry into Viet Nam had also been one of chance. How many of these opportunities were slipping through the cracks because Technophar was not systematically seeking out and evaluating potential markets? Was the same kind of innovation which allowed for simplification and systemization of capsule production required in their approach to international markets?

11 NORA-SAKARI: A PROPOSED JOINT VENTURE IN MALAYSIA

On the morning of Monday, July 13, 1992, Zainal bin Hashim, vice-chairman of Nora Holdings Sdn Bhd[1] (Nora), arrived at his office about an hour earlier than usual. As he looked out the window at the city spreading below, he thought about the previous week's meeting in Kuala Lumpur (KL), Malaysia, with a team of negotiators from Sakari Oy[2] (Sakari) of Finland. Nora was a leading supplier of telecommunications (telecom) equipment in Malaysia while Sakari, a Finnish conglomerate, was a leader in the mobile telecom network. The seven-member team from Sakari was in KL to negotiate with Nora for the formation of a joint venture between the two telecom companies.

This was the final negotiation which would determine whether a joint-venture agreement would materialise. The negotiation had ended late Saturday afternoon, having lasted for six consecutive days. The joint-venture company, if established, would be set up in Malaysia to manufacture and commission digital switching exchanges to meet the needs of the telecom industry in Malaysia and its neighbouring countries, particularly Indonesia and Thailand. While Nora would benefit from the joint venture in terms of technology transfer, the venture would pave the way for Sakari to acquire knowledge and gain access to the markets in Southeast Asia.

The Nora management was impressed by the Finnish capability in using high technology to enable Finland, a small country of only five million people, to become one of the fastest-growing nations in the world. High-tech seemed to be the rule for most Finnish companies. For example, Kone was one of the world's three largest manufacturer of lifts, Vaisala was the world's major supplier of metereological

---

R. Azimah Ainuddin prepared this case under the supervision of Professor Paul Beamish solely to provide material for class discussion. The case is not intended to illustrate either effective or ineffective handling of a managerial situation. Certain names and other identifying information may have been disguised to protect confidentiality. Copyright © 1995, The University of Western Ontario.

[1]Sdn Bhd is an abbreviation for Sendirian Berhad, which means private limited company in Malaysia.

[2]Oy is an abbreviation for Osakeyhtiot, which means private limited company in Finland.

equipment, and Sakari was one of the leading telecom companies in Europe. It would be an invaluable opportunity for Nora to learn from the Finnish experience and emulate their success for Malaysia.

The opportunity emerged when in February, 1990, Peter Mattsson, president of Sakari's Asian regional office in Singapore, approached Zainal[3] to explore the possibility of forming a cooperative venture between Nora and Sakari. Mattsson said:

> While growth in the mobile telecommunications network is expected to be about 40 percent a year in Asia between 1990 and 1994, growth in fixed networks would not be as fast, but the projects are much larger. A typical mobile network project amounts to a maximum of a few hundred million Finnish marks, but fixed network projects can be estimated in billions. In Malaysia and Thailand, billion-mark projects are currently approaching contract stage. Thus it is imperative that Sakari establish its presence in this region to capture a share in the fixed network market.

The large potential for telecom facilities was also evident from the present low telephone penetration rates in the Southeast Asian countries, with the exception of Singapore (see Exhibit 1).

The Telecom Industry in Malaysia

In November, 1990, Syarikat Telekom Malaysia Sdn Bhd (STM), the government-owned telecom company, became a public-listed company, Telekom Malaysia Berhad (TMB). With a paid-up capital of RM2.4 billion,[4] TMB was given the authority to develop Malaysia's telecom infrastructure. It was also given the mandate to provide telecom services that were on par with those available in developed countries.

In a corporate statement, TMB announced that it would be investing in the digitalization of its networks to pave the way for ISDN (integrated services digitalized network), and in international fibre optic cable networks to meet the needs of increased telecom traffic between Malaysia and the rest of the world. TMB would also facilitate the installation of more mobile networks in view of the increased demand for the use of mobile phones among the business community in KL and in major towns.

As the nation's largest telecom company, TMB's operations were regulated through a 20-year license issued by the Ministry of Energy, Telecommunications and Post. In line with the government's Vision 2020 program (a target for Malaysia to become a developed nation by the year 2020), there was a strong need for the upgrading of the telecom infrastructure in the rural areas. TMB estimated that it would spend more than RM6 billion between 1991 and 1995 on the installation of fixed networks, of which 25 percent would be allocated for the expansion of rural telecoms. The objective was to increase the level of telephone penetration rate to 25 percent by the year 2000.

---

[3]The first name is used because the Malay name consists of the name of the individual and the name of his/her father. The word "bin" (for males) or "binti" (for females) separates the name of the individual from that of his/her fathers.

[4]RM is Ringgit Malaysia, the Malaysian currency. As at December 31, 1991, US$1 = RM2.73.

EXHIBIT 1   Telephone Statistics of Selected Countries in 1990.

Country	Area ('000 sq km)	Population (million)	Telephones per 100 population
Canada	9,976	25.3	57
Finland	338	4.9	53
France	552	56.6	48
Germany	249	61.1	67
Indonesia	1,905	179.3	1
Japan	378	121.1	42
Malaysia	330	13.1	11
Philippines	300	60.7	2
Singapore	1	3.0	39
Sweden	450	8.4	68
Thailand	513	54.5	2
United Kingdom	244	55.7	43
United States	9,373	248.7	51

Source: United Nations, *Statistical Yearbook* 1990/91, New York, 1993.

Although TMB had become a large national telecom company, it lacked the expertise and technology to undertake massive infrastructure projects. In most cases, the local telecom companies would be invited to submit their bids for a particular contract. It was also common for these local companies to form partnerships with large multinational corporations, mainly for technological support. For example, Pernas-NEC, a joint-venture company between Pernas Holdings and NEC was one of the companies that had been successful in securing large telecom contracts.

One of the large contracts that was forthcoming from TMB in the near future was the supply of digital switching exchanges for new fixed networks and for existing networks that currently used analog-circuit switches. Digital switches could enhance transmission capabilities, estimated at two million bits per second compared to the 9,600 bits per second on analog circuits. Industry sources predicted the contract would amount to at least RM2 billion.

Nora's Search for a Joint-Venture Partner

Nora was interested in securing a share of the RM2-billion forthcoming contract from TMB and more importantly, in acquiring the knowledge in switching technology from its partnership with a telecom multinational company (MNC). During the initial stages, when Nora first began to consider potential partners in the bid for this contract, telecom MNCs such as Siemens, Alcatel, and Fujitsu seemed appropriate candidates. Nora had previously entered into a five-year technical assistance agreement with Siemens to manufacture telephone sets.

Nora also had the experience of a long-term working relationship with Japanese partners which would prove valuable should a joint venture be formed with Fujitsu.

Alcatel was another potential partner, but the main concern at Nora was that the technical standards used in the French technology were not compatible with the British standards already adopted in Malaysia. NEC and Ericsson were not considered, as they were already involved with other local competitors and were the current suppliers of digital switching exchanges to TMB. Their five-year contracts were due to expire by the end of 1992.

Subsequent to Zainal's meeting with Mattsson, he decided to consider Sakari as a serious potential partner. He was briefed about Sakari's SK33, a digital switching system that was based on an open architecture which enabled the use of standard components, standard software development tools, and standard software languages. Unlike the switching exchanges developed by NEC and Ericsson which required the purchase of components developed by the parent companies, the SK33 used components that were available in the open market. The system was also modular, and its software could be upgraded to provide new services and could interface easily with new equipment in the network. This was the most attractive feature of the SK33 as it would lead to the development of new derivative systems.

Mattsson had also convinced Zainal and other Nora managers that although Sakari was a relatively small player in fixed networks, its networks were easily adaptable, and could cater to large exchanges in the urban areas as well as small ones for rural needs. Sakari's small size, compared to that of AT&T, Ericsson, and Siemens, was an added strength since Sakari could work out customized solutions for its customers. Large telecom companies could not meet such individual demands but had to offer standard products and solutions which sometimes were not consistent with the needs of the customer.

Prior to the July 1992 meeting, at least 20 meetings had been held either in KL or in Helsinki to establish relationships between the two companies. It was estimated that each side had invested not less than RM3 million in promoting the relationship. Mattsson and Ilkka Junttila, Sakari's representative in KL, were the key people in bringing the two companies together. Others who played a role in helping Sakari to understand the Malay/Muslim/Eastern culture and Nora to understand the Finnish/Secular/Western culture were Aziz Majid, a Malay who had been Sakari's manager for more than 12 years in Helsinki; Hussein Gazi, Sakari's senior manager of Egyptian origin, also a Muslim who had worked for Sakari for more than 20 years; and Salleh Lindstrom, Nora's engineer of Swedish origin and a Muslim, who had worked for Nora for almost 10 years. (See Exhibits 2 and 3 for brief background information on Malaysia and Finland respectively.)

Nora Holdings SDN BHD

The Company

Nora was one of the leading companies in the telecom industry in Malaysia. It was established in 1975 by Osman bin Jaafar and his wife, Nora Asyikin binti Yusof, with a paid-up capital of RM2 million. Osman was an electrical engineer trained in the

EXHIBIT 2   Malaysia: Background Information

Malaysia is centrally located in Southeast Asia. It consists of Peninsular Malaysia, bordered by Thailand in the north and Singapore in the south, and the states of Sabah and Sarawak on the island of Borneo. Malaysia has a total land area of about 330,000 sq km, of which 80 percent is covered with tropical rainforest. Malaysia has an equatorial climate with high humidity and high daily temperatures of about 26°C throughout the year.

In 1991 Malaysia's estimated population was 18 million, of which about seven million made up the country's labour force. The population is relatively young, with 40 percent between the ages of 15 and 39 and only 7 percent above the age of 55. A Malaysian family has an average of four children and extended families are common. Kuala Lumpur, the capital city of Malaysia, has approximately 1.5 million inhabitants.

The population is multiracial; the largest ethnic group is the Bumiputeras (the Malays and other indigenous groups such as the Ibans in Sarawak and Kadazans in Sabah), followed by the Chinese and Indians. The Chinese and Indians, originally from China and India respectively, migrated to Peninsular Malaysia in the 18th century to work in the tin mines and rubber plantations owned by the British. When the country achieved independence in 1957 through peaceful negotiations between the Malay leaders and the British government, the immigrants who resided in the country at that time were granted citizenship.

Bahasa Malaysia is the national language but English is widely used in the business circles. Other major languages spoken include the various Chinese dialects and Tamil.

Islam is the official religion in Malaysia but other religions (mainly Christianity, Buddhism, and Hinduism) are widely practiced. Official holidays are allocated for the celebration of Eid, Christmas, Chinese New Year, and Deepavali. All Malays are Muslims, followers of the Islamic faith.

During the British rule, western influence introduced secularism to the country, which led to the separation of the Islamic religion from daily life. In the late 1970s and 1980s, realizing the negative impact of secularism on the life of the Muslims, several groups of devout Muslims such as the Malaysian Muslim Youth Movement (ABIM) undertook efforts to reverse the process using a dynamic and progressive approach to Islam. As a result, changes were introduced to meet the daily needs of the Muslims. Islamic banking and insurance facilities were introduced and prayer rooms were provided in government offices, private companies, factories, and even shopping complexes.

Malaysia is a parliamentary democracy under a constitutional monarchy. The Yang DiPertuan Agung (the king) is the supreme head, and appoints the head of the ruling political party to be the prime minister. In 1992 the Barisan Nasional, a coalition of several political parties representing various ethnic groups, was the ruling political party in Malaysia. Its predominance had contributed to the political stability and economic progress of the country in the late 1980s and early 1990s.

The recession of 1985 through 1986 led to structural changes in the Malaysian economy which had been too dependent on primary commodities (rubber, tin, palm oil and timber) and had a very narrow export base. To reduce excessive dependence on primary commodities, the government directed resources to the manufacturing sector. To promote the establishment of export-oriented industries, generous incentives and relaxed foreign equity restrictions were introduced. A pragmatic approach toward foreign policy and heavy investments in modernizing the country's infrastructure (highways, air and seaports, telecommunications, industrial parks) led to rapid economic growth in 1988 through 1991 (Table 1). In 1991 the manufacturing sector became the leading contributor to the economy, accounting for about 28 percent of gross national product (GNP). Malaysia's major trading partners were Singapore, US, UK, Japan, Korea, Germany and Taiwan.

TABLE 1   Malaysia: Economic Performance, 1988–1991

Economic indicator	1988	1989	1990	1991
Per capita GNP (in RM)	5,065	5,507	6,206	6,817
Real economic growth rate	9.5%	9.3%	11.4%	9.1%
Consumer price index	2.5%	2.8%	3.1%	4.4%

The Malaysian currency is the Ringgit Malaysia (RM). As of December 1991,
US$1 = RM2.73.

Source: *Doing Business in Malaysia,* Ernst & Young International Ltd, 1993.

EXHIBIT 3   Finland: Background Information

Finland is situated in the northeast of Europe, sharing borders with Sweden in the west, Norway in the north and the former Soviet Union in the east. About 65 percent of its area of 338,000 sq km is covered with forest, about 15 percent lakes and about 10 percent arable land. Finland has a temperate climate with four distinct seasons. In Helsinki, the capital city of Finland, July is the warmest month with an average mid-day temperature of 21°C and January is the coldest month with an average mid-day temperature of −3°C.

Finland is one of the most sparsely populated countries in Europe. In 1991 Finland had a population of five million, 60 percent of whom lived in the urban areas. Currently the city of Helsinki has a population of about 500,000. Finland has a well-educated work force of about 2.3 million. About half of the work force are engaged in providing services, 30 percent in manufacturing and construction, and 8 percent in agricultural production. The small size of the population led to scarce and expensive labour resources. Thus Finland had to compete by exploiting its lead in high-tech industries.

Finland's official languages are Finnish and Swedish, although only 6 percent of the population speaks Swedish. English is the most widely spoken foreign language. About 87 percent of the Finns are Lutherans and about 1 percent Finnish Orthodox.

Finland has been an independent republic since 1917, and was previously ruled by Sweden and Russia. A president is elected to a six-year term, and a 200-member, single-chamber parliament is elected every four years.

In the 1980s Finland's economy was among the fastest growing in the world. Other than its forests, Finland has few natural resources but its economic growth was far above that of other countries in Europe. However, Finland experienced a bad recession in 1991 (Table 2).

Finland's economic structure is based on private ownership and free enterprise. However, the productions of alcoholic beverages and spirits are retained as government monopolies. Finland's major trading partners are Sweden, Germany, the former Soviet Union, and UK.

Finland's standard of living is among the highest in the world. The Finns have small, nuclear families with one or two children per family. They have comfortable homes in the cities and one in every three families has a countryside cottage near a lake where they retreat on weekends. Taxes are high, the social security system is efficient, and poverty is nonexistent.

Until recently, the stable trading relationship with the former Soviet Union and other Scandinavian countries led to few interactions between the Finnish and people in the other parts of the world. The Finns are described as rather reserved, obstinate, and serious people. A Finn commented, "We do not engage easily in small talks with strangers. Furthermore, we have a strong love for nature and we have the tendency to be silent as we observe our surroundings. Unfortunately, others tend to view such behaviour as cold and serious."

Visitors to Finland are often impressed by the efficient public transport system, the clean and beautiful city of Helsinki with orderly road networks, scenic parks and lakefronts, quaint museums, and magnificient cathedrals and churches.

TABLE 2   Finland: Economic Performance, 1988–1991

Economic indicator	1988	1989	1990	1991
Per capita GDP (in FIM)	88,308	99,387	104,991	102,083
Increase in GDP	12.8%	12.2%	6.0%	−2.8%
Inflation	5.1%	6.6%	6.1%	4.1%
Unemployment	n.a.	3.5%	3.4%	7.6%

The Finnish currency is the Finnish Markka (FIM). As of December 30, 1991, US$1 = FIM4. 14.

Source: *Doing Business in Finland,* Ernst & Young International Ltd, 1993.

UK in the late 1950s. Upon graduation in 1960 he joined the national Telecom Department in Malaysia, where he held several senior positions.

Ten years later, Osman resigned his position as telecom controller at the Telecom Department to assume the post of executive director of a private company, Asian Auto Works Sdn Bhd (AAW). About five years later, he began to realize his potential as an entrepreneur and decided to start his own business. His boss, Larry Goh, offered him the management of AAW's unprofitable payphone subsidiary which was, coincidentally, under Osman's responsibility at the company. Osman purchased the business, named it Nora, and turned it into a million-dollar company by the 1980s. In 1991 Nora recorded a group turnover of RM320 million. The group consisted of 30 subsidiaries, including two public-listed companies: Multiphone Bhd, and Nora Telecommunications Bhd. As of August, 1991, Nora had 3,081 employees, of which 513 were categorised as managerial (including 244 engineers) and 2,568 as non-managerial (including 269 engineers and technicians).

The Cable Business   Since the inception of the company, Nora had successfully secured two cable-laying projects, one in 1975 and the other in 1983. For the 1983 project worth RM500 million, Nora formed a joint venture with two Japanese companies, Sumitomo Electric Industries Ltd (10 percent) and Marubeni Corporation (5 percent). Japanese partners were chosen in view of the availability of a financial package that came together with the technological assistance needed by Nora. Nora also acquired a 63 percent stake in a local cable company, Selangor Cables Sdn Bhd.

The Telephone Business   Nora had become a household name in Malaysia as a telephone manufacturer. It started in 1975 when the company obtained a contract to supply telephone sets to the Telecom authority, which would distribute the sets to telephone subscribers on a rental basis. The contract, estimated at RM130 million, lasted for 15 years. In 1980 Nora secured licences to manufacture Siemens and Bell telephones, and subsequently began the manufacture of its own telephone models such as the N300S (single line), N300M (micro-computer controlled), and N300V (hands-free, voice-activated).

Upon expiry of the 15-year contract as a supplier of telephone sets to the Telecom authority (STM) in 1989, Nora suffered a major setback when it lost a RM32-million contract to supply 600,000 N300S single line telephones. The contract was instead given to a Taiwanese manufacturer, Formula Electronics, which quoted a lower price of RM37 compared to Nora's RM54. Subsequently, Nora was motivated to move towards the high end feature phone domestic market. The company sold about 3,000 sets of feature phones per month, capturing the Malaysian market that needed more sophisticated sets than the ones supplied by STM.

Nora had ventured into the export market with its feature phones, but industry observers predicted that Nora still had a long way to go as an exporter. The foreign markets were very competitive and many manufacturers already had well-established brands. In 1989, exports amounted to RM2 million and were expected to increase to RM5 million after orders were filled for its N300M and N300V models from Alcatel and Tokyo Telecommunications Network. Nora's N300V had been recently approved in Germany and a shipment of 2,000 sets would be distributed through its subsidiary, Nora GmbH, to test the German market.

The Payphone Business   Nora's start-up in the payphone business had turned out to be one of the company's most profitable lines of business. Other than the cable-laying contract secured in 1975, there was the 15-year contract to install, operate, and maintain payphones in the cities and major towns in the country. More recently, Nora had started to manufacture card payphones under a license from GEC Plessey Telecommunications (GPT) of the UK. The agreement had also permitted Nora to sell the products to the neighbouring countries in Southeast Asia as well as to eight other markets approved by GPT.

While the payphone revenues were estimated to be as high as RM60 million a year, a long-term and stable income for Nora, profit margins were only about 10 percent due to the high investment and maintenance costs.

Other Businesses   Nora was also the sole distributor for Northern Telecom's private automatic branch exchange (PABX) and NEC's mobile telephone sets. The company had ventured into the paging market through a subsidiary, Unikom Sdn Bhd, and was capturing 50 percent of the paging business in Malaysia. It was also an Apple computer distributor in Malaysia and Singapore. In addition, Nora was involved in: distributing radio-related equipment (such as mobile radios, walkie-talkies, alarm systems, and automatic gates); supplying equipment to the broadcasting, meteorological, civil aviation, postal, and power authorities; and manufacturing automotive parts (such as the suspension coil, springs, and piston).

The Management

In the early years, Osman managed the company with seven employees. He was known as a conservative businessman who did not like to dabble in acquisitions and mergers to make quick capital gains. In 1980, Nora's employment had grown to 200 but Osman had yet to find an assistant.

As one of the few experienced engineers and entrepreneurs at that time, Osman sat on the Council of Universiti Teknologi Malaysia (UTM), a local university that emphasized research and teaching in the fields of engineering and applied sciences. Osman was on an interview panel for the recruitment of new faculty when he spotted an applicant, Zainal Hashim, and offered him the position of deputy managing director at Nora.

Zainal, then age 35, held a bachelor's degree in electronic engineering and a master's degree in microwave communications from a British university. Upon graduation in 1972, he served UTM for four years and then left the university to join Pernas-NEC Sdn Bhd, a manufacturer of transmissions equipment, for some practical experience. In 1977, he spent a year in Japan where he trained to be a production and installation engineer. In 1980, he had left Pernas-NEC to return to academia when he was offered a position at Nora.

Zainal recalled that it had been a difficult decision because Nora was then a very small company. However, Osman had been very convincing and Zainal had stayed with Nora since that time. Zainal became Nora's managing director in 1984 and in 1990, the vice-chairman. Osman had also released a 10 percent share of his family holdings to Zainal. It was rumoured in the industry that Zainal had been offered the position as TMB's managing director when the company went public in 1990 but he had turned it down. Osman's son, Ariffin bin Osman was appointed Nora's managing director. At present, Nora's paid-up capital was RM16.5 million.

Industry analysts observed that Nora's success was attributed to the complementary roles, trust, and mutual understanding between Osman and Zainal. While Osman "likes to fight for new business opportunities," Zainal preferred a low profile and concentrated on managing Nora's operations.

Osman and Zainal also felt a responsibility to provide Malay entrepreneurs with a model of a successful Malay company in a high-tech industry. Zainal said:

> The Malays were relatively new in business compared to the Malaysian Chinese. In addition, the financial institutions in Malaysia were also not very supportive of these new entrepreneurs. The banks would require various forms of collateral and guarantees valued as much as the loan. To assist the Malay entrepreneurs, Nora implemented an entrepreneur development programme in which it would undertake feasible projects on a profit-sharing basis by providing the financial support.

Industry observers speculated that Osman, a former civil servant and an entrepreneur, was close to Malaysian politicians, notably the Prime Minister, which in turn, led to easy access to government contracts. Zainal, on the other hand, had been a close friend of the current Finance Minister since the days when they were both active in the Malaysian Muslim Youth Movement (a group that had developed a reputation for idealism, integrity and progressive interpretation of Islam). Zainal disagreed with such allegations and stressed that Nora was already a success even before his friend became the finance minister. He said, "Even now, knowing the minister, I never push for a contract if we don't deserve it." However, he acknowledged that such perceptions in the industry had been beneficial to Nora.

Osman and Zainal had an obsession for high-tech products and made the development of research and development (R&D) skills and resources a priority in the company. About 1 percent of Nora's earnings was ploughed back into R&D activities. Although this amount was considered small by international standards, Nora planned to increase it gradually to 5 to 6 percent in the next two to three years. Zainal said:

> We believe in making improvements in small steps, similar to the Japanese kaizen principle. Over time, each small improvement could lead to a major creation. To be able to make improvements, we must learn from others. Thus we would borrow a technology from others, but eventually, we must be able to develop our own to sustain our competitiveness in the industry. As a matter of fact, Sakari's SK33 system was developed based on a technology it obtained from Alcatel.

To further enhance R&D activities at Nora, Nora Research Sdn Bhd (NRSB), a wholly-owned subsidiary, was formed, and its R&D department was absorbed into this new company. NRSB operated as an independent research company undertaking

R&D activities for Nora as well as for private clients in related fields. The company facilitated R&D activities with other companies as well as government organizations, research institutions, and universities. NRSB, with its staff of 40 technicians/engineers, would charge a fixed fee for basic research and a royalty for its products sold by clients. Thus far, NRSB had developed Nora's Network Paging System, which was the system presently used by the company's paging subsidiary, Unikom Sdn Bhd.

Zainal was also active in instilling and upgrading Islamic values among the Malay employees at Nora. He explained:

> Islam is a way of life and there is no such thing as Islamic management. The Islamic values, which must be reflected in the daily life of Muslims, would influence their behaviours as employers and employees. Our Malay managers, however, were often influenced by their western counterparts, who tend to stress knowledge and mental capability and often forget the effectiveness of the softer side of management which emphasizes relationships, sincerity and consistency. I believe that one must always be sincere to be able to develop good working relationships. A legal agreement signed between two companies which stipulates an obligation on one partner to transfer its technology to the other would not necessarily result in a technology being actually transferred as desired by the recipient partner. It is good personal relationships between engineers and technicians that can actually constitute a technology transfer.

Sakari Oy

Sakari was established in 1865 as a pulp and paper mill located about 200 km northwest of Helsinki, the capital city of Finland. In the 1960s Sakari started to expand into the rubber and cable industries when it merged with the Finnish Rubber Works and Finnish Cable Works. In 1973 Sakari's performance was badly affected by the oil crisis, as its businesses were largely energy-intensive.

However, in 1975 the company recovered when Aatos Olkkola took over as Sakari's president. Olkkola, formerly a paper machinery salesman who held a master's degree in science from Helsinki's University of Technology, was a very active entrepreneur. He led Sakari into competitive businesses such as computers, consumer electronics, and cellular phones via a series of acquisitions, mergers, and alliances. Companies involved in the acquisitions included: the consumer electronics division of Standard Elektrik Lorenz AG; the data systems division of L.M. Ericsson; Vantala, a Finnish manufacturer of colour televisions; and Luxury, a Swedish state-owned electronics and computer concern.

In 1979 a joint venture between Sakari and Vantala, Sakari-Vantala, was set up to develop and manufacture mobile telephones. Sakari-Vantala had captured about a 14 percent share of the world's market for mobile phones and held a 20 percent market share in Europe for its mobile phone handsets. Outside Europe, a 50–50 joint venture was formed with Tandy Corporation which, to date, had made significant sales in the United States, Malaysia, and Thailand.

Sakari first edged into the telecom market by selling switching systems licensed from France's Alcatel and by developing the software and systems to suit the needs of small Finnish phone companies. Sakari had avoided head-on competition with

Siemens and Ericsson by not trying to enter the market for large telephone networks. Instead, Sakari had concentrated on developing dedicated telecom networks for large private users such as utility and railway companies. In Finland, Sakari held 40 percent of the market for digital exchanges. Other competitors included Ericsson (34 percent), Siemens (25 percent), and Alcatel (1 percent).

Sakari was also a niche player in the global switching market. Its SK33 switches had sold well in countries such as Sri Lanka, United Arab Emirates, China, and the Soviet Union. A derivative of the SK33 main exchange switch called SK33XT was subsequently developed to be used in base stations for cellular networks and personal paging systems.

Sakari attributed its emphasis on R&D as its key success factor in the telecom industry. Strong in-house R&D in core competence areas enabled the company to develop technology platforms such as its SK33 system that were reliable, flexible, compatible, and economical. About 17 percent of its annual sales revenue was invested into R&D and product development units in Finland, UK, and France. Sakari's current strategy was to emphasize global operations in production and R&D. It planned to set up R&D centers in leading markets, including Southeast Asia.

Sakari was still a small company by international standards (see Exhibit 4 for a list of the major telecom companies in Europe). It did not have a wide marketing operation and had to rely on joint ventures such as the one with Tandy Corporation to enter the world market, particularly the US. In its efforts to develop market position quickly, Sakari had to accept lower margins for its products, and often the Sakari name was not revealed. In recent years, Sakari decided to emerge from its hiding place as a manufacturer's manufacturer and began marketing the Sakari name.

In 1988 Sakari's revenue increased but margins declined by 21 percent when integration of the acquired companies took longer and cost more than expected. In 1989 Mikko Koskinen took over as president of Sakari when Olkkola died. Koskinen announced that telecommunications, computers, and consumer electronics would be maintained as Sakari's core business, and that he would continue Olkkola's efforts in

---

EXHIBIT 4   Largest Telecommunications Companies in Europe

Name of Company	1988 Sales (US$ billions)
AT&T (U.S.)	10.2
Alcatel (France)	9.4
Siemens (Germany)	6.8
NEC (Japan)	5.8
Northern Telecom (Canada)	5.4
Ericsson (Sweden)	5.0
Motorola (U.S.)	3.0
Philips (Netherlands)	2.8
Fujitsu (Japan)	2.5
Bosch (Germany)	2.2

Source: *Financial Times*, July 25, 1990.

expanding the company overseas. He believed that every European company needed global horizons to be able to meet global competition for future survival. To do so, he envisaged the setting up of alliances of varying duration and designed for specific purposes. He said, "Sakari has become an interesting partner with which to cooperate on an equal footing in the areas of R&D, manufacturing, and marketing."

In 1991 Sakari was Finland's largest publicly-traded industrial company and derived almost 80 percent of its total sales from exports and overseas operations. However, export sales were confined to other Scandinavian countries, Western Europe, and the former Soviet Union. Industry analysts observed that Finnish companies had a privileged relationship with the former Soviet Union, which was considered an easy market with minimal trading costs and high margins. As a result, until recently these companies failed to invest in other parts of the world and were not making the most of their advantage in high-tech industries.

The recession in Finland which had gone on since 1990 led Sakari's group sales to decline substantially from FIM22 billion[5] in 1990 to FIM15 billion in 1991. The losses were attributed to two main factors: weak demand for Sakari's consumer electronic products, and trade with the Soviet Union which had come to almost a complete standstill. Consequently Sakari began divesting its less profitable companies within the basic industries (metal, rubber, and paper), as well as leaving the troubled European computer market with the sale of its computer subsidiary, Sakari Macro. The company's new strategy was to focus on three main areas: telecom systems and mobile phones in a global framework, consumer electronic products in Europe, and deliveries of cables and related technology. The company's divestment strategy led to a reduction of Sakari's employees from about 41,000 in 1989 to 29,000 in 1991.

In June 1992, Koskinen retired as Sakari's president and was replaced by Visa Ketonen, formerly the president of Sakari Mobile Phones. Ketonen appointed Ossi Kuusisto as Sakari's vice-president.

The Nora-Sakari Negotiation

Since mid-May 1990, Nora and Sakari had held at least 20 meetings to discuss the formation of the joint-venture company. Nora engineers were sent to Helsinki to assess the SK33 technology in terms of its compatibility with the Malaysian requirements, while Sakari managers travelled to KL mainly to assess Nora's capability in manufacturing switching exchanges and gaining market access.

In November 1991, Nora submitted its bid for TMB's RM2-billion contract to supply digital switching exchanges consisting of four million lines. Assuming the Nora-Sakari joint venture would materialise, Nora based its bid on Sakari's digital switching exchanges. Nora competed with seven other companies, all offering their partners' technology—Alcatel, AT&T, Fujitsu, Siemens, Ericsson, NEC, and Samsung. In early May 1992, TMB announced five successful companies in the bid. They were companies using technology from Alcatel, Fujitsu, Ericsson, NEC, and

---

[5]FIM is Finnish Markka, the Finnish currency. As of December 30, 1991, US$1 = FIM4.14.

Sakari. Industry observers were critical of TMB's decision to select Sakari and Alcatel. Sakari was perceived to be the least capable in supplying the necessary lines to meet TMB's requirements, as it was alleged to be a small company with little international exposure. Alcatel was criticised for having the potential of supplying an obsolete technology.

The May 21 Meeting

Despite the critics, Nora and Sakari held a major meeting in Helsinki on May 21, 1992, following the successful bid. Zainal led Nora's five-member negotiation team which comprised Nora's general manager for corporate planning division, an accountant, two engineers (including Lindstrom), and Marina binti Mohamed, a lawyer.

Sakari's eight-member team was led by Kunsisto, Sakari's vice-president. His team comprised Junttila, Gazi, Aziz, three other engineers, and Julia Ruola, a lawyer.

The meetings took place every day for long hours and the main issue focused on Nora's capability in penetrating the Southeast Asian market. Apparently there were divided opinions within Sakari's management about pursuing the joint venture with Nora. The group in favour of the Nora-Sakari joint venture held a strong belief that there would be very high growth in the Asia–Pacific region. The joint-venture company in Malaysia was seen as a hub to enter these markets. This group was represented mostly by Sakari's managers positioned in Asia, and engineers who had made several trips to Malaysia, including visits to Nora's facilities. They also had the support of Sakari's vice-president, Kuusisto, who was involved in most of the meetings with Nora, particularly when Zainal was present. Kuusisto had also made efforts to be present at meetings held in KL.

The group at Sakari not in favour of the Nora-Sakari joint venture believed that Sakari should focus its resources on entering the UK, which could be used as a hub to penetrate the European market. There was also the belief that Europe was closer to home and problems arising from cultural differences could be minimized. This group was also particularly concerned that Nora had the potential of copying Sakari's technology and would eventually become a strong competitor.

Zainal felt that the lack of full support from Sakari's management led to a difficult negotiation when new misgivings arose on Nora's capability to deliver its part of the deal. It was apparent that the group in favour of the Nora-Sakari joint venture was under pressure to further justify its proposal and provide counter arguments against the UK proposal. A Sakari manager explained, "We are tempted to pursue both proposals since each has its own strengths, but our current resources are very limited. Thus a choice has to be made, and soon."

The July 6 Meeting

Another meeting to negotiate the joint-venture agreement was scheduled on July 6, 1992. Sakari's eight-member team, which arrived in KL on the afternoon of Sunday, July 5, was met at the airport by key Nora managers involved in the negotiation.

The negotiation started early Monday morning at Nora's headquarters and continued for the next five days, with each day's meeting ending late in the evening. Zainal and Kuusisto did not participate in this negotiation. Members of the Nora team were the same members who had attended the May 21 meeting in Finland. The Sakari team was also represented by the same members in attendance at the previous meeting plus a new member, Solail Pekkarinen, Sakari's senior accountant. Unfortunately, on the third day of the negotiation, the Nora team requested the withdrawal of Pekkarinen from the Sakari team. He was perceived as extremely arrogant and insensitive to the local culture, which tended to value modesty and diplomacy. Pekkarinen left for Helsinki the following morning.

Although Zainal had decided not to participate actively in the negotiation, he followed the process closely and was briefed by his negotiators regularly. Some of the issues which they complained were difficult to negotiate had often resulted in heated arguments between the two negotiating teams. These included:

1. *Equity Ownership.* Sakari had proposed an equity split in the joint-venture company of 49 percent Sakari and 51 percent Nora. Nora, on the other hand, proposed a 30 percent Sakari and 70 percent Nora split. Nora's proposal was based on the foreign equity regulation provided by the Malaysian government, which allowed a maximum of 30 percent foreign equity ownership unless the company would produce a certain percentage of its products for exports (see Exhibit 5 for foreign equity regulation).

   Equity ownership became a major issue, as it was commonly related to control over the joint-venture company. Sakari was concerned over its ability to control the accessibility of its technology. On the other hand, Nora was concerned over its ability to exert control over the joint venture, since it would be used as a spin-off in Nora's long-term strategy to develop its own new high-tech products.

   Nora then offered a counter proposal which was a 60 percent Nora and 40 percent Sakari split. Subsequently the joint-venture company would have to plan for the export of its products in order to qualify for approval from the Malaysian Industrial Development Authority.

2. *Technology Transfer.* Sakari proposed to provide the joint-venture company with the basic structure of the digital switch. The switching exchange would be assembled at the joint-venture plant. On the other hand, Nora proposed that the basic structure of the switch be developed at the joint-venture company so that the joint venture would acquire the switching technology.

   Related to this issue was the payment of a royalty for the technology. Sakari proposed a royalty payment of 5 percent of the joint venture gross sales while Nora proposed a payment of 2 percent of net sales.

   Nora considered the royalty rate of 5 percent as too high. Having to pay a high rate would affect Nora's financial situation as a whole since it would be involved in additional investments in support of the joint venture. In one of the previous meetings, it had been agreed that Nora would invest in a building which would be rented to the joint venture company to accommodate an

---

EXHIBIT 5   An Extract of the Policies on Foreign Investment in Malaysia

---

The level of equity participation for other export-oriented projects are as follows:

For projects exporting between 51 percent to 79 percent of their production, foreign equity ownership up to 51 percent will be allowed; however, foreign equity ownership of up to 79 percent may be allowed, depending on factors such as the level of technology, spin-off effects, size of the investment, location, value-added, and the utilization of local raw materials and components.

For projects exporting 20 percent to 50 percent of their production, foreign equity ownership of 30 percent to 51 percent will be allowed, depending upon similar factors as mentioned above; however, for projects exporting less than 20 percent of their production, foreign equity ownership is allowed up to a maximum of 30 percent.

For projects producing products that are of high technology or are priority products for the domestic market, foreign equity ownership of up to 51 percent will be allowed.

Source: Malaysian Industrial Development Authority (MIDA), 1991, Malaysia: *Your Profit Centre in Asia.*

---

office and the switching plant. Nora would also invest in a plant located close to the joint venture which would supply the switching plant with components (surface mounted devices—SMDs) needed to build the exchanges.

An added bargaining argument posed by the Nora negotiators was that Sakari would receive side benefits from access to Japanese technology used in the manufacture of the SMD components. Apparently the Japanese technology was more advanced than Sakari's present technology.

3. *Expatriates' Salaries and Perks.* Sakari proposed that it would provide eight engineering experts for the joint-venture company on two types of contracts, short-term and long-term. Experts employed on a short-term basis would be paid a daily rate of US$700. The permanent experts would be paid a monthly salary ranging from US$12,000 to US$15,000. Three permanent experts would be attached to the joint-venture company once it was established and the number would gradually be reduced to only one, after two years.

The Nora negotiation team was appalled at the exorbitant amounts proposed by the Sakari negotiators. They were surprised that the Sakari team had not surveyed the industry rates, as the Japanese and other western negotiators would normally have done. Apparently Sakari had not taken into consideration the relatively low cost of living in Malaysia compared to Finland. In 1991, the average monthly rent for a comfortable, unfurnished three-bedroom apartment was US$920 in Helsinki and only US$510 in Kuala Lumpur.[6]

In response to Sakari's proposal, Nora negotiators adopted an unusual "take-it or leave-it stance." They deemed the following proposal reasonable in view of the comparisons made with other joint ventures which Nora had entered into with other foreign parties:

---

[6]IMD & World Economic Forum, 1992, *The World Competitiveness Report.*

Permanent experts' monthly salary ranges to be paid by the joint-venture company were as follows:

1. Senior expert (7-10 years experience). . . . . RM 13,500–15,500
2. Expert (4-6 years experience) . . . . RM 12,500–14,000
3. Junior expert (2-3 years experience). . . . . RM 11,500–13,000
4. Any Malaysian income taxes payable would be added to the salaries.
5. A car for personal use.
6. Annual paid vacation of 5 weeks.
7. Return flight tickets to home country once a year for the whole family of married persons and twice a year for singles according to Sakari's general scheme.
8. Any expenses incurred during official travelling.

Temporary experts are persons invited by the joint-venture company for various technical assistance tasks and would not be granted residence status. They would be paid the following fees:

1. Senior expert. . . . . US$750 per working day
2. Expert . . . . US$650 per working day
3. The joint-venture company would not reimburse the following:
   • Flight tickets between Finland (or any other country) and Malaysia.
   • Hotel or any other form of accommodation.
   • Local transportation.
4. *Arbitration.* Another major issue discussed in the negotiation was related to arbitration. While both parties agreed to the arbitration process in the event of future disputes, they disagreed on the location for resolution. Since Nora would be the majority stakeholder in the joint-venture company, Nora insisted that any arbitration should be located in KL. Sakari, however, insisted on Helsinki since that was the norm practiced by the company.

At the end of the five-day negotiation, many issues could not be resolved. While Nora could agree on certain matters after consulting Zainal, the Sakari team, representing a large private company, had to refer to the company board before it could make any decision that went beyond the limits provided by the board.

The Decision

Zainal sat down at his desk, read through the minutes of the negotiation thoroughly, and was disappointed that an agreement had not been reached. He was concerned about the obligation Nora had made with TMB when Nora was awarded the contract. Nora would be expected to fulfill the contract soon but had yet to find a partner to provide the technology. It was foreseeable that companies such as Siemens, Samsung, and AT&T, which had failed in the bid, could still be potential partners. However, Zainal had also not rejected the possibility of a reconciliation with Sakari. He could start by contacting Kunsisto in Helsinki. But should he?

12   ACCOR (A)

Beginning in 1967 with a single hotel in northern France, ACCOR had become one of the largest lodging, restaurant, and tourist service companies in the world. As of January 1992, ACCOR operated 1,900 hotels with 200,000 rooms, more than 6,000 restaurants, and 1,000 travel agencies, as well as car rental agencies and the world's largest service voucher operation, with 5.4 million daily users. (The list of ACCOR's 46 brands is shown on Exhibit 1.) ACCOR employed 140,000 people in 127 countries, and was opening new hotels at the rate of three per week, and one new restaurant per day. As a giant in lodging, restaurants, and travel services, ACCOR stood alone among European competitors. An equivalent company in the United States would have been the total of Marriott, Ramada Inn, and Motel 6 in lodging, plus Roy Rogers, Pizza Hut, Hardees, and Dairy Queen in restaurants, as well as car rental and travel agencies. (Recent financial results are provided in Exhibit 2.)

The co-chairmen of ACCOR were also the company's founders: Paul Dubrule and Gérard Pélisson. Under their guidance the firm had grown steadily, both through new product introductions and through acquisitions, and had established a strong presence throughout Europe and in many parts of the world. Until 1990, ACCOR's presence in North America had been only moderate, but in July of that year ACCOR took a giant stride with the purchase of the American motel chain, Motel 6, for $2.3 billion. In a single stroke, ACCOR's operations in North America jumped from 3 percent to 16 percent of total company revenues.

The acquisition of Motel 6 was an important strategic move for ACCOR, but it also posed a number of challenges. Dubrule and Pélisson had to determine the best way to integrate Motel 6 into ACCOR's organization. One question was organizational: Where should Motel 6 fit into ACCOR's organization structure? Should it become part of ACCOR North America, or should it be treated as a separate entity?

Assistant Professor Philip M. Rosenzweig and Benoît Raillard (MBA '92) prepared this case as the basis for class discussion rather than to illustrate either effective or ineffective handling of an administrative situation.
Copyright © 1992 by the President and Fellows of Harvard College.

EXHIBIT 1   ACCOR's Brands, 1992

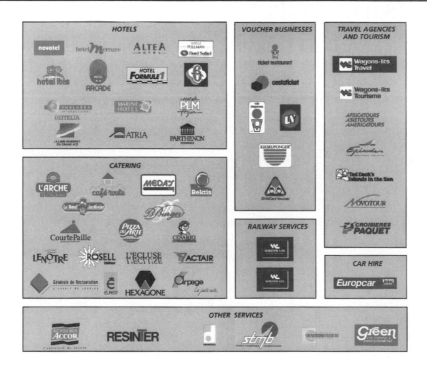

Description of Selected Major Brands

		Total Revenue (million FF)	
Brand	Description	1989	1990
Novotel	National full-service hotels	4,558	4,859
Motel 6	American budget hotels	2,550	2,784
Sofitel	International luxury hotels	1,865	1,986
Mercure	Full-service hotel	1,145	1,322
Formule 1	European budget hotels	200	338
Parthenon residence	Serviced apartment hotels	116	108
Generale de restauration	Institutional catering	2,600	3,000
Le Notre	Gastronomic catering and restaurants	490	535
Courte-paille	Roadside steakhouses	360	369
Pizza del'Arte	Italian restaurants	301	337
L'Arche	Highway restaurants	305	331
Meda's	Highway restaurants	111	99
Le Boeuf Jardinier	Steakhouses	96	114
Ticket restaurant	Meal vouchers	500	570
Croisieres Paquet	Cruises	281	591
Africa/Asie/Americatours	Tour operator	285	252

Source: ACCOR 1991 Annual Report.

EXHIBIT 2   Financial Results of ACCOR (in millions of French francs)

	1991	1990[a]	1989	1988	1987	1986
Total revenue	22,434	22,837	19,919	16,395	14,618	12,935
Net income	949	794	606	469	334	231
	4.23%	3.48%	3.04%	2.86%	2.28%	1.79%
Net income per share	44.15	40.3	34.9	29.2	24.3	21.3
Number of hotels	1,675	1,522	856	773	713	596
Number of rooms	189,911	173,679	98,995	89,691	84,786	71,392
Employees (at year-end)	82,402	81,686	51,502	30,183		

[a]Financial figures for 1990 include six months of Motel 6 results; 1990 totals for hotel rooms and employees include Motel 6.

1990 Financial Performance by Geographic Area

	Revenues		Profits		Operating Margin
France	12,583	55.1%	910	71.4%	7.24%
Rest of Europe	5,549	24.3	339	26.6	6.11
Latin America	1,621	7.1	140	11.0	8.65
United States and Canada	1,598	7.0	−107	(8.4)	−6.70
Africa	662	2.9	−1	(0.1)	−0.19
Asia Pacific	822	3.6	−11	(0.9)	−1.40
Total	22,836	100.0%	1,275	5.6%	5.58%

Approximate exchange rate: $1 = FF5.5; FF1 = $.18.

Source: ACCOR 1992 Annual Report.

Another question involved Motel 6's top manager: How critical was it to retain the CEO, Joseph W. McCarthy, and what could be done to keep him on board? Beyond these immediate challenges, Dubrule and Pélisson were also re-examining the role of general management in a firm that was increasingly large, diverse, and far-flung. Successful integration of Motel 6 and addressing organizational challenges were among the pressing challenges facing Paul Dubrule and Gérard Pélisson.

ACCOR's Early Days: Visions of the Future

Paul Dubrule, born in northern France in 1934, was a graduate of the Institute des Hautes Etudes Commerciales of Geneva University. In the early 1960s he travelled to the United States and spent two years working for NCR. While in the United States, Dubrule was impressed by chains of clean and efficient hotels, such as Holiday Inn, and believed that similar chains could be successful in Europe, where hotels tended to be individually owned and operated. Returning to France in 1963, Dubrule envisioned a chain of hotels, located near airports and alongside the growing national highway system, that could serve the increasing number of business travellers and tourists. But the idea was scoffed at by potential investors, and Dubrule had neither the resources nor the credibility to launch his idea.

Fortunately, Dubrule was introduced by a mutual friend to Gérard Pélisson. Pélisson, born in Lyon in 1932, had graduated from the Ecole Centrale de Paris and subsequently studied industrial management at the Massachusetts Institute of Technology. Pélisson, too, had spent several years in the United States, working with IBM, and returned to France as a manager for IBM Europe. He agreed with Dubrule about the bright prospects for hotel chains in France and, through his business connections, was able to attract investors to secure financing for the new venture.

Dubrule and Pélisson began with an ambitious goal: to open one hotel per year for the next ten years. With a government loan and private start-up capital, the new company, called Novotel, was founded in 1967. The first Novotel was opened near the airport in Lille, a large city near the Belgian border. A second hotel was soon opened in Colmar. The hotels quickly prospered and by 1970 there were seven Novotels, ranging from Lille in the North to Marseilles on the Mediterranean.

Although neither Dubrule nor Pélisson had worked in the hotel industry, they staffed their company almost exclusively with professionals trained in hotel and restaurant management. In their view, the proper role of top management was to liberate these professionals so they could best perform their jobs, rather than to constrain them with tight management controls. They noted: "We decided that we had to decentralize responsibility, and that requires an environment of trust. In the long run, decentralization is less expensive than the excess of centralization. In the service business, delegation of responsibility is necessary—it unleashes initiative." Such an approach stood in contrast to the emphasis on centralization and the reliance on hierarchy that typified many French firms.

Novotel thus exhibited a blend of American and French characteristics. While its basic concept was borrowed from American hotels like Holiday Inn and Hilton, its hands-on approach to service and emphasis on food as a money maker rather than as a sideline business were typically French. And, drawing on American business practices, Novotel introduced the use of cost accounting and financial analysis, something new in an industry that had long been run on a "Mom and Pop" basis.

Growth, Diversification, and Acquisitions

By the early 1970s, Novotel was a well-established brand with hotels spread across the French landscape. The goal of ten hotels in ten years had long since been surpassed. Looking ahead, however, Dubrule and Pélisson foresaw that Novotel could soon reach saturation in France, and decided to diversify into new geographic areas and into new products. A first effort at diversification came in 1973 with the creation of a two-star hotel, called Ibis, aimed at a somewhat lower segment of the lodging industry than Novotel. The following year, Dubrule and Pélisson acquired a small

---

EXHIBIT 3   Milestones in ACCOR's History

1967: Creation of Novotel SIEH (Société d'Investissements et d'Exploitation Hotelière).
Opening of the first Novotel at Lille Airport.

1970: Opening of the seventh Novotel.

1973: Launch of the Ibis two-star hotel chain, in association with the Company La Hénin.

1974: Acquisition of a 44 percent stake in the Courte-Paille restaurant chain.

1975: Acquisition of the Mercure Restaurant-Hotels.

1976: Beginning of operations in Africa, the Middle East and South America.

1980: Acquisition of Sofitel.

1981: Novotel SIEH enters the Paris Stock Exchange.

1983: Creation of ACCOR through the merger of Novotel SIEH and Jacques Borel International.

1984 Paul Dubrule and Gérard Pélisson are named "Manager of the Year" by *Le Nouvel Economiste*.

1985: Opening of the ACCOR Academy. Opening of the first Formule 1 budget hotel.

1987: Paul Dubrule and Gérard Pélisson are awarded "Chevalier de la Légion d'Honneur" by the French
Minister of Industry.

1989: Opening of the 100th Formule 1 budget hotel.

1990: Acquisition of Motel 6 Corporation. With Formule 1 in France and Motel 6 in the United States, ACCOR
becomes the world leader in budget hotels.

1991: Motel 6 buys 9 hotels from Susse Chalet and 53 hotels from Regal Inns.

ACCOR completes the majority acquisition of Compagnie Internationale des Wagons-Lits et du
Tourisme, a FF16 billion company with 54,000 employees, adding Pullman, Altea, Wagons Lits, and
Europcar to ACCOR's product lines.

Source: ACCOR Annual Reports and company documents.

but popular restaurant chain, Courte Paille, and in 1975 they acquired a chain of three-star hotels, Mercure. At the same time, Novotel began to open hotels in foreign lands visited by French tourists, including Africa and the Middle East. Expansion soon followed in other European countries, including Germany, Switzerland, and the United Kingdom. (See ACCOR company history, Exhibit 3.)

Diversification accelerated in the early 1980s. In 1980, Dubrule and Pélisson acquired the luxury hotel chain, Sofitel, from financially troubled Jacques Borel International (JBI). In 1983, they bought the remainder of JBI, acquiring a number of fast-food restaurants and Ticket-Restaurant, a restaurant voucher operation. The merged company was named ACCOR.

Merger with JBI made strategic sense, since JBI's product lines complemented those of Novotel while building on a core competence in hospitality and service delivery, but it posed several managerial challenges. Most difficult was that the management styles of the two companies were diametrically opposed. At Novotel, Dubrule and Pélisson had created a lean and low-overhead company where employees were encouraged to take risks. At JBI, decision making was highly centralized, with headquarters overwhelming product divisions with tight controls and requests for information of all kinds. At Novotel, most managers had been trained in hotel school, and very few had university educations. At JBI, managers tended to come from prestigious schools and were highly sophisticated but, according to one veteran, "they lacked a sense of the field." Given these differences, the integration of JBI and Novotel was complicated and slow. As Dubrule and Pélisson noted: "Jacques Borel's culture was opposite from ours: we were pragmatic and they were tightly controlled. Their reliance on control was understandable because they had been in financial distress for two years. They brought a methodology and a rigor of control, but we brought an approach to decision making and the right to make mistakes."

Little by little members of these two organizations gained confidence in each other. By 1985, ACCOR owned and operated 536 hotels with more than 64,000 hotel rooms, as well as 2,000 restaurants. Revenues had reached FF 10 billion (approximately $2 billion).

Dubrule and Pélisson: Management "Bicéphale"

ACCOR was prominent among French firms for its approach to management as well as for its growth and profitability. In 1984, Paul Dubrule and Gérard Pélisson were named "Managers of the Year" by the French business magazine, *Le Nouvel Economiste*. Their approach to management was called *bicéphale*, or two-headed, with Dubrule the specialist on product strategy and marketing, and Pélisson the expert on administration and finance. They recalled: "At the beginning, we concentrated on our respective fields of expertise, but we always discussed things with each other. That way, after a while, each of us had acquired the expertise of the other." After several years of working closely together, they believed they were almost interchangeable.

In temperament, too, Dubrule and Pélisson were complementary. At times, one would be highly enthusiastic about a project, only to be kept from getting carried away by the sober assessment of the other. "Each of us," observed Dubrule, "benefits from the detached views of the other."

Pélisson noted:

> The combination works because Dubrule and I don't see everything through the same set of spectacles. When we agree on something, I believe we have nine chances out of ten to be right. When we disagree, then we know we have to proceed carefully and take our time. When we ultimately agree, it's because one of us has been able to persuade the other through logic and reasoning.

Dubrule added:

> It's especially important to have two top managers when it comes to dealing with individual personalities. There have been times when I've been very aggravated with a particular manager, and I'm ready to toss him out the window. Then Pélisson comes in and says, "Hey, calm down. Yes, this guy's a real pain, but he also has some good points." So having a partner gives a certain balance. When only one person has all the power, he's tempted to use it.

Despite their long and close collaboration, ACCOR's co-chairmen maintained a sense of professional distance and equality. They noted: "After 25 years of work together we still say *vous* to each other." Equality was sought even in personal matters such as investments. "If one of us finds a good investment opportunity, we always tell the other, and usually go in together or not at all. That way, neither of us becomes much wealthier than the other."

Dubrule and Pélisson explicitly managed ACCOR in the interests of three constituencies: customers, employees and managers, and shareholders (see Exhibit 4). Pélisson asserted:

> We are interested in all three, but if you ask me which comes first, it's the employees and managers. The reason should be clear—everything starts with the employee. If employees are happy, they will provide good service to customers, and we will achieve a good dividend for investors. It's not that investors aren't important—after all, *I* am an investor, too—but in this business, it all has to start with employees.

EXHIBIT 4   ACCOR's Three Constituenices

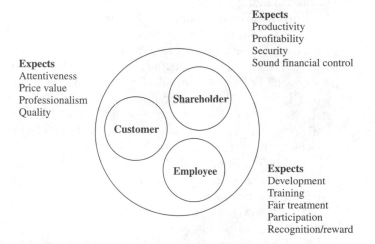

Expects
Productivity
Profitability
Security
Sound financial control

Expects
Attentiveness
Price value
Professionalism
Quality

Expects
Development
Training
Fair treatment
Participation
Recognition/reward

These three—**Employee, Customer,** and **Shareholder**—are like the legs of a tripod. If one is slightly off balance, the tripod is tilted, and all the energy should be directed at restoring balance as soon as possible.

Ideally, we would like to have perfect, permanent balance of the three legs. Realistically, we know this is difficult. The art of management consists of continuously adjusting the tripod to optimize the balance.

The relationship between the legs of the tripod is:

- **Employee** development leads to job satisfaction.
- A satisfied employee gives better service to the customer.
- A satisfied **customer** returns, making the hotel successful.
- A successful unit means satisfactory financial results for the **shareholder,** leading to new investments.
- New investments offer increased opportunities for employee development.

Source: ACCOR North America publication.

ACCOR's Evolving Organization: "Variable Geometry"

ACCOR's organization had evolved over three distinct stages. During the first stage, from 1967 until the acquisition of Jacques Borel International in 1983, the Novotel brand represented the majority of the company's business, and was treated as the center of the firm. Additional brands, such as Courte Paille, were essentially sideline businesses.

With the acquisition of JBI and the addition of several new product lines, ACCOR shifted to a product brand structure. Each of the brands had a president, who reported directly to Dubrule and Pélisson. Brand presidents were responsible for all operating units (hotels or restaurants), which were located almost entirely in France or the Benelux countries. As ACCOR began to expand abroad, it established a series of country organizations that complemented the domestic brand organization. As Dubrule explained, it was important to be closely attuned to country issues during the start-up phase of foreign operations. Country presidents were given full responsibility for all ACCOR units within their lands; they ran both the administrative and the operating aspects of ACCOR's business.

Over time, however, as country operations grew in size and maturity, retaining a primarily country focus became less important, and they began to shift from a country structure to a brand structure. The first country to make this change was Germany; in 1987, the various units in Germany—such as Novotel, and Ibis—began to report directly to their respective brand headquarters in France, leaving the German country manager with only administrative responsibilities. The United Kingdom soon followed, and in 1990, the Middle East and Africa also shifted to a brand organization.

These shifts in reporting lines had the effect of increasing the power of brand management. Consider the example of Novotel. Until 1987, the president of Novotel had operational responsibility for all hotels in France and the Benelux countries, but Novotels elsewhere in the world reported to the various country managers. In 1987, Novotel headquarters took direct operating responsibility for its hotels in Germany and elsewhere in Europe, and in 1989 it gained responsibility for Novotels in the Middle East and Africa. By 1990, the only Novotels that did not report to brand headquarters were in the four remaining country (or geographic) areas: Asia, North America, Brazil, and Italy.

ACCOR retained a regional organization in both Asia and North America because penetration in those regions was relatively recent and a continued regional focus was needed. In Italy the story was different. Although ACCOR's Italian operations were as mature as those in many other parts of Europe, the country organization was retained for a simple reason: the Italian country manager was so capable, and his understanding of management in Italy so strong, that in the view of Dubrule and Pélisson, there was nothing to be gained by shifting operational control to the brands.

The result was not a single, consistent approach to organizational design applied everywhere in the world, nor the simultaneous dual reporting structure of a matrix organization, but what Dubrule and Pélisson called an organization of "variable geometry." A variable structure suited Dubrule and Pélisson: "We are in favor of variable organization structures, because organizations must adapt to the people within them. We are not fond of highly defined organization charts since they engender a certain rigidity."

Key People, Not Key Positions

The approach taken to managing ACCOR's Italian operations exemplified the paramount emphasis that Dubrule and Pélisson put on the person, not on the position. As Dubrule explained:

> You need to design the best job for each person, and not just put people in an existing box. People won't fit in a standardized box—it may be too big or too small, and they'll be cramped or bent out of shape.
>
> We try to tailor the job to fit the person. A job should be like a good suit of clothes. It's more expensive to have a tailor-made suit, but it fits better, and it lasts longer.

Consistent with the emphasis on people, rather than on positions, ACCOR resisted adopting a formal structure that delineated the relationships between various units. In fact, ACCOR intentionally did not publish a formal company organization chart with jobs and names, instead simply providing a list of the company's brands (as shown in Exhibit 1). A senior manager recalled: "A new employee once asked me for a copy of ACCOR's organization chart. I handed him the company phone directory—'Here's the organization,' I told him." This attitude was echoed by managers at all levels, who described ACCOR as an organization of people and not of formal roles. "We don't put people in slots, we build jobs for people," explained Volker Büring, ACCOR's Vice President of Human Resources.

Downplaying the importance of formal structure not only allowed flexibility in tailoring individual positions, but was intended to foster an environment of equality between employees, rather than an environment which emphasized adherence to hierarchical relations. Equality was essential, stressed one manager, for open and free discussions: "It's hard to say to your boss, 'Hey, you're screwing up! *Vous déconnez!* If you want people to talk openly, you have to make them as equal in position as possible. You have to minimize hierarchical distinctions." Dubrule and Pélisson agreed: "We are against the spirit of hierarchy. We are opposed to a caste system and pyramid structures. Flat and lean structures are the key to more efficient organizations."

The lean operation was evident at ACCOR's corporate offices, located in a plain three-story building in Evry, outside Paris. (ACCOR also occupied a floor in the Tour Montparnasse, with a commanding view of Paris, but used these offices primarily to house the Finance Department, which needed to be in close contact with the financial community in Paris.) Paul Dubrule and Gérard Pélisson held the Office of the Chairmen, where they were assisted by one or two other managers, who typically served in the Office of the Chairmen as a rotational assignment before assuming a new position in a product division or country. Also located at headquarters were the key staff functions: finance and administration, technical and construction, human resources, and operations. Each staff function was headed by a vice president. Altogether, ACCOR's corporate offices employed only 150 people.

The presidents of ACCOR's 46 divisions had broad authority for product offerings, pricing, and promotions. According to Volker Büring, "The idea is to transmit the responsibility to the front-line staff in order to increase responsiveness. Each manager has to work with his or her team to meet their plans." Through an annual targeting cycle, divisions formulated targets for revenues, profits, opening new units, quality standards, employee training, and other goals.

ACCOR's emphasis on flat organizations and hands-on management extended to the level of individual hotels. At Novotel New York, in midtown Manhattan, General Manager Bernard Rudler noted that his organization was structured not like a pyramid but like a rake: flat and with a very broad span of control. The hotel had only one secretary for 160 employees, and no manager had a dedicated assistant. Director of Personnel Kathleen Guilford-DeMaiolo confirmed: "All our managers are working managers. Our front desk manager checks in guests. Our restaurant manager seats customers. No one here delegates their job entirely." When Novotel New York opened in 1984, Rudler recalled, some employees thought that the organization was too lean and that employees were stretched too thin. "But when times got tough and other hotels began to lay off employees, they realized that our lean organization helped us preserve jobs," Rudler noted. In addition, the lean overhead structure provided savings that were channelled into employee training.

General Management at ACCOR: Decentralization and Cohesion

Although ACCOR's many brands enjoyed considerable operating autonomy, the company was by no means a loosely connected set of independent operations. Pélisson vigorously denied that ACCOR was a holding company, and stressed that substantial value was added by headquarters. He asserted:

> The more you decentralize day-to-day operations, the more you have to have very strong cohesion at the top level. We may only have 150 people at headquarters, but we have to have very strong expertise at the center. The key is to have expertise at the right level of the organization.

General management at ACCOR concentrated on four responsibilities: finance, human resources, external resources, and external relations.

Finances. Centralized functions undertaken by ACCOR headquarters included raising capital, managing the worldwide flow of cash, and approving major expenditures. "Major financial decisions have to be taken at headquarters," remarked Pélisson. "We can't have each division negotiate independently with bankers. What kind of hotel a division wants to build is up to them, and where they want to put it is up to them, but how to pay for it is a decision taken here."

Human resources. Each brand had wide discretion in its human resource management, but key responsibilities were retained at headquarters. Pélisson described:

> Each product division is responsible for its own hiring, recruiting, firing, and develops its own motivation and compensation plans. The divisions can decide to reward employees on different

---
EXHIBIT 5   ACCOR Statement of Ethics and Management

ACCOR's Values
- Quality
- Profit
- Growth
- Innovation
- Training
- Participation
- Decentralization
- Communication

As an employee of ACCOR:
- I will ensure the profitable and efficient use of resources that are entrusted to me;
- I will protect the people and facilities under my responsibility against accidents, theft, loss, or illicit use;
- I will search for and will suggest improvement in my work organization and will undertake or facilitate the development of new ideas.

With other people:
- I will respect people and I will not display racist, anti-union or sexist behavior;
- I am responsible for the development and the training of my colleagues. Based on their qualifications, their potential and needs, I will facilitate their career within ACCOR;
- I have the duty to inform, explain and listen to my colleagues.

With customers:
- I will honor my promises of quality and service to the customer;
- I will not oversell beyond the customer's budget.

With suppliers:
- I will inform them that it is a group policy not to accept "gifts";
- I will select them based on their quality/price/service performance.

With other members in the industry:
- I will not be arrogant toward smaller competitors.

Political activity:
- I will not engage in any kind of political activity that could be harmful to ACCOR; however, I will try to participate in cultural, social, and humanitarian organizations in my local area.

Toward shareholders:
- I will never lose sight of the fact that I am working with their capital, and that I must strive to retain their confidence.

Source: ACCOR's "Blue Book" on Ethics and Management.

measures—that's up to them. Our concern at headquarters is with establishing consistency in ACCOR's overall culture, the ACCOR ethics, and training at the ACCOR Academy.

One element in establishing a strong set of company ethics was the publication of company principles in ACCOR's "Blue Book of Ethics and Management" (see Exhibit 5). These were reinforced in extensive training sessions. ACCOR emphasized training and continuing education for its employees, and in 1985 established the ACCOR Academy, the first dedicated training complex of its kind in Europe, located in Evry. New general managers participated in an intensive three-week seminar at the Academy. Seminars were organized for heads of departments on such subjects as Marketing, Sales, Human Relations, Team Building. The emphasis on training gave ACCOR an important advantage over smaller competitors that could not provide similar training and educational opportunities. More than 4,500 employees came to the ACCOR Academy each year for training sessions, and local training sessions conducted in each country raised the total number of employees who participated in training sessions to 14,000 per year.

External resources. ACCOR headquarters was closely involved in decisions where central expertise resulted in efficiencies, or where ACCOR's sheer size could bring about cost savings. For example, headquarters had a small staff of experts on contracts and construction management who could help divisions with legal counsel or with technical expertise. "A hotel brand can choose its interior decorator," Pélisson noted, "but if they want to build ten new hotels, they need to work with us on the wording of the contract and on management of construction."

Most supplies and equipment were purchased at the brand level. In some cases, however, the purchase of equipment or even of a consumer good was coordinated centrally to achieve cost savings. "Out of 100 products in a division," said Pélisson, "perhaps only five are worth purchasing on a worldwide level. That still leaves 95 for the divisions." Among the products bought in sufficient volume to merit centralized purchasing included leading brands of soft drinks and mineral water, linens, and consumables.

External relations. The final responsibility of ACCOR's top management concerned external relations: the company's image, its public relations, and its relations with investors. Dubrule and Pélisson acted as ambassadors of ACCOR, giving interviews to the press, and meeting with government officials in host countries. They also counted among their responsibilities the choice and composition of shareholders. In 1991, major institutional investors owned almost 40 percent of ACCOR shares and held nine of eleven seats on the board. These investors included major banks and investors such as the Société Général de Belgique, Caisse Depots et Consignations, Compagnie Général des Eaux, and Caisse Centrale des Mutuelles Agricoles (see Exhibit 6). Pélisson emphasized: "We have never been a slave to capital. We always choose our shareholders. The distribution of our shareholders is very important—we will offer 5 percent to this one, 10 percent to that one." ACCOR's investors supported the long-term vision of Dubrule and Pélisson and tended to remain shareholders for extended periods of time. They had been rewarded by consistent growth: ACCOR dividends rose steadily, and the share price consistently outperformed the Paris Stock Exchange Index (Exhibit 7).

Gérard Pélisson stressed that he and Dubrule were responsible for the company's strategic direction, and were closely involved in these four responsibilities—but *only* these four. They frequently visited individual hotels and restaurants, but did not monitor operations at a detailed level. Pélisson noted:

EXHIBIT 6 ACCOR Composition of Shareholders

Major Shareholders as of December 31, 1991	*Shares (000)*	*Percent of Capital*	*Percent of Votes*
Société Generale de Belgique	2,763	12.7%	16.1%
Caisse Depots et Consignations	1,656	7.6	7.4
Compagnie Generale des Eaux	1,178	5.4	8.7
Caisse Centrale des Mutuelles Agricoles	927	4.3	3.5
Société Generale	837	3.9	4.9
Groupe UAP	739	3.4	2.8
Compagnie d'lnvestissements de Paris (Groupe BNP)	454	2.1	3.3
Total institutional investors	8,555	39.4%	46.6%
Management and employees		42.2	50.4
Remaining shares		18.4	3.0
		100.0%	100.0%

Source: ACCOR 1992 Annual Report.

EXHIBIT 7 Recent Performance of ACCOR Share Price

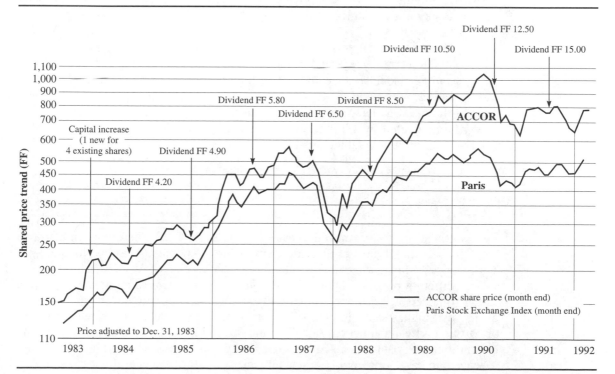

Source: ACCOR 1992 Annual Report.

If a division manager wants to build a hotel in Jamaica, or on an island in the Indian Ocean, that's his business. It's not my problem. Once a manager came to me and asked if I thought he should buy a catering business in Chile. I said: 'You're asking *me?* That's not *my* problem, it's *your* problem.'

Knowing the extent of your autonomy is part of ACCOR's culture. Managers know what they can do, and when they have to ask.

Building and Strengthening the Organization

Managing a far-flung multinational company required managers with a breadth of experience and a versatility of skills, making the task of developing and deploying managers throughout the organization a high priority. For many years, ACCOR had only a minimal centralized human resources function. In 1989, Volker Büring, a German national with experience at Hay Management, was hired to be ACCOR's Vice President of Human Resources. His mission, Büring recalled, was nothing less than the companywide integration of the human resource function.

A common phrase, often repeated by managers and echoed in company publications, emphasized the nature of career development at ACCOR: "A career at ACCOR calls for at least two skills and experience in at least two countries." For example, a manager might move from a hotel division to a restaurant division, or from Germany to Brazil. Dubrule and Pélisson agreed: "Career mobility is essential for a company that operates on all continents. Skills do not belong to any particular country, and careers have no borders."

In order to execute this vision of development and rotation, the careers of roughly 400 top employees were managed from headquarters. "We know them all by name," said Pélisson, "and we know their interests and their motivation." Divisions and operating units of ACCOR worldwide communicated the availability of positions to the headquarters, where every three months, top managers convened for a meeting, moderated by Büring, at which specific openings and careers were discussed. Dubrule described the process:

> Each area identifies its key needs, and also presents its managers who are ready for new assignments. Then it becomes like a stock market, matching people with jobs. We go through the process case by case, person by person. This isn't some theoretical exercise—you have to do it person by person. It only works because we take the time to know all our managers personally.

Although there were no fixed career paths at ACCOR, there was an effort to meet the personal desires of individual employees. As emphasized by Novotel New York General Manager Bernard Rudler, a 20-year veteran of ACCOR who had held several different positions in his career: "There are no planned careers; you build a career for yourself. Maybe an opportunity is suggested to you, but it's up to you to decide if it makes sense to take it." Another manager noted: "With the variety of opportunities available within ACCOR, and the commitment of management to find the appropriate spot for managers, there's really no reason for a good person to want to leave." Indeed, for a company as young as ACCOR, there was already a legion of managers with 15 or 20 years of company experience. Pélisson reflected: "If a person has decided to spend their career with us, or has devoted 20 years or more to ACCOR, then we know we've been successful."

Although Dubrule and Pélisson did not monitor in detail the operating results of each brand, they believed it was their responsibility to know hundreds of managers personally, and if necessary, to intervene directly in matters that affected people. As Dubrule recalled:

> Once we had a manager who had been posted abroad for a long time, and his wife and family really wanted to move back to France. He asked me to find him a job in France, and I said, "Don't worry, I'll take care of it." When you have someone who is 50 years old and has spent 15 of his life with ACCOR, you have to find a place for them. It *has* to be done. I took care of it personally. You have to make an effort—not only for that particular person, but to show others.
>
> After all, financial matters, product matters—they're important, but they're not enough. Most of all, to succeed you need the right people. There's no exact science to managing people. You just have to spend the time to get it right. You have to elevate it in importance, and make sure you lead by example.

Although ACCOR offered employees secure employment, it also placed a major emphasis on individual performance. Many managers received year-end performance bonuses equal to one-third of their salary, an unusually large amount compared to most French firms. Typically there were three performance criteria for receiving bonuses: achieving profit goals, achieving quality goals, and some HRM component, often achieving training goals. Said Michael Flaxman, President of ACCOR North America: "These three bonus criteria reflect our three sets of constituents. Profitability speaks to the needs of our shareholders, quality speaks to the needs of our customers, and training speaks to our employees. Achieving your bonus requires attention to all three constituents, not just meeting revenues or profit targets."

In addition to year-end bonuses for specific achievements, roughly 1,500 employees worldwide were granted stock options that vested over five years. These stock options were not linked with specific achievements, but were granted on a more subjective basis to high-potential employees. "Stock options are not given for past performance, but for the future," explained Volker Büring. "They are designed to ensure the continuing loyalty of our best employees."[1]

ACCOR and the Lodging Industry

Despite continuing to diversify into new areas of travel and tourism, ACCOR remained most dependent on the lodging industry. In 1990, the worldwide lodging industry had sales of about $150 billion. Upon closer inspection, however, lodging was not a single industry, but a set of distinct segments, ranging from luxury hotels to budget motels. The luxury segment accounted for 16 percent of rooms worldwide, and included firms such as Intercontinental, Marriott, Trusthouse Forte, Hyatt Regency, Westin, and others. The luxury segment was global in nature, as customers travelled worldwide, and standards for service were similar in most parts of the world. The middle market segment accounted for 30 percent of rooms worldwide,

---

[1]The use of stock options was especially important given French tax laws. Whereas the marginal tax rate on ordinary income was often more than 50 percent, stock shares held for five years or longer were subjected only to a capital gains tax of 18 percent. Stock ownership was therefore an important way for managers to earn significant personal wealth.

and included well-known American brands such as Holiday Inn, Howard Johnson, and Ramada. The budget or economy segment was the biggest, with 54 percent of rooms worldwide. The great majority of these budget or economy hotels were run by independent operators (85 percent) rather than by wholly-owned chains (15 percent). Competition tended to be local, and customers were mainly domestic. Room rates were often less than $30 per night.

ACCOR was one of the few firms with brands in each of the industry's three segments. For most of its history, ACCOR had operated in the luxury (Sofitel) and middle markets (Novotel, Mercure, and Ibis). In 1985, ACCOR rounded out its product offerings with the launch of Europe's first budget motel chain, called Formule 1. The success of Formule 1 was instantaneous and performance exceeded all expectations. Within three months, the brand had managed to recoup its initial investment and achieved break-even. Part of its success was due to its method of construction: Units were prefabricated and delivered to the site by truck, where they were quickly assembled into a motel. The result: scale economies in construction and consistency in quality. By May 1990, Formule 1 opened its 10,000th room and was recording a 77 percent occupancy rate. It was opening new hotels at the rate of one per week, with new expansion in the United Kingdom and in Germany, and was planning to introduce new units in Poland, Czechoslovakia, and Hungary.

Not only did ACCOR have at least one brand in each segment of the lodging industry, it was also a fully vertically-integrated company, involved in the full range of activities from initial site identification and purchase of real estate, to securing financing, construction, franchising, and finally to the management of hotels. In recent years, many hotel firms had gravitated to one or another specialized niche, focusing on, say, hotel development but not hotel management, or on management of franchised operations but without risking any investment capital. In Pélisson's view, long-term success in the lodging industry depended on mastery of each component activity. Developers and operators who did not share in the financial risk were unlikely to be successful in the long term, he believed, just as financiers who did not understand the operations of the business were unlikely to be successful. Furthermore, involvement at each stage was necessary because at any given time it might be difficult to make money at a particular stage. For example, if real estate was experiencing hard times, it would be essential to earn profits in hotel operations; and if an oversupply of rooms was depressing rates and making it difficult to succeed in hotel operations, it might be very helpful to be able to earn profits in financing.

ACCOR's Entry into North America

The first Sofitel in North America was established in 1979 with the opening of a hotel in Minneapolis. Although ACCOR had expanded into North America only after Europe, the Middle East, and Africa, it was committed to expanding its presence on that continent. Approximately one-third of the world lodging industry was located in North America, and the industry was undergoing a process of globalization. Given these realities, Paul Dubrule noted, "You cannot be successful unless you succeed in North America."

EXHIBIT 8   ACCOR North America Operations, 1990

Brand	Location	Year Opened	Rooms
Novotel	New York City	1984	474
Novotel	Mississauga, Toronto, Ontario	1985	325
Novotel	North York, Ontario	1987	260
Novotel	Toronto Centre, Ontario	1987	266
Novotel	Ottawa, Ontario	1988	283
Novotel	Princeton, NJ	1988	180
Novotel	Meadowlands, NJ	1990	219
Novotel	Toronto Airport, Ontario	1991	196
Novotel	Montreal, Quebec	1991	200
			2,403
Sofitel	Minneapolis, MN	1979	287
Sofitel	Houston, TX	1982	337
Sofitel	Miami, FL	1986	282
Sofitel	Chicago, IL	1987	305
Sofitel	San Francisco, CA	1987	324
Sofitel	Los Angeles, CA	1989	311
			1,846

Source: Novotel and Sofitel company publications.

In 1983, ACCOR appointed Georges Le Mener to become President of ACCOR North America and gave him the responsibility of charting ACCOR's expansion in the United States and Canada. Over the next years, Le Mener closely examined a number of potential large acquisitions but found no suitable deals. Through incremental additions, however, ACCOR's North American operations expanded to include, by 1991, six Sofitels and nine Novotels (locations of these units are provided in Exhibit 8). All reported to ACCOR North America, whose small offices were located in a modest office building in Scarsdale, New York. Because ACCOR maintained a regional organization in North America, the president of ACCOR North America had full responsibility for all brands in Canada and the United States. Assisting the president was a Vice President of Operations, who worked closely with each hotel, and a Vice President of Human Resources, who oversaw training and employee development in each hotel. In April 1990, Le Mener returned to Evry to become Director of the Office of the Chairmen. Michael Flaxman, a British national who had served as Executive Vice President of ACCOR North America since 1987, succeeded Le Mener as president.

The Acquisition of Motel 6

By the late 1980s, the U.S. hotel industry was feeling the effects of a decade of overbuilding, due in part to tax shelters and other government policies that had encouraged construction. An oversupply of rooms helped depress room rates, making it difficult for luxury and middle market hotels to earn a profit. In order to prop up their short-term financial performance, some American hotel companies began to sell real estate or other assets.

ACCOR executives noted the mounting problems of luxury and medium-priced hotels in the United States and, encouraged by the success of Formule 1 in Europe, reasoned that the economy segment held out the brightest prospect for growth in North America. However, success in the economy segment required a substantial size, making the development from scratch of a large chain unfeasible. The acquisition of a large existing network appeared to make more sense as an entry strategy. ACCOR examined the potential acquisition of a number of existing chains, including Days Inn, Motel 6, and Quality Inn. Of these, one emerged as the most attractive candidate: Motel 6.

Motel 6 had been the pioneer of national economy motel chains. The first Motel 6 opened in Santa Barbara, California, in 1962, offering basic accommodations for $6 a night. Its product was a "no-frills" room, without telephones or television, a shower but no bath, and minimal decoration. There was no reservation system, and payment was accepted only in cash. The product was immediately successful and was especially popular among families, older couples, and young people on limited budgets. It grew quickly in the western United States and subsequently spread across the country. By 1982, its 20th year of operation, Motel 6 had 344 locations with more than 37,000 rooms. The occupancy rate was 76 percent, and the average nightly rate stood at $17.

In the 1980s, however, substantial competition from rival economy brands, such as Super 8, Red Roof Inns, and Days Inn, began to erode Motel 6's market share. Occupancy declined to 66 percent. In 1985, with its fortunes sagging, Motel 6 was purchased by Kohlberg Kravis Roberts & Co. (KKR) for $928 million. KKR soon replaced top management, bringing in Joseph W. McCarthy as President and Chief Executive Officer. At 55 years of age, McCarthy was an experienced manager with a long career in the lodging industry. He had served as Director of Marketing of Sheraton, was then president of Quality Inn in the late 1970s, and most recently served as president of Lincoln Hotels, a Dallas-based chain in the 1980s. Under the terms of KKR's offer, McCarthy received a substantial equity position in the company.

Soon after becoming president of Motel 6, McCarthy relocated company headquarters to Dallas and began to install a strong management team. Under his leadership, Motel 6 made significant changes to the product, investing in telephones and televisions, and updating interior design. It also improved its marketing approach, accepting credit cards and implementing a reservation system, and introduced a savvy national radio advertising campaign. Motel 6 revenues began to recover momentum in the late 1980s.

Speaking in 1990, McCarthy summarized the improvement:

> We grew the company from 378 motels with 42,279 rooms and 7,000 employees at the time of the buyout in early 1985 to 554 motels with 63,765 rooms and over 11,500 employees estimated for year-end 1990. In addition, Motel 6's sales have increased from $226 million in 1984 to $475 million estimated for 1990. Operating income increased from $122 million to $220 million for the same period.

By 1990, Motel 6's 554 motels were located in 45 states, offering rooms of a consistent standard. With average room rates of $24.95, Motel 6 prices were 20 to 30 percent below other economy motel chains, and half as much as the average rate for the lodging industry. Occupancy rates were high, averaging around 75 percent. It catered to a local clientele: Of the more than 26 million guests who stayed at a Motel 6 during 1991, more than 90 percent were Americans.

As a potential acquisition, Motel 6 was attractive to ACCOR for several reasons: Its motels were entirely company-owned (none were franchised) allowing for strict control over price and quality; it had a clearly defined and consistent product; it was the market leader in its industry segment; and it had strong management. Compared to other budget motels such as Red Roof Inns and La Quinta, Motel 6 offered rooms at a lower price; and compared to franchised motels such as Comfort Inn and Super 8, Motel 6 had better control over its product.

ACCOR and KKR were both interested in making a deal: ACCOR to take a major position in the North American lodging industry, and KKR to realize a sub-stantial profit after five years of successful management and significant improve-ment. Representatives of ACCOR and KKR held a series of preliminary meetings in the first months of 1990. Once initial issues were settled, further meetings were held in New York in May of 1990, involving principals of KKR, as well as the top man-agement of ACCOR. Paul Dubrule and Gerard Pélisson took direct responsibility for negotiating the acquisition, visiting New York several times during the spring of 1990. Assisting them was Georges Le Mener, whose extensive experience in North America was of considerable value. Providing further help in analysis and negotia-tion was Michael Flaxman, President of ACCOR North America.

A critical issue in the acquisition negotiation was price. A time-honored for-mula, first set forth by hotel baron Conrad Hilton, estimated a hotel's price at 1000 times the daily room rate. By this measure, Motel 6's 63,000 rooms, at an average of $25 per night, would be valued at roughly $1.6 billion. A different rule of thumb placed a hotel's value at between 7 and 10 times EBDIT, which placed Motel 6's value between $1.5 billion and $2.2 billion. In the end, ACCOR agreed to buy Motel 6 for $1.3 billion in equity, plus $1 billion in debt, for a total of $2.3 billion. The price came to $37,000 per room. According to one manager, ACCOR might not make much money on the units it had acquired, but was in an excellent position to make further acquisitions from this initial position and earn considerable returns on these new units.

Challenges in Managing Motel 6

The acquisition of Motel 6 considerably strengthened ACCOR's position in North America, but it also raised a number of challenges. First, and perhaps most impor-tant, Dubrule and Pélisson had to determine who should manage Motel 6. Joseph McCarthy had been highly successful in his five years as president, and his continu-ation with Motel 6 was clearly desirable, but McCarthy was by now 60 years old, and had earned a very significant amount of money with the acquisition by ACCOR. It was not clear if McCarthy would be willing to continue serving as president, but neither was it apparent that ACCOR had internal candidates who could step into the job, taking over a group of entirely American managers without prior experience either in the economy segment or in management of American operations. The question confronting Dubrule and Pélisson was twofold: what could be done to induce McCarthy to remain as CEO, and in the event he would not agree to stay on, should the acquisition still take place?

Second, Dubrule and Pélisson needed to determine how Motel 6 should fit into ACCOR's organization structure. From the inception of its operations in North America, ACCOR had relied on a country structure, with all hotel units reporting to the country manager. If the present structure were retained, Motel 6 could join the North American units of Novotel and Sofitel and report to ACCOR North America. This option had the advantage of adding strength to the regional organization. Another possibility was to treat Motel 6 separately, bypassing ACCOR North America altogether, and reporting as an independent brand directly to Dubrule and Pélisson.

Third, because Motel 6's clientele was almost entirely American and tended not to travel worldwide, it was not clear what synergies existed between Motel 6 and other hotel divisions within ACCOR. Dubrule and Pélisson needed to determine the extent to which Motel 6's operations should be changed, and the extent to which they should be left untouched.

Despite the high price that they paid for Motel 6, Paul Dubrule and Gérard Pélisson remained convinced that the greatest opportunity in the lodging industry was not in the luxury hotels, but in the budget market, where nightly room rates were $30 or less for two people. As they announced upon completion of the deal:

> ACCOR's alliance with Motel 6 helps achieve our strategic plan to establish ACCOR as the preeminent budget hotel company in the world. With the acquisition of Motel 6, we will reach a significant milestone: ACCOR will now own and operate more than 775 economy motels, and we further plan to reach our target of 2,000 budget motels within the next few years.

In the short-term, however, Dubrule and Pélisson confronted specific issues concerning the integration of this new acquisition.

Rethinking the Organization

On the heels of the acquisition of Motel 6 in 1990, ACCOR undertook at the end of 1991 the majority acquisition of Compagnie Internationale des Wagons-Lits et du Tourisme, a venerable Belgian-based company with extensive holdings in hotels (Pullman, Altea) as well as tourism and railway cars, including the legendary Orient Express. Once this acquisition was consolidated in 1992, ACCOR boasted annual revenues of FF 45 billion (roughly $9 billion), and employed 140,000 people in 127 countries.

By the early months of 1992, ACCOR had significantly expanded its presence in North America and had consolidated its leading position in the European lodging industry. Although the financial results for 1991 had not been strong, with a small decline in revenue although an increase in its profit margin (see Exhibit 2), ACCOR had fared better than many competitors in a very difficult year, when the recession, compounded by the Gulf War's depressing effect on travel and tourism, had battered the lodging and tourism industries. ACCOR management believed that it had achieved a reasonably good performance in 1991 precisely because of its product and geographic diversity: Strong results in Italy, Germany, and Belgium had offset weaker performance in France, Great Britain, and the United States; and growth in service vouchers had offset problems associated with tourism.

As a result of ACCOR's rapid growth, however, some executives were re-examining the company's approach to "decentralization and cohesion." Some believed that with the company's greater size, the influence of headquarters should be expanded in order to bring about needed coordination and cohesion. One possibility was to appoint a group vice president for each major product group: lodging, restaurants, service vouchers, and so forth. Another possibility was to devise a system of executive committees that shifted some responsibility from the chairmen to the next tier of brand presidents. Others believed that growth demanded further decentralization and autonomy for the operating divisions, and that brand presidents could continue to report directly to the Office of the Chairmen if additional functions, including finance, were left to the brands.

In weighing these opposing factors, Dubrule and Pélisson kept in mind the overriding vision they had of their company, and the principles they had followed in the company's 25 years:

> ACCOR isn't simply the sum of all the balance sheets and trading accounts of the various brands. ACCOR has a very real existence, its own culture, a corporate image, its ethics, its human resources policy—in short, an identity which goes beyond the financial domain, and which gives ACCOR an important role in the European community, and even in the world economy.

13   WHERE HAVE YOU BEEN? AN EXERCISE TO ASSESS YOUR EXPOSURE TO THE REST OF THE WORLD'S PEOPLES

Instruction:

1. On each of the attached worksheets, note the total number and names of those countries you have visited, and the corresponding percentage of world population which each country represents. Sum the relevant regional totals on page 380.

2. If used as part of a group analysis, estimate the grand total for the entire group. Then consider the following questions.

3. Why is there such a high variability in individual profiles (i.e., high exposure versus low exposure)?

4. What are the implications of each profile for one's career?

5. What would it take to get you to personally change your profile?

Region: Africa

Country	1994 Population (in millions)	Percent of World Total	Country	1994 Population (in millions)	Percent of World Total
1. Nigeria	107.9	1.9	29. Burundi	6.2	.1
2. Egypt	57.5	1.0	30. Chad	6.1	.1
3. Ethiopia	53.4	1.0	31. Benin	5.2	.1
4. Zaire	42.5	.7	32. Libya	5.2	.1
5. South Africa	41.5	.7	33. Sierra Leone	4.5	
6. Tanzania	28.8	.5	34. Togo	4.0	
7. Sudan	27.3	.5	35. Central African Republic	3.2	
8. Algeria	27.3	.5	36. Liberia	2.9	
9. Morocco	26.4	.5	37. Congo	2.5	
10. Kenya	26.0	.5	38. Mauritania	2.2	
11. Uganda	18.5	.3	39. Lesotho	1.9	
12. Ghana	16.9	.3	40. Namibia	1.5	
13. Mozambique	16.6	.3	41. Botswana	1.4	
14. Côte d'Ivoire	13.7	.2	42. Mauritius	1.1	
15. Madagascar	13.1	.2	43. Gabon	1.0	
16. Cameroon	12.8	.2	44. Guinea-Bissau	1.0	
17. Zimbabwe	11.0	.2	45. Gambia, The	1.0	
18. Malawi	10.8	.2	46. Swaziland	.9	
19. Angola	10.6	.2	47. Réunion (Fr.)	.6	
20. Burkina Faso	10.0	.2	48. Dibouti	.5	
21. Mali	9.5	.2	49. Equatorial Guinea	.4	
22. Zambia	9.1	.2	50. Comoros	.4	
23. Somalie	9.0	.2	51. Cape Verde	.3	
24. Niger	8.8	.2	52. Mayotte (FR)	.1	
25. Tunisia	8.8	.2	53. Sáo Tomé and Principe	.1	
26. Senegal	8.1	.2	54. Seychelles	.1	
27. Rwanda	7.7	.1	55. Eritrea (incl. with Ethiopia)	.0	
28. Guinea	6.5	.1	Subtotal	694.4	12.4

Source of all statistics, except for Taiwan: *1996 World Bank Atlas.*

Region: North American and Caribbean

Country	1994 Population (in millions)	Percent of World Total
1. USA	260.5	4.7
2. Mexico	91.8	1.6
3. Canada	29.1	.5
4. Cuba	10.9	.2
5. Guatemala	10.3	.2
6. Dominican Republic	7.6	.1
7. Haiti	7.0	.1
8. El Salvador	5.6	.1
9. Honduras	5.4	.1
10. Nicaragua	4.2	
11. Puerto Rico (U.S.)	3.6	
12. Costa Rica	3.3	
13. Panama	2.5	
14. Jamaica	2.4	
15. Trinidad and Tobago	1.2	
16. Guadeloupe (Fr.)	.4	
17. Martinique	.4	
18. Bahamas	.3	
19. Barbados	.3	
20. Belize	.2	
21. Netherlands Antilles (Neth.)	.2	
22. St. Lucia	.1	
23. Antigua and Barbuda	.1	
24. Aruba (Neth.)	.1	
25. Bermuda (UK)	.1	
26. Dominica	.1	
27. Grenada	.1	
28. Virgin Islands (U.S.)	.1	
29. St. Vincent	.1	
30. St. Kitts and Nevis	.1	
31. Cayman Islands	.1	
Subtotal	448.2	8.0

Region: South America

Country	1994 Population (in millions)	Percent of World Total
1. Brazil	159.1	2.8
2. Colombia	36.3	.6
3. Argentina	34.1	.6
4. Peru	23.3	.4
5. Venezuela	21.3	.4
6. Chile	14.0	.3
7. Ecuador	11.2	.2
8. Bolivia	7.2	.1
9. Paraguay	4.8	.1
10. Uruguay	3.1	
11. Guyana	.8	
12. Suriname	.4	
13. French Guiana (Fr.)	.1	
Subtotal	315.7	5.6

Region: Western Europe

Country	1994 Population (in millions)	Percent of World Total
1. Germany	81.1	1.5
2. United Kingdom	58.0	1.1
3. France	57.7	1.0
4. Italy	57.1	1.0
5. Spain	39.5	.7
6. Netherlands	15.3	.3
7. Greece	10.4	.2
8. Belgium	10.0	.2
9. Portugal	9.8	.2
10. Sweden	8.7	.2
11. Austria	7.9	.2
12. Switzerland	7.1	.1
13. Denmark	5.1	.1
14. Finland	5.0	.1
15. Norway	4.3	
16. Ireland	3.5	
17. Luxembourg	.4	
18. Malta	.4	
19. Iceland	.3	
20. Andorra	.1	
21. Channel Islands (U.K.)	.1	
22. Faeroe Islands (Den.)	.1	
23. Monaco (FR)	.1	
24. Greenland (Den.)	.1	
25. Isle of Man	.1	
26. Liechenstein	.1	
Subtotal	382.3	6.8

Region: Eastern Europe

Country	1994 Population (in millions)	Percent of World Total
1. Russian Federation	148.3	2.7
2. Ukraine	51.4	1.0
3. Poland	38.3	.7
4. Romania	22.7	.4
5. Yugoslavia, Fed. Rep. of	10.7	.2
6. Czech Republic	10.2	.2
7. Belarus	10.2	.2
8. Hungary	10.2	.2
9. Bulgaria	8.8	.2
10. Slovak Republic	5.3	.1
11. Croatia	4.8	.1
12. Bosnia and Herzegovina	4.4	.1
13. Moldova	4.4	.1
14. Lithuania	3.7	
15. Albania	3.4	
16. Latvia	2.6	
17. Macedonia, FYR	2.1	
18. Slovenia	2.0	
19. Estonia	1.5	
Subtotal	345.0	6.2

Region: Central Asia and Indian Subcontinent

Country	1994 Population (in millions)	Percent of World Total
1. India	913.6	16.3
2. Pakistan	126.3	2.3
3. Bangladesh	117.8	2.1
4. Uzbekistan	22.3	.4
5. Nepal	21.4	.4
6. Afghanistan	18.9	.4
7. Sri Lanka	18.1	.3
8. Kazakhstan	17.0	.3
9. Azerbaijan	7.5	.1
10. Tajikistan	5.9	.1
11. Georgia	5.5	.1
12. Kyrgyz Republic	4.7	
13. Turkmenistan	4.0	
14. Armenia	3.7	
15. Mongolia	2.4	
16. Bhutan	1.5	
17. Maldives	.2	
Subtotal	1,290.8	23.1

Region: Middle East

Country	1994 Population (in millions)	Percent of World Total
1. Iran	65.8	1.2
2. Turkey	60.8	1.1
3. Iraq	20.0	.4
4. Saudi Arabia	17.5	.3
5. Syrian Arab Republic	14.2	.2
6. Yemen	13.9	.2
7. Israel	5.4	.1
8. Jordan	4.2	
9. Lebanon	3.9	
10. West Bank and Gaza	2.1	
11. Oman	2.1	
12. United Arab Emirates	1.9	
13. Kuwait	1.7	
14. Cyprus	.7	
15. Bahrain	.5	
16. Qatar	.5	
Subtotal	215.2	3.8

Region: Asia Pacific

Country	1994 Population (in millions)	Percent of World Total
1. China	1,190.9	21.3
2. Indonesia	189.9	3.4
3. Japan	124.8	2.2
4. Vietnam	72.5	1.3
5. Philippines	66.2	1.2
6. Thailand	58.7	1.0
7. Myanmar	45.6	.8
8. South Korea	44.6	.8
9. North Korea	23.5	.4
10. Taiwan	21.0	.4
11. Malaysia	19.5	.3
12. Australia	17.8	.3
13. Cambodia	10.0	.2
14. Hong Kong	5.8	.1
15. Laos	4.7	
16. Papua New Guinea	4.2	
17. New Zealand	3.5	
18. Singapore	2.8	
19. Fiji	.7	
20. Macao (Port.)	.4	
21. Solomon Islands	.4	
22. Brunei	.3	
23. Western Samoa	.2	
24. French Polynesia Fr.)	.2	
25. New Caledonia (Fr.)	.2	
26. Vanuatu	.2	
27. Guam (U.S.)	.1	
28. Micronesia, Fed. Sts.	.1	
29. Tonga	.1	
30. American Samoa (U.S.)	.1	
31. Kiribati	.1	
32. Marshall Islands	.1	
33. Northern Mariana Islands	.1	
Subtotal	1,909.3	34.1

Summary

Region	# of Countries	Which You Have Visited	1994 Population (million)	Region's % of World Population	% of Population You Have Been Exposed To
Africa	55	_____	694.4	12.4	_____
North America and Caribbean	31	_____	448.2	8.0	_____
South America	13	_____	315.7	5.6	_____
Western Europe	26	_____	382.3	6.8	_____
Eastern Europe	19	_____	345.0	6.2	_____
Central Asia and Indian Subcontinent	17	_____	1,290.8	23.1	_____
Middle East	16	_____	215.2	3.8	_____
Asia Pacific	33	_____	1,909.3	34.1	_____
Grand Total	**210**	_____	**5,600.6**	**100.0**	_____

14 STUDDS NOLAN JOINT VENTURE

In February 1995, Mr. Madhu Khurana, the Managing Director of Studds Ltd. (Studds) of Faridabad, India, was considering breaking off Studds' joint venture agreement with Nolan of Italy. The Studds Nolan joint venture was Studds' first equity venture with a foreign partner and the preliminary negotiations for this venture had been completed six months earlier. However, as the two parties worked to finalize the joint venture agreement, they had reached an impasse. The current negotiations were marked by tension and distrust, and Mr. Khurana, while anxious to have a foreign partner for access to world markets, was concerned about several problems which had arisen since the joint venture was initiated. He had serious doubts about the long-term viability of the venture.

Company History

Gadgets India (Gadgets), the first company in the Studds group, was formed by two brothers, Ravi and Madhu Khurana, in 1969. Trained as engineers, the brothers first manufactured, in a house garage, injection and compressed molded engineering items on a custom basis for the automotive, textile, and white goods industries. In 1973, a motorcycle helmet manufacturing process was developed in-house and the first sale was in 1974. The motorcycle helmet line was marketed under the brand name 'Studds.'

381

Studds' development of indigenous technology contrasted with the way in which other companies grew in the regulated environment of India in the 1970s and 1980s. Most large Indian companies formed equity and nonequity alliances to access and acquire foreign technology. As the chairman of one of these conglomerates noted, most of these alliances were cultivated over a period of time and negotiations were often concluded by handshakes.

In the mid-1970s, motorcycle helmet usage was not popular in India. Consequently, early sales were low and only grew slowly. Two competitors existed in this embryonic market: Steelbird, who peddled high-priced helmets, and Concorde, a low-end manufacturer of cheap, industrial helmets. Studds competed in both ends, producing a premium helmet priced 10 percent lower than Steelbird's, and lower quality helmets for more price-conscious consumers. Studds quickly secured a leading position in both the high and low end of the budding motorcycle helmet market. The 'Studds' brand became synonymous with helmets in India, and its market leadership was virtually uncontested through the remainder of the 1970s and into the first half of the 1980s.

Organizational Characteristics

In 1994, Studds consisted of Gadgets and Studds Accessories Pvt Ltd. (Studds Accessories). Studds Accessories, formed in 1984, took over the marketing function for the Studds brand from Gadgets. Thus, Studds Accessories conducted all marketing activities, while Gadgets performed all manufacturing for Studds. By the 1990s, Studds Accessories had established a dealership network that penetrated all the nooks and crannies of the vast, dispersed Indian market; 800 chosen dealers provided Studds Accessories with the extensive network needed to reach into all of India.

These two companies were family-owned and controlled, with equity split equally between the families of the brothers, Ravi and Madhu Khurana. Gadgets remained a partnership, while Studds Accessories was a public-limited company, wholly owned by the two Khurana families, friends and relatives.

Gadgets manufactured all products sold by Studds Accessories. As well, it had testing facilities for ensuring that products complied with the relevant country or regional standard. Gadgets employed 380 people of which 60 were supervisory staff, 145 were skilled labor and 175 were semiskilled or unskilled labor. The main manufacturing facility was located in Faridabad, India and could produce 370,000 bi-wheeler helmets per year when operated at capacity. In 1994, 320,000 helmets were manufactured.

Gadgets was led by Ravi Khurana, the Group Chairman. A General Manager reported to Ravi Khurana and the division of responsibility and control was along functional lines, with six managers reporting directly to the General Manager. Studds Accessories was organized in a similar fashion. Madhu Khurana, the Managing Director, had a general manager and four functional managers reported to him. Twenty-five people were employed in Studds Accessories which had an advertising budget of Rs. 200,000 (in mid-1994, US$ 1 equaled Rs. 30.77).

Managers, responsible for a specific functional area, did not have much cross-communication. Where responsibilities overlapped and conflicts developed, resolution was sought through discussion with either Ravi or Madhu Khurana. Managers were reluctant to assume responsibility for decisions, and the general managers were reluctant to release such responsibility to the managers. Consequently, both Ravi and Madhu Khurana were intimately involved with the day-to-day operations of their companies.

Labour Relations

Employees of Studds were heavily unionized. Unions were active and vocal in India, and possessed considerable bargaining power because of the Indian government's 'no fire' policy. Under the terms of this policy, once an employee had been hired, the company was obligated to employ this individual for the lifetime of the company or employee. Dismissals were rare and were often accompanied by a considerable payout.

Other union activities sporadically disrupted activities inside and outside the Faridabad plant, and consumed upper management time. Studds helmets were distributed throughout India by trucking companies. Deliveries were subject to interruptions based on the relations of the trucker's union with the trucking companies. Also, a 1994 strike by dockworkers at the Bombay port delayed a recent shipment of Studds helmets to the North American market.

The strength of the union made changes in the manufacturing process difficult. In 1992, an injection molding machine was purchased. This machine was to be used for the manufacture of plastic, molded helmets for the lower-end segment of the market. Injection molding was a capital-intensive process, utilizing less labor than that used in the production of fiberglass helmets, a premium product. However, unions resisted the implementation of this process, and the injection molding machine remained idle, inhibiting expansion of Studds helmets in growing lower-end market segments.

Studds' Products

Approximately 70 percent of the revenues for the Studds group came from motorcycle helmet sales. Studds marketed helmets in both the lower and premium segments of the market, though lower-end models were priced higher than inexpensive locally made brands. Studds produced both open-face and full-face helmets. Open-face models ranged from Rs. 248-310, and full-face models were priced between Rs. 434 and 558. The most expensive helmet in the Studds line was priced at Rs. 1,200; however, sales of this model were small. Aerostar's models ranged in price from Rs.100 to 500.

Studds produced seven models in the full-face design and five models in the open-face design. As each model was produced in several color schemes, over 120 designs and colors of bi-wheeler helmets were produced. Both full-face and open-face designs had achieved ISI, ECE22.03, DOT, CSI, SNELL, and ANSI certification. Among a similar range of products, Aerostar had only received ISI certification for two models.

Studds also produced helmets for other user groups. Sales of sports helmets, used in such activities as cycling, canoeing, horseback-riding, skating, and skateboarding, accounted for the remaining 30 percent of revenues. All helmets in this line were manufactured to meet ANSI-Z-90 (a U.S. standard) specifications. Studds' adherence to stringent international quality control laws had enabled its bicycle helmets to receive quality approvals from the U.S., Canada, Mexico, and all of western Europe. Receiving Canadian (CSA) approval was an important benchmark, as companies from only nine nations worldwide had achieved it.

India in 1995

In the 1990s, India was going through a resurgence. Policy reforms, designed by Dr. Manmohan Singh, the Finance Minister, and implemented by the government of P.V. Narasimha Rao in July 1991, had created a feeling of widespread optimism in the country. Despite initial high inflation and a February 1992 stock market scandal, early indications were that the economy had responded positively to economic liberalization. GDP growth increased from less than 1 percent in 1991–92, to a projected 5 percent in 1994–95, and 6 percent in subsequent years. The dollar value of imports and exports grew by 25 percent in this same period, while foreign direct investment tripled. In addition, numerous multinationals had established a presence in India by 1994. Many markets were opened to foreign competitors under the new policy guidelines. Automatic approval existed for the markets in which Studds competed, and in the transportation markets from which the demand for Studds' products was derived. The middle class, the main purchasers of motorcycles and scooters, was expected to reach close to 300 million people by the turn of the century.

Infrastructure was an area of developmental concern. While India possessed an extensive network of railways and roads (there were 1.97 million km of roads of which less than half were paved), the road network was still insufficient for the number of vehicles on the roads. Traffic tie-ups were frequent, and travel by road was complicated by the wide variance in modes of transportation. Motorized trucks, cars, and bi-wheelers shared the nation's highways and urban roads with pedestrians and animal-drawn vehicles. On-time delivery of goods was hampered by road congestion.

Other conditions in India hindered firm efficiency. For example, government approvals were required at several stages in a joint venture setup. Investment (both capital goods and monetary) by foreign partners in a joint venture had to be approved by the Secretary for Industrial Approvals of the Department of Industrial Development, Ministry of Industries. Joint venture agreements had to be approved by the Reserve Bank of India of the Government of India, and permission was required from the Reserve Bank to issue shares to the foreign joint venture participant.

Other regulations governed the remittance of royalties and dividends, and the repatriation of capital. Furthermore, land purchases for industrial use often had an unaccountable component. This informal aspect to the economy was, at times, a reality in doing business in India. While conditions such as these impeded the conduct of

---

FIGURE 1   Motorcycle Demand in India

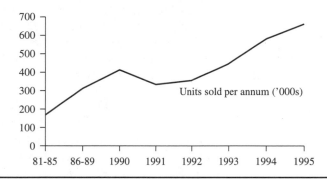

Note: (i) Demand for 1995 is estimated. (ii) Demand for mopeds was similar to that of motorcycles, while demand for scooters was double that of motorcycles.

Source: Government of India documents.

business in India, an overall optimism, reinforced by several years of strong economic growth, prevailed.

The Domestic Market

From its birth in the early 1970s, the helmet market in India had grown to an annual size of nearly one million helmets in the l990s. In 1992, Studds was the market leader, and held a 36 percent share. Aerostar, with a 12 percent share, occupied the number two position. Aerostar, which entered the market in the 1980s, competed directly against Studds' premium product line. Adopting a strategy similar to that used by Studds against Steelbird, Aerostar priced its premium product 10 percent less than Studds', and undercut Studds' prices at the low-end of the market as well. Steelbird, with a 5 percent share, was the number three manufacturer. Vega, which sold about 10,000 helmets per year, led a host of 90 or more other manufacturers who divided the remaining portion of the market among themselves. Helmets from these small manufacturers were low-end models, often sold in temporary roadside stands by individual sellers, independent of any buildings.

A few of these smaller manufacturers infringed on Studds' brand name. These small manufacturers made helmets identical in appearance to the Studds line but at a much lower cost. The duplicates bore the Studds name and could not be distinguished from genuine Studds helmets. Duplicates retailed for Rs. 170, while Studds' cost of manufacture was greater than Rs. 210. Trademark infringement was not legal under Indian law; however, in the past when Studds had tried to prosecute violators of its trademark, the penalty for infringement was not high enough to justify the two-year prosecution period.

The domestic market for helmets, a derived demand from bi-wheeler usage, grew steadily through the early l990s (see Figure 1 above), as did the number of competitors. However, in recent years, Studds' domestic sales had been fairly stagnant. As a result, their market share had declined from its 36 percent level in 1992, to 30 percent in 1994. Regionally, Studds' sales were concentrated in the Northern states of India. However, the final distribution of Studds' helmets was more even than the regional sales figures suggested. Wholesalers were concentrated in Northern India, and helmets sold to these firms were distributed to all regions of India. Thus, Studds helmets were used throughout India.

Market Segmentation

While Studds helmets were popular across India, Studds' market share in individual markets varied dramatically. For example, in New Delhi, Studds had a market share of approximately 10 percent; in Bombay, Studds commanded 75 to 80 percent of the market. Individual buyer behavior and helmet laws explained this trend.

Regions within India had the authority to create their own helmet laws. As a result, helmet use was mandatory in some regions and optional in others. Helmet laws were enacted and retracted frequently, as local governments changed. In 1994, only three cities, Delhi, Calcutta and Bangalore (with an aggregate population of approximately 30 million people, or $\frac{1}{30}$ of India's population) had made helmet use compulsory. These three urban areas accounted for a large fraction of the bi-wheeler market.

Market Segmentation

Studds enjoyed its largest market share in regions which had optional helmet use. Motorcycle and scooter riders, who were safety conscious, were willing to pay for a premium product such as a Studds helmet. Other helmets were perceived not to offer the safety or style desired by voluntary wearers of helmets. In regions in which the rider was forced by law to wear a helmet, the sole criterion for helmet purchase was price. Safety, style and brand name were not important factors in these consumers' minds. As a result, Studds' largest market share was in regions in which helmet use was optional.

Similarly, for market development, Studds was not an advocate of compulsory helmet use. While Studds would gain a few sales should helmet use become mandatory across India, its market share would be eroded. The large increase in sales would be absorbed by low-price, unbranded helmet lines. The long-term trend in India was towards the mandatory use of helmets, especially as national concern for health and safety increased.

High End versus Low End

Currently one in five bi-wheeler drivers wore a helmet voluntarily. Passengers were seldom observed to wear helmets. Even in regions in which helmet use was mandatory, only the driver was required to wear a helmet. Passengers were permitted to travel without a helmet, and at times, the number of riders on a bi-wheeler reached four or five, as a motorcycle or scooter often served as a family's main mode of transportation.

Internationalization

Export Markets

In 1994, exports accounted for 20 percent of the company's sales. Studds had exports to 35 countries in several regions of the world (see Figure 2). Its greatest presence was in South America, followed by South East Asia. Based on large populations and increasing bi-wheeler usage, particularly small motorcycles and scooters, tremendous potential existed in developing country markets. However, as Studds was still new to international markets, a market focus had not been determined.

The Studds group was the only Indian helmet company active in international markets. Studds began to consider foreign markets in 1990 because of a slack in the domestic market and a lot of growth in international markets. In 1991, when Studds decided to go international, the company elected to attend, with the assistance of the India Trade Promotion Organization (ITPO), the IFMA Cologne Motor Show at Milan. The show provided a high profile presence for Studds, as it was the premier trade show for motorcycle and motor-cycle-related products.

In subsequent years, Studds tried to separate its display from other Indian manufacturers and ITPO. Associating with ITPO did not benefit Studds, and Madhu Khurana wished to distance Studds helmets from other Indian products which did not enjoy as good a reputation internationally. Studds helmets were equivalent in quality to leading international manufacturers, and following the first order from

FIGURE 2   Studds' Export Markets

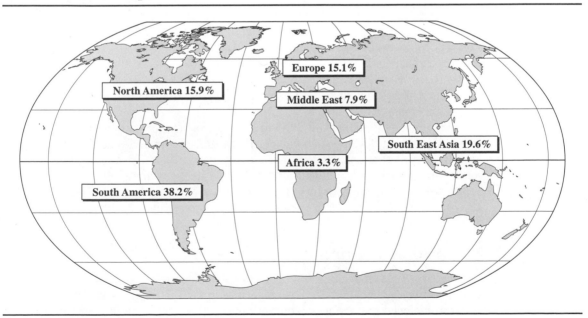

Mauritius, the helmets penetrated world markets rapidly and aggressively. From 1991–92 to 1993–94, export sales quadrupled.

Studds sold to most markets under its brand name. Only in Canada, where Studds helmets were sold under the CKX brand to snowmobilers, and Sri Lanka, were Studds helmets not sold under its brand name. In Germany, helmets for the lower end of the market maintained the Studds brand name; helmets for the upper end of the market were custom-branded. In none of Studds' international markets were funds spent on marketing and advertising. As yet, Studds' international sales were too low to fund such expenditures. Larger companies, such as Arai, were actively involved in developing and maintaining their brands.

Studds' international contacts were made at trade shows where it contacted distributors who would move the helmets to local retailers. Four or five distributors were sufficient to cover a region the size of the United States. The main competitors for Studds in most markets were companies from Taiwan and South Korea. Other India-based competition was non-existent. Studds held a considerable cost advantage over non-Indian competitors. Studds, operating with a 15 to 20 percent gross margin, sold open-face helmets for Rs. 248–310 and full-face helmets for Rs. 434–558. South Korean producers, the next lowest-priced producers, sold full-face models for Rs. 1,550–1,705. Labor costs, particularly in fiberglass models, accounted for Studds' cost advantage. Studds' cost advantage prompted one South Korean firm to offer Studds a subcontract on a North American order.

The Global Market

While export sales growth had been impressive, Studds helmets were still a small component of total world sales. The global market for motorcycle and bicycle helmets was estimated by Madhu Khurana to be approximately Rs. 20 billion and for sports helmets, Rs. 10 billion. Studds covered all three segments, with the strongest sales for motorcycle and bi-cycle helmets in British and South American markets. For bicycle helmets, Studds had identified Canada as a promising market. In the mid-1990s, helmets were expected to be made compulsory for all bicycle riders in Canada, creating a demand for two million helmets. Studds intended to garner 5 percent of this market.

In international markets, firms from Italy and Japan were strongest, and they competed primarily in developed country markets. Italian companies held a 55 to 60 percent share in international markets, and the two main Japanese firms, a 15 to 20 percent share. Companies from Taiwan held a 5 to 7 percent share. The remainder was accounted for by a variety of firms from, for example, South Korea and India (Studds). The Studds Nolan Joint Venture was Studds' first equity venture with a foreign partner.

The Studds Nolan Joint Venture

During early 1994, the management of Studds decided to expand capacity in helmets and motorcycle accessories. To be competitive in international markets, Studds' management believed that the new facilities built in this expansion must incorporate the most modern manufacturing technology. For this reason and the desire to gain access to world markets, Studds decided to partner with one of the world's market leaders.

During March 1994, Studds identified the top ten helmet manufacturers in the world. Each of these manufacturers received a letter from Studds stating its intention to expand capacity and offering the opportunity for a joint venture. Serious responses were received from three companies, two from Italian companies and one from a German company. Figure 3 presents a financial comparison of these three companies.

Representatives from both Italian companies visited Studds in May 1994 and discussed, in depth, the possibility of a joint venture. In July 1994, a team of managers from Studds visited two Italian manufacturers—Bieffe and Nolan—and, on the basis of its market leadership position and well-defined policies, selected Nolan as their joint venture partner. See Appendix A for a description of Nolan.

Letter of Intent

The Studds group and the Nolan group of India signed a Letter of Intent on July 27, 1994, thereby agreeing to establish a joint helmet manufacturing unit in Faridabad, India (see Appendix B for a Summary of the Letter of Intent). Under the terms of the agreement, which were valid until September 1994, Studds Accessories was converted from a closely held to a widely held public limited company. Gadgets remained in the control of the Khurana brothers. The two groups had equal equity participation, with new manufacturing activities added to the existing trading activities of Studds Accessories. The name of Studds Accessories was changed to Studds Nolan Ltd.

While both partners had equal equity (Rs. 10 million) in the venture, each possessed only a 20 percent share. The remaining 60 percent was issued to the public. At the time of the agreement, the current paid-up capital of Studds Accessories was Rs. 2 million. Rs. 8 million more was soon contributed to bring the holdings of Studds to the requisite Rs. 10 million. Nolan invested Rs. 10 million in the form of cash and molds. The total equity of the venture was US$ 1,625,000.

FIGURE 3   A Comparison Between Nolan, FIMEZ, and Bieffe

	Nolan		Fimez		Bieffe	
	1991	*1992*	*1991*	*1992*	*1991*	*1992*
Sales	23	27	11	13	20	21
Net income	1.0	0.8	0.1	(0.1)	0.2	0.1
Cash flow	2.6	2.7	0.5	0.4	0.8	0.3
Number of personnel	184	169	not available	not available	84	84
Debt vs. banks	6.8	6.3	1.7	3.3	7.2	6.7
Investments	1.1	1.4	0.7	0.8	0.2	(0.3)

Note: All monetary figures in US$ millions.

Source: Company documents.

The Joint Venture Agreement

In September 1994, representatives from Nolan visited Studds in India for a second time to work out a final joint venture agreement. During these meetings, most of the discussion centered on operational and control issues. Partner objectives for the joint venture received less attention. As the managers for Studds and Nolan continued to discuss issues related to the management of the joint venture, tension began to enter the relationship. Nolan, which had engaged a local Indian attorney for these negotiations, inserted new clauses into the legal agreements for the joint venture which were not included in the original Letter of Intent. Nolan, keen to proceed with the joint venture, gave Studds the option of framing the basic terms of the final joint venture agreement. The attorney for Studds framed a new agreement which was handed over to Nolan in November 1994.

At this point, both parties became very cautious about the legal aspects of the agreement. The intervention by the attorneys led to increased concern with the exact wording of the legal agreement. Managers from Studds and Nolan wanted to be sure that the agreement would fairly lay out the exact conditions under which the joint venture would be operated. In the words of one Studds manager,

> Representatives from Nolan and Studds were both very cautious about the legal aspects of the agreement. Both parties wanted to read between the lines in the agreement. The lawyers were helping to foster suspicion about the intention of every line written in the agreement.

Implementation

Studds' managers began to implement certain aspects of the agreement in late 1994. The first task was the land purchase. The total cost of the land exceeded the budgeted Rs. 7.2 million. The additional expenditures for the land were related to the informal economy in India. Some of the disbursements made by Studds were necessary to secure the land but were to parties that could not issue a receipt. Nolan became concerned about these payments, and felt that Studds was not being completely veracious in accounting for these expenditures. Other expenditures, too, had nonaccountable components. Nolan's managers expressed a desire to manage more day-to-day operations, contrary to earlier agreements.

In the new agreements put forth by each partner, the offers were largely consistent in their treatment of technology transfer, the location and set-up of the venture, methods of payment, and the transference of molds and dies. However, some divergence emerged concerning the management and administration of the venture. The two sides could not resolve what were to be day-to-day concerns and what were to be long-term concerns.

Nolan's proposal listed 15 decisions that required the approval of the Board of Directors. Many of the decisions were related to strategic concerns; however, others related to operational issues and expenditures. Specifically, real estate property and machines exceeding Rs. 2 million in value could not be bought or sold without prior approval of the Board of Directors. Studds' proposal contained no such provision, though both proposals stated that all day-to-day operating expenses of the joint venture might be incurred by a Director or Official of the company, provided the expenditure fell within the approved budgets and guidelines.

The February 1995 Meeting

In February 1995, Studds' management team visited Nolan in Italy to work through existing concerns about the operation of the venture and to finalize the joint venture agreement. Neither partner felt confident of the other, and much of the discussion concerned the jurisdictional point for the joint venture agreement. Studds insisted on India as the jurisdictional point but Nolan was firm on London or Paris as the place for adjudication.

The meetings continued for three days, and the remaining faith that the parties had in each other continued to deteriorate. Mr. Khurana and others in the Studds management team began to feel that this joint venture could not be salvaged. They began considering breaking off the existing agreement. Doing so would delay Studds in its efforts to become a global leader in helmet manufacturing; however, Bieffe and other helmet manufacturers remained as potential partners for Studds should the agreement be broken off. Other courses of action, such as a go-alone internationalization, could also be taken by Studds. Mr. Khurana and his team evaluated these considerations as they decided on the immediate action to take in their meeting with Nolan.

Appendix A: Nolan–Company Profile

The companies which formed the Nolan Group (Nolan) produced protective helmets for motorcyclists, bicyclists, and other sports enthusiasts. Nolan, formed in the 1970s, began as a supplier of motorcycle and car accessories to a large multinational. In 20 years of operations the company's products were characterized by competitive pricing, high technical performance and consistent quality. Substantial innovations and product developments had improved the esthetic appearance and performance of the helmets, while consistently respecting the regulations and standards which governed safety products.

Nolan's marketing strengths had grown with its technical expertise. Nolan's trademark had increased in importance in principal markets, and was one of the most well-recognized across the world. A network of loyal distributors contributed to Nolan's success. The dealers comprising this network were specialized for sales in this market and adjusted their sales tactics to Nolan's product line changes. Recently, a new line of Nolan products had been developed, but had not yet reached the market. These new items were designed to increase protection to the face, and had excellent mechanical and optical qualities.

Investment supporting continued renovation and improvements in the product lines came to US$ 1.53 million in 1993. For 1994, investment was projected to exceed US$ 1.75 million. These investments, which accounted for 6.4 percent of gross revenues, were for renovations in machinery and products alone. A further 3.6 percent of sales was dedicated to ongoing product design and research. Nolan's performance is summarized below.

	1993 (actual)	1994 (projected)
Turnover	**26.408**	**30.761**
Cost of sales	16.584	19.187
Gross Profit	**9.824**	**11.574**
Less depreciation	1.539	2.137
Less other operating expenses	5.465	6.322
Operating Expense before Interest	**2.819**	**3.115**
Net interest	(1.261)	(847)
Extraordinary items	(0.265)	(233)
Profit before Taxes	**1.294**	**2.035**
Taxes	(0.515)	(1.018)
Accelerated depreciation	(0.285)	0
Net Profit	**.493**	**1.017**

Note: All amount are in US$ millions.
Source: Company documents.

Nolan's 1993 sales were divided between several markets. Exports were larger than domestic sales as depicted in the following table.

Subdivision of Sales	US $ (millions)	
Helmets	24.521	
Optical area (visors)	1.555	
Subdivision of Helmet Sales		% of Total Helmet Sales
Domestic–Italy	4.832	19.71
Exports	19.689	80.29
Subdivision of Export Sales		
Europe	15.051	61.38
North America	2.487	10.14
Other countries	2.151	8.77
Total–55 countries	19.689	

Source: Company documents.

Nolan's products were marketed domestically and in other developed countries using a common advertising strategy. Nolan used standard industry promotional vehicles such as advertising in specialty magazines and sponsoring race car drivers and motorcycle riders. However, the company preferred to concentrate on the commercial end in its marketing strategy. It helped retailers display, promote, and demonstrate its products to the customer. Thus, the company's advertising was less aggressive than its competitors, since Nolan preferred to provide good service to its dealers and customers rather than pay for other, more glamorous, forms of advertising.

The joint venture with Studds would provide Nolan with the opportunity to expand capacity with little capital input. Also, Nolan would lower its cost of production significantly by producing helmets in India. A third but relatively minor benefit of partnering with Studds was the access Nolan would gain to the growing Indian market.

FIGURE 1A   Machinery and Equipment

Machinery:

600 ton injection molding machine	Rs. 7.00 million
400 ton injection molding machine	Rs. 5.50 million
180 ton injection molding machine	Rs. 2.00 million
	Rs. 14.50 million
Assembly equipment	Rs. 0.50 million
Maintenance equipment	Rs. 1.20 million
Sales tax and installation expenses	Rs. 1.95 million
Total machinery and equipment cost:	**Rs. 18.15 million**

Molds and Dies:

Molds and dies imported	Rs. 3.00 million
Custom duty (25%)	Rs. 0.75 million
Freight, insurance, etc.	Rs. 0.40 million
Total molds and dies:	**Rs. 4.15 million**

Generators and Vehicles:

1 no. generator set 500 KVA	Rs. 2.00 million
1 no. generator set 250 KVA	Rs. 1.20 million
Vehicles	Rs. 1.00 million
Total generators and vehicles:	**Rs. 4.20 million**

Factory Workers (annual costs):

Skilled labour (40 @ Rs. 3,500/month)	Rs. 1.680 million
Unskilled labour (30 @ Rs. 2,700/month)	Rs. 0.972 million
Total labour	Rs. 2.652 million
Add: 35% (other associated labour costs)	Rs. 0.928 million
Total annual labour cost:	**Rs: 3.580 million**

Note: All industries installed generators because the electrical supply was not consistent in India.
Source for Figures 1–5: Company documents.

Appendix B: Letter of Intent

The factory of the venture was to be located in Faridabad, Haryana, 6-7 km from the present offices of Studds. The existing offices and sales staff of Studds Accessories were to be used for marketing activities. In the joint venture agreement, land for the factory building and measuring 6000 m³ was to be purchased by February 1995. The land price was estimated to be Rs. 1000/m². With duties, brokerage fees and other set-up costs, the total cost to the company for the land was estimated to be Rs. 7.2 million.

Construction on the factory building was to begin in March 1995, following purchase of the land and receipt of approval from the relevant authorities. The factory building was proposed to consist of 25,000 square feet, with the cost at Rs. 6.25 million. Machinery installation was to occur in November, and production would start in December 1995 (see Figure 1A, all figures are located at the end of Appendix B). The commercial launch date for Studds Nolan helmets was to be January 1996. The figures in this agreement were considered realistic given Studds managers' familiarity with local operating conditions.

Management of the Joint Venture

Studds Nolan Limited was controlled by a Board of Directors which numbered five including the Chairman. The Chairman was from the Studds group, and Nolan and Studds both appointed two other Directors. The Chairman and one Director of the Studds Group were the Working Directors and took care of day-to-day operations of the company.

The Board of Directors would meet quarterly to review the performance of the company. The Nolan directors would be reimbursed for travel to and from India for two of their trips each year. Employees, both skilled and unskilled, were locally available; thus all managers and factory staff were from India. The organization was structured in a form similar to that of Studds Accessories (see Figure 2A).

Projections

Several detailed projections were made concerning production, prices, sales and revenues. Capacity estimates were based on a three-shift operating schedule, during which both full-face and open-face helmets were to be produced. Full-face helmets had a greater market value than open-face helmets; thus more of these would be produced (see Figure 3A).

While close to 400,000 helmets could be produced at capacity, sales were estimated to be less than this amount during the first few years of operations, though early sales would exceed the break-even quantity of 92,000 helmets (see Figure 4A). Helmets would be sold under the 'Studds Nolan' brand name. If sales grew as projected in a market survey, 75% of capacity would be utilized in 1998, the third year of the factory's operation. Most raw materials for production could be sourced locally, though anti-glare visors for the full-face helmets would be procured from Nolan or Korean suppliers depending on the price. The venture was expected to be profitable in its first year of operation (see Figure 5A).

FIGURE 2A   Studds Nolan Organizational Structure

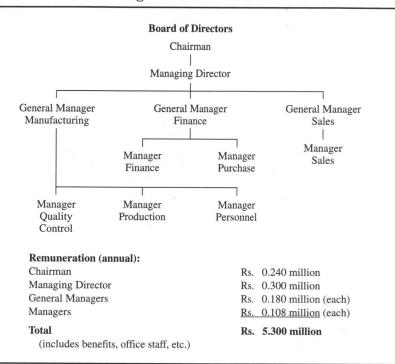

Remuneration (annual):

Chairman	Rs. 0.240 million
Managing Director	Rs. 0.300 million
General Managers	Rs. 0.180 million (each)
Managers	Rs. 0.108 million (each)
Total	**Rs. 5.300 million**

(includes benefits, office staff, etc.)

FIGURE 3A   Capacities and Selling Prices of Products

Product	Capacity	Selling Price (Rs./unit)
Full-face helmet	280,000	750
Open-face helmet	120,000	400
Sunpeaks, visors	120,000	70
Spare visors (full-face)	—	190

FIGURE 4A   Sales Projections (Units)

Product	1995	1996	1997
Full-face helmet	168,000	196,000	210,000
Open-face helmet	72,000	84,000	90,000
Sunpeaks, visors	40,000	50,000	50,000
Spare visors (full-face)	30,000	40,000	50,000

FIGURE 5A   Pro Forma Income Statement

	1995	1996	1997
Sales	163,300	191,700	206,500
Cost of sales	112,900	132,640	143,400
Gross profit	50,400	59,060	63,100
Depreciation	3,381	3,381	3,381
Operating expenses	23,800	27,785	31,137
Operating profit	23,219	27,894	28,582
Interest	5,425	5,600	5,200
Profit before tax	17,794	22,294	23,382
Taxation	4,046	6,230	7,106
Net profit	13,748	16,064	16,276
Dividend	9,400	9,400	9,400
Profit for general reserve	4,348	6,664	6,876
Return on capital	27%	29%	27%

III CASES ON MULTINATIONAL MANAGEMENT

15 Matsushita Industrial de Baja California

Can Mexico Compete with Asia?

Making his daily crossing from San Diego to Tijuana to the offices of Matsushita Industrial de Baja California (MIBA), Mitsuharu Nakata, Sub-Director Administrativo, was personally concerned about the fate of the Mexican plants with the passing of the North American Free Trade Agreement (NAFTA). Approaching the end of 1995, Nakata reflected on the two years since NAFTA was implemented. Before this assignment, Nakata had lived in Central America for 6 years, working for Matsushita in Guatemala and Costa Rica. After San Diego/Tijuana, he knew that he would move wherever the company sent him; the idea of leaving Matsushita was unthinkable. As he swung his car to avoid the potholes in the road leading to Ciudad Industrial just across the commercial border crossing from the United States, he saw the gleaming glass and steel factories belonging to Sanyo, Matsushita's neighbor and worldwide competitor. He had been living in San Diego for 10 years, and he had been concerned that after another 5 years, production of televisions in Mexico would no longer be competitive on the basis of wage costs. But there were many other considerations, beginning with the particular products made in each plant. Matsushita was assembling televisions (TVs) in some plants and manufacturing TV components in others.

Compared to low-cost Asian producers, Mexico in 1994 had offered a 2 percent savings in transportation as a location supplying the U.S. market. There was also a 5 percent duty imposed by the United States on assembled televisions. Together, these two items represented 7 percent; if an Asian country such as Malaysia, Indonesia, or

Situation

Prepared by Stephen Jenner, California State University, Dominguez Hills. This case was prepared as a basis for class discussion rather than to illustrate either effective or ineffective handling of administrative situations.

399

Exhibit 1   China, Trade, and Investment Environment

GENERAL

State role in the economy:
Since 1978, China has been introducing market forces in its centrally planned economy. The current 5-year plan (1991–95) continues to emphasize the primacy of state ownership, but promotes reforms toward the Communist Party's stated goal to achieve a "socialist market economy." Instead of the large-scale privatizations in many other nations, an important approach in China is granting greater autonomy in decision making to state-owned enterprises.

The two principal areas of past liberalization efforts are (1) agriculture and (2) foreign trade. China now has a market economy in food as a result of free prices and the replacement of farming communes by family farms. Results have been excellent in 1992. China was expected to see its 4th straight bumper harvest. With the removal of the central Government's monopoly over foreign trade, and the establishment of 4 "special zones," China benefits from export-led growth. Also, Chinese industry is reducing the dominance of the state. In 1978, state-owned firms accounted for 78 percent of the total; the current comparable share is somewhat above 50 percent.

Exchange rate policy:
China administers a managed, floating official exchange rate linked to a trade-weighted basket of currencies. China also established free adjustment centers (so-called "swap centers") in 1986 to accommodate parallel market rates. The Government is apparently following a strategy of incremental devaluations of the renminbi to eventually unify the official rate of the free market rate.

Intellectual property rights (IPR):
China made some progress in recent years in enacting IPR legislation. Nonetheless, the United States instituted a special Section 301 investigation on China in May 1991 for failing to provide adequate IPR protection. The investigation was resolved in January 1992 when the United States and China reached an agreement and signed a Memorandum of Understanding (MOU) on IPR. In the MOU China pledged to upgrade its IPR regime by amending its patent law, joining the Berne convention, and enacting trade secret legislation.

FOREIGN TRADE

GATT membership:
China's application for GATT membership is under active consideration. Under an October 1992 U.S.-China MOU, China is committed to significantly reducing its multilayered web of import restrictions between 1993 and 1997. The accord was prompted by a huge U.S. trade deficit via-á-vis China.

Transparency:
Under the MOU with the United States, and in accordance with GATT, China is committed to making its trade regime transparent by publishing its heretofore unavailable decrees, rules, and regulations, and halting the use of internal directives on foreign trade.

China had a 10 percent labor cost advantage, then they could compete with Mexico on the basis of assembly and transportation costs. Wages in Indonesia were about two-thirds or 67 percent less, while Chinese wage costs (including dormitories for workers) were one-fourth or 25 percent lower than Mexico's. Malaysian wage costs were about one-third or 33 percent less than Mexico's. (See Exhibits 1–3.)

NAFTA's Rules of Origin stipulated that automobiles must be 62.5 percent North American, but televisions needed only a picture tube worth about 33 percent

EXHIBIT 1   *(concluded)*

Tariffs:
China adopted the harmonized system for customs classification and statistics, effective January 1, 1992, while at the same time reducing duties on 225 items. In April 1992, China eliminated its import taxes. On January 1, 1993, China's most ambitious tariff cuts to date became effective. The cuts, while generally moderate, covered 3,371 items, over half of the goods in China's tariff schedule.

Import restrictions:
China's import licensing system covers 53 broad categories of goods or about half of China's imports by value. Some 75 percent of all import licensing requirements, quotas, and other restrictions will be eliminated by the end of 1994 under the MOU with the United States. In addition to a variety of U.S. industrial exports, import controls on key U.S. agricultural exports, including wheat, other grains, edible oils and fruits will be eliminated. China also agreed to discontinue those standards and testing requirements that serve mainly as trade barriers, i.e., those that do not apply to comparable domestic products.

Export subsidies:
China abolished direct subsidies for exports on January 1, 1991. However, manufactured exports receive many forms of indirect subsidies, including guaranteed provision of energy and raw materials, preferential financing, tax rebates, and duty exemptions on imported inputs. China's swap markets allow exporters to exchange foreign exchange at better than official rates.

FOREIGN INVESTMENT

General policy:
China now stresses the role of foreign investment in promoting structural reforms for the economy. China is reportedly considering measures to attract multinational corporations into the infrastructure, raw material production, and high-technology product development. In 1991, the United States ranked second in China's overall foreign direct investment, behind Hong Kong.

Presently, China does not provide national treatment to foreign investors who are under strong pressure to export, locate in specified areas, and use domestic versus import components. Foreign investors may repatriate profits, as long as they have the foreign exchange to cover the funds to be remitted. Some foreign investors have been permitted to set up their own marketing or service organizations, but most must rely on Chinese state-owned operations.

Services:
China generally does not allow foreign firms in the services sector, including banking, insurance, construction, accounting, and legal services. U.S. lawyers and accountants must largely limit their activities to servicing foreign firms. Recently, however, China began allowing some foreign investors, on an experimental basis, to establish joint ventures in accounting, insurance, and legal services.

Source: Office of the United Sates Trade Representative (USTR), *1993 National Trade Estimate Report on Foreign Trade Barriers,* 1993.

to qualify as North American products. The picture tube (cathode ray tube, or CRT) represented about one-third of costs (actually 30–50 percent, depending on the model), the cabinet accounted for another one-third, and the remaining one-third included printed circuit (PC) boards plus components and assembly. If the CRT was made in the United States, the duty savings were 5 percent compared to a CRT fixed in a cabinet with a tuner, a TV assembled with its chassis. Importing the CRT alone

---

EXHIBIT 2   Indonesia, Trade, and Investment Environment

General

State role in the economy:

The Government controls the oil industry through Pertamina the state-run oil and gas company. State enterprises hold dominant positions in oil refining, petrochemicals, fertilizers, steel. aluminum, cement, basic chemicals, capital-goods manufacturing, and shipbuilding. In most other industries, the Government generally refrains from direct intervention, but has established floor and ceiling prices for certain food items (e.g., rice) and has prohibited exports of goods in short supply.

Exchange rate policy:

Indonesia does not use any foreign exchange restrictions.

Intellectual property rights (IPR):

Though its IPR laws are improving, Indonesia remains on the USTR's Special 301 "watch list" under the provisions of the 1988 Omnibus Trade and Competitiveness Act. An improved trademark law was passed in August 1992 and is expected to provide a legal basis for protection of service and collective marks by April 1, 1993. Indonesia's first patent law came into effect in August 1991. Concerns about the new law remain, including a relatively short term of protection (14 to 16 years), and noncoverage of specific products, such as food and drink products and processes, biotechnology, and integrated circuits.

FOREIGN TRADE

Tariffs:

Tariffs range from 0 percent (raw materials) to 200 percent (sedans and station wagons). Indonesia also imposes 5 to 35 percent surcharges on 255 items (including food, steel, chemical, and pharmaceutical items).

Quotas and licenses:

Strict quotas restrict the importation of certain fruits and vegetables, meats, confectionery items, and alcoholic beverages. Licensing requirements remain for some agricultural commodities, alcoholic beverages, and iron and steel products.

Distribution:

While wholesale distribution is permitted by joint ventures, retail distribution is closed to foreign investors. Furthermore, in several industries, foreign companies are allowed to choose only a single agent to cover the entire country.

---

resulted in a duty of 15 percent; it was the possibility of importing the CRT duty-free into Mexico via Long Beach, California, and bringing it back to the United States as an assembled TV that brought Japanese producers to Tijuana in the first place. Now it was possible that Matsushita and Sanyo would buy CRTs from Samsung in Tijuana. Matsushita's purchasing policies emphasized not only cost, but also quality, on time delivery, and sufficient capacity.

Nakata wondered why the U.S. government didn't seem to care about the television industry in the same way it nurtured the automobile industry. "I guess the car is closer to what America is all about," he said. "The United States government should assist in the development of TV component manufacturing; it's like a growing tree

---

EXHIBIT 2   *(concluded)*

Government procurement:
International competitive bidding practices are followed for most large projects. However, bidding firms are often required to offer concessional financing. Foreign bidders may also be required to purchase and export Indonesian goods equivalent to the contract amount. Government procurement regulations favor locally produced goods and services by a price margin of 15 percent.

FOREIGN INVESTMENT

Foreign ownership:
A May 1992 Investment Regulation permits 100 percent foreign equity in three types of new investments: (1) projects worth at least $50 million; (2) projects located in one of Indonesia's 14 less developed provinces, with divestiture to a maximum of 80 percent foreign ownership within 20 years; and (3) projects in bonded zones that will export 100 percent of production, but must be divested to 95 percent within 5 years. For other industries, foreign investment is limited to joint ventures, usually with a minimum foreign investment of $1 million and a maximum foreign stake of 80 percent to be divested over 20 years to no more than 49 percent ownership. Foreigners are not allowed to own land. The Capital Investment Coordinating Board is responsible for approving all investment in Indonesia. Its chairman has announced plans to reduce the number of sectors closed to foreign investment.

Repatriation of profits:
Indonesia has a long-standing policy of free repatriation of profits, royalties, fees, loan principal and interest, and costs associated with expatriate workers.

Service barriers:
Service trade barriers exist in most sectors. Indonesia has begun to loosen restrictions in the financial sector, allowing foreign banks, security firms, and insurance companies to form joint ventures with local firms. However, these joint ventures are subjected to much higher capitalization requirements than domestic firms. Indonesia strictly limits the practice of foreign lawyers, accountants, advertisers, and express delivery firms. A quota limits the number of foreign films that can be distributed within Indonesia. In addition, films can be imported only by a restricted number of local firms. However, a Government decree that will increase the number of companies permitted to import U.S. films and videos is expected to be implemented in early 1993.

Source: Office of the United States Trade Representative (USTR), *1993 National Trade Estimate Report on Foreign Trade Barriers,* 1993.

---

which needs water and help to reach the size that will allow it to survive a storm. But I guess they don't care about TVs." Any company making TVs has to be concerned with costs and price competition, and production could be moved to the country with the most competitive cost structure.

To Japanese producers of TVs, Mexico was special because it was close to the United States and had good government relations, in addition to low wages, according to Nakata. "But salaries for indirect employees in Mexico are just as high as in the United States, and there are no sources of transistors, integrated circuits (ICs), registers, or raw materials nearby," noted Nakata. "When the United States lost competitiveness, it moved production to Asia, including component manufacturing, which requires 3–5 times the investment of an assembly plant. Now Motorola and Texas Instruments have excellent factories in East Asia, and it makes sense to buy

---

EXHIBIT 3   China and Indonesia—Regimes for Foreign Direct Investment by Transnational Manufacturers

---

Excerpts from "Asians Agree on Disclosure to Halt Crises: Consider Ways to Avoid Mexico-Type Troubles" by David Sanger, *New York Times,* April 17, 1995, p. C1:

The fall of the dollar against the yen has left many Asian countries wondering if American influence in the region will wane despite President Clinton's moves to shape APEC (Asia Pacific Economic Cooperation forum) into a more powerful regional body . . . Moreover, some Asian countries have seen Mexico as a cautionary tale that free trade, deregulation and economic reform can move too fast, and the result can be a loss of economic control. Their preferred model is Japan, which in the last 40 years has used control over foreign investment as a key element of its effort to protect fledgling industries . . . In their joint declaration, the finance ministers said they would attempt to steer clear of reliance on short-term investments that, as Mexico showed, can leave the country as quickly as they enter. Instead, they said they would seek "flows that generate real economic returns and hence are less susceptible to sudden reversal." That chiefly means direct investment in factories and other facilities that are difficult to uproot if investors get nervous. Indonesia, China and several other large Asian nations have been focused on direct investment for years, and thus are considered less susceptible to what Mr. Rubin (United States Treasury Secretary) called a Mexico "contagion."

China

With one-quarter of the world's population and very rapid economic growth in recent years, China is a hugely attractive market. However, key problems in dealing with China include economic inefficiencies, regional inequalities, and environmental degradation. Doing business in China requires dealing with Chinese officials who must deal with multiple bosses, some of whom they obey and some they ignore. Although there is an elaborate Chinese government, officials follow personalistic norms of behavior and there is widespread corruption. The central authorities issue decrees in the authoritarian imperial tradition, but local officials are often petty dictators who are essentially free to take care of their local interests.

China is seeking to join the World-Trade Organization (the successor to the General Agreement on Tariffs and Trade, or GATT), but United States willingness to support China's entry hinges on improving access to the Chinese market. The issue of human rights has also been raised repeatedly by the United States; for example, United States Customs agents want to inspect Chinese prisons and "re-education camps."

High-technology product development is a priority in attracting foreign direct investment. Japanese investment tends to be concentrated on east and northeast China in the form of light industrial production of consumer electronics, although larger scale projects such as cement production and significantly more production of cars and motorcycles are expected. As in other countries taken over by Japan during World War II, there are resentments and unresolved issues which strongly affect bilateral relations with Japan. Poor infrastructure and uncertainty regarding the medium-term political future are expected to moderate foreign investment somewhat. Wage levels for entry-level workers are as low as $50 per month.

(See Figure 1, China's Trade and Investment Environment, USITC, *East Asia: Regional Economic Integration and Implications for the United States,* Publication 2621, May, 1993.)

Indonesia

With over 185 million people, Indonesia has the fifth largest population in the world. As a matter of policy, Indonesia seeks export-oriented, labor-intensive, large-scale investments. Investment incentives include concessions on import duties and a value-added tax for equipment and raw materials. The largest government-owned industrial estate is located on Batam Island, 12 miles from Singapore, where foreigners are permitted to invest without a local Indonesian partner if 100 percent of production is exported. Monthly salaries for unskilled workers can be as low as $50 per month, but investors need to provide training.

The Foreign Investment Law of 1967 opened Indonesia to capital, technology, and management expertise of foreign firms. The President, Major General Suharto, was elected in 1968, following an attempted leftist coup in 1965, and he reversed the antiforeign policies of his predecessor, Sukarno. However, there are sharp ethnic divisions: ethnic Chinese control Indonesia's economic resources, while indigenous "pribumi" dominate the government. Industrial growth inevitably strengthens the Chinese business sector, contrary to the national

---

EXHIBIT 3   *(concluded)*

---

goal of redistributing Chinese wealth to other ethnic groups. The 1974 Matari riots were a protest against the domination of both Japanese and Chinese capital. Strengthened by increased oil revenues, Indonesia shifted to a more restrictive foreign direct investment regime in the mid-1970s.

Declining oil revenues and budget deficits since 1982, along with reduced investment flows, led to a moderate loosening. Suharto's latest five-year plan emphasizes private sector industrial development, and there have been substantial reductions in tariffs and nontariff barriers. However, large state-owned companies linked to the politico-military regime are resisting reforms. The Indonesian Capital Investment Coordinating Board (BKPM) and the Department of Industry work closely with the Chamber of Commerce and Industry (KADIN).

(See Figure 2, Indonesia's Trade and Investment Environment, USITC, *East Asia: Regional Economic Integration and Implications for the United States,* Publication 2621, May, 1993.)

Japan replaced Western Europe and the United States as the leading source of imports, and Japan continues to be the most important market for exports. Indonesia has been the leading site for Japanese investment in East Asia in recent decades. In 1994 alone, Japanese investments in Indonesian assembly lines totaled $1.56 billion, and the United States lists Indonesia as one of the 10 "big emerging markets" in the world.

However, the surge of Japanese investment is overwhelming Indonesia's infrastructure for electrical power generation and distribution, communications, transportation, and waste management.

---

from them. Mexico is very far away from Singapore, Taiwan, Malaysia, Hong Kong, and Japan, where Matsushita sources its components."

Should Matsushita stay in Baja California and continue to import Asian components, while exploring the use of Samsung's picture tubes? Should they locate future plants across from the Texas border (in Ciudad Juárez, for example) where they would be closer to the population center of the United States? Should they make the decision in 1995 to relocate or add new plants in China or Indonesia, where wages were much lower than in Mexico and component plants were close at hand? What about the strategic choice to phase out production of low-end TVs and move up to the higher end of the market, i.e., flat-panel, high-definition TVs, multimedia, and semiconductor production?

Historical Background on the Globalization of the Electronics Industry

The licensing of the transistor by AT&T (Bell Labs had licensed it because of United States antitrust legislation), and subsequently General Electric and RCA, led to fierce competition between Fairchild, Sony, and others. Meanwhile, Hong Kong had lost its role as the trade conduit between the United States, Europe, and China due to the Korean War and China's partnership with the Soviet Union.

Sony began to assemble radios in Hong Kong by subcontracting in 1959; in 1960 the local Hong Kong subcontractor and two other local companies began undercutting the Japanese competition. In 1962, the Japanese government banned the export of transistors to Hong Kong, but they were replaced by British and U.S. imports. In the U.S. market, the shift from military to commercial customers demanded lower costs, either through automation or lower wages. Fairchild was the first U.S. firm to invest and locate its own electronic assembly operations anywhere in the Third World; the first plant was located in Hong Kong in 1961, and by 1966 they had 4,500 workers. One of the little-known secrets of Hong Kong's success was providing low-cost housing, food, and clothing, subsidies totaling half of workers' wages.

During the period of steady growth of world manufacturing production and exports from 1963 to 1981, Japan's performance was spectacular, followed closely by Hong Kong, Singapore, South Korea, Taiwan, Brazil, and Mexico. In the late 1980s, foreign direct investment really took off, and Japan replaced the UK as the largest country source of investment outflows. The biggest investment flow by far was from Europe to North America (U.S. and Canada), followed by the reverse flow, and a much smaller Japanese flow into North America. The flows from North America to Japan, and from Japan to Europe were much smaller, and the flow from Europe to Japan was the smallest among triad members. The explosion of Japanese foreign direct investment (FDI) in the late 1980s was due to higher production costs, because of appreciation of the yen and labor shortages in Japan, and current account surpluses from exports; the more recent slowdown in the early 1990s was due to government stimulus for domestic investment, the collapse of the bubble economy, and tighter reserve requirements for Japanese banks.

In the case of the electrical and electronic equipment industry, Japanese FDI in the United States supported the importation of finished goods and components from Japan and Asia; as of 1992, 99 percent of purchases by U.S. affiliates of Japanese TNCs came from East Asia, and 78 percent from intrafirm supply networks. For Japanese TNCs, production was centered in Japan with strong upstream linkages to an Asian regionally integrated supply network. The Southeast Asian countries provided a low-cost supply network (including Japanese exports) but did not import from North America or Europe.

With very low wages but long distances from the North American or European markets, plant locations in China and Indonesia were best suited to products which required little technical assistance or troubleshooting in the factory, and no contact with the customers, who were sometimes TV producers based closer to their main markets. As Nakata explained, "Sometimes you need to sit down eyeball-to-eyeball with the customer—you can't just send another fax, especially when it's a new, complicated product. You have to decide for each product on a case-by-case basis taking into consideration the market." Being close to the customer simplified delivery of the product and parts, improved customer service, and boosted Matsushita's cash flow. "Business communication grows more difficult with distance," said Nakata.

The Big Picture for Matsushita

Matsushita's long-term response to the appreciation of the yen was to relocate manufacturing outside Japan. In 1994, the company produced 20 percent of its goods abroad, and the goal for 1995 was 25 percent. Nevertheless, many overseas factories

---

EXHIBIT 4   Matsushita at a Glance

Product Category	Major Products
Video Equipment (20% of Total Sales)	Videocassette recorders, video camcorders and related equipment, color TVs, TV/VCR combination units, projection TVs, liquid crystal display TVs, videodisc players, satellite broadcast receivers, satellite-communication-related equipment
Audio Equipment (8%)	Radios, radio cassette recorders, tape recorders, compact disc players, digital compact cassette players, hi-fi stereos, and related equipment, car audio products, electronic musical instruments
Home Appliances (13%)	Refrigerators, room air conditioners, home laundry equipment, dishwashers, vacuum cleaners, electric irons, microwave ovens, rice cookers, electric fans, electric and kerosene heaters, infrared-ray warmers, electric blankets, electrically heated rugs
Communication and Industrial Equipment (25%)	Facsimile equipment, word processors, personal computers, copying machines, CRT displays, telephones, PBXs, CATV systems, measuring instruments, electronic-parts-mounting machines, industrial robots, welding machines, air-conditioning equipment, compressors, vending machines
Electronic Components (12%)	Integrated circuits, discrete devices, charge coupled devices, cathode-ray tubes, image pickup tubes, tuners, capacitors, resistors, speakers, magnetic recording heads, electric motors, electric lamps
Batteries and Kitchen-Related Products (5%)	Dry batteries, storage batteries, solar batteries, solar energy equipment, gas hot-water supply systems, gas cooking appliances, kitchen sinks, kitchen fixture systems, bath and sanitary equipment
Other (8%)	Bicycles, cameras and flash units, electric pencil sharpeners, water purifiers, imported materials and products such as nonferrous metals, lumber, paper and medical equipment
Entertainment (9%)	Filmed entertainment, music entertainment, theme parks, book publishing, gift merchandise, prerecorded video and audio tapes and discs

---

relied heavily on imported components from Japan, and there were concerns about Matsushita's ability to maintain quality.

Although Matsushita's Annual Report for 1994 (see Appendix 1 and Exhibits 4 and 5) was optimistic, their sale of MCA in April 1995 at a big loss after five years, was evidence of a strategic disaster. The assumption of hardware makers Matsushita and Sony (Matsushita's main rival) was that they could gain a competitive advantage by controlling audio and video software. According to industry analysts, Hollywood's entertainment products will increasingly be distributed electronically through cable systems and television networks, which were much more strategically important than the boxes that play the music and movies. Due in part to the changes in U.S. regulations that allowed television broadcasters to enter into program production, Matsushita would have to consider strategic alliances with communications companies and cable television if it were to stay in the movie and music production business.

EXHIBIT 5   Matsushita Group Chart

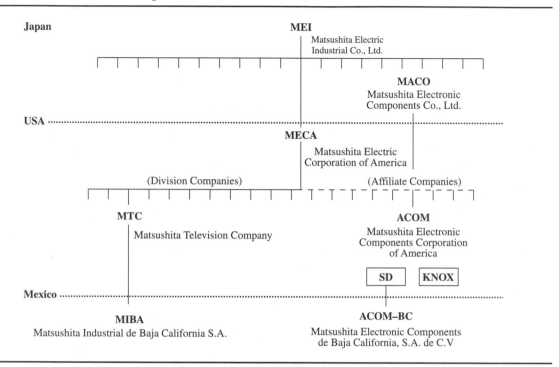

Matsushita planned to spend the money from the sale of MCA to focus more on multimedia and manufacturing key components, such as semiconductors. In order to avoid converting the proceeds back into yen at unfavorable exchange rates, Matsushita expected to spend much of the money in the United States.

Operations in Tijuana, Baja California Mexico

At the end of 1995, MIBA employed 2,600 workers in six buildings in Ciudad Industrial (Tijuana, Baja California, Mexico's industrial city on Otay Mesa adjacent to the United States border). Another 2,200 workers manufactured tuners and other components in two more plants in an industrial park several miles west, overlooking the Pacific Ocean. In addition, there were 2,000 workers making components and cellular telephones at another, newer Matsushita plant in Tijuana. The total of 6,800 workers was more than double the number employed a year before.

Matsushita's goal for the U.S. market was to expand local content, with 50 percent to be manufactured locally, and a 70 percent local-content ratio overall. In the low end of the market, the television was Matsushita's loss leader, and the U.S. market

EXHIBIT 5   (*concluded*) FINANCIAL HIGHLIGHTS
Matsushita Electric Industrial Co., Ltd., and Subsidiaries
Years ended March 31, 1994 and 1993

	Millions of yen, except per share information		Millions of U.S. dollars, except per share information
	1994	*1993*	*1994*
Sales	¥6,623,586	¥7,055,868	$64,307
Percentage of previous year	93.9%	94.7%	93.9%
Income before income taxes	¥ 128,223	¥ 162,207	$ 1,245
Percentage of previous year	79.0%	45.4%	79.0%
Net income	¥ 24,493	¥ 37,295	$ 238
Percentage of previous year	65.7%	27.9%	65.7%
Per share of common stock			
Net income	¥ 11.67	¥ 17.66	$ 0.11
Cash dividends	13.50	12.50	.013
Per American Depositary Share, each representing 10 shares of common stock:			
Net income	¥ 117	¥ 177	$ 1.14
Cash dividends	135	125	1.31
Total assets (at end of period)	¥8,192,632	¥8,754,979	$79,540
Stockholders' equity (at end of period)	3,288,945	3,406,303	31,932
Capital investment	¥ 266,522	¥ 309,097	$ 2,588
R&D expenditures	381,747	401,817	3,706
Employees (at end of period)	254,059	252,075	254,059

Notes:

1. Cash dividends per share are those declared with respect to the income for each fiscal period, and cash dividends charged to retained earnings are those actually paid.

2. U.S. dollar amounts are translated from yen at the rate of ¥103=U.S.$1. the approximate rate on the Tokyo Foreign Exchange Market on March 31, 1994.

3. Beginning with fiscal 1994, the Company adopted SFAS No. 109 (Accounting for Income Taxes), and accordingly, prior year figures have been restated to reflect this change.

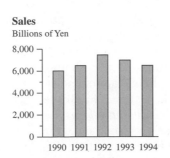

Sales
Billions of Yen

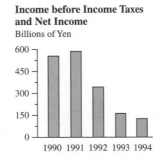

Income before Income Taxes and Net Income
Billions of Yen

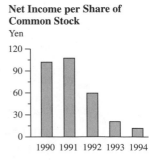

Net Income per Share of Common Stock
Yen

was supplied almost entirely by *maquiladoras* (Mexican companies that assembled, processed, manufactured, and/or repaired materials imported temporarily by others for eventual reexportation). Tijuana TV producers accounted for 5 million sets annually in 1993, or about half of all TVs sold in the United States. If Toshiba, Thompson-RCA, Zenith, and Philips in Ciudad Juárez (opposite El Paso, Texas) were also included, they accounted for most U.S. TV sales. By the end of 1996, the combined MIBA, Sony, Hitachi, Sanyo, JVC, and Samsung plants were expected to churn out one million TVs per month, making Tijuana the world's largest TV-producing region. Many of these Tijuana TV *maquiladoras* were MIBA's customers.

The combination of the twin ports of Long Beach/Los Angeles and factory locations in Baja California allowed better control of the delivery of raw materials and components from Asian sources, as well as lower land transportation costs into the United States. The cost to bring a 40-foot container to Los Angeles from Japan was about $1,900, compared with $3,500 to the East Coast of the United States.

Mexican locations south of Texas—Reynosa in particular—were also attractive alternatives to Tijuana due to the construction of a new superhighway to Detroit. Reynosa was two hours along the superhighway from Monterrey, which was an excellent source of Mexican engineers and technicians already being recruited to work in Tijuana. Furthermore, indirect employees earned salaries about one-half of those in the United States or Tijuana. "Tijuana salaries are high—they've been on a skyrocket the last few years. We're paying the same as in California," observed Nakata. Also, employee turnover in Reynosa was about 2 percent per month versus 10 percent in Tijuana. "Texas is different than California—they are very pro-*maquiladora*. They think that it's part of their business. California is not very friendly with Baja—it's a different mentality," explained Nakata.

With the passage of NAFTA, Asian multinationals faced procurement decisions regarding the future location of TV component manufacturing and assembly, which might be done in Mexico or in East Asia.

The Early Years: The Nelson Era and the Decision to Locate in Tijuana

Chuck Nelson was "very special" compared to other United States managers because he spent five years in Japan after World War II and "he knew the culture." He was also married to a Mexican and knew the Spanish language, and he had experience managing a *maquiladora*/in-bond assembly plant before he came to MIBA. Nelson managed what was once the largest *maquiladora* in Tijuana, Warwick Electronics, a division of Whirlpool, with 1,500 workers assembling Silvertone TVs sold in Sears stores. In 1973, Matsushita bought a Motorola plant in Franklin, Illinois. It was not profitable, and the company sent people to all the U.S.-Mexican border cities, because RCA and Zenith already had *maquiladoras*. Matsushita needed a very competitive price. Tijuana could take material and components from Japan, Malaysia, Taiwan, and Singapore, assemble one standard, high-volume-model TV in Mexico, and send it to the plant in Illinois to finish it. Matsushita began in Mexico

City with a joint venture, and considered a location in Reynosa, Tamaulipas, Mexico (near McAllen, Texas) before deciding to locate in Tijuana.

In 1979, Tijuana was more attractive due to lower transportation costs and proximity to Asian sources of components, although a location along the Texas border was closer to major U.S. markets and distribution centers in the East. According to Nelson, Reynosa also had militant labor unions, and the quality of life for Japanese people living in San Diego, California, was considered far superior to the border regions of Texas. However, Tijuana had the disadvantages of higher costs of labor, energy, and sites, as well as poor telecommunications infrastructure and delays crossing the border. There was also the problem in Tijuana of extremely high employee turnover of around 6 percent per month.

After locating in Tijuana, Nelson reported in 1985 that "overall MIBA encountered very few problems" and it was expected that there would be expansion. Nelson added that the use of the *maquiladora* resulted in a net decrease in the total number of Matsushita's U.S. employees during the first 7 years of operations, "but it saved jobs, and perhaps increased jobs in the United States in the long run" by allowing Matsushita to be more price competitive.

The Evolution of Japanese Investment

According to Yasuo Sasaki, a Brazilian of Japanese ancestry who was deeply involved in Sanyo's move to Tijuana, the location decisions by Japanese TV producers began with the oil crisis in the early 1970s. These Japanese multinationals began investing in the United States and Mexico as part of a trend toward local manufacturing in foreign markets. This globalization was also due to the appreciation of the Japanese yen from 250 to 200 per U.S. dollar, and a shortage of labor in Japan; college graduates did not want factory assembly jobs. Initially, Japanese factories moved to Hokkaido and other more remote islands.

The Japanese pattern of entry into Mexican *maquiladora* was different from that of U.S. firms. "The Japanese start inside and direct by asking questions, starting with other Japanese companies and Mexican local real estate professionals. They test people's credibility by asking the same questions over and over again," Sasaki noted. In contrast, U.S. companies began "outside and indirect, working through lawyers in Mexico City and New York," according to Sasaki. The Mexican government was unknown to most Japanese corporations, and harder to deal with than the U.S. government.

In the case of Sanyo, the original plan was to establish a factory in Mexico City with the involvement of the Mexican government and a Mexican company. Instead, Sanyo decided to go it alone, and originally considered Reynosa just across the Texas border as a location. Zenith was the first TV maker to move to Mexico. Sony established a plant in San Diego, and set up a *maquiladora* in Tijuana, followed by MIBA in 1979.

Sanyo followed Sony and Matsushita to Tijuana, as did Hitachi. "It's part of the Japanese culture and psychology," explained Sasaki, "like the way they play golf together, or go on vacation in Hawaii, always in a group. The fact that the others were there was reason enough—there must be something there."

Japanese companies also chose Tijuana because of its neighbor, San Diego, California, "the only place in the border area with sushi and Japanese schools," he added. "This is important to younger Japanese general managers, production managers, engineers, and technicians working in Mexico," noted Sasaki. According to Sasaki, Japanese investment is always "a one-way ticket." There is a long-term commitment, although it may begin very gradually. "For example, Japanese *maquiladora* buildings were very simple at first, and they could have pulled out easily. Gradually they upgraded." As they became more successful and stronger, Japanese *maquiladoras* increased their level of technology from "screwdriver" assembly operations to manufacturing, and they brought their other divisions and suppliers. "You must keep pedaling the bicycle," says Sasaki. "It's not just profits, but survival."

According to one of the top real estate professionals in Tijuana and landlord for one of Matsushita's factories, Beatrix Sanders, 95 percent of Japanese companies owned the land their *maquiladora* was built on, while only 50 percent of U.S. companies owned their land. Foreigners were allowed to "purchase" Mexican land through a trust held by a Mexican bank and renewable after 30 years. "The Japanese companies want to be around for 200 years," she explained.

The Impact of NAFTA and United States-Mexican Relations in 1994

NAFTA was implemented on January 1, 1994, immediately reducing tariffs and nontariff barriers on many products, while others would be gradually reduced over 5 to 10 years. By 1999, two-thirds of U.S. exports were expected to enter Mexico duty-free, up from one-half in 1994. NAFTA's Rules of Origin (requiring 33 percent North American content, including TV picture tubes) and the restriction of duty drawback (which exempts third-country imports from customs duty) were specific provisions of NAFTA affecting television production (and displays for computers).

NAFTA increased trade and led to a modest increase in U.S. foreign direct investment in Mexico in 1994; there were also massive capital flows into the Mexican stock and bond markets. United States exports to Mexico increased 25 percent (including over 50,000 U.S.-made cars and trucks, a 500 percent increase) as did Mexican exports to the United States. President Clinton boasted of over 100,000 new U.S. jobs created by NAFTA. Japanese and South Korean television producers made massive investments in Tijuana during 1994 (see Exhibit 6).

However, there were also serious concerns about public safety and political stability in Mexico throughout 1994 because of several stunning events. The rebellion in the Mexican state of Chiapas began on January 1, 1994, to coincide with NAFTA's implementation. There were also assassinations of Mexican presidential candidate Luis Donaldo Colosio in Tijuana, and subsequently of a ruling political party leader in Mexico City. The number of kidnappings of businessmen continued to grow, including a *maquiladora* owner/manager in Tijuana in November.

EXHIBIT 6 **New Investments in the San Diego/Tijuana/Mexicali Border Region after Nafta was Implemented 1/1/94**

Name of Firm	Type of Facility
Matsushita	Manufacturing and assembly (200 more workers on car audio, plus 140 more making batteries in addition to 3,000 in Tijuana) Research & development for hemisphere (140 Engineers + admin/support staff in addition to 150 in San Diego)
Sanyo Electric Co.	TV assembly (200 more workers in addition to 1,300 in Tijuana and 6 purchasing in San Diego)
Sony Electronics	Picture tube production (100 more workers in addition to 2,000 in San Diego and 3,000 in Tijuana TV assembly)
Samsung	Picture tube manufacturing ($400 million; 5,000 workers in Tijuana by 1997) Assembly (600 workers in Tijuana)
Goldstar	TV assembly (400 workers in Mexicali)
Daewoo	TV assembly (800 workers near Mexicali)
JVC (announcement expected)	TV assembly (1,000 workers in Tijuana)
Hitachi (existing operation)	TV assembly (1,050 workers in Tijuana and 85 support staff in San Diego)

Source: *San Diego Union-Tribune* as of December 31, 1994.

Most importantly, there was a sudden 40 percent devaluation of the Mexican peso in December, the "Christmas Crisis" for the Mexican government. The Chiapas rebels were still threatening, and it was their false statement to the media that they had broken out of encirclement by the Mexican army which precipitated (but did not cause) the devaluation. The greatest challenge of the decade was to restore the confidence of foreign investors, while responding to the growing popular demands within Mexico for human rights and political reform.

On the positive side, the Mexican elections of August 1994 were the cleanest ever, which was attributed in part to the Chiapas rebellion by a small band of Mexican Indians, and was also due to the introduction of better voter identification cards with photos. There were still instances of unfair tactics by the ruling party, and the election result in the third largest Mexican city, Monterrey, and for the state of Chiapas, were both reversed after an electoral review. Most of the improvements in election processes were at the top or the bottom, with many abuses still prevalent in the middle level of the government apparatus.

The issue of border environmental regulation of *maquiladoras* led to a side agreement to NAFTA and the creation of the Border Environmental Cooperation Commission with $8 billion, and a North American Development Bank (NADBank) to provide additional funding for a deteriorating cross-border infrastructure. However, there was little accomplished in the first year of NAFTA, and critics predicted that increased industrialization on the border would only make things worse. In November of 1994, the United States Environmental Protection Agency (EPA) took steps to enforce U.S. environmental laws against 95 U.S.-owned companies operating in Mexicali, Baja California, Mexico.

In the long term, NAFTA was also expected to cause a diversion of U.S. trade and investment to Mexico from China, Thailand, the Philippines, Malaysia, Indonesia, and other low-wage areas. Nevertheless, Asian countries were often more attractive than Mexico to foreign investors, especially Japanese transnational corporations, because they may offer more favorable government investment incentives, trade administration regimes, and networks for supplying components and other production inputs.

Appendix 1

EXCERPTS FROM MATSUSHITA ELECTRIC ANNUAL REPORT (FOR THE FISCAL YEAR ENDED MARCH 31, 1994)

Profile

Matsushita Electric Industrial Co., Ltd., was founded in Osaka in 1918 as a small producer of home electric products. Today, the Company is one of the world's premier manufacturers of electronic products for home, industrial, and commercial uses. Matsushita's products are marketed under such well-known brand names as National, Panasonic, Technics, and Quasar in more than 160 countries.

Financial Highlights (see graphs of Sales and Income, 1990–94)

In 1994, net sales declined 6 percent, largely reflecting reduced demand and the impact of yen appreciation on overseas revenues when translated into Japanese currency. Although we worked to minimize manufacturing and overhead costs, earnings were negatively affected by lower sales of audiovisual equipment and seasonal products, a shift in consumer preference toward lower-priced items, and the strong yen. Income before taxes fell 21 percent, and net income dropped 34 percent.

There was brisk demand for home facsimile machines and compact read only (CD-ROM) drives in Japan, and in overseas markets, sales of telephones, hard disk drives, and factory automation equipment were firm. Sales of electronic components achieved a level close to that of 1993 as a result of improved demand, especially for semiconductors.

Ten Principal Business Areas (See "Matsushita at a Glance")

To meet the goal of the Revitalization Plan, we have sought to clarify our future direction. To this end, we have identified 10 principal business areas that the Matsushita Group worldwide will develop. These business areas are AV hardware, information and communications, home appliances, housing products, air-conditioning equipment, manufacturing and industrial equipment, components and devices, environmental protection and health care products, systems and networks, and AV software.

Rapid technological advances have prompted us to target three of these areas—AV hardware, information and communications, and components and devices—for intensive, coordinated development by the entire Matsushita Group.

AV Hardware

The transition from analog to digital technology is changing the nature of AV hardware. In the years ahead, high-definition TV, digital videocassette and digital videodisc equipment will lead us into a new era of fully developed digitization.

Toward the Multimedia Age

The Company's response to technological and social change will be to build new businesses around imaginative and innovative products that integrate AV, computer, and communications technologies. In the AV field, for example, Matsushita has to date marketed a broad selection of compact disc (CD) and digital compact cassette (DCC) products. The Company is currently employing its advanced technologies to develop next-generation HDTV, DVC, and DVD equipment.

Matsushita capitalized on its accumulated expertise in the AV, computer, and communications fields in fiscal 1994 to market the Panasonic REAL 3DO Interactive Multiplayer, a 32-bit home entertainment machine that has raised the curtain on the multimedia age, and a notebook-sized PC with built-in CD-ROM drive.

As Matsushita seeks new business opportunities, it will make full use of the extensive resources of the Matsushita Group worldwide. In line with its commitment to strengthening its multimedia technologies, the Company has designated software as a key business area to be cultivated and promoted.

Coexistence with the Earth

Matsushita places great importance on environmental protection in its technological and product development activities. Coexistence with the earth, and harmony with the natural world concerns us in the years ahead as the Company strives to adhere to its philosophy of contributing to society through its business activities.

In 1970, Matsushita established the Environmental Control Office, subsequently renamed the Environmental Protection Promotion Office. Since then, we have broadened our environmental protection efforts. In 1991, the Company published the Matsushita Environmental Control Policy, and we have subsequently set forth environmental rules and procedures to be followed at Matsushita Group sites worldwide.

In line with the tenets of the Matsushita Environmental Control Policy, the Company has devoted considerable efforts to developing technologies that are contributing to the fight against environmental deterioration.

In addition, Matsushita has garnered acclaim from all sectors for its revolutionary no-mercury-added alkaline batteries. Since 1990, the Company has manufactured and marketed these cells, which pose fewer disposal hazards than conventional batteries. Matsushita has also made this technology available to overseas battery manufacturers in the belief that the benefits of such technology should be shared.

Matsushita incorporates concern for the environment into all aspects of production, from product development to waste-conscious packaging practices. A particular focus has been the elimination of CFCs and other ozone-depleting substances from manufacturing processes. CFCs have traditionally been used for washing semiconductors and other electronic components, and Matsushita has devoted significant resources to develop production facilities that do not require CFCs. The Company's achievements have earned praise both in Japan and overseas. The United States Environmental Protection Agency selected Matsushita as a winner of the 1993 Stratospheric Ozone Protection Award in recognition of the Company's efforts to eliminate the use of CFCs.

Matsushita will step up efforts to apply new technologies to the development of products that are safe for the environment and people. By doing so, the Company aims to enhance its contribution to tomorrow's society.

Matsushita is manufacturing environmentally conscious products. All of the Company's domestically produced batteries are no-mercury-added cells. Matsushita's overseas subsidiaries are rapidly switching to this type of battery.

Operations in China

In line with its strategy to localize production in the markets where its products are used, Matsushita plans to conclude a formal contract with the government of the People's Republic of China to establish a joint venture to manufacture VCR mechanisms. Production facilities incorporating the newest technology are already in place. Matsushita is also localizing all aspects of its TV operations, from product planning and design to manufacturing and marketing, in selected major markets to enhance the autonomy of its overseas companies .

In September 1993, Matsushita established its first audio equipment production facility in China for mini-component systems, radios, radio/cassette recorders and portable headphone players. Matsushita will enhance its local presence in the future by having this facility also function as a procurement and supply center for Chinese-manufactured components.

In China, operations progressed smoothly at a joint venture production plant for fully automatic washing machines established in April 1992. Matsushita continues to solidify its operating base in the promising Chinese market: At another joint venture, the Company began manufacturing electric steam irons for the local market in April 1994.

Matsushita is expanding offshore component and material production to bolster overseas procurement and to capitalize on the appreciation of the yen. Following on the success of Beijing Matsushita Color CRT Co., Ltd., Matsushita's first joint venture in China, the Company established two component production joint ventures during the year. One of these companies will manufacture electronic tuners, demodulators, and remote control units for TVs and VCRs, while the other will make feather-touch switches for consumer electronic products.

During the year, Matsushita established a joint venture in Shanghai to produce and market no-mercury-added manganese batteries, primarily for the Chinese market.

International Network: Mexico, China, Indonesia (as of April 1, 1994)

Mexico	Panasonic de Mexico, S.A. de C.V.
	Matsushita Electric de Mexico, S.A. de C.V.
	Matsushita Industrial de Baja California, S.A.
	Matsushita Electronic Components de Baja California
	Kyushu Matsushita Electric de Baja California
China	Beijing-Matsushita Color CRT Co., Ltd.
	Hangzbou KIN MATSU Washing Machine Co., Ltd.
	Beijing Matsushita Communication Equipment Co., Ltd.
	Matsushita-Wanbao (Guangzhou) Electric Iron Co.
	Matsushita-Wanbao (Guangzhou) Air-Conditioner Co.
	Matsushita-Wanbao (Guangzbou) Compressor Co.
	Shunde Matsushita Seiko Co., Ltd.
	Beijing Matsushita Electronic Components Co., Ltd.
	Shanghai Matsushita Battery Co., Ltd.

Qingdao Matsushita Electronic Components Co., Ltd.
Zhuhai Matsushita Electric Motor Co., Ltd.
Matsushita Audio (Xiamen) Co., Ltd.

Indonesia   P.T. National Gobel
P.T. Matsushita Gobel Battery Industry
P.T. Kotobuki Electronics Indonesia
P.T. Asia Matsushita Battery
P.T. Panasonic Gobel Electronic Components
P.T. National Panasonic Gobel
P.T. MET & Gobel

16 P.T. Sekbang Life Insurance (Indonesia)

"What do you mean they want to change the growth strategy?" said Kathleen Parr, executive vice president of operations for the Inter-American Life Insurance Company. "We settled that eight months ago in August, 1994 at the big meeting in Surabaya with the key family members. And they agreed with our whole plan."

"The reason we put $20 million into P.T. Sekbang Life (hereafter called SLI) was because the government said they wanted to professionalize their insurance industry using methods that have worked for us in California: full time agents, steady growth, selling to meet a need. Now they want to get all these part-timers involved? Sure, they'll sell some policies fast, until they run out of relatives and friends."

Nine time zones away, in Jakarta, Alan Stewart agreed. As SLI's vice president of operations, he was responsible for the sales structure of Inter-American Life's first international joint venture. He knew that their 40 percent stake in SLI might not be enough to compel its majority partner to stick with the original growth plan.

Inter-American Life

Inter-American Life (hereafter called IAL) was the largest provider of insurance to individual Californians, holding an estimated 19 percent of that state's market in 1993. The company had been an active participant in the U.S. life insurance industry since its creation in San Francisco following the Gold Rush of 1849.

IAL sold a full range of insurance products to individuals and businesses through a network of more than 6,000 people in 117 offices located throughout the three Pacific Coast states, although the majority of revenues came from California. The

Douglas Reid prepared this case under the supervision of Professor Paul Beamish solely to provide material for class discussion. The case is not intended to illustrate either effective or ineffective handling of a managerial situation. Certain names and other identifying information may have been disguised to protect confidentiality. Copyright © 1996, The University of Western Ontario.

EXHIBIT 1   Excerpts From Inter-American Life's Mission Statement

Our corporate mission is to be the leader in meeting the needs of Americans living on the Pacific Coast for personalized financial security. We want to remove worry about their financial future from their minds. We recognize that corporate integrity and superior service are essential in serving our individual and business customers, and we value the trust and confidence of our customers, our employees, our shareholders, and the communities we serve. Each should share in the success of our enterprise. The following principles guide us in the conduct of our business:

Our customers
...Our field sales organization are the leaders in giving our customers personalized service....we give our customers access to the widest range of financial services available on the West Coast. This is a specialty of our company, and will be key to our future success.

Our people
...We have made a deliberate decision to distinguish ourselves from our competitors by investing in the training and professional education of our people...they are our source of strength and competitive advantage.

Our communities
...Inter-American Life people are known and respected for giving generously of their time, talent and resources to worthwhile community activities. We are part of the communities we serve, and always will be.

The way we work
...We operate through a well-understood, disciplined management process to achieve our corporate goals. We value trust, honesty, and candor in all business relationships, both within the company and most importantly, with our customers who have trusted us with their business.

---

company's core business was life insurance, and it also sold group insurance, retirement planning and income products, and savings and investment products. Over two million Americans owned IAL policies or were covered under its group plans.

IAL had assets of almost $14 billion.[1] It was a major investor in residential and commercial mortgages, real estate, and the financial market and directly held shares in many American companies. The company was chartered as a stock life insurance company, and 98 percent of IAL's stock was owned by the Inter-American Group Ltd. of San Francisco.

IAL's mission was to be the leader in meeting the needs of Pacific Coast residents for personalized financial security. The company believed that corporate integrity and service excellence were essential in serving individual and business customers. Excerpts from IAL's mission statement are given in Exhibit 1.

The company's strategy had been: to sell to well-defined target segments using agents who sold only IAL policies; market policies as products; and differentiate from other companies by offering superior customer service. IAL had also been a cost leader, and ranked among the five lowest cost providers of personal insurance in the U.S. for each of the last 20 years. See Exhibit 2 for the company's financial statements.

IAL had always been committed to a principle called single company representation. That meant that only full-time agents were licensed to sell IAL products, and

---

[1]All figures are quoted in U.S. dollars unless indicated otherwise.

EXHIBIT 2   Inter-American Life Consolidated Balance Sheets
As of December 31 (millions of US dollars)

		1993	1992
Assets			
Bonds		$ 3,741	$ 3,061
Stocks		991	1,151
Mortgages:	Residential	2,476	2,514
	Commercial	1,946	1,977
	Apartment	1,239	1,374
Real Estate:	Income-producing properties	1,139	1,181
	Properties under development	217	254
	Head office premises	49	48
Loans on insurance policies		590	552
Other invested assets		63	67
Cash and short-term deposits		424	378
Other		777	513
		$13,652	$13,070

Liabilities, Participating Policy Owners' Interest and Shareholders' Equity and Minority Interests

		1993	1992
Policy liabilities which together with future premiums and interest earnings provide for the payment of benefits promised on all policies in force		$ 9,312	$ 8,796
Other obligations to policy owners			
Dividends left by policy owners to accumulate with interest		1,156	1,178
Provision for unpaid and unreported claims		68	68
Premiums paid in advance of coverage period		27	42
Policy benefits left on deposit to accumulate with interest		22	27
Reinsurance reserves		473	185
Staff benefit liabilities		131	734
Borrowed funds		504	518
Other liabilities		240	145
Income and other taxes	Current	64	17
	Future	84	139
Net deferred realized gains (losses)		76	(31)
Subtotal		12,157	11,818
Participating interest		581	534
Shareholders' equity and minority interests	Minority interests	186	170
	Shareholders' equity	728	548
		914	718
Other		$13,652	$13,070

that no IAL agent could sell the products of a competitor. Typically, single company representation entailed large training, support and ongoing educational expenses. Most of an agent's formal training occurred during the first 24 months, in addition to on-the-job coaching provided by local management.

Basic courses were supplemented by others, delivered internally, and dealt with estate planning and taxation. Agents could take additional courses sponsored by their

---

EXHIBIT 2 *(concluded)* **Inter-American Life Consolidated Statements of Income**

As of December 31 (millions of US dollars)

	1993	1992
Income		
Insurance premiums	$1,181	$1,186
Retirement and savings premiums	504	516
Reinsurance premiums	621	267
Net investment income	1,065	982
Fee and other income	41	36
Total income	$3,412	$2,987
Policy Owner and Beneficiary Expenses		
Net increases in reserves established for future payment of contract liabilities	547	684
Annuity payments	740	556
Health insurance benefits	251	227
Life insurance benefits	217	190
Life insurance policies surrendered	173	157
Net increases in reserves and payments under reinsurance contracts	613	262
Interest on funds left on deposit	63	76
Experience rating refunds	7	15
Total policy owner and beneficiary expenses	2,611	2,167
Operating expenses	387	370
Taxes and assessments Industry assessments	6	4
Taxes and government levies	72	77
Other	78	81
Net Operating Income	336	369
Division of net operating income Distributed to policyholders	283	284
Undistributed policy owners' income	3	1
Dividends to preferred shareholders	7	—
Net income to common shareholders	$ 43	$ 84

---

industry association, the Life Underwriters Association of California, which were paid for in full by IAL. Managers were selected from agents who had to pass stringent selection criteria before being invited to participate in IAL's management development training program.

The company operated two sales divisions, each focused on selling to a different market:

The Individual Insurance Sales division employed 3,000 salespeople who comprised the largest single life insurance sales force in the Western United States. They were organized into regions. Each region was divided into areas of approximately 3,000–5,000 people, with one agent servicing an area. Areas needed 400 IAL customers to be viable. IAL's individual insurance sales primary target market was persons aged 19–44 with dependents who earned an individual income of between

Target market in U.S.

$15,000–$30,000 a year. Most of the members of this target market were employed in industrial or service occupations.

A secondary target market consisted of individuals who were white-collar managers and professionals under the age of 45 with dependents, whose individual annual income was between $40,000 and $80,000, or whose combined family income was between $50,000 and $100,000. Prospects in this target market were likely to be in a financial building stage, and required life insurance and other financial security products as part of an overall wealth-building plan.

Agents were expected to generate leads and make life insurance sales to anyone, regardless of where they lived, but were to concentrate on making sales in their area. This was done through prospecting households and asking for leads from existing and potential customers. More than 80 percent of a typical agent's annual sales came from referrals. A regional office was headed by a Regional Manager who was supported by four supervisors. A supervisor did not sell insurance, but was responsible for monitoring the work of 7 to 8 agents. Agents were recruited into IAL by field management, usually straight from California universities, though a sizable number (40 percent) were already employed at the time they were hired.

The Employee Benefits Sales and Service organization was composed of 550 people who sold group insurance and other employee products. Their target market was small- and medium-size companies with less than 500 employees. Employee Benefits agents worked in partnership with individual insurance agents, often from the same office, to develop prospects and manage some customer relationships. If an Employee Benefits agent made a sale, it created the strong possibility that other IAL products, such as life insurance, might be cross-sold to the employees of the company purchasing group insurance. An IAL executive estimated that every $1 of new group insurance sales generated $3 worth of new life insurance sales.

A secondary target market consisted of companies with more than 500 employees. Employee Benefits operated four Major Accounts offices, located in Los Angeles, San Francisco, San Diego and Seattle to sell and provide service to larger clients. They also targeted the pension investment sales market, focusing on providing sales and service to pension customers with more than $5 million in assets. Offices located in Los Angeles and San Francisco sold and serviced both large, full-service pension customers and large investment-only pension customers.

These sales channels were supported by units that provided marketing, actuarial, claims handling, information systems, and other corporate services. Exhibit 3 shows IAL's organization chart.

Indonesia

Geography and History

Indonesia is an archipelago of more than 13,000 islands, of which approximately 6,000 are inhabited. The largest are Kalimantan (Indonesian Borneo), Sumatra, Irian Jaya (the western half of New Guinea), Sulawesi, and Java. Approximately two-thirds of Indonesia's 203 million people live on Java, making it one of the most

EXHIBIT 3   Inter-American Life Organization

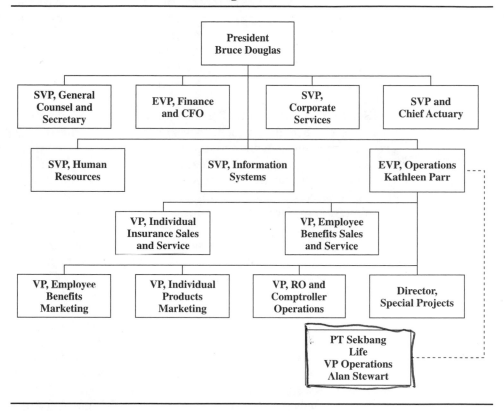

densely populated places on earth. Sumatra has 25 percent of Indonesia's land area and approximately 20 percent of its population. Major cities include Jakarta (estimated population of 10 million), Surabaya (3 million), Bandung (2 million), and Medan (2 million). The republic shares land borders with Malaysia and Papua New Guinea, and sea borders with Australia, India, Singapore, Vietnam, the Philippines, and the U.S.-administered Trust Territory of the Pacific Islands.

Some 1,700 years ago, the islands of what is now called Indonesia were part of a small kingdom under the influence and culture of India. This kingdom, located on Java and called Majapahit, succeeded in gaining control of much of Indonesia and what is now called Malaysia. By the end of the 16th century, Islam was well-established as the dominant religion in most of Indonesia.

The first Europeans to arrive in the islands were the Portuguese, who controlled the eastern half of the island of Timor until, as part of their decolonization initiative, they withdrew in 1975. Far more influential were the Dutch, whose East India Company gained control of the Netherlands East Indies in the 17th century and occupied them as a source of spices, tea, rubber, rice, sugar, and petroleum. In 1799 the Dutch government assumed direct control of the area, which it held until Indonesia gained independence in 1949.

The independence movement began in the early 20th century but did not gain momentum until World War II when the Japanese began stimulating resentment against the Dutch in order to consolidate their control over occupied Indonesia. After the surrender of Japan in 1945, sovereignty over Indonesia was reclaimed by the Dutch with the military support of the Allied forces. In response, Indonesian nationalists led by Sukarno proclaimed the independence of the country from Dutch control. In 1949 Indonesia won independence after four years of intermittent and occasionally heavy fighting.

Sukarno became the first President of Indonesia and moved quickly to establish an authoritarian regime which became exceedingly critical of the West. He also established close ties with the Indonesian Communist Party which, in an attempt to gain control of the army in October, 1965, kidnapped and murdered six senior generals. One of the surviving officers, General Suharto, rallied the army to put down the rebellion. Sukarno became a figurehead leader and transferred effective control of Indonesia to Suharto, who became acting president in 1967. In 1968 Suharto was elected president and was reelected to five-year terms in 1973, 1978, 1983, 1988, and 1993. While Suharto has moved Indonesia closer to the West, he has faced international criticism for limiting dissent and for allegedly using his position of authority to enrich himself and his family.

Suharto remained the dominant figure in Indonesia. He controlled most of the 1,000 members of the Peoples Consultative Assembly, which elects the president and vice president. The president also appoints Indonesia's Cabinet. Due to his own military background, his leading role in suppressing the 1965 coup attempt, and his network of loyalists in senior command positions, Suharto exercised effective control over Indonesia's military. In a similar way, he used the power of appointments to establish a network of supporters within the civil service.

Many members of the civil service were also members of the government's political party, Sekber Golkar. Formed in 1964 by Suharto with the support and assistance of the armed forces, Sekber Golkar's strength stemmed from a broad network of institutional and personal connections in the civil service. It was staffed by government officials, financed by government officials, and dispensed government patronage. More than 25 million Indonesians were members. Sekber Golkar operated a network of party offices in most of Indonesia's major communities to rally support for regularly scheduled elections. Due to its centrality in daily life, Sekber Golkar was expected by most analysts to remain the government party even after Suharto left office.

Indonesia's foreign policy was grounded in its membership in the Association of Southeast Asian Nations (ASEAN), of which it was a founding partner in 1967. Historically, Indonesia had a fear of Chinese influence, arising from Chinese participation in the 1965 coup attempt and because of the disproportionate influence of ethnic Chinese in the Indonesian economy (as 4 percent of the population, they were estimated to control 60 percent of the country's commercial activity). However, growing commerce between the two nations improved relations to the point that Suharto restored diplomatic ties in 1990 after an interruption of 23 years. Relations with the U.S. throughout the early 1990s were considered to be good.

Economy

Indonesia had a mixed economy with many vestiges of central planning and government ownership offset by a growing private sector. While the country has extensive natural wealth, and a large and increasing population, it remained poor.

Real growth in Indonesian GNP averaged 6 percent between 1985–1994 and was expected to remain at this level during 1995. While this was an impressive figure, it was not sufficient to absorb the 2.3 million workers that entered the labour force annually. Indonesia's 1992 GNP was $133 billion, or approximately $680 per capita. This figure was forecast to rise to $1,000 by 1995.[2] In 1992 inflation was 8 percent and official unemployment was 3 percent. However, it was also estimated that 45 percent of the labour force was underemployed. Indonesia's currency, the rupiah, traded at US$1 = Rp2,065 in January, 1993.[3]

Agriculture, including forestry and fishing, had historically been an important sector, accounting for 20 percent of GDP in 1991 but employing approximately 50 percent of the labour force. Industrial output grew significantly in the late 1980s, accounting for 40 percent of GDP in 1991, and was expected to continue increasing steadily due to a ready supply of diverse natural resources, including crude oil, natural gas, timber, metals, and coal. The oil sector dominated the external economy, generating more than 20 percent of government revenues and 40 percent of export earnings (1989 figures). However, future economic growth was expected to be highly dependent on the continuing expansion of non-oil exports. Exports in 1991 were estimated at $30 billion, or 23 percent of GNP. Major trading partners included Japan (37% of all exports), the European Community (13%), the United States (12%) and Singapore (8%). Indonesia had become one of the world's leading debtor nations, with official public debt totalling more than $50 billion in 1992. Private sector external debt was estimated to be more than $16 billion.[4]

The rapid growth and diversification of the economy during the 1980s left Indonesia well-positioned for economic prosperity, especially as growing inflows of foreign direct investment helped shift the country's reliance on oil exports toward manufacturing. Nevertheless, Indonesia faced economic problems far more serious than most of its ASEAN neighbours. Chief among these was a rising but still comparatively low real per capita income. Huge income and wealth disparities made Indonesia home to some of the most wealthy people in the southeast Asia region, as well as to some of the region's most poor. Nevertheless, it was estimated that by 1994, more than 30 million Indonesians earned enough income to benefit from financial planning advice.

The country has also been handicapped by the legacy of government regulation of the economy, a remnant of the Sukarno era, but one that had been only slowly dismantled by the Suharto regime. As well, the extreme price volatility associated with commodity raw materials means that the economy had not known many periods of stability.

---

[2]On a purchasing power parity basis, per capita GNP was $3,090 in 1994.
[3]In March 1995, the exchange rate was US$1 = Rp2,140.
[4]Total external debt in 1994 was $87 billion.

Opportunity

Government Law

Since the mid-1980s, the official attitude toward private enterprise, including foreign business, had become considerably more favourable because Indonesia depended on foreign investment to stimulate and grow its economy. A complex set of regulations aimed to align foreign investment with national development goals. For example, the Capital Investment Co-ordinating Board assumed the responsibility on behalf of various government departments for the flow of domestic and foreign capital to industries other than mining.

The Indonesian economy operated on a 30-year program in accordance with the Broad Outlines of State Policy (Garis Besar Haluan Negara, or GBHN) proposed by the present government in 1966. The program was divided into six five-year plans or *replitas*. The plan called for an annual growth rate of 5 percent a year during the 30-year period. Most major sectors of the economy were open for foreign investment, although investments were preferred in sectors that produced urgently needed goods for export markets or that required relatively large investments and the use of high technology. In return, investment incentives were available to foreign investors, and included unrestricted foreign exchange transfers, indefinite postponement of paying value-added tax on approved imports, exemption from or reduction of import duties, and exemption from capital stamp tax on the initial set-up capital of joint ventures. Most foreign investments were made as joint ventures with Indonesian companies. These ventures were incorporated as limited liability enterprises known as *Perseroan Terbatas* (PT).

Prior to 1994, the maximum foreign equity investment in a financial company was 85 percent. However, if a joint venture had majority Indonesian ownership at the outset, it was treated as a domestic company and received additional privileges including: the direct domestic marketing and distribution of its products, rather than being required to distribute through an Indonesian intermediary; the ability to borrow from state banks; and the ability to operate in business sectors that were closed to majority foreign-owned firms.

Indonesia had a vast, low-cost and broadly literate (more than 80 percent) labour force of some 67 million people. The government expected foreign companies to help train local employees, particularly through the use of expatriates to directly transfer skills to Indonesians. Strikes were usually resolved through the intervention of government to prompt negotiations and called for resolution of the dispute in the spirit of *pancasila,* a state ideology that called for the tolerance and peaceful settlement of differences.

Many business people believed that corruption was widespread, and consequently, relied on well-connected, skillful and reliable local partners or agents to act as intermediaries to help obtain permission to proceed with investments or development initiatives.

Demographic and Social Conditions

Indonesia was a young country: Almost 40 percent of the population were less than 15 years old, and only 5 percent were over 60. The annual growth rate of the population was 1.6 percent. Approximately 45 percent of Indonesians were ethnically

Javanese, 14 percent were Sudanese, 8 percent were Madurese, 8 percent were Malays, and 4 percent were Chinese. It is estimated that 88 percent of Indonesians were Moslem. Bahasa Indonesia was the official language, but as measured by language spoken in the home, the most widespread language was Javanese followed by Sudanese and then Bahasa Indonesia, plus many hundreds of local dialects.

The Javanese culture was dominant. Ethnic Javanese headed most government institutions and their values and accommodating political style provide a unifying cultural force. The majority of Javanese were only nominally Moslem and were both tolerant and flexible in their religious beliefs. The principal division in Indonesian society was between these moderate Muslims located primarily on Java, and their more fundamentalist counterparts from the outer islands. Ethnic and kinship ties were the source of many informal political networks, and Indonesian nationalism persisted as a very strong force in society.

Business activities were dominated by two groups; the *pribumi* and the ethnic Chinese. The former were native traders and Moslem business people who originated from the more devout Islamic communities of urban and coastal Java or the outer islands. Despite decades of government assistance to improve their position in the economy, the *pribumi* remained highly dependent on state help. Many resented the success of the ethnic Chinese in business, and attempted to improve their position in society through political means.

Ethnic Chinese were disproportionately influential in Indonesian business. They constituted a small minority of the population and depended for protection on strong, indirect personal and financial ties to powerful government officials. These ties had been used, together with their links to overseas Chinese in southeast Asia, to obtain investment capital, political protection, and state contracts.

The country was experiencing rapid social change. The migration of rural workers had swelled urban populations and spawned an increase in crime and related social problems. The government responded by initiating job creation and educational opportunity programs. As well, they emphasized the importance of economic development, especially in labour-intensive industries. Nevertheless, there was evidence that a growing and prosperous middle class was emerging, primarily on Java, which had sufficient disposable income to justify the existence of an indigenous life insurance industry.

The concepts of consensus (*mufakat*) and consultation (*musawarah*) were both key to decision-making in Indonesian business or political life. Although these concepts served to dilute the intensity of a particular course of action, to achieve effective execution of an agreement, Indonesians stressed the importance of first obtaining the consent of all interested parties. In practice, the process of consultation required considerable leadership skill so that conflicting viewpoints may be raised constructively and reconciled between parties. The *Bapak* system led to the growth of strong family enterprises in which control tended to reside with the head of the family, who was usually the eldest male.

The Indonesian Insurance Industry

Product Type

Insurance companies in Indonesia sold three types of life insurance policies:

1. *Endowment policies* were the most popular type of insurance by sales and income volume. They represented a form of savings vehicle that also provided coverage to the insured person throughout the life of the policy. At the end of a designated period, the face value of the policy was paid out to the policyholder. Endowment policies had the highest premiums of all types of life insurance.

2. *Whole life* insurance provided coverage to the insured for life, just as in most parts of the world. However, unlike in North America, Indonesian customers preferred to pay for insurance coverage within a known time period. The industry developed policies known as 20-pay or 30-pay, which provided an insured with coverage for life, but were fully paid up in 20 or 30 years respectively. Whole life policies also had a cash surrender value, meaning that an insured could end coverage and receive most or all of the accumulated premiums back from the insurance company. Policyholders could also use their whole life policies as collateral for loans.

3. *Term insurance* provided customers with a fixed amount of insurance coverage for a fixed period of time, and was considered the purest form of insurance since there was no savings component associated with it. Term insurance was less expensive than endowment or whole life policies.

Table 1 shows 1992 product sales and revenues.

	New Sales (1992)		First-Year Premium	
	Number	*Percent (change)*	*Premium (000)*	*Percent (change)*
Endowment	1,237,660	59.5 (−6.0%)	241,149	82.7 (−3.9%)
Whole Life	758,430	36.4 (+5.4%)	37,237	16.0 (+3.4%)
Term	85,337	4.1 (+0.6%)	4,218	1.3 (+0.5%)
Total	2,081,427	100	282,604	100

Competition and Market Entry

Control and supervision of the insurance industry in Indonesia rested with the Ministry of Finance, in the Directorate of Financial Institutions and Accountancy. In principle, all domestic risks were to be insured within Indonesia. At the beginning of 1992, there were 130 insurance companies doing business in Indonesia: 8 state companies, 101 private companies, 17 foreign joint-venture companies, and 4 reinsurance companies. In 1993, there were eight U.S. companies selling insurance in Indonesia.

Some industry executives also believed that Japanese insurance companies were preparing to expand their operations into Indonesia.

[margin note: Possible opportunities and Competition]

Life insurance companies have been successful in developing private pension funds, and their ability to write U.S. dollar-denominated risks has been a further stimulus to market growth. Insurance industry executives expected that Indonesia would continue a pattern of phased deregulation while maintaining liberal market entry rules. However, deregulation would further open the Indonesian market to subsidiaries of other foreign firms, thereby increasing the competitive pressures on existing market participants.

[margin note: Barriers]

Nevertheless, the Indonesian market was still heavily regulated compared to the United States. The Indonesian Ministry of Finance established capital requirements, ownership limits and conditions of license. It also approved the terms of all insurance policies before they could be marketed, and set maximum premiums and mandatory policy dividends based on industry averages of mortality experience and current interest rates. Similar products were grouped into categories, and could only be sold within a narrow band of approved prices for each category. Prices were usually adjusted for inflation each year.

In 1992, the individual life insurance market was dominated by two insurers, P.T. Jakarta Life and P.T. Kaliminta Life, that together accounted for 46 percent of 1992's premium income, a decrease of 2 percent from 1991. These two insurers employed half of Indonesia's 88,520 full- and part-time sales representatives. The government of Indonesia held a substantial stake in both companies. In 1992, Indonesian-owned insurance companies accounted for 94 percent of all policies in force, and 90 percent of all premium income.

In general, foreign joint venture life insurance companies started out selling whole life and term products, but had joined with domestic companies in supplying the market for endowment policies. These foreign joint ventures had minimum capital requirements of $4.5 million, and their overall presence was quite small compared to the domestically-owned market leaders. Exhibit 4 provides data on industry size and sales.

The size of the Indonesian insurance market was conservatively estimated by some industry executives to be $2 to $3 billion of annual premium income. Based on reported 1992 premiums, this meant that further industry growth of some 50 to 80 percent was possible given age and household formation trends, plus a growth in disposable income among the expanding Indonesian urban middle class.

Industry participants expected that as the market opened up, and improved standards of distribution, product design, underwriting and administration became more common, service quality would become a more influential factor in determining the market share held by firms.

Agents

[margin note: Weakness Risks]

The life insurance industry's poor reputation with customers and with the government was due in a significant way to low agent quality. There was high turnover among both part-time and full-time sales representatives. Sales people were not well

---

EXHIBIT 4   Indonesian Life Insurance Industry Profile

	PT Jakarta Life	PT Kaliminta Life	PT First Indonesian	PT Ko-Hong Life	79 Other Indonesian Companies	10 JVs	Total
	Policies in Force[a] *$ policies[b]* *No. of agents*	*Policies in Force[a]* *$ policies[b]* *No. of agents*	*Policies in Force[a]* *$ policies[b]* *No. of agents*	*Policies in Force[a]* *$ policies[b]* *No. of agents*	*Policies in Force[a]* *$ policies[b]* *No. of agents*	*Policies in Force[a]* *$ policies[b]* *No. of agents*	*Policies in Force[a]* *$ policies[b]* *No. of agents*
1992	7,934	6,127	3,067	1,991	9,679	1,838	30,636
	1,098	812	365	350	1,114	415	4,154
	23,015	21,244	9,987	3,750	28,754	1,770	88,520
1991	7,778	5,762	3,169	1,728	8,933	1,441	28,811
	991	763	338	273	997	292	3,654
	20,418	18,759	9,855	3,153	25,084	1,567	78,836
1990	6,852	5,756	2,877	1,507	9,297	1,120	27,409
	817	710	312	215	1,033	162	3,249
	17,370	16,450	8,514	2,871	21,551	1,362	68,118
1989	6,093	5,585	2,856	1,269	8,826	760	25,389
	671	591	284	178	967	112	2,803
	14,985	12,985	7,810	2,346	21,213	1,210	60,549
1988	5,740	5,036	3,045	937	7,969	700	23,427
	560	506	269	118	873	97	2,423
	13,162	11,319	7,471	1,579	18,067	1,053	52,651

[a]Thousands of policyholders.
[b]Dollar value of policies in force, in US$ millions.

trained and received little day-to-day supervision. Consequently, agent productivity as measured by the number of sales was low.

All companies carried out extensive recruiting campaigns, seeking to lure representatives from competitors to facilitate more rapid growth. In fact, senior management and sales force team leaders had been known to take large numbers of representatives with them when they changed companies. Customers tended to follow representatives from company to company, so policy turnover was common.

As of December, 1988, life insurance agents had to be licensed by the Indonesian government. Even so, many licensed representatives were also full-time employees of life insurance companies, meaning that they performed other duties within their companies besides selling insurance. However, being licensed made it possible for them to self-sell at a discount (applying their commission against their premium), and also to sell to friends and family without belonging to the agency system.

A secondary source of distribution was agencies that were headed by individuals called agents who employed their own representatives. They acted as brokers for a variety of companies. Existing immigration regulations made it difficult for foreign life insurance professionals, including actuaries, underwriters and sales managers to qualify for positions in Indonesian companies.

The SLI Joint Venture

Origins and Early History

SLI represented IAL's first entry into a foreign market. The success of this joint venture was integral to the company's plans to expand further into Southeast Asia, an underinsured region that IAL felt would be receptive to its low-key, professional, needs-based selling strategy.

The idea of entering the Indonesian market originated with the former Inter-American Group Chairman Robert Marit. In the late 1980s, IAL's parent made a series of investments in an Indonesian company called P.T. American-Indonesian Development Corporation, which was formed to investigate the possibility of establishing a bank in Indonesia dedicated to trade financing. The board meetings of this company were held in Jakarta. At these meetings, Marit and IAL president Bruce Douglas began to develop relationships with key political and business leaders, including the heads of some of the most prominent Indonesian business families who also were investors in American-Indonesian Development Co.

Several government ministers who met with Marit and Douglas expressed concern that the Indonesian people were not being well-served by the existing life insurance industry. Not only did many Indonesians lack adequate insurance coverage, the industry was poorly run. It was widely believed that benefits were negotiated down by insurance agents from the face value of the policy after a death had occurred. The high turnover and low productivity of part-time sales people meant that growing numbers of middle- and upper-class Indonesians did not trust the insurance industry and were wary of using life insurance as part of a financial security plan.

Consequently, the Indonesian Finance Minister, Satrio Sudraman, wanted to encourage a prominent foreign life insurance company to set up business in Indonesia, sell insurance using full-time agents, provide good service when required, and bring the most advanced analytic methods, sales methods and technology to Indonesia. Based on discussions with Marit and Douglas over several months, Sudraman felt that IAL might offer the right mix of experience, knowledge and willingness to partner with an Indonesian company.

Sudraman suggested to Marit and Douglas that a joint venture be created between IAL and a leading Indonesian family's holding company. He thought that the Suwiro family would be a good match for IAL, as they already had extensive investments in the Indonesian financial industry, and were known and trusted by the government and the military. Sudraman volunteered to contact the head of the Suwiro family and arrange an introduction to IAL. He also noted that the government's own political party, Sekber Golkar, might take a symbolic equity position in the joint venture and subsequently could work to encourage sales among party members.

In December, 1991, Bruce Douglas and Kathleen Parr visited Indonesia for two weeks to investigate the opportunity further. They met with members of the Suwiro family, government officials within the Ministry of Finance, and customers of other companies. They came away believing that Indonesia represented the right first step to begin IAL's Asian expansion strategy, as long as the area sales concept was used to build this new business. Further discussions with the Suwiro group ensued via telephone.

Douglas and Parr made another visit to Indonesia nine months later, but this time stayed for seven weeks. During this time they held an extensive series of meetings to acquire a better sense of Indonesia's market potential and more importantly, consistent with Indonesian norms, to solidify relationships with the Suwiro family. Douglas and Parr came away convinced that IAL's area sales concept would work well in Indonesia. They also believed that IAL's prospective partners felt the same way, and concluded a draft agreement for a joint venture called P.T. Sekbang Life Insurance, which would be capitalized at $50 million. IAL would hold 40 percent of the shares, because the head of the Suwiro family insisted on having majority control of the venture. While Sekber Golkar eventually decided not to invest in SLI, they were willing to make their network of 450 community service offices available to SLI as sales offices should the new venture's management so choose.

The IAL board agreed to the joint venture in July, 1992, but it still had to be approved by IAL's parent. Subsequently, Douglas had several meetings with senior Inter-American officials to discuss the type of ongoing commitment for IAL that an entry into Indonesia would create, and at one critical meeting made a personal commitment to the President of Inter-American to make SLI a success within five years. Inter-American gave IAL its approval for the capital investment and the task of building a new company then began in earnest.

Additional negotiations, which began in October, 1992, and ended in January, 1994, clarified the roles of the parent companies and set out the key elements of SLI's business plan. IAL was to provide expertise in sales and distribution management, and Suwiro would bring local market knowledge, including an understanding of Indonesian culture and norms, plus the ability to obtain the required approvals from the government. Suwiro would also appoint the President of SLI and at least one other senior officer, subject to confirmation by IAL. It was further agreed that while unanimous approval was not required for any matter relating to the joint venture's operation, IAL must approve the business plan. In April, 1994, IAL sent Alan Stewart, an experienced IAL executive who had worked as a deputy to Kathleen Parr, to Jakarta to begin setting up the new company.

Structure and Operating Goals

SLI began operations in October, 1994. See Exhibits 5 and 6 for SLI's Mission and Vision statements and an organization chart.

SLI's business plan listed six corporate objectives:

1. Build and maintain a significant domestic business base through the development of a highly productive distribution system.
2. Provide customers with quality products and service that they perceive to be superior.
3. Rely on well-trained, professional representatives who are paid fairly and have good career opportunities.

[handwritten margin note: Work together to maximize the probability of success.]

[handwritten margin note: Compare these with IAL's objectives]

EXHIBIT 5   P.T. Sekbang Life Mission and Vision

Mission

We will establish P.T. Sekbang Life as a highly productive domestic life insurance company. Our business is providing personalized financial security that will build Indonesia. Everything we do supports our mission. Our success will be determined only by our ability to meet customer needs better than our competitors. We recognize that corporate integrity and superior service are essential in servicing our customers.

Vision

We will distinguish ourselves by having a trust relationship with all P.T. Sekbang Life customers. The basis for that relationship is understanding and satisfying customer needs and expectations throughout their lifetime. Our P.T. Sekbang Life representative initiates and manages the relationship. It builds as all of us, working as a team, provide ongoing superior customer service. Everything we do must enhance our trust relationship in order to earn the privilege to serve our customers for life.

EXHIBIT 6   P.T. Sekbang Life Organization

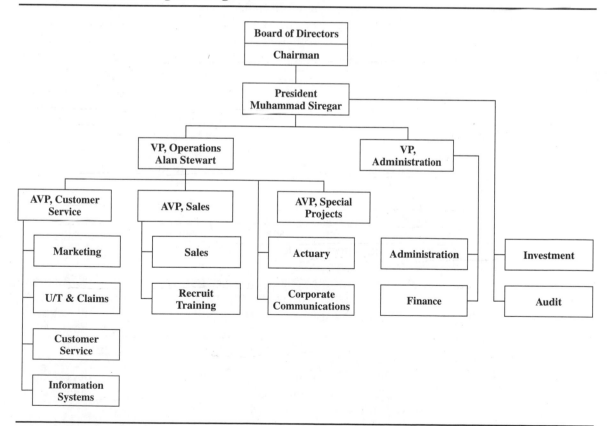

4. Provide the shareholders with excellent returns.

5. Build SLI's image as a leading insurance company while serving the community in a socially responsible way.

6. Be recognized as a low cost producer.

The business plan stated that the primary corporate goal was to build and grow SLI as quickly as possible while maintaining the quality of the insurance operations and meeting the financial plan. In fact, IAL believed that the principal limit to SLI's growth was the speed at which it could recruit and train sales agents. Life insurance would be SLI's core product, with group insurance added after the life business was running successfully. Depending on the existence of a well-defined market, SLI would consider offering financial planning services. See Exhibit 7 for a description of critical success factors as discussed in the business plan.

It was decided that SLI agents needed extensive training at the outset of their careers. This training would be delivered by a manager through a seven-week apprenticeship, during which time the manager would instruct the new agent on all aspects of SLI's product lines and sales processes. A manager could only train one agent at a time. At the end of four years of operations, SLI expected to have 320 agents and 80 managers. This number could be increased if more IAL expatriate managers were made available to SLI. Agents would be recruited from Indonesian universities and from financial institutions.

SLI's source of competitive advantage would be agent productivity. Rather than emulate the Indonesian norm, where agents sold only a handful of policies each year, the SLI agent would be expected to work full-time and sell 80 to 90 policies a year.

The business plan called for SLI to earn an aftertax return on equity of 17 percent after five years, based on accumulated sales of nearly 60,000 policies. An IAL executive noted that because of the obligation to provide for reserves and the country risk involved, this level of return would be acceptable in the United States. He believed his Indonesian counterparts felt that this ROE figure was low, but he did not think they had a firm idea of what constituted an acceptable ROE performance.

The plan also made it clear that SLI was to be operated as an independently managed company. Both parents accepted and agreed that the business plan was the mandate given by both joint venture partners to SLI management, within which they must operate. SLI management would be measured against specific goals and objectives that were set out in the plan.

The plan also called for the creation of an Executive Committee of SLI, composed of the President and the two Vice Presidents of the company. These positions would be filled only with the approval of both parents. The President and one of the Vice Presidents would be Indonesian. This committee would be responsible for developing SLI's business practices and policies. Prior to implementation, these policies would have to be approved by a representative from each joint venture partner. Among other things, the committee would be responsible for developing a proper organizational structure consistent with the joint venture's strategy, along with setting up and closing regional offices.

Exhibit 7   Selected P.T. Sekbang Life Key Success Factors

Based on a situation assessment, the following factors necessary for the success of P.T. Sekbang Life have been identified.

1. Higher Sales Productivity
- Improved sales representative selection
- Training full-time sales representatives, leading to lower rates of sales representative terminations
- Support of Suwiro and Sekber Golkar, with access to corporate resources and party members, respectively
- More effective sales management, using Indonesian managers where possible
- Use of systematic prospect and policy owner follow-up systems through adaptation of Inter-American Life technology/management methods to the needs of Indonesia

2. Higher Policy Persistency
- Increased sales per sales representative by supplying the best sales tools and training
- Selling to meet the needs of our customers
- Pricing aggressively

3. Superior Sales Ability
The goal will be to retain clients for life and to build client and business relations, generation by generation. The sales representatives will have superior sales skills developed through home office training, role playing and regular management training in the branch office. Also, management will be required to provide exceptional on-the-job training and coaching.

4. Exclusive Marketing Territory
Sales representatives will market products in a specific geographical area which shall be their franchise . . . selling and servicing client needs in their area. Representatives will be expected to learn about the residents of their area and work to meet their needs.

5. Management Process
A successful life insurance operation requires the careful integration of all operating functions. . . . P.T. Sekbang Life will develop a unique culture by having its people work as a team in a partnership environment.

6. Continued Training
Sales representatives will continue to develop their marketing skills through ongoing training and education. The results will be a professional sales force with greater productivity.

7. Full Time Sales Force
Sales representatives, dedicated to establishing a successful career in life insurance marketing, will concentrate their efforts on a full-time basis.

  It is our goal to build a solid company with a strong foundation using technology and access to Suwiro employees and Sekber Golkar members. We will have a sound understanding of the market. . . . We will strive to be the leader in establishing the industry standard in professionalism. . . . Marketing through privileged channels, P.T. Sekbang Life will improve its ability to develop into a large and viable company and a low net cost provider.

Marketing and Distribution

The key to SLI's marketing strategy was differentiating itself based on providing superior service. It planned to offer a range of whole life, endowment and term policies, but would innovate by also selling special riders. Riders were additional options that customers could purchase to provide coverage for specific contingencies (e.g., waiver of premium in case of an accident, special health insurance coverage for travel outside

Indonesia, accidental hospitalization benefits, etc.) Each policy would be priced so it could be viable on its own; there would be no loss-leaders or cross-subsidization.

Target markets

SLI saw the primary target market as being members of the growing Indonesian middle class: married individuals, aged 25 to 40, earning the equivalent of household annual incomes between $10,000 to $15,000. There were two secondary markets: individuals aged 40 to 65, interested in savings accumulation, earning household annual incomes between $35,000 and $55,000; and a young adult market, defined as individuals with no dependents, aged 19 to 25 with household incomes of $5,000 or more, working in manufacturing or service industries. Most potential customers lived on the island of Java, especially in the cities of Jakarta and Surabaya.

Distribution

The distribution strategy was built around the area concept. SLI intended to operate as a highly structured home service company, meaning that sales and premium collection would occur at the customer's home. SLI would employ a large full-time sales force selling to target markets located in viable areas (those with sufficiently numbers of prospects within SLI's target markets to eventually support one agent).

The plan also noted that representatives could utilize the network of Suwiro-held businesses to accelerate sales. Area boundaries would be drawn partly based on the location of Suwiro plants and offices. At the insistence of Suwiro representatives, the plan also included an option to develop an early skills training program for interested Suwiro employees, perhaps to support an off-area service strategy. Such a strategy was intended to ensure that SLI's service was available to policy owners who lived in areas, regions or islands not currently serviced by a SLI agent.

Pressures for Growth

Once SLI was licensed to sell insurance in October, 1994, the pressure for faster growth began almost immediately and became quite intense. Some senior family members within the Suwiro group began wondering whether SLI couldn't quickly sell 200,000 individual life policies along with group insurance to 100 leading Indonesian companies, including many in which Suwiro had a controlling interest. At minimum, they believed Suwiro companies should all buy group insurance from SLI, perhaps at a slight discount. This pace of growth would have the advantage of generating large revenues at minimum selling cost, but could not be accomplished without the involvement of considerably more agents than forecast in the business plan. Given the amount of time it took to train an agent, pursuing a fast-paced growth strategy would inevitably mean compromising agent training standards.

Others within Suwiro and Sekber Golkar felt that SLI's links to the Suwiro group and to Sekber Golkar should be used aggressively to create additional sales offices. Specifically, some employees working at the 360 offices and plants scattered around Indonesia that were owned or affiliated with the Suwiro group, and staff working at Sekber Golkar community offices could begin to sell life insurance on a part-time basis, as part of their normal responsibilities.

MAY, 1995

Kathleen Parr took SLI's 5-year business plan out of her desk and scanned its first few pages. The plan was 49 pages long and rich with detail. It was the product of thousands of hours of negotiation, market research and relationship-building. So far, it seemed to be working. Industry reports indicated that SLI's agents were the most productive in the Indonesian insurance industry as measured over an initial six-month period, outpacing their nearest competitors by a factor of three.

She put the plan on her desk, beside a fax sent by Alan Stewart earlier that day. The fax indicated that the Indonesian government's decision to tax premiums remitted to foreign insurance companies at the rate of 20 percent beginning January 1, 1995, had diminished the level of foreign start-up activity within the Indonesian insurance industry.

Parr considered the business plan to be the optimal way to grow SLI along the lines espoused some years before by Minister Sudraman, and for the first time wondered whether her Indonesian partners in Suwiro truly shared this view. Knowing their intentions would be essential to resolving this conflict. If it could not be resolved, Parr wondered if further expansion in the region would be approved by IAL's board.

17 TOPPAN MOORE

In the summer of 1991, the semiannual meeting of the board of Toppan Moore, a joint venture between Toppan Printing of Japan and Moore Corporation of Canada, took place in Tokyo. With sales exceeding US$1 billion, Toppan Moore was a leader in the Japanese business forms industry and widely considered one of the most successful international joint ventures in Japan. While pleased with the venture's recent results, the issue for the board members was how to ensure continued prosperity.

The Parent Companies: Toppan Printing

Founded in 1900, Toppan Printing was one of the world's largest printing companies, with 1990 revenues of US$6.7 billion. The organization had been listed on the Tokyo Stock Exchange since 1908 and had grown through merging several small printing companies and vertically integrating operations. By 1942, Toppan had established a number of wholly owned subsidiaries in China and southeast Asia. Mr. Inoue, who was president at the time, explained:

> We do not construct new plants to fulfill existing and anticipated demands. We establish a plant first and then find clients.

Toppan Printing's growth was halted during World War II when air raids by allied forces caused extensive damage and destroyed its head office and several major plants. The company recovered its momentum in the postwar period when the

This case was prepared by Professor Paul Beamish and Mr. Shigefumi Makino with assistance from Ms. Joyce Miller for the sole purpose of providing material for class discussion at the Richard Ivey School of Business. It is not intended to illustrate either effective or ineffective handling of a managerial situation. Any reproduction, in any form, of the material in this case is prohibited except with the written consent of the School. This case was funded in part through a grant from Foreign Affairs and International Trade Canada. Copyright © 1992, The University of Western Ontario.

demand for general printing increased dramatically. With its superior technology and full line of printing methods, Toppan Printing was able to capture the bulk of orders for colour printing. The company subsequently founded a Technology Institute to create innovative printing technologies, and it established the Toppan Service Centre in 1961 to enhance customer service. Over the following decades, Toppan Printing strengthened its marketing channels throughout Japan and aggressively expanded its business to direct mail, point-of-purchase displays, magnetic printing for credit cards, and so on. By 1991, Toppan Printing operated nine plants in Japan and had subsidiaries in Australia, England, Hong Kong, Indonesia, Korea, Singapore, and the United States.

Moore Corporation

With 1990 sales of over US$2.7 billion, Toronto-based Moore Corporation was the world's largest manufacturer of business forms and a leader in new product development. The company traced its beginnings back to 1882 when Samuel J. Moore acquired the rights to produce a "manifold copying" book that he thought would revolutionize sales management. Inserting a carbon sheet into the binding of accounting books provided receipts for both the customer and the store. This ensured the accurate recording of transactions and represented the birth of the modern business forms industry.

By 1928, nine companies formed the Moore Group, which became Moore Corporation in the following year. While financial issues were discussed in Toronto, the individual companies continued to implement their own marketing and production plans. This autonomy was seen as a strong factor in the organization's growth although it did create some inefficiency in coordinating similar activities. Over time, there were joint efforts in purchasing, human resources, and research and development. However, as most of the affiliated companies produced business forms, they tended to compete with each other. In 1941, Moore saw the need to strengthen the corporation's control over the various companies and integrated their individual activities into a new organizational structure called Moore Business Forms.

Through the 1960s and 1970s, the business forms industry in North America enjoyed real growth rates of roughly double the gross national product, due largely to purchases by business and government of computers that used continuous feeding forms. Numerous small printing companies began producing forms, particularly low-value-added stock items. In the 1980s, the industry's growth slowed with the increased penetration of computers, together with the shift toward personal computers and workstations that used fewer conventional forms products. New printing technologies, plain paper substitution, computer output onto microfilm, and electronic data storage also worked to displace the demand for conventional business forms. The North American forms industry was highly fragmented and was characterized by persistent overcapacity. There were some 550 companies in the United States alone (18 were national in scope) manufacturing and selling over US$7 billion worth of these products. Increasingly, the industry had become more oriented toward satisfying changing customer needs and less toward producing traditional forms products.

Moore responded to the gradual maturing of the North American forms industry by emphasizing high value-added products and diversifying into ancillary fields. While conventional business forms still accounted for the lion's share of sales in 1991, 10 percent of the corporation's revenues were generated from sales of direct marketing products, printing equipment, and database services. Exhibit 1 provides an overview of the current financial status of both parent companies and Toppan Moore.

The Birth of Toppan Moore

Saburota Yamada, Toppan Printing's managing director, first became interested in the business forms area in 1953 when he saw continuous feeding serial forms being used in computers at a U.S. Air Force base in Japan. At the time, Toppan's R&D division concluded that the company did not have the technology to manufacture a product of comparable quality. A few years later, Toppan Printing purchased forms processing equipment from a German firm and began producing simple business forms in a range of sizes, largely for banks and security companies. One such company, Daiwa Security, subsequently established a subsidiary called Asia Business Forms (ABF) to produce its own forms. In 1962, Toppan Printing obtained a 55 percent share in ABF.

In the following year, Yamada travelled to North America with two of his managers to research the business forms industry, which was then worth about US$500 million. Analysts estimated that the Japanese market had the potential to grow to at least one tenth the size of the American market. After visiting several business forms producers, Yamada approached Moore Corporation, the industry's leading manufacturer, about negotiating a joint venture. Yamada believed that the companies had complementary interests. Such an arrangement would enable Toppan Printing to introduce new products into an existing market, while Moore would be able to create a new market with its existing products. Exhibit 2 sets out the initial agreement and Exhibit 3 contains extracts from the final agreement.

At first, it was envisioned that a joint venture would use Moore's technology and equipment to produce business forms, which Toppan Printing's sales force would sell in Japan and other Asian markets. Toppan Printing contended that it had an extensive distribution network, a knowledge of the market, and a well-qualified sales staff. Moore countered that the sales force of the new company should be independent from Toppan Printing, because Moore intended to bring its own sales methods into the venture. Upon further discussion, Toppan Printing acknowledged that the marketing of new products would be quite different from that of existing products. However, Moore recognized that consumer behavior in Japan might be very different from that in North America and that its methods could not always be applied. In the end, an agreement was reached whereby the sales method and production planning would be independent of both parent companies, while cost and pricing principles would generally follow Moore's methods.

In June 1965, Toppan Moore was established as a 55:45 joint venture between Toppan Printing and Moore Corporation. Although Moore had initially insisted on

EXHIBIT 1   Overview of Parent Company and Joint Venture Activities

Moore Corporation	
Total Sales: U.S.	$2.77 billion
Total Assets:	$2.17 billion
Net Income:	$ .121 billion
No. of Employees:	25,021
Shareholders' Equity:	$1.54 billion
Established:	1928

Sales Breakdown

- Business forms   90%
- Data management service
- Direct marketing products   10%
- Packaging

Toppan Printing	
Total Sales:	¥781 billion
Total Assets:	¥928 billion
Net Income:	¥ 31 billion
No. of Employees:	12,393
Shareholders' Equity:	¥425 billion
Established:	1900
Export Ratio:	3%

Sales Breakdown

- General printing   48%
- Books and periodical printing   21%
- Wrapping papers   27%
- Securities paper printing   4%

Toppan Moore

Total Sales:	¥146 billion
Total Assets:	N.A.
No. of Employees:	2,774
Shareholders' Equity:	¥5 billion
Established:	1965

Sales Breakdown

- Business forms   77% (1985)
- Forms processors
- System supply service
- Computer/system machines
- Cards/related equipment
- System houses
- Data entry
- Dispatch or computer staff
- Form processing
- Computer training software
- Video Tex display production
- Video software production

an equal partnership, Japan's Ministry of International Trade and Industry (MITI) was reluctant for a foreign company's ownership to exceed 50 percent. The capital structure chosen reflected the agreement that the venture would use Toppan Printing's sales force (initially) and sell products to Toppan Printing's major customers.

Development of the Internal Organization

Yamada took on the presidency of Toppan Moore after retiring from his position as managing director at Toppan Printing in 1965. Yamada's management team was drawn almost exclusively from Toppan Printing. A vice president was appointed from Moore, but this person remained in Toronto and did not have any substantive responsibility for managing the venture. The Moore vice president explained:

EXHIBIT 2   The 1963* Agreement between Toppan Printing and
Moore Corporation

---

1. Toppan Printing and Moore will set up a new company to produce business forms and sell business machines.

2. The new company's name is "Toppan Moore Business Forms Company, Ltd." The stock of this company will be listed in the security market.

3. The new company will become effective after Asia Business Forms, Inc. (ABF), increases its stock up to ¥150 million.

4. The breakdown of ABF's capital will be assigned as below so that the ownership of the new company will be equal:

Toppan Printing	¥52.2 million (35%)	(+ ¥8.5 million)
Moore Corporation	¥52.5 million (35%)	(+ ¥52.5 million)
Daiwa Security	¥45.0 million (30%)	(+ ¥9.0 million)
Total	¥150.0 million (100%)	(+ ¥70.0 million)

5. Toppan Printing has responsibility for the venture's operation and developing its business plan, while Moore is responsible for supplying the production technology for making business forms.

6. There should be two senior managers from Moore.

7. The royalty allocation will be discussed later.

8. Moore will provide technical assistance and instruction for all of its products.

9. This tie-up is effective in perpetuity, with equal partnership. Either company should not establish relationships with other organizations without the permission of the other company.

10. Moore will provide the venture with printing machines, process machines, and other related equipment.

11. The venture will sell its products with the assistance of Toppan Printing's sales force, at least initially.

12. The sales area includes Japan, Hong Kong, and Asian markets in the ASEAN group.

---

*These agreements were superseded by agreements in 1965 and later. For example, Toppan Moore is not a publicly traded company, the two parents own all of the voting stock, and the royalty rate payable to Moore was later reduced.

I act as a "communications pipeline" between Moore and Toppan Moore. This position was stipulated as part of the joint venture agreement, and my role is to review the venture's results semiannually, independent of Toppan Moore's management, and present a report to the board. I am also one of Moore's five voting members on the board. Actually, the board is dominated by Toppan Moore people, and there are even fewer representatives on the board from Toppan Printing than from Moore.

Moore accepted not having a bigger formal role in the joint venture because we didn't know a lot about the Japanese market in the beginning. We knew that, for Toppan Printing, the joint venture was an outgrowth of what they were doing with Asia Business Forms. We saw our role as bringing proven sales and production methods into the venture, and we were willing to allow Toppan Moore to operate fairly autonomously. Because of the royalty arrangement, we were confident that the people in the joint venture would feel compelled to make it a success.

In the initial stage of operation, Yamada saw the joint venture as being two to three decades behind Moore in terms of technological development. To bridge this gap, Toppan Moore asked its Canadian parent to provide it with a business forms processor. Moore had developed proprietary technology, and both its equipment and production system were highly regarded within the industry. Yamada remarked:

Exhibit 3   Excerpts from the Final Agreement in 1964* between Toppan Printing and Moore Corporation

---

- The new company is responsible for marketing the products that have never been produced by Toppan Printing, such as regi-forms, etc.
- The control centre of the new company is responsible for product price and production cost.
- Discounts above 20% should be reported to and authorized by Moore.
- There will be a royalty of 2% of total sales to Moore during the first five years of operation.

---

*These agreements were superseded by agreements in 1965 and later. For example, Toppan Moore is not a publicly traded company, the two parents own all of the voting stock, and the royalty rate payable to Moore was later reduced.

Moore sent us their newest machine, a high-performance press that cost almost ¥75 million, more than the cash assets (¥70 million) of the whole company. Even though Moore knew that we couldn't afford this, they didn't send a cheaper lower-performance model. Our general managers were very impressed that Moore sent us their best equipment when they didn't have to, and they didn't expect quick payment. In the end, we did somehow raise enough money to pay for it.

Moore was generous with their technology. Over the years, they made a great contribution to Toppan Moore's production technology and production-management skill. The company showed very human feelings. Everyone knows the 1941 story where Moore sent a letter to one of its Japanese salesman who was incarcerated during the war saying "don't worry, we are watching over you; Moore will remain your friend." This is symbolic of the way Moore has always worked. Developing strong human relationships is the most important key to business success.

Moore transferred forms-processing technology and equipment to Toppan Moore under a Technology Assistance Agreement signed in 1965. This agreement also stipulated shared budgets for common R&D activities. Joint efforts on product design, quality, and the manufacturing process resulted in frequent communication at every level between the companies on a whole range of issues. On occasion, engineers were exchanged between the two companies for short periods. A Toppan Moore manager commented:

Moore had particular ideas that they wanted to bring into the joint venture, regarding both sales and production methods. Moore wanted the sales force to work under a territory coverage system based on commissions. As well, Moore wanted to introduce a three-shift system and to control production using cost-based pricing. There was some minor resistance from the plant workers when we added a third shift, but this was largely because of a reduction in net wages.

Moore was a well-established company with good standing in the industry, and we realized there was much to learn from them. We did have some early disagreements over pricing, however. Moore used a highly disciplined pricing scheme based on formal planning and cost-benefit analysis. In Japan, many companies put priority on expanding market share, and prices tended to fluctuate. Under Moore's system, we did much less price cutting. This is just one aspect where we adapted our operating methods. We were never forced. As the company developed, we were able to select which methods we wanted to incorporate into our own practices.

Toppan Printing's contributions were more in the way of intangible assets, the social credit associated with the Toppan name. By comparison, we have less interaction with our Japanese parent. In a sense, there is nothing to learn from Toppan Printing. In the case where we have common clients, there is some opportunity to cooperate; however, there is seldom any sharing of technology. We are not targeting the same markets; therefore, the technology is not so overlapped and the concepts often do not translate back to Toppan Printing. We know Toppan Printing very well; we know our partner's heart. All of our senior managers have come from Toppan Printing. In some instances, it may be that we know too much.

Shortly after Toppan Moore was established, several of the joint venture's managers visited two of Moore's U.S. plants to assess their sales and production systems. Mr. Kawai, who made this trip, offered his impressions:

Moore has achieved the position of being the leading business forms manufacturer in the world through a step-by-step process. Overall, Moore is a well-structured company. The president and plant managers act according to a shared business policy. They do their clearly assigned duties and communicate well with each other and between and across sections. I realized that Moore has a different style than the typical Japanese organization, and although I didn't totally agree with Moore's methods, there were some principles that could be applied to our new organization, such as the emphasis on low waste and high productivity in their production system.

Company Pledge

During the startup phase, Toppan Moore's management began looking for a way to bring people together with the same purpose. Mr. Matsuda, the Hino plant manager, suggested using a company pledge:

Since Adam Smith, it has been thought that the goal of the company is to maximize its profitability. But I believe the time has come to rethink this attitude. I think that the goals of a modern corporation should be to serve the public, to develop the company in a sound way, and to support the employees. Moreover, we have to think of these concepts as inseparable.

Matsuda's basic idea, "tria juncta in uno" (three contributions) was to focus on:

1. Social Community: Let us always be pioneers in the development of Business Forms, and play an important role in the growth of Japan's economy.
2. Company: Let us always be pioneers in the development of Business Forms, and devote ourselves to the prosperity of our Company.
3. Personal Happiness: Let us always be pioneers in the development of Business Forms, and endeavor to achieve the happiness of our people.

This pledge was recited each morning by all employees in every office and plant. Jiro Miyazawa, who succeeded Yamada as president in 1967, was seen as having a strong role in inspiring this philosophy both inside and outside of the company. Moore's vice president remarked:

Miyazawa was a natural leader and he thrived on being a public figure. In fact, over time, he garnered something akin to a cult following in Japan. At one point, he organized an informal association with members from both inside and outside of the company called "Seishun," after Samuel Ullman's poem, "Youth," for people who believed that "youth is not a time of life, it is a state of mind." Miyazawa was an inspiration to many people. He was an extraordinary man, and he was quite driven. He had an eye for detail, and he was very skilled interpersonally. Miyazawa was employee-oriented, and he understood and rewarded superior behavior. He often gave out awards, not for years of service, but to those people who went the extra mile by working on the weekend or calling a customer from home.

TOMOMI-kai: The Employees' Association

Miyazawa believed that having a cooperative relationship between management and labour was critical for the venture. Consequently, Miyazawa and two of his senior managers sketched out the idea of forming an employees' association, TOMOMI-kai ("TO" from Toppan, "MO" from Moore), TOMO, (a combination of "TO" and "MO," means "friendship" in Japanese), "MI" (another Japanese pronunciation of "BU," meaning beautiful, from Business Forms), and "kai" (meaning organization or society). Toppan Moore's managing director, Mr. Ogura, and five other managers were appointed to a steering committee and had the responsibility for the overall management of TOMOMI-kai.

All employees, including top management, joined this association. A company song was composed by one employee, Miyazawa designed a company flag, and several internal statutes were enacted, including the "Ringi rule." A steering committee member explained:

> The Ringi rule is a typical style of decision making in Japan. If someone has an idea, he documents it and passes it up to his boss who checks it. Depending on the issue, the boss may talk to his colleagues in other divisions before handing the paper up to the next level. This consensus approach is used throughout the company.

> TOMOMI-kai acts somewhat like a labour union, but the major difference is that, where a union typically has a position against management, this organization is a place to have communication between managers and employees. The role of the steering committee is to oversee these developments. Often, we find ourselves heatedly discussing what employees really hope for from TOMOMI-kai and why this association should exist.

The Division Control Department and Project Teams

Since its formation, Toppan Moore had focused on expanding its market share and concentrated its capital on establishing plants and merging small, local printing firms. Initially, all sales and production activities were controlled by headquarters in Tokyo. Sections were subsequently established in each plant to coordinate conflicts between the production and sales divisions.

By 1969, Toppan Moore had 850 employees, twice as many as when the venture was established. Many of these people worked in local offices, which operated increasingly independently of the central sales department. In fact, the distinction between headquarters and the local offices had become quite pronounced over the years. Miyazawa worried about this segregation between "brain and body" and thought that a new organizational structure was required. He remarked:

> The growth process of a company resembles that of a child. The whole body does not grow in perfect harmony with its individual parts. Muscles grow rapidly at one time and bones at another

time. Because of this, children are more vulnerable to disease during this period. When a rapidly growing company concentrates its resources on particular functions, the organizational structure grows disharmoniously as a whole. As a result, the company faces many issues of coordination among functions. Our company has reached this stage. The time has come to introduce a control department to overcome the disharmony.

The division control department was formed in 1969. Miyazawa served as the department's director and together with several senior functional managers and two management directors, coordinated cross-functional issues. The division control department had an important role in establishing the company's budget control system and developing five-year business plans. This group was also involved in areas as diverse as devising Toppan Moore's employment exam, selection procedures, and managing the company dormitory.

In May 1970, Miyazawa established a project team within the division control department to look at organizational issues. Miyazawa explained:

> I feel there is a need to restructure, but I'm not sure how to change the organization, so I set up a group of senior managers to look at the issues. I think the project team will become one of the most important functions within the company.

Project teams worked on issues like office work rationalization, research and development, and employee welfare. These teams were required to submit a report within a three-month period. Proposals for office automation, a five-day work week, and the standardization of business forms were subsequently adopted within the company.

Development of the Sales Organization

Early on, Toppan Moore sent several employees to its Canadian parent company as short-term trainees. Moore provided them with information on effective promotion and sales strategy. Moore's sales director, Mr. Seabury, subsequently conducted a training seminar at Toppan Moore for the sales force and managers. One of the participants explained:

> We were not familiar with selling forms. A business form was quite a new product to us. We saw this as an expendable supply for a computer system and focused just on its price. I must admit that we didn't have the attitude that we should join in the customer's form-producing process. We learned that we needed much more "thinking" in our sales activity. Seabury emphasized that Moore did not sell a "thing," but rather the company sold the "value" of a product. He believed that a person selling business forms should, therefore, be a consultant, not merely an order taker. Moore's sales methods emphasized product knowledge, and the company concentrated on educating its sales force. Generally, we continued using the sales methods brought over from Toppan Printing, but, with Moore's help, we changed the tools that our salespeople went out with.

Seabury also introduced territory sales and the sales coverage plan (SCP) as methods to control and implement sales activities. The SCP stressed new orders and new products. Using SCP, Toppan Moore was able to significantly rationalize its sales force. However, some Japanese marketing managers were uneasy about adopting Moore's philosophy and the territory sales method, particularly the "door-to-door" and "walk-in" sales styles that Seabury emphasized. One of the managers elaborated:

The business environment in Japan is different from North America. Our salespeople were used to selling continuous forms for computers in big volumes to large clients who had several regional offices, whereas Moore's clients were typically smaller, family firms. It has been said that the Japanese market is two decades behind the forms industry in North America, and Moore seemed to look upon our market as the same one it faced 20 years ago.

The North American approach is to build business on the basis of market coverage, whereas the Japanese focus on key customers. This is a different task. The approach in North America is different because, for the most part, these firms are not under the same pressure to develop close relationships with customers.

A system of preferred sales was later brought in by Mr. Spencer, who joined Toppan Moore in 1966 after spending 12 years in sales at U.S. Steel. This system focused sales activity on major clients without the territorial constraints of the previous approach.

A Period of Growth

When Toppan Moore was established, the Japanese economy was in a period of unprecedented prosperity. An observer commented:

> The 1950s and 1960s were a time of growth in Japan. GNP was increasing and every economic index was rising. Every industry was growing and every company was aggressively exporting. If a company could make a product, it could sell it. At this time, Japan was seen as a mass producer of low cost goods. MITI encouraged growth through export sales, and Toppan Moore was among the many companies that benefited from its protectionist policies.

The demand for business forms increased dramatically, driven largely by the increasing use of American-made computers that used continuous forms. Over time, developments in information technology created a need for higher-quality forms and more diverse products. Because commercial customs varied across regions, the Japanese forms industry became highly fragmented, with many family companies responding to local needs. Toppan Moore succeeded, to some degree, in standardizing the specifications for business forms and was essentially the only company in the industry that operated on a national scale. Given the strength of the Toppan name in Japan, the salespeople saved time and effort explaining who Toppan Moore was, and they could gain the trust of new prospects more readily. The company experienced a dramatic growth in sales: 136 percent in 1967, 146 percent in 1968, 140 percent in 1969, and 150 percent in 1970. Local offices were added to cover the cities of Sapporo, Sendai, Nagano, Saitama, Chiba, and Kobe (see Exhibit 4). Three regional sales departments were subsequently formed to control the local offices in western Japan, eastern Japan, and the Tokyo area.

A Changing Environment

Toppan Moore's sales growth slowed in the early 1970s due to the "dollar shock." The uncertainty created by U.S. President Nixon's August 15, 1971, announcement that the U.S. dollar would no longer be linked to the gold standard resulted in an

EXHIBIT 4   Toppan Moore Facilities in Japan

appreciation of the Japanese yen. As many Japanese companies depended heavily on exports to the North American market, the strong yen (against the dollar) acted as a brake on the Japanese economy, and the country experienced its first recession in the postwar era. During this time, Toppan Moore's orders and sales fell far short of plan, and the company took emergency measures that had never been used before. All employees who had sales experience, including senior managers, were asked to call on clients. By March 1972, the company finally saw orders increase. In the following year, however, a pulp shortage increased the price of paper. This set off a chain reaction in the other basic materials used to produce forms, such as inks, and Toppan Moore was again obliged to raise the price of its products.

The early 1970s was also a time of rising oil prices, commonly referred to as "oil shock." On October 17, 1973, six Middle East oil producers announced price increases, together with a 5 percent decrease in production levels. Japan had no domestic energy source and the economy was highly dependent on oil imports. These six countries supplied over 90 percent of the oil imported into Japan. As a result, product prices increased across the board. Toppan Moore's prices were soon three times the level they were a year earlier. In 1974, the Japanese government implemented a "Total Demand Control Policy" aimed at controlling price increases. Although this policy reduced inflation, it also dampened demand and increased inventories. At this time, Miyazawa appealed to all Toppan Moore employees to "provide customers with more valuable products than a price increase." A sales manager reflected:

> Miyazawa kept telling us that the hard times wouldn't last and that the customer had to be the priority for all actions. A lot of business forms users looked to Toppan Moore to provide a stable supply, but this was something no manufacturer could guarantee. Many forms makers were, in fact, breaking up with some clients to satisfy the demands of others on more favourable terms. We made a great effort to keep our existing clients. The sales managers, and even board members, called clients to explain the situation we faced and request a 10–20 percent reduction in orders. Most of our clients agreed to this. In daily meetings, our salespeople were told never to show arrogance to the customer, the kind of arrogance that can come from being in a seller's market.

Toppan Moore subsequently established several subsidiaries to disperse headquarter functions and to increase the responsiveness to local markets. These are described in Exhibit 5. Toppan Moore had also entered a number of joint ventures in southeast Asia and became an important link in the global product/service network of Toppan Printing and Moore Corporation.

Once each year, managers from Toppan Moore and Moore met for an open sharing of technical information. Although the joint venture had initially depended heavily on Moore's forms production technology, and still did to some degree, it had altered products to meet the specific requirements of Japanese customers, developed its own production know-how, and was bringing new products to market, such as magnetic forms, single-cut forms, set forms, delivery forms, nonimpact printing forms, envelopes, postcards, and labels.

A notable example of new product innovation was the development by Toppan Moore in cooperation with Moore of a hand-held, intelligent data entry terminal that has been highly successful in eliminating paperwork in the North American parcel delivery market.

Over the years, Toppan Moore had aggressively integrated its operations and automated its manufacturing process. Its system facilitated small lot production without sacrificing product quality, and the company was able to satisfy diverse customer

---

EXHIBIT 5   Toppan Moore's Subsidiaries and Joint Ventures

Toppan Moore Operations (1975) was founded to send skilled operators, programmers, and system engineers to client companies. As well as managing and operating computer systems, this company offered computer programming services on a commission basis and also provided consulting services.

Toppan Moore Learning (1980) was a joint venture between Toppan Moore and Applied Learning International, Inc., a U.S.-based educational information processing company. Several media, including videotapes and textbooks, were used in products aimed at both general and specialized education programs for system engineers.

Toppan Moore-Deltak Company, Ltd. (1980) was a joint venture established between Toppan Moore and Deltak, an American computer training company. This venture offered training packages at both the beginner and advanced levels.

Toppan Moore Systems, Ltd. (1981) offered development services for software systems and application software and assisted clients with hardware selection. The organization provided support on a global scale to Japanese companies setting up overseas operations. As well, Toppan Moore Systems offered services to companies throughout Asia and in Europe and the United States.

Data Card Japan, Ltd. (1981) was established as a joint venture between Toppan Printing Company, Ltd., and U.S.-based Data Card, the leading global manufacturer of card-issuing equipment. This venture had developed a "laser graphic system" and was regarded as the world's first supplier of ID card systems. As well as having a network within Japan, the company operated throughout southeast Asia.

Toppan Moore Forms Handling Centre, Ltd. (1983) was established to process printed business forms on a commission basis. Processing included cutting, binding, sealing, and inserting. The company provided a broad range of support for computer data processing.

---

requirements. Toppan Moore also began manufacturing business forms processors and computer supply equipment. In fact, Moore purchased a forms-processing machine developed by Toppan Moore.

As well, the company had built up a strong service business, which involved dispatching computer operators to customer sites, developing computer software, and processing output forms. A fully automated distribution centre was established in 1982 near Tokyo. The centre was connected with every sales department to enhance the company's delivery capability. By 1990, more than 30 such centres operated throughout Japan, and Toppan Moore had reached over US$1 billion in sales (see Exhibit 6). At this time, the company had about 70,000 customers, although 80 percent of its business was generated by 150 accounts.

A New President

In 1990, Miyazawa retired as chairman (Mr. Kinami became president in 1987), but continued to hold an advisory function within the company. This was a common practice in Japan for retiring executives. Mr. Ogura, who had been Toppan Moore's managing director since 1968, took over as president. There was a great deal of consultation with Moore over Miyazawa's successor. Although Ogura was less of a public

EXHIBIT 6   Japan's GNP and Toppan Moore's Sales and Number of Employees

Year	1965	1970	1975	1980	1985	1990
GNP*	100.7	171.2	212.9	266.5	321.3	404.5
Sales†	8	63	203	433	863	1,485
No. of employees	410	1,028	1,797	1,667	2,229	2,774

*GNP: 100 billion yen.
†Sales: 100 million yen.

figure than Miyazawa had been, he knew the organization and worked well within the company. Ogura considered that he "managed by logic and by developing a network within the company."

Ogura had some strong ideas about the continued evolution of Toppan Moore:

> So far, Toppan Moore has enjoyed immense success. This is not the norm for many joint ventures in Japan. One of the reasons is that Moore provided good circumstances for the development of the company. Moore is a very caring parent. They made a sincere effort to launch the company. They gave us a lot of autonomy. They didn't interfere. We were able to adopt certain managerial methods and arrange them to fit with Japanese business customs.
>
> Moore looks at Toppan Moore as a young company, and they have a long-term view of its growth. For instance, Moore has never asked us to have a detailed strategic plan. We make decisions on personnel, investment, and fund raising without detailed consultation. We are able to manage freely, and we have adopted many Japanese principles, such as a long-term focus, interdependence among companies, business diversification, and a management style based on loyalty and human feeling. Toppan Moore is very much a traditional Japanese company.
>
> Our good relationship with Moore is based on personal communication. A formal agreement is not enough without having good intentions behind it. I believe that the most important way to develop a good relationship is to make the partner company a personal friend. We always try to find opportunities to shake hands with our parent companies. Shaking hands and communicating with partners are the first steps for making a good friend.
>
> There are many examples where Moore and Toppan Printing are learning from Toppan Moore, and we are still learning from our partners. But the relationship between Toppan Printing and Toppan Moore needs to be changed. It is tough for an operating company to manage another operating company. You can't have the manager of a fish shop trying to control the manager of a vegetable shop. An operating company doesn't have an organization to manage a joint venture, and it doesn't have the whole picture, the broader perspective. We should be managed through a holding company, more like how Moore Corporation is set up. But the Japanese government legally prohibits establishing such a structure.
>
> Another important issue is understanding the current product line. Some aspects are maturing, and we need to think about how to maintain growth.

James Saunders, the president and chief operating officer of Moore International–Latin America and Pacific, who was in Tokyo for the semiannual meeting of Toppan Moore's board, shared Ogura's concern for ensuring the venture's continued prosperity. It had been an enormously successful partnership, and recently Saunders had been thinking a lot about the relationship between Moore and the joint venture.

Saunders, 62, had first visited Toppan Moore in 1970 and since 1980 had made at least two trips a year to Japan. Among other possible ideas, Saunders was considering sending Dick Jones, a marketing manager at Moore, into the joint venture for a five-year period. Jones would remain on the Moore payroll. This would presumably provide the opportunity for increased knowledge of, and interaction between, the two organizations.

Twenty-six years of joint venture operations in Japan had resulted in both profits and goodwill. Ultimately for both Ogura and Saunders, the challenge was to build upon the success experienced to date.

18   COLGATE-PALMOLIVE: MANAGING INTERNATIONAL CAREERS

Colgate-Palmolive Company, a leading consumer products company with revenues of more than $7.1 billion in 1993, was best known for brands such as **Colgate** toothpaste, **Palmolive** dishwashing liquid. **Ajax** cleanser, **Irish Spring** soap, and **Hill's Science Diet** pet food.[1] The company (sometimes called "C-P") was also recognized for its comprehensive approach to international career development. Throughout its history, Colgate-Palmolive had relied heavily on expatriates to establish and manage foreign subsidiaries, and in the 1980s developed an explicit policy regarding international assignments. By 1993, it had 170 expatriates in key management positions all over the world. International experience was considered central to career development, and virtually a requirement for anyone aspiring to senior management.

By the early 1990s, however, an increasing number of talented young managers were becoming reluctant to accept international assignments, often because their spouses had careers of their own and could not easily move abroad. As dual-career families became more and more common, C-P began to reconsider its approach. Perhaps, some suggested, greater efforts should be taken to address the concerns of dual-career families. Others wondered if less emphasis should be placed on international experience as a condition for advancement. By the spring of 1994, managers at Colgate-Palmolive were thinking carefully about whether to adjust their approach toward international career development.

Situation

Professor Philip M. Rosenzweig prepared this case as the basis for class discussion rather than to illustrate either effective or ineffective handling of an administrative situation. Copyright © 1994 by the President and Fellows of Harvard College.

[1]Colgate, Palmolive, Ajax, Irish Spring, Hill's, and Science Diet are registered trademarks of Colgate-Palmolive Company.

Colgate-Palmolive Company Background

Colgate-Palmolive was one of America's first major consumer products companies. It traced its roots to two firms founded in the 19th century: Colgate and Company, based in New York City, was the nation's leading toothpaste manufacturer, and the Palmolive-Peet Company was a prominent soap maker based in the Midwest. In 1928 the two firms merged to form Colgate Palmolive-Peet Company, and in 1953 the present name of Colgate-Palmolive Company was adopted.

Following the 1928 merger, Colgate-Palmolive prospered in the United States and expanded abroad. By the late 1930s, the firm had subsidiaries in several European countries, as well as in Argentina, Brazil, India, Mexico, South Africa, and the Philippines. In 1938, foreign sales accounted for 28 percent of company revenues and 41 percent of its profits. Over the next 23 years, under the direction of president E.H. Little, C-P consolidated its position in Europe and further developed its presence in Latin America and Asia. By the time Little retired in 1961, C-P's products were sold in 85 countries around the world. Overseas activities had grown to more than 53 percent of company sales and accounted for fully 78 percent of profits. A description of the Colgate-Palmolive's international expansion is detailed in Exhibit 1.

EXHIBIT 1   Colgate-Palmolive's International Expansion (as of 1993)

More than 50 Years' Experience

Argentina	Denmark	Mexico	South Africa
Australia	France	Netherlands	Sweden
Belgium	Germany	New Zealand	Switzerland
Brazil	India	Norway	United Kingdom
Canada	Italy	Philippines	United States

More than 30 Years' Experience

Austria	Guyana	Morocco	Thailand
Colombia	Hong Kong	Panama	Uruguay
Costa Rica	Ireland	Portugal	Venezuela
Dominican Republic	Jamaica	Puerto Rico	
Guatemala	Malaysia	Spain	

More than 10 Years' Experience

Ecuador	Greece	Kenya	Zambia
Egypt	Honduras	Nicaragua	Zimbabwe
El Salvador	Ivory Coast	Singapore	
Fiji	Japan	Trinidad	

10 Years' and Less Experience

Botswana	Gabon	Poland	Senegal
Brunei	Hungary	Réunion	South Korea
Cameroon	Indonesia	Romania	Taiwan
Chile	Malawi	Russia	Tanzania
China	Pakistan	Rwanda	Turkey
Czech Republic	Papua New Guinea	Saudi Arabia	

Source: Colgate-Palmolive 1992 Annual Report.

EXHIBIT 2   **Colgate-Palmolive's Major Brands**

Oral Care
Colgate® toothpaste
Colgate® Plax® mouthrinse
Colgate Baking Soda® toothpaste
Ultra-Brite® toothpaste
Colgate Plus® and Precision® toothbrushes

Personal Care
Palmolive® soap
Irish Spring® soap
Care® brand baby products, including talcum
   powder, shampoo, and soap
Palmolive Optima® shampoo
Palmolive Neutro Balance® personal care products
Mennen® Speed Stick® deodorant
Mennen® Baby Magic® baby products
Soft Soap® liquid soap

Household Surface Care
Ajax® all-purpose cleanser
Axion® dish cleaner
LaCroix®/Javex® bleach

Fabric Care
Fab® detergent
Dynamo® detergent
Softlan® fabric softener

Pet Dietary Care
Hill's® Science Diet® pet food

Source: Colgate-Palmolive Company documents.

During the 1970s, Colgate-Palmolive undertook a series of acquisitions and became a more diversified company. Revenues grew to 4.9 billion by 1984, but profits lagged. Under the leadership of Reuben Mark, CEO since 1984, the company divested several businesses and focused on five product lines: personal care, oral care, household surface care, fabric care, and pet dietary care. A list of major brands is provided in Exhibit 2.

Although Colgate-Palmolive's strategy shifted during the 1970s and '80s, as it acquired and then divested several companies, its commitment to a strong international position never wavered. C-P continued to found new subsidiaries in Latin America, Africa, and Asia, including in several populous countries such as China, Indonesia, and Pakistan. In the late 1980s C-P entered Eastern Europe, setting up subsidiaries in Poland, Hungary, Russia, Romania, and the Czech Republic. In the early 1990s it expanded many of its existing subsidiaries, starting to manufacture toothpaste in China and Tanzania, enlarging its bar soap factory in Thailand, and producing detergents and bleach in Malaysia, Thailand, and the Philippines.

In 1992, Colgate-Palmolive acquired Mennen, a private firm best known for its line of deodorant products. Bolstered by the Mennen acquisition, worldwide sales topped $7 billion for the first time (see Exhibit 3 for a summary of financial performance). The acquisition also shifted C-P's product mix further toward personal care, as shown in Exhibit 4, and reinforced the company's presence in Latin America, where Mennen had a sizeable market share.[2] International sales were more important than ever, accounting for almost two-thirds of 1993 revenue, with Europe contributing 27 percent, Latin America at 21 percent, and Asia and Africa at 17 percent, as shown in Exhibit 5.

---

[2]Bruce Hager, "Colgate: Oh What a Difference a Year Can Make," *Business Week,* March 23, 1992.

EXHIBIT 3   Colgate-Palmolive Financial Summary, 1982–1992 (million dollars)

	1992	1991	1990	1989	1988	1987	1986	1985	1984	1983	1982
Sales	7,007.2	6,060.3	5,691.3	5,038.8	4,734.3	4,365.7	4,984.6	4,523.6	4,910.0	4,864.8	4,888.0
Cost of goods sold	3,563.6	3,174.1	3,012.7	2,755.5	2,647.4	2,441.5	2,805.2	2,621.9	3,016.0	2,931.1	2,987.7
Gross profit	3,443.6	2,886.2	2,678.6	2,283.3	2,086.9	1,924.2	2,179.4	1,901.7	1,894.0	1,933.7	1,900.3
Selling, general and administrative expense	2,500.2	2,142.4	2,015.6	1,760.3	1,645.6	1,569.7	1,760.0	1,554.0	1,533.8	1,537.9	1,467.5
Operating income before depreciation	943.4	743.8	663.0	523.0	441.3	354.5	419.4	347.8	360.2	395.8	432.8
Depreciation, depletion and amortization	192.5	146.1	126.2	97.0	82.0	70.1	87.1	71.1	65.0	61.7	66.0
Operating profit	750.9	597.7	536.8	426.0	359.3	284.5	332.3	276.7	295.2	334.1	366.8
Interest expense	86.5	114.2	109.2	96.6	116.0	81.3	84.0	64.9	70.5	59.5	54.6
Non-operating income/expense	63.5	74.4	83.8	100.2	65.9	43.0	48.8	63.6	64.7	75.9	65.5
Special items	0.0	−340.0	0.0	17.4	− 59.0	− 205.7	0.0	0.0	−174.0	0.0	0.0
Pretax income	727.9	217.9	511.4	477.0	250.2	40.4	297.0	275.5	115.4	350.5	377.7
Net income	477.0	124.9	321.0	280.0	317.8	54.0	177.5	109.4	71.6	197.8	196.9

Source: Colgate-Palmolive Annual Reports.

Managing International Expansion

Colgate-Palmolive had consistently taken a measured approach toward entering foreign markets. Initially it entered a new country by importing its toothpastes, soaps, and other products. If sales were strong, C-P would set up a country subsidiary and begin to manufacture locally. New subsidiaries were run by experienced C-P managers, sent in from headquarters or from other subsidiaries.

The general managers of foreign subsidiaries, known as country managers, enjoyed a great degree of independence, in part because difficulties in travel and communication in the 1920s and '30s made close contact with headquarters in New York impossible. Some subsidiaries were visited by executives from headquarters only once every two or three years, giving country managers wide latitude for decisions about product offerings and marketing strategies. Following World War II, despite improvements in airplane travel and communication technology, Colgate-Palmolive retained a highly decentralized management style, and continued to allow its country managers to exercise great autonomy.

Colgate-Palmolive initially organized its activities on a country by country basis, with each foreign subsidiary reporting directly to corporate headquarters. In the 1950s, a regional structure was adopted, with subsidiaries reporting to regional presidents, who in turn reported to the COO and CEO. With increasing global competition in consumer goods during the 1970s and '80s, C-P began to seek some of the benefits of worldwide coordination, and shifted away from a strictly geographic approach. In 1981 it created a new unit, Global Business Development, which was responsible for management of certain key equities on a worldwide basis. Global Business Development acted as a global headquarters, gathering consumer and competitive information, developing global strategies, assessing opportunities and risks

EXHIBIT 4   **Colgate-Palmolive: Total Revenue from Principal Products'**
Classes (1990–1993)

	1993	1992	1991	1990
Oral Care	25%	23%	22%	21%
Personal Care	24	23	18	18
Household Surface Care	17	18	20	19
Fabric Care	19	20	23	23
Pet Dietary Care	11%	10%	11%	10%

Source: Colgate-Palmolive Annual Reports.

EXHIBIT 5   **Colgate-Palmolive: Sales and Operating Profit by**
Major Geographic Area (1990–1993)

	Net Sales (million dollars)			
	1993	1992	1991	1990
U.S. and Canada	$2,533.1 (35%)	$2,506.0 (36%)	$2,195.9 (36%)	$2,058.7 (36%)
Europe	1,903.7 (27%)	2,168.4 (31%)	1,968.7 (32%)	1,922.9 (34%)
Latin America	1,525.8 (21%)	1,365.4 (19%)	1,075.4 (18%)	970.4 (17%)
Asia and Africa	1,178.7 (17%)	967.4 (14%)	820.3 (14%)	739.3 (13%)
	$7,141.3	$7,007.2	$6,060.3	$5,691.3

	Operating Profit (million dollars)			
	1993	1992	1991*	1990
U.S. and Canada	$332.3 (38%)	$324.5 (41%)	$252.8 (39%)	$217.4 (39%)
Europe	171.8 (19%)	189.3 (24%)	156.8 (24%)	153.0 (28%)
Latin America	249.6 (28%)	191.6 (24%)	132.8 (21%)	111.5 (20%)
Asia and Africa	134.7 (15%)	90.7 (11%)	79.6 (12%)	72.7 (13%)
	$888.4	$796.1	$643.2	$554.6

*These numbers have been restated to add back the 1991 charge for restructured operations of $340.0. The effects on geographic area data for 1991 had been to reduce the operating profit of United States/Canada, Europe, Latin America, and Asia/Africa by $154.0, $131.0, $19.4, and $14.4, respectively.
Source: Colgate-Palmolive Annual Reports.

around the world, and transferring knowledge among countries. Global Business Development also coordinated the worldwide development and launch of certain new products. During the first stage of product development, regional and country managers worked together to devise a coordinated three-year launch of the product, managing everything from procurement of raw materials to manufacturing to distribution to media advertising. Roll-out took place following a process of concurrent test marketing in multiple countries. At that stage, a manual referred to as a "Bundle Book" was prepared which contained all key information about the product: its concept, formula, packaging, marketing strategy, and advertising. Whereas Global Business

Development managed a number of equities on a global basis, many other products continued to be tailored to the needs or tastes of specific countries, and differed from country to country in terms of pricing, packaging, and market positioning.

In 1994, Colgate-Palmolive's organizational structure could best be described as a hybrid. As shown in Exhibit 6, the primary axis of management remained geographic, with the presidents of the four major regions—North America, Europe, Latin America, and Asia-Pacific—reporting to the COO. Developing regions of the world, including Africa, Eastern Europe, and the Middle East, reported to International Business Development. Other units, including Global Business Development, Worldwide Sales and Marketing Effectiveness, and Corporate Development, provided a complementary structure, coordinating specific activities around the world. With this hybrid structure, Colgate-Palmolive sought the advantages of local responsiveness as well as the benefits of worldwide coordination.

The Role of Expatriate Managers

From its earliest days of international expansion, Colgate-Palmolive made extensive use of expatriate managers. Experienced managers from one country were dispatched to new markets where they were instrumental in founding the subsidiary, hiring and training local employees, introducing C-P products and marketing techniques, and adapting company products and methods to local conditions. After a few years, these expatriate managers usually moved to another country, transferring their expertise and helping to disseminate C-P's management approach. By the 1950s, Colgate-Palmolive had scores of managers working in overseas assignments, including not only Americans posted overseas, but managers from Australia, Holland, Great Britain, and many other countries.

As expatriate managers rose through Colgate-Palmolive's managerial ranks and assumed executive positions, international experience became seen as an essential part of management development. E.H. Little's successor, George Lesch, became CEO in 1961 after heading C-P's European operations and, before that, spent 15 years in C-P's Mexican subsidiary. The CEO during the late '70s and early '80s, Keith Crane, was a New Zealander who began his career in Colgate-New Zealand, became the head of Colgate-Palmolive's operation in South Africa, and then ran Colgate-Australia before moving to headquarters in New York. Before his promotion to CEO in 1984, Reuben Mark served as the Marketing Director for Europe, General Manager of Canada, General Manager of Venezuela, and Vice President of Asia/Pacific. Kathryn Weida, Director of Human Resources Planning for Global Human Resources, commented: "Most of our top executives have worked and lived abroad. Overseas experience is recognized as a path to the top—it's hard to get to top management without international experience."

For most of its history, Colgate-Palmolive handled foreign assignments informally, without any clear policy. John Steel, Senior Vice President of Global Business Development, was an Australian who joined the company in the 1950s and had worked in several subsidiaries. He recalled:

EXHIBIT 6   Colgate-Palmolive Organizational Structure (partial), 1994

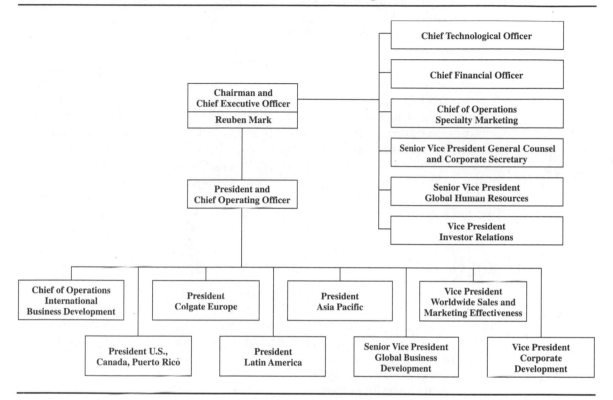

For many years we really didn't have any formal expatriate policy. We would just send a manager in, and give him a salary and an annual bonus. There was no help with housing, with education for children, or with much of anything else. The length of the stay was 22 months, with a two-month leave at the end. During the first year, the manager took two weeks for local leave, but got no home leave.

Once in the foreign country, expatriate managers did their best to adapt to local conditions. Diet, climate, and standard of living were often very different from what they were used to. John Steel recalled the conditions he faced when founding Colgate-Palmolive's Thai subsidiary: Meat and dairy products were in short supply, and the Bangkok heat was oppressive. Although air conditioning was available, Bangkok suffered from frequent power outages. He recalled: "I had to keep the lights down low in order to keep the air conditioning on." In spite of these discomforts, Steel and many other managers relished the challenge of building a foreign subsidiary. They were committed to Colgate-Palmolive, thrived on the variety and stimulation of expatriate life, and often found life overseas to be rewarding personally and for their families.

Colgate-Palmolive's informal approach toward international career management seemed to work well. It not only placed capable people in key overseas positions, but developed for the company an abundance of experienced managers. Over time, however, the lack of a formal expatriate policy became a drawback. One problem had to do with differences in the cost of living. An American salary would allow an expatriate to live very well in some countries, but would not be sufficient to maintain an acceptable standard of living in others. Some foreign assignments were not attractive as managers feared a financial sacrifice—and conversely, other assignments became attractive as a way to save money rather than for the merits of the job. Neither situation was desirable. A second problem had to do with pension planning. If a manager worked for a few years in one country, for several years in another, and for several more in still another country, he or she might not become fully vested for pension purposes in any one. No system existed to credit overall C-P experience, regardless of country, toward a single pension. For these and other reasons, the company decided in the early 1980s to establish a single corporate policy regarding international assignments. One manager remembered: "Colgate-Palmolive had done individual deals with people, but in the early 1980s we wanted to have some consistency. The objective was to have some structure and consistency in our expatriate policy."

Colgate-Palmolive's International Assignment Policy

Colgate-Palmolive's International Assignment Policy was developed in 1983 to provide a standardized set of procedures and entitlements for its expatriate managers. According to a company document, the Policy was intended to be "progressive, comprehensive, and sensitive to employee and family needs." Upon selection to C-P's global management team, the manager—whether an American or a citizen of another country—was formally shifted to "U.S. status" and considered to be an American employee for purposes of pension and benefits. That way, no matter where the manager moved or how long the assignment lasted, he or she received a consistent, U.S.-based compensation and benefits package.[3]

The International Assignment Policy had several important components. (See Exhibit 7 for an abridged version of the 1993 Policy). Before accepting an overseas assignment, managers were allowed to take a 5-day trip, with expenses paid, to visit the assignment location. Upon acceptance of the assignment, the manager and his or her spouse were offered language courses at company expense. Medical examinations were provided for all family members prior to departure and while abroad. While overseas, Colgate-Palmolive reimbursed the cost of private school tuition for children ages 4–19. Employees also received annual home leave so they could return to their home country for an extended visit each year.

Some of the Policy's most important provisions were designed to ensure that expatriate managers had a similar level of disposable income as did their counterparts at corporate headquarters in New York. To ensure financial parity, the firm introduced a goods and services allowance, a housing supplement, and a tax equalization program. The goods and services allowance was calculated by comparing the cost of

---

[3]Colgate at times sent employees on overseas assignments of shorter duration, often lasting a few weeks or even a few months, but these assignments were usually to solve specific technical problems or to meet short-term staffing needs, and did not qualify under the International Assignments Policy.

EXHIBIT 7   **Colgate-Palmolive International Assignment Policy (Abridged)**

Today, more than ever, Colgate is expanding its horizons, powered by talent and committed people around the world.

As a global management expatriate, you can make a real difference to the global Colgate team, while developing your professional and managerial competencies, enhancing your leadership experiences, and enriching your cultural understanding.

To assist you in realizing this world of opportunity, Colgate presents the International Assignment Policy. Through this policy, the Company promotes global career mobility and ensures consistent and equitable treatment to all expatriates, wherever assigned.

In this brochure, we outline the International Assignment Policy and introduce expatriate candidates and their families to the major forms of assistance they will receive during an international assignment for Colgate. Progressive, comprehensive and sensitive to employee and family needs, this policy is one more expression of our commitment to "becoming the best."

Throughout Colgate-Palmolive and its many operating units, opportunity abounds for professional achievement, personal fulfillment, global and cultural enrichment.

As an expatriate, you are part of a world-class team of talented people, performing a key role in the continual development of our global markets. You are also an ambassador, representing your home country as well as Colgate.

For the high potential manager or professional, an expatriate assignment is an important, and often necessary, step in pursuing a global career with Colgate.

In taking this step, you may have some concerns about higher costs of living, currency exchange rates, income tax liabilities, increased housing costs, your spouse's career, adapting to a different culture, and a host of other issues.

The International Assignment Policy seeks to respond to these concerns in a comprehensive manner. The policy provides a standard method of compensation and common entitlements to Global Management Expatriates, regardless of nationality and assignment location. The policy is designed to provide expatriates approximately the same level of net disposable income as their counterparts at headquarters in New York.

Tax Equalization

You may have concerns about being subject to higher foreign taxes and filing foreign and U.S. (if applicable) tax returns.

Your total tax obligation on income earned through the Company will approximate that of a Headquarters-based employee working in New York. Colgate will pay, on your behalf, all income and social insurance taxes on Company-source income due in the assignment country.

To accomplish this, a standard of tax equalization is used that ensures uniformity of treatment for all Company expatriates worldwide.

The mechanism for implementing tax equalization is the Hypothetical Tax, which determines the approximate equivalent of the taxes paid by a NY-based counterpart.

In addition, the Company will engage an external tax advisor to prepare your foreign and U.S. (if applicable) tax returns, and provide an Annual Tax Equalization Calculation. The fees for these services will be paid by the Company.

Goods and Services

If the cost of goods and services in the assignment location are higher than the New York metropolitan area, you will be eligible for a Goods and Services (G&S) Allowance as determined by an independent compensation consultant.

The NY Spendable represents the portion of salary typically spent on goods and services (except housing) in the New York metropolitan area. A Goods and Services Index identifies a standard market basket of goods and services comprising the NY Spendable and measures their costs in the assignment location versus their costs in the New York metropolitan area. A G&S Index of 110, for example, means that the costs of goods and services at the assignment location are 110 percent of New York metropolitan area costs.

The G&S allowance and Assignment Spendable will also be adjusted periodically to reflect changes in salary, family size, and in New York expenditure patterns.

Housing

The Company will normally reimburse the amount by which your actual approved assignment location housing costs, including utilities, exceed your NY Housing Norm. The NY Housing Norm represents typical housing and utility costs for someone with your salary and family size living in the New York metropolitan area. It is determined by an independent compensation consultant and is adjusted when you receive a salary increase.

Reimbursable utility costs include gas, oil, electricity and water, but exclude all telephone-related expenditures.

Housing leased at the assignment location is expected to be comparable in location, standard and size to the housing occupied by other expatriates with similar position responsibilities and similar size families.

EXHIBIT 7   *(continued)*

Availability, proximity to office and school locations, and security requirements are also considered in determining authorized housing.

You will be eligible to receive a Housing Allowance if your actual approved housing costs (including estimated utilities) exceed your NY Housing Norm. This allowance is paid on a net basis and may be adjusted to reflect an increase or decrease in rent or utility costs, or an updated exchange rate.

Making the Move and Settling In
The Company provides extensive assistance with the relocation to the assignment location.

The cost of packing, transporting and unpacking household effects is paid by the Company. Covered expenses include risk insurance and, in certain instances, storage charges for furniture, appliances and personal items.

Colgate will pay any tax liability due as a result of the reimbursement of moving expenses.

Air travel is economy class by the most direct route available. Business class is authorized when published scheduled flight times exceed 10 hours. For such lengthy flights, the Company will normally reimburse for room, meals and taxi expenses incurred for a one day, en route rest stop.

Sale or Rental of Your Principal Residence
If you are renting at the time of transfer, the Company will pay the net costs (up to 3 months of rent) of canceling your lease.

Colgate encourages home owners to keep and rent out their principal residences while on assignment. Toward that end, normal rental brokerage fees up to 15% of the annual rental charges are reimbursable.

Should you elect to sell a principal residence within the first 12 months of a new assignment, Colgate will help protect you against substantial loss through the services of a home sale firm, where available. Such a firm will offer to buy your home based on two independent appraisals. This assures the timely selling of your residence at a fair market price.

Colgate also reimburses for a variety of other expenses associated with the selling of a residence. In all cases, the Company will cover your increased tax liability.

Relocation Allowance
Relocating and acclimating to a foreign living and working environment requires special effort and planning.

Recognizing that there may be unique personal circumstances to your transfer as well as miscellaneous expenses not covered elsewhere, Colgate offers a generous Relocation Allowance. If a full household goods relocation is authorized, the Company provides a lump sum equal to 10% of your new Base Salary, up to a maximum of $10,000. Otherwise, a reduced Relocation Allowance of up to 75% of the standard allowance will be provided.

Temporary Living Expenses
The Company will reimburse temporary living expenses for up to 5 days prior to departure for the assignment location and up to 30 days from your date of arrival. Covered expenses for you and your family include lodging, meals, laundry and valet charges.

The Company will also reimburse any fees or other direct costs related to obtaining suitable housing.

Children Education Reimbursement
Your pre-university school-age dependent children, ages 4 to 19, are entitled to an education equivalent of that available from the U.S. educational system or a comparable international school.

To realize this entitlement, the Company compensates for the costs of full tuition, fees, course texts, laboratory charges and school-provided transportation while overseas. Beginning at age 4 the Company also reimburses the above costs for dependent children enrolled at local schools offering pre-kindergarten programs with a formal educational curriculum.

If adequate schools are unavailable locally, suitable boarding schools in other areas will be identified and utilized. Room and board costs, however, are limited to an 80% reimbursement.

The Company will periodically reimburse you for the round trip costs of transporting dependent children between schools and your foreign assignment home.

Also, dependent children, up to age 23, attending college or university are eligible for one round-trip economy airfare between school and your home at the assignment location each year, for up to 4 years.

Other reimbursable expenses include: special language training; assistance for children with special educational needs; and, in certain cases, tutorial assistance.

EXHIBIT 7   *(concluded)*

Vacation and Leave

Expatriates are eligible for an annual vacation of 30 days (4 weeks of 5 business days each, 4 weekends, and 2 travel days). Where length of service may warrant additional days, the U.S. vacation policy applies.

Vacation for the first year is normally calculated on the basis of 2 working days per month of actual foreign service, plus any remaining vacation from your previous assignment (up to 20 business days).

Legal holidays in the assignment location are in addition to the Expatriate's vacation period. Home Country holidays are not recognized while on international assignment.

Home Leave

The Company reimburses transportation costs for expatriates and family members, including children attending school outside the assignment location, for an annual Home Leave.

This enables the expatriate and family to return to their home country, renew ties with extended family members and friends, and maintain point of origin business contacts.

Home Leave may be taken after at least 7 months of foreign assignment in 12-month intervals thereafter.

Post Allowance

An allowance is paid to expatriates who are assigned to areas of the world where the facilities for family living are considerably less desirable than those in the U.S.

It is considered compensation for enduring unusually difficult conditions such as a harsh climate, political instability, health problems, security risks, and the unavailability of basic goods and services.

The allowance varies according to location, but it generally ranges from 10-20% of Base Salary up to an annual cap. Allowance locations and amounts are reviewed quarterly.

A World of Opportunity

As your career progresses along the Global Management track, Colgate strives to smooth assignment transitions. With each transfer, you are again eligible for the allowances, benefits and reimbursements received during your initial assignment.

With each successive move, the International Assignment Policy is here to assist you and allow you to concentrate on advancing your career, while providing an acceptable quality of life for your family.

Every effort is made to assure that a subsequent position is at least equal to that held at the time of previous transfer.

Assignments are also offered, whenever possible. based on how well they complement your overall career plan.

The International Assignment Policy. It's a vital part of a challenging, rewarding global career, a career full of opportunity with Colgate-Palmolive.

Source: "Your International Assignment Policy: An Overview," Colgate-Palmolive company document, 1993.

---

a standard market basket of goods and services in New York with an equivalent basket in the foreign country. The difference was given to expatriate employees in a cash payment. The housing supplement was calculated to reimburse employees for the amount by which housing costs, including utilities, were expected to exceed housing costs in the metropolitan New York area. In some countries, such as Hong Kong, the housing supplement could amount to several thousand dollars per month. Finally, tax equalization ensured that expatriate managers were not adversely affected by higher tax rates in the foreign country. Colgate-Palmolive calculated the employee's hypothetical tax obligation in New York and, if the tax liability in the foreign country were greater, paid the difference. In countries where the marginal personal income tax rate could reach 65 percent or more, such as Denmark, C-P had to make hefty equalization payments. In addition, the company paid for moving and relocation expenses at the beginning and the end of the assignment, provided a relocation allowance, paid temporary living expenses upon arrival, and protected employees against losses in real estate transactions.

Colgate-Palmolive's International Assignment Policy addressed a wide range of concerns, both personal and financial. Compared to what he had experienced as an expatriate manager, John Steel noted: "We have come light years in dealing with major issues facing expatriates." Industry observers, too, recognized C-P's expatriate policy as a leader among American firms.[4] Yet the Policy was also very costly. Taking all of the Policy's components into consideration, the cost of sending a manager overseas for a five-year assignment ranged from 150 percent to 400 percent of the cost associated with a manager in the United States. Thus, for an American manager with an annual salary of $100,000, the total annual cost to Colgate-Palmolive of an expatriate assignment would be anywhere from $150,000 (for a relatively inexpensive country, perhaps in Latin America) to $400,000. There were, in addition, substantial administrative expenses associated with the Policy, since goods and services indices and tax equalization had to be calculated for dozens of foreign countries. Colgate-Palmolive's New York headquarters employed approximately five full-time professionals to administer the Policy. One manager in New York summed it up: "It's ridiculously expensive to send expatriates abroad."

A Profile of Colgate-Palmolive's Expatriate Managers

Managers were chosen for the International Assignment Policy if they had distinguished themselves in their initial assignments and were judged to be of high potential. A manager's career might begin at age 25 with an entry-level position, followed by advancement through the ranks until a first functional management position was achieved. Once selected for the International Assignment Policy, the manager's career might include a series of overseas assignments, typically for one of the top four positions in a foreign subsidiary: country general manager, director of finance, director of marketing, or director of manufacturing.

After three to five years in one expatriate position, the manager might be offered a new position in another country, either as a promotion or as a rotation. The marketing function had been the most common route to general management, but in recent years, more and more managers were rising to executive positions through the finance and manufacturing functions. Indeed, the promise of advancement to senior management was an important reason why the International Assignment Policy was attractive to professionals in finance and manufacturing.

During the late 1980s, C-P's International Assignment Policy included roughly 150 managers in scores of countries around the world. As the company set up new activities in Eastern Europe following 1989, and as it expanded aggressively its activities in China, it increased the number of expatriates to 170. Of these, 40 percent were Americans, with the rest from a wide number of other countries. This ratio was a significant shift from just a decade before, when 60 percent of expatriate managers had been American, and was evidence of the growing internationalization of C-P's

---

[4]See, for example, Michael Moynihan, *Global Manager: Recruiting, Developing, and Keeping World Class Executives.* New York: McGraw Hill Inc., 1993.

management ranks. Expatriate managers tended to be between 30 and 55 years of age, with most between 35 to 50. Managers under 35 usually had not yet been selected for the International Assignment Policy, and managers over 50 had either settled at corporate headquarters or in a foreign office, or had retired.

Assessing the Policy

Colgate-Palmolive's International Assignment Policy was widely thought to be a success. The company was pleased with its ability to develop and retain talented managers, and for their part, expatriate managers were by and large satisfied with the program. Of course, not all managers were keen to accept a foreign assignment. Common concerns had to do with the host country's religion or social practices, its language, or with matters of health and safety. Sometimes the reasons were personal, such as the family whose child had severe allergic reactions and needed to live in a country where the parents could read food labels. There were also instances where expatriate managers and their families had difficulty adjusting to life in the foreign country and requested to come home after a brief stay. Overall these instances were rare. David Metzler, President of Colgate-Europe and a veteran of almost 30 years at Colgate-Palmolive, 17 of which had been spent abroad, was very satisfied with the International Assignment Policy: "From my experience in the field, I can tell that our expatriate managers feel fairly treated, compensated, recognized, and promoted." Another manager concurred: "We have not had a lot of failures regarding expatriate assignments."

By 1990, however, senior managers began to notice that planning international careers was becoming more difficult. Managers were becoming increasingly selective in accepting foreign assignments. Some positions had to be offered several times before a willing expatriate was found. In an effort to understand changing attitudes toward international assignments, C-P undertook in 1991 an extensive survey of its employees. The objective was to identify the factors that prevented managers from accepting international career moves, and to find ways to make the expatriate program more attractive.

The survey yielded a few important findings. It revealed that the great majority of employees found the International Assignment Policy to be fair and comprehensive. Employees also indicated that they recognized overseas experience to be necessary for advancement to senior management, and that selection for a foreign assignment was a mark of "high potential" status. These findings were welcome evidence that the Policy was well-understood and well-appreciated.

The survey also identified two areas for improvement. First, employees suggested that more could be done to prepare expatriates and their families prior to going abroad. In response, C-P introduced an orientation program to help expatriates and their families anticipate the cultural differences and personal stresses they might experience when living overseas. These programs were offered to all expatriates preparing for their first foreign assignment, and to all expatriates going on assignments that crossed regions, such as a North American manager going to Asia, or an Asian manager to Europe. Second, many expatriates voiced dissatisfaction on the issue of spouse employment, complaining that their spouses were not allowed to work in the foreign country, or that they could not find suitable employment in their chosen professions. The strong concern voiced by many employees prompted the company to take a close look at the matter of spouse assistance.

The Spouse Assistance Program

Until the 1980s, Colgate-Palmolive's expatriate managers had almost all come from a single-career family. Their spouses had typically devoted themselves to supporting the manager's career, and had usually been willing to travel overseas. Whether families were content living abroad was an important element—perhaps *the* most important element—in the success of an expatriate assignment, but never had a special program been devised for the professional concerns of spouses. By the late 1980s, however, a growing number of C-P's managers were reluctant to accept overseas assignments because their spouses had careers of their own. Kathryn Weida stated:

> We have had *many* high-potential people refuse to go overseas because their spouse had a career and they couldn't move. This had never been an issue for us before, and it began to cause a real problem, because at Colgate-Palmolive you can't be a general manager without international operating experience.

Daniel Marsili, Director of Global Succession Planning, added:

> If you turn down a foreign assignment more than once, you may get labelled as not committed to an international career. There are a few exceptions where a person was thought to be quite exceptional and reached a senior position without going abroad, but generally, if you don't agree to go abroad, your career may reach a cap.

The Spouse Assistance Program, introduced in 1992, was aimed at improving professional opportunities for expatriate spouses. Under the terms of the program, an abridged version of which is included in Exhibit 8, C-P provided an orientation program to help spouses identify and take advantage of career opportunities in the host country. It also pledged to use its resources to help spouses gain a work permit, and offered its services in career networking, referring spouses to other multinational companies that might be potential employers. Colgate-Palmolive also provided to spouses a one-time payment of $7,500, either to defray the costs of finding a job or to be used as seed money for starting a new business. Noting that many spouses pursued educational opportunities as an alternative to professional employment, the company also offered a tuition reimbursement plan.

According to one manager, Colgate-Palmolive's Spouse Assistance Program was the first of its kind offered by an American-based multinational company. Soon it was copied by other firms. Within a year of its implementation, one-third of expatriate spouses were taking advantage of the program, usually receiving the $7,500 payment or tuition reimbursement. Several spouses used the seed money to purchase computers and office equipment, setting themselves up as management consultants or in service businesses such as interior design. One spouse used the money to set up a firm that exported U.S.-made quilts to Europe.

EXHIBIT 8   Spouse Assistance Program (Abridged)

In accepting an international assignment, you will be seeking to establish, for a time, a home away from home. That requires a supportive environment, which for many expatriates can best be expressed in one word: family.

Today, more and more expatriates are members of dual-career families. The prospect of a foreign assignment, therefore, often raises professional questions for the spouse of a Colgate expatriate.

To specifically help spouses assess and achieve the transition to a foreign location, Colgate has established an international Spouse Assistance Program.

First, the program endeavors to inform employees and spouses of the career-development opportunities overseas. This is accomplished through orientation sessions and discussions with your functional and/or division management and appropriate human resources representatives.

Colgate may also use its internal and external resources to help secure a spouse work permit in the foreign location if legally possible. All legal expenses for acquiring such a permit are borne by the Company.

In addition, Colgate may provide networking assistance through its membership and high standing in numerous human resources associations throughout the world. In this manner, it may be possible for a spouse's resumé to reach the human resources executives of profit and nonprofit organizations at the assignment location. Employment, however, is not guaranteed.

Spouse Reimbursement Account

To further assist a spouse in locating a job or continuing a career overseas, the Company allocates a Reimbursement Account equivalent to $7,500.

Reimbursable expenses include job-finding and career-counseling services and, if legally permissible, seed money to set up a business or consulting firm and any expenses related to conducting business in a foreign location.

Tuition Reimbursement

Advancing one's education can be a viable alternative to working in a foreign location. Through tuition reimbursement, the Company supports spouses who pursue career-related skill and competency development overseas. Such reimbursement is offered in addition to the language training described earlier.

Source: Colgate-Palmolive company document.

But if C-P's human resource managers were proud of having taken steps to address the needs of expatriate spouses, there was also concern that the Spouse Assistance Program did not go far enough. One executive in New York offered this reflection:

> When it comes to spouse assistance, we've been more creative than most other firms, but I'm not sure the program is really effective. We give money for the spouse to buy a computer, or to set up a business. It sounds nice, but it's not clear that this really works.

Managers were skeptical of the Spouse Assistance Program for a few reasons. First, in more than half the countries where Colgate-Palmolive had subsidiaries, spouses of expatriate managers did not have the legal right to work. Career advice and seed money were of little value if employment were illegal. Second, because many spouses were professionals with high-paying careers, a one-time payment of $7,500 could hardly compensate for lost income. "For a couple with two good salaries," noted one manager, "whether to accept an international assignment becomes a very tough choice."

Human resource managers were especially concerned because they knew that dual-career families were fast becoming the rule rather than the exception. Many young managers who were about to enter the International Assignment Policy had spouses with professional careers. Daniel Marsili commented: "I can think of many examples of 'thirty-something' employees who are facing this issue," and recounted several instances where managers had turned down overseas assignments because their spouses weren't able to move. Occasionally a solution was found, as in the cases of spouses who were professionals in banking or hospital administration, and were able to find suitable positions in the host country, or in the case of a couple who decided to use the expatriate assignment as an opportunity for the wife to stop working and have a second child. "It worked out for these couples," Marsili continued, "but it hasn't worked out for everyone." In the view of one HRM manager, the frequency of dual-career families among C-P's young managers was a reflection of their high quality. "We tend to attract people who have been to graduate school and who often met their spouses at graduate school. Both spouses are educated professionals and both tend to want to pursue their careers."

Looking Ahead: The Future of International Assignments

By 1994, managers at Colgate-Palmolive were becoming aware of a collision between the company's traditional emphasis on international career development and changing social patterns. The importance of international assignments remained an article of faith. A brochure which described marketing careers stated explicitly: "An international operating assignment outside your home country is mandatory before General Management." Senior Vice President John Steel affirmed:

> In the Colgate-Palmolive culture, people know that they have to move if they're going to progress in the corporation. We tell people up front they will move. There are some people who have good careers without going abroad, but it's very much in the culture of the company that if you're going to progress, you have to go abroad.

Haroon Saeed, Director of International Compensation, emphasized the importance of international assignments, stating simply:

> Global mobility is a key value. We want to put the right people in the right jobs at the right time, and anything that hampers that is an impediment to the company's business.

Making the matter even more serious was that Colgate-Palmolive's continuing overseas expansion appeared to call for *more* emphasis on international experience, not less. For example, when C-P set up its new subsidiary in Poland in 1991, it relied on two expatriates to open the Warsaw office.[5] The country general manager, Richard Mener, was a 38-year-old who had emigrated from Poland to Belgium at age 14, and worked for C-P in Belgium and France before being assigned to Warsaw. The director of marketing was a Dutch-born 35-year-old with considerable company experience. Together, they had opened the office, hired local talent, and introduced Colgate-Palmolive products to the Polish market. Without talented managers willing to move to Warsaw, the company might have missed an important opportunity. Nor

---

[5]Gail E. Schares, "Colgate-Palmolive is Really Cleaning Up in Poland," *Business Week.* March 15, 1993.

was Poland an isolated example. Colgate-Palmolive's continuing success in tapping new opportunities in Eastern Europe, Asia, and other promising areas, depended on its ability to send capable expatriates.

If identifying the issue was easy, determining what might be done was proving more difficult. One senior manager thought the underlying problem was essentially financial:

> Anytime a couple goes from two incomes to one income, it's going to be very difficult. If we're going to solve this problem, we've got to zero in on the economic need of the couple. If there's a substantial loss of income, we may have problems.

Several managers shared this view and proposed increasing the benefits offered under the Spouse Assistance Program. One suggestion called for raising the one-time reimbursement payment from $7,500 to $10,000, and for paying child care expenses while the spouse conducted a job search.

A more ambitious suggestion called for "income replacement"—that is, for Colgate-Palmolive to offset a spouse's lost income for up to three months or up to a limit of $50,000. Some felt that income replacement could go a long way toward getting dual-career couples to accept expatriate assignments.

Not all managers were optimistic about a financial solution. Haroon Saeed commented: "I'm not sure the answer is to make expatriate assignments more financially attractive. We'll *never* be able to make up for all the lost income." Rather than trying to overcome the financial shortfall, a different approach was needed. John Steel remarked that it was essential for a spouse to see the foreign assignment not as a sacrifice or a loss, but as something positive, whether as a cultural experience, or in terms of language or education. Non-financial measures might therefore be more effective in making expatriate assignments attractive.

Other managers wondered if Colgate-Palmolive's traditional reliance on overseas assignments was becoming outdated. It may have been reasonable to expect managers to spend long stretches abroad during the 1950s and '60s, but perhaps those days were gone. Perhaps other ways were needed to provide high-potential managers with necessary international experience.

On the other hand, some managers wondered if the problem posed by dual-career families was being exaggerated. They acknowledged that some talented managers might decline a foreign assignment because of their spouse's careers, but expressed confidence that a company as strong as Colgate-Palmolive should be able to find 170 managers who would be glad to pursue an international career. Just because some managers were turning down overseas assignments did not mean that the company needed to make a major change to its traditional approach.

By the spring of 1994, senior managers at Colgate-Palmolive were giving fresh thought to the International Assignment Policy and to the specific issue of dual-career families. Various alternatives were being considered, but none had yet been formally proposed. C-P had long placed a great importance on international career development, and took pride in its expatriate program. How its approach to managing international careers should be changed—if at all—was increasingly a topic of discussion among Colgate-Palmolive's top management.

19 GLOBAL ENTERPRISES, INC.

February 17, 1995

As she prepared for the next day's meeting of the Board of Directors, Jennifer Copperman-Williams, the 49-year-old president and CEO of GLOBAL Enterprises had never felt more frustrated. Despite years of work restructuring the company, Global had just reported a loss of $99 million on sales of $2.55 billion. While Copperman-Williams continued to enjoy the confidence of the Board, she knew that the next day could bring questions for which she did not have answers. In preparing for her presentation, she wondered whether to downplay the company's current problems or turn to the Board for real direction. Almost certainly the Board would push for significant changes in leadership, including the removal of several senior managers. It had become increasingly clear that key individuals stood in the way of the integration efforts that had been ongoing in the company. What was less certain to Copperman-Williams was whether the company's restructuring in fact made sense. As the architect of the company's current integration efforts, Copperman-Williams was clearly in a tough position. With the Board meeting less than 24 hours away, she had little time to spare.

The Early Years—1948–1970

GLOBAL traced its roots back to 1948 in Los Angeles, when Benjamin Copperman started a small company, named Precision Devices, shortly after earning a Ph.D. in mechanical engineering at the California Institute of Technology. During its early years, Precision focused exclusively on designing and manufacturing diagnostic and

---

This fictional case was prepared as the basis for class discussion by Mr. S. M. Steele, Program Director, IBM Leadership Institute, with the assistance of Professor Allen Morrison, American Graduate School of International Management.

control equipment for the medical industry. As a result of several patents, sales grew rapidly, making Copperman a millionaire before he reached the age of 28.

In 1956, Precision acquired Professional Services, Inc. (PSI), for $500,000. PSI provided temporary and contract personnel to the accounting and data processing industry. Jeremy "Joco" Morris, the 26-year-old owner, and close personal friend of Copperman's, stayed on as president. In 1959, Precision spent $2.6 million to buy Best Brands, a Canadian automotive electronics product design and manufacturing company. Best Brands had lucrative OEM contracts with Ford and American Motors for controls, sensors, and sound systems. They also supplied a national chain of retail/wholesale automotive parts stores with after-market products. John Michaels, the owner of Best Brands, also continued as president. In 1963, Copperman paid $11.6 million for New Horizons, a Princeton, New Jersey company that designed and manufactured flight simulators and high resolution video display devices for the aerospace industry. New Horizons also held and licensed key patents for the manufacture of solid state silicon and germanium circuits. The president of New Horizons was Carl Rose, a 34-year-old with separate Ph.D.'s in physics and mathematics. Although somewhat eccentric, he was highly respected in his field and had been able to attract and retain what many regarded as a brilliant young staff.

While Copperman maintained ultimate control of each company, they continued to be managed largely as autonomous ventures. These companies, combined with Precision's core medical equipment operation, generated Group sales of $168 million in 1968.

International Expansion—1970–1975

In the early 1970s, the strong market and growing demand in Europe and Asia began to exceed the distribution capability of Precision's predominantly U.S.-oriented companies. Growth in these geographies seemed to require a dedicated manufacturing, marketing, and service presence. As such, Copperman began a search for international partners.

In 1975, he formed two international partnerships. One was with Nitta Nippon Electronics, a $115 million Japanese distribution company owned by Shinichi Nitta, the 53-year-old founder. The other was with Rhine Mark Products, a $112 million German medical supply company owned by Friedreich Schuller, a hard-driving 50-year-old. The key terms of the agreements were as follows:

1. Precision Enterprises gained 50 percent ownership of both partner companies and the right to purchase the remaining 50 percent when the current owner "retired" or reached the age of 70. For Precision, the purchase price amounted to $31 million over 6 years for one-half of Nitta Nippon's equity and $24 million over 4 years for one-half of Rhine Mark's equity.
2. Nitta Nippon Electronics and Rhine Mark Products were each granted unlimited use of Precision Enterprises' patents, brand names, and technology.
3. Each partner was given exclusive distribution and manufacturing rights for the following geographic areas:

EXHIBIT 1   Organization Chart, 1975

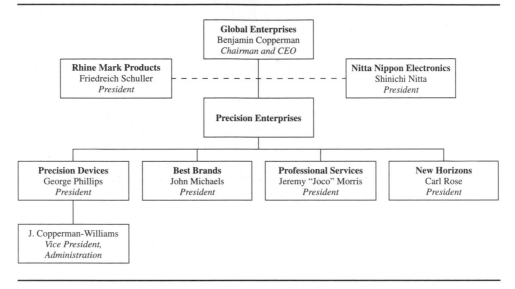

Rhine Mark Distributors—Europe, Middle East, and Africa

Nitta Nippon Electronics—Asia, South Pacific, and Australia

Precision Enterprises—The Americas

Upon ratification of the partnership agreement, GLOBAL Enterprises, Inc., a private holding company, was formed (Exhibit 1).

The Fast Growth Years—1975 to 1990

Precision Enterprises—By 1990, Precision Enterprises had become a $702 million business. Under the direction of Jennifer Copperman-Williams, throughout much of the 1980s Precision was widely regarded for providing excellent installation, maintenance, and facility operations services in the health care industry. In 1988, Precision Enterprises won the prestigious Demming Quality Award and in 1989 the U.S. Commerce Department's Baldrige Award.

Copperman-Williams was generally regarded as a hard-working, no-nonsense manager. She joined the company in 1969 after receiving an MBA (with an emphasis in International Management) from U.C.L.A. and an undergraduate degree in political science from Georgetown University. She worked in a variety of marketing and finance positions and in 1975 was appointed vice president of administration for Precision Devices. Over the next nine years she also served as vice president of marketing and vice president of operation for Precision Devices. In 1984 she was named president of Precision Enterprises.

Rhine Mark Products, Inc.—By 1990, Rhine Mark had grown to $648 million in sales and $44 million in profits. With the political assistance of the European

Development Council, the company opened manufacturing facilities in Germany, Italy, and France. In 1986 and again in 1988, it was honored as the "most admired" company by the European Association of Manufactures. In 1987 Friedreich Schuller was appointed as a commissioner to the European Common Market and, in 1989, was elected to the board of directors of the European Bank of Commerce.

Schuller believed a strong centralized management system should develop strategic direction and control capital investment. He ruled with what many regarded as an iron hand, and on more than one occasion had summarily fired plant managers and vice presidents who questioned his direction or failed to produce results. Ironically, at the same time, he fiercely defended his independence from GLOBAL. He was once quoted as saying "we have to send them half our profits, but we don't have to accept their advice or return their phone calls."

Nitta Nippon Electronics—Initially, the growth in the Asia/Pacific geography outstripped GLOBAL's ability to ship product from the United States. Over time, Nitta Nippon opened manufacturing facilities in Japan, Korea, and Singapore. In each country they were able to negotiate significant concessions on local tariffs, taxes, and administrative regulations. In return, they agreed to limit the import of components and subassemblies. By 1990, Nitta Nippon had profits of $50 million on sales of $670 million.

Shinichi Nitta was a role model for a participative management culture that valued consensus and long-term success over short-term gains. Nitta put a premium on loyalty, quality, and teamwork, He encouraged employees and suppliers to view Nitta Nippon Electronics as part of their family and routinely sent personal notes and gifts when an employee married or had a child. In 1988 he was named as one of the "Outstanding Asian Entrepreneurs" by Fortune magazine. The company was also voted "the most desired place to work" by the Japanese Association of Student Engineers in 1986, 1987, and 1989.

GLOBAL Enterprises—Throughout most of the 1980s, Ben Copperman devoted considerable time to helping Schuller and Nitta establish manufacturing operations in their respective geographies. Despite his best efforts, he continued to find that nationalism represented an enormous barrier to integration. To those who knew him, his biggest disappointment was his inability to effectively exploit the broad geographic scope of GLOBAL. By 1989 the relationship between the partners deteriorated to the point where they frequently would not return each other's phone calls.

Somewhat out of frustration, Copperman began to withdraw from the day-to-day operations of GLOBAL. He became active on several U.S. Presidential Commissions and served on the board of AMTRAK, Bankers Trust, the International Red Cross, and Brunswick.

GLOBAL Goes Public—1990 to 1991

In January 1990, Friedreich Schuller suffered a massive heart attack and died in his office on a Sunday afternoon. GLOBAL acquired the outstanding 50 percent ownership of Rhine Mark for $109 million and named Peter Notehelfer, the former VP of manufacturing, as president.

EXHIBIT 2   Global Common Values

The customer is the center of everything we do.

Performance in the marketplace is the measure of our success.

We work together as a team to provide our customers with the most competitive products and values in the industry.

We act with integrity.

We value diversity and treat each other with respect.

We provide our shareholders, partners, associates, and suppliers with a fair deal and a fair return on their investments.

In September 1990, Shinichi Nitta was appointed as a member of the Japanese delegation to the International Commission on Trade and Tariffs. He retired and quickly reached an agreement to sell GLOBAL the outstanding 50 percent interest in Nitta Nippon Electronics for $124 million. Hajime Takeuchi, the former director general of operations, was appointed president.

GLOBAL engaged Goldman-Sachs to take the company public in order to finance the buyouts. The IPO of 25 million shares at $25 was oversubscribed and on January 1, 1991, the stock was trading at $30/share. When the smoke cleared, the Copperman family had received $255 million in cash and was left with 3 million shares, or 12 percent of the outstanding stock in GLOBAL.

On March 1, 1991, Ben Copperman addressed a special meeting of the top 95 managers, where he announced his retirement from GLOBAL in order to accept an appointment as the Chairman of the U.S. Presidential Commission on Productivity and Quality. In a brief statement he thanked them for their support and said,

> "Your dedication to providing value to the customer, value to the stakeholders, and value to each other has been the foundation for GLOBAL's past success. The future, like the past, will require strength of character and leadership. My legacy to you is my deep faith in your ability to be guided by an unswerving commitment to the GLOBAL Common Values" (Exhibit 2).

Following his announcement, Jennifer Copperman-Williams was named by the board as the new president, CEO, and chairman of GLOBAL.

The New GLOBAL—1991 to Present

Copperman-Williams's succession to the CEO job, while not expected, was not particularly celebrated in EMEA or Asia/Pacific. Although she was highly regarded as a capable and strong leader, she was generally perceived to have a "U.S.-centric" focus. This perception was reinforced by her announcement on April 23, 1991, that GLOBAL would reorganize into international product groups with independent geographic marketing and distribution companies (Exhibit 3). The product groups were as follows:

EXHIBIT 3   Organizational Chart, April 23, 1991

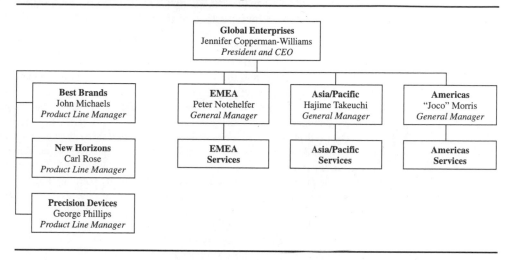

Best Brands—specialized in OEM and after-market automotive sound systems, speakers, and gauges. These were manufactured in the United States, Germany, and Singapore.

New Horizons—built its proprietary visual display and simulation technology into a leadership position in the multimedia entertainment and communications industry, with manufacturing facilities in Mexico, Italy, and Korea.

Precision Devices—specialized in "big ticket" customized medical diagnostic and process control systems with design and manufacturing facilities in the United States, Japan, and France.

Professional Services—provided consulting, programming, and facilities management services to the medical and data processing industries. This product line tended to be regionally unique and, as such, would continue to report directly to the geographies.

Under the new organization, product line managers (PLMs) were paid on market share and sales operating profit. PLMs controlled investments in R&D and all aspects of production. Country-based general managers (GMs) were evaluated on net profit, customer satisfaction, and employee morale. They controlled all marketing, sales, and service activities.

Not surprisingly, many GMs were frustrated because they had lost control of product development and production. Notehelfer and Takeuchi were particularly upset at the perceived loss of power and prestige associated with the reorganization. They were also angry that their input in the restructuring had, for the most part, been ignored.

During this period, the patents on several "cash cows" and New Horizons' licenses on proprietary manufacturing processes expired. This caused intense pressure on prices and manufacturing costs and opened the door to new competition. In 1993, for the first time in history, GLOBAL lost $71 million on $2.4 billion in sales.

Key events from the perspective of the GMs and PLMs include the following:

John Michaels, PLM of Best Brands:

Sales of cars and trucks and the profits of the companies that make them are hitting new highs every quarter. Unfortunately, this is happening at the expense of the independent suppliers who have had to increase productivity and cut costs just to squeeze out razor thin margins. This is particularly true in the automotive sound systems industry which has gone through a blood bath and continues to be a basket case.

The products are all the same under the covers and the only purchase criteria are price and delivery. Brand name, while important in the after market, is of no value in the OEM market. Hell, there are times when I could make more money buying stuff in bulk from our competitors and putting it out under our name than I could by building it in our own factories.

If we are going to succeed in this business we must consolidate our manufacturing and cut our costs. Unfortunately, it has been almost impossible to set the geography GM's to accept this. They give it lip service until it comes time to face the music and close a plant in one of their countries. Then they cry like babies . . . 'it will kill morale, the government will go nuts, I am not going to be the GM to have the first layoff', etc.

We need to face the facts. This is a flat commodity market where we can make some money if we are the low-cost producer and pay attention to balancing demand and production. The first step was closing down our antiquated plant in Europe and doubling our production capacity in the United States. It was painful and expensive, but we are now positioned to be much more competitive and profitable. The next step will be to close the plant in Singapore. I know it will take some time and investment capital, but if we are serious about this market we must do it. If not, we should hand out the pink slips and turn the plants into shopping malls.

Carl Rose, PLM of New Horizons:

The marketplace for interactive entertainment, virtual reality, and multimedia communications is going to explode. It will dwarf the PC boom and the developing nations of Asia and eastern Europe will lead the way. The beauty of it is that we don't have to worry about the infrastructure—cable, optic, glass, cellular, satellite, laser, magnetic, digital, etc.—it doesn't matter. The value added in this market is all in the application. The winner will be the company that can integrate multiple independent complex virtual worlds in a way that brings value to the user, improves the quality of life, and helps people rediscover fun. I call it 'reengineering life,' the ultimate thrill in cyberspace.

We have a good start on this thing, but like any huge new market, it is crowded with deep pocket wanna-be winners. While we fight it out, the demand is going to continue to grow at 15 percent a year with no end in sight. Anyone who misses this, or stands in the way, should be summarily executed. That includes the nay sayers in GLOBAL who just don't get it. I can't ever remember it being so hard getting funding as it is now. The future of GLOBAL is in New Horizons and getting there faster, with more for less, is my mission.

George Phillips, PLM of Precision Devices:

The aging Precision Devices product line, although approaching end of life, continues to be the most profitable for GLOBAL. Over the last four years the impact of managed health care and hospital cost constraints has slowed the industry growth rate from 12 percent per year to 5 percent. Precision has held on to 25 percent of the market by combining continued investment in R&D with highly visible, personalized, value-added marketing. I could grab another 15 points of the market if we had the capital to expand production capacity and took a more aggressive pricing posture.

Unfortunately I have not been able to convince Jennifer or the GMs to make a major investment in Precision Devices. After all, it is a cash cow and is supposed to generate the capital to invest in New Horizons, not consume it. This difference of opinion has become a source of constant frustration and frequent angry debate. I feel that Rose spends too much time in fantasy land, where the rubber meets his dreams, and never comes to grips with the fact that he has yet to show a profit. We have reached the point where continuing with New Horizons is throwing good money after bad.

Jeremy "Joco" Morris, GM, Americas:

You know, at 65, I am one of the youngest senior managers in GLOBAL and although I hate to admit it, I am running out of steam. This business is beating me up. The profit margins are way down and the competition has become fierce. We are all holding our breath for Rose to ride in on his white stallion with another New Horizons blockbuster but, so far, it is not happening. Thank goodness for the services business. While it might not be the most profitable, it is surely the most fun. I really enjoy the personal relationships that have been built over the years.

Despite that, if the truth be known, I want to spend more time being a grandfather and plan to retire as soon as I have finished helping Jennifer clean up the mess that Notehelfer made when he closed his Best Brands plant. I owe her old man that much and, anyway, she has been like a daughter to me.

Peter Notehelfer, GM, Europe, Middle East, Africa:

There is an old German saying, 'the devil is in the details.' That goes to the heart of the problem with the way GLOBAL has gutted the power and capability of the country organizations in favor of centralized U.S. control. Neither Jennifer nor her PLMs have ever had a job outside the United States. What do they know about our culture, about our customers, about our unique market requirements?

Case in point, look at the decision to close my Best Brands plant in favor of doubling capacity in the United States. Michaels thought I should be a good team player and jump at the opportunity to ring up Bonn to tell them we are going to throw a bunch of Germans out of work so that we can import products from America. It sure was convenient that he wanted to double the capacity in Joco's territory and that Joco has an almost mystic ability to influence Jennifer. The whole thing was a little too cozy for me.

To top it off, we lost $58 million on the sale of the plant and paid out another $71 million in severance payments and other extraordinary charges. It was the first layoff in the history of GLOBAL, even dating back to the days of Rhine Mark. It has left me with a huge political problem and has impacted the morale of the entire European operation. It was, in my opinion, one of the dumbest business decisions you could make.

Hajime Takeuchi, GM, Asia/Pacific:

We have a long and proud history of association with GLOBAL from the early days when Nitta-San formed his partnership with Copperman-San. Over the years we have seen the roots of that partnership intertwine and enrich the lives of our employees and their families. Recently, however, the pressure of being a public corporation has caused us to take the seductive road to short-term success at the expense of long-term opportunity.

Perhaps the cultural gap between Japan and the United States is too wide for us to understand each other. We appreciate the pressure to show profits every quarter, but we must not do so at the expense of missing the emerging opportunity in the New Horizons line. We must be patient and make personal sacrifices until we can put these hard times behind us. It is most important during these times that the young woman, who is our CEO, have the wisdom to seek guidance from Copperman-San and Nitta-San as she moves forward on the competitive battlefield.

February 17, 1995:   Copperman-Williams met with her father over dinner to give him a personal preview of the 1994 business results (see Exhibits 4–7). With the Board meeting the next day, she had little choice but to brief her father. Although now 72 years old, Ben Copperman remained the company's biggest single share-holder and a strong supporter of his daughter. Jennifer ran through the events of the last year.

> I backed Michael's plan to consolidate the production of Best Brands to get a cost advantage which would help them grow and become profitable. The gamble worked out well and helped the Best Brands product line show a small operating profit of $30 million on sales of $628 million. In Europe, Notehelfer dragged his feet on closing his Best Brands plant and ended up paying almost $100 million in separation packages and extraordinary charges. As a result, EMEA ended the year with a $115 million loss on sales of $833 million. Thank heavens for George Phillips. He milked the Precision product line to $106 million in profit on sales of $757 million. This all went to help finance Rose, who had promised this would be the year of the big win for New Horizons. The big win turned out to be a $100 million loss on sales of $530 million. Joco squeaked in at $16 million in profit on sales of $357 million in the Americas and Takeuchi-San broke even in Asia/Pacific with $2 million in profit on $854 million in sales.
>
> The PLMs have never been more at each other's throats. The restructuring was supposed to have clarified organizational responsibilities, reduced duplication of effort and cost, and leveraged our global size to make us more competitive. Yet it has only created more conflict. The PLMs and the geographies are ready for war. It's starting to show on the bottom line.

She ended the meeting by asking her father if he thought she was doing the right thing. Copperman listened quietly as his daughter finished speaking. As they stood to leave he said,

> You know, I built this company by taking risks and making investments to bring new technology to the marketplace, faster and better than the competition. That is what you have been doing and it is too early to know if it will pay off. I would say you are in Act II of the opera and the fat lady is scheduled to sing next year. You know I'll support you. But I'm not sure of the other directors. You'll do what's right. Give 'em hell.

Once her father left she resumed to the task at hand, which meant preparing a statement for the Board. By 8:30 p.m., alone in her office, she had penned the following remarks:

> In 1994, GLOBAL generated $2.5 billion in sales and posted a loss of $97 million. I am not here to offer excuses, however, there are several items that need to be brought to your attention to help you put this record in perspective. First, we incurred a one-time $130 million extraordinary charge for closing our Best Brands plant in Germany. Second, we invested an additional $100 million in our continued development of the New Horizons interactive multimedia product. If we had ducked these two tough but strategically necessary investments, we would have shown an annual profit of $130 million, or 5.5 percent net return on sales.

I want to make it very clear that I am personally responsible for our 1994 business results. While disappointing in the short term, they represent an investment in the future and are a tribute to the courage, commitment, and support of my colleagues. Despite the problems we encountered last year, GLOBAL is now well-positioned in every market and has the potential to generate a 10 percent net return on sales in 1995.

I do, however, believe that our potential can best be realized by an infusion of new ideas and new leadership. As such, I have proposed an amendment to our bylaws that would require the retirement of all officers, General Managers, and Product Line Managers upon reaching age 65. In anticipation of board approval of this amendment, I have asked for, and received, the undated letters of resignation of all the GMs and PLMs. I plan to take action later today on several of them. The others, if they are over age 65, will take effect on July 1.

On a personal note, last month marked my 26th year with GLOBAL. I am thankful for the opportunity I have had to work with such a distinguished group of people. However, I too have reached a point where it is time to move on. Therefore, I am offering my resignation to the Board, to become effective on whatever date you choose. In the interim, I will continue my commitment to helping GLOBAL achieve sustained profitability and market leadership.

As Jennifer closed her note pad, she realized that a statement of this sort would provide no opportunity for turning back. Lesser action would no doubt be acceptable to the Board. Would this statement, she wondered, go too far? Or would it not go far enough?

EXHIBIT 4   Global Enterprises Consolidated Income Statement—1994 (in millions)

	Americas	EMEA	Asia/Pacific	Total
Sales revenue	$858	$833	$855	$2,546
Cost of products & services	480	467	487	1,434
Depreciation & inventory charges	65	55	68	188
Gross margin	313	311	300	924
Expenses	288	288	288	864
Operation profit	25	23	12	60
Quality programs	10	10	10	30
Extraordinary charges	0	129	0	129
Net earnings before taxes	15	(116)	2	(99)
Taxes	0	0	0	0
Net earnings	15	(116)	2	(99)

EXHIBIT 5   **Global Enterprises Consolidated Product Income Statement—1994 (in millions)**

	Best Brands	New Horizons	Precision Devices	Services	Total
Sales revenue	$628	$528	$757	$633	$2,546
Cost of goods sold	450	349	251	384	1,434
Depreciation	23	34	108	18	183
Inventory charges	1	3	1	0	5
Gross margin	154	142	397	231	924
Marketing expense	108	198	216	161	683
Research & development	15	46	75	45	181
Operating profit	31	(102)	106	25	60
Quality programs	10	10	10	0	30
Extraordinary charges	129	0	0	0	129
Net earnings before taxes	(108)	(112)	96	25	(99)
Taxes	0	$0	0	0	0
Net earnings	(108)	(112)	96	25	(99)

EXHIBIT 6   **Global Enterprises Consolidated Sources & Uses of Cash—1994 (in millions)**

	Americas	EMEA	Asia/Pacific	Total
Sources:				
Starting cash	$588	$509	$521	$1,618
Sales & receivables	895	759	812	2,466
Extraordinary cash in	0	237	0	237
Loans in	150	0	0	150
Uses:				
Production costs	458	343	449	1,250
Inventory charges	0	1	3	4
Operating expenses	288	288	288	864
Quality programs	10	10	10	30
Investment in plant	556	217	146	919
Loans out	0	150	0	150
Extraordinary cash out	0	71	0	71
Taxes	0	0	0	0
Current cash	321	425	437	1,183

EXHIBIT 7   **Global Enterprises Consolidated Balance Sheet—1994
(in millions)**

	Americas	*EMEA*	*Asia/Pacific*	*Total*
Assets:				
Cash	$321	$425	$437	$1,183
Intercompany Loans	0	150	0	150
Product inventory	5	57	134	196
Receivables	826	794	761	2,381
Plant and services fixed assets	1,695	1,075	1,285	4,055
Total assets	2,847	2,501	2,617	7,965
Liabilities:				
Bank loans	1,000	850	700	2,550
Payables	914	726	826	2,466
Intercompany loans	0	150	0	150
Stockholders' Equity:				
Common stock, par value $25.00 per share				
25 million authorized and issued	208	208	208	624
Accumulated retained earnings	725	567	883	2,175
Total liabilities	2,847	2,501	2,617	7,965

20 NESTLÉ BREAKFAST CEREAL (A AND B)

On a Monday morning in November 1989, Brewster Atwater, chairman of the board and chief executive officer of General Mills, telephoned Helmut Maucher, managing director of Nestlé, to suggest that they meet to discuss the possibility of cooperation between the two companies in the breakfast cereal business. Mr. Maucher agreed, and asked Cam Pagano, an executive vice president, to make a quick study of General Mills and prepare a briefing before the end of the week, when Mr. Atwater and his senior managers were arriving.

Mr. Pagano did better than that. The presentation could be ready in two days, he stated, because he and Bernard Casal, a senior vice president, had recently decided that Nestlé should consider taking a partner in the breakfast cereal business and had collected some information on General Mills. He would also provide samples of about 20 General Mills cereal products, so Mr. Maucher and other Nestlé executives could taste General Mills products for themselves.

Nestlé

With 1988 sales of 40 billion Swiss francs, Nestlé was the world's largest food company. Nestlé's wide range of products was sold under many well-known brand names, including Nescafé, Taster's Choice, Vittel, Maggi, Libby, Stouffer, and Findus. In 1985, Nestlé had dramatically increased its U.S. presence with the purchase of Carnation, and, in 1988, strengthened its chocolate business with the purchase of the British firm Rowntree, adding such brand names as After Eight and Kit Kat to the Nestlé

This case was prepared by Professor Peter Killing for the sole purpose of providing material for class discussion at the Richard Ivey School of Business. Certain names and other identifying information may have been disguised to protect confidentiality. It is not intended to illustrate either effective or ineffective handling of a managerial situation. Any reproduction, in any form, of the material in this case is prohibited except with the written consent of the School. Copyright © 1993, The University of Western Ontario.

EXHIBIT 1   **Nestlé Financial Summary (millions of Swiss francs)**

	1984	1986	1988
Net sales	31,141	38,050	40,600
Operating income	3,156	3,671	4,288
Net income	1,487	1,789	2,038
Total assets	24,474	25,095	33,169

Five-Year Annual Growth Rates (%)		Financial Ratios: Five-Year Average (%)	
Net sales	7.8%	Operating margin	10.2%
Net income	10.1	Net margin	4.8
Total assets	10.1	Return on:	
Employees	7.1	Assets	7.4
Earnings per share	6.5	Equity	14.8
		P/E ratio	14.9x

Source: Worldscope, *Industrial Company Profiles, Europe,* 1990 edition.

lineup. It further acquired the Italian food company Buitoni/Perugina. In 1988, the company operated 428 factories in 60 countries. Total company sales were 46 percent in Europe, 26 percent in North America, with a further 12 percent in Asia and 10 percent in Latin America and the Caribbean. A financial summary is given in Exhibit 1.

To manage its far-flung operations, Nestlé divided the world into five zones: Europe, Asia and Australia, Latin America, North America, and Africa and the Middle East. Each of Nestlé's 75 local operating companies had responsibility for profit and loss in its local market and had a full functional organization. The general manager ("market head") for each operating company reported directly to one of the five zone managers.

As shown in Exhibit 2, local companies were advised by the head office staff in Switzerland, who supplied product marketing, finance, control and administration, technical (production), and research and development services. Headquarters staff acted in an advisory role to the local operating companies. If a Swiss-based product director wanted to launch a new product in a particular market, for example, he or she would have to persuade the market head in that country to make the necessary investment.

The European Breakfast Cereal Market

After showing little growth for many years, the Western European breakfast cereal market began to expand dramatically in the 1980s. It appeared that the French, for example, who traditionally preferred coffee and croissants for breakfast, and the Germans, who preferred bread, meat, cheese, and jam, were turning to cereals. The

EXHIBIT 2   **The Nestlé Organization (partial)**

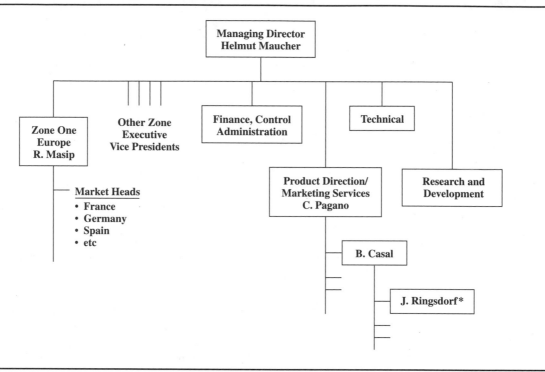

*The product managers reporting to Bernard Casal were responsible for proposing long-term product strategies, for stimulating product innovation, and proposing new products and line extensions to the zones and country managers. They also were responsible for offering marketing advice to the country organizations relating to their respective products.

French cereal market more than tripled between 1983 and 1988, while the German and Italian markets more than doubled. Even the very large and relatively mature British market showed good growth, as sales rose from £440 to £726 million between 1983 and 1988. Most forecasts predicted continuing growth rates of 15–20 percent per annum in European markets. A senior General Mills executive predicted that by the year 2000 the European market would have quadrupled to equal the size of the U.S. market.

Analysts attributed the rapid growth of the European breakfast cereal market to (1) increased demand for convenience foods as more women entered the work force, (2) health and nutritional concerns, and (3) the rise of supermarkets, which allowed a full range of cereal products to be displayed. These trends had also fueled a significant increase in the U.S. breakfast cereal market, which grew from $3.9 billion in 1983 to $6.1 billion in 1988.

The world breakfast cereal market was dominated by the Kellogg Company of Battle Creek, Michigan. Kellogg had a 41 percent share of the U.S., U.K., and German markets, and an even higher proportion of the French and Italian markets. No other firm came close to this level of market penetration. General Mills, led by its successful Cheerios brand, was second in the United States with a 23 percent share but had virtually no sales outside North America. Although Kellogg was an American company, it had moved into the major European markets early, entering France, for example, in 1952 and Germany in 1958.

Nestlé Enters the Market

Nestlé was a relative latecomer in the breakfast cereal business. Cam Pagano commented:

> We looked at the breakfast cereal market 20 years ago and decided that it was not very interesting. The only markets of any size were the United States and the United Kingdom, and there were strong competitors in each. We decided not to enter the business. With hindsight, this was a mistake.

In the early 1980s, Nestlé decided the breakfast cereal market was poised for substantial growth and that it should find a way to enter the market. The company's decision was to simultaneously use its established reputation with the mothers of young infants (built through the company's successful infant food business) and avoid going head to head with Kellogg, by focusing on the cereal market for young children. Jack Ringsdorf commented:

> Our initial decision was to go after the two- to six-year-olds, but when I came into this job I took a close look at the market and concluded that this segment was not large enough for us. As a result, we decided to broaden our target and focus on children up to the age of 14.
>
> Our first entry was Spain. This was not for any particular strategic reason, but because the manager in charge of Spain was interested in trying breakfast cereals and thought he could make a success of them. Kellogg's had only recently entered the Spanish market—via acquisition of a local company—and we were very strong there.

Nestlé began production of cereal in Spain using a new extrusion technology developed by the central technical group. The equipment was installed in an existing multiproduct plant located quite a distance from the principal Spanish markets. Jack Ringsdorf and the technicians who developed the technology were enthusiastic about the new process, as it offered good economics at low volumes, could be started at a small scale and added to as the market expanded, and did not depend on extremely high-quality raw material, the way Kellogg's process depended on very high-quality corn grits. It also, in the words of Jack Ringsdorf, "allowed us to avoid competing head to head with Kellogg on technology. Nobody makes a better, cheaper, corn flake than Kellogg, and we did not think that there was much point in trying." Nestlé's entry to the Spanish breakfast cereal market was initially successful, as the company quickly gained a market share of approximately 10 percent. But after a year or two discouragement set in, as some retailers stopped carrying the Nestlé cereals, market share declined, and the company did not come close to its initial objective of a 20 percent market share. Jack Ringsdorf commented on the disappointing performance:

> A number of important decisions were made when we entered the Spanish market. For instance, the Spanish management team decided to position our cereals head to head against Kellogg's. We had strong distribution and a well-known name, and they argued that with the Nestlé name on the box in big letters we would carry the day. They were right initially, but ultimately we did not prevail.
>
> The Spanish organization also decided to create a cereal suitable for eating with warm milk. They did some market research to support their claim that this was the way to go, but no other markets felt that this was right, and I did not like it myself. A cereal produced to be eaten with warm milk has to be extra hard so it will not turn to mush; but the result is that, if the cereal is eaten with cold milk, it will be as hard as stone.
>
> Although we later came back and reformulated the Spanish products, we never really recovered from this entry, and, in 1989, we are losing money there and sitting with an unsatisfactory market share.

The French Market

Faced with a Spanish market entry that had not lived up to expectations, Jack Ringsdorf decided that the French market, which was showing very rapid growth, would be an ideal second market to enter. However, the situation was complicated by the fact that the French market head was under pressure for profit, and his desire to add a new product line had to be tempered by his need for short-term profit. "Eventually," Ringsdorf said, "we talked him into it," and Nestlé entered the French cereal market in 1984.

Ringsdorf commented on the entry:

> We decided that the two products that we had used in Spain were not enough. We needed a wider product range. We knew that French children, in fact all non-Anglo Saxon children, like to move away from milk as they grow older, so we developed a chocolate cereal product called "Chocapik," which, when milk was added, lightly coloured the milk. Chocapik created a dynamic new segment in the market, and today we have a 42 percent share of that segment, while Kellogg's has 38 percent.
>
> Our initial problem in France was how to organize production. The French wanted their own production unit, but Nestlé was reluctant to invest. So we started producing cereal for the French at a Swiss research operation near the French border. The trouble was that the transfer price from Switzerland into France was the same as the French selling price, so there was no way that France was going to do anything other than lose money as long as they got their supply from Switzerland. We gradually began to supply France from Spain, but Spain could not produce all of the product required by the French market.

The next market that Nestlé entered was Portugal, a small but fast growing market. Here Nestlé entered the market ahead of Kellogg, and the American firm had to import its products into the country over 60 percent tariff barriers. The only local competitor was a government-owned company, which did not make a very good corn flake, and did not cater to the children's segment of the market at all. Nestlé entered the market with, in Ringsdorf's words, "a better corn flake than we had produced in Spain—and, in the absence of Kellogg, we set the standard for what a good corn flake was. We also created a children's segment and we have today a 74 percent share."

Meanwhile, back in France, Nestlé was running into problems. The quality of product coming from the Swiss pilot plant was erratic, in part because producing product for the French market was not a high priority for the researchers in the plant, and partly because small quantities of four different products were required, which called for frequent plant changeovers. In addition, a new manager took charge in France, who did not believe that breakfast cereals could be a profit maker without major changes in packaging and product, and was unenthusiastic about giving the existing line much time or attention. Ringsdorf stated:

> Typical of the problems we face is the question of the sales force. Breakfast cereal is too small a product line to have a dedicated sales force—so who is going to handle us—desserts, milks, baby food? In France we ended up being handled by the baby food sales force, and it is difficult for a sales force also working on another product to give a new product like breakfast cereal the attention it deserves—it is always easier to work with existing products. But we need someone to ensure that our products are at a level on the shelves where kids can reach them. Someone who will fight for an extra half metre of shelf space, not once but continuously.
>
> What I wanted was a small group of key account managers who would handle only breakfast cereal and would spend all their time dealing with the most important accounts, who represent about 70 percent of our volume. I could not, however, convince the French to accept this idea, even when I explained that we did not need such a sales force forever, just to get the product started.

In the spring of 1987, Ramon Masip, the new head of Nestlé's Zone 1 and the previous market head in Spain, asked Jack Ringsdorf to review for him the cereal products business. During his presentation, Ringsdorf stressed the importance of viewing breakfast cereal as pan-European business—with the same products offered in all markets, served by a single large-scale plant. Both men knew that the French were eager to expand their Rumilly plant for cereal products, and the question became one of how large an expansion to build. In making the decision, each country general manager was asked if he would commit to support a new breakfast cereal plant. "The critical answer," Jack Ringsdorf said, "was going to come from Germany. If they committed, we would go for a European-scale plant." The German answer, however, was 'you build the large plant and make product available to us, and then we will see. First we want to do a market test.' The end result was a small addition to the French plant. It was a major disappointment."

Ringsdorf added:

> The Germans went ahead with market tests in two areas of the country. In one they used the chocolate business sales force, and in the other they set up the key account sales force, as I had wanted to do. After eight months, they claimed that the tests were a failure, so I went to have a close look at them myself. I disagreed with them. For one thing, eight months is not long enough for a test. It takes even Kellogg 10 or 11 months to launch a new product here. Furthermore, we achieved a 17 percent market share with the key account sales force, and there was only one of our products that the Germans did not like. The chocolate sales force did not do as well, because they were not as interested in the product.

Bernard Casal's Review

Following the disagreement concerning the German market tests, which was in the fall of 1988, Ramon Masip asked Bernard Casal to undertake a major review of Nestlé's breakfast cereal business. By August 1989, Casal had talked to many Nestlé people in country organizations who had been involved with breakfast cereal products. He made the following observations in his presentation to Mr. Masip.

• The market was indeed attractive. Growth rates were even higher than Mr. Casal had anticipated—France was hitting 20–25 percent per year. He also thought that the German market test had been quite encouraging . . . not a failure.

• The taste and texture of Nestlé's cereal products had not been good enough to pull children or their parents away from Kellogg. Bernard Casal did not believe that Nestlé could beat Kellogg if the company stuck with its current technology. (Jack Ringsdorf agreed with this observation, and he had recommended that Nestlé see if it could license technology from General Mills, which was known to be good.)

• Nestlé's product concept had not been consistent or effective. The company had appealed to parents with a low sugar-added product, and when that did not work, went so far in appealing to children with higher-sugar products that it turned off the adults.

• The country organizations had not put a lot of money or support behind the breakfast cereal products. In fact, managers in individual markets were very outspoken against the breakfast cereal products. They particularly didn't like the packaging, which they said did not appeal to children. Either not enough consumer tests had been done, or the ones that were done were not good enough.

• Nestlé was losing money in virtually every market, for a total loss of SFr 10–15 million per year. Most of the company's financial loss was in France, where the big chains were charging exorbitant stocking fees to keep Nestlé products on the shelves. They were playing Nestlé against Quaker. Kellogg was in a commanding position and avoided such charges.

• Market share, in the 10–12 percent range in France and Spain, was not enough and not increasing.

• It would take Nestlé another five years to develop new technology, acquire the needed marketing skills, and reformulate and reintroduce its cereal product lines. Losses during this time would probably be in the range of $20–30 million per year.

Mr. Masip appeared reluctant to spend so much more time and money on a product line that had enjoyed so little success, but he asked Bernard Casal to return before the end of the year with a carefully thought out course of action.

Intervening Events

Following his August presentation, Bernard Casal set about preparing the specific recommendations that Mr. Masip requested. As he did so, however, several events intervened. The first was that Mr. Pagano acquired for Nestlé the right to sell products at 14 locations in the new Walt Disney park opening near Paris in 1991. As part of the agreement Nestlé could, with Disney's approval, use Walt Disney characters on a number of Nestlé products, including breakfast cereal. Pagano commented that he thought that the Disney characters could provide a powerful unifying force to Nestlé's breakfast cereals throughout Europe.

Jack Ringsdorf did not agree. "Jack does not think that the Disney characters are accepted by the children in many European markets," Bernard Casal explained, "and if it came down to spending an extra couple of percentage points [of sales] on advertising, rather than on a licensing fee to Disney, he would much rather spend it on advertising."

The second event that caught Bernard Casal's attention was the discussion of the breakfast cereal business at Nestlé's 1989 senior management conference. Every year Helmut Maucher and the most senior Nestlé managers met to consider long-range issues facing the company, and a few items of more immediate concern. During the discussion of the breakfast cereal business, which fell in the latter category, Mr. Maucher was very concerned to learn that Nestlé's technology was not considered by his executives to be the equal of Kellogg's, and he suggested that prompt action be taken to rectify the situation.

The third event that influenced Mr. Casal's thinking about the breakfast cereal situation was a letter which Nestlé received in the fall of 1989, from a U.S. advertising agency asking if the company would be willing to allow General Mills to use Quik, Nestlé's powdered chocolate product, in a new cereal that might be formulated for the U.S. market. The request stimulated Cam Pagano and Bernard Casal to examine the publicly available information on General Mills (some of which is reproduced in the Exhibits 3, 4, and 5), and they came to the conclusion that a partnership with General Mills might be a good solution to the difficulties that Nestlé was experiencing in the breakfast cereal business. Jack Ringsdorf did not agree.

Bernard Casal commented:

> Jack does not believe that we need to enter a partnership with General Mills or anyone else, but it looks to Cam and I like it might be a sensible way to go. General Mills has the second largest position in the breakfast cereal market in the United States, and they have the technology and marketing skills that we need. Fortunately, unlike many other companies in this business, there are very few areas in which our two companies are in direct competition.
>
> If we are right, and a partnership makes sense, what kind of partnership should it be? Our guess is that they are interested in a joint venture, probably equally owned between us, which would include all the world except North America. We do not think that they are interested in a licensing agreement.

EXHIBIT 3   Excerpts from "Calling Betty Crocker," in *Forbes*, August 1988

Recent results from General Mills, Inc., the $5.2 billion (sales) Minneapolis restaurant and food company, have been nothing short of astonishing.

In the year ended in May, profits rose 30 percent, to $283.1 million, or $3.25 a share, on a 10 percent sales gain. Return on equity frothed above 41 percent, up 10 points or more above returns of most other food companies. Unit sales of packaged foods, the source of 82 percent of profits, rose 4 percent, double the industry rate. Says H. Brewster Atwater, Jr., 57, chairman and chief executive officer, proudly: "I think you'd have to look at us and say we've done pretty damn well."

Fair enough. But it won't last, and Atwater himself is the first to say so. Repenting 30 years of wandering off into fields as diverse as chemicals, luggage, and two-man submarines, General Mills has sold nearly everything to settle back into the familiar—high-margin mixes and convenience foods, and their restaurant equivalents, for the masses. The company makes Big G brand cereals like Cheerios, Wheaties, and Count Chocula; Betty Crocker desserts; Yoplait yogurt; Gorton's seafood; and snack foods, such as Bugles and Fruit Roll-Ups. Its restaurant group runs Red Lobster, the 410-unit fish house; York's, a weak steak house chain that may be sold or closed; and the Olive Garden, a chain of 100 Italian-style eateries.

Good as the returns on its packaged foods are right now, they are coming in the lowest-growth part of the supermarket. The real action is in "value-added" and fresh groceries—the stuff of bakeries and deli counters. And General Mills is now so big that little less than a string of new product blockbusters would sustain current levels of profitability. This, in a ferociously competitive business, where even one hot new item is something to brag about.

That's why Atwater himself is forecasting sharply lower growth rates in earnings—down to as low as 6 percent annually—and returns on equity in the mid-30s this fiscal year.

EXHIBIT 4   Excerpts from "Big G is Growing Fat on Oat Cuisine," in *Business Week*, September 18, 1989

Kellogg isn't used to playing second banana to anyone. It has dominated the competition in ready-to-eat cereal since W. K. Kellogg founded the company in 1906. But while Kellogg's slice of the $6.6 billion market based on revenues totals about 40 percent, nearly the same as a decade ago, Big G's share has risen steadily from 21 percent in 1979 to almost 27 percent today. Especially impressive are recent figures showing General Mills taking share from Kellogg—not just trouncing weaker rivals such as Ralston-Purina, Nabisco, and General Foods' Post, as it has done in the past.

*****

Health Kick.   Much of Big G's success stems from oat bran. About two years ago, the media were abuzz with reports that eating oat bran could lower blood cholesterol and reduce the risk of heart trouble. Because 40 percent of Big G's cereals, by volume, are made from oats, General Mills benefited more than Kellogg from the resulting craze. Cheerios alone has gained a stunning 3.1 percentage points in market share in just 12 months, from 6.8 to 9.9 percent. Including the Honey Nut and New Apple Cinnamon varieties, oat-rich Cheerios is now the most popular cereal in America, displacing Kellogg's Frosted Flakes.

*****

Full Bellies.   Don't get the idea that Kellogg is starving—the breakfast boom is healthy for the industry, which is a near-oligopoly: Revenues from ready-to-eat cereal are growing 11 percent a year, price hikes are frequent, and gross margins run about 50 percent. Kellogg earned $480.4 million on $4.4 billion in revenues last year.

EXHIBIT 5   General Mills Financial Results (year end May 31) ($ millions)

	1987	*1988**	*1989**
Sales			
Cereal	$1,083.0	$1,140.0	$1,360.0
Other food	2,366.9	2,537.5	2,638.7
Restaurants	1,244.0	1,312.1	1,622.0
Total	$4,693.9	$4,989.6	$5,620.7
Operating Income			
Cereal	$230.0	$230.0	$266.0
Other food	139.5	191.2	186.4
Restaurants	92.5	104.0	127.7
Total	$462.0	$525.2	$580.1
Operating Margins			
Cereal	21.2%	20.2%	19.6%
Other food	5.9	7.5	7.1
Restaurants	7.4	7.9	7.9
Total company	9.8%	10.5%	10.3%

*Restated to exclude Disposals.

Sources: Goldman Sachs; Investment Research; *Packaged Food Quarterly.*

21   WARNER-LAMBERT COMPANY

On August 1, 1991, Melvin Goodes became chairman and chief executive officer of Warner-Lambert Company (WL). In 1990, WL enjoyed the most successful year in its history. Worldwide sales rose 12 percent to $4.7 billion, earnings per share increased 18 percent, and shares in WL stock appreciated by 17 percent. Each of WL's three core businesses—ethical pharmaceuticals, nonprescription health care products, and confectionery—generated increased sales. In international markets, WL continued to make new inroads.

Despite the success of recent years, Goodes was convinced that trouble was looming at WL. In March, the U.S. Food and Drug Administration (FDA) turned down the company's approval application for the Alzheimer's drug *Cognex*. WL had hoped that *Cognex* would be its new blockbuster drug. With the patent expiring on *Lopid,* WL's largest selling drug, in early 1993, the *Cognex* decision was a major blow. At the same time, the growth of private label health care products in the United States was slowing the expansion of powerful brands such as *Listerine* mouthwash and *Schick* razors. Without a major new drug and with domestic sales slowing, restructuring at WL looked unavoidable. Of increasing priority was the need to restructure WL's international operations. Although a proposal to globalize the company had been shelved by the board in 1989, Goodes knew that he could no longer afford to wait. Given the changing configuration of global markets and pressures for increased operating efficiencies, globalization looked like a necessity for WL.

This case was written by Professor Andrew Inkpen with research assistance from Chris Hormann and with assistance from Professor John Zerio, for the sole purpose of providing material for class discussion. It is not intended to illustrate either effective or ineffective handling of a managerial situation. Any reproduction, in any form, of the material in this case is prohibited unless permission is obtained from the copyright holder. Copyright © 1996, Thunderbird–The American Graduate School of International Management.

Product names in italics are registered trademarks of Warner-Lambert Company, its affiliates or licensors.

Warner-Lambert Background

WL's origins can be traced to 1856 when William Warner opened a drugstore in Philadelphia. After 30 years of experimenting with the formulation of pharmaceutical products, Warner closed his retail store and began a drug manufacturing business.

William Warner & Co. was acquired in 1908 by Henry and Gustavus Pfeiffer. Gustavus later wrote that "we changed thinking locally to thinking nationally." For the next 30 years the company made many acquisitions and by 1939, had 21 marketing affiliates outside the United States and several international manufacturing plants. The largest acquisition was Richard Hudnut Company, a cosmetics business, which was eventually sold in 1979.

During the 1950s and 1960s, the company continued to make acquisitions, both in the United States and overseas. In 1952, the company, now known as Warner-Hudnut, acquired Chilcott Laboratories, a pharmaceutical company founded in 1874. In 1955, with sales at $100 million, Warner-Hudnut merged with the Lambert Company to form the Warner-Lambert Pharmaceutical Company. The Lambert Company's largest-selling product was *Listerine* mouthwash, a product developed in 1879.

In 1962, American Chicle was acquired. American Chicle was formed in 1899 with the consolidation of three major chewing gum producers. The *Halls* cough tablets brand was acquired in 1964. In 1970, Schick wet-shave products were acquired. Also in 1970, WL merged with the pharmaceutical firm Parke, Davis, & Company *(Parke-Davis). Parke-Davis* was founded in 1866 in Detroit. In the 1870s, *Parke-Davis* collaborated with the inventor of a machine to make empty capsules for medications. This established the forerunner of WL's Capsugel division, the world's largest producer of gelatin capsules. In 1901, *Parke-Davis* introduced the first systematic method of clinical testing for new drugs. In 1938, *Parke-Davis* introduced the drug *Dilantin* for the treatment of epilepsy, and in 1946 began marketing *Benadryl,* the first antihistamine in the United States. In 1949, *Chloromycetin,* the first broad-spectrum antibiotic, was introduced.

The 1980s was a period of restructuring for WL. During the decade, the company divested more than 40 businesses, including medical instruments, eyeglasses, sunglasses, bakery products, specialty hospital products, and medical diagnostics. The divested businesses accounted for $1.5 billion in annual sales but almost no profit. In 1991, WL had operations in 130 countries and of its 34,000 employees (down from 45,000 in 1981), nearly 70 percent worked outside the United States. WL had 10 manufacturing plants in the United States and Puerto Rico and 70 international plants in 43 countries. Over the previous five years, WL's earnings grew 15 to 20 percent annually. In 1990, sales growth occurred in both the U.S. and international markets and in all worldwide business segments. About 52 percent of company sales were in the United States. Exhibits 1 and 2 provide summary financial information.

Exhibit 1   Warner-Lambert Financial Information

	1990	1989	1988	1987	1986
	(Dollars in millions, except per share amounts)				
Results for Year					
Net Sales	$4,687	$4,196	$3,908	$3,441	$3,064
Cost of Goods Sold	1,515	1,383	1,352	1,170	1,053
Research and Development Expense	379	309	259	232	202
Interest Expense	69	56	68	61	67
Income before Income Taxes	681	592	538	493	446[**]
Net Income	485	413	340	296	309[**]
Net Income per Common Share	$ 3.61	$ 3.05	$ 2.50	$ 2.08	$ 2.09[**]
Year-End Financial Position					
Current Assets	$1,559	$1,366	$1,265	$1,253	$1,510
Current Liabilities	1,101	1,031	1,025	974	970
Working Capital	458	335	240	279	540
Property, Plant, and Equipment	1,301	1,130	1,053	960	819
Total Assets	3,261	2,860	2,703	2,476	2,516
Long-Term Debt	307	303	318	294	342
Total Debt	537	506	512	444	585
Stockholders' Equity	$1,402	$1,130	$ 999	$ 874	$ 907
Common Stock Information					
Average Number of Common Shares Outstanding (in millions)[*]	134.3	135.3	136.1	142.5	148.0
Common Stock Price per Share:[*]					
High	$70⅜	$59⅜	$39¾	$43¾	$31⁹⁄₁₆
Low	49⅝	37¼	29¹⁵⁄₁₆	24⅛	22½
Book Value per Common Share[*]	10.44	8.38	7.36	6.37	6.32
Cash Dividends Paid	204	173	147	127	118
Cash Dividends per Common Share[*]	$1.52	$1.28	$1.08	$.89	$.80
Other Data					
Capital Expenditures	$240	$218	$190	$174	$138
Depreciation and Amortization	$120	$105	$ 96	$ 79	$ 68
Number of Employees (in thousands)	34	33	33	34	31

[*]Amounts prior to 1990 were restated to reflect a two-for-one stock split effected in May 1990.

[**]Includes a net nonrecurring credit of $8 million pretax (after-tax $48 million or $0.32 per share) in 1986.

Source: Warner-Lambert 1990 Annual Report.

Warner-Lambert Business Segments

In 1990, WL had three core business segments: ethical pharmaceuticals, nonprescription health care products commonly referred to as over-the-counter (OTC), and confectionery products. Beyond these segments, WL had several other product sectors: empty gelatin capsules for the pharmaceutical and vitamin industries, wet shave products, and home aquarium products. Exhibit 3 shows sales by region and

EXHIBIT 2   Warner-Lambert Financial Information by Business Segment

	Net Sales (1)			Operating Profit			Research and Development Expense		
	1990	*1989*	*1988*	*1990*	*1989*	*1988*	*1990*	*1989*	*1988*
(Millions of dollars)									
Health Care:									
Ethical Products	$1,555	$1,324	$1,213	$560	$465	$420	$(299)	$(240)	$(204)
Nonprescription									
Products (OTC)	1,526	1,370	1,296	367	311	305	(38)	(35)	(27)
Total Health Care	3,081	2,694	2,509	927	776	725	(337)	(275)	(231)
Confectionery	1,054	1,003	918	208	195	187	(17)	(15)	(13)
Other Products	552	499	481	119	101	92	(25)	(19)	(15)
Research and									
Development Expense				(379)	(309)	(259)	$(379)	$(309)	$(259)
Net Sales and									
Operating Profit	$4,687	$4,196	$3,908	875	763	745			
Interest Expense				(69)	(56)	(68)			
Corporate Expense (2)				(125)	(115)	(139)			
Income Before									
Income Taxes				$681	$592	$538			

	Identifiable Assets			Depreciation and Amortization			Capital Expenditures		
	1990	*1989*	*1988*	*1990*	*1989*	*1988*	*1990*	*1989*	*1988*
Health Care:									
Ethical Products	$1,063	$ 892	$ 916	$ 43	$ 39	$36	$ 88	$ 71	$ 72
Nonprescription									
Products (OTC)	619	513	489	20	16	15	49	37	37
Total Health Care	1,682	1,405	1,405	63	55	51	137	108	109
Confectionery	564	490	459	23	21	20	44	33	33
Other Products	442	406	387	24	20	19	41	42	40
Subtotal	2,688	2,301	2,251	110	96	90	222	183	182
Corporate	573	559	452	10	9	6	18	35	8
Total	$3,261	$2,860	$2,703	$120	$105	$96	$240	$218	$190

Source: Warner-Lambert 1990 Annual Report.

business segment. Exhibit 4 shows a description of the segments and the leading brands in each segment.

The Ethical Pharmaceutical Industry

The ethical pharmaceutical industry involved the production and marketing of medicines that could be obtained only by prescription from a medical practitioner. Seven markets (United States, Japan, Canada, Germany, United Kingdom, France, and Italy) accounted for about 75 percent of the world market, with the largest single

EXHIBIT 3   Warner-Lambert Financial Information by Geographic Segment ($000,000)

	Ethical Pharmaceuticals	Consumer Health Care	Confectionery
United States	$ 871	$1,066	$ 507
Canada	60	95	107
Mexico	11	49	88
Latin America (excluding Mexico)	47	100	127
Japan	80	122	80
Asia/Australia (excluding Japan)	66	115	16
Europe/Middle East/Africa	582	369	129
Total	$1,717	$1,916	$1,054

Note: The figures in Exhibits 2 and 3 show different totals for the ethical pharmaceutical and consumer health care segments. In 1991, WL redefined its business segments. The Capsugel business ($162 million in sales) was reclassified to the Pharmaceutical segment. The wet shave and *Tetra* businesses ($390 million in sales) were reclassified to the Consumer Health Care segment.

market, the United States, accounting for about 30 percent of the total. The pharmaceutical industry was very fragmented, with no single firm holding more than a 4 percent share of the market. The five largest firms—Merck (U.S.), Bristol-Myers Squibb (U.S.), Glaxo (U.K.), SmithKline Beecham (U.K.), and Hoechst (Germany)—accounted for less than 15 percent of world market share.

The pharmaceutical industry was also highly profitable. Between 1986 and 1989, the industry ranked first in the United States on both ROS and ROI. With new medical advances on the horizon and an aging population in the developed countries, the industry was expected to continue growing steadily. However, significant challenges were facing the drug companies. The cost and time to develop new drugs had grown substantially. The drug development cycle from synthesis to regulatory approval in the United States was 10 to 12 years. The average development cost per drug was $230 million (up from $125 million in 1987), with various phases of testing and clinical trials accounting for about 75 percent of the cost.

There was significant risk associated with pharmaceutical R&D. It was estimated that for every 10,000 compounds discovered, 10 entered clinical trials and only one was developed into a marketable product. Of those brought to market, only about 20 percent generated the necessary sales to earn a positive return on R&D expenditures. In 1990, the FDA approved just 23 new drugs, 15 of which were already approved in Europe. Nevertheless, R&D was the lifeblood of the industry, as explained by a senior WL manager:

> Product renewal is critical. Firms must continue to generate a stream of new products. These need not be blockbusters. The key is new products. Eventually, each of these products will become a generic [unbranded] product so in any given year, there must be a certain percentage of new products.

EXHIBIT 4   Warner-Lambert Core Businesses and Primary Products

---

Business Segment	*Leading Brands*

1. Ethical Pharmaceutical Products (Parke-Davis)
- Brand name pharmaceuticals and biologicals, including analgesics, anesthetics, anti-inflammatory agents, antihistamines, anticonvulsants, influenza vaccines, cardiovascular products, lipid regulators, oral contraceptives, psychotherapeutic products

  Dilantin (epilepsy), *Dilzem* (angina and hypertension), *Lopid* (lipid regulating), *Accupril* (hypertension), *Leostrin* (contraceptive), *Ponstan* (analgesic)

- Generic pharmaceuticals (Warner Chilcott), manufacturer of generic pharmaceutical products

2. Nonprescription Health Care (OTC)
- Over-the-counter pharmaceuticals marketed under the *Parke-Davis* name

  Benadryl (antihistamine), *Benylin* (cough syrup), *Sinutab* (sinus medication), *Anusol* (hemorrhoid treatment)

- Other consumer health care products

  Listerine (mouthwash), *Efferdent* (denture cleanser), *Lubriderm* (skin lotion), *Rolaids* (antacid), *Halls* (cough drop)

3. Confectionery (Gums and Mints)
- Chewing gum, breath mints, sugarless gum, bubble gum, chocolate candy

  Chiclets, Dentyne (chewing gum), *Certs, Clorets* (breath mints and chewing gum), *Trident* (sugarless gum), *Bubblicious* (bubble gum), *Junior Mints* (chocolate candy)

4. Other Products
- Empty hard-gelatin capsules for use in pharmaceutical manufacturing (used by Warner-Lambert and other companies)

  Capsugel

- Wet shave products

  Schick

- Home aquarium products

  Tetra

If a firm did come up with a blockbuster drug, the rewards were enormous. New drugs sold at wholesale prices for three to six times their cost. Zantac™, an ulcer drug sold by Glaxo, had worldwide sales of $2.4 billion in 1990. This was Glaxo's only product in the top 200 best-selling prescription drugs. Tagamet™, a competing ulcer drug produced by SmithKline Beecham, had 1990 sales of $1.2 billion.

Two other challenges faced the drug companies. Spiraling health care costs in the major markets were putting increased pressure on the drug companies to hold down their prices. The growing use of price controls and restricted reimbursement schemes in international markets was reducing the flexibility of the drug companies to recoup R&D investments.

Finally, there was competition from generic drugs once a patent expired. Legislation passed in the United States in 1984 made it very easy for generic drugs to enter the market after the patent on the original drug expired. In the United States, 50 percent decreases in sales were not uncommon in the first year after a patent expired. In Europe, the degree of generic erosion was not as dramatic because once a branded drug was on a list of officially sanctioned drugs eligible for state reimbursement, a long lifespan for the drug was reasonably certain.

Although the chemical compounds of the major drugs were the same around the world, the pharmaceutical industry structure varied tremendously from country to country. In Europe, each of the 12 EC member states had different regulations for registering, pricing, and marketing drugs. Government health care systems paid for a majority of the consumer cost of drugs and the prices of drugs were fixed in negotiations between the drug companies and the government. The result was different prices in different countries and a growing problem with parallel imports. Consumers in France and Spain paid about 72 percent of the EC average and in Ireland and the Netherlands, prices were about 130 percent of the average. Most European governments had the legal authority to force the transfer of a drug patent from one firm to another, in the event that the firm with the patent was unwilling to manufacture the drug.

There were also national differences in the type and amount of drugs consumed. In France, the consumption of drugs was the highest per capita in the world. In Japan, physicians made most of their income by dispensing drugs. Moreover, the Japanese government allowed high prices for breakthrough drugs in order to stimulate medical innovation. As well, many of the drugs used in Japan were unique to that market. For example, several best-selling Japanese drugs dilated blood vessels in the brain, on the unproven theory that this reversed senility. In other parts of the world, the lack of controls over intellectual property made it very difficult for drug companies to operate.

WL's Pharmaceutical Business   WL's ethical pharmaceutical line was marketed primarily under the *Parke-Davis* name. Included in the pharmaceutical sector was Warner-Chilcott, a manufacturer of generic prescription drugs primarily for the United States. Sales of WL ethical products were $1.6 billion in 1990, a 17 percent increase over the previous year. WL ranked 17th among the world's leading drug firms by turnover.

WL's largest selling drug, with sales of more than $480 million expected in 1991, was *Lopid,* a cholesterol reducing drug. *Dilantin,* an antiepileptic drug, had sales of $145 million and was a worldwide leader in its category. Other leading drugs were *Loestrin,* a contraceptive, and *Accupril,* a cardiovascular drug. Although the FDA postponed approval of *Cognex* by asking for more data, WL continued to have high expectations for the product and clinical testing continued.

The firm's drug discovery program was focused on two areas: cardiovascular diseases, such as hypertension and congestive heart failure, and disorders of the central nervous system. In recent years, WL had made a major effort to strengthen its pharmaceutical R&D. Over the past five years, the number of scientists had increased 60 percent to 2,600 and 1991 R&D spending for pharmaceuticals was expected to be close to $350 million, an increase of 12 percent over 1990. These efforts were beginning to pay off: WL had several new pharmaceutical products awaiting U.S. FDA approval.

OTC Industry

The OTC health care industry was structured very differently than the ethical drugs industry. With ethical drugs, there was a unique relationship between consumer and decision maker: Consumers paid for the drugs but physicians made the buying decisions. As a result, the marketing of ethical pharmaceuticals was directed at prescribing physicians, who were not particularly concerned about prices. With OTC products, the consumer made the buying decision, although often based on physician or pharmacist advice. To compete successfully with OTC products, significant investments in consumer marketing and distribution were required. Some of the largest drug companies, such as Glaxo, had a corporate policy of staying out of the OTC market on the grounds that selling directly to consumers was very different than the medically oriented marketing of ethical drugs.

There were two broad classes of OTC health care products: (1) drugs that were formerly prescription drugs, and (2) health care products developed for the nonprescription market, such as toothpaste, mouthwash, and skin care products. Moving a prescription drug to the OTC market required regulatory approval in most countries. The shift also required marketing expenditures of as much as $30 million a year and extensive consultation with physicians and pharmacists. Even though a prescription was not required, many OTC drugs would not succeed without continued physician recommendations, particularly in highly controlled retail environments like Germany and Japan. Pharmacists' recommendations were also important. When WL switched the antihistamine *Benadryl* to the OTC market in 1985 after 40 years as a prescription drug, the company devised an extensive program for pharmacists based on product samples and promotional literature.

Between 1982 and 1990, global demand for OTC drugs grew at about 7 percent annually and was expected to remain strong, particularly with increased pressure to reduce health care costs. In the developing nations, shortages of more expensive prescription products made OTC drugs very popular. Among the major types of OTC products were analgesics; antacids; cough, cold, and sinus medicines; skin preparations; and vitamins.

The OTC drug industry was even more fragmented than the ethical pharmaceutical industry, particularly in Europe. According to one report, there were 15,000 registered brands in the European OTC market but only 10 could be purchased in seven or more countries.[1] For example, the Vicks-Sinex™ cold remedy could be purchased in British supermarkets; in Germany it was available OTC but only in pharmacies; and in France it was available only by prescription. In Latin American countries where the state paid for drugs, there was little distinction between ethical pharmaceuticals and OTC drugs. In the United States, nonprescription products could be sold in any retail channel. In Canada, the United Kingdom, and Germany, some nonprescription drugs could be sold only in pharmacies.

WL's OTC Business   Reflecting the increasing global acceptance of nonprescription health care products, WL's OTC sales increased 11 percent in 1990 to $1.5 billion.

---

[1]*The Financial Times,* July 23, 1991, Survey, p. 1.

The largest product lines were *Halls* cough tablets with sales of $320 million and *Listerine* mouthwash with sales of $280 million. Other leading brands included *Rolaids* antacid (number one brand in the United States), *Benadryl* antihistamine (the number one OTC allergy product in the United States), *Lubriderm* skin lotion (number three brand in the United States), and *Efferdent* dental products.

During 1991, WL planned more than 20 new OTC product introductions in non-U.S. markets. It was often necessary to adapt products to local markets to account for differences in product usage and government regulations. For example, there were more than 50 different formulations of *Halls* around the world. *Halls* was considered a cough tablet in temperate climate areas and a confection in tropical areas. In Thailand, *Halls* had a much higher amount of menthol than in most countries because *Halls* was sold as a cooling sweet. In some of the Asian and Latin American countries, a large volume of *Halls* was sold by the individual tablet, as opposed to the package. *Benylin* cough medicine also had more than 50 different formulations, leading to the question raised by a WL manager: "There are not 50 different kinds of coughs, why do we need 50 different formulations?"

The Confectionery Industry

The confectionery industry consisted of four main segments: chocolate products (approximately 53 percent of the industry), nonchocolate products such as chewing gum (23 percent), hard candy (18 percent), and breath mints (6 percent). WL competed primarily in the chewing gum and breath mint segments.

The confectionery industry was highly concentrated on a global basis with the chewing gum segment the most concentrated. Although WL's American Chicle Group had once been the leading firm, the largest chewing gum company in 1991 was William Wrigley Jr. Co. (Wrigley) with $1.1 billion in annual sales in more than 100 countries. Wrigley's strategy had been focused and consistent for many years— sticks of gum sold at low prices. Wrigley's three main brands, Spearmint™, Doublemint™, and Juiceyfruit™, were ubiquitous around the world. In the United States, Wrigley had the largest market share (48 percent), followed by WL (95 percent) and RJR/Nabisco's Beechnut™ brands. Canada was the only English-speaking country in the world where Wrigley products did not have a leading market share. WL had about 55 percent of the Canadian gum market, compared with Wrigley's 38 percent. A major trend in the food market in recent years had been toward healthy eating. This trend was reflected in the shift toward sugarless gum. In the United States, sugarless accounted for 35 percent of the chewing gum market and in Canada, it was 55 percent, the highest percentage in the world.

Although most breath mints were sugared confections, the breath mint category was referred to as candy plus because the mints contained additional breath freshening ingredients. In this segment, RJR/Nabisco was the largest firm, with brands sold by the Lifesavers™ division holding about 40 percent of U.S. market share. WL brands held about 36 percent of the market. Tic Tac™, a brand produced by the Italian company Ferrero, had a 12 percent share of the U.S. market. Several other brands with minimal U.S. sales were strong in international markets, such as Fisherman's

Friend™, a UK product. In other countries such as Germany, Argentina, and Colombia, there were strong local competitors.

Confectionery companies operated on the premise that the majority of sales were by impulse. There were several factors critical to success in this type of market: display and distribution, superb value, and excellent advertising. The most important factor, according to WL confectionery managers, was display and distribution. Thus, there was a strong emphasis on packaging, on developing a wide distribution base, and on in-store display. In the United States, Germany, and France, confectionery distribution to the consumer was dominated by large, efficient retailers (such as Wal-Mart in the United States). In contrast, in Italy, Spain, and Greece, South and Southeast Asia, and Latin America, the retail environment was very fragmented with many kiosks and mom-and-pop stores. A strong retail sales force was essential in these areas.

The major challenge faced by firms producing gums and mints was the threat of new market entrants. Traditionally, gums and mints generated higher profit margins than other confectionery segments. As a result, other firms in the candy industry, as well as snack food companies such as PepsiCo, were making an effort to penetrate the gum and mint markets. In many of the developing countries and in particular Latin America, the imitation of best-selling brands by local firms was a regular occurrence.

WL's Confectionery Business   Although historically focused on chewing gum and breath mints, WL had begun seeking niche opportunities in other confectionery segments in recent years. Sales of WL confectionery products increased 5 percent to $1.1 billion in 1990. The leading brands were *Trident* (sales of $225 million and the world's leading brand of sugarless gum) and *Clorets* gums and breath mints ($130 million). Other major brands were *Adams* brand *Chiclets* (candy coated chewing gum), *Certs* (breath mints), and *Bubblicious* (chewing gum). *Trident* was the product WL would likely lead with in a new market entry. Other brands had regional strengths. *Chiclets* was a major brand in Latin America and French Canada but a minor U.S. brand. The strongest market for *Clorets* was Southeast Asia.

Overall, WL's confectionery business had its largest market shares in the United States, Canada, Mexico, and other countries of Latin America. In Europe, the confectionery business was strongest in Greece, Portugal, Spain, and Italy. The company also had a strong presence in Japan and Southeast Asia. WL's customer mix varied from region to region. In the United States and Canada, customers tended to be adults using products with functional uses, such as breath mints and sugarless gum. In Latin America, where the emphasis was on fun products marketed mainly to young people, *Chiclets, Bubblicious,* and *Bubbaloo* were leading brands.

Global product expansion had been a key objective of recent years. Outside the United States, the *Clorets* brand had become the largest selling confection product. *Clorets* was introduced in the United Kingdom and Portugal in 1990 and in France in 1991. The company had high expectations that *Trident* sugarless gum could be built into a major global brand by capitalizing on concerns for health and fitness. In China, where WL introduced its first three confectionery products in 1991, a new confectionery plant was under construction. Over the previous several years, an aggressive marketing effort in Japan had established a solid market position in chewing gum. To

EXHIBIT 5   Warner-Lambert Organization

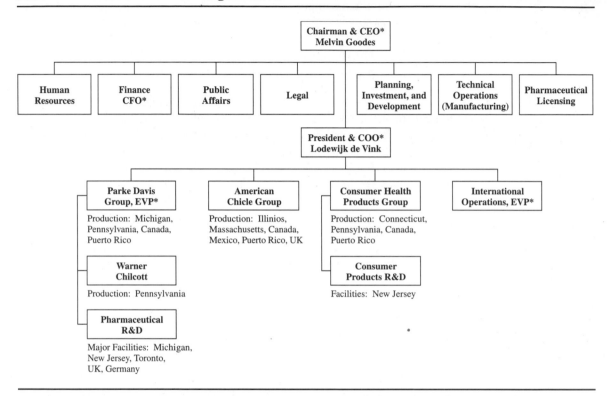

*Member, Office of the Chairman.

increase penetration into the Italian market, a joint venture was formed in 1990. Alivar, the new company, became Italy's second largest nonchocolate confectionery company.

Organizational Structure

WL was organized into four major divisions reporting to the president and COO, Lodewijk de Vink: *Parke-Davis* Group, American Chicle Group, Consumer Health Products Group, and International Operations. All four groups had their headquarters in Morris Plains, New Jersey. See Exhibit 5 for an organization chart and Exhibit 6 for short biographies of the five members of WL's Office of the Chairman.

The *Parke-Davis* Group included the U.S. pharmaceuticals operations, the Warner-Chilcott generics business, and the Pharmaceutical Research Division. The Research Division, based in Ann Arbor, Michigan, operated facilities in Michigan, Canada, the United Kingdom, and Germany. *Parke-Davis* manufactured in three plants in the United States, one in Canada, and two in Puerto Rico. Warner-Chilcott

---

EXHIBIT 6   Members of the Warner-Lambert Office of the Chairman

Melvin R. Goodes was born in Hamilton, Ontario, Canada, and received an MBA from the University of Chicago. After several years at the Ford Motor Company of Canada, he joined WL in 1964 as a new product development manager in confectionery. After various senior international positions, including regional director of European confectionery operations and president of WL Mexico, he was appointed president of the consumer product division in 1979. In 1985, he became WL president, COO and a director of the company and in 1991, chairman and CEO.

Lodewijk J. R. de Vink was a native of Amsterdam, the Netherlands. After completing an MBA at American University, he joined Schering-Plough Corporation in 1969. In 1981, he was appointed vice president of Schering Laboratories and in 1986, president of Schering International. In 1988, he joined WL as vice president, international operations. In 1991, he was appointed president and COO and elected to the board of directors.

Joseph E. Smith was born in Buffalo and earned an MBA from the Wharton School. He worked for several years with International Multifoods and Ross Laboratories before joining Johnson & Johnson in 1965. In 1986, he joined the Rorer Group and held several senior management positions, including executive vice president. He joined WL in 1989 as a vice president and president of the Pharmaceutical Sector and in 1991, became executive vice president and president, *Parke-Davis* Group.

John Walsh, a native of Worcester, Massachusetts, earned an MBA from Seton Hall University. He joined WL as a cost analyst in corporate accounting in 1967. In 1978, he became controller of the American Chicle Division and in 1980, vice president, finance, Consumer Products Group. In 1989, he became president of the Canada/Latin America Group and in 1991, executive vice president of WL and president, international operations.

Robert J. Dircks was born in New York and received an MBA from the City University of New York. He joined WL in 1951 as an accountant in the Nepera Chemical Company. In 1962, he joined the Consumer Products Group as an accounting supervisor. In 1974, he became vice president, finance, *Parke-Davis* Group. In 1986, he was appointed executive vice president and CFO.

---

production came from a plant in the United States. *Parke-Davis* was responsible for U.S. pharmaceutical regulatory affairs.

The American Chicle Group was responsible for the U.S. confectionery business. American Chicle manufactured in two U.S. plants and sourced from plants in Canada, Mexico, Puerto Rico, and the United Kingdom.

The Consumer Health Products Group was responsible for U.S. consumer health care and shaving products. Consumer health care included the OTC pharmaceuticals marketed under the *Parke-Davis* name plus other OTC products such as *Listerine* and *Lubriderm*. Products were manufactured in two U.S. locations, Canada, and Puerto Rico. This group managed a research and development division that performed research for both the Consumer Health Products and American Chicle Groups. The division also performed a significant amount of research for WL's international affiliates.

International Operations was responsible for the manufacture and marketing of WL's pharmaceutical and consumer products outside the United States. Capsugel and *Tetra,* WL's two businesses that were run on a global basis, reported to the International Operations Group.

EXHIBIT 7   Warner-Lambert International Organizations[1]

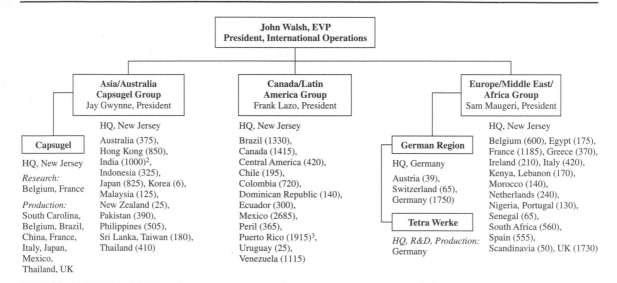

[1]The numbers after each affiliate show the number of employees in the affiliate.

[2]The affiliate in India was a joint venture in which WL had a 40 percent interest.

[3]The Puerto Rico operation was primarily a manufacturing center. The actual affiliate had about 50 employyees.

International Operations

International Operations was divided into three operating groups responsible for 45 operating affiliates: Asia/Australia/Capsugel Group, Canada/Latin America Group, and Europe/Middle East/Africa Group. Exhibit 7 shows the countries in which each of the groups had affiliates and the number of employees in each affiliate. The general manager, or country manager, for each affiliate reported directly to one of the geographic group presidents, who in turn reported to the head of International Operations. Below the geographic group presidents were staff managers responsible for the lines of business, such as the Europe/Middle East/Africa head of pharmaceuticals. Geographic group presidents also had staff functions, like sales and human resources, reporting to them.

In some of the regions, multiple affiliates were grouped together for management and reporting purposes under one general manager. For example, the German general manager was responsible for the Germany, Austria, and Switzerland affiliates. Other grouped affiliates included United Kingdom and Ireland; France, Belgium, and Netherlands; Spain and Portugal; and Italy and Greece.

Across all three of WL's main business segments. acquisitions of confectionery or pharmaceutical firms had accounted for much of WL's international growth. As a result, most of the international affiliates were dominated by either a pharmaceutical or confectionery business. The result was an inconsistent mix of market penetration around the world. For example, the German affiliate had 95 percent of its sales in ethical pharmaceuticals, 5 percent in OTC products, and no confectionery business. In Switzerland, WL was a market leader in several confectionery lines. In the affiliates in France, Italy, and the United Kingdom, pharmaceuticals were dominant but there was also a reasonably strong confectionery presence. In Spain, Portugal, and Greece, confectionery was the primary sector. In Japan, the largest business was *Schick,* with about 65 percent of the wet shave market, by far the highest share in the various countries where Schick was marketed. The affiliate in Canada was unique in that the pharmaceutical, confectionery, and consumer health care businesses were all mature, viable businesses with strong managers in each sector. In that sense, the Canadian unit was very similar to WL's operations in the United States.

Each country manager managed a full functional organization (marketing, finance, human resources, etc.) and was responsible for all WL products marketed in their country. In most of the affiliates, the country manager's background corresponded with the dominant business sector of the affiliate. According to a senior WL manager:

> In our affiliates we have only a handful of country managers capable of managing a diverse business. Very few managers can move from pharmaceuticals to consumer products or vice versa. In one Latin American affiliate, we had a business dominated by confection products. We put in a manager with a pharmaceutical background and the business failed. In Germany, we have tried several times to expand the consumer business and failed each time. In Australia, we have problems with confectionery. Japan is one of the few exceptions. We had a country manager with a pharmaceutical background who successfully grew a confectionery business.

Because the affiliates tended to be dominated by managers from either the confectionery or pharmaceutical side of the business, managers involved in the non-dominant businesses struggled to get resources. As a WL manager commented:

> If, for example, you are a confectionery manager in a country with a small confectionery business, you're treated like the poor stepchild. Because these managers are not given the resources to grow their businesses, there is a tremendous amount of frustration. It is very hard to retain good managers because they are not given the opportunity or the resources to do the things you have to do to be successful.

To illustrate international operations, brief descriptions of the Germany and Brazil affiliates are provided.

Germany

WL's operations in Germany, Austria, and Switzerland were managed from Gödecke, A.G., WL's German affiliate. Gödecke, a pharmaceutical firm founded in 1866, was acquired by WL in 1928. In 1977, *Parke-Davis's* German affiliate was merged with Gödecke. Prior to this, *Parke-Davis* and Gödecke were run as separate organizations.

Within Germany, the Gödecke name was far more well-known than WL. Employees considered themselves Gödecke employees and the Gödecke name, along with Parke-Davis, was prominent in promotional literature and corporate communications. In 1991, Gödecke had about 1,400 employees, with 230 working in pharmaceutical R&D. Gödecke's business was primarily in ethical pharmaceuticals. There was one sales force for OTC and ethical products because in Germany, the OTC market was very small. Because prescription drugs were reimbursable, Germans tended to use drugs that were prescribed by their doctors, even if the drug was available as an OTC product.

Gödecke had no confection business. According to a senior manager in the German affiliate, "WL has never been willing to spend significant long-term money to develop the confection market, which is puzzling since Germany has one of the largest confection markets in the world." Gödecke also had a very limited business in consumer health care products. With respect to the potential of *Listerine* in Germany, the manager commented:

> If you bring a product like that into the market it is not enough to just advertise the product, you have to change people's minds. To do that we would need to spend a lot of money, maybe as much as DM130–140 million . . . People always see Germany as a market with huge potential but what they don't see is that you need to invest in this market first. Another mistake people keep making is thinking that U.S. tastes will work in Germany. Germans are not mouthwash users.

Brazil

American Chicle entered the Brazilian market in the 1940s. When WL acquired American Chicle in 1962, the confectionery business in Brazil was well established under the *Adams* brand. A strong pharmaceutical business based on Parke-Davis products was also established in Brazil. However, the hyperinflation in the 1970s and the government's attempts to control inflation through price controls resulted in significant losses in the pharmaceutical business. WL decided to discontinue manufacturing and marketing pharmaceutical products in Brazil and licensed the *Parke-Davis* line of drugs to another Brazilian company. Since the products were marketed under the *Parke-Davis* name, WL maintained a close relationship with the licensing company for quality assurance purposes. The licensee, however, had complete control over which products to produce and how to manage production, marketing, and distribution.

The Brazil affiliate had about 1,300 employees and virtually all were involved in the confectionery business. The largest brand in Brazil was *Halls,* which was marketed as a confectionery product (a "refreshing experience") rather than a cough tablet. The affiliate had a small consumer health care business; *Listerine* was one of the products sold.

The relationship between headquarters and the affiliate was described by a senior Brazilian manager:

> They are in charge of the strategy and we are in charge of the operations. We have a strategic plan in place, we discuss it with headquarters, they give us direction on which areas to engage in and in which areas not to do anything, and the implementation is left to us.

Aside from product line extensions, such as changes in flavor or packaging, very little new product development was done in Brazil. One exception was the development of a liquid-center chewing gum called *Bubbaloo.* A leading brand in Brazil and several other Latin American countries, *Bubbaloo* was developed by the Brazilian affiliate for the Brazilian market.

The Management of International Operations

The Country Managers

Within WL, the country managers were akin to "kings" because, as one manager explained:

> These people are rulers. They control every asset and every decision that is made. The mindset is "I am managing France or Spain or wherever and I will manage it any way I like."

In the larger affiliates, country managers were usually nationals of that country. In Western Europe, most of the country managers had backgrounds in pharmaceuticals. In other regions, many of the country managers had confectionery backgrounds. In the smaller European countries and in the developing countries, country managers were often expatriates using the country manager position as a training ground for higher level appointments within WL.

Comments from a former country manager illustrate life at the top of an affiliate:

> It was a wonderful life. I was left alone because I was growing the business by 15 percent a year. I learned to run a business from the ground up and I could experiment with ideas very easily. I turned down two promotions because I was having such a great time being king . . . I had a great deal of autonomy and could ride over most of the staff people. I remember one time when we were planning a new product introduction in an area outside our traditional product lines. Someone from the international division told me "you can't do that." I did it anyway. Before we launched the product, I was told that international would send someone down to help us launch the product. I said fine but I won't be here if you do. So they left me alone. The new product outsold the dominant product in the market and was a huge success.

New Product Development

In the pharmaceutical business new product development was critical. Some new product initiatives in the affiliates were the result of coordinated efforts with headquarters. Others occurred independently in the affiliates. Drugs that were successful in the United States did not always achieve success in the affiliates. For example, *Lopid* was a huge success in the United States but only moderately successful internationally, despite a significantly increased international marketing effort in recent years. Nevertheless, *Lopid* represented WL's first truly international pharmaceutical product. Some drugs were introduced outside the United States because of less time-consuming regulatory processes. For example, *Accupril* was available in 23 countries outside the United States; WL anticipated FDA approval for the U.S. market by the end of 1991.

Because WL had a relatively small number of proprietary ethical pharmaceutical products, licensing was an important developmental activity in the United States and in the affiliates. The major affiliates had their own approaches to licensing strategy. According to one manager,

Licensing is an ad hoc process—it is done one way in the United States and one way in each of the affiliates. The affiliates try to find products that work in their region. Germany licenses a drug from Italy, Italy from France, and so on. We've ended up with a hodgepodge of drugs in the different regions.

As an example, WL's largest selling drug in Germany and seventh largest among all drugs was *Valoron N,* a painkiller for chronic and acute pain. This drug was licensed by the German affiliate and was not marketed by WL outside the German region.

Both the background of the country manager and the dominant business segment within the affiliate influenced new product development at the affiliate level. In particular, WL had experienced considerable difficulty in convincing the affiliates with dominant pharmaceutical businesses to adopt new consumer health care or confection products. Germany, for example, with its strong pharmaceutical business, had a series of country managers with pharmaceutical backgrounds. For some time, WL had been interested in introducing *Listerine* in Germany, even though mouthwash was not a recognized product category. The German affiliate leadership believed that the market was too small to justify the $15 million it would take to launch the product, even though *Listerine* was WL's second leading brand worldwide.

Global Integration

There was very little interaction between the senior U.S. pharmaceutical, OTC, and confectionery managers and their international counterparts. For instance, the U.S. head of pharmaceuticals would meet with the European head of pharmaceuticals once a month. There was virtually no other contact between these senior managers. The affiliate managers also rarely interacted. The affiliates reported into one of the three international groups and there were no reporting relationships between the units. Once a year, general managers from the affiliates and the United States would hold an annual meeting attended by about 250 people, characterized by one manager as follows:

> Some silly situations happen at the meetings. For example, Uruguay, an affiliate doing a few million dollars worth of business, might have a new strategic plan. The Uruguay general manager might get the same amount of air time as the head of Consumer Health Care Products in the United States.

The primary objective for country managers was maximizing the performance of their affiliates. A senior WL manager explained:

> Each affiliate is making decisions on a country basis. For example, say there is a strong shaving business in a country where the country manager is focused on building the local pharmaceutical business. If shaving exceeds its profit targets, the country manager could be tempted to shift cash from shaving to pharmaceuticals. The global shaving industry is not his concern. In another country the opposite situation may be happening. The local shaving business is not doing well this year so the country manager borrows money from pharmaceuticals to do some advertising in shaving. This cross borrowing across business lines is sub-optimizing our business lines . . . Country managers are not concerned with company growth; they are concerned with affiliate growth. Strategic decisions are not made about products and brands; the whole thinking process is strictly local—how do I maximize my bonus and my performance?

Manufacturing and raw materials sourcing were largely done locally by the affiliate, particularly in those affiliates that were acquired by acquisition, such as Germany, Spain, Italy, and the United Kingdom. Advertising was also done largely at the affiliate level. Because the affiliates varied so much in size, the quality of the advertising was often less than satisfactory. Although there was an effort to standardize packaging and graphics, particularly with confectionery products, it was not always successful. For example, when *Halls* was introduced in Brazil, a third-party manufacturer was used. Because the firm did not have the proper equipment to manufacture square mints, a rectangular shape was used. As the *Halls* brand grew, the rectangular shape became the standard for mints in Brazil. In the rest of the world, the *Halls* mint was square.

Two lines of business were exceptions to the lack of global integration—the Capsugel and *Tetra* divisions. In the early 1980s, the Capsugel business was organized on a geographic basis with the various international units reporting through the country managers. However, because the gelatin capsule market was essentially a commodity business and extremely competitive on a global scale, the geographic structure was considered ineffective and inconsistent with a fast-moving global business. In the mid1980s, a global structure was created for Capsugel. A similar structure was already in place for *Tetra*.

International Operations Staff

To coordinate WL's far-flung international businesses, there were approximately 950 International Operations staff members working in the New Jersey headquarters. Included in this number was a small headquarters staff for Capsugel and staff for *Tetra's* U.S. operations.

Officially, the role of the International Operations staff was to assist the country managers in implementing strategy by communicating information between HQ and affiliates and consolidating the huge amounts of data that were generated. As one manager commented:

> The staff function is "to make order out of chaos." In New Jersey, the international staff coordinates the three large geographic reporting organizations. Each geographic area has its own hierarchical structure of staff managers: marketing, finance, and so on, working out of New Jersey.

Although the international staff were expected to act in an advisory role to the affiliates, their advice was not always taken, or even wanted. A manager explained:

> If a marketing manager in International Operations wants to launch a new product in a particular country, he or she must convince the country manager to make the investment. The country manager may say "I don't want it." The international manager might be three levels below the country manager in the organizational hierarchy. What can the staff person do?
>
> The country managers run their affiliates like hardware stores. They can have 10 different people telling them we would like you to sell this particular drug or this new confectionery product. The guy leaves and the country manager goes back to doing what he wants to do. Their attitude toward the staff marketing people is "I don't need them, what value are they bringing? Get them out of the mix."
>
> It has always been a blurred vision as to the responsibility of some of the international staff functions. At the international operations level it is supposed to be strategic and visionary—

leave the day-to-day running of the business to the line managers in Europe, Asia, etc. The staff people would be responsible for oversight, monitoring, cross fertilization and linking Germany with what is going on in France, with what is going on in the UK and, hopefully, bringing that knowledge to other geographic areas by feeding that knowledge up to International Operations. The International Operations Group is also supposed to be coordinating with R&D, which is primarily based in the United States.

Earlier Reviews of the International Structure

Concerns that there were problems with the structure of WL's international operations first surfaced in the early 1980s. At that time, a consulting report recommended that the company disband its geographic structure and move to a line of business organization. Although senior management agreed in principle with a global-line-of-business structure, there were concerns that a full-scale reorganization of international operations was too drastic. WL tried a different approach to internationalization several years later. The objective was to put a global strategic planning process in place and merge this with local operating plans. In other words, the strategy would be global and tactics would be local. This approach was largely unsuccessful. Despite the attempt to put global plans into action, the realities were that a global vision had not been established and local objectives took precedence.

In 1989, a task force headed by Mel Goodes was established to develop a globalization plan. The task force was made up of senior managers from the pharmaceutical, confectionery, and consumer segments. A plan based on global lines of business was developed but for several reasons, the plan was not implemented. At some levels in the organization there was the belief that WL was still not ready for major international restructuring. In addition, WL was enjoying record profits with sales growth of 15 to 20 percent per year. Change was viewed as disruptive and unnecessary. There was a sense that "if it is not broken, why fix it?" Given WL's performance, it was not clear that the competitive marketplace had created a strategic imperative for reorganization.

The Next Steps

As the new CEO of WL, Mel Goodes was quite prepared to act and now had the authority. From his perspective, the existing organization was inconsistent with an increasingly competitive global environment. As he explained:

> Our decision making is too slow. For example, we had the opportunity to make an acquisition in Germany. The process started when the German country manager identified the investment opportunity. After he reviewed it, it went to the European Group. It then went to the International Group. Finally, it made its way to corporate in New Jersey. By this time a year had passed and the opportunity was gone.

The next step was to identify priorities and establish an implementation plan. There were many issues to be resolved. Should changes in structure and reporting relationships involve the entire organization? How quickly should change proceed? What would happen to the kings and the international operations staff in a new structure? Should the same international structure be established for each business segment? Should New Jersey remain the headquarters for each business segment?

External Information Sources

Alan Archer, "Alliances Offer a Model: Restructuring the Industry." *Financial Times,* July 23, 1991, Survey, p. 2.

Clive Cookson, "Pharmaceuticals: Successful but Cautious." *Financial Times,* July 23, 1991, Survey, p. 1.

Michael A. Esposito, Gunnar F. Hesse, and Nicholas E. Mellor, "Survival of the Fittest in the EC Pharmaceuticals Market." *The Journal of European Business,* 1991, May/June, pp.31–38.

Matthew Lynn, "Drug Companies in a Fix." *International Management,* 1991, October, pp. 62–65.

Thomas A. Malnight, "Globalization of an Ethnocentric Firm: An Evolutionary Perspective." *Strategic Management Journal,* 1995, 16, pp. 119–141.

Brian O'Reilly, "Drugmakers Under Attack." *Fortune,* July 29, 1991, pp. 48–63.

Melissa Shon, "Pharmaceuticals '94: Industry, Heal Thyself." *Chemical Marketing Reporter,* March 7, 1994, Special Report.

Robert Teitelmann, "Pharmaceuticals." *Financial World,* May 30, 1989, pp. 54–80.

22   RHÔNE-POULENC (A) AND (B) (CONDENSED)

In 1985, Rhône-Poulenc S.A. was France's largest chemical company, with an extensive product line that ranged from basic chemicals to pharmaceuticals. With revenues of $7.48 billion it was the twelfth largest chemical firm in the world, but lagged well behind the leading German and American companies (Exhibit 1). Not only was Rhône-Poulenc smaller than its major competitors, it also had a more restricted geographic presence, as more than 80 percent of its revenues were generated in Europe. Its presence in the United States was minimal, accounting for just 3 percent of total sales.

Seeking to improve its strategic position in an industry that was increasingly characterized by global competition, Rhône-Poulenc undertook an ambitious series of acquisitions, focusing mainly on the United States. From 1986 to 1991, the company made 18 separate purchases in the U.S., ranging from large divisions of major corporations to small entrepreneurial companies. Thanks to these acquisitions, by 1991 Rhône-Poulenc generated 20 percent of its revenues in the United States. In just five years, the U.S. affiliate, known as Rhône-Poulenc Inc., had become the company's single largest foreign affiliate.

Along with its larger U.S. position, however, came a fresh set of managerial challenges. In the spring of 1991, Rhône-Poulenc's senior management had to determine the best way to organize its newly expanded worldwide operations and how best to make key decisions. In short, it was rethinking the role of the U.S. affiliate within the larger operations of the corporation.

Professor Philip M. Rosenzweig prepared this case as the basis for class discussion rather than to illustrate either effective or ineffective handling of an administrative situation. This case combines material from "Rhône-Poulenc (A)," No. 394-040 and "Rhône-Poulenc (B)," No. 394-041. Copyright © 1994 by the President and Fellows of Harvard College.

EXHIBIT 1   **Principal Chemical Manufacturers, 1985**

	Company	Country	Sales ($ billion)
1.	BASF	Germany	18.15
2.	Bayer	Germany	17.79
3.	Hoechst	Germany	16.55
4.	ICI	United Kingdom	15.50
5.	Du Pont	United States	15.04
6.	Dow Chemical	United States	11.54
7.	Shell	United States	9.18
8.	Union Carbide	United States	9.00
9.	Ciba-Geigy	Switzerland	8.85
10.	DSM	Netherlands	8.76
11.	Montedison	Italy	8.49
12.	Rhône-Poulenc	France	7.48
13.	Monsanto	United States	6.75
14.	Exxon	United States	6.67
15.	AKZO	Netherlands	6.54

Source: Compiled from information contained in Rhône-Poulenc company documents and *Chemical Insight.*

Rhône-Poulenc: History and Evolution

The modern chemical industry had its roots in 19th century Germany, where advances in organic chemistry led to a proliferation of new products with important commercial applications.

By the end of the century, the Rhine valley had become the center of the world's chemical industry, and was home to a number of rapidly growing chemical firms. Germany's neighbor to the west, France, was slower to develop its chemical industry, but gradually a number of French firms became active in coal-based chemicals, dyestuffs, and pharmaceuticals. The Lyon region of France, with the Rhône river serving as an important artery for shipping, became the center of French chemical activity.

Rhône-Poulenc was founded in 1928 as the merger of two firms: Société Chimique des Usines du Rhône, a Lyon-based chemicals producer, and Etablissements Poulenc Frères, a Paris-based company specializing in research and pharmaceuticals. Société Chimique des Usines du Rhône brought with it a 50 percent ownership of Rhodiaceta, a producer of artificial fibers, which had a foreign affiliate in Brazil. Etablissements Poulenc Frères also had overseas activities, owning a majority stake in May & Baker, a British manufacturer of fine chemicals and pharmaceuticals. From the start, Rhône-Poulenc was involved in a wide range of products, including man-made fibers, pharmaceuticals, organic intermediates, and fertilizers. By the end of the 1930s, Rhône-Poulenc ranked among the largest French firms.

Following World War Two, the remnants of the German chemical cartel, I.G. Farben, were organized into three firms—Bayer, BASF, and Hoechst—which not only became the dominant chemical companies in Europe but also began to expand abroad. They soon set up operations in the United States, where they established licensing arrangements in the early 1950s, and subsequently created holding companies from which they expanded further through acquisitions and joint ventures. By 1971, Bayer earned 11 percent of its revenues in North America, and Hoechst was close behind at 8 percent. Other chemicals firms, aside from the German giants, were also expanding abroad, including the leading British firm, ICI. In addition to its long-standing activities in Canada, ICI enlarged its presence in the United States, where its products included fertilizers, industrial chemicals, surfactants, and specialty chemicals for paper, rubber, and plastics.

French chemical firms, by contrast, remained narrowly concentrated in Europe. Rhône-Poulenc was typical: Of its $1.8 billion sales in 1969, 53 percent was generated in France and most of the rest came from neighboring European countries. Its foreign affiliates tended to be small and were managed largely as independent operations. Rhône-Poulenc's long-time U.K affiliate, May & Baker, operated with such a high degree of independence that many of its employees were not even aware that it had a French parent. Its other foreign affiliates had a variety of names, reflecting Rhône-Poulenc's lack of a clear worldwide identity: the Swiss affiliate was known as Viscose Suisse; the German affiliate was Deutsche Rhodiaceta AG; and the Spanish affiliate was called SAFA. Meanwhile, Rhône-Poulenc's U.S. presence was insignificant. The U.S. affiliate, known until 1978 as Rhodia Inc., had sales of about $120 million, amounting to just 2 percent of the firm's total. An industry analyst concluded simply: "The U.S.A. plays an unimportant role in the business of Rhône-Poulenc."

As global competition in the chemical industry intensified during the 1970s, Rhône-Poulenc found itself under pressure on several fronts. Its textile and fertilizer products were attacked by low cost imports, often from Asia. In addition, the oil shocks of the 1970s led to higher prices for petroleum, squeezing the profit margins of petrochemical products. By 1978, the company was losing money in each of these product lines and was in serious financial difficulty overall. It responded by cutting costs and reducing headcount, and began to shift its portfolio towards products with higher profit margins and less vulnerability to business cycles, such as specialty chemicals and pharmaceuticals. Jean-Marc Bruel, an Executive Vice President and member of Rhône-Poulenc's six-man Executive Committee, explained:

> In the late 1970s, we decided the skill of Rhône-Poulenc lay in research and high added-value products. We decided that we had to get out of commodities—petrochemicals, polymers, and fertilizers.[1]

As a first step toward repositioning its portfolio, in November 1980, Rhône-Poulenc sold its petrochemicals and polymers assets to the French oil companies, Elf-Aquitaine and Compagnie Française des Petroles (CFP).

---

[1]"The Global Reach of Rhône-Poulenc," *Director,* March 1989, p. 77.

EXHIBIT 2   **Rhône-Poulenc S.A. Financial Results, 1982-1989 (million French francs)**

	1982	1983	1984	1985	1986	1987	1988	1989
Total sales	37,196	43,117	51,207	56,402	52,694	56,160	65,334	73,068
Net income	(844)	98	1,989	2,312	2,008	2,360	3,457	4,092

Source: Rhône-Poulenc Annual Reports.

Nationalization and "Refocusing"

In 1981, François Mitterand was elected president of France, marking the ascendancy of the Socialists to power after years of Gaullist rule. Fulfilling part of the Socialist campaign platform, in early 1982 the Mitterand government nationalized five large industrial groups, including Rhône-Poulenc. The following year, the French government undertook a second phase of its economic program, "refocusing" several key industries, including chemicals. As a result, the product portfolios of France's three major chemical firms were juggled. Rhône-Poulenc's fertilizer activities were moved to CdF Chimie, and it received in return pharmaceutical assets from other French companies. The firm emerged from the restructuring in much-improved shape, no longer burdened by petrochemicals or fertilizers, and with a strengthened pharmaceuticals business. Rhône-Poulenc now had what one industry analyst called "one of the most attractive portfolios in the European chemicals industry."[2] Thanks to this improved portfolio, and in part due to better economic conditions around the world, the company's financial performance began to pick up (Exhibit 2).

Even with a stronger portfolio and improved financial performance, Rhône-Poulenc's lack of a strong overseas presence continued to be a problem, as competition in the world chemical industry was becoming global in scope. A strong position in the United States was especially critical. A first reason was scale. The United States was by far the largest single national market for chemicals, representing 40 percent of sales in the Triad countries of Europe, North America, and Japan (Exhibit 3). A chemical firm could not achieve global scale economies without a substantial presence in the United States. A second reason was strategic balance: being represented in each major world market reduced dependence on any single market. A firm that derived most of its sales from EEC countries was highly vulnerable to recession in Europe, and at a disadvantage vis-à-vis competitors with better geographic balance. A third reason was proximity to market leadership. Although the United States was not the technical leader in all segments of the chemical industry, it was important in a number of segments including agrochemicals, specialty chemicals, pharmaceuticals, as well as applied R&D. One Rhône-Poulenc executive noted that because

---

[2]Stuart Wamsley, quoted in *Chemical Week*, December 3, 1986, p. 18.

EXHIBIT 3   Chemical Consumption in the Triad, 1977, ($ million)

North America	
United States	$109,390
Canada	6,921
Subtotal	$116,311
Western Europe:	
West Germany	27,818
United Kingdom	21,484
France	18,078
Italy	15,141
Subtotal	$111,935
Japan:	$ 36,198
Total	$264,444

Source: "The Chemical Industry 1977," Organization for Economic Cooperation and Development.

technical and marketing innovations often originated in the United States, companies without a strong position there were at a competitive disadvantage worldwide.

Of course, the largest European chemical firms had long recognized the importance of the American market and continued to expand their positions there. By 1982, Bayer, Hoechst, and BASF derived from the United States 20, 13, and 12 percent of their respective sales. Their presence continued to expand through the 1980s, at times through major acquisitions, such as BASF's $1 billion acquisition of United Technology's Inmont Corporation, a producer of inks and coatings. Rhône-Poulenc, although it had recognized the need for an American presence, did not have sufficient financial resources to expand in the United States.

Building an American Presence

In 1986, with the backing of the French government, Rhône-Poulenc's new CEO, Jean-René Fourtou, articulated a strategic direction with two main components. First, its activities were grouped into five product lines, or Sectors: Agrochemicals, Organic and Inorganic Intermediates, Specialty Chemicals, Films and Fibers, and Health. *Agrochemicals* were crop protection chemicals including insecticides, herbicides, and fungicides. These products tended to be the same all around the world and could be marketed globally. *Organic and Inorganic Intermediates* included basic chemicals such as sulfuric acid, phosphates, and soda ash. The economics of basic chemicals effectively precluded global competition: transportation was too expensive to make the worldwide shipment of these products economically feasible. Rather, these chemicals tended to be extracted, processed, and sold locally in many regions of the world. *Specialty Chemicals* included such things as food ingredients and flavorings, additives for paints and inks, and fine chemicals. They were tailored for specific customers, and therefore tended to be local in nature. *Films and Fibers* included synthetic fabrics and materials. Finally, *Health* included pharmaceuticals and other life science products. Although Rhône-Poulenc sought to grow in each of these five Sectors, it anticipated a shift towards specialty chemicals and pharmaceuticals, which were less vulnerable to business cycles and tended to generate higher margins.

Second, with regard to geographic position, Rhône-Poulenc was determined finally to build its presence in the United States. One executive noted: "All our European competitors have more than 20 percent of their turnover in the United States, and we would not want to go further than five to seven years before we reach that level." Another put it simply: *"Les Etats-Unis est un 'must.'"*

Fourtou and his top managers set an explicit goal: to expand U.S. sales from 3 percent of total revenues to at least 20 percent. Jean-Marc Bruel explained:

> We analyzed the U.S. very precisely as a potential market for every line of our products. The results showed that the U.S. represented 40% of our potential markets. So you can see that a 3% share was just ridiculous.

Expanding U.S. sales from 3 percent to 20 percent called for a complete transformation of Rhône-Poulenc's U.S. operations, developing it from a small trading outpost to a large manufacturing operation. A work force of 1,300 employees would have to grow to several times that size. These challenges were compounded by the firm's lack of confidence regarding the U.S. market. Many French firms had experienced severe difficulties in trying to enter the American market, and Rhône-Poulenc was no exception. One of Rhône-Poulenc's top executives, Philippe Desmarescaux, recalled:

> For 30 years we had tried to get into the U.S., but without success. So the question would always come up: "Why try now? Why will this time be any better?"
>   We had to overcome a sense of fatalism. We had to combat the complex—French in general, but Rhône-Poulenc in particular—that we always fail in the U.S.

To position itself for growth in the United States, Rhône-Poulenc first sold some of its losing American ventures. It then undertook a few small acquisitions in early 1986, including U.S. Ethicals, an $8 million New York-based drug company; Purification Engineering, a biotechnology research group; and Williams Metals Industries, a rare earths company. But these purchases were only appetizers. In October 1986, Rhône-Poulenc undertook a more significant acquisition, purchasing Monsanto's vanillin division, making Rhône-Poulenc the world's largest producer of that food ingredient. Then came rumblings of a far larger deal, one that would change the scale of Rhône-Poulenc's U.S. operations in a single stroke.

Acquiring Union Carbide Agrochemical Products

At first glance, Union Carbide Agrochemical Products (UCAP) was an unlikely object of interest—its image still suffered from the Bhopal disaster of December 1984, when an accident at a plant in India killed hundreds of people. But upon analysis of UCAP's products, and guided by a desire to achieve a leadership position in the world agrochemical market, Rhône-Poulenc decided to go ahead. On December 16,

1986, Rhône-Poulenc acquired for $575 million the worldwide agricultural products business of Union Carbide Company, excluding the operations of Union Carbide India Limited, which operated the Bhopal facility, and a few other foreign units.

Explaining the acquisition, one Rhône-Poulenc manager commented: "The two product lines were very complementary in terms of functionality." UCAP's leading products were insecticides, whereas Rhône-Poulenc's Agrochemical Sector was strong in herbicides and fungicides. Together they formed a strong family of products that could be used for crop protection around the world. Furthermore, Rhône-Poulenc generated 68 percent of its agrochemical sales in Europe, whereas UCAP generated 52 percent of its sales in North America and was represented in parts of Latin America and South East Asia where Rhône-Poulenc was not yet strong. The possibility therefore existed for Rhône-Poulenc's herbicides and fungicides to reach the U.S. market through UCAP's distribution system. Rhône-Poulenc was upbeat in announcing the deal: "The complementarity between Rhône-Poulenc's and Union Carbide's agrochemicals business is remarkable and a total synergy exists between their networks."

Even so, integration of UCAP posed immense challenges. In contrast to Rhône-Poulenc's small U.S. operation, called Rhône-Poulenc Inc., UCAP was a manufacturing operation with more than 3,000 employees. Its headquarters and R&D center were located at Research Triangle Park, North Carolina, with manufacturing plants spread across the country. One of these plants, at Institute, West Virginia, employed 1,500 and was the largest chemical plant east of the Mississippi. Rhône-Poulenc Inc. had neither experience in managing a large manufacturing plant nor the infrastructure to handle an acquisition three times its size. In addition, Rhône-Poulenc was not well-known to UCAP employees. Rhône-Poulenc Inc.'s newly hired vice president of human resources, Robert C. (Bob) Machin, recalled his first encounters with UCAP employees:

> What I heard most of all from people at Union Carbide was "*Who* is Rhône-Poulenc? *What* is it? We've heard about this company in France and in Europe, but what is it here in the U.S.?" That was very enlightening to me, because it showed what we needed to do. If people didn't understand who we were, we had to be able to respond. Because it wasn't okay if people said "Rhône-Poulenc is this and this in Europe, but we don't know who we are in the U.S."

Managing the Integration Process

Philippe Desmarescaux, head of Rhône-Poulenc's Agrochemical Sector, took a lead role in managing the integration process. On January 5, 1987, Desmarescaux sent a letter to UCAP employees announcing the formation of an interim organization, drawing on managers from both organizations. He also announced the creation of a Steering Committee whose aim was to integrate UCAP into the worldwide activities of Rhône-Poulenc's Agrochemicals Sector. Soon afterwards, Desmarescaux visited the Institute plant where he explained to employees the motive for the acquisition and outlined his plans for the future. His goal was to express confidence and to ensure a sense of continuity. Desmarescaux feared that if he did not make a good impression, many valuable employees might decide to take an early retirement, in which case *"Nous nous serions retrouvés en culottes courtes"*—we would have found ourselves wearing nothing but our shorts.[3]

Assisting Desmarescaux as vice president and general manager of the interim organization was a veteran French executive, Jean Lefebvre. Whereas Desmarescaux continued to handle worldwide responsibility for the Agrochemical Sector from Lyon, Lefebvre moved to the United States where he played a key role, serving as an on-site representative and liaison between the Americans and their new French managers. Tom Dille, an American who had joined Rhône-Poulenc Inc. from Monsanto, joined the management team and was groomed to eventually take over as CEO of the newly-acquired division.

Managing the Matrix

UCAP took its place within Rhône-Poulenc's worldwide matrix organization. Before the acquisition, UCAP had been the worldwide headquarters for Union Carbide's agrochemical products; now it was one part of a larger structure. As part of Rhône-Poulenc's U.S. organization, it reported to Rhône-Poulenc Inc. headquarters in Princeton, N.J., and to its president, Bertrand Louvet. As part of Rhône-Poulenc's Agrochemical Sector, it reported to Sector headquarters in Lyon and became one part, albeit a large one, of a worldwide agrochemical operation. For members of UCAP, becoming part of a matrix structure was at times difficult, as it was not always clear what their relationship should be with these two entities. One manager recalled: "We would ask: 'What is Rhône-Poulenc Inc. doing? What is Sector doing? How do I relate to one, and how do I relate to the other, and how do I serve the information needs and requirements of each?' It was a very difficult transition. Very, very difficult."

Following the acquisition of UCAP, Rhône-Poulenc's Agrochemical Sector adopted an organizational structure consisting of three regional units (Exhibit 4). Reporting to the head of the Sector, Philippe Desmarescaux, were Tom Dille, division head of agrochemicals in the United States (henceforth called Rhône-Poulenc Ag Co.); Bruce Drew, head of U.K. and Commonwealth (May and Baker Agrochemicals); and Alain Godard, with responsibility for France plus the rest of the world (Rhône-Poulenc Agrochimie SA). Staff functions, including strategy, marketing, finance, and R&D, were located in Lyon and reported to Desmarescaux. Although Sector headquarters in Lyon had formal responsibility for all worldwide operations, Rhône-Poulenc Ag Co. retained a large measure of independence. One French executive remembered that Desmarescaux had warned French managers against overwhelming the newly acquired division:

> Philippe was very clear about that. He said: "You've got to respect the Americans because they were here before and they know better than you do. Don't come up with a rigid mindset and try to impose what you think is the best. You don't know better than the Americans."

---

[3]"Le Nouveau Monde de Rhône-Poulenc," *L'Expansion,* May 1990, p. 120.

EXHIBIT 4   **Organization of Rhône-Poulenc Agrochemical Sector, September 1987**

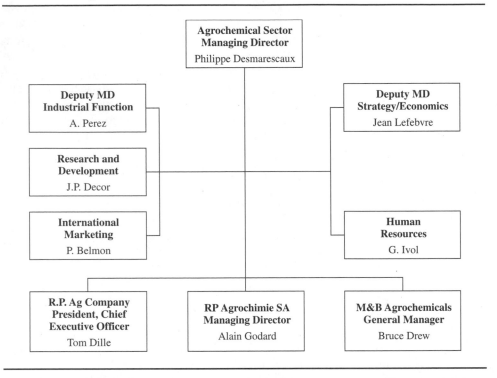

Another French manager concurred, recalling: "At the beginning the Sectors were fairly shy." According to Alain Godard, the relationship between Philippe Desmarescaux, the Sector head, and Tom Dille, head of Rhône-Poulenc Ag Co., could be described as only a "dotted line." Some members of the Sector staff in Lyon were frustrated that the U.S. operation saw itself as semi-independent, and did not always defer to strategic plans formulated at Sector headquarters in Lyon, but a conservative approach was deemed best.

Building Rhône-Poulenc Inc.

In 1987, Bertrand Louvet, president of Rhône-Poulenc Inc., returned to France to become president of the Specialty Chemicals Sector. The search began for a successor to head the U.S. affiliate. Unlike previous heads of Rhône-Poulenc Inc., who had been French, top management decided that the next one would be an American. According to Desmarescaux, it made no sense to put a Frenchman in charge of an affiliate that needed to become an integrated part of the American economy—it was *"impensable,"* unthinkable. Beyond nationality, they sought an individual with considerable skill and experience. Rhône-Poulenc Inc. was no longer a small trading outpost, but was striving to become a strong manufacturing operation, and would need at its head a solid operating manager who could offer stability and professionalism to a growing organization. This person should represent *"la permanence,"* and should be able to personify *"Rhône-Poulenc aux U.S.A."* for the next 10 years.

Following an extensive search, top management selected Peter J. Neff, a chemist with experience at Exxon and most recently at St. Joseph Minerals, which had then been acquired by Fluor. Neff knew the chemical industry and had first-hand experience about managing acquisitions. In order to attract a manager of Neff's caliber, Desmarescaux recalled telling him: "We've proven our commitment to the United States by investing $600 million [in the Union Carbide deal], and we're committed to growing much bigger."

Neff accepted the job and became president of Rhône-Poulenc Inc. in 1987. He was given a simple mandate: "To make Rhône-Poulenc Inc. a success." That involved more than expanding sales; it also required building a viable local organization, establishing a clear identity, and creating "an American Rhône-Poulenc culture." It was Neff's job to develop Rhône-Poulenc in the United States, and toward this end corporate executives in Paris expressed their intention to give him wide latitude.

In addition to Neff, Americans were sought for other key positions, including vice president of administration and vice president for human resources. These Americans were attracted by many features of the job, but voiced a number of concerns about working for a foreign-based firm. The experience of Bob Machin, hired in 1987 as Rhône-Poulenc Inc.'s vice president for human resources, was typical:

> When I joined the company, I tried to get clarity on two things. One: How much influence would come out of France, and how much autonomy would we have? And two: How important was it for me to speak French?

Machin received satisfactory answers to both questions. Regarding autonomy, he was assured that the human resource function would be run locally, since it dealt mainly with American employees and had to contend with local laws and labor practices. Regarding language, Machin recalled, "I was told it was a non-issue: "Don't worry about French. It's not important at all." Pete Neff had similarly inquired about the importance of learning French. He recalled: "They told me 'You've got more important things to do than learn French.'"[4] These assurances reflected Rhône-Poulenc's belief that it could not impose a French management style on its growing U.S. affiliate. "To be successful in different parts of the world," Desmarescaux concluded, "you have to manage in a different way. When it comes down to it, it's up to *us* to become more *American.*"

Acquiring Stauffer's Basic Chemicals Division

Encouraged by its acquisition in agrochemicals, Rhône-Poulenc looked toward other acquisitions in the United States. The Organic and Inorganic Intermediates Sector set its sights on acquiring the basic chemicals division of an eminent American chemical firm, Stauffer Chemical, and in September 1987, Rhône-Poulenc acquired Stauffer's

---

[4]"A New Era at Rhône-Poulenc: Banking on Success in the U.S.," *Chemical Week,* March 22, 1989.

basic chemicals business for $522 million. In announcing the deal, CEO Jean-René Fourtou stated that the acquisition gave to Rhône-Poulenc what it had long sought—a "solid industrial and commercial base in the United States"—and reinforced Rhône-Poulenc's position in inorganic chemicals.

The Stauffer acquisition rivaled the Union Carbide purchase in size, adding 3,600 employees and annual sales of $530 million, but in other ways it was very different. Whereas UCAP's insecticides complemented Rhône-Poulenc Agrochemical Sector's existing herbicide and fungicide products, Stauffer's capabilities in phosphates, sulfuric acid, and soda ash, overlapped the products that Rhône-Poulenc already had in Europe. Unlike agrochemicals, which had global applications and could be sold around the world, these three basic chemicals were produced, marketed, and distributed in the United States. They were, commented one manager, "a commodity business, totally bound by the East Coast and the West Coast." Thus, Stauffer's operations were not closely integrated within the worldwide activities of the Organic and Inorganic Intermediates Sector, but remained relatively more self-sufficient and independent.

Consolidating the U.S. Organization

With the acquisitions of UCAP and Stauffer Basic Chemicals, Rhône-Poulenc now generated 12 percent of its worldwide sales in the United States, or about $1.4 billion of $11 billion. Sales in the United States surpassed those in Brazil or in Germany, making Rhône-Poulenc Inc. the firm's single largest foreign affiliate. Meanwhile, at the Princeton, NJ, headquarters of Rhône-Poulenc Inc., efforts were taking place to forge a strong country organization. The newly acquired units—formerly divisions of Union Carbide, of Stauffer, as well as earlier acquisitions from firms such as Monsanto—were being molded into a single organization with a clear identity and a consistent approach to management. Pete Neff, president of Rhône-Poulenc Inc., played a vital role in this process. Jean-Marc Bruel recalled:

> When we were integrating the acquisitions it was necessary to have unity of command. We had to have someone in the U.S. who could carry out the acquisitions and initially manage their operations. That was Pete Neff.
>
> From 1987 to 1991, Pete Neff executed the acquisitions, then consolidated them, and put together an organization. In all of these things, he was *terriblement actif*—deeply involved.

For Neff and his team of managers, some of the most pressing demands lay in health and safety, environmental regulation, and human resources. Rhône-Poulenc had acquired a large number of plants from several different firms, each of which had its own approach to safety and environmental matters. Some plants needed considerable upgrading, and all had to be brought into line with a company standard of excellence. Integrating the human resources function was also required, as each of the acquired units had its own approach to compensation, pensions and benefits, and employee progression and succession.

Neff and his top managers also sought to develop a clear sense of corporate identity. Thousands of Americans who had joined U.S. firms now found themselves working for a large French company about which they knew little. Under the guidance of Bob Machin, vice president for human resources, employees from the newly acquired units came together and developed a mission statement and a statement of values (Exhibit 5). In addition, Rhône-Poulenc Inc.'s corporate affairs department began publication of a quarterly magazine that highlighted the contributions of each division, communicated strategic priorities, and built a sense of common purpose. Other efforts, ranging from safety awards to scholarships for employees' children to initiatives aimed at quality improvement, sought to foster a sense of cohesion and unity within Rhône-Poulenc Inc.

As they built the U.S. organization, the newly-hired American managers at Rhône-Poulenc Inc. enjoyed great autonomy. With regard to the human resource function, Bob Machin recalled, French managers at corporate headquarters took a restrained approach:

> They were very, very hands off. They said: "We're not going to get involved. We don't know how to handle the human resource function in the American way. You just ask for what you need, and we'll provide it if we can, but we're not going to look over your shoulder."

In contrast to the hands-off approach in human resources, there was somewhat more direct interaction in strategic planning and R&D between the U.S. divisions (Rhône-Poulenc Ag Division, formerly UCAP, and Rhône-Poulenc Basic Chemicals Division, formerly of Stauffer Chemical) and their respective Sector headquarters in France. For example, the divisions worked with Sector headquarters to set strategic direction and annual targets. Once these targets were approved, however, responsibility for execution rested with each division working with Pete Neff at Rhône-Poulenc Inc. As Neff described it, the division presidents, Tom Dille (Rhône-Poulenc

---

EXHIBIT 5   Rhône-Poulenc Inc. Mission and Value Statements

Rhône-Poulenc Mission

Rhône-Poulenc Inc. is a provider of high-value products and services in the fields of chemistry and life sciences. Using the core skills and technologies of Rhône-Poulenc worldwide, we will grow and succeed by building profitable businesses that satisfy the evolving needs of our customers, challenge our employees, and establish us as a recognized and respected market leader.

As an integral part of Rhône-Poulenc's global organization, we will lead our international affiliates in capitalizing on opportunities in the U.S. market, contribute unique U.S. capabilities to Rhône-Poulenc Group, and maximize our contribution to Rhône-Poulenc's overall profitability.

Rhône-Poulenc Values

Fundamental to our mission are five shared values that will shape our goals, guide our conduct, and promote a sense of pride in Rhône-Poulenc Inc.

Integrity	**Safety**	**Quality**	**Innovation**	**Partnership**

Source: Rhône-Poulenc company publication.

Ag Co.) and Sam Russo (Rhône-Poulenc Basic Chemicals), had a dotted-line relationship to their Sectors and a solid-line relationship to Rhône-Poulenc Inc.

Further Acquisitions, 1989–1990

By 1987, two of Rhône-Poulenc's Sectors, Agrochemicals and Organic and Inorganic Intermediates, had acquired a significant presence in the United States. The firm now turned its attention to a third Sector: Specialty Chemicals. The Specialty Chemicals Sector had activities in France that included fine chemicals and latex resins, but had very little volume in the United States.

To boost its position in specialty chemicals, Rhône-Poulenc in 1989 undertook a flurry of acquisitions, including Monsanto's analgesics divisions; RM Industries, a specialist in the production of an additive for polymers; the U.S. operations of RTZ, a British firm with worldwide revenues of FF 6 billion; the surfactants and specialty chemicals divisions of the American firm GAF, with U.S. revenues of FF 1.2 billion; and Miranol Inc., a New Jersey-based firm whose surfactants were used in, among other products, Johnson's Baby Shampoo. The new holdings in surfactants were especially exciting because they represented a new direction for the company—Rhône-Poulenc previously had only a minor position in surfactants.

At first, the several specialty chemicals acquisitions were organized into four divisions: Surfactants, Food Ingredients, Fine Organics, and Performance Resins and Coatings (PRC). Each division was led by a vice-president, some of whom had joined Rhône-Poulenc through the acquisition. For example, the new head of the Surfactants Division, Frank Sheeder, had been the head of surfactants at GAF, and the head of PRC, Dennis Kerrison, had come from RTZ. Each division vice-president took a place on the executive committee of Rhône-Poulenc Inc., reporting to Pete Neff. Thus, in 1990, Rhône-Poulenc Inc. consisted of two large divisions, Agrochemicals and Basic Chemicals, plus four smaller divisions, all reporting to Neff (Exhibit 6).

In March of 1990, Rhône-Poulenc made a bold move in the Health Sector, offering to buy 51 percent of Rorer Group Inc., a Pennsylvania-based pharmaceuticals company best known as the producer of Maalox. Rhône-Poulenc's CEO, Jean-René Fourtou, noted: "If we succeed in the Rorer acquisition, we will have resolved the totality of our great strategic dilemmas."[5] When the deal was completed in July of 1990, Rhône-Poulenc had bought 66.7 percent of Rorer for $1.7 billion, 32 times earnings. Unlike earlier acquisitions, which had been acquired in full and reported to Rhône-Poulenc Inc., Rorer was renamed Rhône-Poulenc Rorer and reported directly to the Health Sector in France. Thanks to this acquisition, Rhône-Poulenc acquired a majority stake in a large pharmaceuticals firm with foreign affiliates from Asia to Europe. The company announced with pride:

> [This acquisition] enables Rhône-Poulenc to meet its strategic objectives in the Health Sector, which are to penetrate the United States market, accelerate its development in Japan, and reach critical mass worldwide. Rhône-Poulenc Rorer becomes one of the world's ten largest pharmaceutical companies.

---

[5]"Rhône-Poulenc: Hey Big Spender," *Chemical Week*, March 14, 1990, p. 42.

Exhibit 6   Organizational Structure of Rhône-Poulenc Inc., 1990

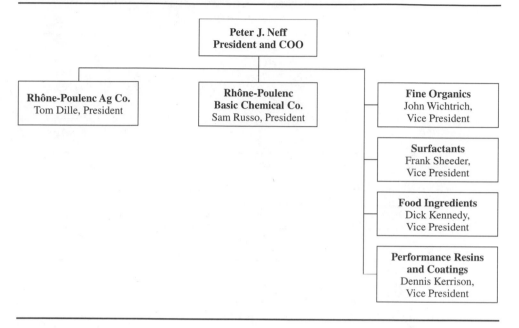

Rhône-Poulenc in 1991: Pondering Reorganization

By 1991, Rhône-Poulenc had undertaken a breathtaking series of acquisitions in the United States. With the acquisition of Rorer, the company's portfolio shifted increasingly toward pharmaceuticals (Exhibit 7). The company now generated 20 percent of its revenues in the United States, a dramatic shift from just a few years before (Exhibit 8). It had, in addition, become the seventh largest chemical firm in the world (Exhibit 9).

Rhône-Poulenc's U.S. activities now consisted of Rhône-Poulenc Rorer, which reported directly to Health Sector headquarters in France, and Rhône-Poulenc Inc., which consisted of three divisions—Rhône-Poulenc Ag Co., Rhône-Poulenc Basic Chemicals Co., and Rhône-Poulenc Specialty Chemicals Co.[6] Each of these divisions reported on one hand to Rhone-Poulenc Inc. headquarters and on the other to its Sector headquarters in France. Strategy was set in consultation with Sector headquarters, but responsibility for meeting annual targets rested with Rhône-Poulenc Inc. The operating results of these three divisions were consolidated into Rhône-Poulenc Inc.'s profit and loss statement, for which Pete Neff and his staff were responsible.

Although Rhône-Poulenc's Sector headquarters worked closely with managers at their U.S. divisions to develop strategy and to share technical expertise, they had

---

[6]The final Sector, Films and Fibers, had never expanded in the United States, in part because domestic competition from Du Pont and other firms was thought to make success unlikely. Thus, four of Rhône-Poulenc's five Sectors were represented in the U.S.

EXHIBIT 7   **Percentage of Sales by Sector**

	1989	1990	1991
Organic and inorganic intermediates	24.5%	20.6%	17.8%
Specialty chemicals	13.5	17.4	16.9
Fibers and polymers	21.4	17.5	15.7
Health	24.3	30.2	34.8
Agrochemicals	14.3	12.8	13.0
Other	2.0	1.5	1.8
Total	100.0%	100.0%	100.0%

Source: Rhône-Poulenc Annual Reports.

EXHIBIT 8   **Distribution of Sales by Country (FF billion)**

	1989	1990	1991
France	18.4	18.1	19.0
United States	9.7	14.8	16.9
Germany	5.8	6.9	7.8
United Kingdom	4.0	5.5	5.4
Asia	3.4	5.3	6.2
Brazil	6.9	4.5	4.4
Italy	3.4	4.1	4.5
Spain	3.6	3.2	2.9
Other	17.6	16.0	16.7
Total	72.8	78.4	83.8

Source: Rhone-Poulenc Annual Reports.

until now refrained from managing the U.S. operations directly. In part, Rhône-Poulenc's French managers had been reluctant to manage closely their newly-acquired U.S. operations because they lacked experience and confidence in managing in the United States. Furthermore, they recognized that the United States was a unique market and they respected the need for American managers to retain a substantial degree of autonomy.

By 1991, however, the need to respect the independence of the U.S. affiliate was matched by a perceived need to view the corporation's activities as an integrated whole. Jean-René Fourtou remarked that the firm had undergone a fundamental transformation:

> Over the past four years, Rhône-Poulenc has profoundly modified its business base, spending FF 40 billion on acquisitions while disposing of nearly sixty companies or affiliates. In the process, we have gained considerable size in the global marketplace. Expressed in dollars, our sales have practically doubled since 1986.

EXHIBIT 9   **Principal Chemical Manufacturers, 1990**

	Company	Country	Sales ($ billion)
1.	BASF	Germany	31.20
2.	Hoechst	Germany	30.02
3.	Bayer	Germany	27.86
4.	ICI	United Kingdom	24.91
5.	Du Pont	United States	22.27
6.	Dow Chemical	United States	19.77
7.	Rhône-Poulenc	France	15.48
8.	Ciba-Geigy	Switzerland	15.46
9.	Shell	United States	12.70
10.	Atochem	France	10.41
11.	AKZO	Netherlands	10.23
12.	Exxon	United States	9.59
13.	Monsanto	United States	9.00
14.	Solvay	Belgium	8.32
15.	Sumitomo Chemicals	Japan	7.87

Source: Compiled from information contained in Rhône-Poulenc company documents and *Chemical Insight.*

> We have now achieved our primary strategic goal: to rank, in each of our businesses and in each of our products, among the world's five leading companies, in order to enjoy the critical mass so vital to creating sustainable competitive advantage. The aggressive implementation of this strategy has completely reshaped our corporate profile, in terms of both business portfolio and geographical reach.[7]

Now that the firm had achieved its "primary strategic goal," Rhône-Poulenc shifted its emphasis from acquiring additional units to improving the operations of existing units. Fourtou described his goal as the "continued blending of recently acquired activities into our existing business organization," and "streamlining" the firm's activities.

As part of this "blending" and "streamlining," some managers in France suggested that the time had come to rethink the corporation's overall organization. Now that each of the Sectors had reached a critical size and possessed substantial operations around the world, perhaps Sector headquarters should assume primary decision-making responsibility for all activities worldwide. Accordingly, a proposal was set forth in which Sector management would be responsible not just for the formulation of strategy but for its execution, as well. The Sectors would take a more active role in all product-line related issues, ranging from R&D to manufacturing to marketing. Rhône-Poulenc's many country organizations would give up direct strategic oversight and evolve toward primarily administrative and support responsibilities.

---

[7]Rhône-Poulenc 1990 Annual Report, p. 3.

Shifting the primary locus of power to the Sectors seemed attractive because it would, at least in theory, allow for each product line to be optimized on a global basis. But in practice, moving toward a Sector-based structure might not be an easy matter. In the United States, for example, a strong country organization had been developed following the acquisitions of the late 1980s. The president of Rhône-Poulenc Inc., Pete Neff, had become the "single voice" who represented Rhône-Poulenc in the United States, and had provided an essential unity of command during the phase of organization building and acquisition assimilation. He had been hired to build the U.S. organization, to personify Rhône-Poulenc in the United States, and by all accounts had performed those tasks well. How Pete Neff's role would change under the proposed re-organization was unclear. In addition to Neff, other U.S. managers had joined Rhône-Poulenc with assurances of autonomy and freedom from Paris. Their reaction to greater decision-making power located at Sector headquarters was uncertain.

As Rhône-Poulenc's top officers pondered their options, several were concerned that a move toward greater power at the Sector level might undo precisely what had been built during the preceding years. Rhône-Poulenc Inc. was a large and growing operation, of high importance to the firm as a whole, yet it was still a young organization. Corporate management was hesitant to make changes that would disrupt the progress of the U.S. affiliate.

23   PHIL JOHNSON

Saturday, September 26, 1992. "We're getting there!" thought Phil Johnson as the Sabena flight took off from Brussels on its way to Lagos, Nigeria. Phil Johnson was the vice president, marketing, of Basic Furniture, a middle-sized Columbus, Ohio, office furniture manufacturer. He was going to Lagos to close a business deal that Martha Langford, the owner of Basic Furniture, had been negotiating in the preceding weeks. Phil had left his home in Columbus 26 hours earlier and he looked forward to reaching his final destination.

Phil decided to go over the specifics of the deal one more time and review the strategy that he would follow in the next day's meeting with his Nigerian partners. This was his first trip to Africa and he was uncertain about local business practices. Since he would be in Lagos for a short stay, he wanted everything to go smoothly.

The Deal

The deal required Basic Furniture to facilitate a financial transaction involving an international transfer of funds and would earn the company over $5.0 million, their 35 percent share of the $14.3 million deal. Martha Langford had been approached a month earlier by Tokunbo Jacobs with the business proposal (see Exhibit 1 for a copy of Mr. Jacobs' initial letter to Ms. Langford). Intrigued by the prospect, she entered into discussions with Mr. Jacobs. Ms. Langford was in the process of negotiating a sale in Bahrain on the Persian Gulf and thought that Africa could offer additional prospects for her company:

This case was prepared by Professor J. Nyeri, of The University of Northern Nigeria as a basis for class discussion, rather than to illustrate either effective or ineffective handling of an administrative situation. Copyright © 1993 by J. Nyeri.

Exhibit 1   Initial Letter Sent by Tokunbo Jacobs to Martha Langford*

26th August 1992   Tokunbo Jacobs
                                                        32 Falkar Street, Lagos, Nigeria
                                                     Tel. 234-1-874235, FAX 234-1-442157
                                                            TELEX 37854 RT NG

Dear Mr. President,

I am Mr. Tokunbo Jacobs, a staff of Nigerian National Petroleum Corporation (NNPC) and a member of the "Tender Committee" of same corporation. I got your contact address through a close relation who is the corporate affairs manager of Nigerian Export Promotions Council. The transaction which is detailed below is being presented to you based on mutual trust and confidentiality.

After due consultation with other members of the Tender committee, I have been specifically mandated to arrange with you the remittance of $14.3M. being an over estimated sum resulting from contract executed by an expatriate contractor. The original value of this contract was purposely over inflated by us (Tender Committee) with the sum of $14.3M. Now that the firm has received their supposed payments accordingly and the projects commissioned, I want you to nominate an account into which this money will be paid for division between us and you.

Sharing terms are:—35% to you as the owner of the account into which the money will be paid. 55% to the officials of the three parastatals. 10% is set aside for contingencies. The big bosses of the three parastatals involved in this transaction namely:—Nigerian National Petroleum Corporation (NNPC), Federal Ministry of Finance (FMF), and Central Bank of Nigeria (CBN) are aware and behind the deal.

Meanwhile, you are required to indicate your interest through my *FAX LINE* or *TELEX* by *personal call.* Please in your reply include your personal telephone, fax and telex numbers for easy communications.

You can be rest assured that within few weeks of my receipt of your positive reply this amount will be remitted into your nominated account.

May I demand with *the* highest respect for the code of business morality and secrecy that under no circumstance should you circumvent or share with any uninvolved person the contents of this letter and other vital documents that may arise in the course of this noble transaction until it is accomplished.

I look forward to your pragmatic conformity to this mutual proposition.

Yours faithfully,

TOKUNBO JACOBS

*The text of the letter is original. The address, phone, fax, and telex numbers have been disguised.

Business is all over the world for us. You have to adapt yourself to the fact that conditions are different in other countries from how they are here. This is just part of living in today's world.

In response to her inquires, she received further details on the deal (see the two faxes in Exhibit 2 and Exhibit 3) and decided to send Phil Johnson to Nigeria to complete the negotiations with the Nigerians.

EXHIBIT 2   September 12 Fax from Jacobs to Langford

FAX: 12 September 1992
FROM: TOKUNBO JACOBS
ATTENTION: MARTHA LANGFORD

Thanks for your fax of 9 September 1992 accepting to do this business with us. As you rightly mentioned there must be some responsibilities from your company to see this deal through. As a matter of fact you will be required to send to us some basic documents regarding your company to enable us to process payment to your account.

The requirements are:

1. Two of your company's letter headed papers
2. Two of your company's proforma invoices
3. Bank particulars in which the said money will be transferred to:—the name of the bank, the account number, the telex number of the bank

On receipt of these above requirements the money will be remitted within twenty one working days.

Martha, I will suggest you visit us with the requirements to expedite this deal and to enable the officials involve in this transaction meet with you person to person for more confidence and to enable to meet who we are entrusting our money. Furthermore I want your personal home phone number for easy communications. Remember we will not hesitate to ask for your assistance financially if the need arises which will be dually deducted from the 10% set aside as contingencies during the process of this transaction. All request needed by you will be given proper attention.

Note: There is no risk whatsoever in this transaction putting into consideration our good home work and calibre of people involved in this deal.

Acknowledge receipt of this message through my fax number 442157.

Thanks and God bless.

TOKUNBO JACOBS

The Nigerian Context

Nigeria offered significant business opportunities (for a profile on Nigeria, see Exhibit 4). *Marketing Force News*[1] described Nigeria's potential as follows:

> Nigeria, this African giant and Africa's greatest hope, a country where Christians and Muslims form a homogeneous group, a country possessing great assets with a population of more than 90 million inhabitants, including the greatest of Africa's elite, is often referred to as an example for its commercial liberalization policy, and its democratization process.

---

[1]September 1992, p. 1.

EXHIBIT 3   September 21 Fax from Jacobs to Langford

FAX: 21 September 1992
FROM: TOKUNBO JACOBS
ATTENTION: MARTHA LANGFORD
  Consequent to our telephone discussions, these are the required information. When you despatch those documents via DHL courier service, including your company's catalogues, fax the air way bill number to me to enable me to pick them up in earnest.

  I want you to realize that there are some expenses which we cannot afford to ignore if this transaction *must* succeed highfreely. We will need US$48,000.00 in order to off-set these expenses. We therefore solicit you to assist us with the already set aside amount. As regards the account:

Beneficiary:	Larry Oluntigo
Bank Name:	National First Bank of Nigeria PLC
	Broad Street, Branch Lagos
	Nigeria
Account Number:	1554

Below is the format for the attorney:

The Governor of Central Bank of Nigeria
Tinubu Square Lagos

Dear Sir,

Letter of Authority

  I wish to inform you that I Mrs. Martha Langford, the president of Basic Furniture Company of U.S.A. hereby authorize barrister Eze Bakoto to sign on my behalf for the release of the sum of US$14.3 million U.S. dollars being payment for contract completed in 1990 for N.N.P.C. This is due to my present indisposed condition.
  I look forward to your anticipated cooperation.

Yours faithfully,

Martha Langford (President)

N.B.: The about format should be typed on your company's letter-headed paper and should be included with the courier documents.

  Nigeria's gross domestic product was the largest on the African continent (in 1990, it amounted to U.S. $119 billion at constant 1987 prices and exchange rates, while the GDP for the rest of sub-Saharan Africa combined was $148 billion). The country was endowed with significant resources. For example, Nigeria was the world's sixth-largest producer of peanuts and the eight-largest producer of rubber. It also produced important quantities of cotton, cocoa, yams, cassava, sorghum, corn, and rice.

EXHIBIT 4   Nigerian File

October 1st, 1963:	The establishment of the Republic of Nigeria.
January 5th, 1966:	Military coup. The Biafran war begins, lasting two years and causing several million deaths of which approximately 2 million were Biafran.
December 31st, 1983:	Military coup. Benral Buhari overturns President Shagari and seizes power.
April 23rd, 1984:	Demonetization operations: bank notes are no longer in circulation and are replaced by a new currency.
August 27th, 1985:	State coup. General Ibrahim Babangida replaces General Buhari as head of the country.
September 26th, 1986:	End of the flat exchange rate and the implementation of a controlled flexibility in currency auction sales resulting in a 70% devaluation of the naira and in a currency fluctuation.
April 22nd, 1990:	Unsuccessful state coup againt president Babangida.
July 27th, 1990:	42 military shot after aborted state coup of April 22nd, 1990.
April 22nd, 1991:	Riots provoked by Shiite fundamentalists causing two hundred deaths.

GNP per habitant: $360 US/1990, United Nations Development Programs, The World Bank.
Population: Approximately 90 million inhabitants
Area: 923,768 sq km
Density: 117 persons/sq km
Capital: Lagos—10,000,000 inhabitants
Educational attainment: 47%
Agricultural land: 34%
Languages spoken: English and approximately 200 dialects

Source: Adapted from *Marketing Force News,* September 1992, p. 6.

Nigeria was the eighth-largest producer of petroleum in the world and the fifth-largest exporter (second-largest exporter of petroleum to the United States). Oil revenues were channeled toward the creation of an industrial base and the strengthening of the agricultural sector. Other important industries included mining (natural gas, coal) and processing (oil, palm, peanuts, cotton, petroleum).

Phil's Position

Phil Johnson wondered how to approach the negotiations with the Nigerians and to resolve a few issues that had not been addressed. He wanted the deal to go through without upsetting his partners. Phil had just read during the stopover in Brussels a business publication that emphasized the need to be "skillful in the art of bargaining" when dealing with Nigerians (see Exhibit 5).

Phil and Martha had agreed on what should be obtained from the Nigerians. They believed that 5 percent (i.e., $715,000) was more than sufficient to cover the contingencies associated with the completion of this deal. They wanted the contingency fund reduced from 10 to 5 percent and their share raised from 35 to 40 percent.

Phil's plan was to negotiate the financial commitments to be made by both sides prior to the release of funds so as to minimize Basic Furniture's exposure. In order to have a clear picture of the expenses to be incurred in the implementation of the deal and of the respective contributions expected from each side, he wanted to examine the pro forma financial statements prepared by Mr. Tokunbo. His objective was to modify them to Basic Furniture's advantage.

In a phone conversation with Mr. Tokunbo, Phil had found that, to do business with the Nigerian government and its agencies, it was necessary to be registered in the official list of prequalified suppliers. Various approvals and stamps were required in the registration process. The $48,000 requested in the September 21 fax were for that purpose.

Phil also wanted to obtain a written commitment that all expenses and advances incurred by Basic Furniture would be reimbursed from the contingency fund, including his travel and accommodation expenses that amounted to just over $5,000.

Phil brought with him all the documents requested by the Nigerian partners, including a power of attorney signed by Martha Langford, which authorized him to conclude the deal on behalf of Basic Furniture.

As he closed the Nigerian file and put it back in his briefcase, Phil wondered how he should conduct the negotiations in order to achieve his objectives and without jeopardizing the relationship.

EXHIBIT 5   Doing Business in Nigeria

Greetings: In Nigeria, greetings are highly valued among the different ethnic groups. Refusing to greet another is a sign of disrespect. Due to the diversity of customs, cultures, and dialects that exist among the different ethnic groups in Nigeria, English is widely used in exchanging greetings throughout the country. Visitors are advised and encouraged to greet while in Nigeria. "Hello" is the most popular greeting. More formal greetings, such as "Good Morning," "Good Afternoon," and Good Evening" are also appropriate. Avoid the use of casual or colloquial greetings and phrases such as "Hi" or What's happening?" In addition, visitors are also encouraged to be courteous and cheerful when exchanging greetings. Do not be arrogant. Nigerians treat visitors with respect and, in return, expect to be treated with respect. Personal space between members of the same sex is much closer than in North America. This may cause discomfort to those not accustomed to conversing at close quarters.

Visiting: Nigerians try very hard to please their guests. Although Nigerians are generally not too concerned with time, they know about the western habit of punctuality and expect their western friends to arrive at the appointed time. Most Nigerians prefer "African time" to western punctuality. Nigerians treat their guests with congenial respect and expect their guests to respond in the same manner. Nigerians possess a rich heritage and hope for a bright future as a modern African nation, and thus can be offended by a "superior" attitude of some visitors.

Tipping: A dash (from the Portuguese word das, meaning "give") is a common Nigerian form of compensation in money, goods, or favours for services rendered. With the exception of services performed by waiters or bellhops, a "dash" is normally paid before the service is given. If the service offered is not desired, a firm refusal is usually necessary. The government is officially committed to discouraging certain kinds of dash that resemble bribery, such as payments for help in clearing customs, getting visas, or obtaining preferential treatment from government officials. But the custom is widespread and one has to be skillful in the art of "bargaining."

Personal Appearance: Dress varies according to the area and the culture. In the Muslim north, dress is very conservative for both men and women. Dress is more casual in the non-Muslim east and west. Shorts are not considered appropriate attire for Nigerian adults. For men, a shirt and tie are appropriate for formal and most other semi-formal occasions. Visitors will be most comfortable in cotton clothing—polyester is too warm. Traditional Nigerian men's dress is loose and comfortable. Although women in the cities and young girls often wear western dress, most women wear traditional long wraparound skirts, short-sleeved tops, and head scarves. The fabric is renowned for its color and patterns.

Gestures: Nigeria is a multicultural nation and gestures differ from one ethnic group to another. Generally, pushing the palm of the hand forward with the fingers spread is a vulgar gesture and should be avoided. One should not point the sole of the foot at a

EXHIBIT 5   (concluded)

person. Using the left hand in eating (unless left-handed) or in receiving something from someone has a bad connotation. The Yorubas (a large major ethnic group), in addition to the Ibibios and Igbos (two smaller, although major ethnic groups), will wink if they want their children to leave the room.

General Attitudes: Individual Nigerians are proud of the unique cultural heritage of their particular ethnic group. There is some ethnic tension, but continuing efforts are gradually unifying the nation. The Nigerians are striving to create a modern industrial society that is uniquely "African," and not "western." Because of negative connotations attached to the word "tribe," Nigerians avoid its use and "ethnic group" is often used in its place. Life in Nigeria moves at a relaxed pace with exception to Lagos which can be very frenzied. People are generally not as time conscious as in the west.

Language: English is the official language in Nigeria. However, because of the Nigerian mother tongue influence, spoken English may be difficult to understand. Pidgin English (broken English) is widely spoken by uneducated Nigerians, although even educated people widely use Pidgin English as a medium of informal conversation among themselves. Each of the over 250 ethnic groups also has it own distinct language. Hausa, Yoruba, and Ibo are widely spoken. Educated Nigerians usually are fluent in several languages.

Religion: In very general terms, Nigeria can be said to be divided between the Muslim North (47%) and the Christian South (34%), with a strong minority of traditional religions throughout the country (18%). However, it is important to note that both the Christians and the Muslims have strong missionary movements all over the whole country making the division of faiths to a particular region not exactly accurate. In addition, Nigerians may claim membership in a particular religion but may also incorporate traditional worship practices and beliefs into their daily life.

Family: Although the technical details of family structure vary from culture to culture, Nigerian families are generally male-dominated. The practice of polygamy is common throughout the country. The protected status of Muslim women in Nigeria is similar to other Muslim countries, however, most other Nigerian women enjoy a great degree of freedom by influencing family decisions and engaging in open trade at the market place, where the money they make is their own. Large families traditionally help share the workload at home. Nigerians pay deep respect to their elders. Children are trained to be quiet, respectful, and unassertive in their relations with adults. Marriage customs vary, but the payment of bridal wealth (money, property, or service traditionally given to the family of the bride by the husband) is common throughout the country.

Social and Economic Levels: Nigerians have the third highest average income in sub-Sahara Africa, but are still very poor by western standards. The average home consist of 1.4 rooms and more than 3 people per room. About 30% of the people live in absolute poverty. Nigeria once had the ninth lowest crime rate in the world, but without current statistics, it is difficult to determine the country's rank today.

Business Schedules: Most businesses are open from 8:00 am to 12:30 pm, and then reopen from 2:00 to 4:30 pm. Government offices are open from 7:30 am to 3:30 pm Monday through Friday. Many establishments and shops are also open on Saturdays with shorter hours. Every fourth Saturday is "Sanitation Day" (where no one is allowed on the street before 10:00 am) and shops normally are not ready to receive business before noon. Sunday is the normal day of rest. Business appointments must be made in advance. Due to the poor telephone communications, business is often discussed on a person-to-person basis versus via the telephone. Westerners are expected to be prompt, even though they may have to wait for some time after arriving.

Source: Canadian High Commission, Lagos, 1991.

24   LARSON IN NIGERIA–1994

David Larson, Vice-President of International Operations for Larson Inc., was mulling over the decisions he was required to make regarding the company's Nigerian operation. He was disturbed by the negative tone of the report sent to him on January 4, 1994, by the Chief Executive Officer of the Nigerian affiliate, George Ridley (see Exhibit 1). Larson believed the future prospects for Nigeria were excellent and was concerned about what action he should take.

Company Background

Larson Inc. was a New York-based multinational corporation in the wire and cable business. Wholly-owned subsidiaries were located in Canada and the United Kingdom, while Mexico, Venezuela, Australia, and Nigeria were the sites of joint ventures. Other countries around the world were serviced through exports from the parent or one of its subsidiaries.

The parent company was established in 1925 by David Larson's grandfather. Ownership and management of the company remained in the hands of the Larson family and was highly centralized. The annual sales volume for the corporation worldwide approximated $575 million in 1993. Revenue was primarily generated from the sale of power, communication, construction and control cables.

Technical service was an important part of Larson Inc.'s product package; therefore, the company maintained a large force of engineers to consult with customers and occasionally supervise installation. As a consequence, licensing was really not a viable method of serving foreign markets.

Professor I.A. Litvak of York University prepared this case solely to provide material for class discussion. It was revised by Professor Paul W. Beamish of The University of Western Ontario, with the assistance of Mr. Harry Cheung. The case is not intended to illustrate either effective or ineffective handling of a managerial situation. Certain names and other identifying information may have been disguised to protect confidentiality. Copyright © 1995, The University of Western Ontario.

EXHIBIT 1   The Ridley Report

In response to the request from head office for a detailed overview of the Nigerian situation and its implications for Larson Inc., George Ridley prepared the following report in December, 1993. It attempts to itemize the factors in the Nigerian environment that have contributed to the problems experienced by Larson's joint venture in Nigeria.

The Nigerian Enterprises Promotion Decrees

1. There can be no doubt that the Nigerian Enterprises Promotion Decree of 1977 represents very severe and far-reaching indigenization legislation. The cumulative damaging effects of the decree have been exacerbated by some aspects of its implementation. In particular, the valuation of companies by the Nigerian Securities and Exchange Committee has in many cases been unrealistically low. This has represented substantial real-capital asset losses to the overseas companies concerned, which had no opportunity of appeal to an independent authority. Although the Decree was amended in 1989 to remove some of these problems, companies have experienced difficulties and delays in obtaining foreign currency for the remittance of proceeds from the sale of shares. A disquieting feature has been the enforced imposition, in certain cases, of a requirement to issue new equity in Nigeria instead of selling existing shares, with the consequent ineligibility to remit even part of the proceeds from Nigeria and dilution of value to both Nigerian and foreign shareholders. Another aspect causing great concern is related to the time constraint for compliance, particularly as the Nigerian authorities concerned appear to be literally snowed under with applications.

Remittance

2. In addition to the problems of remittances of the proceeds from the sale of shares, there has been a steadily increasing delay in the granting of foreign exchange for remittances from Nigeria, such as payment for supplies and services from overseas. Whereas early this year delays of about one year were being reported, delays of up to five years or even more are now not unusual. Larson Nigeria cannot continue to operate effectively if it is unable to remit proceeds and pay bills in a reasonable time frame. It is in the position of importing $5.5 million in products and services annually. These delays in remittances, coupled with delays in payments (see paragraph 4 (a) below), also raise problems related to export guarantees, which normally are of limited duration only.

3. A problem regarding remittances has arisen as a result of the Nigerian Insurance Decree No. 59, under which cargoes due for import to Nigeria have to be insured with a Nigerian-registered insurance company. For cargoes imported without confirmed letters of credit, claims related to cargo loss and damage are paid in Nigeria; however, foreign exchange for remittance to pay the overseas suppliers is not being granted on the grounds that the goods have not arrived.

Problems Affecting Liquidity and Cash Flow

4. A number of problems have arisen during the last two years that are having a serious effect upon liquidity and cash flow, with the result that local expenses can be met only by increasing bank borrowing, which is not only an additional cost but also becoming more difficult to obtain.

   (a) Serious delays exist in obtaining payment from federal and state government departments for supplies and services provided, even in instances where payment terms are clearly written into the contract concerned. This is particularly true for state governments where payment of many

---

EXHIBIT 1   *(continued)*

---

accounts is 12 months or more in arrears. Even after payment, further delays and exchange-rate losses are experienced in obtaining foreign currency for the part that is remittable abroad. This deterioration in cash flow from government clients has, in turn, permeated through to the private clients.

(b) There is a requirement that a 100 percent deposit be made on application for foreign currency to cover letters of credit.

(c) In order to clear the cargo as soon as possible and to avoid possible loss at the wharf, importers normally pay their customs duty before a ship arrives.

(d) Under the current FIFO inventory system, net earning after tax (35 percent income tax + 2 percent education tax) is insufficient to cover increased working capital requirements and to maintain an adequate inventory.

Incomes and Prices Policy Guidelines

5. Many of the guidelines issued by the Productivity, Prices and Incomes Board are of direct discouragement, as they make operations in Nigeria increasingly less attractive in comparison with other areas in the world. Although these guidelines were removed in 1987, increases for wage, salary, fees for professional services and auditing are still subject to final government approval.

Dividends

6. While Larson Inc. welcomed the raising of the level of dividend restriction from 30 percent gross (16.5 percent net) to 40 percent gross (20 percent net) of issued capital, the exclusion of script/bonus issues past October 1, 1976, is still a matter of concern where profits that would otherwise have been available for remittance have been reinvested. It seems inequitable that investors, both indigenous and foreign, should not receive a return on this reinvestment. Furthermore, it results in an artificial dilution of share value for both indigenous and overseas shareholders.

7. The regulations regarding interim dividends are also a matter of concern. The requirement to pay advance income tax on such dividends prior to the due date for payment of tax on the full year's income is unreasonable, and the rule under which remittance to overseas shareholders has to await final account is discriminatory.

Offshore Technical and Management Services

8. Restrictions on the reimbursement of expenses to the parent company for offshore management and technical services are a cause of great concern, since such services are costly to provide.

Professional Fees

9. The whole position regarding fees for professional services provided from overseas is most unsatisfactory. Not only are the federal government scales substantially lower than those in most other countries, but also the basis of the project cost applied in Nigeria is out of keeping with normally accepted international practice. The arbitrary restriction on the percentage of fees that may be remitted is a further disincentive to attracting professional services. Moreover, payment of professional fees in themselves produces cash flow problems exacerbated by long delays in payments and remittance approvals (referred to above).

EXHIBIT 1   *(continued)*

Royalties and Trademarks

10. The Nigerian government's apparent unpreparedness to permit payment of royalties for the use of trademarks for a period of more than 10 years is out of keeping with the generally accepted international practice.

Expatriate Quotas, Work Permits, and Entry Visas

11. It must be recognized that expatriate expertise is a very important element for this business, but an expatriate staff is very costly. Unfortunately, at the present time there are a number of difficulties and frustrations, such as the arbitrary cuts in expatriate quotas, the delays in approving quota renewal, and in some cases, the refusal of entry visas and work permits for individuals that are required for work in Nigeria.

Expatriate Staff

12. In general, the conditions of employment and life in Nigeria are regarded as unattractive when compared with conditions in many other countries competing for the same expertise. These differences are due to: the general deterioration in law and order; the restrictions on salary increase and home remittance; the difficulties in buying air tickets; the poor standard of health care; the unsatisfactory state of public utilities such as electricity, water, and telecommunications; the harassment from the police, airport authorities and other government officials; the general frustrations related to visas and work permits mentioned above. The situation has now reached a stage where not only is recruitment of suitably qualified skilled experts becoming increasingly difficult, but we are also faced with resignations and refusals to renew contracts even by individuals who have worked and lived here for some years. Furthermore, the uncertainty over the length of time for which employment in Nigeria will be available (due to doubts whether the necessary expatriate quotas will continue to be available to the employer) is most unsettling to existing staff. This and the restriction of contracts to as little as two years are important factors in deterring the more highly qualified applicants from considering posts in Nigeria. These factors are resulting in a decline in the quality of the expatriate staff it is possible to recruit.

Local Staff

13. Nigeria has one of the strongest national unions in Africa. Its National Labor Congress (NLC) basically operates in every joint venture employing over 100 workers. It is almost impossible to discipline a worker without attracting confrontation with the union. On certain occasions, some union members can be very militant. The union is also continuously attacking the employment of expatriates and trying to replace them with Nigerian staff.

14. Inadequate local technical training leads to low quality workers who tend to be lazy and not quality conscious.

15. The desirability of maintaining a tribal balance in the work force limits the options in recruiting the best workers.

16. Nigerian companies suffer heavily from pilferage, which normally accounts for 2 percent of sales.

Exhibit 1   (concluded)

Public Utilities

17. The constant interruption in public utility services not only affects the morale of all employees but also has a very serious impact upon the operation of the business itself. Unless reasonable and continuing supplies of electricity, water, petroleum products and telecommunications can be assured, and the highway adequately maintained, the costs related to setting up and operating escalate.

Continuity of Operating Conditions

18. The general and growing feeling of uncertainty about the continuity of operating conditions is a matter of considerable concern. It would seem that this uncertainty is engendered by a whole range of matters related to: short notice changes (sometimes even retrospective) in legislation and regulations; imprecise definition of legislation and regulations, which leads to long periods of negotiation and uncertainty; delays between public announcement of measures and promulgation of how they are to be implemented; and sometimes inconsistent interpretation of legislation and regulations by Nigerian officials.

Government Officials

19. Foreign partners have to rely on their Nigerian counterpart to handle the government officials. But it is impossible to measure its performance nor to control its expenses in these activities. In addition, carefully cultivated relationships with officials could disappear, as they are transferred frequently.

Bribery

20. Surrounding many of the problems previously listed is the pervasive practice of bribery, known locally as the *dash*. Without such a payment, it is very difficult to complete business or government transactions with native Nigerians.

Background on Nigeria

Nigeria is located in the west-central part of the African continent. With 105 million people in 1993, it was the most populous country in Africa and the ninth most populous nation in the world. From 1970 to 1993, population had grown by 2.4 percent annually. About 47 percent of the population was under 15 years of age.

Seventy-five per cent of the labour force in Nigeria worked in agriculture. About 20 percent of the population lived in urban centres.

The gross national product in 1993 was about $33-billion. While per capita GNP was only about $310, on a purchasing power parity basis it was substantially higher at $1,480. GNP had grown from 1987 to 1993 at over 5 percent annually—one of the highest rates in the world. This increase was fueled in part by the export sales of Nigeria's large oil reserves.

During the 1988 to 1992 period, Nigeria's annual inflation rate had ranged between 8 and 51 percent. This fluctuation had contributed to the change in the value of the naira from 4.5 to the US dollar in 1988 to 17.3 to the U.S. dollar in 1992.

The Nigerian Operation

Larson Inc. established a joint venture in Nigeria in 1984 with a local partner who held 25 percent of the joint venture's equity. In 1989, Larson Inc. promised Nigerian authorities that the share of local ownership would be increased to 51 percent within the next five to seven years. Such indigenization requests from developing country governments were quite common.

Sales revenue for the Nigerian firm totaled $28 million in 1993. Of this revenue, $24.5 million was realized in Nigeria, while $3.5 million was from exports. About 40 percent of the firm's Nigerian sales ($10 million) were made to various enterprises and departments of the government of Nigeria. The company was making a reasonable profit of 10 percent of revenue, but with a little bit of luck and increased efficiency, it was believed it could make a profit of 20 percent.

The Nigerian operation had become less attractive for Larson Inc. in recent months. Although it was widely believed that Nigeria would become one of the key economic players in Africa in the 1990s and that the demand for Larson's products would remain very strong there, doing business in Nigeria was becoming more costly. Furthermore, Larson Inc. had become increasingly unhappy with its local partner in Nigeria, a lawyer who was solely concerned with quick "paybacks" at the expense of reinvestment and long-term growth prospects.

David Larson recognized that having the right partner in a joint venture was of paramount importance. The company expected the partner or partners to be actively engaged in the business, "not businesspeople interested in investing money alone." The partner was also expected to hold a substantial equity in the venture. In the early years of the joint venture, additional funding was often required and it was necessary for the foreign partner to be in a strong financial position.

The disillusionment of George Ridley, the Nigerian firm's CEO, had been increasing since his early days in that position. He was an expatriate from the United Kingdom who, due to his background as a military officer, placed a high value upon order and control. The chaotic situation in Nigeria proved very trying for him. His problems were further complicated by his inability to attract good local employees in Nigeria, while his best expatriate staff requested transfers to New York or Larson Inc.'s other foreign operations soon after their arrival in Nigeria. On a number of occasions, Ridley was prompted to suggest to head office that it reconsider its Nigerian commitment.

The Decision

David Larson reflected on the situation. He remained convinced that Larson Inc. should maintain its operations in Nigeria; however, he had to design a plan to increase local Nigerian equity in the venture to 51 percent. Larson also wondered what should be done about Ridley. On the one hand, Ridley had been with the company for many years and knew the business intimately; on the other hand, Larson felt that Ridley's attitude was contributing to the poor morale in the Nigerian firm and wondered if Ridley had lost his sense of adaptability. Larson knew Ridley had to be replaced, but he was unsure about the timing and the method to use, since Ridley was only two years away from retirement.

Larson had to come to some conclusions fairly quickly. He had been requested to prepare an action plan for the Nigerian operation for consideration by the board of directors of Larson Inc. in a month's time. He thought he should start by identifying the key questions, whom he should contact, and how he should handle Ridley in the meantime.

25 YUTAKA NAKAMURA: A FOREIGNER IN HIS NATIVE LAND

As he neared the top of the stairs that would lead him to the subway train and his hour and a half commute to his office, Yutaka Nakamura hesitated and then quickly moved aside to allow the mass of morning commuters to push their way down to the most punctual and safe mass transit system in the world. As he stood there at the top of the stairs watching the mass of humanity before him, he reflected on the past six months since he and his family had returned to Japan from their overseas assignment in the United States. Once again, this morning his wife had cried and asked him to request another transfer overseas. After listening to his wife, Yutaka pushed back the carefully prepared breakfast his wife had made. Like most mornings lately, he left for work without eating much and with a throbbing headache left over from the previous night's drinking and socializing. As he stood there knowing that he needed to hurry down the stairs in order to catch the train that would put him into Tokyo and at his office precisely ten minutes before nine o'clock, Yutaka wondered what direction his life should take.

Background

Yutaka, 44, prior to being sent to a key subsidiary in California four years ago, was in the sales department in a large electronics firm. He was hired directly after graduating from Tokyo University, the most prestigious university in all of Japan. His wife Chizuru, 40, was a graduate of Sofia University and the daughter of a former parliament member of Japan's Lower House. Yutaka and Chizuru met when they were both employees in the same department of the electronics firm. After they were married, they waited a few years to have their first child, Kenichi, now 14 and a very bright and outgoing teenager. Three years after Kenichi was born, they had their daughter,

This case was prepared by Associate Professor J. Stewart Black to provide the basis for class discussion rather than to illustrate effective or ineffective administration.

Yukimi. Yutaka felt he had a fairly typical middle-class Japanese life. Given that he worked in one of the largest electronics firms in the world, with operations in over 100 different countries, it was not surprising that Yutaka was asked to fill an overseas position in the marketing and sales department in southern California. He was given the position of co-vice president of marketing. Although it took some effort, Yutaka adjusted to living and working in southern California with its much more leisurely paced life and work style compared to Tokyo.

At first Chizuru had trouble adjusting to living in the United States. It took her several months before her English was sufficiently proficient for her to go grocery shopping, driving, and otherwise to take care of various family needs. Chizuru's English was much more labored than that of the other family members, but she eventually reached the point where she felt comfortable talking with the various neighbors who lived around them.

The children, on the other hand, quickly adjusted to the California lifestyle. In particular, Kenichi enjoyed whatever time he could at the beach, where he learned how to surf. Both children did extremely well in school and after their first year were completely age-proficient in English. The children attended normal American schools during the weekday, but on weekends spent one and a half days in a special Japanese school. Chizuru also had correspondence work sent from Japan and spent weekends helping the children with math, science, and Japanese reading and writing.

In general, the Nakamuras enjoyed their new lifestyle, the three-bedroom, 2600 sq. ft. house, the two cars, the weekends of picnics, museums, and camping, the evenings spent together barbecuing in the backyard, and the yearly holiday back to Japan.

In spite of the fact they enjoyed their life in America, when it came time to return to Japan, all of the family members were excited to return. Other than checking on schools back in Tokyo, little thought was given to preparing for the re-entry and re-adjustment back to Japan. After all, they were going home.

Problems since Return

Unfortunately, things had not gone as smoothly as they had anticipated since their return to Japan. The kids, Chizuru, and Yutaka had their own particular problems in adjusting to life back in Japan.

The Children

Although Kenichi and Yukimi had spent weekends in a special Japanese school while they were overseas, when they returned, it became very clear they were somewhat behind in several key areas. In particular, they were behind in math, science, and written Japanese. As a consequence, Chizuru hired a special private tutor to help the children with these subjects. She was most concerned that Kenichi was not adequately prepared for the upcoming high school exam. She hoped he would be able to enter an "escalator" high school (i.e., those particularly well-known for facilitating their graduates in entering a prestigious Japanese university). However, soon after their return. Chizuru began to get phone calls from the children's teachers and school administrators. In particular, Kenichi's teacher commented that he asked too many questions during class, and that his memorization skills seemed to be quite poor. Kenichi also seemed unwilling to accept facts as stated by the teacher, and constantly wanted to know the logic behind various statements.

Yukimi adjusted somewhat more easily than Kenichi to school. However, not long after they returned to Japan, she complained that her classmates were calling her *Gaigin,* which translated means foreigner.

Both children commented that their peers ridiculed some of their clothes, which they had purchased while they were in California. Some of their teachers commented that both Yukimi and Kenichi were not as proficient as they should be in the variations of their speech needed when speaking to individuals of differing status. Kenichi also complained several times that he didn't get jokes told at school because he didn't understand the particular slang expression that was being used. Chizuru was disappointed to find that the children's English ability actually worked against them in their English classes. In particular, Kenichi had difficulty because he felt his English teacher had terrible pronunciation. A couple of times Kenichi offered a correct pronunciation, only to be ridiculed by his teacher and his classmates. Eventually, Kenichi had to consciously try to forget correct English pronunciation, and pronounce English words with a strong Japanese accent.

One Sunday morning, before going off to a special weekend class at a nearby *Juku,* or cram school, Kenichi asked his mother if his father would play catch with him with the half hour he had before he needed to go. Chizuru replied that his father was asleep and tired from the long hours of work. At this Kenichi exploded and burst out that his father was never around. They used to go to museums and the park and camping when they lived in the United States, now it was clear his father loved his job more than he loved his children. In tears, Kenichi ran out of the house and off to his cram session.

Above all these developments, one of the most disturbing had only recently emerged. Chizuru knew that both of the children had enjoyed much of their experience in the U.S.; however, lately she found them criticizing California and the U.S. to their friends. In fact, one day she overheard Yukimi telling a classmate that she hated America; she hated Americans; and she hated her parents for making her live in that foreign country. This 180-degree turn in attitude seriously troubled Chizuru, but she didn't know what to do about it or what it meant.

Chizuru Nakamura

Chizuru had her own difficulties adjusting to Japan. It had taken her about a year to begin to feel comfortable in the United States, but she now missed many things about their life in California. One of the most interesting aspects of life in the U.S. was the parties she and Yutaka attended and hosted together. When they hosted parties at their California home, her role was quite different than back in Japan. In the U.S. when they hosted a party, both she and Yutaka would plan the event and then greet the guests at the door. Throughout the night guests would comment to Chizuru how lovely her home was, how wonderful the dinner was, and how beautiful she looked. These compliments were, at first, somewhat strange to her, but over time became a very important source of pride and satisfaction. In addition, during dinners, as was customary, Chizuru rarely sat by her husband. Instead she was often placed next to other spouses as well as other executives and clients with whom her husband associated. Many of these guests commented directly and indirectly about Chizuru's intelligent insights concerning international affairs. After some time, Chizuru found that she quite enjoyed both attending and hosting these social interactions. Instead of simply being relegated to the kitchen and bringing in various dishes for the guests only to quickly disappear again as was the custom in Japan, Chizuru found she played an important role in the social standing of her husband, and that she had an importance in her own right.

When she returned to Japan, of course, these social interactions were completely out of the question. Yutaka rarely brought friends home, and when he did, he brought them without their wives. Her role was not that of hostess as much as it was that of waitress. Chizuru longed for her life back in the U.S. On top of losing her broader role in life, Chizuru felt she lost her husband upon returning to Japan. During their time in the United States, Chizuru had felt that she had rediscovered the man she had fallen in love with and married over 17 years ago. Many times they would talk together at night or take walks in their quiet suburban neighborhood. Especially during the last two years of their overseas assignment, Chizuru and Yutaka would often go out for dinner, see a show, or attend a cultural event. Unfortunately, those times were long gone now.

When Chizuru had first returned to Japan, she tried to re-establish relationships with some of her friends. However, whenever she tried to tell them of her experiences in the U.S., they quickly seemed disinterested and on some occasions actually accused her of showing off. This hurt Chizuru deeply. In her heart, she was simply trying to share something that was very important to her with her friends in order to reconnect with them after the long absence.

In addition to these social difficulties, Chizuru often found herself depressed because of the difficulties the children were having at school. Chizuru had prided herself on the fact that she had kept the children involved in Japanese curriculum during their stay in the U.S. through correspondence work and the weekend Japanese classes. She was very disappointed and frustrated to find that once they had returned, the children were still somewhat behind in critical areas. Also, despite her best efforts, the children had not yet adjusted well to the new schools, and it was becoming increasingly doubtful that Kenichi would be able to pass the test and enter one of the more prestigious high schools. She was convinced that women in her neighborhood were talking about what a poor mother she was, and the disservice she had brought upon her children by not keeping them up-to-date in their schoolwork while overseas.

Chizuru had also found many other points of frustration during the six months since they had returned to Japan. Although she was unaware of it at first, many of the Western clothes she had purchased while in California had brighter colors than those in Japan. It had first occurred to her that her style of dress had changed when she had visited the market the first week after their return. As she was in the market buying fruits and vegetables for dinner that evening, she overheard one of her neighbors whisper to another that she must think herself better than the Japanese. After all, she was not wearing a traditional apron that all the women in that neighborhood wore when visiting the market.

The daily visits to the market were by themselves another irritant to Chizuru. In America, she had been able to shop once a week, or once every two weeks, because the refrigerator she had was large enough to store plenty of food. Going to the grocery store only once every week or two reduced the time she spent shopping and gave her more time to enjoy various activities. Now she had to spend two hours every day grocery shopping and had to spend nearly twice as much money on food because of its high cost in Japan. The high cost caused her to change the family's diet. For example, Yutaka, as well as the children, had come to like steak and other meats, but they were so expensive in Japan that Chizuru had to cut back dramatically on their purchase.

Another frustration concerned Chizuru's English language ability. In an effort to keep her language ability that she had worked so hard to achieve from declining, Chizuru joined an English class a month or so after returning to Japan. She very much enjoyed the classes until one day her sister-in-law commented that it was perhaps her attending English classes that was contributing to her children's difficulty in school. The fact that her sister-in-law would think such a thing made Chizuru wonder if she really was at the heart of her children's difficulties at school.

Her sister-in-law was not the only one with whom Chizuru had had difficulties since her return. Recently Chizuru's mother-in-law had asked her to come over. Although the request had seemed rather innocent at the time and her mother-in-law wanted nothing more than to chat, Chizuru discovered that it was a test of her loyalty. Her delay in going to visit her mother-in-law caused serious problems for a period of about two weeks. Yutaka had strongly criticized her for being so self-centered and not visiting his mother until the day after she called.

The cumulative effect of all these incidents was almost more than Chizuru could bear. One night after her husband arrived home at about 11:30 p.m., Chizuru in tears complained that she felt like Cinderella in reverse. All the wonderful things that she had come to enjoy were suddenly taken away from her, including her Prince Charming. When Yutaka replied that there was nothing that could be done, she begged him to seek another international assignment.

Yutaka Nakamura

Incidents big and small had taken their toll on Yutaka since his return to Japan. Often he had difficulty sleeping, and most mornings he headed to work with a throbbing headache. His wife was also worried because of his poor appetite. Yet, by many standards these were the typical ailments of a Japanese salaryman. Still, Chizuru encouraged Yutaka to take better care of himself. Yutaka was a little resentful of her concern and complaints. It seemed to him that on Sundays, his only free day at home, when he wanted to sleep, all he received was complaints from the family about his unwillingness to spend time with them. No matter what he did, someone was complaining.

Complaints also showed up rather frequently at work. For example, not long after he had returned home to Japan, he was reading a *Newsweek* on the train into work, just as he had often done before his assignment to America. However, once he got in his office, several of his peers chided him for showing off his language skills and reading an English news magazine instead of reading one of the more traditional Japanese news magazines. Surprised and hurt by this, Yutaka decided that from then on, even though he would continue to read *Newsweek* in order to pass the time on the train, he would hide it before entering the office so as not to offend his peers.

He was also frustrated about the slow decision-making process in Japan. In the U.S., it had been uncomfortable at first to make important decisions on his own, but he soon grew to enjoy the autonomy and responsibility. Back in Japan, even simple decisions, such as approving a minor promotion budget, required him to talk to dozens of people. In fact, the more people he talked to, the more people that were suggested for him to talk to. Often the people who were suggested seemed totally unrelated to the issue on which Yutaka was working. However, he was reminded that in Japan relationships are what makes businesses function. As a consequence, even though someone's opinion may not always directly bear on a particular project, it was important to stay connected with that person and for that person to feel that their opinion would be considered.

This emphasis on relationships also required after-hours socializing at least three nights a week until approximately 11:30 or 12 midnight. This socializing was particularly difficult for Yutaka to readjust to. The frequency was nothing short of exhausting. Twice he had fallen asleep on the train and had to stay in a hotel at the end of the line until he could take an early train home the next morning.

The commute in Japan was a far cry from his 20-minute commute in his comfortable car in California. Although he resented the complaints of his family about the time he spent at work, Yutaka was also frustrated with the long hours he spent away from his family. In fact, some days it felt as though he were wasting his entire life traveling on cram-packed, noisy trains.

Some days the train was so crowded that Yutaka could doze off without any worry of falling over. Some days after the long commute to or from work, life back in California seemed like a fading dream. Memories of going to museums, going to the beach, camping, and barbecues on the back patio were harder to recall. Now, it seemed to him that he was stuck in "no man's land." He no longer had the love and companionship of his family, and he also didn't feel completely accepted by his Japanese coworkers. It seemed to him that whatever direction he turned, any effort to try to please one group would alienate and displease another group. It was like being caught in an ever-tightening vice and there was no way out.

He felt frustrated almost on a daily basis at work because the marketing and negotiation skills that he had worked so hard to develop in the U.S. were going virtually unutilized back in Japan. Yutaka had gained great knowledge and insights into methods of integrating promotion print media and electronic media into unified marketing strategies. Unfortunately, in the general affairs department, these skills were not needed. Yutaka had also gained a great knowledge of how to negotiate effectively with Americans. He had mentioned his insights in this area several times to various people throughout the organization, but the only time he was allowed to utilize these skills was simply as a translator in a high-level meeting between a potential American supplier and the purchasing department. Yutaka had thought to himself that he had not worked so hard at understanding Americans' negotiation tactics and thinking only to simply translate words, rather than to formulate negotiation strategy.

Yutaka was rudely awakened from these reflections as someone crashed into him in their hurry down the steps to the subway. Unavoidably, Yutaka found himself running down the steps in order not to lose his balance. As he paid for his ticket and headed through the turnstile toward the tracks, he couldn't help but feel isolated and alone, despite being surrounded by 120 million Japanese.

Suddenly over the loudspeaker came the announcement that the train was arriving. As Yutaka looked down the track he saw the solitary beam of the approaching train. He wondered to himself how he should resolve these feelings he felt inside.

Should he ask for a transfer to another overseas assignment? If he did, he might become a permanent international assignee, rotating from one international assignment to another. This would virtually lock him out of any major advancement. Also, if he ever chose to return to Japan, it would probably be much more difficult the next time. Each time away would likely contribute to a deeper chasm between him and his home country and coworkers. Also, if the children went away again, this time it would be impossible for them to pass the entrance exams and get into a prestigious Japanese university. This would virtually guarantee that they would have to enter a foreign university. However, even if they went to a prestigious foreign university, such as Oxford, Harvard, or one of the grand ecoles in France, Yutaka doubted that they would ever be able to work for a large Japanese corporation. If they were given such a job, he doubted if they would ever be able to reach a position of any significance.

Yutaka worried that another overseas assignment would take his children away from both sets of grandparents. He had already heard enough from his mother about the pain she had suffered while the children were away. On the other hand, an international transfer could bring back the lifestyle and time together he and his wife and children had once enjoyed.

Part of him wanted to request a transfer, but another part of him deep inside recalled various stories he heard as a youth in Japan—a story of a 40-year-old son who dressed in a diaper and crawled across the floor so his parents would not feel old, a story of a son who laid naked beside his parents so that the mosquitoes would only attack him. These and other stories of self-sacrifice—for many the essence of the Japanese spirit—caused him to think about the responsibility he had to simply *gammon* or "hang in there."

As the train grew near, its flickering light sparked another alternative that would free him from disappointing someone no matter what choice he made. Yutaka flirted with this image longer than he had ever done before.

26   SCOTCH-BRITE (3M)

In June 1990, the 3M operating committee met in world headquarters in St. Paul, Minnesota, to consider a proposal to rationalize the North American production and distribution of "SCOTCH-BRITE" hand scouring pads. Due to increased consumer demand, the decision had been made to upgrade the equipment which converted the jumbo-sized rolls into consumer and industrial-sized packages and quantities. At issue was where this upgraded processing equipment would be located.

Currently, most of the conversion took place in Alexandria, Minnesota from jumbo rolls supplied from Perth, Ontario. The Alexandria facility then shipped finished goods to eight distribution centres around the United States. (See Exhibit 1.)

The Canadian division of 3M was now proposing that all production and distribution for "SCOTCH-BRITE" hand pads take place from Perth. This would mean $4 million in new equipment would go to Perth, the current "SCOTCH-BRITE" workforce in Alexandria would be shifted to different responsibilities, and Perth would now ship directly to the various distribution centres. (See Exhibit 2.) This proposal to grant a regional product mandate to Perth had not gone unopposed. The Alexandria plant felt it would be preferable to place the new converting equipment in their facility, and to maintain the existing relationship with Perth.

3M Background

3M was a multinational enterprise with 80,000 employees, subsidiaries and operations in 50 countries, and worldwide annual sales in excess of US$10 billion. During the past decade, 3M's outside-the-U.S. (OUS) sales had climbed from about one-third

This case was prepared by Professor Paul W. Beamish for the sole purpose of providing material for class discussion at the Richard Ivey School of Business. Certain names and other identifying information may have been disguised to protect confidentiality. It is not intended to illustrate either effective or ineffective handling of a managerial situation. Any reproduction, in any form, of the material in this case is prohibited except with the written consent of the School. This case was made possible through the support of the Task Force on Investment from The Ontario Premier's Council on Economic Renewal. Copyright © 1993, The University of Western Ontario and The Ontario Premier's Council on Economic Renewal.

EXHIBIT 1   Present Scotch-Brite Product Flowchart

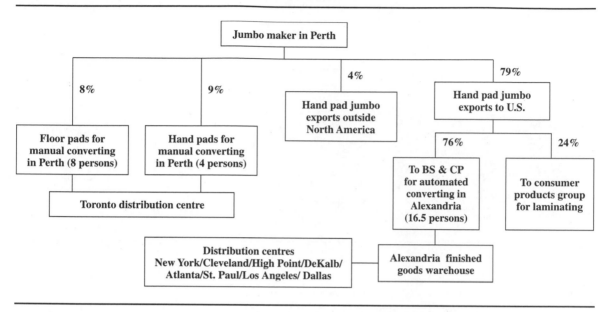

to nearly one-half of total sales. This growth was a result of a conscious strategy of global expansion. The company was organized into four divisions: Industrial and Consumer, Electronic and Information Technologies, Life Sciences, and Graphic Technologies.

Among the more familiar products were "SCOTCH" Brand transparent tapes, magnetic tapes, cassettes, and cartridges. Abrasives and adhesives were early products of the company and still formed a very important portion of the business.

Developing other technologies and applying them to make problem-solving products was the basis on which 3M had been able to grow. So many new products were produced on an ongoing basis that 25 percent of any year's sales were of products that did not exist five years before.

Like its parent company, 3M Canada Inc. was a highly diversified company which manufactured thousands of different products for industry, business, the professions, and the consumer. The head office and main plant were located in London, Ontario with sales and service centres across the country. 3M Canada was established as part of the newly founded International Division in 1951. Additional subsidiaries were set up at that time in Australia, Brazil, France, West Germany, Mexico, and the United Kingdom. 3M Canada employed about 2,000 people. In addition to operations in London and Perth, the company had manufacturing plants in Toronto, Havelock, and Simcoe, Ontario and Morden, Manitoba. Canada was the sixth largest of 3M's subsidiaries.

With the exception of two or three people from the worldwide organization, everyone working for 3M Canada was Canadian. The Canadian subsidiary annually

EXHIBIT 2   Proposed Scotch-Brite Product Flowchart (all hand pad)

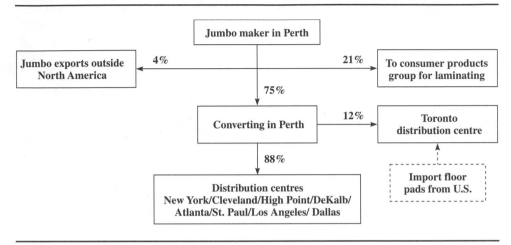

lost 10 to 15 people to the worldwide organization. Although a high proportion of the professional management group in Canada had a career goal to work in the worldwide organization at some stage, this was not a requirement. For example, several managers at the plant manager level and above had indicated a preference to stay in Canada despite offers within the worldwide organization.

The Canadian subsidiary, under the direction of its president, Jeffery McCormick, was expected to generate sales growth and to produce an operating income on Canadian sales. Increasingly, emphasis was being placed on achieving certain target market share levels.

Within Canada, the 25 individual business units were split among 8 groups, each of which operated as a profit centre. Variability existed in each with respect to the amount of divisional input from the United States.

The headquarters perception of the competencies of the Canadian subsidiary varied according to the business and functional area. For example, Canadian manufacturing and engineering had a solid reputation for getting things done.

In terms of research, Canada specialized in three, somewhat narrow areas. These dealt with polymer chemistry, materials science, and electro-mechanical telecommunications. Several dozen scientists pursued research in these areas within Canadian laboratories.

The Canadian subsidiary did not have a critical mass in R&D for all the technologies necessary to support "SCOTCH-BRITE". In addition it was not deemed feasible to move (or build) a pilot plant to Canada for "SCOTCH-BRITE" testing purposes since pilot plants tended to serve a multitude of products.

Partly as a consequence of the 1988 Canada-U.S. Free Trade Agreement, the overall level of company harmonization between the two countries had risen. Some U.S. divisions were asking for more direct control over their businesses in Canada.

EXHIBIT 3   3M Canada Inc.

Consolidated Statement of Earnings and Retained Earnings for the Year Ended October 31, 1989

	1989	1988
	(Dollars in Thousands)	
Revenue		
Net sales*	$561,406	$516,663
Other income	8,823	3,536
	570,229	520,199
Costs and Expenses		
Cost of goods sold and other expenses	451,298	412,826
Depreciation and amortization	16,908	15,921
Interest	312	239
Research and development	1,876	2,010
	470,394	430,996
	99,835	89,203
Provision for Income Taxes	41,636	38,339
Net Earnings for the Year	58,199	50,864
Retained Earnings – Beginning of Year	215,960	185,496
	274,159	236,360
Dividends	28,046	20,400
Retained Earnings–End of Year	246,113	215,960
* Includes net sales to parent and affiliated companies of . . .	$106,773	$ 89,709

The Canadian president needed to deal with these issues and to develop the necessary organizational response.

The Canadian subsidiary had placed a lot of importance on building intercompany sales. Over 20 percent of its sales were of this type, and further increases were intended.

3M Canada sales in 1990 were over $500 million while after-tax earnings were in the range of 10 percent. (See Exhibits 3 and 4 for financial statements.)

The Perth Scotch-Brite Plant

The $5 million Perth plant went into operation in 1981, employing 22 people. The plant covered 36,000 square feet on a 78-acre site and was the first Canadian production facility for this product line. It was built to supplement the jumbo output of

EXHIBIT 4   3M Canada Inc.
Consolidated Balance Sheet as at October 31, 1989

Assets

	1989	1988
	(Dollars in Thousands)	
Current Assets		
Interest bearing term deposits	$ 66,998	$ 52,896
Accounts receivable	73,524	69,631
Amounts due from affiliated companies	18,050	13,670
Other receivables and prepaid expenses	5,472	4,592
Inventories -		
Finished goods and work in process	67,833	63,745
Raw materials and supplies	9,321	10,601
	241,198	215,135
Fixed Assets		
Property, plant and equipment - at cost	180,848	164,313
Less accumulated depreciation	85,764	75,676
Other Assets	9,590	8,856
	$345,872	$312,628

Liabilities

Current Liabilities		
Accounts payable - trade	$ 21,600	$ 18,388
Amounts due to affiliated companies	18,427	17,985
Income taxes payable	9,394	12,437
Deferred payments	1,437	1,422
Other liabilities	20,832	18,367
	71,690	68,599
Deferred Income Taxes	14,669	14,669
	$ 86,359	$ 83,268

Shareholders' Equity

Capital Stock		
Authorized -		
Unlimited shares		
Issued and fully paid -		
14,600 shares	13,400	13,400
Retained Earnings	246,113	215,960
	259,513	229,360
	$345,872	$312,628

Alexandria, which was nearing capacity. The plant was designed with sufficient capacity to produce enough hand pads and floor pads to eliminate imports, but with exports in mind. In 1981, the Canadian duty on shipments from the United States to Canada was 13.5 percent, while shipments from Canada could enter the United States duty free.

Over the next decade, the plant was expanded several times, and employment grew to 80 people. Throughout this period, the plant exclusively produced "SCOTCH-BRITE". "SCOTCH-BRITE" was a profitable, growing product line in a core business area. The total scouring pad market in which "SCOTCH-BRITE" competed was estimated to be $60 million in the United States and nearly $5 million in Canada.

"SCOTCH-BRITE" material was a web of nonwoven nylon or polyester fibres impregnated throughout with abrasive particles. The result was a pad, disk, or wheel used to scour, clean, polish, or finish materials such as wood, metal, plastic, and many other surfaces.

As "SCOTCH-BRITE" material wears down it exposes more abrasives so that it continues to be effective all through its life. Because it is made of a synthetic fibre it does not rust or stain. Some types of "SCOTCH-BRITE" have a sponge backing so that both scouring and washing can be done with the one product. Other versions of this material have integral backing pads and handles made of strong plastic to enable the user to scour and clean flat surfaces and corners with ease.

"SCOTCH-BRITE" products were made in sheet, roll, and wheel shapes, and used in a wide variety of applications in the metal-working, woodworking, and plastics industries, as well as in the hotel and restaurant trade, and the home.

Floor and carpet cleaning companies, schools, hospitals, and building maintenance personnel used a wide variety of "SCOTCH-BRITE" disks and pads for floor maintenance. Other smaller handheld pads were used for cleaning painted surfaces such as door frames, stairs, walls, sinks, and tiles surfaces. "SCOTCH-BRITE" products were used in hotels and restaurants for griddle and grill cleaning, deep fat fryer scouring, as well for carpet and floor maintenance. Several types of "SCOTCH-BRITE" products were available for home use. These ranged from a gentle version designed for cleaning tubs, sinks, tile, and even fine china, to a rugged scouring pad with a built-in handle for scouring barbecue grills.

The Perth Proposal

During the 1980s as the Perth plant grew in size and experience, its reputation as a workforce with a demonstrated ability to work effectively began to develop. With increased confidence came a desire to assume new challenges. An obvious area for potential development would be to take on more of the SCOTCH-BRITE value-added function in Perth, rather than to ship semi-finished goods to the United States.

In the mid 1980s, the Perth managers advocated that they should now supply finished goods to the U.S. for certain mandated products. The SCOTCH-BRITE Manufacturing Director during this period opposed this approach. He claimed that nothing would be saved as all the finished goods would have to be sent to Alexandria anyway, for consolidation and distribution to the customer.

The U.S.-based manufacturing director also argued that mandating products could reduce the utilization of the larger, more expensive maker at Alexandria which would increase the unit burden costs on other products there. During this period, the Perth maker operated as the swing maker with utilization cycling in order to keep the Alexandria maker fully loaded.

With a change in management came a willingness to take a fresh look at the situation. The new manager, Andy Burns, insisted that a more complete analysis of all the delivered costs be provided. To that end, a study was initiated in December 1989 to determine the cost of converting and packaging SCOTCH-BRITE hand pads in Perth, rather than shipping jumbo to Alexandria for converting and packaging.

The task force struck in Canada was led by Len Weston, the Perth Plant Manager. Procedurally, any proposal would first go to Gary Boles, Manufacturing Director for Canada, and Gord Prentice, Executive Vice President of Manufacturing for Canada. Once their agreement had been obtained, the Perth plant manager would continue to champion the project through the 3M hierarchy, although people such as Prentice would facilitate the process.

The proposal would next go to the Building Service and Cleaning Products (BS + CP) division for review and agreement. If successful, the proposal would then be sent back to Canadian engineering to develop an Authority for (capital) Expenditure, or AFE. It would then be routed through senior Canadian management and U.S. division and group levels. The final stage was for the AFE to go to the Operating committee at

EXHIBIT 5   3M International – Partial Organization Chart

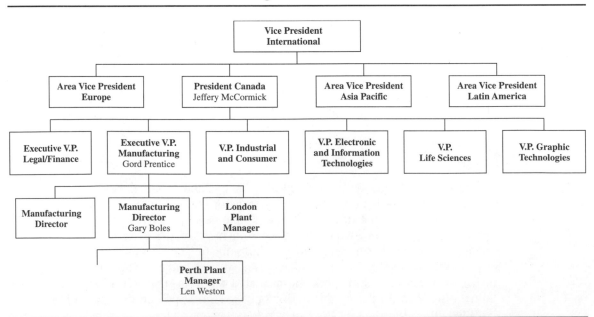

EXHIBIT 6   3M Worldwide – Partial Organization Chart

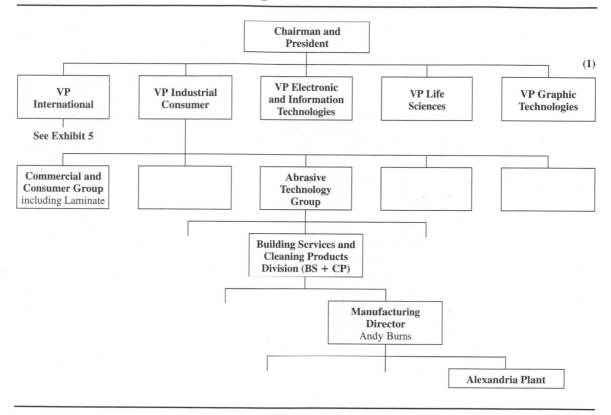

Note: (1) Operating Committee made up of the four sector vice-presidents, the V.P. International, and several other key executives.

the sector level for assessment. See Exhibits 5 and 6 for partial organization charts for 3M Worldwide and International.

The Perth proposal acknowledged that Alexandria was a competently managed plant and that putting the new equipment in either location would reduce costs from their current levels. At issue was where the greater cost savings would be generated. The Perth proposal argued that these would occur in Perth (see Exhibit 7) through a combination of reduced freight and storage costs, and faster and more efficient manufacturing. The Perth proposal's overall approach was to emphasize what was best for shareholders on the basis of total delivered costs.

Overall employment needs were expected to increase by 8 in Canada yet decline by at least double that in Alexandria. (See Table 1.)

Some of the modest employment increases in Canada could be traced to the fact that the small amount of manual converting in Perth would now be automated. It had been viable to convert a small quantity of hand pads in Canada, even manually, when shipping costs and duties were factored in.

EXHIBIT 7   Sample Unit Cost Comparison (US Dollars per Case)

	Current Alexandria Operation	Upgraded Cutter Alexandria	Upgraded Cutter Perth
Jumbo Cost Ex Perth	$6.20	$6.20	$6.20
Jumbo Freight to Alexandria	$0.70	$0.70	—
Jumbo Storage	$0.70	$0.70	$0.05
Jumbo Burden Absorption	—	—	($0.20)[1]
Input Cost to Converting	**$7.60**	**$7.60**	**$6.05**
Converting Waste	$0.95	$0.65	$0.45
Converting Labour	$1.35	$0.30	$0.15[2]
Variable Converting Overhead	$0.60	$0.45	$0.30
Fixed Converting Overhead	$1.00	$0.55	$0.85[3]
Packaging Supplies	$1.20	$1.20	$1.20
Fin Goods Whse/Mat Hand	$0.45	$0.45	$0.25
Fin Goods Direct Charges	$1.15	$1.15	$0.90
Cost Including Converting	**$14.30**	**$12.35**	**$10.10**
Freight to Branch	$0.90	$0.90	$1.05
Cost Delivered to Branch	**$15.20**	**$13.25**	**$11.15**

[1]Volume savings through equipment usage.

[2]Lower than Alexandria due to faster equipment speed and smaller production teams.

[3]Higher than Alexandria due to larger investment in equipment.

Source: Perth proposal.

TABLE 1   Changes in Staffing for Each Proposal

Perth Proposal	
Add in Perth	1 Maintenance
	3 Shippers
	<u>4 Production Operators *</u>
Total	8 Persons @ Labour Rate U.S. $13.18/hr
Delete in Alexandria	Maintenance ?
	Shipping / Receiving ?
	16.5 Production Operators
Alexandria Proposal	
Add in Alexandria	6 Operators @ $15.43

*In addition, eight persons in floor pad manual conversion, and four persons in hand pad manual conversion would now be shifted to hand pad automated conversion in Perth.

The biggest reason for the small number of proposed new hires in Canada was the plan to discontinue floor pad manual converting in Perth and to shift those operators to the automated hand pad area. The initial response to this in Canada, in several quarters, had been less-than-enthusiastic.

The Canadian floor pad business manager felt that he might now have to pay a premium if purchasing from the United States. As well, he was concerned that some of his customers might notice a difference in performance. He felt the manually converted floor pads from Perth were of a slightly higher quality than the automatically converted ones from Hutchison, Minnesota. The Canadian business manager had built a higher market share for 3M floor pads in Canada than his U.S. counterparts, and he did not wish to see this jeopardized.

A shift from floor pad manual converting to hand pad automated converting would also have immediate implications for the operators. Currently most of the manual floor pad (and hand pad) jobs were on a one shift (day) basis. A second, evening shift was sometimes required, but no one worked the midnight-to-morning shift. With automation, all operators would now need to work a three shift rotation in order to maximize machine utilization. In a nonunion plant, with a 10-year tradition of day jobs in converting, and with a no-layoff policy, this could be an emotional issue. The task of selling it to the operators would fall to Weston.

The Alexandria Response

The Alexandria response was less a proposal, and more a reaction to the Perth initiative. A variety of concerns, some old and some new, were raised.

- First, the increased production volume in Canada and the resultant re-exports to the United States would cause an increased vulnerability to currency fluctuations.
- Second, lengthening the supply distance would make it more difficult to guarantee delivery to U.S. customers.
- Third, the Perth plant would now need to be interfaced with the 3M-USA computer-based materials management system in order to have effective transportation. This would require the Canadian information technology group to work with the logistics people in order to develop a program which would allow for cross-border integration of information.
- Fourth, cost of shipping finished goods to the branches would increase in both Perth and Alexandria. In Perth it would be due to the smaller volumes, and increased distances associated with shipping a single product line. In Alexandria it would now take longer to make up a truckload without the hand pads.
- Fifth, since SCOTCH-BRITE converting was already well established in Alexandria, and there would be savings wherever the new equipment was located, it was safer to keep it where the manufacturing experience already existed rather than to rely on optimistic projections from Perth.

Conclusion

In part, due to the distances involved, regional production mandates on various products had been granted as early as the 1970s by 3M in Europe. SCOTCH-BRITE, in fact, was already also being produced in Europe, Asia, and Mexico. However, unlike these other production mandates, the Perth proposal was to supply the core U.S. market. For the operating committee, the decision would come down to how much confidence they had in the Perth proposal.

27 ENRON DEVELOPMENT CORPORATION

On August 3, 1995, Rebecca Mark, chairman and CEO of Enron Development Corporation (EDC), hurried to the airport to catch a flight from Houston to Bombay. Earlier that day she had received word from India that EDC's $2.8 billion Dabhol power plant project in India had been canceled. Given the political situation in the state of Maharashtra, the cancellation was not completely unexpected. However, if the decision could not be reversed, EDC's potential financial losses were significant. More importantly, EDC was counting on Dabhol as a beachhead that would lead to further projects in India. India's power-generating capacity was forecast to triple in the next 15 years. The cancellation of the Dabhol project could seriously undermine EDC's participation in this massive development.

Enron Corporation

Houston-based Enron Corporation (Enron), formed in 1985 in a merger between InterNorth, Inc., and Houston Natural Gas Corp., was a leading firm in the worldwide energy industries. The firm's new slogan was "Creating Energy Solutions Worldwide" and its stated vision was to become "The World's Leading Energy Company—creating innovative and efficient energy solutions for growing economies and a better environment worldwide."

Enron was the largest natural gas company in the United States and operated the largest gas pipeline system in the world outside of Gazprom in Russia. The firm was involved in developing more natural-gas-fired independent power plants than any

This case was written by Professor Andrew Inkpen with research assistance from Katherine Johnston and assistance from Professor Arvind Phatak, Temple University, for the sole purpose of providing material for class discussion. It is not intended to illustrate either effective or ineffective handling of a managerial situation. Any reproduction, in any form, of the material in this case is prohibited unless permission is obtained from the copyright holder. Copyright © 1996, Thunderbird–The American Graduate School of International Management.

TABLE 1   Enron Financial Summary

(Dollars in Millions, Except per Share Amounts)	Year Ended December 31,				
	1994	1993	1992	1991	1990
Revenues	$ 8,894	$ 7,986	$ 6,415	$ 5,698	$5,460
Income before Interest, Minority Interest and Income Taxes	$ 944.4	$ 797.7	$ 767.2	$ 715.3	$662.1
Income before Extraordinary Items	$ 453.4	$ 332.5	$ 328.8	$ 232.1	$202.2
Earnings per Common Share	$ 1.70	$ 1.46	$ 1.21	$ 0.98	$ 0.86
Total Assets	$11,966	$11,504	$10,312	$10,070	$9,849
Return on Shareholders' Equity	16.5%	15.0%	14.9%	12.4%	11.2%
NYSE Price Range					
High	$ 34⅝	$ 37	$ 25	$ 19⅛	$ 15⅝
Low	$ 27	$ 22⅛	$ 15¼	$ 12⅜	$ 12½
Close December 31	$ 30½	$ 29	$ 23³⁄₁₆	$ 17½	$ 13⅝

other company in the world. Enron owned and operated energy facilities in 15 countries and had projects underway in 15 additional countries. In 1994, the firm had revenues of $9 billion and an operating profit of $944 million. Enron's international operations had earnings before interest and taxes of $148 million in 1994, an increase of 12 percent over the previous year. International operations represented 15 percent of the company's total sales and operating income. Table 1 provides a financial summary for Enron.

Enron had five operating divisions:

- Enron Operations Corp. was responsible for U.S. interstate natural gas pipelines, operated the company's worldwide physical assets (except those owned by Enron Oil & Gas), and provided engineering, construction, and operating services expertise across all business lines.
- Enron Capital & Trade Resources Corp. conducted the majority of the firm's worldwide marketing activities for natural gas, liquids, and electric power and was responsible for U.S. power development.
- Enron Oil & Gas was involved in exploration and production activities in natural gas and crude oil.
- Enron Global Power & Pipelines owned and operated natural gas pipelines in emerging market countries. Enron Corporation held a 52 percent ownership interest in Enron Global Power & Pipelines.
- Enron Development Corporation (EDC) was involved in the development of international energy infrastructure projects such as power plants, pipelines, fuel transportation, and natural gas processing plants.

Enron Development Corporation. EDC's focus was on natural gas projects. The firm had an international reputation as a reliable provider of turnkey natural gas projects on a timely basis. All of EDC's projects were project-financed and had long-term contracts with pricing agreements reached in advance. Revenues were tied to the U.S. dollar, and the host government or an outside agency held responsibility for currency conversions.

EDC's projects spanned the globe. On Hainan Island in China, EDC was constructing a $135 million, 150 megawatt (MW) power plant. This independent power plant was the first developed by a U.S. company in China. After completion by late 1995, Enron would be the operator and fuel manager. In the Dominican Republic, EDC was completing the first phase of a 185 MW power plant. This project had a 20-year power purchase agreement with the government. In Colombia, EDC was constructing a 357-mile natural gas pipeline for the state-owned oil company. Other projects in active development included a 478 MW gas-fired power plant in Turkey, a 1,120 mile natural gas pipeline from Bolivia to São Paulo, Brazil, a 500 MW gas-fired power plant in Java, Indonesia, and a $4 billion liquefied natural gas processing plant in Qatar.

There was a close relationship between EDC and Enron Global Power & Pipelines (EPP). The parent firm had granted EPP a preferential right to acquire all of EDC's ownership interests in completed power and gas projects outside the United States. The projects under construction in which EPP had preferential rights included the firm's interest in the Dominican Republic power project, the Hainan Island power project, the Colombia pipeline, and the first and second phases of the 2,015 MW Dabhol project in India.

Market Reform in India

India gained its independence in 1947. From that time until the mid-1980s, the government pursued an economic policy of self-sufficiency. This policy was often referred to as *swadeshi,* a Hindi word meaning "indigenous products" or "made in India." The term was first used by Mahatma Gandhi during the independence movement to encourage people to buy native goods and break the British economic stranglehold on India. To many Indians, *swadeshi* evoked images of patriotism and Indian sovereignty.

After decades of socialist-oriented/statist industrial policy focused on achieving self-sufficiency, India was financially strapped and bureaucratically bloated. High tariffs kept out imports and official government policy discouraged foreign investment. In the 1970s, Coca-Cola and IBM were among the multinational firms that pulled out of India. During the period 1985 to 1990, foreign investment in India averaged only about $250 million annually.

Efforts to reform the Indian economy began after the 1991 federal elections. The Indian government was on the verge of bankruptcy and foreign exchange reserves were sufficient for only three months of imports. After considerable prodding by the IMF and Finance Minister Manmohan Singh, Prime Minister Rao introduced free-market reforms in July 1991. Singh urged that India follow the free-market models of South Korea and Taiwan in achieving rapid economic development. India's economic liberalization plan moved the economy away from its traditionally protectionist policies toward actively encouraging foreign participation in the economy. As part of the plan, the prime minister's office set up a special "fast track" Foreign Investment Promotion Board to provide speedy approval for foreign investment proposals. In October 1991, the government of India opened the power industry to private-sector foreign direct investment. In February 1992, the Indian government allowed the rupee to become partially convertible. In 1994, India ratified the World Trade Organization agreement on intellectual property laws.

The economic reform program had a powerful effect. By 1995, the Indian economy was growing at an annual rate of more than 8 percent. Exports were up by 27 percent over the previous year in the April–June quarter. The country had more than $20 billion in foreign reserves, up from $13.5 billion in 1994 and only $1 billion in 1991. Food stocks were at an all-time high and inflation was under 10 percent. Tariffs, while still high and ranging from 30 to 65 percent, were only about one-fifth of what they were before liberalization. By some estimates, the government's policies had produced up to $100 billion in new entrepreneurial projects in India since 1992. In January 1995, a delegation of U.S. executives accompanied U.S. Commerce Secretary Ron Brown on a visit to India. During the trip, Brown was asked if the CEOs from the energy sector had expressed any fears about doing business in India. Brown replied "if they had any [fears] before they came, they certainly have been dissipated by this visit."[1]

Despite these efforts to encourage market reform and economic development, many hurdles remained. In 1995, foreign direct investment in India was only $1.3 billion, as compared to $33.7 billion in China. About 40 percent of the industrial economy remained government-owned. Perhaps the greatest impediment to both rapid growth and attracting foreign investment was the lack of infrastructure that met international standards. In particular, India suffered from a substantial electricity shortage.

Demand for Electricity

The Indian population was starved for electricity. It was estimated that many of India's industries were able to operate at only half their capacity because of a lack of electric power. Frequent power outages were taken for granted. In New Delhi, the government-owned power company imposed rotating one- to two-hour blackouts periodically during the summer, when demand for electricity peaked and temperatures were often as high as 115 degrees. More-remote areas had no power at all. India's current annual electrical generating capacity was about 80,000 MW. Demand was expected to nearly triple by 2007[2], as shown in Table 2.

Virtually all of India's power was generated and managed by state-owned electricity boards (SEBs). It was widely acknowledged that these boards suffered from chronic managerial, financial, and operational problems.[3] As much as a quarter of the electricity generated was stolen. Government-run power plants typically operated at about 50 percent capacity. In comparison, the private power plants run by Tata Steel, an Indian company, operated at around 85 percent capacity.

TABLE 2   **Power Demand Projections (at March 1995)**

Current capacity	78,900 MW
Estimated growth rate of demand to 2007	Approximately 9% per year
Total requirements by 2007	220,000 MW
Likely rate of addition to 2007	3,000 MW per year
Total capacity by 2007	115,000 MW
Likely shortfall in 2007	107,000 MW
Additional investment needed	Rs 5 trillion ($160 billion)

Indian power rates were among the lowest in the world. Farmers paid less than 15 percent of the cost of electricity generated by new thermal power plants. In several states, small farmers paid nothing for electricity. Although the SEBs had been trying to raise rates, this had proved to be very difficult. In 1994, in the state of Gujarat, the opposition government encouraged farmers to blockade roads and burn government property after rural power rates were increased. The government was forced to back down and lower the amount of the increase.

Because of these problems and because all levels of government were so short of funds, the central government decided to turn to the private sector. The Electricity Act was amended in October 1991 to make this possible. However, the response from the private sector was poor so the act was amended again in March 1992 to provide further incentives, including a 16 percent rate of return to investors. In comparison, the Chinese government in 1994 announced a 12 percent rate of return cap on private power projects.

Still, potential investors remained skeptical of the central government's commitment to reform and were doubtful of the SEBs' ability to pay for privately generated power. The government took one more step. In May 1992, a delegation of Indian central government officials visited the United States and the United Kingdom to make a pitch for foreign investment in the power sector. The delegation included then power secretary S. Rajagopal, finance secretary K. Geethakrishan, and cabinet secretary Naresh Chandra. The visits were a major success. Many independent power producers (IPPs) immediately sent executives to India. By July 1995, more than 130 Memorandums of Understanding (MoUs) had been signed by the government of India with IPPs. Twenty-three of the 41 pending electricity projects that were bid on by non-Indian companies were led by American firms.

The Dabhol Project

In turning to the private sector for power plant development, the Indian government decided to give the first few private sector projects the status of pioneer projects; later these projects became known as "fast-track" projects (of which eight such projects were eventually signed). For the fast-track projects, the central government decided not to follow the standard public tendering process. Instead, it would negotiate with IPPs for individual projects. The rationale was that the government was not in a strong negotiating position and therefore, the financial risk to the IPPs had to be reduced to entice them to invest in India. At a press conference, power secretary S. Rajagopal said the first few projects "would not be allowed to fail."

EDC's Rebecca Mark met with the Indian delegation when it visited Houston. In June 1992, Mark and several other EDC managers, at the Indian government's invitation, visited India to investigate power plant development opportunities. Within days, Enron had identified a potential site for a gas-fired power plant on the western coast of India in the port town of Dabhol, 180 miles south of Bombay in the state of Maharashtra. Maharashtra was India's richest state and the center of Indian industrialization. The huge port city of Bombay was the capital and the headquarters of most of India's major companies, including Air India and Tata Enterprises, the largest Indian industrial conglomerate. Firms based in Bombay generated about 35 percent of India's GNP.

EDC, acting on the government's assurances that there would not be any tendering on the first few fast-track projects, submitted a proposal to build a 2,015 MW gas-fired power plant. The proposed project would be the largest plant EDC had ever built, the largest of its kind in the world, and at $2.8 billion, the largest foreign investment in India. The liquefied natural gas needed to fuel the Indian power plant would be imported from a plant EDC was constructing in Qatar. The proposal was very favorably received by both the central government and officials in the Maharashtra state government. The Maharashtra State Electricity Board (MSEB) had long wanted to build a gas-fired plant to reduce its dependence on coal and oil. Other countries with limited petroleum reserves, such as Japan and Korea, had followed a similar strategy and built coastal gas-fired power plants.

EDC was the first IPP to formally submit a proposal. Later in June 1992, EDC signed an MoU with the MSEB. A new company called Dabhol Power Company was formed. Enron held 80 percent of the equity in Dabhol and its two partners, General Electric and International Generation Co., each held 10 percent. International Generation was a joint venture between Bechtel Enterprises Inc. (Bechtel) and San Francisco-based Pacific Gas & Electric formed in early 1995 to build and operate power plants outside the United States. General Electric was contracted to supply the gas turbines and Bechtel would be the general contractor. Exhibit 1 lists the various individuals involved with the Dabhol project and Exhibit 2 shows the timing of the various events.

Following the signing of the MoU, EDC began a complex negotiation process for proposal approval, followed by more negotiations on the actual financial details. Officially, no power project could be developed without technical and economic clearance from the Central Electricity Authority. Typically, this process could take many months, or possibly years. The Foreign Investment Promotion Board (FIPB) was the central government's vehicle for a speedy approval process. The FIPB asked the Central Electricity Authority to give initial clearance to the Dabhol project without the detailed information normally required. However, final clearance would still be necessary at a later date.

EXHIBIT 1   Individuals Involved in the Dabhol Project

Lal Krishna Advani President of the Federal BJP Party
Manohar Joshi Chief minister of Maharashtra, deputy leader of Shiv Sena
Kenneth Lay CEO of Enron Corporation
Rebecca Mark Chairman and CEO of EDC
Gopinath Munde Deputy chief minister of Maharashtra with direct responsibility for the state energy
  ministry, BJP Party member
Ajit Nimbalkar Chairman and managing director of Maharashtra State Electricity Board
Sharad Pawar Former chief minister of Maharashtra, voted out of office March 1995; known as the
  Maratha strongman
P.V. Narasimha Rao Prime minister of India.
N.K.P. Salve Federal power minister
Manmohan Singh Federal finance minister, architect of free market reforms and economic advisor to PM Rao
Robert Sutton EDC managing director
Balashaheb "Bal" Thackeray Leader of Shiv Sena

EXHIBIT 2   Timing of Events Associated with the Dabhol Project

October 1991	Government of India invites private sector participation in the power sector.
May 1992	Indian delegation visits UK and U.S.; EDC invited to India by government of India.
June 1992	Maharashtra State Electricity Board signs MoU with EDC.
February 1993	Foreign Investment Promotion Board (FIPB) grants approval.
March 1993	Power Purchase Agreement negotiations start.
November 1993	Central Electricity Authority clears Dabhol project.
February 1994	Government of Maharashtra signs counter guarantee.
September 1994	Government of India signs counter guarantee.
March 1995	Dabhol financing completed.
March 1995	Maharashtra state election results announced.
April 1995	Construction begins; government of Maharashtra orders a review; Munde Committee set up to investigate Dabhol project.
August 1995	Project canceled by government of Maharashtra.

In November 1992, EDC made a detailed presentation at a meeting chaired by the central government finance secretary[a] and attended by various other senior government officials, including the chairman of the MSEB. From this meeting came a recommendation to the FIPB to approve the project. In turn, the Central Power Ministry, acting on the advice of the FIPB, asked the Central Electricity Authority to expedite the approval process. The Central Electricity Authority gave an in-principle

---

[a]The finance secretary was the senior civil servant in the finance department and reported directly to the finance minister.

(not final) clearance to proceed with the project, since the Ministry of Finance had found the project satisfactory.

In March 1993, with the necessary government approvals largely in place, EDC was in a position to negotiate the financial structure of the deal. The most critical element was a Power Purchasing Agreement (PPA) with the MSEB. The PPA was the contract under which EDC, as the owner of the power plant, would supply power to the MSEB electric grid. Over the next year or so, Rebecca Mark visited India 36 times. Ajit Nimbalkar, chairman and managing director of MSEB, described the negotiations:

> This is the first project of this kind that we are doing. MSEB did not have any experience in dealing with international power developers. It was a complicated exercise, for the money involved is large, and so the negotiations took a long time.[4]

MSEB turned to the World Bank for advice in the negotiations. The World Bank offered to fund a team of international consultants. The MSEB chose Freshfields, a British law firm, and the British office of the German Westdeutsche Landesbank Girozentale as consultants in the PPA negotiations.

In addition to negotiating the project financial structure and gaining state and central government approvals, EDC had to obtain dozens of other government approvals, some of which dated back to British colonial times. For example, to get permission to use explosives on the construction site, EDC had to visit the western Indian town of Nagpur, where British imperial forces once stored munitions.[5]

In November 1993, the Central Electricity Authority officially cleared the Dabhol project. In December 1993, the MSEB signed the Dabhol PPA. The state government of Maharashtra signed a financial, or counter, guarantee in February 1994 and the central government signed a counter guarantee in September 1994. The central government counter guarantee, which was to become very controversial, was signed with EDC before the government's guarantee policy was announced publicly.

Structure of the Dabhol Project

Although the original plans were for a 2,015 MW project, the Maharashtra government decided to break the project into two phases. Phase I would be a 695 MW plant using distillate fuel instead of natural gas, and Phase II would be a 1,320 MW gas-fired plant. The capital cost for Phase I would be $920 million, with an estimated turnkey construction cost of $527 million.[6] The second phase would cost about $1.9 billion.

Dabhol was broken into two phases because EDC had been unable to finalize its gas contracts and because the government had become concerned about the mounting criticism of the project. The shift from gas to distillate was done because distillate, a fuel indigenous to India, could be sourced from local refineries, helping deflect the criticism that gas imports would be a persistent drain on India's foreign exchange. Furthermore, using distillate instead of gas eliminated the need to build a port facility for Phase I.

The capital cost for Phase I included some costs for infrastructure items that would normally have been provided by the state, such as a pipeline. If these costs were deducted from the total capital cost, the cost per MW was comparable with the other fast-track power plant projects. However, Dabhol was the only project that had been finalized. The other projects were still going through planning and approval stages.

The Indian government generally followed what was known as a fixed rate of return model. Investors were assured a 16 percent rate of return on net worth for a plant load factor of up to 68.5 percent. Beyond 68.5 percent, the rate of return on equity would increase by a maximum of 0.70 percent for each 1 percent rise in the plant load factor. Net worth was based on the total costs of building the power plant. The main objection against this model was that it provided no incentive to minimize the capital costs of investment.

The Dabhol project used a different model. A tariff of Rs2.40 ($1 equaled about 36 rupees) per unit (kilowatt/hour) of electricity was established. The tariff consisted of a capacity charge of Rs1.20 based on the capital cost of the plant and an energy charge of Rs1.20 for the price of fuel. By using a fixed tariff, the problems of a cost-plus system were eliminated and consumers would not be affected by increases in the capital cost of the project. For EDC and its partners, there was an incentive to become more efficient to improve shareholder returns. Based on the capital costs per MW, Dabhol was comparable to other proposed projects in India. As to the tariff of Rs 2.40, other fast-track power projects had similar tariffs, as did several recently approved public sector projects. Several existing public sector plants were selling power in the Rs2.15 range (although the average tariff for state electricity boards in India was Rs1.20). Enron's estimated internal rate of return on the project after adjusting for inflation was 19 percent. Dabhol was granted a five-year tax holiday.

Nevertheless, because there was no competitive bidding on the Dabhol project, critics argued that the Rs2.40 per unit was too high and that the company would be making huge profits. Kirit Parekh, director of the Indira Gandhi Institute of Development and Research, was an ardent critic:

> In the United States, power generated from gas-based plants is sold to utilities at 3–4 cents at the bus bar while Enron is charging 7 cents. It is a rip-off. The China Power Company, which is setting up a 2000 MW power plant in Hong Kong, and which will go on stream in 1996, is doing so at 15 percent less capital than Enron.[7]

Further criticism was directed at the company's lack of competitive bidding for its principal equipment supplier, General Electric, and its construction partner, Bechtel. Although General Electric and EDC had worked closely in the past, some critics suggested that foreign equipment suppliers were favored over Indian suppliers. EDC countered with the argument that it had awarded more than 60 contracts worth more than $100 million (Rs360 crore) to Indian companies.

EDC was also subject to criticism because of its plan to import gas for Phase II from its gas processing plant in Qatar. When completed, this plant would be owned by a joint venture between Enron Oil & Gas and the Qatar government. Although Enron vigorously denied it, critics suggested that Enron would make excessive profits through transfer pricing and charging arbitrary prices for the fuel. From EDC's perspective, taking responsibility for fuel supply was a means of reducing its risk, since the contract specified penalties when the plant was not able to generate electricity. Fuel supply failure would not constitute sufficient grounds for being unable to generate electricity.

The federal counter guarantees also came in for criticism. A World Bank report questioned the counter-guarantee arrangement because in its opinion, it was nothing more than a loan made by the federal government on behalf of the MSEB if it could not cover its payments to Enron. EDC's Sutton countered:

> It is only after the government of India decided as a policy to give counter guarantees that we also decided to ask. It would have been impossible to raise money from international bankers at competitive rates without the guarantee when others are approaching the same bankers with guarantees in their pockets.[8]

The Political Situation in India

India's political process was based on a parliamentary system. At the national, or central level as it was referred to in India, the Congress (I) Party formed the government, and its leader, P. V. Narasimha Rao, was prime minister. The Congress (I) Party was the descendant of the Indian National Congress, which was formed in 1855 and became the major vehicle of Indian nationalism. From 1947 to 1989, some form of the Congress Party ruled India in an unbroken string of governments. Indira Gandhi, who had been prime minister since 1964, founded the Congress (I) Party after her defeat in the 1977 election. In 1980, Indira Gandhi and the Congress (I) party regained power. After Indira Gandhi was assassinated in 1984, her son Rajiv became prime minister. In the 1989 election, Congress (I) lost and turned power over to a minority Janata Dal government. During the 1991 election campaign, Rajiv Gandhi was assassinated and P. V. Narasimha Rao became Congress (I) party leader. Congress (I) regained power in a minority government and although Rao was not considered to be a strong leader by opponents or supporters, he had proven to be surprisingly resilient. The next election was scheduled for May 1996. Predictions in August 1995 were that three parties, Congress (I), Left Front, and BJP, would each get about 150 of the 543 available seats in the Lok Sabha (House of the People).

The official opposition party was the Bharatiya Janata Party (BJP). In English, this translated to the Indian People's Party. The BJP platform emphasized support for traditional Hindu goals and values, making the party less secular than the Congress (I) Party. Many of its members belonged to the urban lower middle class and distrusted the free market reforms and modern cultural values. The BJP believed it could build support among the business community that sought decentralization and deregulation but resented intervention on the part of foreign multinationals. The BJP was considered to be the front party for a Hindu fundamentalist movement led by Rajendra Singh. It was known as Rashtriya Swayamsevak Sangh (RSS; translation: National Volunteers Core). The RSS supported economic nationalism and promoted anti-Muslim, anti-feminist, and anti-English-language views. In 1990, the RSS formed the Swadeshi Jagaran Manch, or National Awakening Forum, to promote economic nationalism. The Forum deemed the marketing of Western consumer goods frivolous and wasteful ("India needs computer chips, not potato chips"). According to the Forum's Bombay representative, "Soft drinks and instant cereals do not serve the mass of Indian people. We are not pleased with the way [Coke and Pepsi] are demolishing their rivals."[9]

The Maharashtra Election. The political parties at the state level mirrored those at the central level, although the Congress (I) was less dominant. In two states, West Bengal and Kerala, politics had long been dominated by the Communist Party. The BJP was particularly strong in the industrial, heavily populated, and largely Hindu northern states. Decision making was decentralized in India and many of the states had a substantial amount of power and autonomy. For example, the World Bank had secured an agreement to lend directly to individual states.

On February 12, 1995, a state election was held in Maharashtra. Results were to be announced about four weeks later because the chief election commissioner in Maharashtra had a policy of delinking voting from the counting of votes. The incumbent Congress (I) Party and an alliance between the BJP and Shiv Sena parties were the primary contestants. State elections were normally held every five years. In the previous election in 1990, the Congress (I) Party had formed a majority government under Chief Minister Sharad Pawar. Pawar was confident of retaining power in the 1995 election.

The BJP Party was closely aligned with the national BJP Party. Shiv Sena was a Maharashtra-based party with the stated objective of protecting the economic interests and identity of Maharashtrians and safeguarding the interests of all Hindus. The official leader of Shiv Sena was Manohar Joshi, but he had limited power and openly admitted that the real authority was Bal Thackeray (sometimes referred to as Mr. Remote Control for his ability to control the party from an unofficial capacity). Thackeray was a newspaper cartoonist before he become a right-wing activist. A talented organizer and rousing orator, he set up the Shiv Sena Party in the mid 1960s to appeal to poor Hindus who resented the influence of foreigners and non-Maharashtrians, particularly those from South India. Thackeray was prone to provocative and somewhat threatening statements. He wanted to change the name of India to Hindustan and during the Maharashtra election, talked about chasing non-Maharashtrians out of the state.

The Dabhol power project was a major campaign issue leading up to the election. Election Commission norms in India prohibited a state government from making decisions on vital matters in the run-up to an election. However, the BJP and Shiv Sena did not make this an issue in February. Had they done so, the Election Commission might have ordered the state government to defer the decision on Dabhol.

The BJP/Shiv Sena election campaign rhetoric left little doubts as to their sentiments— one of their slogans was "Throw Enron into the Arabian Sea." The BJP platform promoted economic nationalism and sovereignty and denounced the Dabhol project. The BJP attempted to isolate Chief Minister Pawar as the only defender of Enron. The Dabhol project was described as a typical case of bad government—the failure of the ruling party to stand up to pressure from multinationals, corruption, and compromising on economic sovereignty. The BJP had always been opposed to the project for various reasons: the social and environmental aspects, alleged bribes, the project's cost, and the lack of competitive bidding. The BJP/Shiv Sena campaign strategy painted the Congress (I) Party as anti-poor, corrupt, and partial to foreign firms. This platform evidently appealed to Maharashtrians. On March 13 the election results were announced. The BJP/Shiv Sena coalition won 138 of 288 seats election and with the help of several independent members, formed the new government. The Shiv Sena's Manohar Joshi became the new chief minister.

Not long after the election, Enron CEO Kenneth Lay noted, "If something happens now to slow down or damage our power project, it would send extremely negative signals to other foreign investors."[10] Other firms with power projects underway or in planning included the Swiss firm ABB, the U.S. firms AES Corp. and CMS Energy, and Hong Kong's Consolidated Electric Power Asia.

Construction Begins

On March 2, 1995, EDC completed the financing for the Phase I of the Dabhol project. Phase I financing would come from the following sources:

- A 12-bank syndication led by the Bank of America and ABN-Amro (loans of $150 million)
- U.S. Export-Import Bank ($300 million; arranged by GE and Bechtel)
- Overseas Private Investment Corp. ($298 million)
- Industrial Development Bank of India ($98 million)

Construction was soon underway. But, almost simultaneously, the new state government in Maharashtra, in keeping with its campaign promises, decided to put the project under review.

The Munde Committee

The Munde Committee was formed by the Maharashtrian state government to review the process and details of the Dabhol project. The committee had two members from the BJP and two from the Shiv Sena. The chairman of the committee was deputy chief minister and state BJP president Gopinath Munde, a known critic of Dabhol. An open invitation to individuals to appear before the committee was followed up by letters to the MSEB and Dabhol Power Company. The committee was scheduled to submit its report by July 1.

Over the next few months, the committee held more than a dozen meetings and visited the site of the power plant. The committee was assisted by five state government departments: energy, finance, industries, planning, and law. All requests for appearances before the committee were granted. Among those making depositions were: environmental groups, energy economists, a former managing director of the Bombay Suburban Electric Supply Company, representatives of other IPPs, and representatives of the IPP Association. The Industrial Development Bank of India, a prime lender to the project, representatives from the former state government, and the Congress (I) Party did not appear before the committee.

During the committee hearings, the BJP continued its public opposition to Dabhol. The issue of irregularities—a euphemism for bribes—was raised. According to a senior BJP official:

> Though it is impossible to ascertain if kickbacks were paid to [former Maharashtra chief minister] Anwar, even if we can obtain circumstantial evidence it is enough. The project has been padded up and if the review committee can establish that, it is sufficient to cancel the project.[11]

Allegations of bribery were vigorously denied by EDC. Joseph Sutton, EDC's managing director in India, had told delegates at India Power '95, a conference on the power sector held in New Delhi in March, "during the three years we have been here, we have never been asked for, nor have we paid any bribes."[12]

On June 11, the RSS (the Hindu fundamentalist group) issued a directive to the BJP that it would like the party to honor its commitment to the *swadeshi* movement. The economic advisor to the Central BJP Party, Jay Dubashi said:

> We think canceling this project will send the right signals. It will demonstrate that we are not chumps who can be taken for a ride. Enron probably never imagined that Sharad Pawar [former Maharashtra chief minister] would go out of power. They thought he would see the deal through.[13]

Pramod Mahajan, the BJP's All-India secretary, was also fervently against Dabhol, stating that "we will go to court if necessary and decide in the long-term interest of the country."[14] Mahajan also ruled out paying penalties to EDC if the project were scrapped.

Meanwhile, EDC officials were shuttling back and forth between New Delhi and Bombay, trying to convince the press and the government of the viability of the Dabhol project. At one point, the U.S. ambassador to India, Frank Wisner, met with BJP president, L. K. Advani. Advani refused to meet Enron officials. The issue was even discussed during U.S. Treasury Secretary Robert Rubin's visit to India in April. According to the Assistant Secretary of the Treasury, "We pushed for resolution of the issue."[15] In May 1995, the U.S. Department of Energy warned that failure to honor the contract would jeopardize most, if not all, other private projects proposed for international financing in India. Maharashtra had attracted more than $1 billion of U.S. investment and more than half of all foreign direct investment projects in India were in this state. Furthermore, more than 25 percent of all FDI in India was from the United States.

In the meantime, Bechtel had not stopped construction. A spokesman for Bechtel said the company can't afford to have its 1,300 workers idled during a month-long review. "We have to meet a schedule; we have to provide power according to the power purchase agreement."[16]

Cancellation of the Dabhol Project

The Munde Committee report was submitted to the Maharashtra government on July 15, 1995. Prior to the release of the report, N.K.P. Salve, India's power minister, stressed that the "Enron contract can be canceled only if there is a legal basis for doing so, not for any arbitrary or political reason."[17] On August 2, the Indian

Supreme Court dismissed a petition by a former Maharashtra legislator challenging the Dabhol project on the grounds of secrecy.

On August 3, Chief Minister Joshi (who had visited the United States in the previous month to attract investment to India) announced to the Maharashtra legislature that the cabinet unanimously agreed to suspend Phase I of the project and scrap Phase II. The following are excerpts from Chief Minister Joshi's lengthy statement in the Assembly:

> The Enron project in the form conceived and contracted for is not in the best interests of the state. Being conscious of the deception and distortion in the Enron-MSEB deal which have caused grave losses, the subcommittee is clear that the project must not be allowed to proceed. The subcommittee wholeheartedly recommends that the Enron-MSEB contract should be canceled forthwith . . . Considering the grave issues involved in the matter and the disturbing facts and circumstances that have emerged pointing to extracommercial considerations and probable corruption and illegal motives at work in the whole affair, immediate action must be initiated under the penal and anticorruption laws by police.
>
> The wrong choice of LNG [liquefied natural gas] as fuel and huge inflation in capital costs, along with unprecedented favors shown to Enron in different ways, including in the fuel procurement [had all resulted in an] unreasonable fuel cost to the consumers . . . The documentary evidence obtained by the committee shows beyond any reasonable doubt that the capital cost of Enron Plant was inflated and jacked up by a huge margin. The committee believes that the extent of the inflation may be as high as $700 million . . . Being gas-based, this project should have been cheaper than coal-based ones but in reality, it turns out to be the other way about.
>
> I am convinced that Enron, Bechtel, and GE will sell off at least 50 percent of their equity for the recovery of their expenditures on the project plus profits, and the government would be a helpless spectator. The government should have sought some part of this for itself . . . This contract is anti-Maharashtra. It is devoid of any self-respect; it is one that mortgages the brains of the state which, if accepted, would be a betrayal of the people. This contract is no contract at all and if by repudiating it, there is some financial burden, the state will accept it to preserve the well-being of Maharashtra.[18]

Other grounds were given for cancellation: There had been no competitive bidding; EDC held secret negotiations and used unfair means to win its contract; there was potential environmental damage to a region that was relatively unpolluted; the guaranteed return was well above the norm; and there were concerns about the $20 million earmarked by EDC for education and project development. The BJP government charged that concessions granted to EDC would cause the state of Maharashtra to lose more than $3.3 billion in the future. The committee was also outraged that loose ends in the Dabhol project were being tied up by the Maharashtra government as late as February 25, almost two weeks after the state election. In effect, the contract had been made effective by an administration that had already been rejected by voters.

When the decision was announced, Prime Minister Rao was on a trade and investment promotion trip to Malaysia. He indicated that the economic liberalization policies initiated by his government would not be affected by this decision. Sharad Pawar, the chief minister of Maharashtra at the time the original agreement was signed with Enron, criticized the BJP's decision to cancel the Dabhol power project:

If the government of Maharashtra was serious about the industrialization of Maharashtra, and its power requirements for industrialization and agriculture, they definitely would have appointed an expert group who understands the requirement of power, about overall projection, about investment which is coming in the fields of industry and agriculture, legal sides, but this particular angle is totally missing here and that is why I am not so surprised for this type of decision which has been taken by the government of Maharashtra.[19]

On the day after the government's cancellation announcement, the *Saamna* newspaper, known as the voice of the nationalist Shiv Sena Party, published a headline that read, "Enron Finally Dumped into the Arabian Sea." Later that week, *The Economic Times* in Bombay reported that local villagers celebrated the fall of Enron (see Exhibit 3).

EDC's Next Steps

About 2,600 people were working on the Dabhol power project and it was nearly one-third complete. More than $300 million had been invested in the project and estimated costs per day if the project were shut down would be $200,000 to $250,000. Cancellation of Phase II was less critical because EDC had not yet secured financing commitments for this portion of the project.

A few days before the Munde Committee report was made public and anticipating a cancellation recommendation, Rebecca Mark had offered publicly to renegotiate the deal. She told the media that the company would try to meet the concerns of the MSEB. On August 3, EDC announced that while it was aware of the reported announcement in the Maharashtra Assembly on the suspension of Dabhol, the company had received no official notice to that effect. The statement, issued in Houston, said:

> [EDC] remains available for discussions with the government on any concerns it may have . . . [EDC] has very strong legal defenses available to it under the project contracts and fully intends to pursue these if necessary. The DPC [Dabhol Power Company] and the project sponsors would like to reiterate that they have acted in full compliance with Indian and U.S. laws.[20]

EXHIBIT 3   Excerpts from *The Economic Times,* Bombay, August 7,1995

Villagers Celebrate "Fall" of Enron

The "Fall" of Enron was celebrated with victory marches, much noise of slogans, firecrackers and dancing outside the gates of the Dabhol Power Project and in the neighboring villages of Guhagar, Veldur, Anjanvel and Katalwadi on Sunday.

The march was led by local BJP MLA, the boyish Mr. Vinay Natu, whose father, a former MLA, is said to have originally brought the Enron project to its present site. The younger Natu denies this and says it is Enron propaganda to defame his father.

Much action was expected at the project site by the accompanying police escort. If nothing else, the celebrators were expected to pull down the Dabhol Power Company signboards on the gates of the high fence. They had earlier done this in Guhagar when women pulled down a DPG signpost indicating the way to the site and trampled it with fury.

Instead, the processionists danced, threw gulai in the air, and burst long strings of firecrackers before moving on to the next gate. Behind the wire fences at the site stood the tense security staff of the project; in the distance on higher ground could be seen site engineers observing the proceedings through binoculars.

Lining the fence inside were hundreds of construction workers who came to see the show. These workers too came from the neighboring villages, including those where the celebrations were being held. And even among the processionists were many who on other days worked inside the fence area on pay much higher than anything they can get in their villages. The paradox of benefiting by the Enron project as well as protesting against it has been the most striking aspect of the controversy.

The local Congress leader, 'Mama' Vaidya, was most unimpressed by the show or the opposition to the project. "This backward area needs the project." he said. As to any Congress efforts in the area to muster support for the project or economic development of the area, Mr. Vaidya said there was infighting in the party and coordinated action was not possible.

At DPC itself work goes on. There's worry on the faces of engineers, but they are determined to go on until they are told by their bosses to stop. No such order has been served yet.

References

1   N. Chandra Mohan, New Beginnings, *Business India,* January 30–February 12, 1995, p. 135.

2. The Economist Intelligence Unit, *India: 3rd Quarter Report, EIU,* 1995. p. 22.

3. Michael Schuman, "India Has a Voracious Need for Electricity: U.S. Companies Have a Clear Inside Track," *Forbes,* April 24, 1995.

4. Bodhisatva Ganguli & Tushar Pania, "The Anatomy of a Controversial Deal," *Business India,* April 24–May 7, l995, p. 57.

5. Marcus W. Brauchli, "A Gandhi Legacy: Clash Over Power Plant Reflects Fight in India for Its Economic Soul," *The Wall Street Journal,* April 27, 1995, A6.

6. Ganguli & Pania, p. 59.

7. Ganguli & Pania, p. 58.

8. Ganguli & Pania, p. 56.

9. "India Power Down: A Major Blow to Rao's Reform Drive," *Asia Week,* August 18, 1995.

10. Emily MacFarquhar, "A Volatile Democracy," *U.S. News and World Report,* March 27, 1995, p. 37.

11. Ganguli & Pania, p. 56.

12. Ganguli & Pania, p. 55.

13. Ganguli & Pania, p. 55.

14. Ganguli & Pania, p. 55.

15. Ganguli & Pania, p. 55.

16. *San Francisco Business Times,* May 5, 1995 Sec. 1, p. 1.

17. "Foreign Investment in India: The Enron Disease," *The Economist,* July 29, 1995, p. 48.

18. "Indian State Axes $2.8 BN Dabhol Power Project," *International Gas Report, The Financial Times,* August 4; Mahesh Vijapurkar, "Enron Deal Scrapped, Ongoing Work Halted," *The Hindu,* August 4, p. 1. 1995

19. All-India Doordarshan Television, 3 August 1995.

20. Vijapurkar, p. 1.

28   INTERNATIONAL SOURCING IN ATHLETIC FOOTWEAR: NIKE AND REEBOK

More than 374 million pairs of athletic shoes were sold to U.S. consumers in 1992—mountains of shoes for basketball, jogging, fitness, tennis, golf, and for everyday wear.[1] Sales of athletic footwear in the United States, the largest single market in the world, totalled $11.6 billion, three times the level of 1982. The leading athletic footwear firms were Oregon-based Nike, Inc., with 31.8 percent of the U.S. branded footwear market, and Massachusetts-based Reebok International Ltd., with 21.1 percent of the market. Other prominent athletic footwear companies included Converse, Adidas, LA Gear, and Avia. Their shares of the U.S. branded footwear market are shown in Exhibit 1.

Nike and Reebok were household names, thanks to highly visible marketing campaigns and endorsements from some of the world's best known athletes. They were also very profitable. In 1993, Nike earned $365 million on sales of $3.9 billion and had a return on equity of 24.5 percent. Reebok earned $223 million on 1993 sales of $2.9 billion, and boasted an ROE of 27.2 percent. Selected financial data for Nike and Reebok are presented in Exhibit 2 and Exhibit 3, respectively. According to one study, the Nike brand name was estimated to be worth $3.5 billion, the Reebok brand name $2.3 billion.[2]

Nike and Reebok concentrated on product design and product marketing, but did not actually produce the shoes. Instead they relied on a network of contractors in South Korea, Taiwan, China, Indonesia, Thailand, and the Philippines, who built shoes to exact specifications and delivered a high-quality good according to precise delivery schedules.[3] They also helped Nike and Reebok keep their costs down, since low-cost Asian labor was plentiful. By working with contractors, Nike and Reebok did not have to manage directly a manufacturing operation, and did not have to tie up

EXHIBIT 1   U.S. Branded Athletic Footwear Sales by Major Brand (Estimated in millions of dollars at wholesale)

Rank	Company	1993 sales	% in 1993	1992 sales	1991 sales
1	Nike	$1,990	31.8%	$1,817	$1,693
2	Reebok	1,320	21.1%	1,475	1,336
3	Keds	360	5.8%	370	345
4	LA Gear	290	4.6%	311	492
5	Converse	265	4.2%	215	187
6	Fila	250	4.0%	200	77
7	ASICS	234	3.7%	225	165
8	Adidas	190	3.0%	185	177
9	K-Swiss	120	1.9%	99	92
10 (tie)	Avia	110	1.8%	110	135
10 (tie)	New Balance	110	1.8%	95	95
	Totals	$6,251		$6,029	$5,707

Source: Adapted from *Sporting Goods Intelligence,* December 17, 1993.

working capital in raw materials or work in process inventory. The only inventory on their books was for finished goods. Finally, by shifting demand among contractors as economic conditions changed, Nike and Reebok were able to minimize their input costs. An estimated cost breakdown for an average athletic shoe in 1993 is presented in Exhibit 4.

Sourcing from Asian contractors was in many ways beneficial, but it also raised sensitive questions about worker exploitation and human rights. In the early 1990s, several journalists and industry "watchdog" groups wrote exposés about Asian athletic footwear factories, depicting grim working conditions and thousands of workers toiling long hours for exceedingly low wages. While Nike and Reebok rejected such charges, international sourcing posed a basic question: How could firms derive the full advantage of low cost labor and the benefits of flexible contractor relationships, while also respecting the rights of workers in developing countries?

Athletic Shoe Manufacturing

The use of Asian contractors to produce athletic footwear increased sharply in the early 1970s, when Nike first began to design and market track shoes. The primary attraction was low cost labor. Nike's founder and CEO, Philip H. Knight, an accountant by training but a track enthusiast by avocation, had noted the success of Japanese cameras in the 1950s against the higher-priced German models, and believed the same approach might succeed in athletic footwear, where the leading brands, Adidas and Puma, were German.

At the outset, Nike operated small manufacturing plants in New Hampshire and Maine, but sourced most of its shoes from factories in Taiwan and South Korea. One manager stated that Nike was successful in working with Asian contractors because

EXHIBIT 2   Nike, Inc., Financial Performance, 1988–1993 (Year ended May 31) ($ million)

	1993	1992	1991	1990	1989	1988
Revenues	3,931	3,405	3,004	2,235	1,711	1,203
Cost of sales	2,387	2,089	1,851	1,384	1,075	803
%	61%	61%	62%	62%	63%	67%
Gross profit	1,544	1,316	1,153	851	636	400
%	39%	39%	38%	38%	37%	33%
Selling & administrative	922	761	664	455	355	247
Interest & other	27	33	27	3	10	(13)
Income before taxes	595	522	462	393	271	166
%	15%	15%	15%	18%	16%	14%
Net income	365	329	287	243	167	102
%	9.3%	9.7%	9.6%	10.9%	9.8%	8.5%
Geographic Revenues						
United States	2,529	2,271	2,141	1,755	1,362	900
Europe	1,086	920	665	334	341	233
Asia/Pacific	178	76	56	29	32	21
Canada, Latin American, and other	138	138	141	116	75	48

Source: Nike Annual Reports.

EXHIBIT 3   Reebok International Ltd., Financial Performance, 1988–1993 ($ million)

	1993	1992	1991	1990	1989	1988
Revenues	2,894	3,023	2,734	2,159	1,822	1,786
Cost of sales	1,720	1,809	1,645	1,288	1,072	1,122
%	59%	60%	60%	60%	59%	63%
Gross profit	1,174	1,214	1,089	871	750	664
%	41%	40%	40%	40%	41%	37%
Selling	516	552	441	354	279	261
General & administrative	254	255	225	202	175	149
Interest & other	41	149	33	20	5	23
Income before taxes	363	258	390	295	391	231
%	14%	9%	14%	14%	16%	13%
Net income	223	115	235	177	175	137
%	7.7%	3.8%	8.6%	8.2%	9.6%	7.7%
Geographic Revenues						
United States	1,775	1,982	1,883	1,655	1,584	1,587
United Kingdom	434	415	380	*	*	*
Europe	466	425	296	385	117	106
Other	218	200	176	119	121	93

*United Kingdom revenues were included in European revenue totals through 1990.

Source: Reebok Annual Reports.

EXHIBIT 4   Estimated Cost Breakdown of an Average Athletic Shoe, 1993

Labor (approx. 20%)	$ 2.28
Materials (approx. 60%)	6.84
Overhead (approx. 20%)	2.28
Total cost of sales:	$11.40
Approximate average wholesale price:	$19.60
Average price at retail:	$31.00

Source: Casewriter estimate based on several sources including Sporting Goods Manufacturer's Association, Footwear News, Nike 1992 Annual Report, and personal communications from industry analysts.

---

it developed good relationships and worked closely with contractors to ensure product quality. Nike posted technicians at the factory site to collaborate with local managers. "This has been the real key," a Nike executive explained. "Our people living there and working with the factories as the product is going down the lines. This is a lot different from accepting or rejecting the product at the end of the line—especially at the end of a three-month pipeline to the United States."[4] Sourcing from Asian firms worked so well that by 1982, Nike imported 70 percent of its shoes from South Korea, 16 percent from Taiwan, 7 percent from Thailand, Hong Kong, and the Philippines, and manufactured only 7 percent in the United States. Soon the New Hampshire and Maine plants were shut down altogether.

As sales of athletic shoes boomed during the 1970s and 1980s, other U.S. firms entered the market and also began to source their shoes from Asia. The greatest concentration of athletic shoe manufacturing sprang up in Pusan, South Korea's second largest city. Scores of companies, large and small, produced millions of athletic shoes for export. A single factory run by Samyang Tongsang, one of South Korea's largest footwear manufacturers, produced up to 4 million pairs of shoes a year.[5] In time, athletic shoes became an important component of South Korea's total exports, with exports to the United States alone reaching 125 million pairs in 1988.[6] Contractors such as Samyang Tongsang proved enormously valuable to U.S. athletic footwear companies as they carried out the full range of manufacturing activities: They built the factories, bought raw materials and other inputs such as rubber and leather, hired and trained workers, set local wages and working conditions, and managed the operations.

The Athletic Shoe Manufacturing Process

The manufacture of athletic shoes was a labor intensive process that transformed rubber, leather, and plastic into high-quality shoes. The shoe had three main parts: the outsole, the midsole, and the upper. Rubber, mixed with chemicals and pigments, was rolled and pressed into sheets, then cut to form the shoe's outsole. Polyurethane or ethylene-vinylacetate, mixed with chemicals and pigments, was rolled into sheets and foamed in an oven, then cut to create the shoe's midsole. Outsoles and midsoles were glued together to form a complete sole unit. The shoe's upper consisted of several parts cut from leather or plastic and sewn together. The upper was then joined to the sole unit, using glue and air pressure, to form the complete shoe. Finally, the shoe was trimmed, polished, labelled, and packaged.

Much of the work was done by hand. Machines also played an important role, but overall the degree of automation was low. The manufacturing process also used various chemicals and volatile organic compounds (VOCs). Although there were concerns about worker exposure to chemicals, the overall environmental impact, compared to many other industries, was not especially high.

The Evolution of Supplier Networks

By the 1980s, Nike worked with its contractors through a sophisticated system that combined high-tech design in the United States with low-cost Asian labor. Nike designers in Oregon created more than one hundred new styles and colors of athletic shoes per year. Designs were relayed by satellite to their contractors' CAD/CAM systems in Taiwan, where prototypes were developed and tested. Once approved, blueprints could be faxed to factories in South Korea and elsewhere in Asia, where new production would begin almost at once.[7]

To avoid dependence on a small number of contractors, Nike and other U.S. firms developed relations with several manufacturers in a number of countries. For their part, large South Korean and Taiwanese contractors often produced for more than one athletic shoe firm. A single plant might have production lines turning out Nikes alongside production lines making shoes for Converse or other companies. Other contractors were dedicated to a single company.

Reebok, too, developed an extensive network of overseas contractors. In the late 1980s, Reebok's shoes were manufactured in forty factories located in several countries. Most of the volume came from South Korea and Taiwan, but plants in China, Thailand, the Philippines, and Indonesia also produced for Reebok. The company explained: "This diversity makes us more flexible as national pricing structures and supply conditions change. At Reebok, we are manufacturers without the burden of plant ownership."[8]

Virtually all U.S. athletic footwear companies relied on overseas manufacturing. There were only a few exceptions, one of which was New Balance Athletic Shoe Inc., a niche producer with a small share of the U.S. market that specialized in width sizing, offering shoes ranging from AA to EEEE. It operated four U.S. plants: two in Maine, one in Lawrence, Massachusetts, and one in Brighton, a district of Boston. Employees at the Brighton plant, many of whom were recent immigrants from Latin America, earned a base wage of $7.50 an hour. With benefits, wages for manufacturing workers ranged from $8 to $12 per hour.[9] Given these labor costs, New Balance reported that it was unable to profitably produce shoes that retailed for less than $50.[10]

Rising Labor Costs, Shifting Factories

As South Korea and Taiwan prospered in the 1980s, wages for manufacturing workers rose sharply. The Korean Ministry of Labor reported that workers in shoe factories earned an average of $24.40 per day in 1990 compared to just $9.71 per day in 1986.[11]

. **EXHIBIT 5   Hourly Labor Costs, Production Workers in the Textile and Apparel Industries—Selected Countries, 1993**

Country	Hourly Labor Cost—Textile (in US$)	Hourly Labor Cost—Apparel (in US$)	Normal Equivalent Days Worked, Textile (per operator per year)
North America			
United States	$11.61	$ 8.13	241
Canada	13.44	9.14	237
Mexico	2.93	1.08	286
Europe			
Denmark	21.32	17.29	226
France	16.49	14.84	233
Germany	20.50	17.22	232
Greece	7.13	5.85	231
Ireland	9.18	7.44	243
Netherlands	20.82	15.41	207
Asia			
China (PRC)	0.36	0.25	306
Hong Kong	3.85	3.85	294
India	0.56	0.27	289
Indonesia	0.43	0.28	297
Japan	23.65	10.64	261
South Korea	3.66	2.71	312
Malaysia	1.18	0.77	261
Philippines	0.78	0.53	288
Singapore	3.56	3.06	284
Taiwan	5.76	4.61	291
Thailand	1.04	0.71	341
Vietnam	$ 0.37	$ 0.26	287

Source: Compiled by Jane Palley Katz, Research Associate, based on data from Werner International Management Consultants, New York, New York.

Labor costs in South Korea and Taiwan had become significantly higher than in other Asian countries. A comparison of 1993 wages for textile and apparel workers in several Asian, North American, and European countries is presented in Exhibit 5.

Rising labor costs were a major concern to Nike and Reebok. On a visit to South Korea in 1990, Reebok CEO Paul Fireman told his contractors that Reebok would continue to buy from them only if productivity were boosted.[12] Despite efforts to improve efficiency through automation, South Korean factories found it difficult to overcome the disparity in labor costs. The production of athletic footwear remained heavily labor-intensive. Commented one manufacturer, "There are only so many operators that you can replace with machines."[13]

As the relative cost of labor shifted among Asian nations, athletic shoe manufacturers studied the advantages of relocating production. "We're always looking for new manufacturing sources," said David Taylor, Nike's vice president of manufacturing.[14]

Especially attractive were China and Indonesia, countries with large populations and low labor costs. In 1992, a South Korean shoe factory worker earned close to $10,000 per year, compared to $1,200 per year for a Chinese worker and even less for an Indonesian.

Hoping to maintain their working relationships with Taiwanese and South Korean contractors, Nike provided incentives for them to move their operations to countries with lower labor costs. Neal Lauridsen, a Nike vice president, explained the system:

> We say, "We're in a position to give you 'x' amount of orders" to take the uncertainty out of this move. They go to the country. They bring management. That formula has worked really well.[15]

Thanks in part to such guarantees, several of Nike's contractors dismantled their production lines and shifted to new countries. Many Taiwanese contractors moved across the Taiwan Strait to China's Fujian and Guangdong provinces, where they built spacious new plants and equipped them with sophisticated machinery. More importantly, these plants were staffed by diligent Chinese workers who were significantly less costly than their Taiwanese counterparts.[16] By 1992, annual footwear production in China reached 700 million pairs, a 400 percent increase from 1988.[17] Meanwhile, the number of footwear companies in Taiwan fell by almost half, from 1,245 in 1988 to 745 in 1992.[18]

While Taiwanese contractors moved to China, many South Korean contractors closed shop in Pusan and moved to Indonesia. The result, according to a senior researcher at the Korea Institute of Footwear Technology, was that employment in Pusan's shoe manufacturing industry fell from nearly 500,000 in 1990 to 120,000 at the end of 1993, putting 380,000 people out of work.[19] Nike's imports from South Korea dropped by one-third in four years, from 66 percent of its total imports in 1988 to 42 percent in 1992. Further cutbacks were expected. In January 1994, the factory director of one leading South Korean manufacturer commented: "During the last three years, we closed more than 90 percent of our production lines. All of our overseas customers, such as Nike Inc. and Reebok International Ltd., have left us for manufacturers in countries with cheap labor like China and Indonesia."[20] An industry source predicted that by the mid-1990s only a few South Korean shoe exporters would survive.

Indonesia was a particularly attractive place to set up athletic footwear factories because of its large population (180 million) and a labor force that was growing by 2.4 million per year. Unemployment was a serious problem. In an effort to find jobs for its citizens, the Indonesian government not only sought to attract foreign investors but sponsored programs that sent workers overseas, including 300,000 who went to Saudi Arabia in the late 1980s. Although some government officials had visions of attracting modern industry, such as aircraft manufacturing, most recognized that the average Indonesian had little more than a basic education and could perform only unskilled labor. "Industrialization in Indonesia will be a tenuous, gradual, step-by-step process, always affected by a huge oversupply of labor," said Dorotjatun Kuntjoro-Jakti, an economist at the University of Indonesia.[21] Given the need for employment, Indonesian government planners welcomed the influx of athletic shoe manufacturers. From 1988 to 1991, more than $350 million was invested in Indonesian shoe factories, much of it from contractors that supplied Nike, Reebok, and other U.S. athletic footwear companies.

Nike in Indonesia

By 1990, Nike sourced shoes from six Indonesian factories, four owned by South Korean firms and two owned by Indonesians. Together, these factories employed more than 24,000 Indonesians and supplied Nike with more than 6 million pairs of shoes, or 8 percent of its worldwide volume.[22] But as athletic footwear factories expanded in Indonesia, they came under careful scrutiny. Reports compiled in 1991 by an Indonesian research institute, Institut Teknology Bandung (ITB), and by the Asian-American Free Labor Institute (AAFLI), alleged that Nike's system of procuring shoes in Indonesia was rife with exploitation and cited the firm for a range of labor abuses.[23] It accused South Korean-owned factories, in particular, of paying less than the minimum daily wage, which was only 2,100 rupiah, or about $1. The AAFLI also charged Nike's contractors with forcing employees to work overtime, violating child-labor laws, and not respecting special work rules for women. Employees, usually young women, complained of an atmosphere of fear. One worker at Nagasakti Para Shoes, a Nike contractor, said that she and other Indonesians were "terrified" of their South Korean managers: "They yell at us when we don't make the production quotas, and if we talk back they cut our wages." Workers were not allowed to leave the factory during the workday, she added.

Some observers charged that Nike created these problems by pressuring contractors to meet very aggressive cost and volume targets. Jeffrey Ballinger, AAFLI's representative in Jakarta, described Nike's approach in Indonesia:

> Nike's strategy is to pit six factories against each other and have them compete for orders based on who produces the cheapest shoe. The government doesn't protect the workers, the union is complacent, and Nike looks the other way. Is it any wonder the workers are getting screwed?[24]

In January 1992, the Indonesian government raised the official minimum daily wage from 2,100 rupiah to 2,500 rupiah, approximately $1.25.[25] At prevailing food prices, however, 2,500 rupiah could purchase only 70 percent of an individual's daily minimum physical caloric needs.[26] Furthermore, the "official" minimum wage tended to be a guideline rather than a strict requirement. Some employers said they could not afford to pay the minimum wage, while others combined a lower basic wage with a food allowance and incentive payments.[27] Either way, workers received less than the officially mandated wage. Given widespread unemployment, however, many Indonesian workers tolerated low wages and poor working conditions. One reporter commented: "For every disgruntled worker, employers can hire 100 willing to work for a pittance."[28]

Nike executives deflected these accusations by noting that the factories were owned and operated by independent contractors, not by Nike. Nike had no control over the labor practices of its contractors, they maintained. According to Neal Lauridsen, Nike's vice president for Asia, "We don't know the first thing about manufacturing. We are marketers and designers."[29] John Woodman, Nike's general manager in Jakarta, explained: "They are our subcontractors. It's not within our scope to investigate [allegations of labor violations.]" Woodman was aware of problems in the factories that produced Nike shoes, but had not investigated them, adding: "I don't know that I need to know."[30] Overall, he maintained, Nike was a positive force in Indonesia: "We've come in here and given jobs to thousands of people who wouldn't be working otherwise."[31]

Nike's Memorandum of Understanding

In late 1992, Nike developed a Memorandum of Understanding for its contractors and suppliers. Under the terms of the Memorandum, shown in Exhibit 6, Nike directed its contractors to certify their compliance with "all applicable local laws" for labor regulations, for occupational safety and health, and for worker insurance. In addition, Nike's contractors had to certify they did not use forced labor and did not discriminate on the basis of gender, race, or other differences. Regarding environmental pollution, contractors were required to adhere to Nike's environmental practices, including a prohibition on any use of chlorofluorocarbons (CFCs). By accepting Nike's Memorandum of Understanding, contractors agreed to maintain on file documentation that provided evidence of compliance with each of the points, and agreed to make such evidence available to Nike upon request. The Memorandum of Understanding was codified in late 1992 and formally adopted in January 1993.

The effects of Nike's Memorandum of Understanding were not yet apparent in July 1993, when CBS reported on the working conditions at one of Nike's contractors in Indonesia. CBS found that workers were paid 19 cents an hour, a sum insufficient to buy basic necessities. Women lived in barracks which they were allowed to leave only on Sunday, and then only with a letter of permission from management. Commenting on these conditions, AAFLI representative Jeffrey Ballinger said: "It would take roughly 1 percent of Nike's advertising budget, which is about $180 million a year, to put 15,000 workers above the poverty line."[32]

Responding to these and similar charges, Nike's chairman, Phil Knight, denied that his company engaged in any exploitation of workers. Instead he emphasized Nike's contribution to Indonesia:

> We're not gouging anybody. Our gross profits are around 39 percent, right on the industry standard. We make our profit on volume. A country like Indonesia is converting from farm labor to semiskilled—an industrial transition that has occurred throughout history. There's no question in my mind that we're giving these people hope.[33]

Reebok in Indonesia

Nike was not the only U.S. company to be criticized for working conditions in Indonesian factories. In 1991 the International Labor Rights Education and Research Fund (ILRERF) criticized Reebok for manufacturing its shoes with child labor, for poor working conditions, for paying subminimum wages, and for violating workers' rights.[34] While applauding many of Reebok's efforts on behalf of human rights, ILRERF's director, Pharis Harvey, was critical of the company: "Reebok's corporate integrity would be far better served if the company utilized its moral energy to clean up its own industry, before looking for human rights heroes elsewhere."[35] Reebok's

---

EXHIBIT 6   Nike's Memorandum of Understanding

---

1. Government Regulation of Business

(Subcontractor/supplier) certifies compliance with all applicable local labor government regulations regarding minimum wage, overtime, child labor laws, provisions for pregnancy, menstrual leave, provisions for vacations and holidays, and mandatory retirement benefits.

2. Safety and Health

(Subcontractor/supplier) certifies compliance with all applicable local government regulations regarding occupational health and safety.

3. Worker Insurance

(Subcontractor/supplier) certifies compliance with all applicable laws providing health insurance, life insurance, and worker's compensation.

4. Forced Labor

(Subcontractor/supplier) certifies that it and its suppliers and contractors do not use any form of forced labor—prison or otherwise.

5. Environment

(Subcontractor/supplier) certifies compliance with all applicable local environmental regulations and adheres to Nike's own broader environmental practices, including the prohibition of the use of chlorofluorocarbons (CFCs), the release of which could contribute to depletion of the earth's ozone layer

6. Equal Opportunity

(Subcontractor/supplier) certifies that it does not discriminate in hiring, salary, benefits, advancement, termination, or retirement on the basis of gender, race, religion, age, sexual orientation, or ethnic origin.

7. Documentation and Inspection

(Subcontractor/supplier) agrees to maintain on file such documentation as may be needed to demonstrate compliance with the certifications in this Memorandum of Understanding and further agrees to make these documents available for Nike's inspection upon request.

Source: Nike company document.

---

chairman, Paul Fireman, responded with a letter questioning the merits of these allegations, and stated his belief that charges concerning Reebok's contractors "contain serious errors in fact."[36]

Reebok had, in fact, long taken a strong public position in support of human rights. To protest apartheid, Reebok in 1986 terminated a distribution agreement in South Africa and subsequently refused to do business there. In 1988, The Reebok Foundation created the Reebok Human Rights Award, given annually to people under the age of 30 who were active in support of human rights. The first Reebok Human Rights Awards were presented on December 7, 1988, during the week that commemorated the 40th Anniversary of the United Nations Universal Declaration of Human Rights. Honorees in 1988 included Janet Cherry, a 27-year-old champion of racial equality in South Africa; Arn-Chorn Pond, a 20-year-old survivor of genocide in Cambodia who founded "Children of War"; and Winona LaDuke, 29-year-old advocate of Native American rights. In subsequent years, Reebok gave the award to many other young people who had struggled to advance human rights.[37] Also in 1988, Reebok donated $10 million to support Amnesty International's "Human Rights Now!" concert tour. Following the Tiananmen Square massacre of pro-democracy students in 1989, Reebok issued a policy in support of human rights and governing workplace conditions in all its overseas operations. The policy is presented in Exhibit 7.

Reebok's Human Rights Production Standards

Partly in response to the concerns raised by the ILRERF in 1991, Reebok worked with a human rights lawyer to develop a policy that addressed worker health and safety in the factories of its contractors. For guidance, Reebok turned to the U.N. Universal Declaration on Human Rights, which included several articles about work and employment. Some key articles from the Declaration are presented in Exhibit 8. In May 1993, Reebok unveiled a comprehensive set of principles regarding workplace conditions for Reebok's many suppliers and contractors. In presenting its production standards, the company declared:

> Tens of thousands of people around the world are involved every workday in manufacturing Reebok products. While the company has been monitoring the conditions under which they work, Reebok has recently established a set of guidelines, called "Reebok Human Rights Production Standards."[38]

These standards, presented in Exhibit 9, barred the use of child labor or compulsory labor (such as prison workers), declared that no one should be discriminated against or forced to work excessive overtime without compensation, required fair compensation for all workers, guaranteed freedom of association, and called for a safe and healthy work environment. In announcing the policy, Reebok's Director of Human Rights Programs, Douglas Cahn, stated:

> Reebok's devotion to human rights worldwide is a hallmark of our corporate culture. We are a corporation operating in a global economy and cannot be indifferent to the standards of our business partners around the world.[39]

Reebok's Human Rights Production Standards called for the firm to conduct regular on-site inspections, or audits, of contractor factories. Contractors that did not meet Reebok's standards would be terminated. Cahn explained: "I think corporations are increasingly finding that you need to be more than good business people. You have to be responsible business citizens." Reebok's executive vice president of operations and finance, Ken Watchmaker, added: "Consumers today hold companies accountable for the way products are made, not just the quality of the product itself."[40] Reebok's CEO, Paul Fireman, explained the logic:

> We have learned in our brief corporate history that our success very much depends on the participation of our employees. If they care passionately about their company, it will be a better company in every way. Our commitment to human rights is something many employees feel passionate about. It engenders pride, loyalty, and spirit that goes beyond whatever we do in a commercial sense.

**EXHIBIT 7   Reebok International Ltd., Human Rights Policy
(Adopted November 1990)**

---

1. Reebok will not operate under martial law conditions or allow any military presence on its premises.
2. Reebok encourages free association and assembly among its employees.
3. Reebok will seek to ensure that opportunities for advancement are based on initiative, leadership and contributions to the business, not political beliefs. Further, no one is to be dismissed from working at its factories for political views or nonviolent involvement.
4. Reebok will seek to prevent compulsory political indoctrination programs from taking place on its premises.
5. Reebok affirms that it deplores the use of force against human rights.

Source: Diane F. Orentlicher, and Timothy A. Gelatt, "Public Law, Private Actors: The Impact of Human Rights on Business Investors in China," Reprinted by special permission of Northwestern University School of Law, Volume 14, Issue 1, *Northwestern Journal of International Law & Business,* p. 108 (1993).

**EXHIBIT 8   United Nations Universal Declaration of Human Rights
(Selected articles)**

Article 23

6. Everyone has the right to work, to free choice of employment, to just and favorable conditions of work, and to protection against unemployment.
7. Everyone, without any discrimination, has the right to equal pay for equal work.
8. Everyone who works has the right to just and favorable remuneration insuring for himself and his family an existence worthy of human dignity, and supplemented, if necessary, by other means of social protection.
9. Everyone has the right to form and join trade unions for the protection of his interests.

Article 24

Everyone has the right to rest and leisure, including reasonable limitation of working hours and periodic holidays with pay.

Article 25

1. Everyone has the right to a standard of living adequate for the health and well-being of himself and of his family, including food, clothing, housing, and medical care, and if necessary, social services and the right to security in the event of unemployment, sickness, disability, widowhood, old age, or other lack of livelihood in circumstances beyond his control.
2. Motherhood and childhood are entitled to special care and assistance. All children, whether born in or out of wedlock, shall enjoy the same social protection.

Reebok was aware that conducting regular audits of contractor factories would be costly. Levi Strauss, the California-based apparel maker, had recently initiated a similar policy of contractor standards and had found that audits required considerable staff time to conduct inspections and to prepare reports, imposed significant travel costs, called for training for contractors, and required financial incentives to upgrade facilities.[41] In 1993 a Reebok task force conducted the first audit of factory working conditions. The investigation included interviews with workers and managers, as well as an inspection of workspace, living quarters, and cafeterias at 45 separate factories in Indonesia, Thailand, the Philippines, China and South Korea. After

EXHIBIT 9   Reebok's Human Rights Production Standards

A Commitment to Human Rights

Reebok's devotion to human rights worldwide is a hallmark of our corporate culture. As a corporation in an ever-more global economy we will not be indifferent to the standards of our business partners around the world.

We believe that the incorporation of internationally recognized human rights standards into our business practice improves worker morale and results in a higher quality working environment and higher quality products.

In developing this policy, we have sought to use standards that are fair, that are appropriate to diverse cultures and that encourage workers to take pride in their work.

Nondiscrimination

Reebok will seek business partners that do not discriminate in hiring and employment practices on grounds of race, color, national origin, gender, religion, or political or other opinion.

Working Hours/Overtime

Reebok will seek business partners who do not require more than 60 hour work weeks on a regularly scheduled basis, except for appropriately compensated overtime in compliance with local laws, as we will favor business partners who use 48 hour work weeks as their maximum normal requirement.

Forced or Compulsory Labor

Reebok will not work with business partners that use forced or other compulsory labor, including labor that is required as a means of political coercion or as punishment for holding or for peacefully expressing political views, in the manufacture of its products. Reebok will not purchase materials that were produced by forced prison or other compulsory labor and will terminate business relationships with any sources found to utilize such labor.

Fair Wages

Reebok will seek business partners who share our commitment to the betterment of wage and benefit levels that address the basic needs of workers and their families so far as possible and appropriate in light of national practices and conditions. Reebok will not select business partners that pay less than the minimum wage required by local law or that pay less than prevailing local industry practices (whichever is higher).

Child Labor

Reebok will not work with business partners that use child labor. The term "child" generally refers to a person who is less than 14 years of age, or younger than the age for completing compulsory education if that age is higher than 14. In countries where the law defines "child" to include individuals who are older than 14, Reebok will apply that definition.

Freedom of Association

Reebok will seek business partners that share its commitment to the right of employees to establish and join organizations of their own choosing. Reebok will seek to assure that no employee is penalized because of his or her nonviolent exercise of that right. Reebok recognizes and respects the right of all employees to organize and bargain collectively.

Safe and Healthy Work Environment

Reebok will seek business partners that strive to assure employees a safe and healthy workplace and that do not expose workers to hazardous conditions.

Application of Standards

Reebok will apply the Reebok Human Rights Production Standards in our selection of business partners. Reebok will seek compliance with these standards by our contractors, subcontractors, suppliers, and other business partners.

To assure proper implementation of this policy, Reebok will seek business partners that allow Reebok full knowledge of the production facilities used and will undertake affirmative measures, such as on-site inspection of production facilities, to implement and monitor these standards.

Reebok takes strong objection to the use of force to suppress any of these standards and will take any such actions into account when evaluating facility compliance with these standards.

Source: Reebok company document.

a year of such audits, Reebok acknowledged in 1994 that it had ceased working with at least one contractor, and that it could document improvements in contractors' factories, particularly in the areas of health and safety. Regular inspections were scheduled for the future.

The Athletic Footwear Industry in 1994

Nike's Memorandum of Understanding and Reebok's Human Rights Production Standards were announced just as the U.S. athletic footwear industry was experiencing a slowdown. Following a peak year in 1990, when sales reached $11.9 billion on 392 million pairs, revenues fell back slightly. Branded athletic footwear continued to grow but at a slower rate, as shown in Exhibit 1. After fifteen years of explosive growth a slowdown could hardly have been unexpected—by 1992, the average wearer of athletic shoes owned three pairs.[42] Also changing was the willingness of consumers to pay high prices. In 1992, the average price paid for a pair of athletic shoes edged slightly lower.

Faced with slowing demand in the United States, Nike and Reebok looked for new ways to grow. Both firms emphasized international sales, and made steady inroads into European and Asian markets. Both firms branched into related footwear products, including hiking shoes and other outdoor wear. They also continued to invest in product design, seeking new models that would be lighter, more durable, and more comfortable. Reebok, for example, refined its "PUMP" technology, which filled the shoe's upper with air for superior support and comfort, and introduced GraphLite, a graphite composite in the arch which replaced part of the sole and reduced up to 10 percent of the shoe's weight. Reebok also sponsored special events and stepped up its endorsements from athletes including basketball star Shaquille O'Neal, Super Bowl MVP Emmitt Smith, golfer Greg Norman, and figure skater Nancy Kerrigan. Nike continued to rely on endorsements of stars, featuring Michael Jordan and Olympic gold medalist Jackie Joyner-Kersee in extensive television campaigns, and also worked to improve its distinctive technologies.

Competition in athletic footwear remained fierce in 1994, with firms scrambling to keep growing and maintain profitability in a maturing market. Advertising was crucial. In early 1994, Paul Fireman disclosed an exclusive agreement with the World Football League under which Reebok would supply footwear to all of its athletes. Fireman also announced a deal in which Reebok and Nike would be the exclusive footwear advertisers on NBA telecasts. Fireman observed: "This means that Converse, Fila, Adidas and others will have to find another way to reach their consumers."[43] With advertising expenses increasing and development costs rising, and with consumers becoming more price sensitive, Nike and Reebok remained vitally concerned with controlling their costs.

Endnotes

1. 1992 Footwear (Athletic) Market, *Sporting Goods Manufacturers Association.*

2. "Brands," *Financial World,* September 1, 1993, p. 41.

3. Overseas producers of athletic shoes are called "contractors" by some industry observers and "subcontractors" by others. This case will use the term "contractor" because it more accurately captures the direct relationship between the producer and the U.S. company, except in instances of direct quotation, as in Exhibit 6.

4. Adam Klein, "Phil Knight: CEO at Nike (1983)," Harvard Business School Case 9-380-038.

5. Mark Clifford, "Pain in Pusan," *Far Eastern Economic Review,* November 5, 1992, p. 58.

6. Rich Wilner, "Revival Tactics," *Footwear News,* March 21, 1994.

7. Mark Clifford, "Spring in Their Step," *Far Eastern Economic Review,* November 5, 1992, p. 57.

8. Reebok 1989 Annual Report, p. 16.

9. Diane E. Lewis, "Delicate Balance: Running Shoe Company Weighs Commitment to Manufacturing in Urban American Against Efforts to Organize its Boston Workers," *Boston Globe,* February 23, 1993

10. Jay Finegan, "Surviving in the Nike/Reebok Jungle," *Inc.,* May 1993, p.l02.

11. Elliott Blair Smith, "K-Swiss in Korea: Stirrings in Chosun Land," *California Business,* October 1991.

12. Mark Clifford, "Pain in Pusan," op. cit., p. 59.

13. Ibid.

14. Mark Clifford, "Spring in Their Step," op. cit., p. 56.

15. Ibid., p. 57.

16. Josephine Bow, "China's Shoe Sourcing Builds into Dynasty," *Footwear News,* September 6, 1993.

17. Ibid.

18. Mark Clifford, "The China Connection," *Far Eastern Economic Review,* November 5, 1992, p. 60.

19. Myong-Hwan Kim, "Costs Drive South Korean Shoemakers Out of Business," *The Reuters European Business Report,* January 24, 1994.

20. Ibid.

21. Adam Schwarz, "Low-tech and Labour Driven" *Far Eastern Economic Review,* April 2, 1992, p. 53.

22. Adam Schwarz, "Running a Business," *Far Eastern Economic Review,* June 20, 1991, p. 16.

23. Ibid.

24. Ibid.

25. According to Reebok's Doug Cahn, in early 1994 the minimum daily wage in Indonesia was raised to 3,800 rupiah, or roughly $2.

26. Suhaini Aznam, "The Toll of Low Wages," *Far Eastern Economic Review,* April 2, 1992.

27. Ibid.

28. Ibid., p. 50.

29. Mark Clifford, "Spring in Their Step," op. cit., p. 57.

30. Adam Schwarz, "Running a Business," op. cit., p. 16.

31. *Boston Globe,* December 30, 1991.
32. Deborah Leipziger, "The Denim Revolution: Levi Strauss & Co. Adopts a Code of Conduct," *Council on Economic Priorities,* February 1994.
33. Donald Katz, "Triumph of the Swoosh," *Sports Illustrated,* August 16, 1993, p. 64.
34. "Reebok Awards Hypocritical, International Group Charges," *AFL-CIO News,* January 6, 1992.
35. Ibid.
36. Letter from Paul Fireman to Pharis Harvey, January 8, 1992, Reebok company document.
37. Reebok International Ltd., *Corporate Backgrounder,* April 1993, p. 14.
38. "Human Rights Production Standards Set in Worldwide Reebok Initiative," *Reebok: Making a Difference,* Vol. 3, Number 3, June 1993.
39. Mark McSherry, "Reebok Slams Home Point on Human Rights," *Hong Kong Sunday Morning Post,* May 16, 1993.
40. *Reebok: Making a Difference,* Volume 3, Number 3, June 1993.
41. Deborah Leipziger, op. cit.
42. 1992 Footwear (Athletic) Market, *Sporting Goods Manufacturing Association.*
43. Mark Tedeschi, and Rich Wilner, "Athletics Seek Control at Crossroads," *Footwear News,* February 7, 1994.